CENTURY 21®
ACCOUNTING

ROBERT M. SWANSON

Ball State University
Muncie, Indiana

KENTON E. ROSS

East Texas State University
Commerce, Texas

ROBERT D. HANSON

Central Michigan University
Mount Pleasant, Michigan

LEWIS D. BOYNTON

Formerly, Central Connecticut State College
New Britain, Connecticut

B30

Published by

SOUTH-WESTERN PUBLISHING CO.

CINCINNATI WEST CHICAGO, ILL. DALLAS PELHAM MANOR, N.Y. PALO ALTO, CALIF.

THIRD EDITION
CENTURY 21
ACCOUNTING

First-Year
Course

ISBN: 0-538-02300-7

Library of Congress Catalog Card Number: 80-50308

10 11 12 13 14 15 16 17 18 19 20 K 1 0 9 8 7 6

Printed in the United States of America

Preface

This textbook is the first in a two-volume series available for use in a complete two-year high school accounting program. CENTURY 21 ACCOUNTING, First-Year Course, is followed by CENTURY 21 ACCOUNTING, Advanced Course. The first-year text is for students who have a variety of career objectives. Some students desire beginning vocational preparation for careers in accounting. Other students look forward to careers in related business fields for which mastery of some accounting knowledge and skill is needed. Some students seek a foundation on which to continue studying business and accounting at the collegiate level.

The revisions made for this third edition of CENTURY 21 ACCOUNTING, First-Year Course, are based on suggestions received from classroom teachers, accounting students, and businesses surveyed, and on changes occurring in the accounting profession.

FROM SIMPLE TO COMPLEX

This edition of CENTURY 21 ACCOUNTING retains the spiral approach to learning. Greater emphasis is focused on forms of business ownership. The study of accounting in Part 2 is based on a service business organized as a sole proprietorship. In Part 3 a merchandising business organized as a partnership is used. All learnings from Parts 2 and 3 are used in Part 4 for the study of accounting practices for a partnership using automated procedures. In Parts 5 and 6, the text is based on businesses organized as corporations. Partnership and corporation accounting had been described in two separate chapters in previous editions. The material from these two chapters is now distributed throughout the text. This new organization presents the complete accounting cycle for each form of business ownership. Study progresses from the complete accounting cycle for a sole proprietorship to the accounting cycle for a partnership to the accounting cycle for a corporation.

The spiral approach also is used to introduce accounting forms and records. Part 2 describes a business using a simple two-column general journal and a simple multi-column cash journal. The learnings from Part 2 are applied in Part 3 to the use of an expanded multi-column combination journal. In Part 5 special journals are introduced as an extension of the learnings about multi-column journals.

STUDENT-CENTERED LEARNING

This text is student-centered. The basic objective is helping students acquire accounting knowledges, understandings, and skills.

Competency-based organization and content

This edition has been revised according to pre-determined general behavioral goals, terminal performance objectives, and enabling performance tasks. A complete section of the Teacher's Reference Guide is devoted to the specific types of behavior students are expected to demonstrate at the end of each learning experience. In addition, general behavioral goals are listed on each part opener of the text. Enabling performance tasks are listed at the beginning of each chapter.

Easy reading level

The reading level (as determined by *A Formula for Predicting Readability*, by Edgar Dale and Jeanne S. Chall, Bureau of Educational Research, Ohio State University) is appropriate for the typical high school student. The authors have made a special effort to meet the criteria of this readability formula as applied to the exacting and specialized technical field of accounting.

Practice material for varying levels of students

The end-of-chapter practice materials provide various levels of difficulty. For example, chapters include drills and application problems for all students. Students with varying abilities are provided for through mastery and challenge problems. Also, recycling problems (formerly called review problems) are provided for those students who need additional practice. Reinforcement activities (formerly called projects) are provided to strengthen the basic learnings.

Flexible organization

Because of differences from school to school in class period length, student ability, and length of school term, an accounting text must be flexible. Versions of the text are available for quarter-year courses, half-year or semester courses, and one-year or two semester courses. An advanced text is available for schools offering three or four semesters of high school accounting.

Visual and learning aids

Appropriate, realistic illustrations and the use of four-color photographs aid student motivation and learning. A CENTURY 21 Trans-Vision® insert in Chapter 14 assists students in learning how to prepare an eight-column work sheet.

Many supplemental learning aids are available to be used with this text. Materials such as working papers and study guides and business simulations provide the students an opportunity for individual learning activities. Supplemental learning packages are also available for use with microcomputers. These materials provide the students an opportunity to perform automated accounting tasks.

Testing program

The testing program has been expanded, reorganized, and completely revised. Each testing instrument measures student performance specified in the terminal performance objectives.

Objective tests are available for use at convenient times each semester. In addition, two semester examinations are provided. The objective tests are a continuation of the very popular testing program available with previous editions.

Problem tests have been expanded, and a problem test is now available for each chapter except Chapter 1. A single problem test can be administered as students finish each chapter or combined for use after several chapters have been completed.

Use of published objective and problem tests assures evaluation of important knowledges, understandings, and skills described in pre-determined terminal performance objectives. The published tests combine easily with teacher-prepared quizzes and tests to provide for differences in course organization and objectives for individual schools.

Chapter content

Chapter 1 is a new chapter that contains information about accounting careers. This chapter is useful as a springboard for a more detailed study of accounting career possibilities in local communities. Chapter 1 also includes eleven commonly accepted accounting concepts that guide professional accountants. Throughout this text, reference is given each time an application of one of these accounting concepts occurs.

Part 6 of this text is new and contains information about accounting control systems. One chapter is provided for each control system — a voucher system, a petty cash system, and an inventory system.

ACKNOWLEDGMENTS

This third edition of CENTURY 21 ACCOUNTING follows the traditions established over the more than 75 years since its predecessor, 20TH CENTURY BOOKKEEPING AND ACCOUNTING was first published. However, this edition updates tradition and provides a more learnable, practical, and realistic tool for teachers and students. Combined with the supplementary materials, this text is a complete learning package for all high school accounting curricula. This revision is based on the efforts of a large number of persons including high school teachers, professional accountants, students, and others who have offered suggestions, provided information, and worked with the authors in creating new materials. The authors express their sincere appreciation to all those persons who have contributed to this third edition of CENTURY 21 ACCOUNTING.

Robert M. Swanson
Kenton E. Ross
Robert D. Hanson
Lewis D. Boynton

Contents

PART 1 ACCOUNTING AS A CAREER

PART 2 ACCOUNTING FOR A SERVICE BUSINESS

PART 4 AN AUTOMATED ACCOUNTING SYSTEM

PART 5 AN ACCOUNTING SYSTEM WITH SPECIAL JOURNALS

ACKNOWLEDGMENTS

For permission to reproduce the photographs on the pages indicated, acknowledgment is made to the following:

11	Courtesy of Armco, Inc.
112	Editorial Photocolor Archives, Inc.
120	Courtesy of A. E. Staley Mfg. Co.
136	Courtesy of Moore Business Systems
170	Courtesy of Amdahl Corporation
247	Monroe, The Calculator Company (A Division of Litton Industries)
293	Reprinted through the courtesy of New York Life Insurance Company
327	Photograph courtesy of Burroughs Corporation
328	Photo by Jim Ayers, American Business Products, Inc.
331	Courtesy of Prudential Insurance Company
345	Kidde, Inc., 1979 Annual Report
346	Photo Courtesy of IBM
347	Courtesy of Bell & Howell Company
348	Photos Courtesy of IBM
349	Photo Courtesy of Boise Cascade Corporation
352	Courtesy of National, a Division of Dennison Mfg. Co.
370	Courtesy of Cabot Corporation
394	Courtesy of Apple Computer, Inc.
454	Courtesy of Reynolds + Reynolds
508	Courtesy of Philip Morris Incorporated
519	Freelance Photographers Guild
526	Freelance Photographers Guild
533	Courtesy of Digital Equipment Corporation
540	Courtesy of Moore Business Systems
566	Photo by Tom Tracy, © The Image Bank
603	Photo Courtesy of Mohawk Data Sciences, Parsippany, New Jersey
605	Courtesy of Reynolds + Reynolds

1 ACCOUNTING AS A CAREER

GENERAL BEHAVIORAL GOALS

1. Know terminology related to accounting careers.
2. Understand entry-level positions, advancement-level positions, educational requirements, and career opportunities in accounting.
3. Understand basic accounting concepts.

1

Accounting Careers and Concepts

ENABLING PERFORMANCE TASKS

After studying Chapter 1, you will be able to:

a. Define terminology related to accounting careers.
b. Identify how accounting is a foundation for careers and personal financial life.
c. Identify the differences in the work of accountants, bookkeepers, accounting clerks, and general office clerks.
d. Identify applications of eleven basic accounting concepts.

One important decision a person makes in a lifetime is how to earn a living. Citizens must earn a living and successfully manage their personal finances. In the United States there are many careers for which people can prepare. The accounting field has many career opportunities for young persons.

WHAT IS ACCOUNTING?

Every business manager and owner needs *good* financial information to make *good* business decisions. Orderly records of businesses' financial activities are called accounting records. Planning, keeping, analyzing, and interpreting financial records is called accounting.

Both large and small profit-making organizations use accounting information to make decisions. Managers and owners use accounting information to decide if the profits are sufficient. Should selling prices be increased or decreased? How many workers should be employed? Should different or additional products be sold? Should the size of a business be increased or decreased? Non-profit organizations, such as churches, social clubs, and city governments must keep expenditures within available income. Directors of non-profit organizations must decide on spending priorities to stay within the funds available. City governments must plan carefully to assure that tax rates are sufficient to provide adequate tax revenues. At the same time, city governments keep financial records to restrict expenditures to priority items. Thus, non-profit organizations also need accounting information as the basis for making decisions.

Inaccurate accounting records often contribute to business failure. Failure to *understand* accounting information can result in poor business decisions. Accounting training helps business owners and managers avoid business failure.

Business speaks an accounting language

Accounting is often referred to as the language of business. Everyone in business must be able to use this language. Typists use accounting terms in typing financial statements and other accounting reports. Sales clerks or general office clerks prepare basic accounting papers. Secretaries use basic accounting language in taking dictation and preparing correspondence. These workers do their jobs better if they have some accounting knowledge and can use accounting terms. Many common accounting terms are used in all phases of business.

Accounting in everyday life

Wage earners must prepare and submit personal federal income tax reports. Many states and cities require that wage earners submit similar tax reports. Everyone must plan ways to balance expenses with available income. Persons who know basic accounting principles and concepts are better able to plan and keep adequate personal records.

Some persons use a knowledge of accounting as a means of earning a living. Almost all persons use a knowledge of accounting in personal financial activities.

OCCUPATIONAL OPPORTUNITIES IN ACCOUNTING

The many available accounting jobs can be grouped into major categories. The four major accounting job categories are: accountants, bookkeepers, accounting clerks, and general office clerks.

Persons who plan, summarize, analyze, and interpret accounting information are called accountants. Persons who do general accounting work plus some summarizing and analyzing are often called bookkeepers. Persons who record, sort, and file accounting information are often called accounting clerks. Persons doing general kinds of office tasks, including some accounting tasks, are called general office clerks.

The U.S. Department of Labor has reported that over 1,800,000 persons are employed as bookkeeping workers and accountants. In addition, many hundreds of thousands of general office clerks do some accounting tasks. Many more persons are employed in areas where some accounting knowledge is needed. Some of these areas include banking, teaching, finance, automated processing, and management.

In 1978, the U.S. Department of Labor reported that 1,800,000 persons were employed as accountants or bookkeeping workers. In 1980, the Department of Labor estimated that there would be approximately 150,000 job openings for accountants and bookkeeping workers *every year* through 1990.

An increasing amount of future accounting work will be done using automated equipment. However, the estimated future personnel needs show that use of automated processing is not decreasing the need for accounting workers. The need for accountants and bookkeepers is expected to rise in spite of the expanded use of office machines. Business continues to need accountants, bookkeepers, and accounting clerks.

Accountants

Accountants plan accounting systems used by business. Accountants also interpret financial information and check the accuracy of that information. Accountants often supervise work of other accounting workers. In medium to large businesses, accountants help owners and managers make financial decisions.

Some accountants work as members of accounting firms that sell accounting services to other businesses. For example, a small grocery store may not need a full-time accountant. The owner or an employee normally does the day-to-day accounting tasks. These tasks include recording, summarizing, and reporting basic accounting information. To plan, summarize, analyze, and interpret accounting information, the owner hires an accounting firm. A business selling accounting services to the general public is called a **public accounting firm**. Public accounting firms provide a variety of accounting services to other businesses and individuals. Accounting services may include all accounting tasks as well as planning an accounting system. Accounting firms may periodically check the accuracy of a business' records and prepare annual statements and reports.

> person
> coordination of payroll activities. Salary depends on training and experience.
>
> **ACCOUNTANT.** Local mfgr. has opening for accountant to supervise gen'l and cost accounting.
>
> **ACCOUNTANT NEEDED.** Seeking person with degree and 2-3 yrs. experience. Duties include credit and general accounting. Advancement to supervisory position possible.
>
> **ACCOUNTS PAYABLE CLERK**
> Immediate opening for an accounts payable clerk. Retail. Automated

The help-wanted advertisements shown in this chapter are typical of those found daily in newspapers throughout the U.S.

Some accountants are employed by a single business. Private accountants' work is similar to that done by public accounting firms. However, a private accountant works for only one business.

Bookkeepers

A bookkeeper's tasks include recording, summarizing, and reporting basic accounting information. In a few businesses, bookkeepers may help owners and managers interpret accounting information. Many small or medium businesses employ a public accountant to plan an accounting system. However, a bookkeeper does all the remaining accounting tasks.

Bookkeepers in small firms also may do additional general office work. Many businesses want bookkeepers with typing and filing skills. These two general office skills are closely related to the preparation of accounting reports.

FULL CHARGE BOOKKEEPER
Research company needs accurate bookkeeper. Work without supervision. Experience must include ledger and payroll.

BOOKKEEPER/CLERICAL
Accts. receivable, ledger, and general office experience. Accurate typing a must.

Accounting clerks

Some businesses have large quantities of day-to-day accounting tasks to be done. These businesses do not want their highly-trained accountants doing the routine work. Instead, accounting clerks are responsible for day-to-day accounting tasks. Accountants are then free to plan and interpret financial information as well as supervise other accounting workers.

Accounting clerks' job titles often describe the accounting records on which they work. For example, an accounting clerk working with payroll records is sometimes known as a payroll clerk. Other common job titles include accounts receivable clerk, cash receipts clerk, inventory clerk, and vouchers clerk. These accounting clerks work with a small part of the total accounting activities. However, accounting clerks who know the total accounting system understand the importance of the work being done. Also, knowledge of a total accounting system helps an accounting clerk earn promotion to more responsible positions.

office experience. Accurate typing a must.

ACCOUNTS PAYABLE CLERK
Immediate opening for an accounts payable clerk. Retail. Automated systems. Will train right person.

PAYROLL CLERK
Immediate opening for a responsible person in payroll dept. Duties include coordination of payroll activities. Salary depends on training and experience.

General office clerks

Most office workers do some accounting work. A secretary may handle cash payments from a small cash fund. A typist may type accounting reports. A salesperson may prepare sales invoices.

Accounting tasks performed by general office clerks must be done according to basic accounting concepts and procedures. All persons performing some accounting tasks need to understand a business' basic accounting system. General office clerks with a knowledge of accounting better understand the importance of the accounting tasks they do.

SECRETARY. For our sales dept. 4 yrs secl expr., type 60 wpm, and at least 1 yr bkkpg training or experience needed.

WANTED. Typist with bookkeeping background for all phases of office work.

BUILDING CAREERS IN ACCOUNTING

An important reason for studying accounting is to prepare for a career in accounting. A career in accounting may begin immediately upon graduation from high school. Also, many students use their high school study as preparation for continued accounting study at the college level.

Accounting career ladder

The first jobs that individuals get are called entry-level jobs. Persons completing high school accounting study may get entry-level jobs as bookkeepers, accounting clerks, or as general office clerks. Persons with accounting study beyond high school may get entry-level jobs as bookkeepers or accountants.

The illustration below represents careers in accounting. The bottom step of the ladder represents those office jobs which are not primarily accounting. These jobs do however include some accounting tasks.

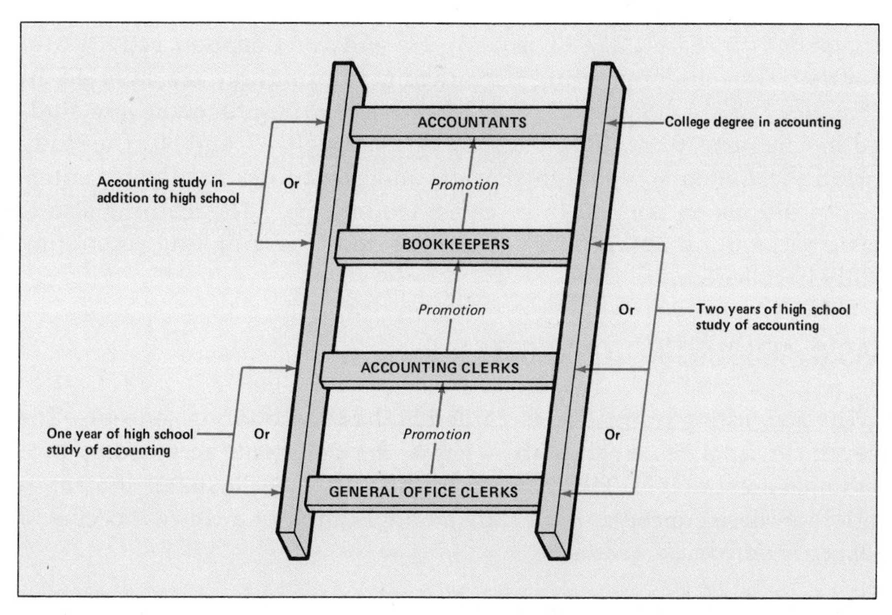

Accounting career ladder

The second career ladder step, accounting clerks, is where most persons with one year of high school accounting study may find entry-level jobs. Some individuals with two years of accounting study can obtain entry-level jobs as bookkeepers, the third career ladder step. With experience, accounting clerks often can earn promotion to the next career ladder step. However, persons with both high school accounting study and experience are preferred when promotions are made.

Persons with college accounting education usually obtain entry-level jobs on the top career ladder step as accountants. Many professional ac-

countants also earn the Certified Public Accountant (CPA) designation. Each state sets standards that persons must meet to earn the CPA. These standards usually include passing a rigorous examination and having a specified amount of accounting experience. In some states, college accounting study can be substituted for some of the required experience. The CPA designation is important to professional accountants. The public knows that CPA's are accounting professionals. Public accounting firms often require that accounting employees earn a CPA to be eligible for promotion to top positions. Many businesses also require that top accounting persons earn the CPA designation.

Starting a career in accounting

High school accounting study is an important step to an accounting career. Students completing study using this textbook will have a broad background in accounting principles, skills, and concepts. The study will include day-to-day accounting tasks such as analyzing and recording financial information. Various typical accounting records are studied in Chapters 2, 5, 6, 11, 12, 13, 20, 21, 22, and 23. Common activities in summarizing and reporting accounting information are studied in Chapters 7, 8, 14, 15, and 27. Specialized accounting functions are studied in Chapters 10, 17, 18, 19, 22, 23, 24, 25, 26, 28, 29, and 30. The study includes common accounting concepts and procedures needed for entry-level positions on the first three career ladder steps. The learning also is basic background for earning promotions and for continuing accounting study in college.

BASIC ACCOUNTING CONCEPTS

The accounting profession is guided by basic accounting concepts. The eleven concepts described in this chapter are commonly accepted by professional accountants. The material in this textbook illustrates the application of these concepts. Each time an application of a concept occurs, a concept reference is given.

CONCEPT: Accounting Period Cycle

Financial changes are reported for a specific period of time in the form of financial statements.

Accounting records are summarized periodically and reported to business owners or managers. The reports or statements are prepared for a specific period of time. The period of time may be once every month, every three months, every six months, or every year. Most individuals summarize personal financial information once every year in order to prepare tax reports.

CONCEPT: Adequate Disclosure

Financial statements should contain all information necessary for a reader to understand a business' financial condition.

Many persons need financial information about a business. These persons include owners, managers, bankers, and other executives. *All* financial information *must be* reported if good business decisions are to be made. A financial statement with incomplete information is similar to a book with some of the pages missing. The complete story is not told.

CONCEPT: Business Entity

A business' financial information is recorded and reported separately from the owner's personal financial information.

A person can own a business and also own a personal house and car. However, a business' financial records should *not* show information about personal houses and cars. Financial records for a business and for its owner's personal belongings should not be mixed. One bank account is used for the owner and another for the business. A business exists separately from its owner.

CONCEPT: Conservatism

When more than one accounting method is acceptable, the one used should result in the least amount of reported earnings or value of assets.

A business sells items to customers. What is the value of the items on hand for sale? Murray's Lumber Company paid 45¢ each for fence posts which are for sale to customers. The posts were bought a month ago. Today, Murray's would have to pay 50¢ each for the same posts. What is the value of the fence posts to Murray's? A common accounting practice is to use the lower of the price paid (cost) or what items now cost (market). In Murray's case, the cost is 45¢ and the current market price is 50¢. Therefore, Murray's will value the fence posts at 45¢, the more conservative value. At the same time, Murray's paid $11.00 each for wooden storm doors for sale to customers. The current market price is $10.00. Murray's would value the storm doors at the lower value, market, $10.00.

CONCEPT: Consistent Reporting

In the preparation of financial statements, the same accounting principles are applied in the same way in each accounting period.

Sally Holland walked to school this year. Last year Sally drove a car to school. Sally tells friends that getting to school cost less this year than last. Without knowing that a different method of getting to school was used, the friends cannot really understand Sally's report.

Owners and managers use information on financial statements when making business decisions. Financial information for one year is often compared to the previous year as a basis for making decisions. If accounting information is recorded differently from one year to the next, information reported on financial statements cannot be compared. Unless changes make information more easily understood, changes in accounting methods or statements are not made.

CONCEPT: Going Concern

Financial statements are prepared with the expectation that a business will remain in operation indefinitely.

Businesses are started with the expectation that they will be successful. Owners expect to continue operating their businesses well into the future. For example, Harry Landon starts a grocery store expecting to continue the business until he retires. Upon retirement, Mr. Landon expects to sell the business. He expects the new owner to continue the store's operation. All accounting records and statements are prepared as though the business will continue even after the present owner is gone. Even though the opposite eventually may be true, Mr. Landon expects his grocery store to continue in business indefinitely.

CONCEPT: Historical Cost

The actual amount paid or received is the amount recorded in accounting records.

A delivery truck is advertised at a sale price of $9,000.00. However, a business arranges to buy the truck for $8,500.00. The truck is recorded at a value of $8,500.00.

John Chan buys a used sports car in 1978 for $5,000.00. He spends an additional $4,000.00 customizing the car. His total historical cost is $9,000.00. John believes he can sell the customized car in 1982 for $11,000.00. The car has become a collector's item. However, the only definite value John knows is the actual amount paid, $9,000.00. Accounting practice requires that all things be recorded at a historical value that is known. John's records should show the car's value as $9,000.00.

CONCEPT: Matching Expenses with Revenue

Revenue from business activities and expenses associated with earning that revenue are recorded in the same accounting period.

Jane Piedmont operates a home decorating service. In November, she spends $30.00 for gasoline driving back and forth to a customer's home. She also spends $270.00 for supplies. These amounts are expenses for her business. Ms. Piedmont receives $400.00 for her services to this customer. She should record the revenue ($400.00) and the expenses

($300.00) in the same accounting period. Ms. Piedmont's financial statements for November will show how much she earned ($400.00) and how much it cost her to earn it ($300.00).

CONCEPT: Objective Evidence

Each transaction is described by a business document that proves the transaction did occur.

Only business transactions that actually did occur should be recorded if accurate financial statements are to be prepared. The amounts recorded also must be accurate and true. Nearly all business transactions result in the preparation of a business form. One way to check the accuracy of accounting records is to look at the business papers giving details for transactions. For example, checks are prepared for cash payments. Receipts are prepared for cash received. Sales slips are prepared for goods sold. Every accounting entry is supported by a business form or paper. When accounting information needs to be checked, accountants can look at the supporting business paper or form.

CONCEPT: Realization of Revenue

Revenue from business transactions is recorded when goods or services are sold.

Some businesses sell goods or services for cash only. Other businesses sell goods or services on one date but receive payment on a later date. For example, Marilyn Muldoon buys some personal items on credit. On October 25 she buys a dress from Junior Tops for $65.00. On November 15 she pays her account at the store. Junior Tops records the dress as sold for $65.00 on October 25. Revenue is recorded when the sale is made, not necessarily when the cash is received.

CONCEPT: Unit of Measurement

All business transactions are recorded in a common unit of measurement — the dollar.

Accounting records are used to prepare financial reports. Reports would not be clear if part of the information were in dollars and part in pesos. A hamburger shop could report the number of hamburgers sold. However, the owner would not know if the shop was earning a profit. Also, a financial report might show that 50 hamburgers and 30 ham sandwiches were sold. The owner would not know which kind of food was bringing in the most money. A record might be kept showing that the expenses were 50 dozen hamburger buns and 13 pounds of meat. The revenue is shown as 45 hamburgers. The report still does not show if the shop is earning a profit. All values are reported in a common unit of measurement.

In the United States, accounting records are kept in dollar values. (Of course, in Mexico, the accounting records are kept in pesos.) When financial statements are prepared, the values are all reported in a common unit — the dollar. In this way the hamburger shop knows it sold $59.50 in hamburgers and $58.50 in ham sandwiches. The amount received from each kind of food sale can be compared.

ACCOUNTING TERMS

What is the meaning of each of the following?

1. accounting records
2. accounting
3. accountants
4. bookkeepers
5. accounting clerks
6. general office clerks
7. public accounting firm
8. entry-level jobs

QUESTIONS FOR INDIVIDUAL STUDY

1. What is one of the most important things that a person does in a lifetime as described in this chapter?
2. What must a business manager or owner have in order to make good business decisions?
3. What two things are stated in this chapter as reasons for business failures?
4. Why must wage earners know accounting concepts for personal reasons?
5. What are the four major categories of jobs in accounting? 6 - 5 - 4 - 2
6. What is happening in the United States to the need for persons with accounting education?
7. What effect will the expanded use of office machines have on the estimated need for accounting workers?
8. What three kinds of things do accountants do?
9. What do public accounting firms do?
10. What is the difference between a public accountant and a private accountant?
11. What kind of accounting work do bookkeepers do?
12. What is described by actual job titles for accounting clerks?
13. Why should general office clerks also study accounting?
14. What kinds of jobs may be obtained by persons with high school accounting study?
15. What must a person do to earn the Certified Public Accountant designation?
16. Which accounting concept states that financial reports should be prepared periodically?
17. Which accounting concept states that all financial information should be reported?
18. Which accounting concept states that a business and its owner are not the same?
19. Which accounting concept states that accounting information should be reported in the same way each year?
20. Which accounting concept is based on the expectation that a business will continue to operate indefinitely?
21. Which accounting concept is based on the idea that information recorded in accounting records comes from details on a business paper?
22. Which accounting concept is being followed when financial information in a Japanese business is recorded in yen?

CASES FOR MANAGEMENT DECISION

CASE 1 Michael and Vinney, two high school students, are discussing possible careers they might go into. Michael's brother graduated from high school last year. His brother obtained an entry-level job as an accounting clerk. Michael says that he is not going to study accounting in high school. His reason is that he does not want to spend the rest of his life as an accounting clerk, like his brother. Michael wants a job supervising other workers. Vinney has the same career objective as Michael. However, he is planning to study high school accounting. Is the reasoning of Michael or Vinney better?

CASE 2 Arlene is planning her high school course selections. She would like to do accounting work as a career after she completes high school. For this reason she plans to take two years of high school accounting study. However, she is not planning to take any other business courses. Arlene's parents suggest that she also plan to take a typewriting course. Whose thinking is better in this matter? Explain.

CASE 3 Holder Company needs a new typewriter. Business A offers to sell a new typewriter for $630.00. Business B's price for a new typewriter is $550.00. Business C offers a price of $690.00. After considering the cost and features of the three typewriters, Holder Company buys a typewriter from Business A for $630.00.What value should be recorded by Holder Company for the typewriter? Explain.

CASE 4 Linda Morrison starts a new business. During the first year, Mrs. Morrison sometimes uses the family car for business purposes. All expenses for operating the car are paid by and recorded as expenses of the business. These expenses include license plates, gasoline, oil, tune-up, and new tires. Are Mrs. Morrison's procedures acceptable? Explain.

CASE 5 Charles Brown does the accounting work for his own business. When money is received from customers, Mr. Brown usually prepares a cash receipt form. Sometimes, when Mr. Brown is very busy with customers, he does not take time to prepare a receipt form for each amount of cash received. Instead, he writes the amounts received on a sheet of paper which he carries in his pocket. At the end of the day he records all the amounts written on the sheet of paper. Do you approve of Mr. Brown's procedures? Explain.

2 ACCOUNTING FOR A SERVICE BUSINESS

GENERAL BEHAVIORAL GOALS

1. Know accounting terminology related to a service business organized as a sole proprietorship.
2. Understand accounting principles and practices for a service business organized as a sole proprietorship.
3. Demonstrate accounting procedures for a service business organized as a sole proprietorship.

Putt Around, the business for Part 2, is a miniature golf facility.

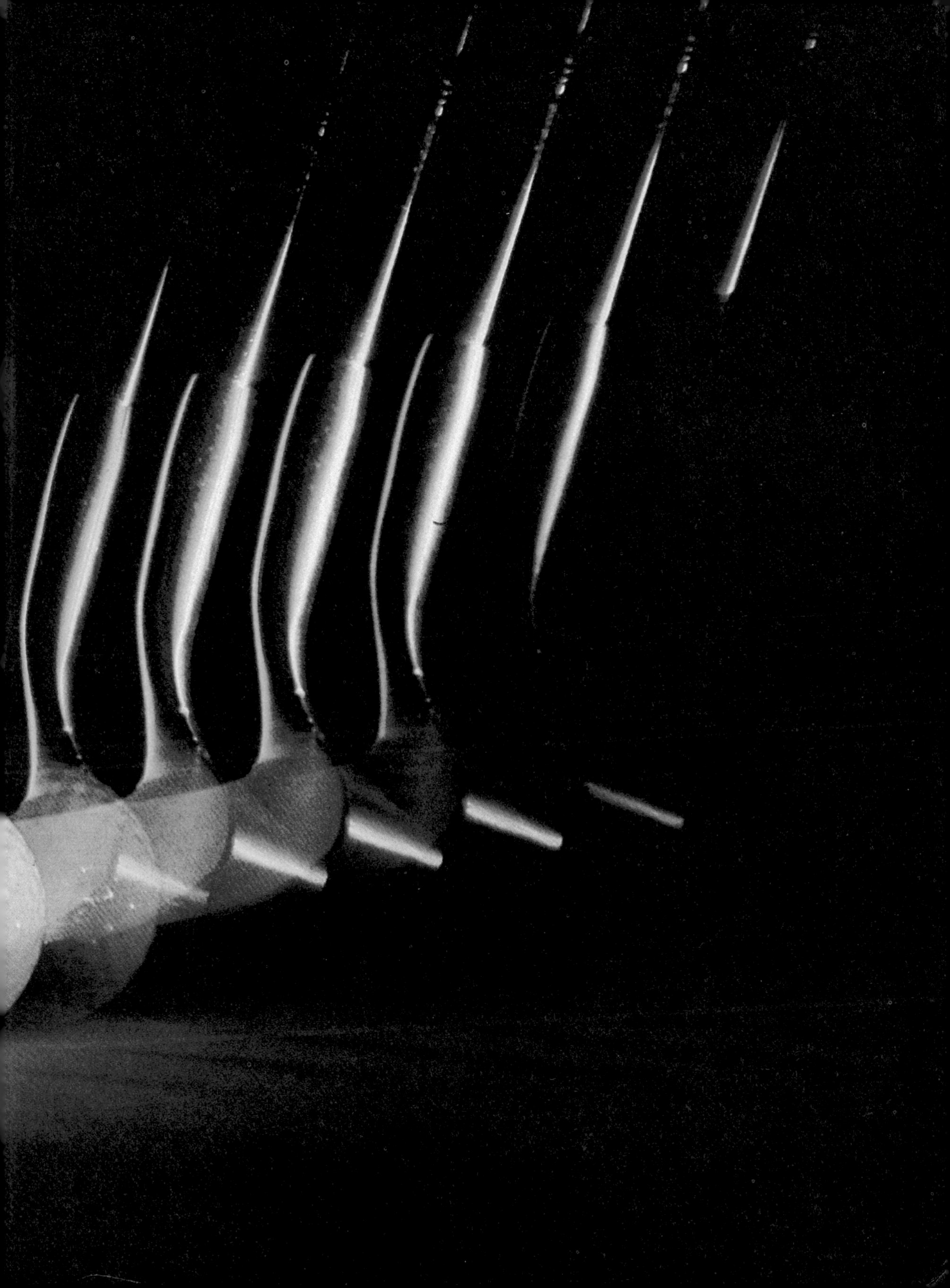

PUTT AROUND
Chart of Accounts

(1) ASSETS	Account Number
Cash	11
Supplies	12
Golf Equipment	13
Maintenance Equipment	14
(2) LIABILITIES	
Melcor Equipment Company	21
Sasson Supply Company	22
(3) CAPITAL	
Harry Rossi, Capital	31
Harry Rossi, Drawing	32
Income Summary	33

(4) REVENUE	Account Number
Sales	41
(5) EXPENSES	
Advertising Expense	51
Miscellaneous Expense	52
Rent Expense	53
Utilities Expense	54

The chart of accounts for Putt Around is illustrated above for ready reference as you study Part 2 of this textbook.

2 Starting an Accounting System

ENABLING PERFORMANCE TASKS

After studying Chapter 2, you will be able to:

a. Define accounting terms related to starting an accounting system.
b. Identify the accounting concepts and principles used in deciding on the procedures for starting an accounting system.
c. Classify financial items as assets, liabilities, or capital.
d. Prepare a beginning balance sheet for a small service business.
e. Record an opening entry in a two-column general journal.
f. Open accounts in a ledger guided by a chart of accounts.
g. Post an opening entry from a journal to a ledger.

Accounting records are needed to manage a business properly and to prepare financial reports. Accounting information may be recorded by hand, on accounting machines, or on automated equipment. The kind and size of a business determines how its accounting records are best kept. Regardless of the methods used, the accounting concepts and principles are the same.

THE ACCOUNTING EQUATION

The value of what a business owns equals the financial rights people have in the business. Anything of value that a business owns is called an asset. The financial rights to the assets of a business are called equities. The records and financial reports of a business are kept separate from the records of the persons supplying the assets. *(CONCEPT: Business Entity)*

A concept reference indicates an application of a specific accounting concept. For a complete statement and description of the concept, refer to pages 8–12 of Chapter 1.

In accounting, assets always equal equities. There are two kinds of equities. (1) *Equity of persons outside a business to whom amounts are owed.* An amount owed by a business is called a liability. (2) *Equity of the owner of a business.* The owner's equity is what remains when the value of liabilities is subtracted from the value of assets. The value of the owner's equity, or share of a business, is called capital.

An equation showing the relationship between the assets and equities of a business is called the accounting equation. The basic accounting equation is most often written as:

ASSETS = LIABILITIES + CAPITAL

STARTING AN ACCOUNTING SYSTEM

Harry Rossi operates a miniature golf business known as Putt Around. A business owned by one person is called a sole proprietorship. The property used by the business is rented. The business does furnish the equipment and supplies. Putt Around is expected to make money and to continue in business indefinitely. *(CONCEPT: Going Concern)*

Mr. Rossi decides to start a new accounting system for his business. To start a new system, he needs to list the assets and equities of the business. He lists these items on July 1, 1982.

What is owned (assets)	
Cash on hand and in bank.	$1,100.00
Supplies	500.00
Golf Equipment	2,200.00
Maintenance Equipment	900.00
Total owned	$4,700.00

What is owed (liabilities)	
Melcor Equipment Company	$ 650.00
Sasson Supply Company	550.00
Total owed	$1,200.00

Mr. Rossi figures his equity (capital) as: Assets, $4,700.00, *minus* liabilities, $1,200.00, *equals* capital, $3,500.00. The information for the new accounting system in equation form is below.

ASSETS	=	LIABILITIES	+	CAPITAL
$4,700.00	=	$1,200.00	+	$3,500.00

Information in the records of a business is recorded in a common unit. In the United States the common unit of measurement is the dollar. *(CONCEPT: Unit of Measurement)*

A BALANCE SHEET

Details about the assets and equities, expressed as an accounting equation, are reported on a business form. A business form that reports the assets, liabilities, and capital on a specific date is called a balance sheet. A balance sheet presents a complete and accurate report of a business' assets and equities. *(CONCEPT: Adequate Disclosure)* The balance sheet for Putt Around prepared on July 1, 1982, is below.

Putt Around
Balance Sheet
July 1, 1982

Assets		Liabilities	
Cash	1100 00	Melcor Equipment Co.	650 00
Supplies	500 00	Sasson Supply Co.	550 00
Golf Equipment	2200 00	Total Liabilities	1200 00
Maintenance Equip.	900 00	Capital	
		Harry Rossi, Capital	3500 00
Total Assets	4700 00	Total Liab. and Capital	4700 00

Heading of a balance sheet

The heading of a balance sheet includes three lines. (1) The name of the business. (2) The name of the report. (3) The date for which the report is prepared.

Body of a balance sheet

The body of the balance sheet prepared for Putt Around is in the shape of a capital T. The report has three major sections.

BALANCE SHEET	
Assets	Liabilities and Capital

1. **Assets.** Assets are listed on the left side of the report.

2. **Liabilities.** The liabilities are listed on the right side of the report.

3. **Capital.** The amount of the capital is listed beneath the liabilities on the right side of the report.

The right side of the balance sheet for Putt Around shows the equities of the business. The liabilities have first claim against the assets of a business. If the assets were to be sold and distributed, the liabilities owed would be paid first. Then the owners would be paid. For this reason the liabilities are listed on a balance sheet before the owner's capital.

On a completed balance sheet, the total of the left side must be the same as the total of the right side. A balance sheet shows the same relationship between assets and equities as does the accounting equation.

BALANCE SHEET			
Total Assets	=	Total Equities	
		Liabilities	1,200.00
		+ Capital	3,500.00
4,700.00	=		4,700.00

STEPS IN PREPARING A BALANCE SHEET

Five steps are followed in preparing the balance sheet, page 19.

1 Write the heading on three lines. Center each line.

2 Prepare the assets section on the left side.

- Write the word *Assets* in the center of the first line of the left wide column. List the name and amount of each asset beginning on the next line.

3 Prepare the liabilities section on the right side.

- Write the word *Liabilities* in the center on the first line of the right wide column. List the name and amount of each liability. Rule a single line across the amount column directly under the last amount. Write the total amount of the liabilities in the amount column. Write the words *Total Liabilities* in the wide column on the same line.

4 Prepare the capital section immediately below the liabilities section on the right side.

- Write the word *Capital* in the middle of the wide column on the next line. Write the name of the owner and the word *Capital* on the next line. Write the amount of the owner's equity on the same line in the same amount column.

5 Determine that the balance sheet is "in balance" and complete the form.

- Draw a single line across both the left and right amount columns under the last amount in the right amount column. Add both the left and right amount columns. The two column totals must be the same. Write the words *Total Assets* in the left wide column on the same line as the total. Write the words *Total Liabilities and Capital* in the right wide column. Rule double lines across both amount columns directly under each final amount. The double lines show that the work is completed and the balance sheet is "in balance."

If necessary to fit the space available, the words written on any line of the balance sheet may be abbreviated. However, if space is available, words are not abbreviated in accounting records. Limited use of abbreviations makes reading easier by other persons.

RECORDING A BEGINNING BALANCE SHEET

Financial information about a business is first recorded in chronological order. This means that the information is recorded according to dates or in the order that it happens. A beginning balance sheet is the first information to be recorded in a new accounting system.

A journal

The record in which accounting information is recorded in chronological order is called a journal. Each item recorded in a journal is called an entry. An entry to record information from a beginning balance sheet is called an opening entry. There are different kinds of journals. The nature of a business and the number of entries to be made determine the kind of journal to be used.

A general journal. A journal with two amount columns in which all kinds of entries can be recorded is called a general journal. The two-column general journal used by Putt Around is below.

GENERAL JOURNAL PAGE

	DATE		ACCOUNT TITLE	POST. REF.	DEBIT	CREDIT	
1							1
2							2
3							3

Standard form of two-column general journal

Source document for an entry. When an entry is made in a journal, there should be some written business form to support the entry. The business paper from which information is obtained for a journal entry is called a source document.

The source document for the opening entry of Putt Around is the beginning balance sheet on page 19. (CONCEPT: Objective Evidence) The amounts on the left side of a balance sheet are recorded in the left or Debit column of a general journal. The amounts on the right side of a balance sheet are recorded in the right or Credit column of a general journal.

The meaning of the amount column headings, *Debit* and *Credit*, is explained later in this chapter.

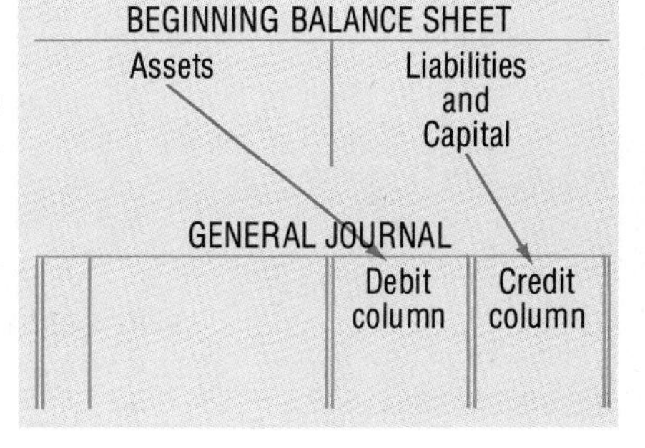

Relationship of items on beginning balance sheet to general journal columns

A journal entry. Every journal entry has four parts. (1) The date of the entry. (2) The debit part of the entry. (3) The credit part of the entry. (4) An explanation or source document number.

Recording an opening entry

Each of the four parts of an opening entry is recorded as explained below.

1 ***Date of entry.*** Write the date of the opening entry in the Date column of the journal. The year and month are written only once on a general journal page in the Date column.

GENERAL JOURNAL PAGE 1

	DATE		ACCOUNT TITLE	POST. REF.	DEBIT	CREDIT	
1	1982 July	1	Cash		1 100 00		1
2			Supplies		500 00		2
3			Golf Equipment		2 200 00		3
4			Maintenance Equipment		900 00		4
5			Melcor Equipment Company			650 00	5
6			Sasson Supply Company			550 00	6
7			Harry Rossi, Capital			3 500 00	7
8			Balance sheet, July 1, 1982.				8
9							9
10							10
11							11

Complete opening entry for Putt Around

2 ***Debit part of entry.*** Write the debit part of the opening entry. Write the name of each asset at the left edge of the Account Title column. Write the amount of each asset in the Debit column.

3 ***Credit part of entry.*** Write the credit part of the opening entry. Write the name of each liability and the name of the owner in the Account Title column. Write the word *Capital* after the owner's name. Indent the liability and capital account names about 1 centimeter (about one-half inch) from the left edge of the Account Title column. Write the amount of each credit item in the Credit column.

Indenting the names of the credit items helps to separate the debit and credit parts of the entry.

4 ***Reason for entry.*** Write the words *Balance Sheet, July 1, 1982*. For most entries, write the name or number of the source document as the fourth part of the entry. Persons who need more information can refer to the source document for details. The explanation is indented about 2 centimeters (about one inch) from the left of the Account Title column. This indentation helps separate the explanation from the credit part of the entry.

The use of the Post. Ref. column in the journal will be explained later in this chapter.

Checking an entry for accuracy

The total of the left side of a balance sheet is the same as the total of the right side. Also, the total debit amounts in a journal entry must be the same as the total credit amounts.

In the opening entry on page 22, the total of the debit amount column is $4,700.00. The total of the credit amount column is also $4,700.00. The debit part of the entry is equal to the credit part. The entry is in balance. As each entry is recorded in a journal, the equality of debits and credits must be checked.

POSTING TO A LEDGER

As a business conducts daily activities, changes occur in the value of balance sheet items. Goods and services are bought and sold. Cash is received. Cash is paid out. Supplies are bought. For example, Putt Around receives cash each time a customer plays a game of miniature golf. Accounting records should show any changes that occur.

A ledger

A separate record is kept of each asset, each liability, and the capital of a business. Changes in each of these items must be brought together in one place. This separate record will show how each item has changed. An accounting form used to sort and summarize changes in a specific item is called an account. A group of accounts is called a ledger. The separate accounts in a ledger may be on ledger cards, ledger sheets, or on sheets bound in book form.

Two-column account form. Account forms are printed in various ways. One form has two amount columns: a Debit amount column and a Credit amount column. The two-column account form is below.

ACCOUNT — ACCOUNT NO.

DATE	ITEM	POST. REF.	DEBIT	DATE	ITEM	POST. REF.	CREDIT
	Entries on the left side are debit entries				Entries on the right side are credit entries		

Two-column account form

The two-column account form has two sides, each with the same ruling. The left side of a two-column account form is called the debit side. The right side of a two-column account form is called the credit side.

When an entry is made on the left side of an account, it is referred to as a debit. An entry on the right side is referred to as a credit. The abbreviations *Dr.* for Debit and *Cr.* for Credit are commonly used in accounting.

Chart of accounts. Each account in a ledger is given a name and a number. A name given to a separate ledger account is called an account title. A number given to an account is called an account number. An account number usually shows the account's location in a ledger. The ledger contains an account for each item on the beginning balance sheet.

A list of account titles and numbers showing the location of the accounts in a ledger is called a chart of accounts. A partial chart of accounts for Putt Around is below.

Putt Around
Chart of Accounts

(1) Assets	Account Number	(2) Liabilities	Account Number
Cash	11	Melcor Equipment Company	21
Supplies	12	Sasson Supply Company	22
Golf Equipment	13		
Maintenance Equipment	14	(3) Capital	
		Harry Rossi, Capital	31

Partial chart of accounts

The complete chart of accounts for Putt Around is on page 16.

The first digit of each account number shows in which division of the ledger the account is located. The chart of accounts above shows three divisions of the ledger. (1) Assets. (2) Liabilities. (3) Capital. All asset account numbers begin with *1* to show that the accounts are in the first division of the ledger. All liability account numbers begin with *2*. The capital account number begins with *3*.

The second digit of each account number shows the order in which an account is listed in each division. For example, in Putt Around's chart of accounts above Cash is numbered *11*. The second digit of this number shows that Cash is the first account in the asset division. The account number for Sasson Supply Company is *22*. The second digit of this number shows that Sasson Supply Company is the second account in the liabilities division.

Some businesses use more than two digits for account numbers. Charts of accounts with more than two digits are used and explained in later chapters.

Opening accounts in a ledger

Writing an account title and account number on the heading of an account form is called opening an account. An account is opened in the ledger for each item listed in a chart of accounts. Accounts are opened in the ledger in the same order that they appear on a chart of accounts.

Cash is the first account on the chart of accounts for Putt Around, page 24. The cash account is opened as explained below.

1 Write the name of the account, *Cash*, after the word Account in the heading of the account.

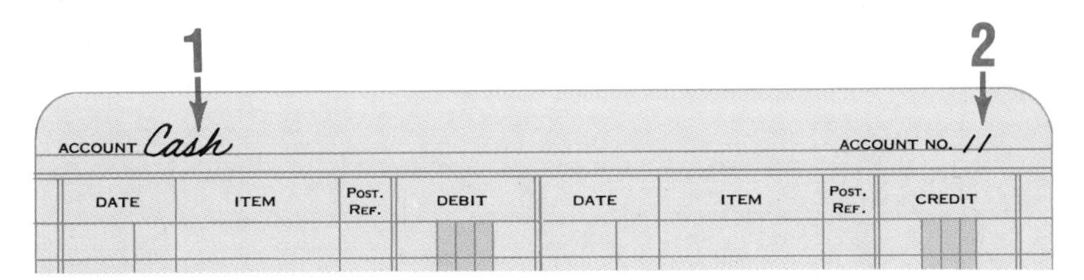

Opening the cash account

2 Write the account number, *11*, after the words Account No.

This procedure is used in opening all accounts on Putt Around's complete chart of accounts, page 16.

Posting an opening entry

Each amount in an opening entry is transferred to a ledger account. Transferring information from journal entries to ledger accounts is called posting. Posting sorts the information so that all activities affecting a single account are brought together in one place. For example, all information about changes in Cash are brought together in the cash account.

Posting the debit items of an opening entry. The steps in posting the debit items of an opening entry are below.

1 Write the *amount* of the cash debit, *$1,100.00*, in the Debit column of the cash account.

2 Write the *date* of the journal entry, *1982, July 1,* in the Date column. The year and the month are written only once on the same side of an account. The day is written once for each entry posted to an account.

3 Write the word *Balance* in the Item column of the account. The word Balance helps to separate the beginning balance in the account from other entries posted later.

GENERAL JOURNAL PAGE 1

	DATE		ACCOUNT TITLE	POST. REF.	DEBIT	CREDIT	
1	1982 July	1	Cash		110000		1
2			Supplies		50000		2
3			Golf Equipment		220000		3
4			Maintenance Equipment		90000		4
5			Melcor Equipment Company			65000	5
6			Sasson Supply Company			55000	6
7			Harry Rossi, Capital			350000	7
8			Balance sheet, July 1, 1982.				8
9							9

ACCOUNT Cash ACCOUNT NO. 11

DATE		ITEM	POST. REF.	DEBIT	DATE		ITEM	POST. REF.	CREDIT
1982 July	1	Balance		110000					

First three steps in posting a debit entry to a ledger account

The final two steps in posting are to cross-reference the information. One part of the cross-reference tells where the entry in an account came from. The other part shows in the journal the account number to which the amount was posted. This cross-referencing is below.

GENERAL JOURNAL PAGE 1

	DATE		ACCOUNT TITLE	POST. REF.	DEBIT	CREDIT	
1	1982 July	1	Cash	11	110000		1
2			Supplies		50000		2
3			Golf Equipment		220000		3
4			Maintenance Equipment		90000		4
5			Melcor Equipment Company			65000	5
6			Sasson Supply Company			55000	6
7			Harry Rossi, Capital			350000	7
8			Balance sheet, July 1, 1982.				8
9							9

ACCOUNT Cash ACCOUNT NO. 11

DATE		ITEM	POST. REF.	DEBIT	DATE		ITEM	POST. REF.	CREDIT
1982 July	1	Balance	G1	110000					

Posting references in accounts and journals

4 Write *G1* in the Post. Ref. column of the cash account. The *G1* shows that the entry came from page 1 of the general journal.

> The *G* is used to show that this entry is posted from the *G*eneral journal.

5 Return to the journal and write the account number, *11*, in the Post. Ref. column of the journal. This notation shows to which account the item in the journal was posted.

> A person checking the records knows at a glance which items in a journal have not been posted. The items without account numbers in the Post. Ref. column have not been posted. For this reason, placing the account numbers in the journal Post. Ref. column *must* be the last step in posting.

The same five steps are used in posting all debit items in an opening entry.

Posting the credit items of an opening entry. The same five steps used to post debit items are used to post credit items of an opening entry. However, the items are posted to the *credit* side of the accounts involved.

GENERAL JOURNAL — PAGE 1

	Date		Account Title	Post. Ref.	Debit	Credit	
1	1982 July	1	Cash	11	1100 00		1
2			Supplies	12	500 00		2
3			Golf Equipment	13	2200 00		3
4			Maintenance Equipment	14	900 00		4
5			Melcor Equipment Company	21		650 00	5
6			Sasson Supply Company			550 00	6
7			Harry Rossi, Capital			3500 00	7
8			Balance sheet, July 1, 1982.				8

ACCOUNT Melcor Equipment Company — ACCOUNT NO. 21

Date	Item	Post. Ref.	Debit	Date		Item	Post. Ref.	Credit
				1982 July	1	Balance	G1	650 00

Steps in posting a credit entry to a ledger account

A ledger after all items in an opening entry are posted. The ledger accounts on the next page are shown after all posting of the opening entry, page 22, is completed.

ACCOUNT *Cash* ACCOUNT NO. *11*

DATE		ITEM	POST. REF.	DEBIT	DATE		ITEM	POST. REF.	CREDIT
1982 July	*1*	*Balance*	*G1*	*1100 00*					

ACCOUNT *Supplies* ACCOUNT NO. *12*

DATE		ITEM	POST. REF.	DEBIT	DATE		ITEM	POST. REF.	CREDIT
1982 July	*1*	*Balance*	*G1*	*500 00*					

ACCOUNT *Golf Equipment* ACCOUNT NO. *13*

DATE		ITEM	POST. REF.	DEBIT	DATE		ITEM	POST. REF.	CREDIT
1982 July	*1*	*Balance*	*G1*	*2200 00*					

ACCOUNT *Maintenance Equipment* ACCOUNT NO. *14*

DATE		ITEM	POST. REF.	DEBIT	DATE		ITEM	POST. REF.	CREDIT
1982 July	*1*	*Balance*	*G1*	*900 00*					

ACCOUNT *Melcor Equipment Company* ACCOUNT NO. *21*

DATE		ITEM	POST. REF.	DEBIT	DATE		ITEM	POST. REF.	CREDIT
					1982 July	*1*	*Balance*	*G1*	*650 00*

ACCOUNT *Sasson Supply Company* ACCOUNT NO. *22*

DATE		ITEM	POST. REF.	DEBIT	DATE		ITEM	POST. REF.	CREDIT
					1982 July	*1*	*Balance*	*G1*	*550 00*

ACCOUNT *Harry Rossi, Capital* ACCOUNT NO. *31*

DATE		ITEM	POST. REF.	DEBIT	DATE		ITEM	POST. REF.	CREDIT
					1982 July	*1*	*Balance*	*G1*	*3500 00*

Ledger accounts with all items in the opening entry posted

SUMMARY OF STARTING AN ACCOUNTING SYSTEM

A diagram showing the sequence of steps involved in a procedure is called a flowchart. The flowchart below summarizes the activities involved in starting an accounting system.

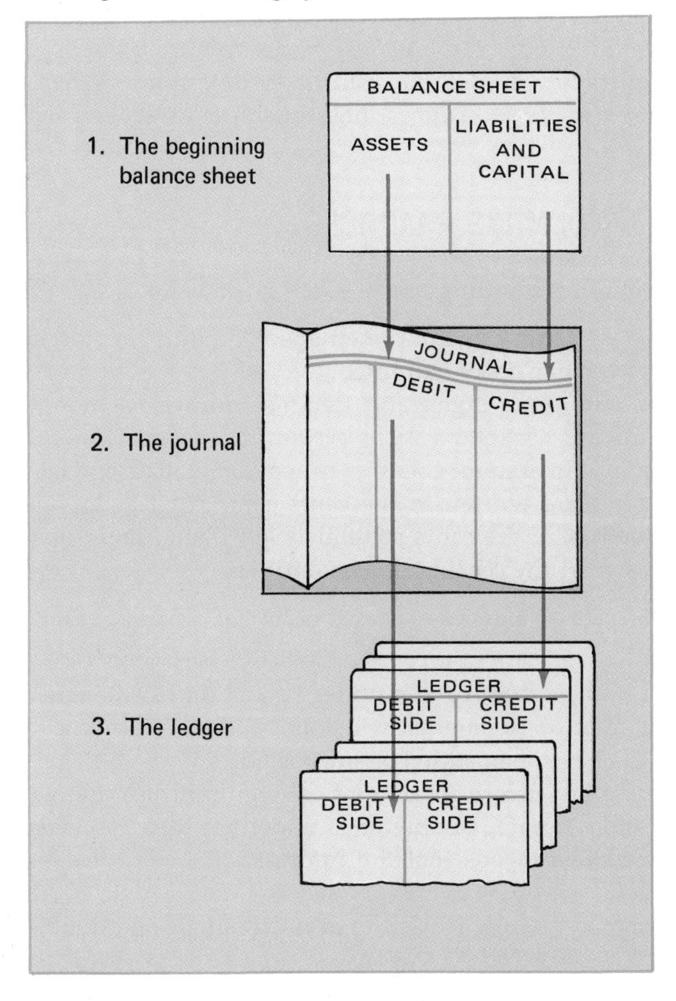

Flowchart for starting an accounting system

1. A beginning balance sheet is prepared listing the accounting equation as of the day the new accounting system is started.
2. The information on a beginning balance sheet is recorded as an opening entry. The opening entry is recorded in a journal. The assets are recorded as debits, and the equities (liabilities and capital) are recorded as credits.
3. The items recorded in the opening entry are posted to individual ledger accounts.

KEEPING BUSINESS AND PERSONAL RECORDS SEPARATE

The owner of a business has both personal and business assets. The owner also has both personal and business liabilities. The personal and business financial information must be kept separate. *(CONCEPT: Business Entity)* If the records are not kept separate, the owner will have difficulty determining how the business is doing. The owner's personal financial condition will also be difficult to determine. When a balance sheet is prepared for a business, only business assets and liabilities are listed.

COMMON ACCOUNTING PRACTICES

Some common accounting practices are given below.

1. Words are written in full when space permits. Words may be abbreviated when space is limited.
2. Dollar and cents signs and decimal points are not used when amounts are written on ruled accounting paper. Sometimes a color tint is used in amount columns to separate dollars and cents.
3. Two zeros are written in the cents column when an amount is in even dollars. If the cents column is left blank, there may be doubt later whether the cents had been omitted.

   Sometimes a dash (—) is used instead of two zeros to indicate "no cents."

4. When a single line is ruled under an amount, the single line means that a total or remainder will follow. The single line means that amounts have been added or subtracted.
5. A double line across an amount column indicates that work is complete and accurate. Double lines under the total assets amount on a balance sheet means that the information before the lines is completed.
6. For neatness, a ruler is used in drawing single and double lines.

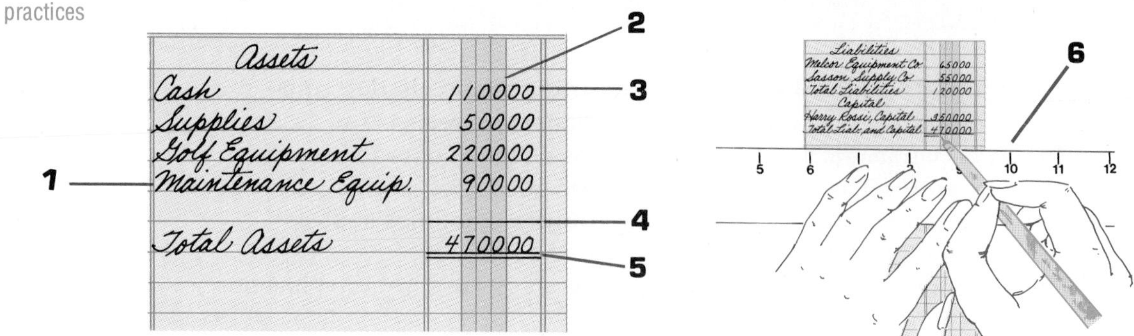

Some common accounting practices

ACCOUNTING TERMS

What is the meaning of each of the following?

1. asset
2. equities
3. liability
4. capital
5. accounting equation
6. sole proprietorship
7. balance sheet
8. journal
9. entry
10. opening entry
11. general journal
12. source document
13. account
14. ledger
15. debit side
16. credit side
17. account title
18. account number
19. chart of accounts
20. opening an account
21. posting
22. flowchart

QUESTIONS FOR INDIVIDUAL STUDY

1. Why are liabilities and capital referred to as equities?
2. Why is the basic accounting equation written *Assets = Liabilities + Capital*?
3. What three items are included in the heading of a balance sheet?
4. What kind of information is placed on the left side of a balance sheet as described in this chapter? On the right side of a balance sheet?
5. Why are double lines ruled across both amount columns of the balance sheet, page 19?
6. Why are abbreviations usually *not* used in accounting?
7. What is meant by "recording information in chronological order"?
8. What are the column headings of the two-column general journal described in this chapter?
9. In which column of a general journal should the asset amounts of the beginning balance sheet be recorded?
10. In which column of a general journal are the liability amounts of the beginning balance sheet recorded?
11. In which column of a general journal is the amount of the capital from the beginning balance sheet recorded?
12. What are the four parts of a journal entry?
13. Why are account titles with credit amounts in the opening entry, page 22, indented in the Account Title column?
14. How can the accuracy of the opening entry, page 22, be checked?
15. Why are ledger accounts used?
16. What is the purpose of an account number?
17. The account numbers described in this chapter have two digits. What is shown by the first digit? By the second digit?
18. What does the account number 14 mean?
19. In what order are accounts opened in the ledger?
20. Why are journal entries posted?
21. Why is writing the account number in the journal Post. Ref. column the last step in posting?
22. What are the three basic activities in starting an accounting system?

CASES FOR MANAGEMENT DECISION

CASE 1 Michael Morgan started a summer lawn care business which is successful and he decides to continue it indefinitely. He realizes that he needs an accounting system to maintain necessary records. He asks your advice in starting the system. What would you do first? Where would you get the information needed to start Mr. Morgan's system for him?

CASE 2 Matilda Hormeyer is the owner of a plumbing business. Her balance for the year just ended shows her capital to be $26,000.00. The balance sheet for the end of the previous year showed her capital to be $27,500.00. What are some reasons for this decrease in capital?

CASE 3 Alice Martin started a new accounting system for her business. In the chart of accounts, she numbered all the accounts consecutively. The four asset accounts are numbered 1 to 4. The two liability accounts are numbered 5 and 6. The capital is numbered 7. Why is Miss Martin's system of numbering accounts not as satisfactory as the system described in this chapter?

DRILLS FOR UNDERSTANDING

DRILL 2-D 1 Classifying assets, liabilities, and capital

This drill gives you practice in classifying balance sheet items. The drill also gives you practice in deciding which general journal columns are used for an opening entry. Use a form similar to the one below to record your answers.

1	2	3	4	5
	Balance Sheet		General Journal	
Balance Sheet Items	Left-hand side	Right-hand side	Column in which amount in opening entry is recorded	
			Debit column	Credit column
1. Delivery equipment............	*Asset*		√	

Instructions: 1. Classify each item listed below. Write *asset, liability,* or *capital* in Columns 2 or 3 showing where on a balance sheet the item is listed.

(1) Delivery Equipment
(2) Mannies Supply Company
(3) Cash
(4) Office Equipment
(5) Office Supplies
(6) Zapata Equipment Company
(7) Dry Cleaning Equipment
(8) Supplies
(9) Golf Equipment
(10) Any amount owed
(11) Anything owned
(12) Bryan Dooley, Capital

Instructions: 2. Decide which general journal columns are used for an opening entry for each item listed in Instruction 1. If an amount goes in the debit amount column, place a check mark in Column 4. If an amount goes in the credit amount column, place a check mark in Column 5.

3. Cover your answers on the form. See how rapidly you can do this drill mentally without looking at your answers. Repeat this drill several times to increase your speed and accuracy.

DRILL 2-D 2 Preparing a chart of accounts

Fashion Barn has the items on page 33 listed on its beginning balance sheet.

Cash
Supplies
Store Equipment
Office Equipment
Delivery Equipment
A-1 Finance Company
Beulah's Garage and Repairs
Metro Office Equipment Company
Isaac Bloom, Capital

Instructions: Prepare a partial chart of accounts similar to the one on page 24.

APPLICATION PROBLEMS

PROBLEM 2-1 Preparing a beginning balance sheet

The following are assets and liabilities of Wilson's Self-Serve Laundry, owned and operated by Walter Wilson.

Assets		Liabilities	
Cash	$1,100.00	Miller's Repair Shop	$ 85.00
Supplies	320.00	Professional Appliances Company	2,900.00
Drying Equipment	3,000.00	O.K. Supply Company	150.00
Washing Equipment	5,000.00		

Instructions: 1. Prepare a beginning balance sheet for Wilson's Self-Serve Laundry. Use the date September 1 of the current year. Follow the steps in preparing a balance sheet given on page 20.

2. Check the accuracy and completeness of your work with the questions given below.

a. Is each of the items in the heading centered and on a separate line?
b. Is each of the sectional headings in the body of the balance sheet centered?
c. Are each of the assets, liabilities, and capital listed in the correct section of the balance sheet?
d. Is the amount of total assets on the same line as the amount of total liabilities and capital?
e. Are the totals at the bottom of the balance sheet the same?
f. Are the single and double lines drawn across only the amount columns?
g. Is the work neat? Is the handwriting legible?

PROBLEM 2-2 Recording an opening entry

Instructions: 1. Record an opening entry on page 1 of a general journal using the information on the balance sheet below. Use the date of August 1 of the current year.

Chu Realty Agency
Balance Sheet
August 1, 19--

Assets		Liabilities	
Cash	700 00	Mabel Allison Company	170 00
Supplies	300 00	Michael Daniels Company	550 00
Automobile Equipment	6 000 00	Teri McIntyre Company	2 000 00
Office Equipment	1 000 00	Total Liabilities	2 720 00
		Capital	
		Yi Chu, Capital	5 280 00
Total Assets	8 000 00	Total Liabilities and Capital	8 000 00

Instructions: 2. Check the accuracy of your work by asking yourself the questions given below.

a. Are the year, month, and day written at the top of the Date column in the journal?
b. Is each debit item written at the extreme left edge of the Account Title column?
c. Is each credit item in the Account Title column indented about 1 centimeter?
d. Is the indication of the source document given at the end of the opening entry? Is it written in the Account Title column? Is it indented about 2 centimeters?
e. Does the total of the debit amounts equal the total of the credit amounts?

The solution to Problem 2-2 is needed to complete Problem 2-3.

PROBLEM 2-3 Posting an opening entry

The solution to Problem 2-2 is needed to complete Problem 2-3.

Instructions: 1. Open the accounts as shown in the partial chart of accounts below.

Account Title	Account Number
Cash	11
Supplies	12
Automobile Equipment	13
Office Equipment	14
Mabel Allison Company	21
Michael Daniels Company	22
Teri McIntyre Company	23
Yi Chu, Capital	31

Instructions: 2. Post the opening entry recorded in Instruction 1 of Problem 2-2.

PROBLEM 2-4 Preparing a partial chart of accounts; preparing a beginning balance sheet; recording and posting an opening entry

Lester Sheng, a veterinarian, starts Westdell Animal Clinic. The information for the beginning balance sheet on September 1 of the current year is given below.

Assets: Cash $1,530.00; Medical Supplies, $1,350.00; Office Supplies, $810.00; Automobile, $4,860.00; Medical Equipment, $4,600.00; Kennel Equipment, $2,000.00.

Liabilities: Veterinary Supply Company, $3,000.00; Masson's Pet Store, $50.00; Medical Drug Company, $1,540.00. Capital 10560

Instructions: 1. Prepare a partial chart of accounts similar to the one on page 24.

2. Prepare a beginning balance sheet for Westdell Animal Clinic.

3. Record the opening entry for Westdell Animal Clinic. Use page 1 of a general journal.

4. Open ledger accounts for all items on the chart of accounts prepared in Instruction 1 above.

5. Post the opening entry.

ENRICHMENT PROBLEMS

MASTERY PROBLEM 2-M Preparing a beginning balance sheet; recording and posting an opening entry

Marilyn Lukens starts Lukens' Delivery Service. The information on page 35 is listed by Ms. Lukens for her beginning balance sheet.

Assets: Cash, $2,700.00; Truck Equipment, $5,300.00; Office Equipment, $2,900.00.
Liabilities: Russo's Supply Company, $2,000.00; Milton's Equipment Company, $1,200.00; Bullocks' Service Station, $96.00.

Instructions: 1. Prepare a beginning balance sheet for Lukens' Delivery Service. Use the date of September 1 of the current year. After you have prepared the beginning balance sheet, check it by asking the same questions listed in Instruction 2, Problem 2-1.

2. Record the opening entry for Lukens' Delivery Service. Use page 1 of a general journal. When you have completed the opening entry, check it by asking the same questions listed in Instruction 2, Problem 2-2.

3. Open ledger accounts for the partial chart of accounts below.

Account Title	Account Number
Cash	11
Truck Equipment	12
Office Equipment	13
Russo's Supply Company	21
Milton's Equipment Company	22
Bullocks' Service Station	23
Marilyn Lukens, Capital	31

Instructions: 4. Post the opening entry recorded in Instruction 2 above.

CHALLENGE PROBLEM 2-C Preparing a balance sheet; recording an opening entry; keeping business and personal records separate

John Botsworth has operated a dry cleaning business, Welldone Dry Cleaning, for the past month. During this time he failed to keep any records of either his dry cleaning business or his personal affairs. The following information includes both his business and personal financial data.

Assets: Cash in Mr. Botsworth's personal checking account, $625.00; cash in the business' checking account, $1,248.00; delivery truck, $5,552.00; furniture in the family home, $5,540.00; dry cleaning equipment, $4,220.00; store equipment, $2,680.00; family automobile, $6,400.00; family home, $39,000.00; building in which business is located, $16,000.00; land on which business building is located, $12,000.00.

Liabilities: Auto Finance Company, owed on delivery truck, $3,200.00; Collier County National Bank, owed on family automobile, $1,600.00; Haskins Supply Company, owed on dry cleaning equipment, $2,000.00; Merchants National Bank, mortgage on home, $8,000.00; Citizens National Bank, mortgage on business building, $9,000.00.

Instructions: 1. Prepare a balance sheet for Welldone Dry Cleaning. Use July 1 of the current year.

2. Record an opening entry on page 1 of a general journal.

3

Changes Caused by Business Transactions

ENABLING PERFORMANCE TASKS

After studying Chapter 3, you will be able to:

a. Define accounting terms related to changes caused by business transactions.
b. Explain accounting principles and practices related to changes caused by business transactions.
c. Analyze business transactions to show how these transactions affect items on an expanded accounting equation.
d. Figure new balances after increases and decreases are shown in basic accounting equation items.
e. Determine that after each transaction's changes are shown on an expanded accounting equation, the basic equation is still "in balance."
f. Prepare a balance sheet from information on an expanded accounting equation after changes caused by a series of transactions are shown.

Each time a business conducts a business activity, the amounts in the accounting equation are changed. A normal business activity that changes assets, liabilities, or owner's equity is called a transaction. For example, a transaction may be a sale of services or goods. Also, a transaction may occur when a business buys supplies.

HOW TRANSACTIONS CHANGE THE BASIC ACCOUNTING EQUATION

As described in Chapter 2, the basic accounting equation for Putt Around is:

Assets	=	Liabilities	+	Capital
$4,700	=	$1,200	+	$3,500

Each time a transaction occurs two or more of the amounts in the basic equation will change. For example, Putt Around sells an old lawn mower for $50.00. The change in the equation is below.

	Assets		=	Liabilities	+	Capital
Beg. Balances	$4,700		=	$1,200	+	$3,500
Transaction	−50	(old equipment)				
	+50	(new received cash)				
New Balances	$4,700		=	$1,200	+	$3,500

The net change in the basic accounting equation is made in two items on the same side of the equation. The net change to the left side is zero (−50, +50). The business has less equipment but more cash. Because the net change on the left side of the equation is zero, the same zero change affects the right side.

As another example, the business pays part of the liability owed, $200.00. The change in the basic equation is below.

	Assets		=	Liabilities		+	Capital
Balances	$4,700		=	$1,200		+	$3,500
Transaction	−200	(paid cash out)		−200	(paid liability)		
New Balances	$4,500		=	$1,000		+	$3,500

As a result of this transaction to pay a liability, the basic accounting equation is changed. The total amount of assets is reduced, $200.00. The new amount of assets becomes $4,500.00. The total amount owed to other persons is reduced, $200.00. The new amount of liabilities becomes $1,000.00. The amount of the capital is not affected and remains the same, $3,500.00. After the effect of the transaction is shown, the basic accounting equation is still in balance. The total assets, $4,500.00, equal the total liabilities plus capital, $4,500.00 ($1,000.00 + 3,500.00).

As a third example, the business receives cash from customers. The cash register shows that a total of $250.00 has been received from customers during the day. Rather than record each individual daily transaction, the business treats all the day's sales as one transaction. Cash from sales increases a business' capital. An increase in capital resulting from the operation of a business is called revenue. The change in the equation is below.

	Assets		=	Liabilities	+	Capital	
Balances	$4,500		=	$1,000	+	$3,500	
Transaction	+250	(received cash)				+250	(revenue)
New Balances	$4,750		=	$1,000	+	$3,750	

In this transaction the total amount of assets is increased by $250.00, the amount of cash received from customers. This transaction does *not* affect liabilities. Therefore, the amount of liabilities is not changed. The owner's equity (capital) is increased by this transaction, $250.00. After the effect of this transaction is shown, the equation is still in balance. The total amount of assets, $4,750.00, equals the total liabilities plus capital, $4,750.00 ($1,000.00 + 3,750.00).

The following summarizes the effect of the three transactions on the basic accounting equation.

Transaction 1. The left side of the equation (assets) is both increased and decreased, $50.00. The net change in assets is zero. Therefore, the net change for the right side (liabilities, capital) is also zero.

Transaction 2. The left side of the equation (assets) is decreased, $200.00. The right side of the equation (liabilities) is also decreased, $200.00. Both sides of the equation are decreased by the same amount.

Transaction 3. The left side of the equation (assets) is increased, $250.00. The right side of the equation (capital) is increased, $250.00. The same net change to both sides is an increase of $250.00.

A summary of the changes caused by the three transactions is below.

How transactions change the basic accounting equation

	Assets	=	**Liabilities**	+	**Capital**
Beg. Balances	$4,700	=	$1,200	+	$3,500
Transaction 1	−50				
	+50				
	$4,700	=	$1,200	+	$3,500
Transaction 2	−200		−200		
	$4,500	=	$1,000	+	$3,500
Transaction 3	+250				+250
New Balances	$4,750	=	$1,000	+	$3,750

HOW TRANSACTIONS CHANGE THE DETAILS IN THE EXPANDED ACCOUNTING EQUATION

The basic equation for Putt Around can be expanded to show details of each of the elements.

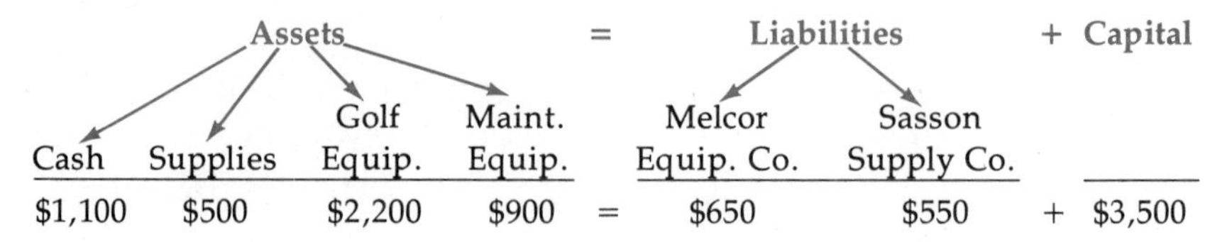

The expanded accounting equation shows more details than does the basic accounting equation, page 36. The beginning balances are taken from the balance sheet, page 19. Each transaction will change at least two items in the expanded accounting equation.

Transaction 1: Received cash from sale of equipment

Received cash from sale of a lawn mower, $50.00.

The effect of Transaction 1 on the expanded accounting equation is below.

	Assets				=	Liabilities		+	Capital
	Cash	Supplies	Golf Equip.	Maint. Equip.		Melcor Equip. Co.	Sasson Supply Co.		
Beg. Balances	$1,100	$500	$2,200	$900	=	$650	$550	+	$3,500
Transaction 1	+50			−50					
New Balances	$1,150	$500	$2,200	$850	=	$650	$550	+	$3,500

After Transaction 1 is recorded in the expanded equation above, the accounting equation is still in balance. The total of the left side of the equation is $4,700.00 ($1,150 + 500 + 2,200 + 850). The total of the right side of the equation is also $4,700.00 ($650 + 550 + 3,500).

Transaction 2: Paid cash for an amount owed to liabilities

Paid cash to Sasson Supply Company, $200.00.

The effect of Transaction 2 on the expanded equation is below.

	Assets				=	Liabilities		+	Capital
	Cash	Supplies	Golf Equip.	Maint. Equip.		Melcor Equip. Co.	Sasson Supply Co.		
Balances	$1,150	$500	$2,200	$850	=	$650	$550	+	$3,500
Transaction 2	−200						−200		
New Balances	$ 950	$500	$2,200	$850	=	$650	$350	+	$3,500

The amount of cash is decreased on the left side, $200.00. The amount owed Sasson Supply Company is decreased on the right side, $200.00. The same amount of decrease is made on both sides of the equation. After Transaction 2 is recorded in the expanded equation, the equation is still in balance. The total of the left side is $4,500.00. The total of the right side is also $4,500.00.

Transaction 3: Received cash from sales

Received cash from the daily sales, $250.00.

The effect of Transaction 3 on the equation is below.

	Assets				=	Liabilities		+	Capital
	Cash	Supplies	Golf Equip.	Maint. Equip.		Melcor Equip. Co.	Sasson Supply Co.		
Balances	$ 950	$500	$2,200	$850	=	$650	$350	+	$3,500
Transaction 3	+250								+250
New Balances	$1,200	$500	$2,200	$850	=	$650	$350	+	$3,750

The amount of cash is increased on the left side, $250.00. The amount of the capital is increased on the right side for the same amount, $250.00. The same amount of increase is made on both sides of the equation. The equation is still in balance. The left-side total is $4,750.00. The right-side total is also $4,750.00.

Transaction 4: Paid cash for an expense

Paid cash for July rent, $600.00.

A decrease in capital resulting from the operation of a business is called an expense. Business expenses are the costs of items and services used to produce revenue.

The effect of Transaction 4 on the equation is below.

	Assets				=	Liabilities		+	Capital	
	Cash	Supplies	Golf Equip.	Maint. Equip.		Melcor Equip. Co.	Sasson Supply Co.			
Balances	$1,200	$500	$2,200	$850	=	$650	$350	+	$3,750	
Transaction 4	−600								−600	(expense)
New Balances	$ 600	$500	$2,200	$850	=	$650	$350	+	$3,150	

The amount of cash is decreased on the left side, $600.00. The amount of capital is decreased on the right side for the same amount, $600.00. The same amount of decrease is made on both sides of the equation. After Transaction 4, the equation is still in balance. The left side totals $4,150.00. The right side also totals $4,150.00.

Transaction 5: Received cash from the owner as an additional investment in the business

Received cash from the owner, Harry Rossi, as an additional investment in the business, $500.00.

The effect of Transaction 5 on the equation is below.

	Assets				=	Liabilities		+	Capital	
	Cash	Supplies	Golf Equip.	Maint. Equip.		Melcor Equip. Co.	Sasson Supply Co.			
Balances	$ 600	$500	$2,200	$850	=	$650	$350	+	$3,150	
Transaction 5	+500								+500	(invest.)
New Balances	$1,100	$500	$2,200	$850	=	$650	$350	+	$3,650	

Transaction 5 increases the left side of the equation (cash) by $500.00 and increases the right side (capital) by $500.00. Transaction 5 increases the *total* amount of assets. With each increase in total assets, there also must be a similar increase in total equity. The amount of liabilities is not changed by Transaction 5. Therefore, the change on the right side must be in the owner's equity (capital).

Transaction 6: Paid cash for supplies

Paid cash for supplies, $50.00.

The effect of Transaction 6 on the equation is below.

	Assets				=	Liabilities		+	Capital
	Cash	Supplies	Golf Equip.	Maint. Equip.		Melcor Equip. Co.	Sasson Supply Co.		
Balances	$1,100	$500	$2,200	$850	=	$650	$350	+	$3,650
Transaction 6	−50	+50							
New Balances	$1,050	$550	$2,200	$850	=	$650	$350	+	$3,650

The amount of cash is decreased and the amount of supplies is increased by $50.00. Both the increase and decrease are on the left side of the equation. Transaction 6 does not change the *total* amount of assets. Therefore, there is no change in the equity on the right side. No items are changed on the right side of the equation.

Transaction 7: Paid cash for an expense

Paid cash for telephone bill, $25.00.

The effect of Transaction 7 is below.

	Assets				=	Liabilities		+	Capital
	Cash	Supplies	Golf Equip.	Maint. Equip.		Melcor Equip. Co.	Sasson Supply Co.		
Balances	$1,050	$550	$2,200	$850	=	$650	$350	+	$3,650
Transaction 7	−25								−25
New Balances	$1,025	$550	$2,200	$850	=	$650	$350	+	$3,625

After Transaction 7, the equation is still in balance. The left side totals $4,625.00. The right side also totals $4,625.00.

Transaction 8: Paid cash to buy new equipment

Paid cash for a new lawn mower, $400.00.

The effect of Transaction 8 is below.

	Assets				=	Liabilities		+	Capital
	Cash	Supplies	Golf Equip.	Maint. Equip.		Melcor Equip. Co.	Sasson Supply Co.		
Balances	$1,025	$550	$2,200	$ 850	=	$650	$350	+	$3,625
Transaction 8	−400			+400					
New Balances	$ 625	$550	$2,200	$1,250	=	$650	$350	+	$3,625

Cash is decreased and maintenance equipment is increased on the left side, $400.00. The *total* amount of assets is not changed by Transaction 8. Therefore, no change is made in the equities on the right side of the equation.

Transaction 9: Paid cash to owner for personal use

Paid cash to the owner, Harry Rossi, for personal use, $100.00.

Assets taken out of a business for the personal use of the owner are called withdrawals. The owner might withdraw any kind of asset. For example, the owner might withdraw cash or supplies for personal use at home. In a few situations the owner might withdraw equipment for personal use. However, owners seldom withdraw equipment. The equipment is needed to operate the business and might be too expensive for the business to replace.

The effect of Transaction 9 is below.

	Assets				=	Liabilities		+	Capital
	Cash	Supplies	Golf Equip.	Maint. Equip.		Melcor Equip. Co.	Sasson Supply Co.		
Balances	$625	$550	$2,200	$1,250	=	$650	$350	+	$3,625
Transaction 9	−100								−100
New Balances	$525	$550	$2,200	$1,250	=	$650	$350	+	$3,525

Cash is decreased on the left side, $100.00. The owner's equity (capital) is decreased on the right side, $100.00. The *total* amount of assets is decreased. There must be a similar decrease in equity on the right side. The amount owed to liabilities is not affected by Transaction 9. Therefore, the decrease is in the owner's equity (capital).

Transaction 10: Paid cash for repairs

Paid cash for repair of a broken window, $10.00.

A business may have many kinds of expenses. As described on page 41, Putt Around paid a telephone bill. Cost of utilities is one kind of expense. Rent is another expense. Cost of repairs is also an expense. The repair transaction is the same as the telephone bill and rent transactions. All are expense transactions.

The effect of Transaction 10 on the accounting equation is below.

	Assets				=	Liabilities		+	Capital
	Cash	Supplies	Golf Equip.	Maint. Equip.		Melcor Equip. Co.	Sasson Supply Co.		
Balances	$525	$550	$2,200	$1,250	=	$650	$350	+	$3,525
Transaction 10	−10								−10
New Balances	$515	$550	$2,200	$1,250	=	$650	$350	+	$3,515

Cash is decreased on the left side, $10.00. The amount of the owner's equity is decreased on the right side, $10.00.

The effect of Transaction 10, above, is the same as the effect for Transaction 7, page 41. *Total* assets and the owner's equity are decreased.

SUMMARY OF HOW TRANSACTIONS CHANGE THE ACCOUNTING EQUATION

The illustration below summarizes the effect of Transactions 1 to 10 on the expanded accounting equation.

	Assets				=	Liabilities		+	Capital
	Cash	Supplies	Golf Equip.	Maint. Equip.		Melcor Equip. Co.	Sasson Supply Co.		
Beg. Balances	$1,100	$500	$2,200	$ 900	=	$650	$550	+	$3,500
Transaction 1	+50			−50					
	$1,150	$500	$2,200	$ 850	=	$650	$550	+	$3,500
Transaction 2	−200						−200		
	$ 950	$500	$2,200	$ 850	=	$650	$350	+	$3,500
Transaction 3	+250								+250
	$1,200	$500	$2,200	$ 850	=	$650	$350	+	$3,750
Transaction 4	−600								−600
	$ 600	$500	$2,200	$ 850	=	$650	$350	+	$3,150
Transaction 5	+500								+500
	$1,100	$500	$2,200	$ 850	=	$650	$350	+	$3,650
Transaction 6	−50	+50							
	$1,050	$550	$2,200	$ 850	=	$650	$350	+	$3,650
Transaction 7	−25								−25
	$1,025	$550	$2,200	$ 850	=	$650	$350	+	$3,625
Transaction 8	−400			+400					
	$ 625	$550	$2,200	$1,250	=	$650	$350	+	$3,625
Transaction 9	−100								−100
	$ 525	$550	$2,200	$1,250	=	$650	$350	+	$3,525
Transaction 10	−10								−10
New Balances	$ 515	$550	$2,200	$1,250	=	$650	$350	+	$3,515

How transactions change the expanded accounting equation

On July 1 the expanded accounting equation above shows that Mr. Rossi's equity was $3,500.00. After Transaction 10, on July 2, the expanded equation shows the owner's equity to be $3,515.00. The amount of capital increased $15.00. The change in capital resulted from the transactions below.

Transaction	Kind of Transaction	Amount of Change
3	Sales	+250
4	Rent expense	−600
5	Additional investment	+500
7	Telephone expense	−25
9	Withdrawal of cash	−100
10	Repair expense	− 10
Net change		+15

An increase in capital resulting from the operation of a business is known as revenue. Most of the increases in capital are from revenue. Sometimes capital will be increased by additional investment. An increase because of investment is not due to the usual operations of the business. An investment is *not* revenue.

Most of the decreases in capital for a service business are because of expense transactions. Sometimes capital is decreased by withdrawals. A withdrawal occurs when an owner removes equity from the business. Withdrawals are *not* expenses of the business.

The following basic rules summarize how transactions affect the accounting equation.

1. Each transaction changes at least two items in the expanded accounting equation. For example, Transaction 1 changed Cash and Maintenance Equipment. Transaction 2 changed Cash and Sasson Supply Company. Transaction 3 changed Cash and Capital.

2. When a transaction changes two asset items, equity is not changed. For example, Transaction 1 changed two assets, Cash and Maintenance Equipment. Neither the liabilities nor the capital were changed.

3. When a transaction changes only one asset item, at least one equity item is changed. For example, Transaction 2 changed only one asset item, Cash. The *total* amount of assets is changed. Thus, an equity item on the right side of the equation must be changed. The equity item changed by this transaction is Sasson Supply Company. Because the liability is changed, no change is made in capital.

REPORTING A CHANGED ACCOUNTING EQUATION ON A BALANCE SHEET

The owner of a business can prepare a balance sheet on any date to report the accounting equation. *(CONCEPT: Accounting Period Cycle)* For example, Harry Rossi prepared a beginning balance sheet on July 1. This beginning balance sheet reports the accounting equation on July 1. This balance sheet is shown on page 19.

Mr. Rossi may want to know how his business stands after the ten transactions have occurred. A balance sheet could be prepared for Putt Around after ten transactions have been recorded. The information for the balance sheet is on the last line of the illustration, page 43. The balance sheet is prepared using the same steps described in Chapter 2, page 20.

The balance sheet prepared on July 2 is on page 45.

Putt Around
Balance Sheet
July 2, 1982

Assets		Liabilities	
Cash	515 00	Melcor Equipment Co.	650 00
Supplies	550 00	Sasson Supply Co.	350 00
Golf Equipment	2200 00	Total Liabilities	1000 00
Maintenance Equip.	1250 00	Capital	
		Harry Rossi, Capital	3515 00
Total Assets	4515 00	Total Liab. and Capital	4515 00

A comparison of the July 2 and the July 1 balance sheets on the basic accounting equation is below.

	Assets	=	Liabilities	+	Capital
July 1, 1982	$4,700	=	$1,200	+	$3,500
July 2, 1982	4,515	=	1,000	+	3,515
Net changes	−185	=	−200	+	+15

The same basic principles are followed in preparing each balance sheet for Putt Around. The principle used is that the assets always equal the liabilities plus the capital. *(CONCEPT: Consistent Reporting)* The two balance sheet equations show that the total assets decreased by $185.00. Also the total equity decreased by $185.00 (+15.00 capital, −200.00 liabilities).

A balance sheet can be prepared on any date. In practice, most owners and managers of businesses have balance sheets prepared infrequently. The periodic preparation of balance sheets is described in more detail in Chapter 8.

ACCOUNTING TERMS

What is the meaning of each of the following?

1. transaction **2.** revenue **3.** expense **4.** withdrawals

QUESTIONS FOR INDIVIDUAL STUDY

1. What is the basic accounting equation?

2. In what way does the sale of an old piece of equipment for cash change the basic equation?

3. What must be the condition of amounts in the basic accounting equation after each transaction?

4. In Transaction 1, page 39, why is the amount of equity *not* changed?

5. What is the effect of Transaction 2, page 39, on the accounting equation?
6. Why was capital increased by Transaction 3, page 39, and Transaction 5, page 40?
7. Why is capital decreased by Transaction 7, page 41?
8. What kinds of things might be withdrawn from a business by the owner for personal use?
9. Why are Transaction 4, page 40, and Transaction 10, page 42, similar?
10. Why did Mr. Rossi's capital increase from $3,500.00 on July 1 to $3,515.00 on July 2 as shown on page 43?
11. What two kinds of increases in capital are described in this chapter?
12. What two kinds of decreases in capital are described in this chapter?
13. What are the three basic ways that transactions change the expanded accounting equation?
14. What net change is shown in the accounting equations reported on the balance sheets, pages 19 and 45?

CASES FOR MANAGEMENT DECISION

CASE 1 West End Car Wash and Downtown Car Emporium both have assets totaling $20,000.00. Maria Lugo's equity in West End Car Wash is $18,000.00. Peter Donoski's equity in Downtown Car Emporium is $9,000.00. Based on this information, which of the two businesses might find it easier to get a $5,000.00 loan at a bank? Why?

CASE 2 Marion Doyle owns Riverside Golf. The business pays part of the amount owed to Compton Supply Company, $350.00. Mrs. Doyle analyzes the change caused by the transaction. What two accounting factors has Mrs. Doyle overlooked in making her analysis?

	Assets			=	Liabilities	+	Capital
	Cash	Supplies	Equipment		Compton Supply Co.		
Balances	$5,000	$300	$600	=	$500	+	$5,400
Transaction	−350						
New Balances	$4,650	$300	$600	=	$500	+	$5,400

DRILLS FOR UNDERSTANDING

DRILL 3-D 1 Determining how transactions change the basic accounting equation

For each transaction below, indicate how each element in the basic accounting equation is affected: increased or decreased. Use a form similar to the following. Place a check mark in the appropriate columns. Transaction 1 is shown as an example.

Trans. No.	Assets		= Liabilities		+ Capital	
	Increased	Decreased	Increased	Decreased	Increased	Decreased
1.	√	√				

Transactions

1. Received cash from sale of an old piece of equipment.
2. Paid cash to Mizer Company (liability) for amount owed.

3. Received cash from week's sales.
4. Paid cash for month's rent.
5. Received cash from the owner as an additional investment in the business.
6. Paid cash for supplies.
7. Paid cash for the water bill.
8. Paid cash for a new piece of equipment.
9. Paid cash to the owner for personal use.
10. Paid cash for a miscellaneous expense.

DRILL 3-D 2 Determining how transactions change the expanded accounting equation

Use a form similar to the one below. Decide which items on the expanded accounting equation are affected by each transaction listed in Drill 3-D 1. Show your decisions for each transaction by checking the + column if the item is increased and the − column if the item is decreased. Transaction 1 is given as an example.

Trans. No.	Assets						= Liabilities				+ Capital	
	Cash		Supplies		Equipment		Mizer Co.		Seitz Co.			
	+	−	+	−	+	−	+	−	+	−	+	−
1.	√					√						

APPLICATION PROBLEMS

PROBLEM 3-1 Determining how transactions change the expanded accounting equation

Speedy Delivery Service uses the items shown on the expanded accounting equation in the form below. The transactions below and on page 48 are a sample of those completed by the delivery service during one week. Use a form similar to the one below.

Trans. No.	Assets				=	Liabilities		+	Capital
	Cash	Supplies	Truck Equip.	Office Equip.		Sayles Equip. Co.	Truck Supply Co.		
Bal. 1.	1,200 *+100*	100	7,000	300 *−100*	=	200	50	+	8,350
Bal. 2.	*1,300*	*100*	*7,000*	*200*	=	*200*	*50*	+	*8,350*

Transactions

1. Received cash from the sale of an old desk, $100.00.
2. Received cash from the week's sales, $500.00.
3. Paid cash for month's rent, $100.00.
4. Paid cash to owner for personal use, $100.00.

5. Paid cash for repair of an office chair, $20.00.
6. Received cash from the week's sales, $400.00.
7. Paid cash to Sayles Equipment Company for part of amount owed, $100.00.
8. Paid cash for supplies, $75.00.
9. Paid cash for a new office desk, $300.00.
10. Paid cash for the heating bill, $55.00.
11. Paid cash for gasoline bill, $75.00.

Instructions: Complete steps a, b, and c for each transaction. (a) Analyze the transaction and show the amount increased (+) and the amount decreased (−) for the items affected on the equation. Transaction 1 is shown as an example. (b) Figure the new balance for each item and write it on the next line. (c) Check that *Assets* = *Liabilities* + *Capital* for each new balance line.

PROBLEM 3-2 Determining how transactions change the expanded accounting equation

Lucy Prince operates a small motel, Middletown Gardens. The transactions below are a sample of those completed by the motel during one week. Use a form similar to the one below.

Trans. No.	Assets				=	Liabilities		+	Capital
	Cash	Supplies	Motel Equip.	Maint. Equip.		Motel Supply Co.	Melmer Laundry		
Bal. 1.	4,200 *−700*	500	8,000	2,000	=	4,000	1,000	+	9,700 *−700*
Bal. 2.	*3,500*	*500*	*8,000*	*2,000*	=	*4,000*	*1,000*	+	*9,000*

Transactions

1. Paid cash for the month's rent, $700.00.
2. Received cash from day's sales, $1,500.00.
3. Paid cash for a supply of business forms, $150.00.
4. Received cash from the owner as an additional investment in the business, $2,000.00.
5. Paid cash for repair to an office door, $25.00.
6. Paid cash to Motel Supply Company for part of amount owed, $2,000.00.
7. Received cash from day's sales, $1,200.00.
8. Paid cash for the electric bill, $200.00.
9. Received cash from the sale of unused chairs, $250.00.
10. Paid cash for supply of towels used in guest rooms, $325.00.
11. Received cash from day's sales, $850.00.
12. Paid cash for new equipment to be used in guest rooms, $1,000.00.
13. Paid cash to the owner for personal use, $150.00.
14. Paid cash for the telephone bill, $200.00.
15. Paid cash for amount owed to Melmer Laundry, $1,000.00.
16. Paid cash for repainting office door, $35.00.
17. Received cash from day's sales, $1,100.00.
18. Paid cash for heating oil used to heat hot water, $300.00.

Instructions: Complete steps a, b, and c for each transaction. (a) Analyze the transaction and show the amount increased (+) and the amount decreased (−) for the items affected on the equation. Transaction 1 is shown as an example. (b) Figure the new balance for each item and write it on the next line. (c) Check that *Assets = Liabilities + Capital* for each new balance line.

The solution to Problem 3-2 is needed to complete Problem 3-3.

PROBLEM 3-3 Preparing a balance sheet based on a changed accounting equation

The solution to Problem 3-2 is needed to complete Problem 3-3.

Instructions: Prepare a balance sheet using the information on the last balance line of the solution to Problem 3-2. Use the date, September 4 of the current year. Review the steps in preparing a balance sheet, Chapter 2, page 20, before starting to work.

ENRICHMENT PROBLEMS

MASTERY PROBLEM 3-M Determining how transactions change the expanded accounting equation

Isabel Cardona operates a small service business known as The Conference Reporter. The transactions below are a sample of those completed during one week by the business. Use a form similar to the one below.

Trans. No.	Assets			=	Liabilities	+	Capital
	Cash	Supplies	Equipment		Gates Supply Co.		
Bal. 1.	3,000 −300	200	600	=	100	+	3,700 −300
Bal. 2.	*2,700*	*200*	*600*	=	*100*	+	*3,400*

Transactions

1. Paid cash for month's rent, $300.00.
2. Paid cash for repair and cleaning of a typewriter, $45.00.
3. Paid cash for supplies, $50.00.
4. Received cash from day's recording services at a local conference, $200.00.
5. Paid cash for electric bill, $50.00.
6. Paid cash for part of the amount owed to Gates Supply Company, $50.00.
7. Paid cash to printer for a supply of business letterheads, $25.00.
8. Received cash from day's services, $175.00.
9. Paid cash to Ms. Cardona, owner, for personal use, $100.00.
10. Paid cash for a new piece of equipment, $150.00.
11. Received cash from the sale of an old piece of equipment, $25.00.
12. Paid cash for the telephone bill, $45.00.
13. Received cash from day's services, $225.00.
14. Paid cash for a new piece of equipment, $200.00.
15. Received cash from day's services, $125.00.

Instructions: 1. Complete steps a, b, and c for each transaction. (a) Analyze the transaction and show the amount increased (+) and the amount decreased (−) for the items affected on the equation. Transaction 1 is shown as an example. (b) Figure the new balance for each item and write it on the next line. (c) Check that *Assets* = *Liabilities* + *Capital* for each new balance line.

2. Prepare a balance sheet using the information on the last balance line of the solution to Instruction 1. Use the date September 11 of the current year.

CHALLENGE PROBLEM 3-C Figuring the missing amounts in the basic accounting equation

The information below shows two of the three amounts in a basic accounting equation.

1. Liabilities, $1,000.00; Capital, $4,500.00.
2. Assets, $5,000.00; Liabilities, $2,000.00.
3. Assets, $6,000.00; Capital, $5,500.00.
4. Assets, $7,500.00; Liabilities, $1,500.00.
5. Liabilities, $2,500.00; Capital, $6,500.00.
6. Assets, $10,000.00; Capital, $7,000.00.
7. Liabilities, $3,000.00; Capital, $6,200.00.
8. Assets, $1,000.00; Liabilities, $200.00.
9. Assets, $2,000.00; Capital, $800.00.
10. Assets, $1,900.00; Liabilities, $500.00.
11. Liabilities, $600.00; Capital, $1,200.00.
12. Assets, $7,500.00; Liabilities, $400.00.
13. Assets, $4,650.00; Capital, $2,925.00.
14. Liabilities, $1,800.00; Capital, $3,600.00.
15. Assets, $8,500.00; Liabilities, $1,700.00.

Instructions: 1. Use a form similar to the one below. Write the amounts shown above in the correct columns. The amounts for line 1 above are shown as an example.

Line	Assets	=	Liabilities	+	Capital
1.		=	1,000.00	+	4,500.00

Instructions: 2. For each line, figure the missing amount. Write the amount in the correct column on that line. For example, line 1 in the form above needs an amount for Assets to complete the equation. The amount for line 1 is found by adding the amounts of Liabilities and Capital: $1,000.00 + $4,500.00 = $5,500.00. The amount, $5,500.00, is written in the Assets column on the first line.

Line	Assets	=	Liabilities	+	Capital
1.	*5,500.00*	=	1,000.00	+	4,500.00

3. After all lines have been completed, check that the equality of the basic equation has been maintained on each line. Do *Assets* = *Liabilities* + *Capital*?

4

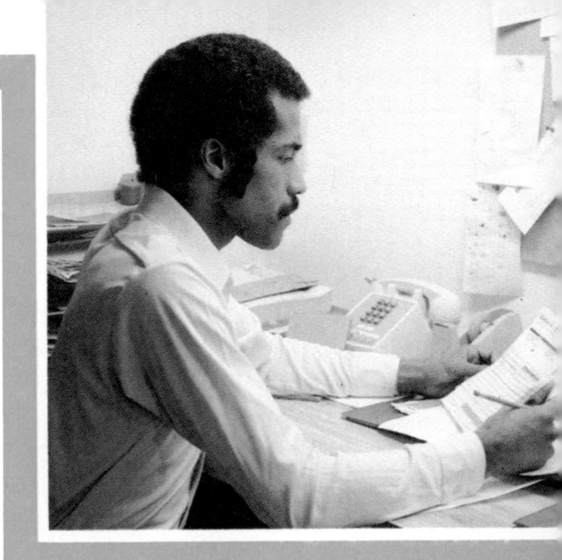

Analyzing Transactions into Debit and Credit Parts

ENABLING PERFORMANCE TASKS

After studying Chapter 4, you will be able to:

a. Define accounting terms related to analyzing transactions into debit and credit parts.
b. Explain accounting principles and practices related to analyzing transactions into debit and credit parts.
c. Use T accounts to analyze transactions showing whether accounts are debited or credited for each transaction.
d. Recognize and check that debits equal credits for each transaction.

The analysis of transactions described in Chapter 3 shows how transactions affect items in an expanded accounting equation. Using the expanded accounting equation in an accounting system is not practical. The equation analysis does not show quickly in one place all the changes in any one specific item. To see how all the transactions have changed cash, for example, the entire equation record must be checked. For this reason, businesses use ledger accounts to show in one place all the changes to a single item.

The opening entry for Putt Around is described in Chapter 2. The items in the opening entry are posted to ledger accounts as described on pages 25–27. The changes in each of these items are recorded first in a journal and then posted to the ledger accounts. Before the transactions can be recorded in a journal, the transactions are analyzed to determine how the accounts are changed.

ACCOUNT BALANCES

The difference between the totals of the amounts recorded on the two sides of an account is called the account balance. Each account has a balance after the opening entry is posted as shown in Chapter 2, page 28.

Each asset account has a beginning balance on its debit side. Each liability account has a beginning balance on its credit side. The capital account has a beginning balance on its credit side.

Balance side of an account

The balance side of an account may be determined by an account's location on the balance sheet as shown below.

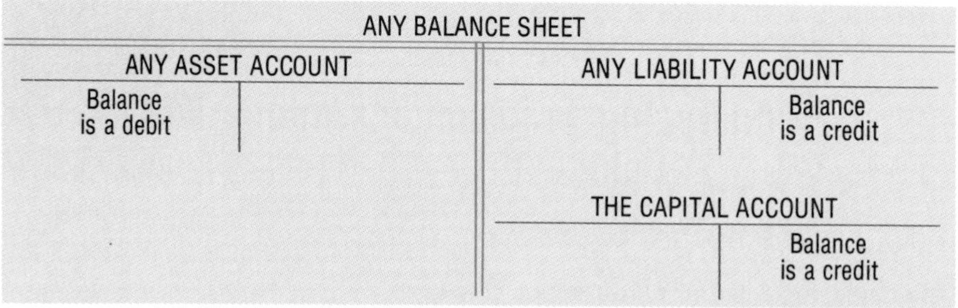

ANY BALANCE SHEET

ANY ASSET ACCOUNT		ANY LIABILITY ACCOUNT	
Balance is a debit			Balance is a credit
		THE CAPITAL ACCOUNT	
			Balance is a credit

Normal balances of balance sheet accounts

The left side of an account is known as the debit side. The right side of an account is known as the credit side. An entry made on the left side of an account is called a debit. An entry made on the right side of an account is called a credit.

An account has two sides with amount columns headed *Debit* and *Credit*. The purpose of the debit and credit sides of an account is to show increases and decreases in account balances. If an account balance is increased, the amount is shown on the balance side. If an account balance is decreased, the amount is shown on the side opposite the balance side. The illustration below shows how changes are recorded to show increases or decreases in asset accounts.

ANY ASSET ACCOUNT

Debit side		Credit side	
a. Balance	1,800.00	c. Decreases	−600.00
b. Increases	+50.00		

a. Beginning balance is $1,800.00; shown on the debit or balance side.
b. The account is increased, $50.00; shown on the balance or debit side.
c. The account is decreased, $600.00; shown on the side opposite the balance side, or credit side.

A skeleton form of account showing the account title and the debit and credit sides is called a T account.

After the credit entry is recorded in the T account above, the new balance is figured by finding the difference between total debits and total credits.

Total debits ($1,800.00 + 50.00)	$1,850.00
Total credits	−600.00
New debit balance	$1,250.00

When an account has only one item recorded, this single amount is the account balance. This is shown in the illustration of Putt Around's ledger, page 28. Only one item has been recorded in each account and this single amount is each account's balance.

When the total debit amounts in an account are greater than the total credit amounts, the balance is a debit. This debit balance is shown in the illustration on page 52. When the total credit amounts in an account are greater than the total debit amounts, the balance is a credit. This credit balance is shown below.

ANY LIABILITY ACCOUNT			
Debit side		Credit side	
Decrease	−20.00	Balance	50.00
Decrease	−70.00	Increase	+100.00

Total credits ($50.00 + 100.00)	$150.00
Total debits ($20.00 + 70.00)	−90.00
New credit balance	$ 60.00

The account balance when the total debits exceed the total credits is called a debit balance. The account balance when the total credits exceed the total debits is called a credit balance.

Transactions change at least two account balances

Each transaction increases or decreases the balances of two or more accounts. For example, Putt Around receives cash for a piece of old maintenance equipment, $50.00. Two accounts are affected by this transaction: Cash and Maintenance Equipment. Cash is increased because the business has more cash than before. Maintenance Equipment is decreased because the business has less maintenance equipment. This change is shown in the two T accounts below.

Cash			
Beg. Bal.	1,100.00		
Increase	+50.00		

Maintenance Equipment			
Beg. Bal.	900.00	Decrease	−50.00

After this transaction, the balance of Cash is $1,150.00. The balance of Maintenance Equipment is $850.00.

ANALYZING TRANSACTIONS

Every transaction is recorded in a journal before being recorded in a ledger account. The reason for this procedure is to first provide a record of transactions in chronological order. The information from the beginning balance sheet, page 19, is first recorded in a journal, page 22. Second, the information is posted to ledger accounts providing a record of

all changes in each account in one place. The information from the opening entry, page 22, is posted to ledger accounts, page 28.

Before a transaction is recorded in a journal, the transaction is analyzed into its debit and credit parts. The analysis shows which accounts are increased and which accounts are decreased. This analysis shows which accounts will be debited and which will be credited. When analyzing the effect of a transaction on accounts, the following three questions are answered.

1 *What are the names of the accounts affected?*

2 *What is the classification of each of these accounts?* The answer to this question helps determine which is the balance side of the account. When the balance side of an account is known, the increase and decrease sides can be determined.

3 *How is the balance of each account affected?* If the account is increased, is this shown by a debit or a credit? If the account is decreased, is this shown by a debit or a credit?

ANALYZING TRANSACTIONS AFFECTING ASSETS, LIABILITIES, AND CAPITAL

Each business transaction must be analyzed to determine the asset, liability, or capital accounts increased or decreased by the transaction.

Transaction: Two assets affected

July 1, 1982. Received cash from sale of an old lawn mower, $50.00.

1 *What are the names of the accounts affected?* Cash and Maintenance Equipment.

2 *What is the classification of each of these accounts?* Cash is an asset with a debit balance. Maintenance Equipment is an asset with a debit balance.

3 *How is the balance of each account affected?* Cash is increased by a debit, $50.00. Maintenance Equipment is decreased by a credit, $50.00.

Cash		
Beg. Bal.	1,100.00	
Increase	+50.00	

The T account at the left for Cash shows a debit balance of $1,100.00 before this transaction. The transaction increases the balance, $50.00. The new balance of Cash is $1,150.00.

The T account at the right for Maintenance Equipment shows a debit balance of $900.00 before this transaction. The transaction decreases the balance by a credit of $50.00. The new balance of Maintenance Equipment is $850.00.

Maintenance Equipment			
Beg. Bal.	900.00	Decrease	−50.00

The basic meaning of *debit* and *credit* is related to the two sides of a two-column ledger account form. This is why a skeleton T account is used to analyze a transaction into debit and credit parts.

The debit and credit parts of a transaction are always equal. The debit amount, $50.00, in the transaction, page 54, equals the credit amount, $50.00. Also, for the accounting equation, the total of asset account balances always equals the total of liability and capital balances. These two guides provide a check on the accuracy of accounting records.

Transaction: One asset and one liability affected

July 1, 1982. Paid cash to Sasson Supply Company, $200.00.

1 ***What are the names of the accounts affected?*** Sasson Supply Company and Cash.

2 ***What is the classification of each of these accounts?*** Sasson Supply Company is a liability with a credit balance. Cash is an asset with a debit balance.

3 ***How is the balance of each account affected?*** Sasson Supply Company is decreased by a debit, $200.00. Cash is decreased by a credit, $200.00.

The T account at the right for Sasson Supply Company shows that there is a credit balance before this transaction. The transaction decreases the balance on the opposite or debit side, $200.00.

The T account for Cash shows a debit balance. Cash decreases on the opposite or credit side. Cash is credited, $200.00.

One account is debited and one account is credited for $200.00. The equality of debits and credits for this transaction is maintained.

Sasson Supply Company			
Decrease	200.00	Beg. Bal.	550.00

Cash			
Beg. Bal.	1,100.00	Decrease	200.00
Increase	50.00		

Transaction: One asset and the capital affected

July 1, 1982. Received cash from the owner, Harry Rossi, as an additional investment in the business, $500.00.

1 ***What are the names of accounts affected?*** Cash and Harry Rossi, Capital.

2 ***What is the classification of each of these accounts?*** Cash is an asset with a debit balance. Harry Rossi, Capital is a capital account with a credit balance.

3 ***How is the balance of each account affected?*** Cash is increased by a debit, $500.00. Harry Rossi, Capital is increased by a credit, $500.00.

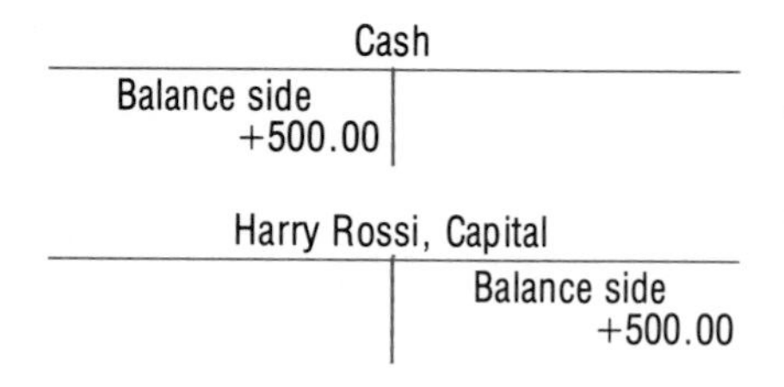

The T accounts at the left show how this transaction affects the two accounts. Cash is increased on its balance or debit side. Harry Rossi, Capital is increased on its balance or credit side. Both accounts are increased $500.00. The equality of debits and credits is maintained for this transaction.

Transaction: Two assets affected

July 2, 1982. Paid cash for supplies, $50.00.

1 ***Accounts affected?*** Supplies and Cash.

2 ***Account classifications?*** Supplies is an asset with a debit balance. Cash is an asset with a debit balance.

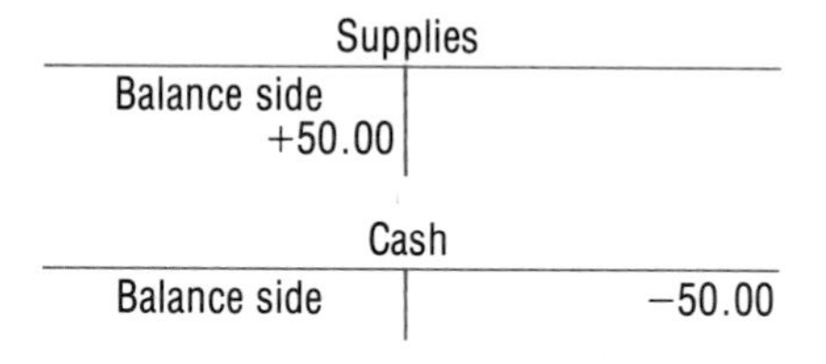

3 ***How affected?*** Supplies is increased by a debit, $50.00. Cash is decreased by a credit, $50.00.

The T accounts at the left show the effect of this transaction on ledger accounts. The equality of debits and credits is maintained for this transaction.

Transaction: Two assets affected

July 2, 1982. Paid cash for a new lawn mower, $400.00.

1 ***Accounts affected?*** Maintenance Equipment and Cash.

2 ***Account classifications?*** Maintenance Equipment is an asset with a debit balance. Cash is an asset with a debit balance.

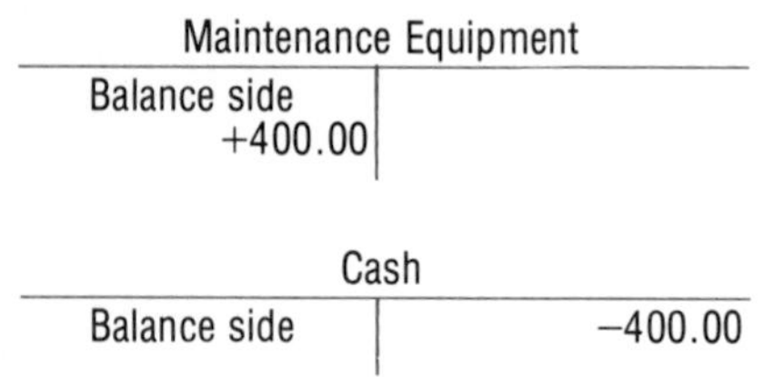

3 ***How affected?*** Maintenance Equipment is increased by a debit, $400.00. Cash is decreased by a credit, $400.00.

The T accounts at the left show the effect of this transaction on ledger accounts. One asset, Maintenance Equipment, is increased and another asset, Cash, is decreased. The debit, $400.00, is the same as the credit, $400.00. The equality of debits and credits is maintained.

Transaction: One asset and the capital affected

July 2, 1982. Paid cash to the owner, Harry Rossi, for personal use, $100.00.

Assets taken out of a business for an owner's personal use are known as withdrawals. The value of withdrawals could be recorded as debits directly in the owner's capital account. However, common accounting practice is to record withdrawals in a separate account titled Drawing. The balance of the drawing account easily shows the total amount of assets taken out of a business. Putt Around's ledger has an account titled Harry Rossi, Drawing for recording withdrawals.

A drawing account shows decreases in an owner's capital account. Thus, a drawing account has a debit balance. A drawing account is increased by debits and decreased by credits. The cash withdrawal transaction is analyzed below.

1 ***Accounts affected?*** Harry Rossi, Drawing and Cash.

2 ***Account classifications?*** Harry Rossi, Drawing is a capital account with a debit balance. Cash is an asset with a debit balance.

3 ***How affected?*** Harry Rossi, Drawing is increased by a debit, $100.00. Cash is decreased by a credit, $100.00.

The T accounts at the right show the effect of this transaction on ledger accounts. The drawing account is debited and the cash account is credited for $100.00. The equality of debits and credits is maintained.

Harry Rossi, Drawing	
Balance side +100.00	

Cash	
Balance side	−100.00

ANALYZING TRANSACTIONS AFFECTING REVENUE AND EXPENSES

All revenue transactions increase capital. This is shown in the illustration, Chapter 3, page 37. When cash is received from sales, the amount of revenue is increased. The entry for this transaction on the expanded equation below shows that revenue increases capital.

Assets				=	Liabilities		+	Capital
Cash	Supplies	Golf Equip.	Maint. Equip.		Melcor Equip. Co.	Sasson Supply Co.		
+250								+250

Revenue increases the total amount of assets a business has. When the *total* assets increase, an equity is also increased. Revenue accounts show increases in an owner's equity or capital. As described in Chapter 3, increases in an owner's equity *could* be shown directly as increases in the capital account. When equity increases are shown in a capital account, the records do not show clearly what caused all the changes. Rather than record all increases and decreases in the capital account, separate revenue accounts are used.

Businesses use a variety of titles for revenue accounts. The account title should describe the kind of information recorded in the account. A bank receives revenue from interest on loans. A bank might use the account title Interest Income or Interest Revenue. A doctor has revenue from fees collected from patients and might use the account title Fees. The owner of an apartment building receives revenue from rent. The account title could be Rent or Rent Income or Rent Revenue. Putt Around has only one source of revenue and uses the account title Sales. At Putt Around, the title Sales is understood to mean "sales revenue."

Expenses decrease the total amount of assets a business has. For each decrease in *total* assets, there is also a decrease in equities. Expenses decrease the owner's equity or capital. Rather than record all the separate expense transactions in the capital account, separate expense accounts are used. In this way, the total amount of each kind of expense can be easily seen. *(CONCEPT: Adequate Disclosure)* Putt Around has several major kinds of expenses. The account titles for these expense accounts are shown on the chart of accounts, page 16.

The relationship of revenue and expense accounts to the owner's capital account is shown in the diagram below.

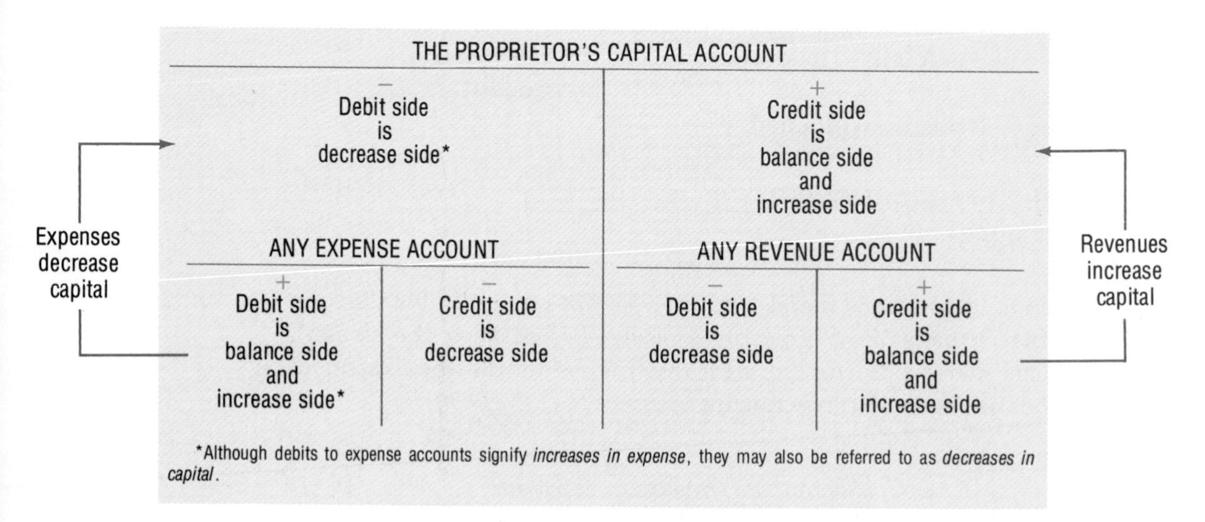

The principles of debit and credit for revenue and expense accounts and their relationship to the capital account

An expense account shows decreases in the owner's capital. Decreases are shown on the debit side of a capital account. Therefore, expense accounts have debit balances. A revenue account shows increases in the owner's capital. Increases are shown on the credit side of a capital account. Therefore, revenue accounts have credit balances.

Transaction: Revenue — daily sales

July 1, 1982. Received cash from daily sales, $250.00.

The amount of revenue from *each* sale could be recorded as cash is received. The procedure would result in a large number of revenue transactions being recorded daily. To reduce the number of entries, Putt Around totals the sales revenue for each day. The *total* daily sales revenue is recorded as a single transaction at the end of each day. *(CONCEPT: Realization of Revenue)* The revenue transaction is analyzed below.

1 ***Accounts affected?*** Cash and Sales.

2 ***Account classifications?*** Cash is an asset with a debit balance. Sales is a revenue account with a credit balance.

3 ***How affected?*** Cash is increased by a debit, $250.00. Sales is increased by a credit, $250.00.

The T accounts at the right show the effect of this transaction on ledger accounts. One account is debited, $250.00, and one account is credited, $250.00. The equality of debits and credits is maintained.

Cash	
Balance side +250.00	

Sales	
	Balance side +250.00

Transaction: Expense — rent

July 1, 1982. Paid cash for July rent, $600.00.

1 ***Accounts affected?*** Cash and Rent Expense.

2 ***Account classifications?*** Cash is an asset with a debit balance. Rent Expense is an expense account with a debit balance.

3 ***How affected?*** Cash is decreased by a credit, $600.00. Rent Expense is increased by a debit, $600.00.

The T accounts at the right show the effect of this transaction on ledger accounts. One account is debited and one account is credited for $600.00. The equality of debits and credits is maintained.

Rent Expense	
Balance side +600.00	

Cash	
Balance side	−600.00

Transaction: Expense — utility

July 2, 1982. Paid cash for telephone bill, $25.00.

Putt Around has transactions to pay for several kinds of utilities. The utilities are telephone, electricity, and water. Each of the utilities transactions is recorded as described on page 60 for the telephone bill.

1 *Accounts affected?* Cash and Utilities Expense.

2 *Account classifications?* Cash is an asset with a debit balance. Utilities Expense is an expense account with a debit balance.

Utilities Expense	
Balance side +25.00	

Cash	
Balance side	−25.00

3 *How affected?* Cash is decreased by a credit, $25.00. Utilities Expense is increased by a debit, $25.00.

The T accounts at the left show the effect of this transaction on ledger accounts. One account is debited and one account is credited for $25.00. The equality of debits and credits is maintained.

Transaction: Expense — miscellaneous

July 2, 1982. Paid cash for repair of a broken window, $10.00.

Some expense transactions occur so infrequently that a separate account is not kept in the ledger. One of these expenses is for the minor repairs to facilities and equipment. When a specific expense account is not kept for an expense, the amount is recorded in the miscellaneous expense account. The miscellaneous expense transaction is analyzed below.

1 *Accounts affected?* Cash and Miscellaneous Expense.

2 *Account classifications?* Cash is an asset with a debit balance. Miscellaneous Expense is an expense account with a debit balance.

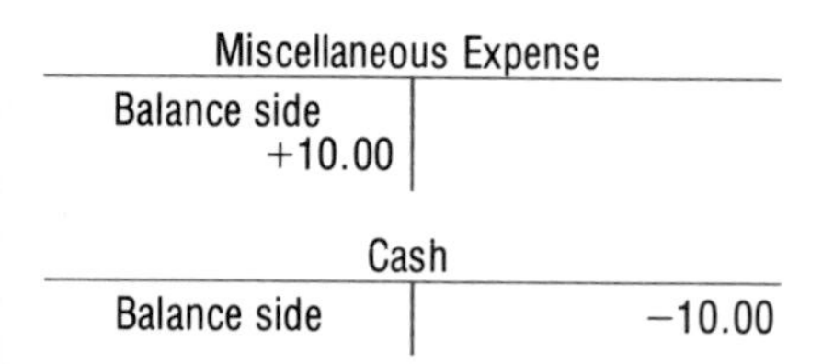

3 *How affected?* Cash is decreased by a credit, $10.00. Miscellaneous Expense is increased by a debit, $10.00.

The T accounts at the left show the effect of this transaction on ledger accounts. One account is debited and one account is credited for $10.00. The equality of debits and credits is maintained.

SUMMARY OF HOW DEBITS AND CREDITS CHANGE LEDGER ACCOUNT BALANCES

Each ledger account kept by Putt Around has two sides, a debit side and a credit side. Each account has a balance side. An account's balance side is determined by an account's classification. Increases are recorded on an account's balance side. Decreases are recorded on the side opposite an account's balance side.

Changes in balances of asset accounts

The balance of any asset account is normally a debit. Increases in asset accounts are shown on the balance or debit side. Decreases in asset accounts are shown on the credit side opposite the balance side.

ANY ASSET ACCOUNT	
+	−
Debit side is balance side and increase side	Credit side is decrease side

ANY LIABILITY ACCOUNT	
−	+
Debit side is decrease side	Credit side is balance side and increase side

The principles of debit and credit for asset and liability accounts

Changes in balances of liability accounts

The balance of any liability account is normally a credit. Increases in liability accounts are shown on the balance or credit side. Decreases in liability accounts are shown on the debit side opposite the balance side.

Changes in balances of capital accounts

The balance of a proprietor's capital account is normally a credit. Increases in the capital account are shown on the balance or credit side. Decreases are shown on the debit side opposite the balance side.

The drawing account shows decreases in the proprietor's capital account. Therefore, the owner's drawing account has a debit balance. Increases in the drawing account are shown on the balance or debit side. Decreases are shown on the credit side opposite the balance side.

THE PROPRIETOR'S CAPITAL ACCOUNT	
−	+
Debit side is decrease side	Credit side is balance side and increase side

THE PROPRIETOR'S DRAWING ACCOUNT	
+	−
Debit side is balance side and increase side	Credit side is decrease side

The principles of debit and credit for the proprietor's capital and drawing accounts

Changes in balances of revenue accounts

All revenue transactions cause an increase in capital. Rather than crediting the proprietor's capital account directly, a revenue account is credited for revenue transactions.

The balance of a revenue account is normally a credit. Increases in revenue are shown on the balance or credit side. Decreases in revenue are shown on the debit side opposite the balance side.

The principles of debit and credit for revenue and expense accounts

ANY REVENUE ACCOUNT	
− Debit side is decrease side	+ Credit side is balance side and increase side

ANY EXPENSE ACCOUNT	
+ Debit side is balance side and increase side	− Credit side is decrease side

Changes in balances of expense accounts

All expense transactions cause a decrease in capital. Rather than debiting the proprietor's capital account directly, expense accounts are debited for expense transactions. The balance of any expense account is normally a debit. Increases in expense accounts are shown on the balance or debit side. Decreases in expense accounts are shown on the credit side opposite the balance side.

Temporary capital accounts

The use of separate revenue and expense accounts provides detailed information needed for the best management of a business. The use of separate accounts keeps the proprietor's capital account from becoming cluttered with many debit and credit entries. Revenue and expense accounts used to store information until transferred to the capital account are called temporary capital accounts.

How information is summarized and transferred to the capital account is described in Chapter 9.

Debits and credits in each transaction

Each transaction has a debit part and a credit part. The total debit amount equals the total credit amount in each transaction.

ACCOUNTING TERMS

What is the meaning of each of the following?

1. account balance
2. debit
3. credit
4. T account
5. debit balance
6. credit balance
7. temporary capital accounts

QUESTIONS FOR INDIVIDUAL STUDY

1. Why are ledger accounts used in accounting records?
2. What is done with information for a transaction before it is recorded in a ledger account?
3. In what way are the balances of asset accounts related to a balance sheet?
4. In what way are the balances of liability accounts related to a balance sheet?

5. In what way is the balance of the proprietor's capital account related to a balance sheet?
6. Why does a two-column ledger account have a debit and credit side?
7. On which side of an account is an increase recorded?
8. On which side of an account is a decrease recorded?
9. What kind of balance does an account have if the total debit amounts exceed the total credit amounts?
10. What kind of balance does an account have if the total credit amounts exceed the total debit amounts?
11. How many accounts are affected by each transaction?
12. What must be done with a transaction before it is recorded in a journal? Why?
13. What is the relationship of debit and credit parts for each transaction?
14. Why are increases in capital because of revenue recorded in separate revenue accounts instead of in the capital account?
15. Why do revenue accounts have credit balances?
16. Why do expense accounts have debit balances?
17. Why are revenue and expense accounts often known as temporary capital accounts?

CASES FOR MANAGEMENT DECISION

CASE 1 Wilbur Mooney owns a small business for which he bought an electric typewriter for $520.00. He analyzes this transaction as shown in the T accounts at the right. Did Mr. Mooney analyze the transaction correctly? Explain your answer.

Cash	
520.00	

Equipment	
520.00	

CASE 2 Vincente Delgado owns a beauty salon. The business receives revenue from services rendered to customers and from the sale of cosmetics. Revenue from both sources is recorded in an account titled *Sales*. Mr. Delgado would like to know how much revenue is being received from the services and how much from cosmetics. What changes in this accounting system would you suggest, and why?

CASE 3 Emi Iwasaki just bought a sports store. She finds that the former owner recorded all cash received as revenue. Miss Iwasaki believes that this is incorrect. Is the procedure correct or incorrect? Why?

DRILLS FOR UNDERSTANDING

DRILL 4-D 1 Determining the balance side, increase side, and decrease side of ledger accounts

Instructions: 1. Make a T account for each account title below. The T account for Cash is shown as an example.

Cash	

Account Titles

Cash
Office Furniture
Office Supplies
Garage Equipment
Midland National Bank (liability)
Moser Equipment Company (liability)
Paul Richardson, Capital
Paul Richardson, Drawing
Sales
Advertising Expense
Delivery Expense
Miscellaneous Expense
Utilities Expense

Instructions: 2. Write *Debit side* and *Credit side* in each T account as in the example at the right.

Cash	
Debit side	Credit side

3. Write the words *Balance side* on the debit side of accounts that normally have debit balances. Write the words *Balance side* on the credit side of accounts that normally have credit balances. The T account at the right is an example.

Cash	
Debit side Balance side	Credit side

4. In each T account place a (+) on the increase side of the account. Place a (−) on the decrease side. The T account at the right is an example.

Cash	
Debit side Balance side +	Credit side −

DRILL 4-D 2 Analyzing the effect of transactions on ledger accounts

The following transactions are typical of those described in Chapter 4.

1. Received cash from sale of an old piece of golf equipment.
2. Paid cash to Sasson Supply Company for amount owed.
3. Received cash from the owner as an additional investment in the business.
4. Paid cash for supplies.
5. Paid cash for a new piece of maintenance equipment.
6. Paid cash to the owner for personal use.
7. Received cash from day's sales.
8. Paid cash for month's rent.
9. Paid cash for the telephone bill.
10. Paid cash for a small repair bill.

Use a form similar to the one below.

1	2	3	4	5	6	7	8	9
Trans. No.	Account Title	Change In Account	Account Classifications					Debit or Credit
			Assets	Liabilities	Capital	Revenue	Expenses	
1.	*Cash*	+	√					*Dr.*
	Golf Equip.	−	√					*Cr.*

Instructions: 1. Use Putt Around's chart of accounts, page 16, for account titles. For each transaction, write in Column 2 the names of the two accounts affected. Transaction 1 is given as an example.

2. For each account title written in Column 2, place a (+) or a (−) in Column 3. The (+) or (−) shows whether the account is increased or decreased.

3. For each account title written in Column 2, place a check mark in one classification column 4-8. The check mark shows the classification of the account.

4. For each account title written in Column 2, write *Dr.* (for debit) or *Cr.* (for credit) in Column 9. The abbreviations show on which side of an account the amount is written.

APPLICATION PROBLEMS

PROBLEM 4-1 Analyzing transactions into debit and credit parts

Ms. Sarah Plunkett operates an insurance agency. The business' ledger contains the accounts below.

Cash	Will's Garage (liability)	Sales
Office Supplies	Dolan's Stationery Store (liability)	Advertising Expense
Automobile	Jane's Equipment Company (liability)	Miscellaneous Expense
Office Furniture	Sarah Plunkett, Capital	Rent Expense
Office Machines	Sarah Plunkett, Drawing	Utilities Expense

The following are selected transactions completed by Ms. Plunkett's insurance agency:

1. Received cash from the sale of an old typewriter, $50.00.
2. Paid cash for a new electric typewriter, $640.00.
3. Paid cash for the telephone bill, $36.00.
4. Received cash from day's sales, $780.00.
5. Paid cash for office supplies, $30.00.
6. Paid cash to Dolan's Stationery Store for part of amount owed, $100.00.
7. Received cash from the sale of an old desk, $45.00.
8. Received cash from day's sales, $275.00.
9. Paid cash for repairs to tiles on the office floor, $21.00.
10. Paid cash for the electric bill, $60.00.
11. Paid cash to the owner for personal use, $100.00.
12. Paid cash for newspaper advertising, $85.00.
13. Paid cash for a new office chair, $65.00.
14. Received cash from Ms. Plunkett as an additional investment, $1,000.00.
15. Paid cash to Jane's Equipment Company for part of amount owed, $250.00.

Instructions. Use a pair of T accounts for each transaction. Complete steps a, b, and c for each transaction. (a) Write the account titles affected on the T accounts. The T accounts at the right are examples. (b) Write the debit amount in the account to be debited. (c) Write the credit amount in the account to be credited.

1.

Cash	
50.00	

Office Machines	
	50.00

PROBLEM 4-2 Analyzing transactions into debit and credit parts

Linda Russel operates a small quick-service repair shop. Some of the ledger accounts and their balances are below. When no amount is shown, the account has no beginning balance.

Cash, $1,800.00	Linda Russel, Capital, $3,980.00
Supplies, $700.00	Linda Russel, Drawing
Repair Equipment, $2,500.00	Sales
Office Equipment, $1,500.00	Advertising Expense
Bilmay Company (liability), $120.00	Miscellaneous Expense
Fell Equipment Company (liability), $2,000.00	Rent Expense
Reynolds Supply Company (liability), $400.00	Utilities Expense

Instructions: 1. Prepare T accounts for the accounts listed on page 65. Write the account balance in the T accounts for those accounts that have a balance.

2. Analyze each of the following transactions into debit and credit parts. Write the amounts in the correct T accounts for each transaction. The T accounts at the right show the accounts affected by Transaction 1 as an example.

Rent Expense			
(1)	450.00		

Cash			
Balance	1,800.00	(1)	450.00

Transactions

1. Paid cash for month's rent, $450.00.
2. Received cash from sale of an old piece of repair equipment, $30.00.
3. Received cash from sale of old broken chairs used in the office, $50.00.
4. Received cash from day's sales, $120.00.
5. Paid cash for part of amount owed to Reynolds Supply Company, $200.00.
6. Paid cash for new repair equipment, $245.00.
7. Received cash from day's sales, $235.00.
8. Paid cash for part of amount owed to Bilmay Company, $60.00.
9. Received cash from sale of an old adding machine, $20.00.
10. Paid cash for a new electronic calculator, $195.00.
11. Received cash from day's sales, $312.00.
12. Paid cash for the water bill, $48.00.
13. Paid cash for advertising placed in local newspapers, $45.00.
14. Received cash from day's sales, $275.00.
15. Paid cash for electric bill, $120.00.
16. Received cash from day's sales, $318.00.
17. Paid cash for telephone bill, $52.00.
18. Paid cash to the owner for personal use, $100.00.
19. Received cash from day's sales, $238.00.
20. Received cash from the owner as an additional investment in the business, $300.00.

ENRICHMENT PROBLEMS

MASTERY PROBLEM 4-M Analyzing transactions into debit and credit parts

William Alpine operates Makeway Delivery Service.

Instructions: 1. Prepare a T account for each of the ledger accounts used by the business. Cash; Delivery Equipment; Office Equipment; Creditable Motors (liability); William Alpine, Capital; William Alpine, Drawing; Delivery Revenue; Advertising Expense; Delivery Truck Expense; Miscellaneous Expense; and Telephone Expense.

2. For each of the following accounts, write the balance on the correct side of the T account. Cash, $1,350.00; Delivery Equipment, $8,640.00; Office Equipment, $1,520.00; Creditable Motors, $3,780.00; William Alpine, Capital, $7,730.00.

3. Analyze each of the transactions on page 67 into debit and credit parts. Write the amounts in the correct T accounts. The T accounts at the right are an example for Transaction 1.

Telephone Expense			
(1)	45.90		

Cash			
Balance	1,350.00	(1)	45.90

Transactions

1. Paid cash for telephone bill, $45.90.
2. Received cash from day's delivery revenue, $532.00.
3. Paid cash for gas and oil used in the delivery truck, $22.50.
4. Paid cash for a new office desk and chair, $297.00.
5. Received cash from the owner as an additional investment in the business, $1,000.00.
6. Paid cash for washing the delivery truck, $6.00.
7. Received cash from day's delivery revenue, $484.00.
8. Paid cash for leather gloves used by Mr. Alpine as part of his work, $10.00.
9. Paid cash for part of amount owed to Creditable Motors, $500.00.
10. Paid cash for new electronic calculator for use in the office, $225.00.
11. Paid cash for the electric bill, $75.00.
12. Received cash from day's delivery revenue, $560.00.
13. Paid cash for gas and oil used in the delivery truck, $117.00.
14. Paid cash to the owner for personal use, $100.00.
15. Paid cash for advertising in local newspaper, $60.00.
16. Paid cash for month's rent, $400.00.
17. Received cash from day's delivery revenue, $540.00.

CHALLENGE PROBLEM 4-C Analyzing transactions already recorded in T accounts

Nancy Withers operates a car wash. The T accounts below show the beginning account balances and the debit and credit parts of transactions completed by the car wash.

Cash

Balance	360.00	(1)	19.00
(3)	400.00	(2)	280.00
(6)	2,960.00	(4)	16.00
(8)	400.00	(5)	18.00
(11)	120.00	(7)	3,600.00
		(9)	36.00
		(10)	6.00
		(12)	160.00

Nancy Withers, Capital

		Balance	3,680.00
		(3)	400.00

Car Wash Sales

		(8)	400.00
		(11)	120.00

Truck

Balance	2,960.00	(6)	2,960.00
(7)	3,600.00		

Advertising Expense

(1)	19.00		
(5)	18.00		

Car Wash Equipment

Balance	680.00		
(2)	280.00		

Car Wash Expense

(9)	36.00		

Robert Mercer Equipment Co.

(12)	160.00	Balance	320.00

Miscellaneous Expense

(4)	16.00		
(10)	6.00		

Use a form similar to the one below.

1	2	3	4	5	6	7	8
Trans. No.	Account Debited			Account Credited			Description of the Transaction
	Title	Classification	Effect	Title	Classification	Effect	
1.	*Advertising Expense*	*Expense*	+	*Cash*	*Asset*	−	*Paid cash for advertising expense*

Instructions: 1. For each transaction, write the title of the account debited in Column 2. Write the title of the account credited in Column 5. Transaction 1 is recorded as an example. Transaction 1 can be identified with the (1) before the two amounts in the T accounts.

2. For each transaction, write the debited account's classification in Column 3. Write the credited account's classification in Column 6.

3. For each transaction, write in Column 4 whether the debited account is increased (+) or decreased (−). Write the same symbols in Column 7 to show whether the credited account is increased or decreased.

4. Write in Column 8 a brief description of each transaction.

5

Journalizing Business Transactions

ENABLING PERFORMANCE TASKS

After studying Chapter 5, you will be able to:

a. Define accounting terms related to journalizing business transactions.
b. Explain accounting principles and practices related to journalizing business transactions.
c. Record transactions in a multi-column cash journal.
d. Prove cash.
e. Prove equality of debits and credits in a cash journal.
f. Total, rule, and forward totals from one page to another in a cash journal.
g. Rule a cash journal.

Before a transaction can be recorded, the transaction is analyzed into its debit and credit parts. The procedure for analyzing transactions is described in Chapter 4. After each transaction is analyzed into its debit and credit parts, the transaction is recorded in a journal. Recording a business transaction in a journal is called journalizing.

Reasons for recording transactions in journals

As described in Chapter 4, information about each transaction could be recorded on a form showing an expanded accounting equation. However, generally accepted accounting practice requires a more permanent record of each transaction. A journal provides an orderly record from which information is posted to accounts in a ledger. The reasons why transactions are recorded first in a journal and not recorded directly in ledger accounts are below.

1. Accuracy. A journal entry shows the debit and credit parts of each transaction in one place. The equality of the debit and credit amounts is readily seen by looking at a journal entry. If only part of a transaction is recorded in one place, the omissions may not be easily seen. Errors in recording a transaction can be corrected in a journal before the information is posted to ledger accounts.

2. Chronological record of transactions. A journal contains the day-to-day transactions listed according to the date of the transactions. When facts about a transaction are needed some months or days afterwards, the journal is an easy source to use.

If transactions are recorded first in ledger accounts, the debit and credit parts will be on different pages. This procedure makes it difficult to find both the debit and credit parts of a single, specific transaction.

Double-entry accounting is complete accounting

The recording of the debit and credit parts of a transaction is called double-entry accounting. Double-entry accounting, used in most well-organized businesses, provides a complete record of each transaction. Complete accounting *is* double-entry accounting.

JOURNALIZING TRANSACTIONS IN A GENERAL JOURNAL

A two-column general journal is used by Putt Around for recording an opening entry. This procedure is described in Chapter 2, pages 22 and 23. A two-column general journal *could* be used to record all transactions of a business. For example, the five July 1 transactions described in Chapter 4 appear below.

GENERAL JOURNAL PAGE 1

	DATE		ACCOUNT TITLE	POST. REF.	DEBIT	CREDIT	
9		1	Cash		50 00		9
10			Maintenance Equipment			50 00	10
11			Receipt No. 10.				11
12		1	Sasson Supply Company		200 00		12
13			Cash			200 00	13
14			Check No. 20.				14
15		1	Cash		250 00		15
16			Sales			250 00	16
17			Cash Register Tape No. 1.				17
18		1	Rent Expense		600 00		18
19			Cash			600 00	19
20			Check No. 21.				20
21		1	Cash		500 00		21
22			Harry Rossi, Capital			500 00	22
23			Receipt No. 11.				23
24							24

Entries recorded in a two-column general journal

Using *only* a two-column general journal has a disadvantage. Much space and time is required to record many transactions in a two-column general journal. To save time and space, Putt Around uses a cash journal described in this chapter.

A CASH JOURNAL

All but a few of the entries made in Putt Around's journals are cash transactions. Therefore, Putt Around uses one journal in which to record only cash transactions. Entries for other than cash transactions are recorded in a two-column general journal. The opening entry for Putt Around, described in Chapter 2, is not a cash transaction. For this reason the opening entry is recorded in a two-column general journal. A journal used to record only one kind of transaction is called a special journal. A special journal used only for cash transactions is called a cash journal.

Other kinds of special journals are described in Part 5.

Form of a cash journal

The cash journal used by Putt Around is shown below.

CASH JOURNAL PAGE 1

	1	2					3	4	5	
	CASH		DATE	ACCOUNT TITLE	DOC. NO.	POST. REF.	GENERAL		SALES CREDIT	
	DEBIT	CREDIT					DEBIT	CREDIT		
1			1982 July 1	Balance on hand, $1,100.00		✓				1
2	50 00		1	Maintenance Equipment	R10			50 00		2
3		200 00	1	Sasson Supply Company	C20		200 00			3
4	250 00		1	✓	T1	✓			250 00	4
5		600 00	1	Rent Expense	C21		600 00			5
6	500 00		1	Harry Rossi, Capital	R11			500 00		6
7										7

Entries recorded in a cash journal

The five transactions recorded in the cash journal above are the same as those in the general journal, page 70.

The entry on line 1 of the cash journal above is not for a business transaction. This entry is explained later in this chapter on page 73.

The form of a cash journal is different from that of a general journal. The cash journal has additional amount columns. The additional amount columns have account titles in the column headings. A journal amount column headed with an account title is called a special amount column. A special amount column is provided for each account for which many entries are made each month. For example, most of Putt Around's transactions result in either a debit or a credit to Cash. For this reason, the cash journal has both *Cash Debit* and *Cash Credit* special amount columns. Also, Putt Around has many entries for sales. Sales transactions result in a credit to Sales. For this reason, the cash journal has a *Sales Credit* amount column. The General Debit and General Credit amount columns are used for accounts that are affected infrequently by transactions.

The Cash Debit and Cash Credit columns are placed at the left of the Date column in the cash journal, page 71. These amount columns could have been placed at the right along with the other amount columns. However, with the Cash columns at the left, the amount of cash on hand can be easily checked.

Putt Around's first transaction in July is for cash received from the sale of equipment, $50.00. This entry is shown in the general journal, page 70, lines 9–11. The entry requires three lines in the general journal. The same entry is shown in the cash journal, page 71, line 2. The entry requires only one line in the cash journal. The account title, Cash, is written on line 9 of the general journal, page 70. On line 2 of the cash journal, page 71, only the amount is written in the Cash Debit column. The name of the account is not written because it is already in the column heading.

Advantages in using a cash journal

A cash journal with special amount columns has several advantages.

1. *Less space is required for recording* journal entries in a cash journal than in a two-column general journal. For example, the first transaction in both journals records $50.00 for the sale of an old piece of equipment. Each entry records the same information. The entry in the general journal requires three lines. The entry in the cash journal requires only one line. Thus, if used for all transactions, a two-column general journal is bulkier than a cash journal.
2. *Less time is required for recording* transactions in a cash journal than in a two-column general journal. A general journal entry requires that at least two account titles be written in the Account Title column. One account title is for the debit part and one is for the credit part of the entry. A cash journal entry requires that usually no more than one account title be written. The "cash" part of the transaction is recorded in one of the special Cash columns. For some transactions, both the debit and credit amounts are recorded in special amount columns. Using special amount columns eliminates the need to write an account title in the Account Title column. On line 4 of the cash journal, page 71, both the debit and credit amounts are recorded in special columns. A check mark (√) is placed in the Account Title column. The check mark shows that no account title needs to be written. The check mark also shows that the writing of an account title has not been overlooked.
3. *Less time is required for posting* from a cash journal than from a general journal. Every amount recorded in a two-column general journal is posted individually. The amounts entered in special columns

of the cash journal are not posted individually. Only the total of a special column is posted. Posting from a cash journal is described in Chapter 6.

Each business plans for amount columns in its cash journal to fit its needs. Examples of journals with various special columns are described in Chapters 11, 12, 20, and 21.

JOURNALIZING TRANSACTIONS IN A CASH JOURNAL

Before a transaction is recorded in any journal, the transaction is analyzed into its debit and credit parts. The procedure for analyzing transactions is described in Chapter 4.

Recording the cash on hand in a cash journal

A business sometimes needs to know the amount of cash that was on hand at the beginning of a month. The first line of a cash journal is used each month to record this information. This entry is not posted since this information is already in the cash account. This procedure avoids having to check the cash account in the general ledger to find the beginning cash balance.

On July 1, 1982, Putt Around's cash balance on hand, $1,100.00, is recorded on line 1 of the cash journal, page 71. The entry, including the amount, is written in the Account Title column. The year, month, and day are written in the Date column. A check mark is placed in the Post. Ref. column. The check mark shows that nothing is to be posted from this line. Nothing is written in the amount columns.

Source documents used for journalizing transactions

A business paper is prepared describing a transaction in detail. For example, a check stub is prepared for each check issued. Check stubs are the source documents for cash payments transactions. *(CONCEPT: Objective Evidence)*

When cash is received from sales, the amount is entered on a cash register. The cash register prints the amount on a paper tape inside the register. The paper tapes are the source documents for cash sales transactions. When cash is received from sources other than sales, a written receipt is prepared. This written receipt is the source document. A business paper from which information is obtained for any journal entry is known as a source document.

Journalizing a sale of an asset

July 1, 1982. Received cash from the sale of an old lawn mower, $50.00. Receipt No. 10.

Source document for a sale of an asset. A written acknowledgement given when cash is received is called a receipt. When Putt Around receives cash other than from sales, a receipt is prepared. Before preparing a receipt, a receipt stub is prepared. The receipt stub is the source document for a cash received transaction. *(CONCEPT: Objective Evidence)* Journal entries are made from information on the receipt stub. The receipt is given to the person from whom the cash is received. The receipt stub is kept by Putt Around.

The receipt stub and receipt issued by Putt Around for the $50.00 received for an old lawn mower are below.

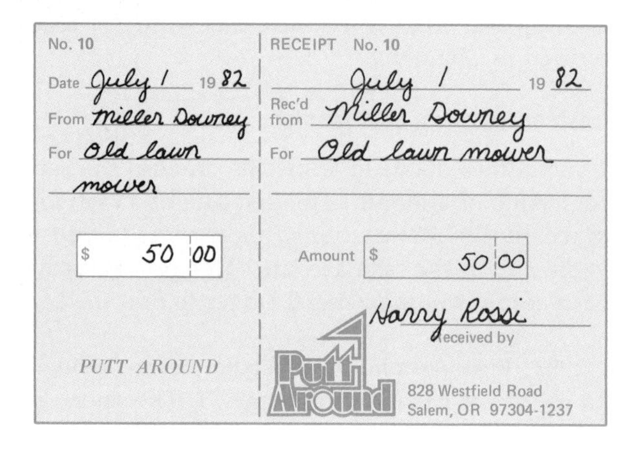
No. 10
Date July 1 19 82
From Miller Downey
For Old lawn mower
$ 50 00
PUTT AROUND

RECEIPT No. 10
July 1 19 82
Rec'd from Miller Downey
For Old lawn mower
Amount $ 50 00
Harry Rossi
Received by
Putt Around
828 Westfield Road
Salem, OR 97304-1237

Receipt stub and receipt

Recording a sale of an asset. This transaction is analyzed into debit and credit parts before it is recorded in a journal. The analysis of this transaction is described on pages 54 and 55. The results of the analysis are repeated in the T accounts at the left.

Cash	
50.00	

Maintenance Equipment	
	50.00

For this transaction, the balance of the asset Cash is increased by a debit, $50.00. The balance of the asset account Maintenance Equipment is decreased by a credit, $50.00. The entry to record this transaction is on line 2 of the cash journal, page 71.

This transaction is recorded in the cash journal as described below.

1 ***Date of entry.*** Write the date in the Date column. The year and month have already been written on this page. Therefore, only the day, *1*, needs to be written.

2 ***Debit part of entry.*** Debit the cash account by writing *$50.00* in the Cash Debit column on line 2. Writing *Cash* in the Account Title column is *not* necessary. The column heading, *Cash Debit*, shows that all amounts are debits to the cash account.

3 ***Credit part of entry.*** Credit the maintenance equipment account by writing *$50.00* in the General Credit column. Also, write *Maintenance Equipment* in the Account Title column.

The General Debit and Credit columns are used for accounts for which there are no special columns. The account title is written for each amount recorded in a General amount column.

4 ***Indication of source document.*** Write *R10* in the Doc. No. column to show that Receipt No. 10 is issued in this transaction. The letter *R* stands for *receipt*. The number *10* shows that this is Receipt No. 10. The number is obtained from the receipt stub.

The journal entry does not show what item of maintenance equipment was sold. *R10* in the Doc. No. column of the cash journal shows where detailed information can be obtained. Therefore, such details are not repeated in the journal entry.

Journalizing a part payment of a liability

July 1, 1982. Paid cash to Sasson Supply Company for part of the amount owed, $200.00. Check No. 20.

Source document for a part payment of a liability. A business form ordering a bank to pay cash from a depositor's bank account is called a check. Most businesses use checks to make all major cash payments. Checks are safer than money to send through the mail. After a check is cashed and processed, the bank returns it to the business that wrote it. The returned check shows that payment has been made.

The source document for recording a cash payment transaction is a check stub. *(CONCEPT: Objective Evidence)* Each check stub should be filled out completely. A check stub should contain all the information needed for journalizing a cash payments transaction.

The check stub and check prepared by Putt Around for the part payment to Sasson Supply Company are below.

Check stub and check

NO. 20 $ 200.00
DATE July 1 19 82
TO Sasson Supply Co.
FOR Payment on account

BAL. BRO'T. FOR'D	1100	00
AMT. DEPOSITED (DATE)		
TOTAL	1100	00
AMT. THIS CHECK	200	00
BAL. CAR'D. FOR'D.	900	00

828 Westfield Road
Salem, OR 97304-1237
Putt Around
NO. 20 96-523/1232
July 1 19 82
PAY TO THE ORDER OF Sasson Supply Company $ 200.00
Two hundred and no/100 DOLLARS
Security National Bank
SALEM, OREGON
FOR Payment on account BY Harry Rossi
⑆1232052321⑆ 68⑈545⑈09⑈

Recording a part payment of a liability. The analysis of this transaction into its debit and credit parts is explained on page 55. Line 3 of the illustration, page 71, shows how this transaction is recorded in a cash journal.

The steps in journalizing this transaction in a cash journal are below.

1 ***Date of entry.*** Write the day of the month, *1*, in the Date column.

2 ***Debit part of entry.*** Debit the Sasson Supply Company account by writing *$200.00* in the General Debit column. Also, write *Sasson Supply Company* in the Account Title column.

3 ***Credit part of entry.*** Credit Cash by writing *$200.00* in the Cash Credit column. The column heading, *Cash Credit*, shows the account to be credited. There is no need to write the account title.

4 ***Indication of source document.*** Write *C20* in the Doc. No. column to show that Check No. 20 is issued for this transaction. *C* stands for *check*. The check number is obtained from the check stub. The check number in the Doc. No. column shows which check stub contains additional details about the transaction. Since this information can be located quickly, these details are not recorded in a journal.

Journalizing a revenue transaction

July 1, 1982. Received cash from daily sales, $250.00. Cash Register Tape No. T1.

Source document for a revenue transaction. All cash sales for each day are totaled at the end of the day. To save time, only one transaction is recorded for the total daily sales. *(CONCEPT: Realization of Revenue)* At the end of each day, Putt Around's cash register prints the total amount of the day's sales. A paper tape inside a cash register on which details of transactions are printed is called a detail tape. The tape for the day is removed from the cash register and numbered with an abbreviation, *T1*. The letter *T* is used by Putt Around as an abbreviation for *cash register tape*. The number *1* is the date on which the tape was printed by the cash register. The cash register tape is used as the source document for daily cash sales transactions. *(CONCEPT: Objective Evidence)*

Recording a revenue transaction. The July 1 daily cash sales transaction is analyzed as described on page 59. The result of this analysis is recorded in Putt Around's cash journal, line 4, page 71.

The steps in journalizing this transaction in a cash journal are below.

1 ***Date of entry.*** Write the day of the month, *1*, in the Date column.

2 ***Debit part of entry.*** Debit the cash account by writing *$250.00* in the Cash Debit column.

3 ***Credit part of entry.*** Credit the sales account by writing *$250.00* in the Sales Credit column. Writing the account title *Sales* is not necessary. The heading of the special column shows clearly that the sales account is to be credited. Place a check mark in the Account Title column. A check mark shows that no account title needs to be written for this entry.

> Revenue from sales occurs almost daily at Putt Around. Thus, a special column for *Sales Credit* is provided in the cash journal. This special column saves time in journalizing.

4 ***Indication of source document.*** Write *T1* in the Doc. No. column. *T1* shows which cash register tape is the source document for this entry.

5 ***For CASH sales only.*** Place a check mark in the Post. Ref. column. This check mark shows that no separate amounts are to be posted from this line of the journal. Posting from special amount columns is described in Chapter 6.

Journalizing an expense transaction

July 1, 1982. Paid cash for July rent, $600.00. Check No. 21.

Source document for an expense transaction. The source document for this expense transaction is the check stub for Check No. 21. *(CONCEPT: Objective Evidence)*

Recording an expense transaction. This rent expense transaction is analyzed into debit and credit parts as described on page 59. The entry is on line 5 of the cash journal below.

CASH JOURNAL — PAGE 1

	1 Cash Debit	2 Cash Credit	Date	Account Title	Doc. No.	Post. Ref.	3 General Debit	4 General Credit	5 Sales Credit	
5		600 00	1	Rent Expense	C21		600 00			5
6	500 00		1	Harry Rossi, Capital	R11			500 00		6
7		50 00	2	Supplies	C22		50 00			7
8		25 00	2	Utilities Expense	C23		25 00			8
9		400 00	2	Maintenance Equipment	C24		400 00			9
10		100 00	2	Harry Rossi, Drawing	C25		100 00			10
11		10 00	2	Miscellaneous Expense	C26		10 00			11
12										12
13										13

Cash journal

The steps in recording this transaction in a cash journal are below.

1 ***Date of entry.*** Write the day of the month, *1*, in the Date column.

2 ***Debit part of entry.*** Debit the rent expense account by writing *$600.00* in the General Debit column. Also, write *Rent Expense* in the Account Title column.

3 ***Credit part of entry.*** Credit the cash account by writing *$600.00* in the Cash Credit column.

4 ***Indication of source document.*** Write *C21* in the Doc. No. column to show that Check No. 21 is issued for this transaction.

Journalizing an additional investment by an owner

July 1, 1982. Received cash from Harry Rossi, owner, as an additional investment in the business, $500.00. Receipt No. 11.

Source document for an additional investment by an owner. Cash received from a sales transaction is recorded on a cash register by Putt Around. Cash received from all other sources is recorded on printed receipt forms. The preparation of receipt forms is described on page 74. The source document for an additional investment transaction is the receipt stub prepared when the cash is received. *(CONCEPT: Objective Evidence)*

Recording an additional investment by an owner. This transaction is analyzed into debit and credit parts as described on pages 55 and 56. The entry to record this transaction is on line 6 of the cash journal, page 77.

The steps in recording this transaction in a cash journal are below.

1 ***Date of entry.*** Write the day of the month, *1*, in the Date column.

2 ***Debit part of entry.*** Write the debit amount, *$500.00*, in the Cash Debit column. The name of an account need not be written in the Account Title column. The name of the account is already in the amount column heading.

3 ***Credit part of entry.*** Write the credit amount, *$500.00*, in the General Credit column. This amount is written in the General Credit column because there is no special amount column for Capital Credit. Write the name of the account, *Harry Rossi, Capital*, in the Account Title column. This account title is needed to show to which account the amount in the General Credit column will be posted.

4 *Source document.* Write the abbreviation for the source document, *R11*, in the Doc. No. column.

Journalizing a buying of supplies transaction

July 2, 1982. Paid cash for supplies, $50.00. Check No. 22.

Source document for a buying of supplies transaction. The check stub written for Check No. 22 is the source document for this transaction. *(CONCEPT: Objective Evidence)*

Recording a buying of supplies transaction. This transaction is analyzed into debit and credit parts as described on page 56. The entry to record this transaction is on line 7 of the cash journal, page 77.

The steps in recording this transaction in a cash journal are below.

1 *Date of entry.* Write the date, *2*, in the Date column.

2 *Debit part of entry.* Write the debit amount, *$50.00*, in the General Debit column. Also, write *Supplies* in the Account Title column.

3 *Credit part of entry.* Write the credit amount, *$50.00*, in the Cash Credit column.

4 *Source document.* Write the abbreviation for the source document, *C22*, in the Doc. No. column.

Journalizing a utilities expense transaction

July 2, 1982. Paid cash for telephone bill, $25.00. Check No. 23.

Source document for a utilities expense transaction. The source document is the check stub for Check No. 23. *(CONCEPT: Objective Evidence)*

Recording a utilities expense transaction. This transaction is analyzed into its debit and credit parts as described on pages 59 and 60. The entry to record this transaction is shown on line 8 of the cash journal, page 77.

The steps in recording this transaction in a cash journal are below.

1 *Date.* Write the day of the month, *2*, in the Date column.

2 *Debit part.* Write the debit amount, *$25.00*, in the General Debit column. Also, write *Utilities Expense* in the Account Title column.

3 *Credit part.* Write the credit amount, *$25.00*, in the Cash Credit column.

4 ***Source document.*** Write *C23* in the Doc. No. column.

Journalizing a buying of equipment transaction

July 2, 1982. Paid cash for a new lawn mower, $400.00. Check No. 24.

Source document for a buying of equipment transaction. The source document for this transaction is the check stub for Check No. 24. *(CONCEPT: Objective Evidence)*

Recording a buying of equipment transaction. This transaction is analyzed into debit and credit parts as described on page 56. The entry to record this transaction is on line 9 of the cash journal, page 77.

The steps in recording this transaction in a cash journal are below.

1 ***Date.*** Write the day of the month, *2*, in the Date column.

2 ***Debit part.*** Write the debit amount, *$400.00*, in the General Debit column. Also, write *Maintenance Equipment* in the Account Title column.

3 ***Credit part.*** Write the credit amount, *$400.00*, in the Cash Credit column.

4 ***Source document.*** Write *C24* in the Doc. No. column.

Journalizing a cash withdrawal transaction

July 2, 1982. Paid cash to the owner, Harry Rossi, for personal use, $100.00. Check No. 25.

Source document for a cash withdrawal transaction. The check stub for Check No. 25 is the source document for this transaction. *(CONCEPT: Objective Evidence)*

Recording a cash withdrawal transaction. This transaction is analyzed into debit and credit parts as described on page 57. The entry to record this transaction is on line 10 of the cash journal, page 77.

The steps in recording this transaction in a cash journal are below.

1 ***Date.*** Write the date, *2*, in the Date column.

2 ***Debit part.*** Write the debit amount, *$100.00*, in the General Debit column. Also, write *Harry Rossi, Drawing* in the Account Title column.

3 ***Credit part.*** Write the credit amount, *$100.00*, in the Cash Credit column.

4 ***Source document***. Write the abbreviation, *C25*, in the Doc. No. column.

Journalizing a miscellaneous expense transaction

July 2, 1982. Paid cash for repair of broken window, $10.00. Check No. 26.

Some expenses occur infrequently. Separate expense accounts are used only for the frequently occurring expenses. Those expenses occurring infrequently are recorded in an account titled Miscellaneous Expense.

Source document for a miscellaneous expense transaction. The source document for this transaction is the check stub for Check No. 26. *(CONCEPT: Objective Evidence)*

Recording a miscellaneous expense transaction. This transaction is analyzed into debit and credit parts as described on page 60. The entry to record this transaction is shown on line 11 of the cash journal, page 77.

The steps in recording this transaction in a cash journal are below.

1 ***Date.*** Write the date, *2*, in the Date column.

2 ***Debit part.*** Write the debit amount, *$10.00*, in the General Debit column. Also, write *Miscellaneous Expense* in the Account Title column.

3 ***Credit part.*** Write the credit amount, *$10.00*, in the Cash Credit column.

4 ***Source document.*** Write *C26* in the Doc. No. column.

Journalizing other business transactions

Putt Around's transactions for the remainder of July are similar to those described in this chapter. The complete July cash journal for Putt Around is on pages 82 and 83.

Each transaction recorded by Putt Around during July requires a single line in the cash journal. Much time and space is saved by using a multi-column cash journal instead of a two-column general journal.

PROVING THE ACCURACY OF A CASH JOURNAL

The accuracy of recording in a cash journal must be checked. The procedures for verifying the accuracy of accounting work are known as proving.

CASH JOURNAL PAGE 1

	1	2					3	4	5	
	CASH						GENERAL			
	DEBIT	CREDIT	DATE	ACCOUNT TITLE	DOC. NO.	POST. REF.	DEBIT	CREDIT	SALES CREDIT	
1			1982 July 1	Balance on hand, $1,100.00		✓				1
2	5000		1	Maintenance Equipment	R10			5000		2
3		20000	1	Sasson Supply Company	C20		20000			3
4	25000		1	✓	J1	✓			25000	4
5		60000	1	Rent Expense	C21		60000			5
6	50000		1	Harry Rossi, Capital	R11			50000		6
7		5000	2	Supplies	C22		5000			7
8		2500	2	Utilities Expense	C23		2500			8
9		40000	2	Maintenance Equipment	C24		40000			9
10		10000	2	Harry Rossi, Drawing	C25		10000			10
11		1000	2	Miscellaneous Expense	C26		1000			11
12	10000		2	✓	J2	✓			10000	12
13	20000		3	✓	J3	✓			20000	13
14		6000	5	Utilities Expense	C27		6000			14
15	10000		5	✓	J5	✓			10000	15
16		2500	6	Advertising Expense	C28		2500			16
17	10000		6	✓	J6	✓			10000	17
18		1000	7	Miscellaneous Expense	C29		1000			18
19	8000		7	✓	J7	✓			8000	19
20	4500		8	✓	J8	✓			4500	20
21	5500		9	✓	J9	✓			5500	21
22	15000		10	✓	J10	✓			15000	22
23		7500	12	Supplies	C30		7500			23
24		10000	12	Golf Equipment	C31		10000			24
25	5200		12	✓	J12	✓			5200	25
26	168200	165500	12	Carried Forward		✓	165500	55000	113200	26
27										27

Completed cash journal

Proving the accuracy of each entry in a cash journal

Each transaction has an equal debit and credit part. After a transaction is recorded in any journal, the equality of debits and credits must be checked for that transaction. For example, the transaction on line 2 of the cash journal above has both a $50.00 debit and a $50.00 credit. Debits and credits are equal.

Proving the entire cash journal

The equality of all debits and credits for all entries in any journal must also be proved. Also, cash must be proved. These proofs are made before a cash journal is completed at the end of each month.

Proving cash. Determining that the amount of cash on hand agrees with the accounting records is called proving cash. Cash on hand includes the money in the bank plus all cash not deposited in the bank. Cash is proved daily in many businesses. Cash is always proved at the end of a month. Putt Around finds that proving cash once a month is sufficient. The amount of cash received is not great enough to require more frequent proof.

CASH JOURNAL — PAGE 2

	1 CASH DEBIT	2 CASH CREDIT	DATE	ACCOUNT TITLE	DOC. NO.	POST. REF.	3 GENERAL DEBIT	4 GENERAL CREDIT	5 SALES CREDIT	
1	168200	165500	1982 July 12	Brought Forward		✓	165500	55000	113200	1
2	6000		13	✓	J13	✓			6000	2
3	8000		14	✓	J14	✓			8000	3
4		1500	15	Miscellaneous Expense	C32		1500			4
5	5000		15	✓	J15	✓			5000	5
6	10000		16	✓	J16	✓			10000	6
7	15000		17	✓	J17	✓			15000	7
8	4000		19	✓	J19	✓			4000	8
9		3200	20	Utilities Expense	C33		3200			9
10	4500		20	✓	J20	✓			4500	10
11	5100		21	✓	J21	✓			5100	11
12		1800	22	Miscellaneous Expense	C34		1800			12
13	4300		22	✓	J22	✓			4300	13
14		5000	23	Harry Rossi, Drawing	C35		5000			14
15	7500		23	✓	J23	✓			7500	15
16		10000	24	Supplies	C36		10000			16
17	17500		24	✓	J24	✓			17500	17
18	3000		26	✓	J26	✓			3000	18
19		500	27	Miscellaneous Expense	C37		500			19
20	4500		27	✓	J27	✓			4500	20
21	4000		28	✓	J28	✓			4000	21
22	5000		29	✓	J29	✓			5000	22
23		1200	30	Miscellaneous Expense	C38		1200			23
24	8800		30	✓	J30	✓			8800	24
25	17500		31	✓	J31	✓			17500	25
26	297900	188700	31	Totals			188700	55000	242900	26
27										27

Completed cash journal

Putt Around proves cash at the end of July as explained below.

Beginning cash balance	$1,100.00
(This is the amount of cash on hand at the beginning of July. The amount is taken from line 1 of the cash journal, page 82.)	
Plus cash received during the month	2,979.00
(This amount is the total of the Cash Debit column in the cash journal. The amount is found by using an adding machine to add the column.)	
Equals total	$4,079.00
Less cash paid out during the month	1,887.00
(This amount is the total of the Cash Credit column in the cash journal.)	
Equals cash on hand at the end of the month	$2,192.00

The last amount in the cash proof, $2,192.00, should be the same as the amount of cash on hand. On July 31, 1982, all cash receipts have been deposited in the bank by Putt Around. Check Stub No. 39 in Putt Around's checkbook shows a balance of $2,192.00. The cash proof agrees with the checkbook balance. Cash is proved.

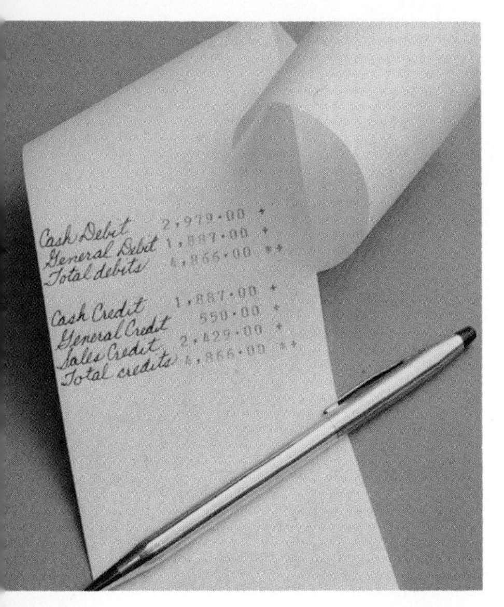

Totaling a cash journal. At the end of each month, an adding machine is used by Putt Around to total all columns of the cash journal. Then, the totals of all debit columns are added. Also, the totals of all credit columns are added. The adding machine tape at the left shows this work for the cash journal, page 83. The column headings from the cash journal are handwritten on the tape to help identify each amount.

As shown on the adding machine tape, the total of the debit columns is $4,866.00. The total of the credit columns is also $4,866.00. The equality of the debits and credits in the complete journal has been maintained. Therefore, Putt Around assumes that the journal is accurate.

If the total of all debits is not equal to the total of all credits, an error has been made. The error or errors must be found and corrected. No more work should be done until the errors are corrected.

Proving a journal

Three accuracy checks of the cash journal are made by Putt Around.

1. As each transaction is recorded, the equality of debits and credits is checked.
2. At the end of each month, cash is proved.
3. At the end of each month, the equality of debits and credits for the entire cash journal is checked.

RULING A CASH JOURNAL

When the three accuracy checks are made and proved, the cash journal is ruled.

Ruling a cash journal at the end of a month

At the end of each month, Putt Around's cash journal is ruled as shown below.

CASH JOURNAL PAGE 2

	1 CASH DEBIT	2 CASH CREDIT	DATE	ACCOUNT TITLE	DOC. NO.	POST. REF.	3 GENERAL DEBIT	4 GENERAL CREDIT	5 SALES CREDIT	
25	175 00		31	✓	T31	✓			175 00	25
26	2 979 00	1 887 00	31	Totals			1 887 00	550 00	2 429 00	26
27										27

Cash journal totaled, proved, and ruled

The steps in ruling Putt Around's cash journal are below.

1 Draw a single line across all amount columns. The single line shows that the columns are being added.

2 Write the total of each column below the single line. The totals are taken from the adding machine tape, page 84, prepared to prove the cash journal.

If an adding machine is not available, the columns may be added mentally. The totals are then written on a separate piece of paper.

3 Write the last day of the month in the date column.

4 Write the word *Totals* in the Account Title column.

5 Draw double lines across all amount columns below the column totals. The double lines show that the work of totaling and ruling is completed.

Forwarding totals to a new page

Sometimes a page in a cash journal is filled before the end of a month. If this happens, the page is totaled and the totals forwarded to a new page. The illustration below shows page 1 of Putt Around's cash journal with totals prepared for forwarding.

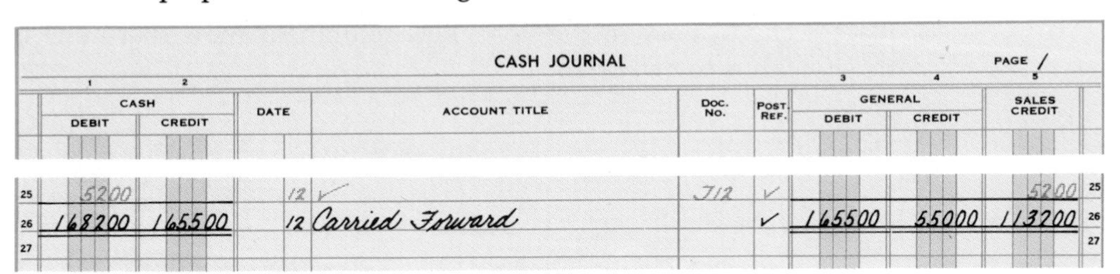

CASH JOURNAL — PAGE 1

	1	2					3	4	5	
	CASH						GENERAL			
	DEBIT	CREDIT	DATE	ACCOUNT TITLE	DOC. NO.	POST. REF.	DEBIT	CREDIT	SALES CREDIT	
25	5200		12	✓	312	✓			5200	25
26	168200	165500	12	Carried Forward		✓	165500	55000	113200	26
27										27

Column totals prepared for forwarding to a new page of a cash journal

The steps in forwarding totals to a new journal page are below.

1 Total all columns of the completed page.

2 Prove the equality of the debits and credits.

3 Draw a single line across all amount columns.

4 Write the total of each column below the single line.

5 Write the date in the Date column.

6 Write the words *Carried Forward* in the Account Title column.

7 Place a check mark in the Post. Ref. column to show that none of these totals is to be posted.

8 Draw double lines across all amount columns.

The illustration below shows page 2 of Putt Around's cash journal with totals carried forward.

CASH JOURNAL — PAGE 2

	Cash Debit (1)	Cash Credit (2)	Date	Account Title	Doc. No.	Post. Ref.	General Debit (3)	General Credit (4)	Sales Credit (5)	
1	1682 00	1655 00	1982 July 12	Brought Forward		✓	1655 00	550 00	1132 00	1
2										2

Column totals brought forward to a new page of a cash journal

The steps in entering totals brought forward to a new journal page are below.

1 Write the date in the Date column.

2 Write the words *Brought Forward* in the Account Title column.

3 Write the totals from the preceding page in each amount column.

Prove that the debit totals equal the credit totals again to be sure the totals are forwarded correctly.

4 Place a check mark in the Post. Ref. column to show that none of these totals is to be posted.

MAKING CORRECTIONS

Sometimes the debit amounts will not equal the credit amounts in an entry. If an entry is not in balance, the errors must be found and corrected. If an error is made in writing an amount, cancel the error by drawing a line through the amount. The correct amount is then written immediately above the canceled item. Also, if an error is made in any part of an entry, draw a line through the error. Then the correction is written immediately above the canceled part of the entry. Corrections are shown in the illustration below.

CASH JOURNAL — PAGE 5

	Cash Debit (1)	Cash Credit (2)	Date	Account Title	Doc. No.	Post. Ref.	General Debit (3)	General Credit (4)	Sales Credit (5)	
16	250 00		8	✓	T8	✓			250 00 (corrected from ~~2500 00~~)	16
17		15 00	8	Supplies (corrected from ~~Miscellaneous Expense~~)	C92		15 00			17
18										18

Making corrections

On line 16 above, an error was made in writing an amount. On line 17 an error was made in writing an account title.

ACCOUNTING TERMS

What is the meaning of each of the following?

1. journalizing
2. double-entry accounting
3. special journal
4. cash journal
5. special amount column
6. receipt
7. check
8. detail tape
9. proving cash

QUESTIONS FOR INDIVIDUAL STUDY

1. Why is accounting information first recorded in a journal?
2. Why is double-entry accounting said to be complete accounting?
3. Why does Putt Around use a cash journal?
4. Why did Putt Around record the opening entry in a general journal instead of a cash journal?
5. For which accounts are special amount columns included in a multi-column journal? What are the special amount columns in Putt Around's cash journal?
6. What must be done with a transaction's information before it is recorded in a journal?
7. What are the two kinds of *source documents* used by Putt Around for receipt of cash transactions?
8. Why is the account title *Sales* not written in a cash journal's Account Title column for a cash sales transaction?
9. What is the source document for a cash payments transaction?
10. What kinds of transactions are recorded in a miscellaneous expense account?
11. What is the procedure for proving cash?
12. How is the accuracy of the cash journal proved?
13. How is a cash journal ruled?
14. Why might a cash journal be totaled and ruled before the end of a month?
15. If an error is made in writing an account title in a journal, how should a correction be made?

CASES FOR MANAGEMENT DECISION

CASE 1 Mrs. Malloy uses a two-column general journal to record all transactions for her business. She is thinking of changing to a multi-column cash journal similar to the one described in this chapter. Mr. Malloy recommends that she continue to use the two-column general journal for two reasons. (a) The equality of debits and credits can be checked more easily than in a cash journal. (b) The two-column general journal does not need to be totaled and ruled. Do you agree with Mr. or Mrs. Malloy? Why?

CASE 2 Nicole Weatherby owns a small bus service that carries young children to and from a nursery school. Ms. Weatherby refers to all cash payments of the business as "my expenses." Is Ms. Weatherby correct in referring to all cash payments as expenses? Why?

CASE 3 When Mr. Minot prepares a check, he fills in the check stub first and then writes the check. When Mr. Billingsly prepares a check, he writes the check first and then fills in the stub. Which is the preferred procedure? Why?

DRILLS FOR UNDERSTANDING

DRILL 5-D 1 Analyzing transactions

Before transactions can be recorded in a journal, the transactions are analyzed into debit and credit parts. This drill provides practice in analyzing transactions. Use Putt Around's chart of accounts, page 16, for needed account titles.

Transactions

1. Received cash from week's sales, $100.00.
2. Paid cash for month's rent, $150.00.
3. Paid cash for telephone bill, $25.00.
4. Received cash from the owner as additional investment in the business, $500.00.
5. Paid cash for advertising, $40.00.
6. Paid cash for having store windows washed, $10.00.
7. Received cash from sale of worn out golf clubs, $30.00.
8. Paid cash to Melcor Equipment Company for amount owed, $100.00.
9. Paid cash for supplies, $20.00.
10. Paid cash for new maintenance equipment, $300.00.
11. Paid cash to the owner for personal use, $100.00.

Instructions: 1. Use two T accounts for each transaction. Write the name of the accounts affected on the T accounts. T accounts for Transaction 1 are at the right.

2. Use the T accounts prepared in Instruction 1. Write the debit amount on the debit side of the correct account. Write the credit amount on the credit side of the correct account. The T accounts for Transaction 1 are at the right.

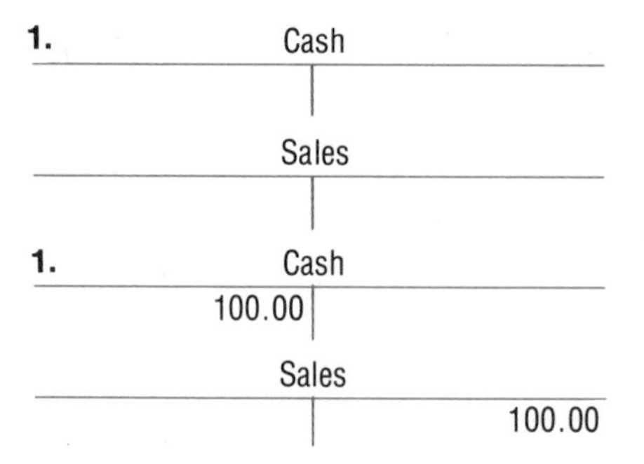

DRILL 5-D 2 Analyzing transactions

A selected list of transactions is given below for a business.

Transactions

1. Received cash for fees from customers.
2. Paid cash for advertising in local newspaper.
3. Paid cash for month's rent.
4. Paid cash for telephone bill.
5. Received cash from sale of an old office chair.
6. Paid cash to owner for personal use.
7. Paid cash for gas and oil used in automobile.
8. Paid cash for postage stamps used in office.
9. Paid cash to Pfitzer Company for part of amount owed.
10. Paid cash for electric bill.
11. Paid cash for new electronic calculator to use in office.
12. Received cash from owner as additional investment in business.
13. Paid cash for supplies.

Some of the account titles on the business' chart of accounts are below.

Cash
Supplies
Office Equipment
Pfitzer Company (liability)
Donna Major, Capital
Donna Major, Drawing
Fees Revenue
Advertising Expense
Automobile Expense
Miscellaneous Expense
Rent Expense
Utilities Expense

Use a form similar to the one below. Transaction 1 is given on the form as an example.

	1	2	3	4	5	6
Trans. No.	Account Titles Affected	Account Classification	Account is		Balance of Account is	
			Debited	Credited	Increased	Decreased
1	*Cash*	*Asset*	√		√	
	Fees Revenue	*Revenue*		√	√	

Instructions: 1. In Column 1, write the names of the two accounts affected by each transaction.

2. In Column 2, write the account classification for each account title written in Column 1.

3. In either Column 3 or 4, place a check mark (√) to show if the account is debited or credited for this transaction.

4. In either Column 5 or 6, place a check mark (√) to show if the account balance is increased or decreased.

APPLICATION PROBLEMS

PROBLEM 5-1 Recording transactions in a cash journal

Ema Langhorn is a registered architect. She receives revenue from fees charged to clients. Mrs. Langhorn does not use a cash register. The receipt of all cash is first recorded on receipt forms. The receipt forms are the source documents for all cash received transactions.

The following accounts are used by Mrs. Langhorn's business. *Assets*: Cash, Automobile, Drafting Equipment, Office Equipment. *Liabilities*: Mixer Equipment Company. *Capital*: Ema Langhorn, Capital; Ema Langhorn, Drawing. *Revenue*: Fees. *Expenses*: Automobile Expense, Miscellaneous Expense, Rent Expense, Utilities Expense.

The following transactions were completed during May of the current year.

Transactions

May 1. Paid cash for office rent, $350.00. C201.
1. Paid cash for minor repairs to business' automobile, $36.00. C202.
2. Received cash from sale of an old office desk, $45.00. R110.
2. Received cash from fees, $1,170.00. R111.
2. Paid cash for gas and oil used in business' automobile, $11.50. C203.
3. Paid cash for new office desk, $400.00. C204.
4. Received cash from fees, $1,160.00. R112.

May 7. Received cash from fees, $810.00. R113.
9. Paid cash for new drafting equipment, $175.00. C205.
15. Received cash from fees, $360.00. R114.
18. Paid cash to Mixer Equipment Company for amount owed, $864.00. C206.
22. Paid cash for electric bill, $38.50. C207.
28. Received cash from fees, $810.00. R115.
28. Paid cash for telephone bill, $60.75. C208.
30. Received cash from fees, $270.00. R116.
31. Paid cash to owner for personal use, $2,000.00. C209.

Instructions: 1. Use a pair of T accounts for each transaction. Analyze each transaction into its debit and credit parts in the T accounts.

2. Use page 9 of a cash journal similar to the one on page 83. Record the beginning cash balance for May 1 of the current year, $720.00.

3. Record each transaction. Follow the T account analysis completed in Instruction 1.

4. Prove cash. The ending balance on Check Stub No. 209 is $1,409.25.

5. Prove the equality of debits and credits in the journal.

6. Rule the cash journal.

The solution to Problem 5-1 is needed to complete Problem 6-1 in the next chapter.

PROBLEM 5-2 Recording transactions in a cash journal

Richard Connelly operates a delivery service. The business uses a cash register to record revenue from the delivery services. All other cash received is recorded on receipt forms.

The following accounts are used by Connelly's Delivery Service. *Assets*: Cash, Supplies, Delivery Equipment, Office Equipment. *Liabilities*: Community Bank, Gotman's Garage. *Capital*: Richard Connelly, Capital; Richard Connelly, Drawing. *Revenue*: Sales. *Expenses*: Advertising Expense, Automobile Expense, Miscellaneous Expense, Rent Expense, Utilities Expense.

Instructions: 1. Record the beginning cash balance for May 1 of the current year, $1,045.00. Use page 1 of a cash journal.

2. Record the transactions in the cash journal.

May 1. Received cash from sales, $375.00. T1.
1. Paid cash for month's rent, $600.00. C109.
3. Paid cash for telephone bill, $62.30. C110.
3. Received cash from sales, $250.00. T3.
4. Received cash from sales, $125.00. T4.
5. Paid cash for supplies, $60.00. C111.
5. Received cash from sales, $60.00. T5.
6. Received cash from sales, $75.00. T6.
7. Received cash from sale of old office chairs, $25.00. R4.
7. Received cash from sales, $210.00. T7.
10. Paid cash to local newspaper for classified advertising, $75.00. C112.
10. Received cash from sales, $100.00. T10.
11. Received cash from sales, $215.00. T11.
12. Received cash from sales, $95.00. T12.
13. Paid cash to Gotman's Garage for part of amount owed, $200.00. C113.
13. Received cash from sales, $80.00. T13.

May 14. Received cash from sales, $60.00. T14.
17. Paid cash for automobile gasoline and oil expense, $240.00. C114.
17. Received cash from sales, $325.00. T17.
18. Paid cash for expense of fixing lock on office door, $30.00. C115.
18. Received cash from sales, $115.00. T18.
19. Paid cash for new office chairs, $140.00. C116.
19. Received cash from sales, $50.00. T19.

Instructions: 3. Prepare page 1 of the cash journal for forwarding. Total the amount columns and prove the equality of debits and credits. Record the totals to be carried forward and rule the journal.

4. Record the totals brought forward on line 1 of page 2 of the cash journal. Prove the equality of debits and credits again.

5. Continue recording the transactions for May.

May 20. Received cash from sales, $70.00. T20.
21. Received cash from sales, $135.00. T21.
24. Received cash from sales, $115.00. T24.
25. Paid cash to the owner for personal use, $700.00. C117.
25. Received cash from sales, $50.00. T25.
26. Received cash from sales, $65.00. T26.
27. Paid cash for automobile gasoline and oil, $325.00. C118.
27. Paid cash for tune up of automobile, $130.00. C119.
27. Received cash from sales, $55.00. T27.
28. Paid cash for supplies, $120.00. C120.
28. Received cash from sales, $70.00. T28.
31. Received cash from sales, $75.00. T31.
31. Paid cash for electric bill, $125.00. C121.
31. Paid cash for minor repairs to an office chair, $25.00. C122.

Instructions: 6. Prove cash. The balance on Check Stub No. 122 is $1,007.70.

7. Prove page 2 of the cash journal.

8. Rule page 2 of the cash journal.

ENRICHMENT PROBLEMS

MASTERY PROBLEM 5-M Recording transactions in a cash journal

Neiman Townsend operates Blue Dart Taxi Service. The business' revenue account is titled *Fares Earned*. The business does not use a cash register. At the end of each day the fares are totaled and recorded on a receipt form. The receipt form is the source document for all cash received transactions.

The following are accounts used by the business. *Assets*: Cash, Supplies, Taxi Equipment. *Liabilities*: Jerry's Garage, Merchants Bank. *Capital*: Neiman Townsend, Capital; Neiman Townsend, Drawing. *Revenue*: Fares Earned. *Expenses*: Advertising Expense, Gas and Oil Expense, Rent Expense, Repairs and Maintenance Expense, Utilities Expense.

Instructions: 1. On page 3 of a cash journal, record the beginning cash balance on hand, $1,153.00. Use September 1 of the current year.

2. Record the transactions in the cash journal.

Sept. 1. Received cash from fares, $110.00. R1.
2. Paid cash for rent, $300.00. C21.

Sept. 2. Paid cash for gas and oil, $12.75. C22.
3. Received cash from fares, $138.50. R2.
4. Paid cash for telephone bill, $23.80. C23.
6. Received cash from fares, $180.20. R3.
6. Paid cash to Jerry's Garage for part of amount owed, $75.00. C24.
7. Received cash from fares, $110.00. R4.
8. Paid cash for repairs to taxi, $55.00. C25.
9. Paid cash for gas and oil, $12.50. C26.
11. Paid cash to Merchants Bank for amount owed, $170.00. C27.
13. Paid cash for electric bill, $27.20. C28.
15. Received cash from fares, $75.00. R5.
16. Paid cash for gas and oil, $15.90. C29.
18. Received cash from fares, $36.50. R6.
20. Paid cash for supplies, $80.00. C30.
21. Received cash from fares, $36.50. R7.
23. Paid cash for gas and oil, $11.20. C31.
25. Received cash from fares, $188.70. R8.
27. Paid cash for newspaper advertising, $12.75. C32.
29. Received cash from fares, $62.00. R9.
30. Paid cash to owner for personal use, $50.00. C33.

Instructions: 3. Prove cash. The ending balance on Check Stub No. 33 is $1,244.30.
4. Prove the cash journal.
5. Rule the cash journal.

CHALLENGE PROBLEM 5-C Recording transactions in a cash journal

Sue Lozier operates Pacific Travel Agency. The cash journal used by the business is similar to the one on page 83. However, the arrangement of the columns is not the same. The business' cash journal is below.

CASH JOURNAL								Page 2
Date	Account Title	Doc. No.	Post. Ref.	General		Cash		Commissions Revenue Credit
				Debit	Credit	Debit	Credit	

The following are some of the ledger accounts used by the business. Cash; Supplies; Office Equipment; Sue Lozier, Capital; Sue Lozier, Drawing; Commissions Revenue; Advertising Expense; Automobile Expense; Miscellaneous Expense; Rent Expense; Utilities Expense.

Instructions: 1. Record the beginning cash balance on hand, $2,475.00, on page 2 of the cash journal. Use October 1 of the current year.
2. Record the transactions in the cash journal.

Oct. 1. Received cash as commissions, $292.00. R10.
1. Received cash from owner as additional investment in business, $1,000.00. R11.
2. Paid cash for gas and oil for automobile, $78.65. C101.
4. Paid cash for month's rent, $260.00. C102.
5. Received cash as commissions, $455.00. R12.

Oct. 6. Received cash as commissions, $150.00. R13.
8. Paid cash for supplies, $20.00. C103.
11. Paid cash for advertising in local newspaper, $15.60. C104.
13. Paid cash to have office cleaned, $25.00. C105.
15. Paid cash for gas and oil, $23.70. C106.
18. Received cash as commissions, $747.50. R14.
20. Received cash as commissions, $625.00. R15.
22. Received cash from sale of old piece of office furniture, $50.00. R16.
25. Paid cash for telephone bill, $75.00. C107.
28. Paid cash for advertising in local newspaper, $15.60. C108.
29. Received cash as commissions, $1,040.00. R17.
31. Paid cash to owner for personal use, $300.00. C109.

Instructions: 3. Prove cash. The ending balance on Check Stub No. 109 is $6,020.95.

4. Prove the cash journal.

5. Rule the cash journal.

Posting

ENABLING PERFORMANCE TASKS

After studying Chapter 6, you will be able to:

a. Explain accounting principles and practices related to posting.
b. Arrange accounts for a small service business in a chart of accounts.
c. Post amounts from General amount columns of a cash journal.
d. Post column totals of a cash journal.

The financial position of a business for a specific date is shown on a balance sheet. As transactions occur the balances of accounts listed on a balance sheet change. Therefore, each business transaction changes the financial position of a business.

The balance sheet in Chapter 2, page 19, shows the financial position of Putt Around on July 1, 1982. The transactions from July 1 to July 31 change the account balances for Putt Around. Thus, Putt Around's financial position is not the same on July 31 as it was on July 1. *(CONCEPT: Accounting Period Cycle)*

Putt Around records each transaction in a cash journal as described in Chapter 5. A cash journal does not show in one place the account balances on a specific date. To show how transactions change account balances, information is posted from journals to ledgers. The debits and credits in each account are used to determine a new account balance. The

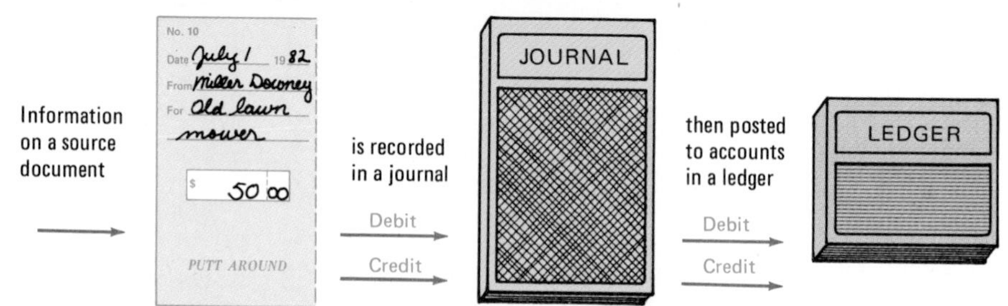

new account balances on a specific date provide the information for an up-to-date balance sheet. *(CONCEPT: Adequate Disclosure)*

ARRANGING ACCOUNTS IN A LEDGER

Accounts in a ledger are arranged in the same order as they will appear on financial reports. Because the order is the same, information from the ledger accounts is easily transferred to financial statements. Putt Around's ledger accounts are listed in the order given at the right.

1 Assets
2 Liabilities
3 Capital
4 Revenue
5 Expenses

Each group of similar accounts is a division in the ledger. For example, asset accounts are in the first division of Putt Around's ledger. Expense accounts are in the last ledger division.

A list of account titles and numbers showing the location of accounts in a ledger is known as a chart of accounts. Putt Around's complete chart of accounts, page 16, has five divisions. Putt Around uses a two-digit numbering system for ledger accounts. The asset division accounts are numbered from 11 to 19. The cash account is numbered 11. The first digit, *1*, shows the division of the ledger, Assets. The second digit, *1*, shows the order of the account in the division. Thus, Cash is the first account in the assets division. Maintenance Equipment is numbered 14. The first digit, *1*, shows that the account is in the assets division. The second digit, *4*, shows that this is the fourth account in the assets division.

Ledgers for some businesses have more than five divisions. Some businesses use more than two-digit account numbers. Ledgers with more than five divisions and more than two-digit account numbers are described in later chapters.

POSTING FROM A CASH JOURNAL

Line 1 of the cash journal, page 96, shows the cash balance on hand at the beginning of July. This entry is not for a transaction. A check mark is placed in the Post. Ref. column at the time the entry is recorded. The check mark shows that the entry for the July 1, 1982, beginning cash balance is not posted. The beginning cash balance is already recorded in the cash account.

Posting general amount columns

For each amount in a General Debit or General Credit column, an account title is written in the Account Title column. The amount is posted to the account written in the Account Title column.

Posting an amount from a General Credit column. The entry on line 2 of the cash journal, page 96, includes an amount in the General Credit column.

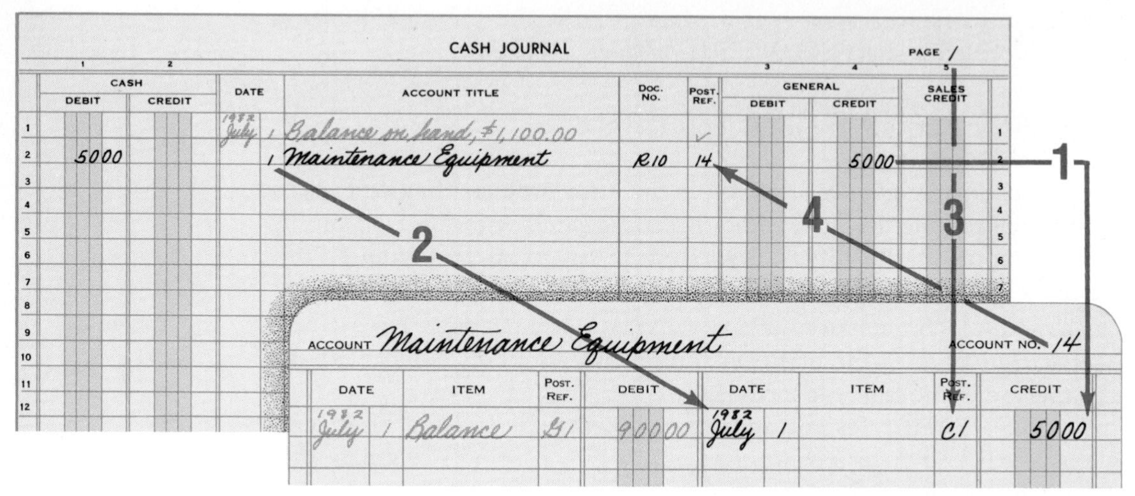

Posting from the General Credit column of the cash journal

The steps in posting the credit amount on line 2 are below.

1 Write the credit amount, *$50.00*, in the Credit column of the account Maintenance Equipment.

2 Write the date of this journal entry, *1982, July 1*, in the Date column of the ledger account.

This is the first entry on the credit side of the account. For this reason, the entire date must be written in the Date column.

3 Write the journal page number, *C1*, in the Post. Ref. column of the ledger account.

When written in a Post. Ref. column, *C* is the abbreviation for the cash journal. When more than one journal is used, the page number is coded with a journal abbreviation. Thus, *G1* means page 1 of a General journal. *C1* means page 1 of a Cash journal.

4 Return to the cash journal. Write the account number, *14*, in the cash journal's Post. Ref. column.

The posting reference numbers serve three purposes. (1) An entry in an account can be traced to its source in a journal. (2) An entry in a journal can be traced to where it is posted in an account. (3) If posting is interrupted, it is easy to see which entries still need to be posted. The entries with no posting references in the journal have not been posted. *The posting reference is always placed in the journal as the last step in the posting procedure.*

Posting an amount from a General Debit column. The entry on line 3 of the cash journal on page 97 includes an amount in a General Debit column.

CASH JOURNAL — PAGE 1

Cash Debit	Cash Credit	Date	Account Title	Doc. No.	Post. Ref.	General Debit	General Credit	Sales Credit
		1982 July 1	Balance on hand, $1,100.00		✓			
50 00		1	Maintenance Equipment	R10	14		50 00	
	200 00	1	Sasson Supply Company	C20	22	200 00		

ACCOUNT Sasson Supply Company — ACCOUNT NO. 22

Date	Item	Post. Ref.	Debit	Date	Item	Post. Ref.	Credit
1982 July 1		C1	200 00	1982 July 1	Balance	G1	550 00

Posting from the General Debit column of a cash journal

The steps in posting the debit amount from line 3 are below.

1 Write the debit amount, *$200.00*, in the Debit column of the account Sasson Supply Company.

2 Write the date of this entry, *1982, July 1*, in the Date column of the ledger account.

This is the first entry on the debit side of the account. For this reason, the complete date is written in the Date column.

3 Write the journal page, *C1*, in the Post. Ref. column of the ledger account.

4 Return to the cash journal. Write the account number, *22*, in the cash journal's Post. Ref. column.

Completing the posting of the two General columns of a cash journal. Each amount in the General Debit column is posted as described for line 3. Each amount in the General Credit column is posted as described for line 2. The amounts in the General Debit and General Credit columns are posted at frequent intervals. Frequent posting keeps accounts up to date and avoids doing all the posting at the end of a month. *(CONCEPT: Accounting Period Cycle)*

Each amount in a General Debit or a General Credit column is posted individually. Therefore, the totals of the General amount columns are *NOT* posted. The total of a journal column is posted only when an account title is listed in the column heading. A check mark (✓) is placed in parentheses under each General amount column total. The check mark shows that the total of a column is not posted. The placing of the check marks below column totals is on page 98.

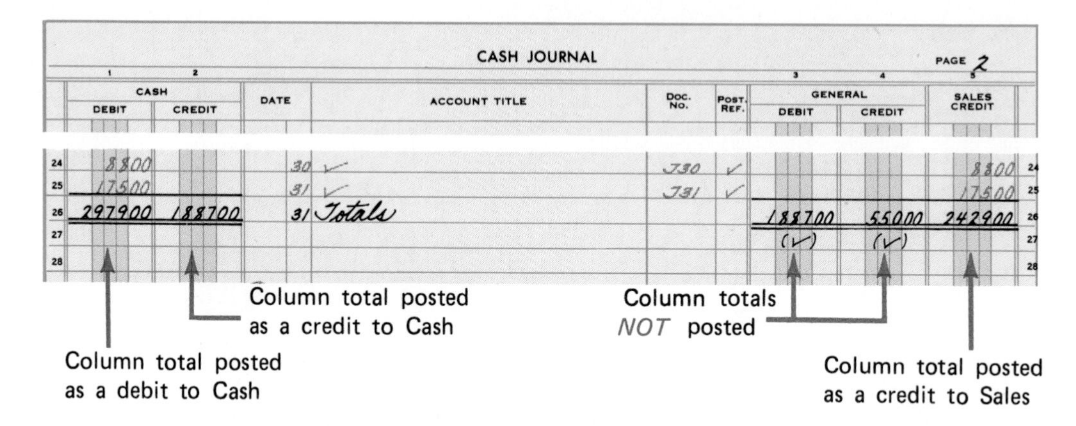

Posting special amount columns of a cash journal

Putt Around's cash journal has three special amount columns. The separate amounts written in these special amount columns are *NOT* posted individually. Only the total of a special amount column is posted. This procedure saves time in posting. For example, Putt Around's Cash Debit column for July has 29 entries recorded in it. Twenty-nine separate postings would be required to post these entries individually. Posting only the total means a savings of 28 postings.

The total of each special amount column *IS* posted to the account listed in the column heading. The total of the Cash Debit column is posted as a debit to Cash. The total of the Cash Credit column is posted as a credit to Cash. The total of the Sales Credit column is posted as a credit to Sales.

Posting the total of a Cash Debit column. Only the total of a Cash Debit column is posted. The separate amounts in this column are not posted individually.

Posting a Cash Debit column total

The posting of a Cash Debit column total is below.

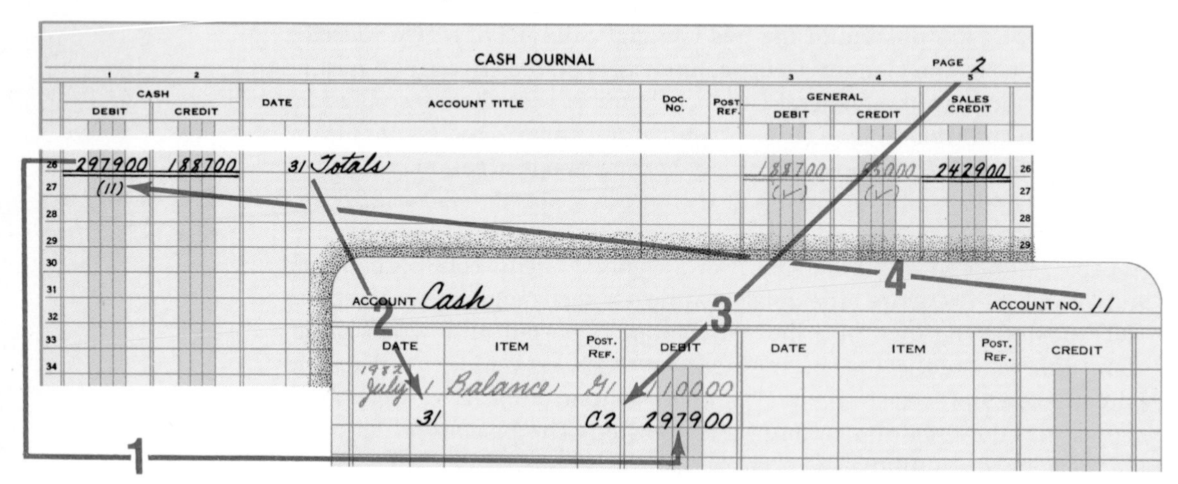

The steps in posting the Cash Debit column total are below.

1 Write the debit amount, *$2,979.00*, in the Debit column of the cash account.

2 Write the date, *31*, in the Date column of the cash account.

Only the day of the month needs to be written. The year and the month have already been written in the Date column on the debit side.

3 Write *C2* in the Post. Ref. column of the cash account.

4 Return to the cash journal. Write the account number, *11*, in parentheses immediately below the Cash Debit column total.

Posting the total of a Cash Credit column. Only the total of a Cash Credit column is posted. The posting of a Cash Credit column total is below.

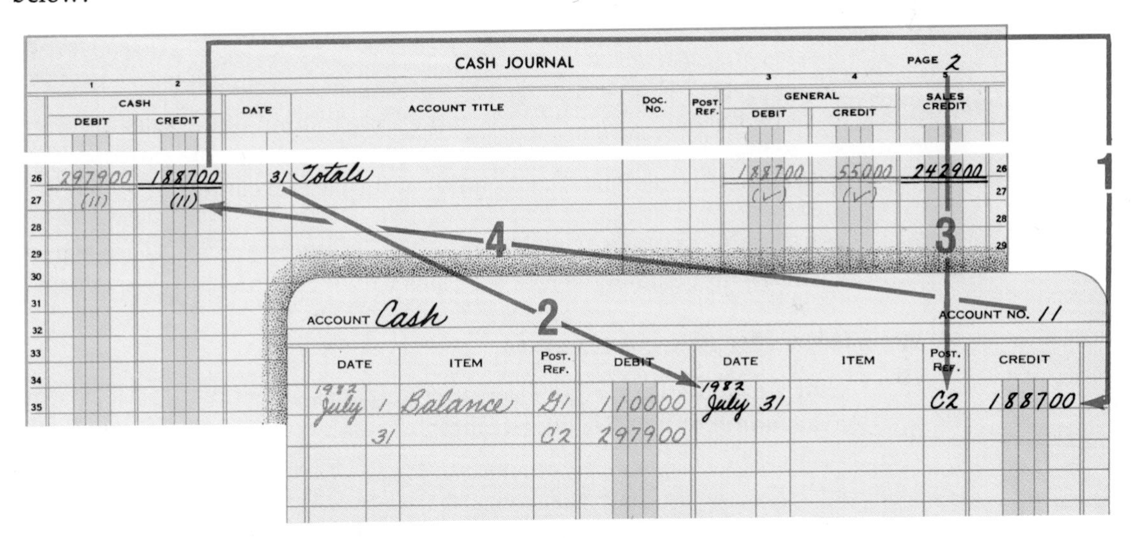

Posting a Cash Credit column total

The steps in posting the Cash Credit column total are below.

1 Write the amount of the total, *$1,887.00*, in the Credit column of the cash account.

2 Write the date, *1982, July 31*, in the Date column of the cash account.

3 Write *C2* in the Post. Ref. column of the cash account.

4 Return to the cash journal. Write the account number, *11*, in parentheses immediately below the Cash Credit column total.

Posting the total of a Sales Credit column. Only the total of a Sales Credit column is posted. The posting of a Sales Credit column total is below.

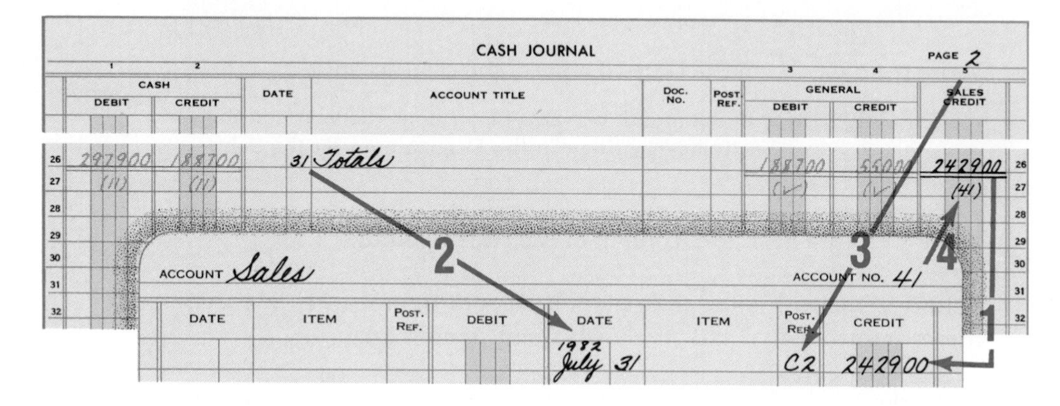

Posting a Sales Credit column total

The steps in posting the Sales Credit column total are below.

1 Write the amount of the total, *$2,429.00*, in the Credit column of the sales account.

2 Write the date, *1982, July 31*, in the Date column of the sales account.

3 Write *C2* in the Post. Ref. column of the sales account.

4 Return to the cash journal. Write the account number, *41*, in parentheses immediately below the Sales Credit column total.

A ledger after posting is completed

Putt Around's ledger is below and on pages 101 and 102. All posting for the month of July has been completed.

ACCOUNT Cash — ACCOUNT NO. 11

DATE	ITEM	POST. REF.	DEBIT	DATE	ITEM	POST. REF.	CREDIT
1982 July 1	Balance	G1	110000	1982 July 31		C2	188700
31		C2	297900				

ACCOUNT Supplies — ACCOUNT NO. 12

DATE	ITEM	POST. REF.	DEBIT	DATE	ITEM	POST. REF.	CREDIT
1982 July 1	Balance	G1	50000				
2		C1	5000				
12		C1	7500				
24		C2	10000				

Ledger after posting is completed

Ledger after posting is completed (continued)

ACCOUNT *Golf Equipment* ACCOUNT NO. 13

DATE		ITEM	POST. REF.	DEBIT	DATE		ITEM	POST. REF.	CREDIT
1982 July	1	Balance	G1	220000					
	12		C1	10000					

ACCOUNT *Maintenance Equipment* ACCOUNT NO. 14

DATE		ITEM	POST. REF.	DEBIT	DATE		ITEM	POST. REF.	CREDIT
1982 July	1	Balance	G1	90000	1982 July	1		C1	5000
	2		C1	40000					

ACCOUNT *Melcor Equipment Company* ACCOUNT NO. 21

DATE		ITEM	POST. REF.	DEBIT	DATE		ITEM	POST. REF.	CREDIT
					1982 July	1	Balance	G1	65000

ACCOUNT *Sasson Supply Company* ACCOUNT NO. 22

DATE		ITEM	POST. REF.	DEBIT	DATE		ITEM	POST. REF.	CREDIT
1982 July	1		C1	20000	1982 July	1	Balance	G1	55000

ACCOUNT *Harry Rossi, Capital* ACCOUNT NO. 31

DATE		ITEM	POST. REF.	DEBIT	DATE		ITEM	POST. REF.	CREDIT
					1982 July	1	Balance	G1	350000
						1		C1	50000

ACCOUNT *Harry Rossi, Drawing* ACCOUNT NO. 32

DATE		ITEM	POST. REF.	DEBIT	DATE		ITEM	POST. REF.	CREDIT
1982 July	2		C1	10000					
	23		C2	5000					

ACCOUNT *Sales* ACCOUNT NO. 41

DATE		ITEM	POST. REF.	DEBIT	DATE		ITEM	POST. REF.	CREDIT
					1982 July	31		C2	242900

ACCOUNT *Advertising Expense* ACCOUNT NO. 51

DATE		ITEM	POST. REF.	DEBIT	DATE		ITEM	POST. REF.	CREDIT
1982 July	6		C1	2500					

ACCOUNT *Miscellaneous Expense* ACCOUNT NO. 52

DATE		ITEM	POST. REF.	DEBIT	DATE	ITEM	POST. REF.	CREDIT
1982 July	2		C1	10 00				
	7		C1	10 00				
	15		C2	15 00				
	22		C2	18 00				
	27		C2	5 00				
	30		C2	12 00				

ACCOUNT *Rent Expense* ACCOUNT NO. 53

DATE		ITEM	POST. REF.	DEBIT	DATE	ITEM	POST. REF.	CREDIT
1982 July	1		C1	600 00				

ACCOUNT *Utilities Expense* ACCOUNT NO. 54

DATE		ITEM	POST. REF.	DEBIT	DATE	ITEM	POST. REF.	CREDIT
1982 July	2		C1	25 00				
	5		C1	60 00				
	20		C2	32 00				

Ledger after posting is completed (concluded)

SUMMARY OF PROCEDURES FOR POSTING FROM A CASH JOURNAL TO A LEDGER

The procedures for posting from a cash journal are much the same as posting from any journal. A summary of the posting procedures is given below.

Posting from General amount columns

The procedures for posting from General amount columns of a cash journal are below. *Separate amounts in General Debit and General Credit*

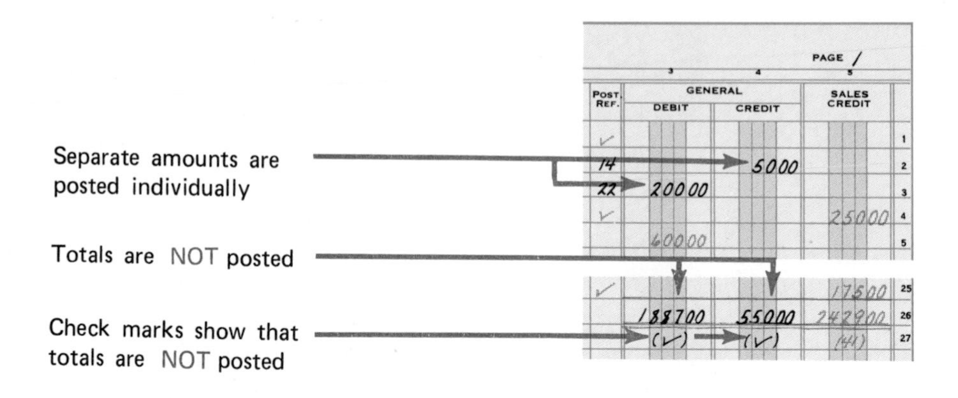

columns ARE posted individually to accounts listed in the Account Title column. The account number is written in the Post. Ref. column of a cash journal.

The totals of General Debit and General Credit columns ARE NOT posted to a ledger account. A check mark (√) is placed in parentheses under a General column total. This check mark shows that the column total is not posted.

Posting from special amount columns

The procedures for posting from special amount columns of a cash journal are below. *Separate amounts in special amount columns ARE NOT posted individually.* A check mark (√) is placed in the Post. Ref. column of a cash journal. The check mark shows that these individual amounts are not posted.

The totals of special amount columns ARE posted to the account listed in the column heading. An account number is written in parentheses immediately below a special amount column total. This account number shows to which account the total was posted.

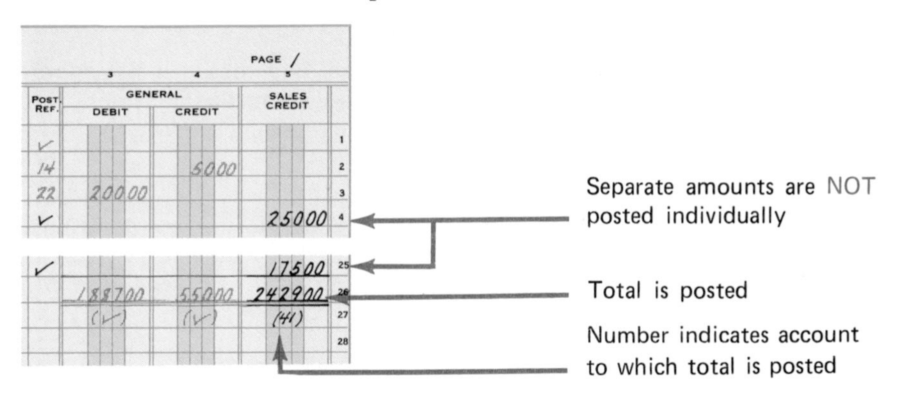

Writing account numbers in Post. Ref. column of a cash journal

The account number is written in a journal as the last step in posting each amount. These account numbers are written last to show that posting of the item is completed. Also, if work is interrupted, the item without a posting reference is the next item to be posted.

QUESTIONS FOR INDIVIDUAL STUDY

1. Why is Putt Around's balance sheet prepared on July 1, 1982, not the same as the balance sheet prepared on July 31, 1982?
2. What guide is used by Putt Around in arranging accounts in its ledger?
3. What are the major divisions of the ledger used by Putt Around?
4. What is the meaning of the ledger account number *52* used by Putt Around? What account is numbered 52?

5. Why is the entry on line one of the cash journal, page 96, not posted?
6. What are the four steps in posting an amount from a cash journal's General Credit column?
7. What three purposes are served by the posting of reference numbers?
8. Why is posting of individual amounts in General Debit and General Credit columns done frequently during a month by Putt Around?
9. How does Putt Around determine if a column total in a cash journal needs to be posted?
10. Why are check marks placed under General Debit and General Credit amount column totals?
11. Why can it be determined by looking at the cash journal, page 98, that posting of the two General columns is completed?
12. What are the two rules for posting from General amount columns?
13. What are the two rules for posting from special amount columns?
14. Why are posting reference numbers placed in the journal as the last step in posting?

CASES FOR MANAGEMENT DECISION

CASE 1 Ken Wilovich does accounting work for a small business. When posting from a journal to a ledger, he records all the information in the ledger accounts first. Then, he goes back to the journal and writes all the account numbers in the Post. Ref. column at one time. Is this procedure satisfactory? Why?

CASE 2 Mildred Humphrey keeps records of her business much as is described in this chapter for Putt Around. Her husband recommends that she stop using a cash journal and record information directly in ledger accounts. Which procedure do you recommend? Why?

CASE 3 Winston Malby posts individually all separate amounts in all columns of a cash journal used in his business. He does not post any column totals. The cash journal is similar to the one described in this chapter for Putt Around. Do you agree with Mr. Malby's procedures? Why?

CASE 4 Jackie Bellinger keeps accounting records for a business. The ledger has dozens of accounts in it. Many pages of the journal are used each month. Ms. Bellinger needs to find information from a source document for one entry in the miscellaneous expense account. How would you suggest she go about finding the specific source document she needs?

DRILLS FOR UNDERSTANDING

DRILL 6-D 1 Assigning account numbers

The list below refers to the location of accounts in a ledger.

1. The first asset account
2. The first liability account
3. The owner's capital account
4. The first revenue account
5. The first expense account
6. The third asset account

7. The second liability account
8. The owner's drawing account
9. The fourth expense account
10. The second asset account
11. The third expense account

Instructions: 1. Use a form such as the one below. Indicate the account number for each of the items listed. Item 1 is shown as an example.

Item	Account Number
1. *The first asset account*	*11*
2.	

Instructions: 2. Cover the Account Number column. See how rapidly you can recall the account numbers.

3. As a check, use Putt Around's chart of accounts, page 16. Check which account fits the description of each item above. Also, check if that account has the same account number you listed on the form. For example, on the chart of accounts, page 16, Putt Around's first asset account is *Cash*. The account number shown for Cash is 11.

DRILL 6-D 2 Analyzing posting from a cash journal

Use the cash journal on pages 82 and 83, Chapter 5. Answer the questions below.

1. Which amounts on line 3 of the cash journal, page 83, are posted separately?
2. Which amounts on line 12 of the cash journal, page 83, are posted separately?
3. Which totals on line 26 of the cash journal, page 83, are posted?
4. Which totals on line 26 of the cash journal, page 83, are not posted?
5. What was the cash balance on hand, July 1, according to information in the cash journal, page 82?
6. How would you figure the amount of cash on hand, July 31, 1982?

Use the ledger accounts on pages 100–102. Answer the questions below.

7. What item or transaction is represented by each of the three amounts in the cash account, page 100?
8. Why is there only one amount recorded for all of July in the sales account, page 101?
9. Where will you find complete details for the transaction dated July 2, $400.00, in the maintenance equipment account, page 101? How did you decide where to find the details for this transaction?

APPLICATION PROBLEMS

PROBLEM 6-1 Posting from a cash journal

The cash journal prepared in Problem 5-1 is needed to complete Problem 6-1.

Instructions: 1. Open ledger accounts for each of the following accounts. Write the account title and number at the top of the form. Record the account balance if the account has a balance. Write the word *Balance* in the Item column and place a check mark in the Post. Ref. column. Use May 1 of the current year.

Account Title	Acct. No.	Account Balance	Account Title	Acct. No.	Account Balance
Cash	11	$ 720.00	Fees	41	——
Automobile	12	5,350.00	Automobile Expense	51	——
Drafting Equipment	13	875.00	Miscellaneous Expense	52	——
Office Equipment	14	900.00	Rent Expense	53	——
Mixer Equipment Co. (liability)	21	864.00	Utilities Expense	54	——
Platt Company (liability)	22	600.00			
Ema Langhorn, Capital	31	6,381.00			
Ema Langhorn, Drawing	32	——			
Income Summary	33	——			

Instructions: 2. Post the individual amounts recorded in the General Debit and General Credit columns of the cash journal. Place check marks in parentheses under the General Debit and Credit columns. The check marks show that these column totals are not posted.

3. Post the special amount columns of the cash journal. Write an account number in parentheses under each special amount column total.

Solution to Problem 6-1 is needed to complete Problem 7-1 in Chapter 7.

PROBLEM 6-2 Posting from a cash journal

A completed cash journal and ledger accounts for Robinson Repair Service are given in the working papers for this textbook.

Instructions: 1. Prove cash as of June 30 of the current year. The balance on Check Stub No. 114 is $2,153.90.

2. Total, prove, and rule the cash journal.

3. Post the amounts from the General Debit and Credit columns of the cash journal.

4. Post the special amount column totals of the cash journal.

ENRICHMENT PROBLEMS

MASTERY PROBLEM 6-M Journalizing and posting using a cash journal

Dr. Milton Benson uses the ledger accounts below.

Account Title	Acct. No.	Account Balance	Account Title	Acct. No.	Account Balance
Cash	11	$ 8,841.00	Professional Fees	41	——
Automobile	12	8,820.00	Automobile Expense	51	——
Office Furniture	13	7,056.00	Miscellaneous Expense	52	——
Medical Equipment	14	9,450.00	Rent Expense	53	——
Grossman Furniture Co. (liability)	21	3,927.00	Utilities Expense	54	——
Health Supplies Co. (liability)	22	7,182.00			
Milton Benson, Capital	31	23,058.00			
Milton Benson, Drawing	32	——			

Instructions: 1. Open the accounts in a ledger. Record the balance for each account with a balance. Use July 1 of the current year.

2. Record the following transactions on page 7 of a cash journal similar to the one on page 100. The heading for the revenue column is *Professional Fees Credit* instead of Sales Credit. Source documents are abbreviated as: check, C; receipt, R.

July 1. Record cash balance on hand, $8,841.00.
1. Paid cash for July rent, $500.00. C230.
2. Received cash from professional fees, $283.50. R351.
5. Paid cash for new office furniture, $375.00. C231.
6. Paid cash for stamps, $15.00. C232.
9. Received cash from professional fees, $1,428.00. R352.
12. Paid cash to Grossman Furniture Company, $966.00. C233.
15. Paid cash for electric bill, $200.00. C234.
16. Paid cash for automobile expense, $168.00. C235.
19. Received cash from professional fees, $1,302.00. R353.
20. Received cash from sale of old office furniture, $225.00. R354.
21. Paid cash to Health Supplies Company, $1,400.00. C236.
23. Paid cash to Dr. Benson for personal use, $2,000.00. C237.
26. Paid cash for miscellaneous expense, $24.00. C238.
26. Received cash from professional fees, $1,400.00. R355.
27. Received cash from professional fees, $935.00. R356.
29. Paid telephone bill, $51.50. C239.
31. Received cash from professional fees, $374.00. R357.
31. Paid cash for automobile expense, $103.00. C240.

Instructions: 3. Prove cash. The balance on Check Stub No. 240 is $8,986.00.
4. Total, prove, and rule the cash journal.
5. Post from the cash journal to the ledger.

CHALLENGE PROBLEM 6-C Journalizing and posting using a cash journal

Peter Roselle operates a business called Speedy Service Company. The cash journal used by the business is below.

CASH JOURNAL

1	2					3	4	5
Cash Debit	General Debit	Date	Account Title	Doc. No.	Post. Ref.	General Credit	Sales Credit	Cash Credit

The following are ledger accounts used by the business. Cash, $4,631.00; Delivery Truck, $4,200.00; Office Furniture, $3,696.00; Delivery Equipment Company (liability), $3,762.00; Holliday Supply Company, (liability), $4,950.00; Peter Roselle, Capital, $3,815.00; Peter Roselle, Drawing; Sales; Delivery Expense; Miscellaneous Expense; Rent Expense; Utilities Expense.

Instructions: 1. Use page 8 of a cash journal similar to the one above. Record the beginning cash balance on hand, $4,631.00, on line 1 of the journal. Use August 1 of the current year.

2. Record the following selected transactions for August. Number all checks beginning with C201. Number all receipts beginning with R370.

Aug. 1. Paid cash for August rent, $500.00.
2. Received cash from sales, $150.00.
3. Paid cash for new office furniture, $200.00.

Aug. 4. Paid cash for miscellaneous expense, $33.50.
9. Received cash from sales, $750.00.
10. Paid cash to Delivery Equipment Company for part of amount owed, $550.00.
15. Paid cash for utilities expense, $200.00.
16. Paid cash for delivery expense, $90.00.
19. Received cash from sales, $700.00.
20. Received cash from the sale of an old piece of office furniture, $88.50.
21. Paid cash to Holliday Supply Company for part of amount owed, $800.00.
23. Paid cash for miscellaneous expense, $16.00.
24. Received cash from sales, $800.00.
31. Received cash from sales, $675.00.
31. Paid cash for delivery expense, $253.00.
31. Paid cash for miscellaneous expense, $54.70.
31. Paid cash to Mr. Roselle for personal use, $500.00.

Instructions: 3. Prove cash. The balance on Check Stub No. 211 is $4,597.30.
4. Total, prove, and rule the cash journal.
5. Post from the journal to the ledger accounts.

Reinforcement Activity 1

PART A

An Accounting Cycle for a Sole Proprietorship Using a Cash Journal

Reinforcement activities strengthen the learning of accounting concepts and procedures. Reinforcement Activity 1 is a single problem divided into four parts. Part A includes learnings from Chapters 2 to 6. Part B, page 129, includes learnings from Chapter 7. Part C, page 142, includes learnings from Chapter 8. Part D, page 160, includes learnings from Chapter 9. An accounting cycle is completed in Parts A to D for a single business: Wilson's Secretarial Service.

WILSON'S SECRETARIAL SERVICE

Anthony Wilson has been earning money part-time doing typing work for various businesses and individuals. Mr. Wilson decides to start a full-time secretarial service offering the same services. The services include typing of letters, employment resumes, and reports. In addition, the business will provide bulk mailing and typing of some legal documents. Mr. Wilson rents a one-room office with a minimum of office furniture. Mr. Wilson also owns some of his own office equipment.

Chart of accounts

The chart of accounts for Wilson's Secretarial Service is below.

WILSON'S SECRETARIAL SERVICE
Chart of Accounts

(1) ASSETS	Account Number	(4) REVENUE	Account Number
Cash	11	Secretarial Fees	41
Supplies	12		
Office Equipment	13	(5) EXPENSES	
		Advertising Expense	51
(2) LIABILITIES		Cleaning Expense	52
Evans Stationery	21	Electricity Expense	53
Mansoori Equipment Company	22	Miscellaneous Expense	54
		Rent Expense	55
(3) CAPITAL		Telephone Expense	56
Anthony Wilson, Capital	31		
Anthony Wilson, Drawing	32		
Income Summary	33		

Beginning financial condition

On October 1 of the current year, Mr. Wilson prepares the beginning balance sheet below.

Wilson's Secretarial Service
Balance Sheet
October 1, 19--

Assets		Liabilities	
Cash	2000 00	Evans Stationery	100 00
Supplies	170 00	Mansoori Equip. Co.	200 00
Office Equipment	700 00	Total Liabilities	300 00
		Capital	
		Anthony Wilson, Capital	2570 00
Total Assets	2870 00	Total Liabilities + Capital	2870 00

Recording and posting an opening entry

On October 1, Mr. Wilson begins to record entries in the business' new records.

Instructions: 1. Record an opening entry on page 1 of a general journal. The source document is the balance sheet for October 1 of the current year.

2. Open a ledger account for each account on the chart of accounts, page 109.

3. Post the opening entry from the general journal to the accounts.

Recording transactions

Instructions: 4. Record each of the following transactions beginning on page 1 of a cash journal. Source documents are abbreviated as: checks, C; receipts, R.

Oct. 1. Record the cash on hand, $2,000.00.
1. Paid cash for October rent, $300.00. C100.
1. Paid cash for a business license, $25.00. C101.
1. Paid cash for a new typewriter, $800.00. C102.
4. Paid cash for advertising in local newspaper, $75.00. C103.
4. Received cash for secretarial fees, $25.00. R10.
5. Received cash for secretarial fees, $34.00. R11.
6. Paid cash for notary seal (miscellaneous expense), $50.00. C104.
6. Received cash for secretarial fees, $40.00. R12.
7. Received cash for secretarial fees, $60.00. R13.
8. Received cash for secretarial fees, $80.00. R14.
11. Paid cash for direct mail advertising, $85.00. C105.
11. Received cash for secretarial fees, $45.00. R15.
12. Received cash for secretarial fees, $65.00. R16.
13. Paid cash for sign painted on office door, $25.00. C106.
13. Received cash for secretarial fees, $80.00. R17.
14. Paid cash to Mansoori Equipment Company for part of amount owed, $100.00. C107.

Oct. 14. Received cash for secretarial fees, $45.00. R18.
15. Paid cash for supplies, $200.00. C108.
15. Received cash for secretarial fees, $95.00. R19.
18. Paid cash for advertising in local newspaper, $80.00. C109.
18. Received cash for secretarial fees, $30.00. R20.
19. Received cash for secretarial fees, $100.00. R21.

Instructions: 5. Total, prove, and rule page 1 of the cash journal. Forward the totals to page 2 of a cash journal.

6. Post individual items from the cash journal's General Debit and Credit columns.

7. On page 2 of a cash journal record the transactions given below.

Oct. 20. Paid cash to Evans Stationery for part of amount owed, $50.00. C110.
20. Received cash for secretarial fees, $50.00. R22.
21. Received cash for secretarial fees, $10.00. R23.
22. Received cash for secretarial fees, $90.00. R24.
25. Paid cash for direct mail advertising, $100.00. C111.
25. Received cash for secretarial fees, $60.00. R25.
26. Paid cash for telephone bill, $90.00. C112.
26. Received cash for secretarial fees, $80.00. R26.
27. Received cash for secretarial fees, $75.00. R27.
28. Paid cash for supplies, $100.00. C113.
28. Received cash for secretarial fees, $55.00. R28.
29. Paid cash for electric bill, $60.00. C114.
29. Received cash for secretarial fees, $100.00. R29.
31. Paid cash to owner for personal use, $500.00. C115.

Instructions: 8. Prove cash. The balance on unused Check Stub No. 116 is $579.00.

9. Total, prove, and rule page 2 of the cash journal.

10. Post individual items from the cash journal's General Debit and Credit columns.

11. Post the cash journal's special amount column totals.

The ledger prepared in Reinforcement Activity 1, Part A, is needed to complete Parts B and D. The general journal used in Part A is needed to complete Part D.

7

Six-Column Work Sheet

ENABLING PERFORMANCE TASKS

After studying Chapter 7, you will be able to:

a. Define accounting terms related to a six-column work sheet.
b. Explain accounting principles and practices related to a six-column work sheet.
c. Sort account balances on a six-column work sheet.
d. Prepare a trial balance on a six-column work sheet using information from ledger accounts.
e. Figure the net income or net loss on a six-column work sheet.
f. Complete a six-column work sheet.
g. Find and correct errors made in accounting records.

Managers and owners of businesses must know whether a profit or a loss is being made. Information needed to figure if a profit or loss is being made is contained in ledger accounts. Ledger accounts need to be analyzed and information reported to the manager and owner of a business. Managers and owners need up-to-date information to make wise business decisions.

A business analyzes its financial information at regular intervals. The length of time for which a business analyzes business information is called a fiscal period. *(CONCEPT: Accounting Period Cycle)* A fiscal period is sometimes known as an accounting period. Each business chooses the fiscal period that meets its own needs. Some businesses, such as Putt Around, use a one-month fiscal period. Other businesses may use fiscal periods of three months, six months, or one year.

Putt Around's fiscal period begins on the first day of a calendar month and ends on the last day of the same month. For example, a fiscal period begins on July 1, 1982, and ends on July 31, 1982. Not all fiscal years begin and end with a calendar year. For example, a business might begin a fiscal year on July 1 of one year. The fiscal year would then end on June 30 of the following year.

For tax purposes, most individuals begin a personal fiscal period on January 1 of a calendar year. The personal fiscal period ends on December 31 of the same year.

Before financial reports can be prepared, ledger accounts are summarized and reports planned. Accounting paper with a number of amount columns used in analyzing ledger accounts is called analysis paper. Analysis paper on which the financial condition of a business is summarized is called a work sheet. A work sheet is used to plan the information to be put on financial reports. Putt Around's work sheet at the end of July, 1982, is on page 121.

The preparation of financial statements for Putt Around is described in Chapters 8 and 9.

PREPARING A SIX-COLUMN WORK SHEET

Preparation of a six-column work sheet achieves three objectives. (1) Summarizing ledger account information on a trial balance. (2) Sorting ledger information according to financial reports to be prepared. (3) Figuring the amount of net income or net loss for a fiscal period.

Heading on a work sheet

The heading on a work sheet is similar to the heading of any accounting report. The illustration at the right shows the heading for Putt Around's work sheet prepared on July 31, 1982.

Line 1: Name of the business.
Line 2: Name of the report.
Line 3: Date of the report.

Putt Around
Work Sheet
For Month Ended July 31, 1982

The date shows that the work sheet covers the fiscal period from July 1 to July 31, 1982. Thus, the report is for the month ended July 31, 1982. *(CONCEPT: Accounting Period Cycle)*

Heading on a work sheet

Preparing a trial balance

Proof of the equality of debits and credits in a ledger is called a trial balance. To prepare a trial balance, account balances are figured for each account. Then, all the debit balances are added and all the credit balances are added. The sum of all debit balances must equal the sum of all credit balances.

Figuring account balances. Putt Around uses a two-column ledger account form. The form does not show the account balances. Account balances must be figured when needed. The illustration below shows how the account balance for Cash is figured.

ACCOUNT *Cash* ACCOUNT NO. *11*

DATE		ITEM	POST. REF.	DEBIT	DATE		ITEM	POST. REF.	CREDIT
1982 July	1	Balance	G1	1 100 00	1982 July	31		C2	1 887 00
	31		C2	2 979 00					
		2,192.00		4 079 00					

Ledger account with pencil footings

The steps in figuring the cash account balance are below.

1 ***Pencil foot the debit and credit amount columns.*** Write the total of each column in small pencil figures immediately below the last amount. In the illustration above the total of the debit column is $4,079.00. This pencil figure is written immediately below the last amount in the debit column.

Pencil figures are written very small so that space can be used for recording another posted amount. Pencil figures do not occupy the entire space on the line.

The cash account's credit column has only one amount recorded in it, $1,887.00. There is no need to add this column to find the total. There is no need to write the total in small pencil figures on the credit side.

2 ***Figure the account balance.*** Subtract the smaller column total from the larger column total. Cash debit, $4,079.00, *minus* Cash credit, $1,887.00, *equals* account balance, $2,192.00.

The debit column total is larger than the credit column total. Thus, the balance is a debit.

3 ***Record the account balance in the account.*** Write the account balance in the Item column on the debit side of Cash. In the illustration above the account balance, *$2,192.00*, is written in the Item column. The balance is written in small pencil figures on the same line with the column total.

The cash account balance should also be compared with the cash proof previously figured. The cash proof, page 83, is $2,192.00. This amount is the same as the balance shown in the cash account. If the two amounts do not agree, an error has been made.

This same procedure is followed to figure the balances of all accounts with entries on both sides. If an account has two or more entries on one side only, that side alone is footed. The account balance is not placed in the Item column. The footing of the single column is the account balance. If an account has only one entry, pencil footing is not necessary. The single amount in the account is the account balance.

ACCOUNT *Golf Equipment* ACCOUNT NO. 13

DATE	ITEM	POST. REF.	DEBIT	DATE	ITEM	POST. REF.	CREDIT
1982 July 1	Balance	G1	220000				
12		C1	10000				
			230000				

ACCOUNT *Melcor Equipment Company* ACCOUNT NO. 21

DATE	ITEM	POST. REF.	DEBIT	DATE	ITEM	POST. REF.	CREDIT
				1982 July 1	Balance	G1	65000

Putt Around's ledger with all account balances figured is below and on pages 116 and 117.

Ledger with all account balances figured

ACCOUNT *Cash* ACCOUNT NO. 11

DATE	ITEM	POST. REF.	DEBIT	DATE	ITEM	POST. REF.	CREDIT
1982 July 1	Balance	G1	110000	1982 July 31		C2	188700
31		C2	297900				
	2192.00		407900				

ACCOUNT *Supplies* ACCOUNT NO. 12

DATE	ITEM	POST. REF.	DEBIT	DATE	ITEM	POST. REF.	CREDIT
1982 July 1	Balance	G1	50000				
2		C1	5000				
12		C1	7500				
24		C2	10000				
			72500				

ACCOUNT *Golf Equipment* ACCOUNT NO. 13

DATE	ITEM	POST. REF.	DEBIT	DATE	ITEM	POST. REF.	CREDIT
1982 July 1	Balance	G1	220000				
12		C1	10000				
			230000				

ACCOUNT *Maintenance Equipment* ACCOUNT NO. *14*

DATE	ITEM	POST. REF.	DEBIT	DATE	ITEM	POST. REF.	CREDIT
1982				1982			
July 1	Balance	G1	900 00	July 1		C1	50 00
2	1250.00	C1	400 00				
			1300 00				

ACCOUNT *Melcor Equipment Company* ACCOUNT NO. *21*

DATE	ITEM	POST. REF.	DEBIT	DATE	ITEM	POST. REF.	CREDIT
				1982			
				July 1	Balance	G1	650 00

ACCOUNT *Sasson Supply Company* ACCOUNT NO. *22*

DATE	ITEM	POST. REF.	DEBIT	DATE	ITEM	POST. REF.	CREDIT
1982				1982			
July 1		C1	200 00	July 1	Balance 350.00	G1	550 00

ACCOUNT *Harry Rossi, Capital* ACCOUNT NO. *31*

DATE	ITEM	POST. REF.	DEBIT	DATE	ITEM	POST. REF.	CREDIT
				1982			
				July 1	Balance	G1	3500 00
				1		C1	500 00
							4000 00

ACCOUNT *Harry Rossi, Drawing* ACCOUNT NO. *32*

DATE	ITEM	POST. REF.	DEBIT	DATE	ITEM	POST. REF.	CREDIT
1982							
July 2		C1	100 00				
23		C2	50 00				
			150 00				

ACCOUNT *Income Summary* ACCOUNT NO. *33*

DATE	ITEM	POST. REF.	DEBIT	DATE	ITEM	POST. REF.	CREDIT

ACCOUNT *Sales* ACCOUNT NO. *41*

DATE	ITEM	POST. REF.	DEBIT	DATE	ITEM	POST. REF.	CREDIT
				1982			
				July 31		C2	2429 00

Ledger with all account balances figured (continued)

Ledger with all account balances figured (concluded)

ACCOUNT *Advertising Expense* ACCOUNT NO. 51

DATE		ITEM	POST. REF.	DEBIT	DATE		ITEM	POST. REF.	CREDIT
1982 July	6		C1	25 00					

ACCOUNT *Miscellaneous Expense* ACCOUNT NO. 52

DATE		ITEM	POST. REF.	DEBIT	DATE		ITEM	POST. REF.	CREDIT
1982 July	2		C1	10 00					
	7		C1	10 00					
	15		C2	15 00					
	22		C2	18 00					
	27		C2	5 00					
	30		C2	12 00					
				70 00					

ACCOUNT *Rent Expense* ACCOUNT NO. 53

DATE		ITEM	POST. REF.	DEBIT	DATE		ITEM	POST. REF.	CREDIT
1982 July	1		C1	600 00					

ACCOUNT *Utilities Expense* ACCOUNT NO. 54

DATE		ITEM	POST. REF.	DEBIT	DATE		ITEM	POST. REF.	CREDIT
1982 July	2		C1	25 00					
	5		C1	60 00					
	20		C2	32 00					
				117 00					

The income summary account will be discussed in Chapter 9.

Recording account balances in a trial balance. Account titles and account balances are recorded on a work sheet form. All accounts in a ledger are listed even if some accounts have no balances. This procedure assures that no accounts with balances are omitted. Account balances are written in either the Trial Balance Debit or Credit columns. The column in which an amount is recorded shows the kind of balance an account has.

The steps in preparing and completing the work sheet Trial Balance columns are given below and on the next page.

1 Write the account titles in the Account Title column.

2 Write the account balances in either the Trial Balance Debit or Credit columns.

Putt Around
Work Sheet
For Month Ended July 31, 1982

	ACCOUNT TITLE	1 TRIAL BALANCE DEBIT	2 TRIAL BALANCE CREDIT	3 INCOME STATEMENT DEBIT	4 INCOME STATEMENT CREDIT	5 BALANCE SHEET DEBIT	6 BALANCE SHEET CREDIT	
1	Cash	219200						1
2	Supplies	72500						2
3	Golf Equipment	230000						3
4	Maintenance Equipment	125000						4
5	Melcor Equipment Company		65000					5
6	Sasson Supply Company		35000					6
7	Harry Rossi, Capital		400000					7
8	Harry Rossi, Drawing	15000						8
9	Income Summary							9
10	Sales		242900					10
11	Advertising Expense	2500						11
12	Miscellaneous Expense	7000						12
13	Rent Expense	60000						13
14	Utilities Expense	11700						14
15		742900	742900					15

Trial balance on work sheet

3 Check the trial balance for accuracy.

- Rule a single line across the two Trial Balance columns below the last amount. This single line shows that the two columns are to be added.
- Add the Trial Balance Debit and Credit columns. Write the total of each column below the single line. (Use an adding machine to do the arithmetic if one is available.)
- Compare the totals of the two columns. The totals must be the same if equality of debits and credits is maintained in the ledger. If the totals are not the same, an error has been made. If the totals are not the same, recheck the work to find the error or errors.
- Rule double lines across both columns immediately below the totals. The double lines are ruled only if the totals are the same. The double lines show that the two columns are in balance and assumed to be correct.

Other parts of a work sheet are not completed until the Trial Balance columns are in balance.

Extending account balances to Balance Sheet columns

Extend balance sheet account balances to the Balance Sheet columns.

1 Extend each asset account balance from the Trial Balance Debit column to the Balance Sheet Debit column.

2 Extend each liability account balance to the Balance Sheet Credit column.

3 Extend the owner's capital account balance to the Balance Sheet Credit column.

4 Extend the owner's drawing account balance to the Balance Sheet Debit column.

The extension of these account balances is below.

Putt Around
Work Sheet
For Month Ended July 31, 1982

	ACCOUNT TITLE	1 TRIAL BALANCE DEBIT	2 TRIAL BALANCE CREDIT	3 INCOME STATEMENT DEBIT	4 INCOME STATEMENT CREDIT	5 BALANCE SHEET DEBIT	6 BALANCE SHEET CREDIT	
1	Cash	219200				219200		1
2	Supplies	72500				72500		2
3	Golf Equipment	230000				230000		3
4	Maintenance Equipment	125000				125000		4
5	Melcor Equipment Company		65000				65000	5
6	Sasson Supply Company		35000				35000	6
7	Harry Rossi, Capital		400000				400000	7
8	Harry Rossi, Drawing	15000				15000		8
9								9

Extending account balances to Income Statement columns

Asset, liability, and capital accounts extended to work sheet Balance Sheet columns

Extend the revenue and expense account balances to the Income Statement columns.

1 Extend each revenue account balance to the Income Statement Credit column.

Putt Around has only one revenue account, Sales. Thus, only one revenue account balance is extended.

2 Extend each expense account balance to the Income Statement Debit column.

Revenue and expense accounts extended to work sheet Income Statement columns

The extension of these account balances is below.

Putt Around
Work Sheet
For Month Ended July 31, 1982

	ACCOUNT TITLE	1 TRIAL BALANCE DEBIT	2 TRIAL BALANCE CREDIT	3 INCOME STATEMENT DEBIT	4 INCOME STATEMENT CREDIT	5 BALANCE SHEET DEBIT	6 BALANCE SHEET CREDIT	
10	Sales		242900		242900			10
11	Advertising Expense	2500		2500				11
12	Miscellaneous Expense	7000		7000				12
13	Rent Expense	60000		60000				13
14	Utilities Expense	11700		11700				14

Figuring net income or net loss on a work sheet

Figure the net income or net loss and complete a work sheet as described below.

1 Rule a single line across the Income Statement and Balance Sheet columns.

2 Add the amounts in the Income Statement and Balance Sheet Debit and Credit columns. Write each column total below the single line.

3 Figure the net income or net loss. Net income for Putt Around is figured below.

Total of Income Statement Credit column	$2,429.00
Minus Total of Income Statement Debit column	812.00
Equals Net Income	$1,617.00

When the amount of revenue is greater than the total expenses, the difference is called net income. When the total expenses are greater than the revenue, the difference is called net loss.

The information shows a net income for Putt Around. The Income Statement Credit column total (revenue) is larger than the Income Statement Debit column total (expenses). If the Debit column is larger than the Credit column, there is a net loss.

4 Write the amount of net income below the Income Statement Debit column total. For Putt Around's work sheet, page 121, write *$1,617.00* below the column total, *$812.00*. Write *Net Income* on the same line in the Account Title column. The words Net Income identify the amount on this line as net income.

If there is a net loss, write the amount in the Income Statement Credit column. Write *Net Loss* in the Account Title Column.

5 Write the amount of net income, *$1,617.00*, in the Balance Sheet Credit column. Write this amount on the same line as the words *Net Income*.

A net loss amount is written in the Balance Sheet Debit column.

6 Rule a single line across the Balance Sheet and Income Statement columns.

7 Add the subtotal and the net income amount to get new column totals. Write each new column total below the single line.

Putt Around
Work Sheet
For Month Ended July 31, 1982

	ACCOUNT TITLE	TRIAL BALANCE (1) DEBIT	TRIAL BALANCE (2) CREDIT	INCOME STATEMENT (3) DEBIT	INCOME STATEMENT (4) CREDIT	BALANCE SHEET (5) DEBIT	BALANCE SHEET (6) CREDIT	
1	Cash	2192 00				2192 00		1
2	Supplies	725 00				725 00		2
3	Golf Equipment	2300 00				2300 00		3
4	Maintenance Equipment	1250 00				1250 00		4
5	Melcor Equipment Company		650 00				650 00	5
6	Sasson Supply Company		350 00				350 00	6
7	Harry Rossi, Capital		4000 00				4000 00	7
8	Harry Rossi, Drawing	150 00				150 00		8
9	Income Summary							9
10	Sales		2429 00		2429 00			10
11	Advertising Expense	25 00		25 00				11
12	Miscellaneous Expense	70 00		70 00				12
13	Rent Expense	600 00		600 00				13
14	Utilities Expense	117 00		117 00				14
15		7429 00	7429 00	812 00	2429 00	6617 00	5000 00	15
16	Net Income			1617 00			1617 00	16
17				2429 00	2429 00	6617 00	6617 00	17
18								18
19								19
20								20
21								21
22								22

Completed six-column work sheet

8 Check that the totals of the two Income Statement columns are the same. Check that the totals of the two Balance Sheet columns are the same.

The totals of each pair of columns must be the same. If the column totals are not the same, an error has been made.

9 Rule double lines across all Income Statement and Balance Sheet columns as shown on the work sheet above. Double lines show that the columns are in balance and are assumed to be correct.

FINDING ERRORS ON A WORK SHEET

Each pair of columns on a work sheet must be in balance. If any pair of columns does not balance, add the columns again. Use an adding machine, if available, to assure greater accuracy. If adding the columns again does not correct the error, use the procedures described below.

Check amounts recorded in Balance Sheet and Income Statement columns

1. Have amounts been copied correctly when extended from Trial Balance columns?

2. Has each amount in the Trial Balance *Debit* column been extended to the correct *Debit* column? Has each amount in the Trial Balance *Credit* column been extended to the correct *Credit* column?
3. Has the amount of net income or net loss been figured and recorded correctly?

Check account balances recorded in Trial Balance columns

1. Have *all* account balances been transferred from the ledger to the work sheet Trial Balance columns?
2. Have all *debit* account balances been recorded in the Trial Balance *Debit* column? Have all *credit* account balances been recorded in the Trial Balance *Credit* column?
3. Have the ledger account balances been figured correctly?

If an error is found in account pencil footings, erase the error. Write the correct amount in pencil figures. If an amount is incorrect on a work sheet, erase the error. Write the correct account balance on the work sheet. The pencil footings and the work sheet are not permanent parts of the records. Thus, the work sheet may be completed in pencil. Only permanent records, such as journals and ledgers, *must* be done in ink.

Check that posting to ledger accounts is correct

Have all amounts that need to be posted actually been posted? Have the amounts been posted to the correct side of an account?

Each item is checked in the journal to assure that it has been posted. As the amount is checked, place a check mark next to the amount. This check mark shows that the posting has been checked.

For an amount posted to the wrong side of an account, draw a line through the incorrect item in the account. Record the posting correctly as shown below.

ACCOUNT Maintenance Equipment ACCOUNT NO. 14

DATE		ITEM	POST. REF.	DEBIT	DATE		ITEM	POST. REF.	CREDIT
1982 Sept.	1	Balance	G1	1 100 00	1982 Sept.	1		C1	80 00
	2		C1	350 00		~~2~~		~~C1~~	~~350 00~~

Corrected posting to wrong side of account

For an amount posted to a wrong account, draw a line through all of the incorrect item. Record the posting in the correct account. Make the correction as shown on the next page.

ACCOUNT *Supplies* ACCOUNT NO. 12

DATE		ITEM	POST. REF.	DEBIT	DATE	ITEM	POST. REF.	CREDIT
1982 Sept.	1	Balance	G1	700 00				
	2		C1	75 00				
	13		C1	60 00				
	~~15~~		~~C2~~	~~95 00~~				
	23		C2	150 00				

ACCOUNT *Miscellaneous Expense* ACCOUNT NO. 52

DATE		ITEM	POST. REF.	DEBIT	DATE	ITEM	POST. REF.	CREDIT
1982 Sept.	2		C1	5 00				
	9		C1	15 00				
	15		C2	6 00				
	24		C2	12 00				
	15		C2	95 00				

Corrected posting to wrong account

For an amount that has not been posted, complete the posting to the correct account. In all cases where posting is corrected, refigure the account balance. When an omitted posting is recorded as described above, the dates in the account may be out of order. This procedure is better than not having the amount posted at all.

Errors in permanent records should *never* be erased. Erasures in permanent records raise questions about whether the information has been altered.

Check journals to assure that correct entries have been made

If errors discovered on a trial balance are not found by doing the procedures previously described, check the journal entries. For each journal entry, do debits equal credits? For each journal entry, are the amounts recorded in the correct journal columns? For each journal entry, is the information in the journal Account Title column correct?

For the completed journal, are the columns added correctly? Does the sum of debit column totals equal the sum of credit column totals? Have all the transactions been recorded?

Guides to finding typical arithmetic errors

When a pair of work sheet columns are not in balance, subtract the smaller total from the larger total. Check the difference between the column totals with the guides on the next page.

1. *The difference between column totals is an even 1.* (Such as $.01, $.10, $1.00, or $10.00). The error most often is in addition. Add the columns again.
2. *The difference between column totals can be divided evenly by 9.* (Such as $54.00 can be divided by 9 an even 6 times.) Look for a number involving a "slide" or a transposition. A "slide" is when numbers "slide" to the left or right in an amount column. (Such as $1.00 is recorded as $10.00, or $100.00 is recorded as $10.00.) A transposition is when two digits are reversed during recording. (Such as $45.00 is recorded as $54.00, or $236.00 is recorded as $326.00.)
3. *Look for an amount equal to the difference between column totals.* An amount may have been omitted from the trial balance. If the difference is $26.00, look for a $26.00 amount that has been omitted. The $26.00 amount may be an account balance not recorded on the trial balance. The $26.00 amount may be an amount not posted to a ledger account.
4. *Divide the difference between column totals by 2.* Look for the resulting number. (If the difference is $53.00, divide $53.00 by 2 which equals $26.50.) A debit amount may have been recorded or transferred as a credit. Look for a $26.50 *debit* amount recorded in a *credit* column. Also, look for a $26.50 *credit* amount recorded in a *debit* column.

The best way to prevent errors is to work carefully at all times. Check the work at each step in the accounting procedures. Most errors occur in doing the required arithmetic, especially in adding columns. Use an adding machine if one is available. When an error is discovered, do no more work until the error is found and corrected.

ACCOUNTING TERMS

What is the meaning of each of the following?

1. fiscal period
2. analysis paper
3. work sheet
4. trial balance
5. net income
6. net loss

QUESTIONS FOR INDIVIDUAL STUDY

1. How long are typical fiscal periods of businesses?
2. What are the three lines in the heading of a work sheet?
3. What are the steps in figuring account balances in Putt Around's ledger?
4. Why are *all* ledger accounts listed in the work sheet Trial Balance columns even if an account has no balance?
5. How are a work sheet's Trial Balance columns checked for accuracy?
6. To what columns are the asset, liability, and capital account balances extended on a work sheet?
7. To what columns are the revenue and expense account balances extended on a work sheet?
8. How is the net income figured for Putt Around's work sheet, page 121?
9. In the answer to question 8, how do you know there is a net income?
10. What is the relationship of the two

amounts written on line 16 of the work sheet, page 121?

11. Why are double lines ruled across all amount columns on a work sheet?
12. What is the first thing to do if the totals of any pair of work sheet columns do not balance?
13. What should be done if all the work on a work sheet appears correct, but columns are not in balance?
14. Why should errors in posting be corrected without erasing the incorrect items?
15. The totals of a work sheet's Trial Balance columns are: Debit, $4,321.00; Credit, $4,221.00. What kind of error probably has been made?
16. The totals of a work sheet's Trial Balance columns are: Debit, $4,345.00; Credit, $4,336.00. What kind of error probably has been made?

CASES FOR MANAGEMENT DECISION

CASE 1 Which of the following errors would *not* be indicated by Putt Around's work sheet trial balance? Why?

(a) A July 2 debit, $50.00, for supplies is posted as a debit to Miscellaneous Expense.

(b) A July 1 *credit* to Maintenance Equipment is posted as a *debit* to Maintenance Equipment.

(c) A July 31 balance of Utilities Expense, $117.00, is not recorded in the work sheet Trial Balance columns.

(d) A July 31 balance of Advertising Expense, $25.00, is written in the work sheet Trial Balance *Credit* column.

CASE 2 How would you correct each of the errors described in Case 1?

DRILLS FOR UNDERSTANDING

DRILL 7-D 1 Sorting account balances on a work sheet

The following accounts are used by Superior Lawncare Company. Advertising Expense; Brownstone Supply Company (liability); Cash; Entertainment Expense; Miscellaneous Expense; Office Equipment; Rent Expense; Roger Reynolds, Capital; Roger Reynolds, Drawing; Sales; Utilities Expense.

Use a form similar to the one below.

	1	2	3	4	5	6
Account Title	Trial Balance		Income Statement		Balance Sheet	
	Debit	Credit	Debit	Credit	Debit	Credit
1. *Advertising Expense*	✓		✓			

Instructions: 1. Write each account title on a separate line in the Account Title column of the form.

2. Place a check mark in either Column 1 or 2 to show what kind of balance each account normally has. Line 1 is shown in the form above as an example.

3. Place a check mark in Column 3, 4, 5, or 6 showing where the account balance is extended on a work sheet. The example above shows that the advertising expense account balance is extended to Column 3.

DRILL 7-D 2 Figuring net income or net loss on a work sheet

Totals from work sheet columns for four businesses are below.

	Income Statement		Balance Sheet	
	Debit	Credit	Debit	Credit
Company 1	$4,500.00	$5,300.00	$36,670.00	$35,870.00
Company 2	974.00	2,186.00	7,937.00	6,725.00
Company 3	4,050.00	3,994.00	25,669.00	25,725.00
Company 4	4,192.00	5,265.00	33,442.00	32,369.00

Instructions: 1. Use a form similar to the one below. Record the column totals for Company 2. The information for Company 1 is shown on line 1 as an example.

COMPANY 1

	Income Statement		Balance Sheet	
	Debit	Credit	Debit	Credit
1.	$4,500.00	$5,300.00	$36,670.00	$35,870.00
2. *Net Income*	*800.00*			*800.00*
3.	*$5,300.00*	*$5,300.00*	*$36,670.00*	*$36,670.00*

Instructions: 2. Figure the amount of net income or net loss for Company 2. Write the amount in the correct columns on line 2 of the form. Line 2 for Company 1 is shown above as an example. Label the amount on line 2 to show if it is a net income or a net loss.

3. Check the accuracy of your arithmetic by adding the four amount columns. Write the new column totals on line 3 of the form. Line 3 for Company 1 is shown above as an example. If each pair of columns does not balance, check your arithmetic.

4. Repeat Instructions 1, 2, and 3 for Company 3.

5. Repeat Instructions 1, 2, and 3 for Company 4.

APPLICATION PROBLEMS

PROBLEM 7-1 Preparing a trial balance on a work sheet

The ledger prepared for Problem 6-1 is needed to complete Problem 7-1.

Instructions: 1. Pencil foot the ledger accounts and figure account balances.

2. Prepare the heading of a work sheet for Ema Langhorn, Architect. The business uses a one-month fiscal period.

3. Record a trial balance in the Trial Balance columns of the work sheet.

4. Total the Trial Balance columns. Check that the two columns are in balance. Rule the Trial Balance columns.

The solution to Problem 7-1 is needed to complete Problem 7-2.

PROBLEM 7-2 Completing a work sheet

The solution to Problem 7-1 is needed to complete Problem 7-2.

Instructions: 1. Use the work sheet with the trial balance completed in Problem 7-1. Extend the asset, liability, and capital account balances to the Balance Sheet columns.

2. Extend the revenue and expense account balances to the Income Statement columns.

3. Total the Income Statement and Balance Sheet columns.

4. Figure the amount of net income or net loss for the Income Statement columns. Record the net income or net loss in the correct Income Statement column. Identify the amount by writing *Net Income* or *Net Loss* in the Account Title column.

5. Write the amount of net income or net loss in the correct Balance Sheet column.

6. Total the Income Statement and Balance Sheet columns. Check that each pair of column totals is in balance. If the columns *are* in balance, rule double lines across the four columns. If the columns *are not* in balance, find and correct the errors.

The solution to Problem 7-2 is needed to complete Problem 8-1 in Chapter 8.

PROBLEM 7-3 Finding errors in accounting records

Robert Evans has completed a monthly work sheet for his business, Window Kleen. Window Kleen's ledger accounts and the work sheet are given in the working papers available with this textbook.

Mr. Evans asks you to check his work sheet to make sure he has not made any mistakes. He asks you to redo the work sheet and any other work that may be wrong.

Instructions: 1. Use the work sheet as a starting point. Check the work sheet for accuracy. Also check the ledger for errors that would affect amounts on the work sheet. Make a list of the errors you find.

2. Prepare a correct work sheet for Window Kleen.

PROBLEM 7-4 Completing a work sheet

Northwest Mall Cinema uses the following ledger accounts. Balances are shown for those accounts that have balances on October 31 of the current year.

Account Title	Balance	Account Title	Balance
Cash	$ 6,920.00	Admissions Revenue	$21,260.00
Seating Equipment	18,000.00	Vending Machine Revenue	3,260.00
Projection Equipment	59,000.00	Advertising Expense	3,862.00
Sound Equipment	28,840.00	Electricity Expense	2,928.00
Movies, Inc. (liability)	7,788.00	Film Rental Expense	5,204.00
Theater Sound Service (liability)	1,672.00	Maintenance Expense	540.00
National Studios (liability)	4,772.00	Miscellaneous Expense	444.00
Wilma Mercer, Capital	95,528.00	Rent Expense	7,000.00
Wilma Mercer, Drawing	700.00	Utilities Expense	842.00
Income Summary	——		

Instructions: 1. Prepare the heading for a work sheet. Northwest Mall Cinema uses a monthly fiscal period. Prepare a trial balance on the work sheet from the account information above.

2. Extend all account balances to the correct Income Statement and Balance Sheet columns.

3. Figure the net income or net loss and complete the work sheet.

ENRICHMENT PROBLEMS

MASTERY PROBLEM 7-M Completing a work sheet

County Delivery Service's ledger accounts and balances on March 31 of the current year are shown below.

Account Title	Account Balance	Account Title	Account Balance
Cash	$ 3,432.00	Sales	$3,120.00
Delivery Truck	10,000.00	Advertising Expense	218.00
Office Equipment	1,644.00	Miscellaneous Expense	86.00
Boulder Supply Company (liability)	903.00	Rent Expense	540.00
Sisselman Motors (liability)	3,360.00	Truck Expense	300.00
Welman Company (liability)	1,712.00	Utilities Expense	362.00
Malcolm Vincent, Capital	7,727.00		
Malcolm Vincent, Drawing	240.00		
Income Summary	——		

Instructions: Prepare a work sheet for County Delivery Service. The business uses a one-month fiscal period.

CHALLENGE PROBLEM 7-C Preparing a trial balance and a work sheet

On December 31 of the current year, Weller Service Company had a small fire in its office. Some of the business' accounting records were destroyed. The information below was reconstructed from the remaining records.

Reconstructed information from remains of the ledger

Account Title	Account Balance	Account Title	Account Balance
Supplies	$1,315.00	Advertising Expense	$ 414.00
Equipment	8,000.00	Rent Expense	378.00
James Weller, Drawing	192.00	Utilities Expense	289.00
Fees Revenue	2,496.00		

Reconstructed information from the business' checkbook

Cash balance on last unused check stub, $2,745.00.
Total payments made for miscellaneous expenses, $68.00.

Reconstructed information through inquiries to liabilities

Owed to Justin Supply Company, $2,688.00.
Owed to Richards Equipment Company, $1,551.00.

Instructions: 1. From the information above, prepare a trial balance on work sheet paper. Use the date December 31 of the current year. The business uses a one-month fiscal period.

2. Complete the work sheet.

Reinforcement Activity 1

PART B

An Accounting Cycle for a Sole Proprietorship Using a Cash Journal

The ledger used in Part A is needed to complete Part B.

Reinforcement Activity 1, Part B, includes the accounting activities needed to prepare a six-column work sheet for Wilson's Secretarial Service.

Preparing a work sheet

Instructions: 12. Pencil foot the ledger accounts. Figure the account balance for each account.

13. Prepare a trial balance on work sheet paper. Use a fiscal period of one month ended October 31 of the current year.

14. Complete a work sheet for Wilson's Secretarial Service.

The work sheet used in Reinforcement Activity 1, Part B, is needed to complete Parts C and D. The ledger used in Part B is needed to complete Part D.

8

Financial Statements

ENABLING PERFORMANCE TASKS

After studying Chapter 8, you will be able to:

a. Define accounting terms related to financial statements.
b. Explain accounting principles and practices related to financial statements.
c. Prepare an income statement using information from a six-column work sheet.
d. Prepare a balance sheet using information from a six-column work sheet.

Business owners and managers need up-to-date financial information to make decisions about future operations. A business' financial information is recorded in ledger accounts. Transactions occurring during a fiscal period change the balances of ledger accounts. These changes should be reported periodically in the form of financial statements. *(CONCEPT: Accounting Period Cycle)*

Financial statements summarize the financial information contained in ledger accounts. *(CONCEPT: Adequate Disclosure)* A financial statement showing the assets and equities of a business on a specific date is known as a balance sheet. A financial statement showing the revenue, expenses, and net income or net loss of a business is called an income statement.

A balance sheet and an income statement can be prepared any time that the financial information is needed. Businesses always prepare these two statements at the end of a fiscal period. Financial statements prepared at the end of a fiscal period are called fiscal period statements. Financial statements prepared for periods shorter than a fiscal period are called interim statements. For example, Putt Around uses a one-month fiscal period. Putt Around prepares fiscal period statements at the end of each month. Financial statements that might be prepared on other dates during a month are interim statements for Putt Around.

An income statement shows financial information *over a specific period of time*. A balance sheet shows financial information *on a specific date*.

(CONCEPT: Accounting Period Cycle) Financial *progress* of a business in earning a net income or a net loss is shown by an income statement. Financial *condition* of a business on a specific date is shown by a balance sheet.

1982 JULY

S	M	T	W	T	F	S
				1	2	3
4	5	6	7	8	9	10
11	12	13	14	15	16	17
18	19	20	21	22	23	24
25	26	27	28	29	30	31

Income Statement
reports financial *progress* from July 1 through July 31, 1982.

Balance Sheet
reports financial *condition* on July 31, 1982.

Information needed to prepare financial statements is contained in a business' ledger accounts. However, to assist in preparing financial statements, ledger information is summarized and sorted on a work sheet. Preparation of Putt Around's work sheet is described in Chapter 7.

AN INCOME STATEMENT

Revenue is a business' earnings from business activities. Expenses are what a business pays to run the business and earn the revenue. An income statement shows the total expenses of earning the revenue for a fiscal period. Thus, expenses are matched with revenue earned for a specific fiscal period. *(CONCEPT: Matching Expenses with Revenue)*

Source of information for an income statement

Information needed to prepare Putt Around's income statement is obtained from two places on the work sheet below.

Putt Around
Work Sheet
For Month Ended July 31, 1982

	ACCOUNT TITLE	3 INCOME STATEMENT DEBIT	4 INCOME STATEMENT CREDIT
10	Sales		242900
11	Advertising Expense	2500	
12	Miscellaneous Expense	7000	
13	Rent Expense	60000	
14	Utilities Expense	11700	
15		81200	242900
16	Net Income	161700	
17		242900	242900
18			

Part of work sheet used in preparing income statement

First, account titles are taken from the Account Title column of the work sheet. Second, amounts are taken from the Income Statement columns of the work sheet.

Preparing an income statement

Based on the information obtained from the work sheet, Putt Around prepares the income statement below.

Putt Around Income Statement For Month Ended July 31, 1982		
Revenue:		
Sales		2429 00
Expenses:		
Advertising Expense	25 00	
Miscellaneous Expense	70 00	
Rent Expense	600 00	
Utilities Expense	117 00	
Total Expenses		812 00
Net Income		1617 00

Income statement

An income statement heading. All financial statements have the same three lines of information in the heading.

Income statement heading

1. *Name of the business.*
2. *Name of the statement.*
3. *Date of the statement.*

Putt Around
Income Statement
For Month Ended July 31, 1982

An income statement revenue section. Some businesses might have revenue from more than one source. Thus, gasoline stations might have revenue from sales of gas and oil as well as from repair services. Some businesses, such as Putt Around, receive revenue from only one source, sales of services.

Putt Around lists the heading for the revenue section of the income statement as shown below. The heading *Revenue* is written on the first line beginning at the left of the wide column.

Income statement revenue section

Revenue:		
Sales		2429 00

The title of the revenue account Sales is written on the next line. The account title is indented about 1 centimeter. This account title is taken from the Account Title column, line 10, of the work sheet, page 131. The account balance, *$2,429.00*, is written in the second amount column of the income statement. This amount is taken from the Income Statement Credit column, line 10, of the work sheet, page 131.

If there is more than one source of revenue, account balances are written in the first amount column. The amounts are added. The total revenue is written in the second amount column of the income statement.

An income statement expenses section. All expenses from operating the business are listed in the expenses section of the income statement. Putt Around lists the heading for the expenses section of the income statement as shown below. The heading *Expenses* is written on the next blank line at the left of the wide column.

Expenses:		
Advertising Expense	25 00	
Miscellaneous Expense	70 00	
Rent Expense	600 00	
Utilities Expense	117 00	
Total Expenses		812 00

Income statement expenses section

The title of each expense account is written in the wide column indented about 1 centimeter. Account titles are taken from the Account Title column, lines 11–14, of the work sheet, page 131. The account balance for each expense account is written in the first amount column. Amounts are taken from the work sheet's Income Statement Debit column, lines 11–14, page 131.

The words *Total Expenses* are written on the next blank line indented about 1 centimeter. The expense amounts are added. The total, *$812.00*, is written in the second amount column.

Figure the net income. A single line is ruled across the second amount column. Net income for Putt Around's income statement is figured as shown below.

Total revenue	$2,429.00
Less total expenses	812.00
Equals net income	$1,617.00

If the expenses were greater than the revenue, a net loss would result. This is figured as shown below.

Total expenses	$932.00
Less total revenue	745.00
Equals net loss	$187.00

The words *Net Income* are written at the left of the wide column on the income statement. The amount of net income, *$1,617.00*, is written in the second amount column as shown on the next page.

Income statement net income line

Total Expenses		81200
Net Income		161700

Completing an income statement

The amount of net income on an income statement must be the same as that shown on a work sheet. The amount of net income figured for Putt Around's income statement is $1,617.00. This amount is the same as shown on line 16 of the work sheet, page 131.

When the amount of net income or net loss agrees with the work sheet, the income statement is ruled. Double lines are ruled across both amount columns of the income statement. Double lines show that amounts are correct and the statement is completed. The completed income statement for Putt Around is on page 132.

A BALANCE SHEET

The procedure for preparing Putt Around's balance sheet on July 1, 1982, is described in Chapter 2, page 20. The same procedure is used to prepare all balance sheets for Putt Around.

Source of information for a balance sheet

Information needed by Putt Around to prepare a July 31 balance sheet is contained in ledger accounts. However, to assist in preparing a balance sheet, Putt Around sorts the ledger information on a work sheet. Information needed to prepare Putt Around's balance sheet is found in two places on the work sheet below.

Putt Around
Work Sheet
For Month Ended July 31, 1982

	Account Title	5 Balance Sheet Debit	6 Balance Sheet Credit	
1	Cash	219200		1
2	Supplies	72500		2
3	Golf Equipment	230000		3
4	Maintenance Equipment	125000		4
5	Melcor Equipment Company		65000	5
6	Sasson Supply Company		35000	6
7	Harry Rossi, Capital		400000	7
8	Harry Rossi, Drawing	15000		8
15		661700	500000	15
16	Net Income		161700	16
17		661700	661700	17
18				18
19				19

Part of work sheet used in preparing balance sheet

First, account titles are obtained from the Account Title column of the work sheet. Second, amounts are obtained from the Balance Sheet columns of the work sheet.

Preparing a balance sheet

Putt Around's July 31 balance sheet is below.

Putt Around
Balance Sheet
July 31, 1982

Assets		Liabilities	
Cash	2192 00	Melcor Equipment Co.	650 00
Supplies	725 00	Sasson Supply Co.	350 00
Golf Equipment	2300 00	Total Liabilities	1000 00
Maintenance Equip.	1250 00	Capital	
		Harry Rossi, Capital	5467 00
Total Assets	6467 00	Total Liab. and Capital	6467 00

Balance sheet

A balance sheet heading. The three-line heading for the balance sheet is shown at the right.

1. *Name of the business.*
2. *Name of the statement.*
3. *Date of the statement.*

Putt Around
Balance Sheet
July 31, 1982

Balance sheet heading

A balance sheet reports financial information on a specific date. Thus, a balance sheet states the date on which it is prepared. A balance sheet *does not* report information covering a period of time as does an income statement.

A balance sheet assets section. Asset account titles are obtained from the Account Title column of the work sheet, page 134. Amounts are obtained from the Balance Sheet Debit column of the same work sheet.

Assets	
Cash	2192 00
Supplies	725 00
Golf Equipment	2300 00
Maintenance Equip.	1250 00

Balance sheet assets section

The section heading, *Assets*, is written in the middle of the wide column as shown above. Immediately below this section title, the asset account titles are listed. The balance of each account is listed in the amount column.

The line for *Total Assets* is not prepared at this time. The total line is prepared later when the total liabilities and capital is determined.

A balance sheet liabilities section. Liability account titles are obtained from the Account Title column of the work sheet, page 134. Amounts are obtained from the Balance Sheet Credit column.

The section heading, *Liabilities*, is written in the middle of the wide column as shown below.

Balance sheet liabilities section

Liabilities	
Melcor Equipment Co.	650 00
Sasson Supply Co.	350 00
Total Liabilities	1 000 00

Immediately below the section heading, each of the liability account titles is listed. The account balance for each liability account is listed in the amount column. A single line is drawn across the amount column. The words *Total Liabilities* are written on the next blank line. The liability amounts are added and the total written in the amount column.

A balance sheet capital section. Capital account titles are obtained from lines 7–8 of the work sheet's Account Title column, page 134. The amounts obtained are below.

Balance of capital account, line 7	$4,000.00
Balance of drawing account, line 8	150.00
Amount of net income, line 16	1,617.00

The amount of capital reported on the balance sheet is figured as shown below.

Capital account balance, line 7 of work sheet	$4,000.00
Plus net income, line 16 of work sheet	+1,617.00
Equals total	$5,617.00
Less drawing account balance, line 8	− 150.00
Equals capital, July 31, 1982	$5,467.00

The section heading, *Capital*, is written in the middle of the wide column. The account title Harry Rossi, Capital is written on the next line. The amount of the capital, *$5,467.00*, is written in the amount column as shown below.

Balance sheet capital section

Capital	
Harry Rossi, Capital	5 467 00

Completing a balance sheet

The balance sheet is completed by preparing the final lines for both the left and right sides of the statement. *On the same line* write the total lines as shown below.

		Harry Rossi, Capital	5467 00
Total Assets	6467 00	Total Liab. and Capital	6467 00

Balance sheet total lines and final rulings

On the left side, write the words *Total Assets* in the wide column. On the right side write the words *Total Liabilities and Capital* in the wide column. In the amount columns write the total amounts.

The two final totals on the balance sheet must be the same. The two totals above are $6,467.00. Thus, the assets equal the equities.

If the two totals are the same, double lines are drawn across the amount columns. Double lines show that the statement is completed.

> If the two final totals on a balance sheet are not equal, errors must be found and corrected. Only when the two final totals are equal is the statement double ruled.

The completed balance sheet for Putt Around is on page 135.

Another method of reporting capital on a balance sheet

Putt Around's balance sheet, page 135, shows the ending capital on one line. How this amount is figured is not shown on the balance sheet. Some businesses prefer to show all the details on a balance sheet. When all the details are included, the capital section of a balance sheet appears as shown below.

Capital			
Harry Rossi, Capital,			
July 1, 1982		3,500.00	
Additional investment,			
July 1, 1982		500.00	
Total invested capital		4,000.00	
Net Income for			
July, 1982	1,617.00		
Less Harry Rossi, Drawing	150.00	1,467.00	
Harry Rossi, Capital,			
July 31, 1982			5467 00

Figuring amount of capital with a net loss

If a net loss results from business operations, the current capital would be figured as shown on the next page.

Capital, June 1, 1982	$2,500.00
Less net loss shown on work sheet	900.00
Equals total	$1,600.00
Less drawing account balance	200.00
Equals capital, June 30, 1982	$1,400.00

The amount of ending capital to be shown on the balance sheet is $1,400.00.

ACCOUNTING TERMS

What is the meaning of each of the following?

1. income statement **2.** fiscal period statements **3.** interim statements

QUESTIONS FOR INDIVIDUAL STUDY

1. What is the major difference between the time covered by a balance sheet and an income statement?

2. What is the source of information needed to prepare Putt Around's income statement?

3. What are the three parts of a heading for an income statement?

4. For Putt Around's income statement, page 132, what is the information for each line of the statement heading?

5. What are the two main sections in the body of Putt Around's income statement?

6. If the total revenue is $3,500.00 and the total expenses are $1,950.00, what is the net income?

7. If the total revenue is $2,400.00 and the total expenses are $2,450.00, what is the net income or loss? How did you figure the amount?

8. How is the accuracy proved for the net income figured on an income statement?

9. What is the source of information needed to prepare a balance sheet?

10. What are the three main sections in the body of a balance sheet?

11. What can be done to check the accuracy of the figures and arithmetic on a balance sheet?

CASES FOR MANAGEMENT DECISION

CASE 1 Miss Melinda Boxer owns her own business. Net income reported on the income statement for the month ending October 31, 1982, was $2,950.00. Net income reported on the income statement for the next month ending November 30, 1982, is $2,800.00. What might have caused the change in the amount of net income from one month to the next?

CASE 2 Martha Wexler earns a salary for managing Family Miniature Golf. The business is owned by Maggie Malone. Mrs. Malone wants to sell the business and retire. What information should Miss Wexler obtain about the business before deciding if she will buy?

CASE 3 Roy Carlson owns and manages a business. The business has earned an average monthly net income of $1,500.00 for the past two years. Mr. Carlson has been offered a position as manager in a similar business at a monthly salary of $1,800.00. What information should Mr. Carlson consider before selling his current business and accepting a position with the new business?

DRILLS FOR UNDERSTANDING

DRILL 8-D 1 Classifying accounts

Use a form similar to the one below.

1	2	3	4	5	6	7	8
Account Title	Kind of Account					Financial Statement	
	Asset	Liab.	Capital	Revenue	Expense	Income Statement	Balance Sheet
1. *Cash*	√						√

Instructions: 1. In Column 1 copy the following list of account titles.

1. Cash
2. Alice Osborn, Capital
3. Advertising Expense
4. Central Supply Company (liability)
5. Miscellaneous Expense
6. Office Equipment
7. Page Company (liability)
8. Professional Fees
9. Rent Expense
10. Sales
11. Supplies
12. Thomas Tate, Drawing
13. Utilities Expense

Instructions: 2. Place a check mark in either Column 2, 3, 4, 5, or 6 to show each account's classification. The first account is given as an example.

3. Place a check mark in either Column 7 or 8 to show on which financial statement each account is reported. The first account is given as an example.

DRILL 8-D 2 Figuring net income or net loss

Information is given below for several companies.

	1	2	3	4	5	6
Business	Total Assets	Total Liabilities	Balance of Capital	Balance of Drawing	Total Revenue	Total Expenses
A	$2,500.00	$ 900.00	$1,050.00	$ 50.00	$1,000.00	$ 400.00
B	3,250.00	1,170.00	1,265.00	65.00	1,400.00	520.00
C	4,750.00	1,440.00	2,430.00	80.00	1,600.00	640.00
D	4,250.00	1,260.00	2,220.00	70.00	1,400.00	560.00
E	4,750.00	1,710.00	1,795.00	95.00	2,100.00	760.00
F	7,125.00	2,565.00	2,567.00	142.00	3,275.00	1,140.00
G	6,056.00	2,180.00	2,185.00	120.00	2,780.00	969.00
H	9,690.00	3,500.00	6,432.00	190.00	4,448.00	4,500.00

Instructions: 1. Use the information in Columns 5 and 6. Figure the amount of net income or net loss for each company. As an example: Company A, Revenue, $1,000.00, *less* Expenses, $400.00, *equals* net income, $600.00.

2. Use the amount figured for Instruction 1 and the information in Columns 1 to 4. Figure the amount of ending capital for each business. As an example: Company A, Capital, $1,050.00, *plus* net income, $600.00, *less* drawing, $50.00, *equals* ending capital, $1,600.00.

APPLICATION PROBLEMS

PROBLEM 8-1 Preparing an income statement

The solution to Problem 7-2 is needed to complete Problem 8-1.

Instructions: Use the work sheet from Problem 7-2. Prepare an income statement. Use the illustration on page 132 as your guide.

PROBLEM 8-2 Preparing a balance sheet

The solution to Problem 7-2 is needed to complete Problem 8-2.

Instructions: Use the work sheet from Problem 7-2. Prepare a balance sheet. Use the illustration on page 135 as a guide.

PROBLEM 8-3 Preparing financial statements

A work sheet for the Westside Bowling Lanes is given in the working papers for this chapter.

Instructions: 1. Prepare an income statement.

2. Prepare a balance sheet.

ENRICHMENT PROBLEMS

MASTERY PROBLEM 8-M Preparing a work sheet and financial statements

The ledger accounts and balances for Masterson's Miniature Golf business on December 31 are below.

Account	Balance	Account	Balance
Cash	$ 2,252.00	Sales	$ 6,408.18
Supplies	3,009.00	Advertising Expense	149.76
Golf Equipment	45,900.00	Miscellaneous Expense	58.68
Maintenance Equipment	2,278.00	Rent Expense	1,530.00
Allison Company (liability)	2,040.00	Utilities Expense	242.78
Gentry Equipment Co. (liability)	4,622.98		
Uniform Supply Co. (liability)	521.82		
Sally Dorton, Capital	42,327.24		
Sally Dorton, Drawing	500.00		
Income Summary	——		

Instructions: 1. Prepare a work sheet for the three months ending December 31 of the current year.

2. Prepare an income statement.

3. Prepare a balance sheet.

CHALLENGE PROBLEM 8-C Preparing a work sheet and financial statements

The ledger accounts and balances for Mensona Service Company on December 31 are below.

Cash	$2,400.30	Sales	$1,260 00
Supplies	88.48	Advertising Expense	58.80
Equipment	1,972.68	Miscellaneous Expense	242.90
Alsop Equipment Company (liability)	3,385.25	Rent Expense	840.00
Lawrence Company (liability)	224.28	Repairs Expense	131.04
Windfall Company (liability)	92.96	Utilities Expense	46.20
Jane Ruso, Drawing	500.00		
Income Summary	——		

Instructions: 1. Figure the balance of the owner's capital account for the list of accounts.

2. Prepare a work sheet for the month ending December 31 of the current year.

3. Prepare an income statement.

4. Prepare a balance sheet. Show all details for figuring ending capital as described on page 137. (The owner made an additional investment of $500.00 on December 28.)

Reinforcement Activity 1

PART C

An Accounting Cycle for a Sole Proprietorship Using a Cash Journal

The work sheet prepared for Part B is needed to complete Part C.

Reinforcement Activity 1, Part C, includes the accounting activities needed to prepare the financial statements for Wilson's Secretarial Service.

Preparing financial statements

Instructions: 15. Use the work sheet to prepare an income statement.

16. Prepare a balance sheet.

The work sheet used in Reinforcement Activity 1, Part C, is needed to complete Part D.

Closing the Ledger

ENABLING PERFORMANCE TASKS

After studying Chapter 9, you will be able to:

a. Define accounting terms related to closing a ledger.
b. Explain accounting principles and practices related to closing a ledger.
c. Analyze closing entries for a service business.
d. Record closing entries for a service business.
e. Post closing entries.
f. Prepare a post-closing trial balance.

A work sheet is prepared at the end of a fiscal period to sort and summarize a business' ledger accounts. From the completed work sheet, a business' financial progress and condition are reported in the form of financial statements. An income statement is prepared to report financial progress *over* a fiscal period. A balance sheet is prepared to report financial condition at the *end* of a fiscal period. *(CONCEPT: Accounting Period Cycle)*

Financial progress reported on an income statement is the amount of net income or loss resulting from business operations. The net income or loss affects a business' capital. Net income increases capital. Net loss decreases capital. After an income statement is prepared, the amount of net income or loss is transferred to a capital account. The new balance of the capital account is reported on a business' balance sheet. *(CONCEPT: Adequate Disclosure)*

NEED FOR CLOSING TEMPORARY CAPITAL ACCOUNTS

Separate revenue and expense accounts are used to record a business' financial progress. These revenue and expense accounts are known as temporary capital accounts. Balances of these temporary capital accounts provide the information needed to prepare an income statement. The difference between the balances of the revenue and expense accounts equals the net income or net loss.

Revenue and expenses are recorded separately for each fiscal period. *(CONCEPT: Matching Expenses with Revenue)* Therefore, each revenue and expense account must have a zero balance at the beginning of a new fiscal period. After an income statement is completed, the temporary accounts have served their purpose. The balance of each revenue and expense account is transferred to one ledger account. This single account summarizes the increases and decreases in capital. The journal entries transferring the revenue and expense account balances clear these accounts for the next fiscal period. An account that has its balance transferred to another account is called a closed account. Journal entries used to prepare temporary capital accounts for a new fiscal period are called closing entries.

INCOME SUMMARY ACCOUNT

To close a temporary capital account, an amount equal to its balance is transferred out of the account. Temporary capital account balances are transferred to a summarizing account. The balances are not transferred directly to the owner's capital account. This procedure avoids having a capital account that is cluttered with many debit and credit entries.

The summarizing account used to close revenue and expense accounts is titled Income Summary. Accountants assume that a business will continue indefinitely and will earn a net income. *(CONCEPT: Going Concern)* For this reason, the title generally given the account is Income Summary. Income Summary is sometimes titled Income and Expense Summary.

After the temporary account balances are transferred, Income Summary shows the total revenue and total expenses for a fiscal period. The resulting balance of Income Summary is the net increase or decrease in capital from business operations. The balance of the income summary account is transferred to the owner's capital account. The chart below shows the flow of information in closing the revenue and expense accounts.

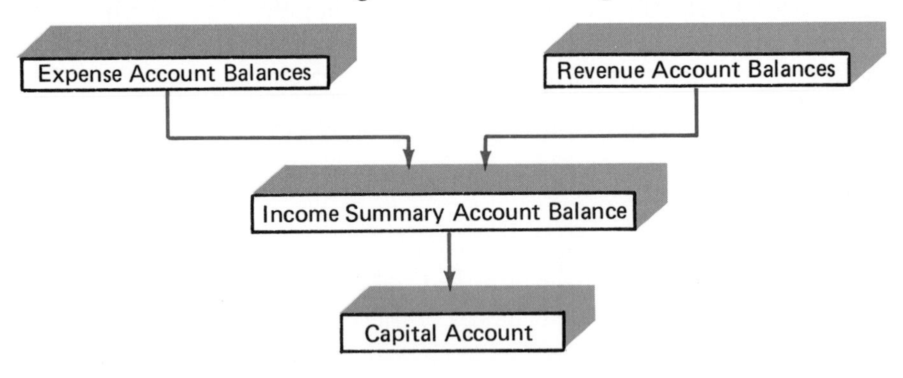

Chart showing the closing of temporary capital accounts

CLOSING ENTRIES

Putt Around's closing entries accomplish four things.

1. Close all revenue accounts.
2. Close all expense accounts.
3. Close income summary account and record net income in owner's capital account.
4. Close the owner's drawing account.

Account balances at the end of a fiscal period are summarized on a work sheet. The information needed to record closing entries is taken from a work sheet.

Closing revenue accounts

Information needed to close revenue accounts on July 31, 1982, is taken from line 10 of Putt Around's work sheet.

	ACCOUNT TITLE	1 TRIAL BALANCE DEBIT	2 TRIAL BALANCE CREDIT	3 INCOME STATEMENT DEBIT	4 INCOME STATEMENT CREDIT	5 BALANCE SHEET DEBIT	6 BALANCE SHEET CREDIT	
10	Sales		2429 00		2429 00			10

Before closing entries are posted, the accounts affected appear as shown below.

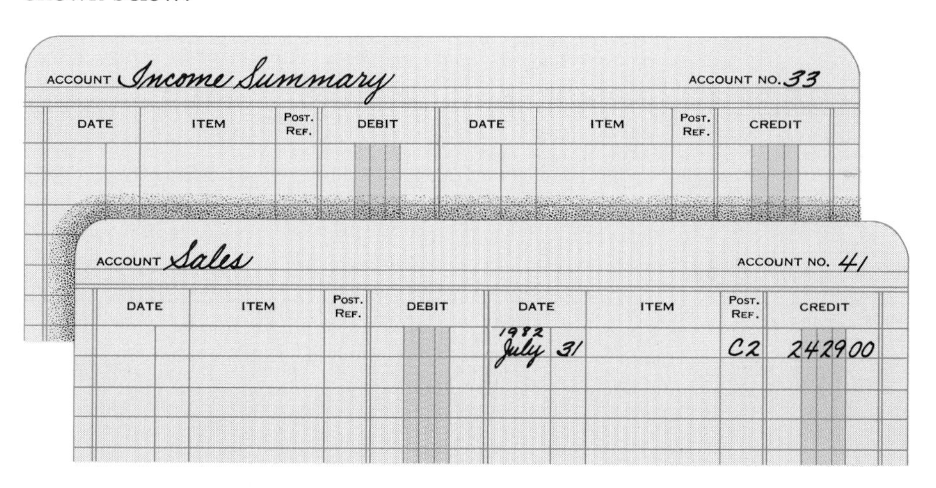

Sales has a *credit* balance of $2,429.00 before a closing entry is posted. The closing entry removes this credit balance and clears the sales account. Sales is debited for $2,429.00.

Sales			
Closing	2,429.00	Balance	2,429.00

Income Summary			
		Closing	2,429.00

The entry is not complete without equal debits and credits. Thus, a credit of $2,429.00 is made to Income Summary.

The general journal entry to record the closing entry for Putt Around's revenue is on the next page.

	GENERAL JOURNAL				PAGE 1
	DATE	ACCOUNT TITLE	POST. REF.	DEBIT	CREDIT
9		Closing Entries			
10	31	Sales		242900	
11		Income Summary			242900

Closing entry for revenue account

The words *Closing Entries* are written in the journal's Account Title column. Closing entries are not based on information from a source document. The heading in the Account Title column is the explanation for all closing entries. Thus, no source document number needs to be written for each of the entries.

The complete entry is written immediately following the heading for closing entries. In the journal above, the date, *31*, is written in the Date column. The account title, *Sales*, is written on the same line in the Account Title column. The amount, *$2,429.00*, is written in the Debit column. On the next line, indented about 1 centimeter, *Income Summary* is written in the Account Title column. The amount, *$2,429.00*, is written in the Credit column.

After Putt Around's closing entry for the revenue account is posted, the ledger accounts appear as shown below.

ACCOUNT Income Summary — ACCOUNT NO. 33

DATE	ITEM	POST. REF.	DEBIT	DATE	ITEM	POST. REF.	CREDIT
				1982 July 31		G1	242900

ACCOUNT Sales — ACCOUNT NO. 41

DATE	ITEM	POST. REF.	DEBIT	DATE	ITEM	POST. REF.	CREDIT
1982 July 31		G1	242900	1982 July 31		C2	242900

The sales account has a zero balance. The original credit balance, $2,429.00, now appears as a credit in the income summary account.

If there were other revenue accounts, their balances also would be closed. The balances would be recorded in the income summary account.

Closing expense accounts

Information needed to close expense accounts is taken from Putt Around's work sheet, lines 11–14.

	ACCOUNT TITLE	TRIAL BALANCE DEBIT (1)	TRIAL BALANCE CREDIT (2)	INCOME STATEMENT DEBIT (3)	INCOME STATEMENT CREDIT (4)	BALANCE SHEET DEBIT (5)	BALANCE SHEET CREDIT (6)	
11	Advertising Expense	2500		2500				11
12	Miscellaneous Expense	7000		7000				12
13	Rent Expense	60000		60000				13
14	Utilities Expense	11700		11700				14

Expense accounts are all closed in a single entry. An entry that contains two or more debits or two or more credits is called a combined entry. A separate closing entry could be made for each expense account. This procedure would result in separate postings to Income Summary for each expense account balance. A combined entry results in only one posting to Income Summary. Thus, time is saved in recording and posting a combined entry.

Putt Around's opening entry, Chapter 2, page 22, is another example of a combined entry.

The total of all expense account balances is figured. Putt Around's total expenses are $812.00. Income Summary is debited for this amount, $812.00.

Each expense account is credited for the amount of its balance. For example, Advertising Expense's balance is $25.00. This account is closed with a credit for $25.00.

The general journal entry to close the expense accounts is below.

Income Summary			
Closing	812.00		

Advertising Expense			
Balance	25.00	Closing	25.00

Miscellaneous Expense			
Balance	70.00	Closing	70.00

Rent Expense			
Balance	600.00	Closing	600.00

Utilities Expense			
Balance	117.00	Closing	117.00

GENERAL JOURNAL PAGE 1

	DATE		ACCOUNT TITLE	POST. REF.	DEBIT	CREDIT	
12		31	Income Summary		81200		12
13			Advertising Expense			2500	13
14			Miscellaneous Expense			7000	14
15			Rent Expense			60000	15
16			Utilities Expense			11700	16

Closing entry for expense accounts

After Putt Around's closing entry for expenses is posted, the ledger accounts appear as shown below and on page 148.

ACCOUNT Income Summary ACCOUNT NO. 33

DATE		ITEM	POST. REF.	DEBIT	DATE		ITEM	POST. REF.	CREDIT
1982 July	31		G1	81200	1982 July	31		G1	242900

ACCOUNT *Advertising Expense* ACCOUNT NO. 51

DATE		ITEM	POST. REF.	DEBIT	DATE		ITEM	POST. REF.	CREDIT
1982 July	6		C1	25 00	1982 July	31		G1	25 00

ACCOUNT *Miscellaneous Expense* ACCOUNT NO. 52

DATE		ITEM	POST. REF.	DEBIT	DATE		ITEM	POST. REF.	CREDIT
1982 July	2		C1	10 00	1982 July	31		G1	70 00
	7		C1	10 00					
	15		C2	15 00					
	22		C2	18 00					
	27		C2	5 00					
	30		C2	12 00					
				70 00					

ACCOUNT *Rent Expense* ACCOUNT NO. 53

DATE		ITEM	POST. REF.	DEBIT	DATE		ITEM	POST. REF.	CREDIT
1982 July	1		C1	600 00	1982 July	31		G1	600 00

ACCOUNT *Utilities Expense* ACCOUNT NO. 54

DATE		ITEM	POST. REF.	DEBIT	DATE		ITEM	POST. REF.	CREDIT
1982 July	2		C1	25 00	1982 July	31		G1	117 00
	5		C1	60 00					
	20		C2	32 00					
				117 00					

Each expense account now has a zero balance. The total amount of all expense account balances, *$812.00*, is a debit in Income Summary.

Closing income summary account and recording net income

After all revenue and expense accounts are closed, Putt Around's income summary account has a credit balance of $1,617.00. This balance is Putt Around's net income for the month ended July 31, 1982. The balance is checked with the amount of net income on the work sheet, page 121. The two amounts are the same. The first two closing entries are assumed to be correct.

The third closing entry closes Income Summary. The amount of net income is also recorded as an increase in the owner's capital account. Income Summary has a credit balance, $1,617.00. Income Summary is debited, *$1,617.00*, to close the account. Harry Rossi, Capital is credited, *$1,617.00*, to record the net income. Putt Around's third closing entry is shown in the journal below.

GENERAL JOURNAL PAGE 1

	DATE	ACCOUNT TITLE	POST. REF.	DEBIT	CREDIT	
17	31	Income Summary		1617 00		17
18		Harry Rossi, Capital			1617 00	18

Entry to close Income Summary and record net income in owner's capital account

If a business has a net loss, Income Summary would have a debit balance. Income Summary would be credited to close the account. The owner's capital account would be debited to record the net loss.

The effect of this closing entry to record net income is shown in the T accounts at the right. The income summary account has a zero balance. The income summary account is a temporary account used only to summarize other temporary capital accounts. *(CONCEPT: Matching Expenses with Revenue)* The account is used to make closing entries only at the end of a fiscal period. The use of Income Summary avoids the need to record all the information in the capital account. Only the net income or net loss is recorded in an owner's capital account each fiscal period.

Income Summary

Expenses	812.00	Revenue	2,429.00
Closing	1,617.00		

Harry Rossi, Capital

		Balance	4,000.00
		Closing	1,617.00

Closing an owner's drawing account

Withdrawals represent capital that an owner has taken out of a business. At the end of a fiscal period, the drawing account is closed. The drawing account balance is also recorded as a decrease in the owner's capital account. The balance of the drawing account is obtained from the work sheet's Balance Sheet Debit column. Putt Around's fourth closing entry is shown in the journal below.

GENERAL JOURNAL PAGE 1

	DATE	ACCOUNT TITLE	POST. REF.	DEBIT	CREDIT	
19	31	Harry Rossi, Capital		150 00		19
20		Harry Rossi, Drawing			150 00	20

Closing entry for owner's drawing account

On July 31, Putt Around's drawing account has a $150.00 debit balance. The account is closed with a $150.00 credit. Harry Rossi, Capital is debited for $150.00 to show the decrease in that account. The effect of this closing entry is shown in the T accounts at the right.

Harry Rossi, Capital

Closing	150.00	Balance	4,000.00
		Closing	1,617.00

Harry Rossi, Drawing

Balance	150.00	Closing	150.00

The drawing account has a zero balance. Information about withdrawals for the next fiscal period will be separated from information about previous fiscal periods.

The new balance of Harry Rossi, Capital is $5,467.00. This new balance is the amount of equity the owner has in Putt Around at the end of the fiscal period. This balance is the same as the amount of capital on the balance sheet, page 135.

Summary of closing entries

The following diagram summarizes the use of Income Summary to make closing entries.

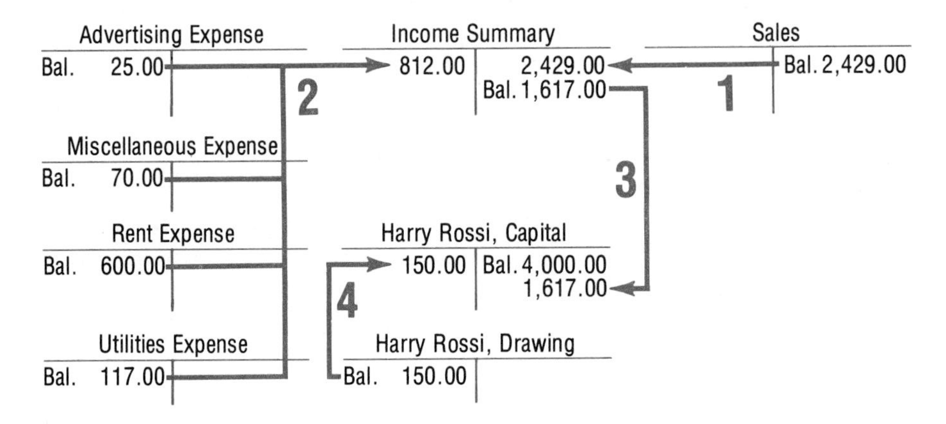

Complete ledger after closing entries are posted

Putt Around's complete ledger after all closing entries are posted is below and on pages 151 and 152.

ACCOUNT *Cash* ACCOUNT NO. 11

DATE		ITEM	POST. REF.	DEBIT	DATE		ITEM	POST. REF.	CREDIT
1982 July	1	Balance	G1	1,100 00	1982 July	31		C2	1,887 00
	31	2,192.00	C2	2,979 00 4,079 00					

ACCOUNT *Supplies* ACCOUNT NO. 12

DATE		ITEM	POST. REF.	DEBIT	DATE		ITEM	POST. REF.	CREDIT
1982 July	1	Balance	G1	500 00					
	2		C1	50 00					
	12		C1	75 00					
	24		C2	100 00 725 00					

Ledger after closing entries are posted

Ledger after closing entries are posted (continued)

ACCOUNT Golf Equipment — ACCOUNT NO. 13

DATE		ITEM	POST. REF.	DEBIT	DATE		ITEM	POST. REF.	CREDIT
1982 July	1	Balance	G1	2200 00					
	12		C1	100 00					
				2300 00					

ACCOUNT Maintenance Equipment — ACCOUNT NO. 14

DATE		ITEM	POST. REF.	DEBIT	DATE		ITEM	POST. REF.	CREDIT
1982 July	1	Balance	G1	900 00	1982 July	1		C1	50 00
	2	1250.00	C1	400 00					
				1300 00					

ACCOUNT Melcor Equipment Company — ACCOUNT NO. 21

DATE		ITEM	POST. REF.	DEBIT	DATE		ITEM	POST. REF.	CREDIT
					1982 July	1	Balance	G1	650 00

ACCOUNT Sasson Supply Company — ACCOUNT NO. 22

DATE		ITEM	POST. REF.	DEBIT	DATE		ITEM	POST. REF.	CREDIT
1982 July	1		C1	200 00	1982 July	1	Balance 350.00	G1	550 00

ACCOUNT Harry Rossi, Capital — ACCOUNT NO. 31

DATE		ITEM	POST. REF.	DEBIT	DATE		ITEM	POST. REF.	CREDIT
1982 July	31		G1	150 00	1982 July	1	Balance	G1	3500 00
						1		C1	500 00
									4000 00
						31	5467.00	G1	1617 00
									5617 00

ACCOUNT Harry Rossi, Drawing — ACCOUNT NO. 32

DATE		ITEM	POST. REF.	DEBIT	DATE		ITEM	POST. REF.	CREDIT
1982 July	2		C1	100 00	1982 July	31		G1	150 00
	23		C2	50 00					
				150 00					

ACCOUNT *Income Summary* ACCOUNT NO. 33

DATE		ITEM	POST. REF.	DEBIT	DATE		ITEM	POST. REF.	CREDIT
1982 July	31		G1	812 00	1982 July	31		G1	2429 00
	31		G1	1617 00					

ACCOUNT *Sales* ACCOUNT NO. 41

DATE		ITEM	POST. REF.	DEBIT	DATE		ITEM	POST. REF.	CREDIT
1982 July	31		G1	2429 00	1982 July	31		C2	2429 00

ACCOUNT *Advertising Expense* ACCOUNT NO. 51

DATE		ITEM	POST. REF.	DEBIT	DATE		ITEM	POST. REF.	CREDIT
1982 July	6		C1	25 00	1982 July	31		G1	25 00

ACCOUNT *Miscellaneous Expense* ACCOUNT NO. 52

DATE		ITEM	POST. REF.	DEBIT	DATE		ITEM	POST. REF.	CREDIT
1982 July	2		C1	10 00	1982 July	31		G1	70 00
	7		C1	10 00					
	15		C2	15 00					
	22		C2	18 00					
	27		C2	5 00					
	30		C2	12 00 70 00					

ACCOUNT *Rent Expense* ACCOUNT NO. 53

DATE		ITEM	POST. REF.	DEBIT	DATE		ITEM	POST. REF.	CREDIT
1982 July	1		C1	600 00	1982 July	31		G1	600 00

ACCOUNT *Utilities Expense* ACCOUNT NO. 54

DATE		ITEM	POST. REF.	DEBIT	DATE		ITEM	POST. REF.	CREDIT
1982 July	2		C1	25 00	1982 July	31		G1	117 00
	5		C1	60 00					
	20		C2	32 00 117 00					

Ledger after closing entries are posted (concluded)

After all closing entries are posted, revenue accounts, expense accounts, Income Summary, and the drawing account all have zero balances. The capital account is footed again. The new balance, *$5,467.00*, is recorded as a pencil footing in the account's Credit column.

POST-CLOSING TRIAL BALANCE

After closing entries are posted, a trial balance is prepared to test that debits still equal credits in the ledger. A trial balance prepared after the closing entries are posted is called a post-closing trial balance. Putt Around's post-closing trial balance, prepared on July 31, 1982, is below.

Putt Around
Post-Closing Trial Balance
July 31, 1982

ACCOUNT TITLE	DEBIT	CREDIT
Cash	2192 00	
Supplies	725 00	
Golf Equipment	2300 00	
Maintenance Equipment	1250 00	
Melcor Equipment Company		650 00
Sasson Supply Company		350 00
Harry Rossi, Capital		5467 00
	6467 00	6467 00

Post-closing trial balance

Only accounts with balances at the end of a fiscal period are listed on a post-closing trial balance. For Putt Around, these accounts are assets, liabilities, and the owner's capital account. Accounts are listed in the same order that they appear in the ledger. Revenue and expense accounts are not listed because they have zero balances. Harry Rossi, Drawing and Income Summary are not listed because they also have zero balances.

The post-closing trial balance above has both debit and credit totals of $6,467.00. The equality of debits and credits in the ledger is proved. The ledger is in balance and ready for the next fiscal period.

SUMMARY OF THE ACCOUNTING CYCLE FOR A SERVICE BUSINESS

Chapters 3 to 9 include a description of Putt Around's accounting activities for a fiscal period. The fiscal period was one month in length. The fiscal period started on July 1 and ended on July 31, 1982. The complete series of accounting activities followed in recording financial information for a fiscal period is called an accounting cycle. *(CONCEPT: Accounting Period Cycle)* Putt Around's accounting cycle is summarized in the flowchart below.

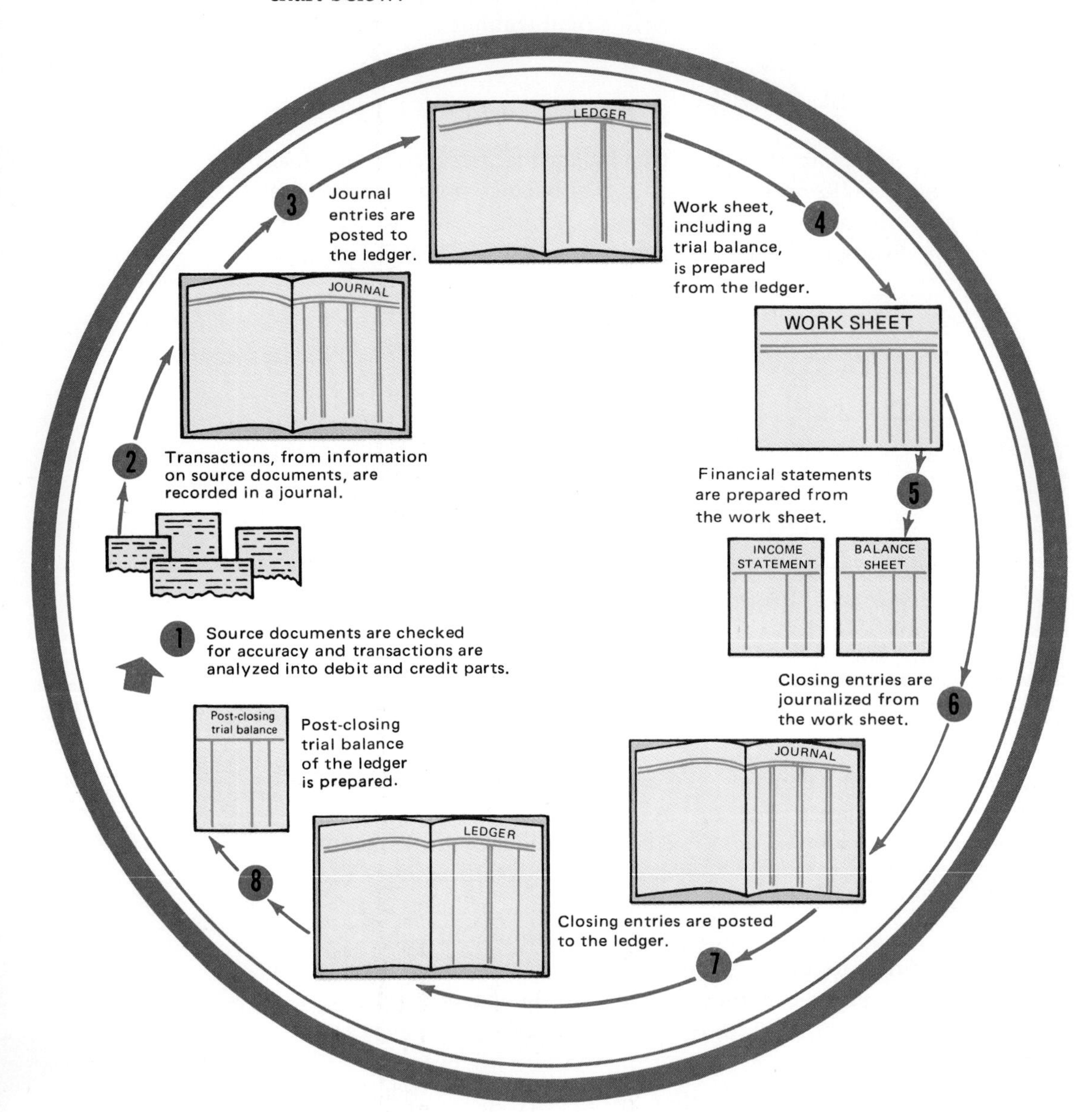

Flowchart of the steps in the accounting cycle

Putt Around's accounting cycle starts with an analysis of source documents and ends with a post-closing trial balance. The parts of the accounting cycle are listed below.

1. Check source documents for accuracy and analyze transactions into debit and credit parts.
2. Record transactions in a journal.

3. Post entries from a journal to a ledger.
4. Prepare a work sheet.
5. Prepare financial statements.
6. Record closing entries in a journal.
7. Post closing entries to a ledger.
8. Prepare a post-closing trial balance.

Some accountants also balance and rule ledger accounts. This is done after the post-closing trial balance is prepared. An increasing number of accountants *do not* balance and rule accounts, however. Balancing and ruling procedures are described in the Appendix.

ACCOUNTING TERMS

What is the meaning of each of the following?

1. closed account
2. closing entries
3. combined entry
4. post-closing trial balance
5. accounting cycle

QUESTIONS FOR INDIVIDUAL STUDY

1. Why are closing entries recorded?
2. Why is an income summary account used in making closing entries?
3. What four things are achieved by Putt Around's closing entries?
4. What accounts are affected by Putt Around's closing entry for revenue? How are they affected?
5. Why is no source document recorded in Putt Around's general journal for closing entries?
6. What effect does Putt Around's closing entry for revenue have on the balance of the sales account?
7. Why does Putt Around make a combined entry to close expense accounts?
8. What accounts are affected by Putt Around's closing entry for expenses? How are they affected?
9. What effect does Putt Around's closing entry for expenses have on the expense account balances?
10. After Putt Around's closing entries for revenue and expenses are posted, what name can be given to the balance of Income Summary?
11. If the business has a net income, what accounts are affected by the entry to close Income Summary? How are they affected?
12. If Putt Around has a net loss, what accounts are affected by the entry to close Income Summary? How are they affected?
13. What accounts are affected by Putt Around's entry to close the drawing account? How are they affected?
14. Why is a post-closing trial balance prepared by Putt Around on July 31, 1982?
15. What ledger accounts are listed on a post-closing trial balance?
16. What are the parts of Putt Around's accounting cycle?

CASES FOR MANAGEMENT DECISION

CASE 1 Helen Moore records and posts closing entries for her business at the end of each fiscal period. She carefully checks the equality of debits and credits in each closing entry. Therefore, she does not prepare a post-closing trial balance. Frank Long does not prepare and post closing entries at the end of each fiscal period. He claims that his ledger has only 25 accounts and they do not need to be closed. Who is following the better accounting procedures, Ms. Moore or Mr. Long? Why?

CASE 2 When Roger McPierson records his closing entries, he does not close his drawing account. What effect will this have on his capital account?

CASE 3 The post-closing trial balance for Peckeral Company on September 30, 1982, shows the capital account balance to be $5,130.00. The post-closing trial balance on August 31, 1982, shows the capital account balance to be $4,330.00. What could cause the balance of this account to increase by $800.00?

DRILLS FOR UNDERSTANDING

DRILL 9-D 1 Identifying accounts affected by closing entries

The ledger accounts used by Mickleson Delivery Service are given below.

1. Advertising Expense
2. Baxter Company (liability)
3. Cash
4. Delivery Equipment
5. Delivery Expense
6. Delivery Revenue
7. Foxworthy Garage (liability)
8. Income Summary
9. Miscellaneous Expense
10. Office Equipment
11. Rent Expense
12. Sally Mickleson, Capital
13. Sally Mickleson, Drawing
14. Utilities Expense
15. Warehouse Equipment
16. Wilson Trucking Company (liability)

Use a form similar to the one below.

1	2	3	4
Account Title	Account is affected by a closing entry	After closing entries are posted, account has	
		a zero balance	a balance
1. *Advertising Expense*	√	√	

Instructions: 1. List the account titles in Column 1 of the form. The first account is given as an example.

2. For each account title, place a check mark in Column 2 if the account is affected by a closing entry. The first account is given as an example.

3. Determine if each account will have a balance or not after closing entries are posted. Place a check mark in either Column 3 or 4 to show your decision. The first account is given as an example.

DRILL 9-D 2 Analyzing the effect of net income or net loss and withdrawals on capital

Information about 10 businesses is given on the next page.

1	2	3	4	5
Business	Account balances on trial balance		Net income or loss for fiscal period	Balance of capital account on post-closing trial balance
	Capital	Drawing		
1	$ 18,000.00	$ 500.00	$5,568.00	?
2	33,600.00	none	?	$ 31,740.00
3	54,720.00	2,000.00	7,740.00	?
4	24,960.00	800.00	4,056.00	?
5	67,800.00	2,500.00	?	63,800.00
6	46,620.00	none	?	51,840.00
7	44,256.00	?	3,168.00	43,824.00
8	111,000.00	5,000.00	?	106,144.00
9	?	500.00	2,844.00	31,696.00
10	5,600.00	250.00	750.00	?

Instructions: On a separate sheet of paper, figure the amount that is missing for each business. Businesses 1 and 2 are given as examples.

Business 1: Beginning capital (Column 2), $18,000.00, + net income (Column 4), $5,568.00 = total, $23,568.00. Total, $23,568.00 − drawing (Column 3), $500.00 = capital on post-closing trial balance (Column 5), $23,068.00.

Business 2: Capital on post-closing trial balance (Column 5), $31,740.00 − beginning capital (Column 2), $33,600.00 = −$1,860.00, net loss for Column 4. (A negative number indicates that there is a net loss. The amount should be written in Column 4 as *−$1,860.00* to show that it is a net loss.)

APPLICATION PROBLEMS

PROBLEM 9-1 Recording closing entries

The solution to Problem 7-2 is needed to complete Problem 9-1.

Instructions: Use the work sheet completed in Problem 7-2. Record the closing entries on page 1 of a general journal.

The solution to Problem 9-1 is needed to complete Problem 9-2.

PROBLEM 9-2 Posting closing entries

The solutions to Problem 7-1 and Problem 9-1 are needed to complete Problem 9-2.

Instructions: Use the ledger completed in Problem 7-1 and the solution to Problem 9-1. Post the closing entries.

The solution to Problem 9-2 is needed to complete Problem 9-3.

PROBLEM 9-3 Preparing a post-closing trial balance

The solution to Problem 9-2 is needed to complete Problem 9-3.

Instructions: 1. Use the ledger completed in Problem 9-2. Pencil foot the capital account to figure the new account balance.

2. Prepare a post-closing trial balance.

PROBLEM 9-4 Recording closing entries

Parts of Miracle-Kleen's work sheet are given below.

Miracle-Kleen
Work Sheet
For Month Ended October 31, 19--

Account Title	Income Statement Debit	Income Statement Credit
Sales		1 820 00
Advertising Expense	86 80	
Electricity Expense	76 00	
Miscellaneous Expense	36 80	
Rent Expense	500 00	
Repairs Expense	37 00	
Water Expense	70 40	
	807 00	1 820 00
Net Income	1 013 00	
	1 820 00	1 820 00

The balance of the account Jerald Bessemer, Drawing on October 31 is $500.00.

Instructions: 1. Use page 1 of a general journal. Record the closing entry for revenue.

2. Record the closing entry for expenses.

3. Record the closing entry to close Income Summary and record net income in the capital account.

4. Record the closing entry to close the drawing account.

ENRICHMENT PROBLEMS

MASTERY PROBLEM 9-M Recording closing entries

Parts of Continental Travel Agency's work sheet are given on the next page. The account Teresa Jason, Drawing has a balance of $1,000.00 on June 30.

Instructions: Use page 1 of a general journal. Record the four closing entries.

Continental Travel Agency
Work Sheet
For Month Ended June 30, 19--

Account Title	Income Statement Debit	Income Statement Credit
Sales		5 293 65
Advertising Expense	335 25	
Automobile Expense	627 00	
Electricity Expense	486 00	
Miscellaneous Expense	160 20	
Rent Expense	2 025 00	
Utilities Expense	450 00	
	4 083 45	5 293 65
Net Income	1 210 20	
	5 293 65	5 293 65

CHALLENGE PROBLEM 9-C Preparing a work sheet; recording and posting closing entries; preparing a post-closing trial balance

Middletown Company's ledger accounts are given in the working papers accompanying this textbook.

Instructions: 1. Foot the ledger accounts. Prepare a trial balance on a work sheet form.

2. Complete the work sheet.
3. Prepare the closing entries. Use page 1 of a general journal.
4. Post the closing entries.
5. Foot the capital account. Prepare a post-closing trial balance.

Reinforcement Activity 1

PART D

An Accounting Cycle for a Sole Proprietorship Using a Cash Journal

The work sheet prepared in Part B and used in Part C is needed to complete Part D. Also needed are the ledger used in Parts A and B and the general journal used in Part A.

Reinforcement Activity 1, Part D, includes the accounting activities needed to complete the end-of-fiscal-period work for Wilson's Secretarial Service.

Completing the end-of-fiscal-period work

Instructions: 17. Use the work sheet. Record closing entries on page 1 of the general journal.

18. Post the closing entries to the ledger.

19. Pencil foot accounts that need to have new balances figured. Figure the new balances.

20. Prepare a post-closing trial balance.

SUMMARY

The accounting cycle for Wilson's Secretarial Service is now complete. The activities listed below were included.

Part A
- Recording an opening entry in a general journal.
- Opening ledger accounts.
- Posting an opening entry.
- Recording transactions in a cash journal.
- Proving cash.
- Totaling, proving, ruling, and posting a cash journal.

Part B
- Footing ledger accounts and figuring account balances.
- Preparing a trial balance on work sheet paper.
- Completing a work sheet.

Part C
- Preparing financial statements (income statement; balance sheet).

Part D
- Recording and posting closing entries.
- Preparing a post-closing trial balance.

10

Checking Account and Reconciling the Bank Statement

ENABLING PERFORMANCE TASKS

After studying Chapter 10, you will be able to:

a. Define accounting terms related to a checking account and reconciling a bank statement.
b. Explain accounting principles and practices related to checking accounts.
c. Prepare a bank deposit slip.
d. Endorse checks to transfer ownership.
e. Prepare check stubs and write checks.
f. Prepare a bank statement reconciliation.
g. Record a bank service charge in a cash journal.
h. Record a dishonored check in a cash journal.

All money kept at a place of business plus money in a bank is usually referred to as cash on hand. Money is less safe than most other assets for several reasons. (1) Money can be transferred from one person to another without ownership being questioned. Usually, cash is considered owned by the person possessing it. (2) Money can be lost because of mistakes in making change. (3) Errors can be made in recording cash receipts or cash payments.

Cash transactions occur in most businesses more frequently than other kinds of transactions. Thus, there are more chances to make recording errors affecting cash. Also, money can be lost or stolen. Therefore, most businesses deposit all cash receipts and make most cash payments by issuing checks.

If all cash receipts are placed in a bank, a business has more evidence that accounting records for cash are accurate. The amount of cash received will equal the cash placed in a bank. Also, the amount of cash withdrawn from a bank equals the amount of cash payments. These procedures give some control over a business' cash.

OPENING A CHECKING ACCOUNT

Placing cash in a bank account is called making a deposit. The person or business in whose name cash is deposited is called a depositor. A bank account from which payments can be ordered by a depositor is called a checking account. A business paper used to make payments from a checking account is known as a check.

Sometimes depositors wish to leave cash in a bank for a period of time to earn interest. A bank account on which a bank pays interest to a depositor is called a savings account. Some checking accounts may also earn interest. These interest-bearing checking accounts are known as NOW accounts.

A signature card

Depositors must tell a bank which persons are authorized to sign checks. A form signed by each person authorized to sign checks is called a signature card. Putt Around's signature card signed by Harry Rossi is below.

Security National BanK

Authorized Signatures For:

PUTT AROUND

Address: 828 Westfield Rd.
Salem, OR 97304-1237
Telephone: 364-9377

Date Opened: June 2, 1982
Checking ☒ Savings ☐
Initial Deposit: $900.00
Account Number: 68-545-09

Name and Title (please print)	Specimen Signature
Harry Rossi, Manager	Harry Rossi

Signature card for a checking account

When more than one person is authorized to sign checks, each person's signature must appear on the signature card. Banks use signature cards to verify signatures on checks presented for payment.

Checks must always be signed with the same signatures shown on signature cards. Sometimes businesses need to change the persons authorized to sign checks. When this occurs, a new signature card is prepared.

Signature cards are also prepared for personal checking accounts. A business owner should keep personal and business cash separate. *(CONCEPT: Business Entity)* For family joint checking accounts, both husband and wife sign a signature card.

A deposit slip

When making deposits, depositors prepare forms showing what is being deposited. A bank form on which a depositor lists all cash and checks being deposited is called a deposit slip. Two forms of deposit slips are below.

Community State Bank PORTLAND, OREGON

THE SPORTS SHOP
PLEASE PRINT EXACT TITLE OF ACCOUNT

ACCOUNT NUMBER
254-88450

July 9 19 82
PLEASE LIST EACH CHECK SEPARATELY

CURRENCY	50	00
COINS	15	00
CHECKS M. Downs	20	00
J. Sherman	12	00
S. Pollis	16	00
K. Mettle	5	00
TOTAL	118	00

Deposit slip showing checks identified by person from whom received

Security National Bank SALEM, OREGON

96-523 / 1232

For deposit to the account of

PUTT AROUND
828 Westfield Road
Salem, OR 97304-1237

Date July 31 19 82

Currency	253	00
Coin	164	00
Checks 96-464	5	00
96-523	6	00
TOTAL	428	00

⑆1232052321⑆ 68⑈545⑈09⑈

Deposit slip showing checks identified by ABA numbers

Checks may be listed on deposit slips in either of two ways. (1) The bank number on which a check is drawn can be listed. (2) The name of the person or business issuing the check can be listed. Depositors should ask which method of preparing deposit slips a bank prefers.

Deposit slips used by one bank may differ from deposit slips used by another bank. Each bank designs its own deposit slips to fit the bank's recording machines. When a deposit is made, a bank gives a depositor a written receipt. This receipt may be a copy of the deposit slip with a stamped verification. The bank may also use a receipt form printed on a bank machine.

The form below is a deposit receipt issued to Putt Around. The bank has verified the form with the printed line across the top showing *July 31 82 D 428 00.*

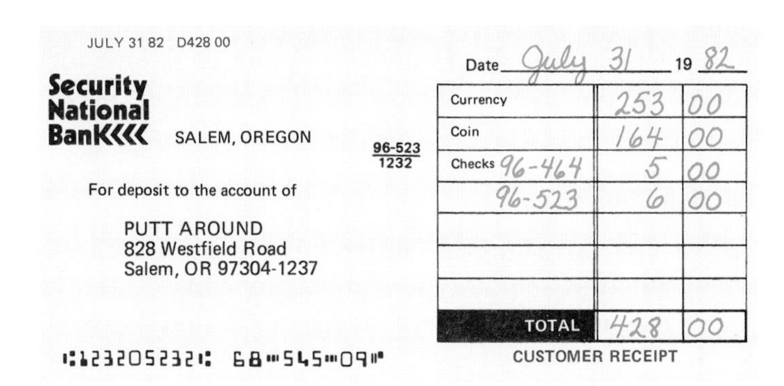

JULY 31 82 D428 00

Security National Bank SALEM, OREGON

96-523 / 1232

For deposit to the account of

PUTT AROUND
828 Westfield Road
Salem, OR 97304-1237

Date July 31 19 82

Currency	253	00
Coin	164	00
Checks 96-464	5	00
96-523	6	00
TOTAL	428	00

CUSTOMER RECEIPT

⑆1232052321⑆ 68⑈545⑈09⑈

Receipt for bank deposit

Recording deposits on check stubs

NO. 39 $
DATE 19
TO
FOR

BAL. BRO'T. FOR'D.	1,764	00
AMT. DEPOSITED 7/31/82 DATE	428	00
TOTAL	2,192	00
AMT. THIS CHECK		
BAL. CAR'D. FOR'D.		

Deposit recorded on a check stub

Putt Around records a deposit on the next unused check stub. Putt Around's July 31 deposit is on the check stub at the left.

Putt Around's cash receipts are recorded in a journal as cash is received. Thus, no journal entry is made to record a deposit. However, some journals have a special column for recording the amount of deposits. This deposit column information can be used to check that all cash received has been deposited.

ABA numbers

Identification numbers assigned to banks by the American Bankers Association are called ABA numbers. ABA numbers are printed on checks and may be printed on deposit slips. The ABA number for Security National Bank, $\frac{96\text{-}523}{1232}$, is on the check below.

828 Westfield Road
Salem, OR 97304-1237
Putt Around
NO. 20
96-523
1232
July 1 19 82
PAY TO THE ORDER OF Sasson Supply Company — $ 200.00
Two hundred and no/100 DOLLARS
Security National Bank
SALEM, OREGON
FOR Payment on account BY Harry Rossi
⑆123205232⑆ 68⑈545⑈09⑈ ⑇0000020000⑇

Check with ABA number and magnetic ink characters

The ABA number is a code including three kinds of information.

1. The *96* is the number assigned to all banks located in the Salem, Oregon area.
2. The *523* is the number assigned specifically to Security National Bank.
3. The number *1232* is a check routing symbol. This number helps the banking system route checks to the area and bank on which drawn. The check routing symbol is not used when listing checks on a deposit slip.

Magnetic ink characters

Banks print special numbers along the bottom of checks. These numbers are printed in special type and magnetic ink. The numbers are referred to as magnetic ink characters. Magnetic ink characters can be "read" by a bank's automated equipment. Using magnetic ink characters speeds a bank's sorting and recording of checks. The numbers are preprinted along the bottom of blank checks received from a bank by a depositor.

When a bank receives a check, the amount is printed along the bottom in the same type and ink. The bank's automated equipment reads this bottom line and records the amount in the depositor's checking account. Magnetic ink characters are printed along the bottom of the check, page 164.

The check digit is used by the automated equipment to verify the accuracy of the routing symbol and bank number.

TRANSFERRING CHECKS

The name of the person to whom a check is issued is written on a check. The person to whom a check is issued becomes the owner of the check. Ownership of a check can be transferred. The check's owner transfers ownership by signing on the check's back. A signature or stamp on a check's back transferring ownership is called an endorsement.

Several endorsements are commonly used. Each endorsement has a specific use in transferring ownership.

Blank endorsement

An endorsement consisting only of the endorser's signature is called a blank endorsement. A lost or stolen check with a blank endorsement can be cashed by anyone who has the check. Ownership can be transferred without further endorsement. Blank endorsements should be used only when a depositor is at a bank ready to cash or deposit checks.

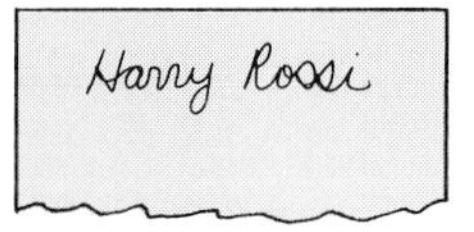

Blank endorsement

Special endorsement

An endorsement stating to whom a check is to be paid is called a special endorsement. Special endorsements are sometimes known as endorsements in full. Only the person or business named in a special endorsement can cash or transfer a check.

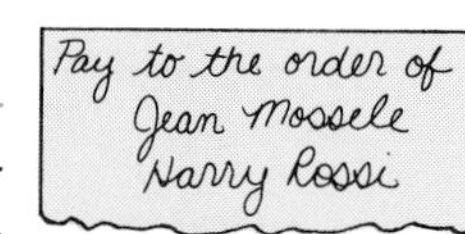

Special endorsement

Restrictive endorsement

An endorsement restricting transfer of a check is called a restrictive endorsement. Restrictive endorsements are often used when checks are prepared for deposit. The endorsement can be either written or stamped on the check as shown at the right.

When using blank, special, or restrictive endorsements, endorsers guarantee payment of checks. If a bank does not receive payment for a check, the endorser must pay the bank.

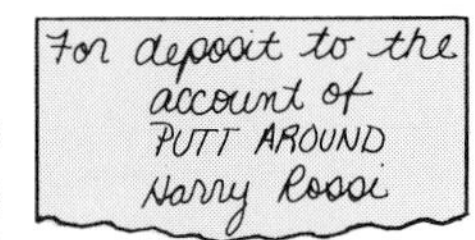

Pay to the
Security National Bank
For Deposit Only
Putt Around

Restrictive endorsement

Putt Around stamps restrictive endorsements on checks at the time they are received from customers. This procedure prevents unauthorized persons from cashing any checks that might be lost or stolen.

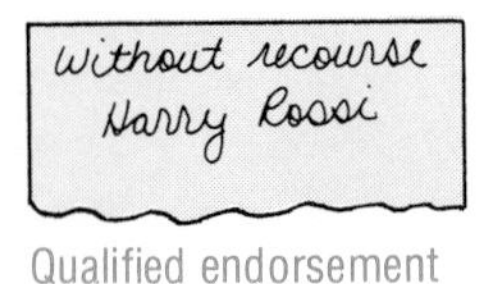

Qualified endorsement

Qualified endorsement

An endorsement showing that the endorser assumes no responsibility for payment is called a qualified endorsement. If a bank does not receive money for the check, a qualified endorser does *not* have to pay the bank.

WRITING CHECKS

Most checks used by businesses are prenumbered as part of the printing process. If check numbers are not printed, the numbers must be written on the checks. Putt Around uses prenumbered checks ordered from its bank. Consecutive numbers provide an easy way to identify each check. Also, the numbers help Putt Around assure that no blank checks are lost or misplaced.

Preparing check stubs

A person or business issuing a check is called a drawer. A person or business to whom a check is issued is called a payee. A bank on which a check is drawn is called a drawee. Putt Around's Check No. 20 is below.

NO. 20 $ 200.00
DATE July 1 19 82
TO Sasson Supply Co.
FOR Payment on account

BAL. BRO'T. FOR'D.	1,100	00
AMT. DEPOSITED (DATE)		
TOTAL	1,100	00
AMT. THIS CHECK	200	00
BAL. CAR'D. FOR'D.	900	00

828 Westfield Road
Salem, OR 97304-1237
Putt Around
NO. 20 96-523/1232
July 1 19 82
PAY TO THE ORDER OF Sasson Supply Company $ 200.00
Two hundred and no/100 DOLLARS
Security National BanK<<<
SALEM, OREGON
FOR Payment on account BY Harry Rossi
⑆123205232⑆ 68⑈545⑈09⑈

Completed check stub and check

The following information is placed on Check Stub No. 20.

1. Amount of the check, *$200.00.*
2. Date of the check, *July 1, 1982.*
3. Payee, *Sasson Supply Company.*
4. Purpose of the check, *Payment on account.*

The check's amount is subtracted from the check stub total to figure the new checking account balance. (Total, $1,100.00, *less* amount of this check, $200.00, *equals* balance carried forward, $900.00.) The new balance, *$900.00*, is written on Check Stub No. 21.

Preparing a check

After a check stub is completed, a check is prepared. The procedure described below is for the check on page 166.

1 The date is written in the space for the date, *July 1, 1982*.

The date written on a check should be the month, day, and year on which the check is issued. Most banks will not accept checks that have a future date. A check with a future date on it is known as a postdated check.

2 The name of the payee is written following the words "Pay to the Order of," *Sasson Supply Company*.

If a payee is a business, use the business' name rather than the owner's name. If a payee is a person, use the person's name.

3 The amount is written following the dollar sign, *$200.00*.

The figures are written close to the printed dollar sign. This procedure prevents anyone from writing another figure in front of the amount.

4 The amount is written in words on the line with the word "Dollars," *Two hundred and no/100*.

This written amount verifies the amount written in figures. The words begin at the extreme left of the line provided. A line is drawn through the remaining space to the printed word *Dollars*. This line prevents anyone from inserting additional words to change the amount. If the amounts in figures and in words are not the same, a bank often will pay the amount in words. Sometimes, when the amounts do not agree, a bank will refuse to accept a check.

Some businesses use a check writing machine to prepare checks. The amount is perforated into the check paper on the Dollar line. The amount perforated into the check cannot be changed without destroying the check.

5 The purpose of a check is written in the space provided, *Payment on account*.

Some checks have a small detachable slip on which to write the purpose. Many businesses use a check with a detachable slip so all details of the payment can be noted.

6 The check is signed by an authorized person, *Harry Rossi*.

The last thing to do in preparing a check is to sign it. Before a check is signed, each item on the check and stub is verified. A check should *not* be signed until it has been verified for accuracy.

Voiding a check

Banks usually refuse to accept altered checks. Banks often refuse to accept checks when the amounts written in figures and words do not agree. Also, most banks refuse to accept postdated checks. If any kind of error is made on a check, a new check is prepared. A check that is not issued should still be filed for the records. This procedure helps account for all prenumbered checks and assures that no check is lost or misplaced.

If a check is not issued, the word *Void* is written across the face of the check. Marking a check so that it cannot be used is called voiding a check. A similar notation is placed on the check stub for a voided check.

Putt Around records all checks in a cash journal. Inspection of the cash journal's Doc. No. column, pages 82 and 83, shows all check numbers in numerical order. If a check number is missing from the Doc. No. column, not all checks are accounted for. Thus, Putt Around also records voided checks in a cash journal. The words *Voided check* are written in the Account Title column. A dash is placed in the Cash Credit column. The check number is written in the Doc. No. column. A check mark is placed in the Post. Ref. column.

RECONCILING A BANK STATEMENT

Banks keep separate records for each depositor. Deposit slips and checks are recorded in depositors' accounts on the day received by a bank. Many banks use automated machines to record items daily in depositors' accounts. This procedure keeps depositors' accounts up to date at all times. The up-to-date balance appearing on a depositor's bank records is called a bank balance.

A bank statement

A copy of a depositor's bank records usually is sent to the depositor each month. A report of deposits, withdrawals, and bank balance sent to a depositor by a bank is called a bank statement.

> For some kinds of personal checking accounts, banks send bank statements only once every two or three months. This procedure is used because relatively few deposits and checks are recorded in these checking accounts.

Putt Around received the bank statement, page 169, on August 1, 1982. The last amount in the Balance column, $1,897.00, is the ending bank balance for this statement.

Some banks mail bank statements to all depositors at the end of each month. Many banks have a large number of depositors. Mailing all bank statements at the end of a month requires that all work be done at one

Security National Bank
SALEM, OREGON

STATEMENT OF ACCOUNT FOR
PUTT AROUND
828 WESTFIELD ROAD
SALEM OR 97304-1237

ACCOUNT NUMBER
68-545-09

STATEMENT DATE
7/30/82

BALANCE FROM PREVIOUS STATEMENT	NO. OF CHECKS	AMOUNT OF CHECKS	NO. OF DEPOSITS	AMOUNT OF DEPOSITS	SERVICE CHARGES	STATEMENT BALANCE
1,190.00	18	1,842.00	5	2,551.00	2.00	1,897.00

DATE	CHECKS	DEPOSITS	BALANCE
6/30/82			1,190.00
7/1/82	25.00	800.00	1,965.00
7/2/82	60.00 5.00 600.00		1,300.00
7/3/82	400.00 25.00 50.00	300.00	1,125.00
7/5/82	10.00 100.00 200.00		815.00
7/8/82	25.00 60.00		730.00
7/9/82	10.00		720.00
7/10/82		530.00	1,250.00
7/16/82	75.00		1,175.00
7/17/82	15.00 100.00	492.00	1,552.00
7/24/82	50.00 32.00	429.00	1,899.00
7/30/82	SC 2.00		1,897.00

PLEASE EXAMINE AT ONCE — IF NO ERROR IS REPORTED WITHIN 10 DAYS THE ACCOUNT WILL BE CONSIDERED CORRECT AND VOUCHERS GENUINE. REFER ANY DISCREPANCY TO OUR ACCOUNTING DEPARTMENT IMMEDIATELY.

Bank statement

time. Banks may use a system of preparing and mailing statements throughout the month. The schedule at the right is used by Security National Bank. The bank prepares and mails Putt Around's bank statement on the 30th of each month. Putt Around receives the bank statement sometime around the first of the next month.

Initials of last name of depositors	Day of month on which statements are mailed
A–H	10th
I–O	20th
P–Z	30th

Checking the accuracy of a bank statement

Banks seldom make errors in depositors' bank records. However, a check might be charged to a wrong account. If errors are discovered on bank statements, depositors should notify the bank at once.

Errors may be made by depositors. The most common error is in arithmetic. However, businesses may make errors in entries for checks issued or cash deposited. When depositors receive bank statements, the information should be verified with the business' accounting records.

All checks charged to a depositor's account are returned by a bank with the bank statement. Checks paid by a bank and returned to a de-

positor are called canceled checks. Checks issued by a depositor but not yet received by a bank are called outstanding checks. Not all deposits may be listed on the latest bank statement received by a depositor. Deposits made but not yet shown on a bank statement are called outstanding deposits.

Some banks charge a fee for maintaining depositors' checking accounts. A charge made by a bank for maintaining a checking account is called a bank service charge. Banks deduct bank service charges from depositors' checking accounts. Bank service charges are listed on bank statements. Putt Around's bank statement, page 169, includes a service charge of $2.00.

> Some banks do not make a service charge if a depositor's checking account balance is large enough. Each bank has its own regulations about service charges.

A bank's records and depositor's records may not agree for the reasons listed below.

1. A bank service charge is not recorded on a depositor's accounting records.
2. The bank statement does not show outstanding deposits.
3. A bank has not received outstanding checks.
4. A depositor may have made errors in recording entries affecting cash.
5. The bank may have made an error.

In good accounting practice, a business' accounting records are verified to assure that they agree with the bank statement.

Reconciling a bank statement

Bringing bank statement and checkbook balances into agreement is called reconciling a bank statement. Putt Around reconciles its bank statement as soon as the statement is received from the bank. Before the reconciliation is prepared, Putt Around proves cash. A procedure for proving cash is described on page 83.

Canceled checks are arranged in numerical order. A check mark is placed on the check stub for each canceled check. Check stubs with no check marks show that checks were outstanding at the time the bank statement was prepared.

The reconciliation is prepared as shown on page 171. The procedure for reconciling Putt Around's bank statement is described below.

1 *Figure adjusted check stub balance.*

- List in the left amount column the balance shown on the next unused check stub. Check Stub No. 39 shows an ending balance of $2,192.00.

Putt Around
Reconciliation of Bank Statement
August 1, 1982

Balance on Check Stub No. 39, August 1, 1982	2192 00	Balance on bank statement, July 30, 1982		1897 00
Deduct:		Add:		
Service charge for July	2 00	Outstanding deposit, July 31, 1982		428 00
		Total		2325 00
		Deduct:		
		Outstanding checks,		
		No. 34	18.00	
		No. 36	100.00	
		No. 37	5.00	
		No. 38	12.00	135 00
Adjusted check stub balance, Aug. 1, 1982	2190 00	Adjusted bank balance August 1, 1982		2190 00

Reconciliation of a bank statement

- List the bank service charge, *$2.00*. Putt Around's bank service charge is obtained from the bank statement, page 169.
- Subtract the bank service charge from the check stub balance. List the difference, *$2,190.00*, on the reconciliation. Label this amount *Adjusted check stub balance, August 1, 1982.*

2 *Figure adjusted bank balance.*

- List in the right amount column the bank statement balance, $1,897.00. This is the last amount in the bank statement's Balance column, page 169.
- List any outstanding deposits not shown on the bank statement. Check Stub No. 39 shows a deposit of $428.00 that is not listed on the bank statement.
- Add the outstanding balance to the bank statement balance. Write the total, *$2,325.00*, in the right amount column.
- List the number and amount of each outstanding check. Four checks are outstanding according to the verification of canceled checks.
- Add the amounts of all outstanding checks. List the total, *$135.00*, in the right amount column.
- Subtract the total amount of outstanding checks from the previous total. Write the difference, *$2,190.00*, in the amount column. Label this amount *Adjusted bank balance, August 1, 1982.*

3 ***Compare adjusted balances.*** Verify that the two adjusted amounts are the same. Putt Around's adjusted check stub balance is $2,190.00. The adjusted bank statement balance is the same amount. The two adjusted balances are the same. The bank statement is reconciled.

If the two adjusted balances are not the same, an error has been made. The error must be found and corrected.

Printed form for reconciliation of bank statement

Sometimes banks print suggested reconciliation forms on the back of bank statements. A suggested printed reconciliation form is below.

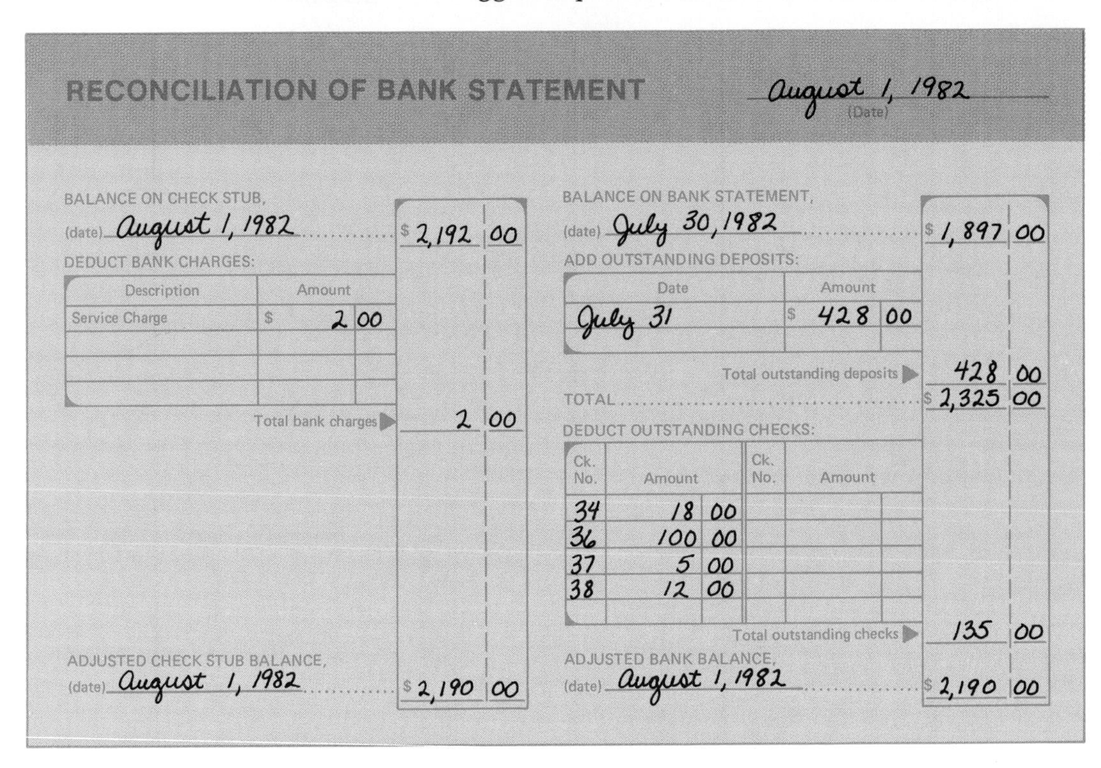

RECONCILIATION OF BANK STATEMENT   August 1, 1982 (Date)

BALANCE ON CHECK STUB, (date) August 1, 1982 .... $ 2,192 00

DEDUCT BANK CHARGES:

Description	Amount
Service Charge	$ 2 00

Total bank charges ▶ 2 00

ADJUSTED CHECK STUB BALANCE, (date) August 1, 1982 .... $ 2,190 00

BALANCE ON BANK STATEMENT, (date) July 30, 1982 .... $ 1,897 00

ADD OUTSTANDING DEPOSITS:

Date	Amount
July 31	$ 428 00

Total outstanding deposits ▶ 428 00

TOTAL .... $ 2,325 00

DEDUCT OUTSTANDING CHECKS:

Ck. No.	Amount	Ck. No.	Amount
34	18 00		
36	100 00		
37	5 00		
38	12 00		

Total outstanding checks ▶ 135 00

ADJUSTED BANK BALANCE, (date) August 1, 1982 .... $ 2,190 00

RECORDING A BANK SERVICE CHARGE

NO. 39	$	
DATE	19	
TO		
FOR		
BAL. BRO'T. FOR'D.		1764 00
AMT. DEPOSITED	7/31/82 (DATE)	428 00
TOTAL	July S.C. 2.00	2192 00 / 2,190 00
AMT. THIS CHECK		
BAL. CAR'D. FOR'D.		

Service charge recorded on a check stub

The bank service charge, *$2.00*, is deducted from Putt Around's checking account by the bank. Putt Around must also record this payment on its check stubs and in its cash journal.

Recording a bank service charge in a checkbook

Putt Around records the service charge on the next unused check stub, Check Stub No. 39. The words *July S. C.* are written on the check stub to identify the amount. The amount is subtracted from the total on the check stub. The difference, *$2,190.00*, is written on the check stub at the left. The balance on the check stub, *$2,190.00*, is now correct. The balance is the same as the adjusted check stub balance on the bank reconciliation.

Recording a bank service charge in a cash journal

Putt Around's bank service charge is one cash payment for which no check is written. However, the bank service charge must still be recorded in the cash journal. A form is prepared describing the reason for the entry. A form on which a brief message is written is called a memorandum. Sometimes transactions occur for which there is no business paper. For the service charge entry, Putt Around prepares a memorandum as the source document. *(CONCEPT: Objective Evidence)* Putt Around's Memorandum No. 1 is below.

MEMORANDUM

NO. 1

DATE August 1, 1982

Record the bank service charge, $2.00, per bank statement dated July 30, 1982.

Putt Around

Signature Harry Rossi

Memorandum

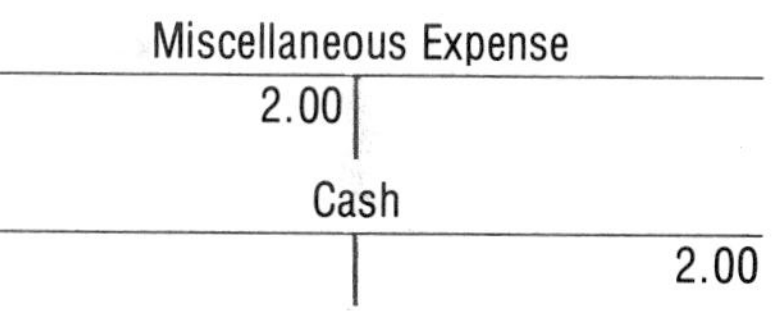

The effect of the bank service charge entry is shown in the T accounts at the right.

The entry increases Putt Around's expenses. Miscellaneous Expense is debited for $2.00. The entry also decreases the cash account. Cash is credited for $2.00.

Putt Around's Memorandum No. 1 is the source document for the entry to record the bank service charge. *(CONCEPT: Objective Evidence)* Putt Around's cash journal entry for the August 1 bank service charge is below.

Entry to record a bank service charge

CASH JOURNAL — PAGE 3

	1 Cash Debit	2 Cash Credit	Date		Account Title	Doc. No.	Post. Ref.	3 General Debit	4 General Credit	5 Sales Credit	
1			1982 Aug.	1	Balance on hand $2,192.00		✓				1
2		200		1	Miscellaneous Expense	M1		200			2

The date, *1*, is written in the Date column. The debit to Miscellaneous Expense, *$2.00*, is written in the General Debit column. The credit to Cash, *$2.00*, is written in the Cash Credit column. The account title, *Miscellaneous*

Expense, is written in the Account Title column. The source document number, *M1*, is written in the Doc. No. column.

> The abbreviation for memorandums is *M*. Thus, the abbreviation *M1* means that the source document is Memorandum No. 1.

RECORDING DISHONORED CHECKS

Banks may not accept checks for a number of reasons. (1) The amount on the check appears to have been altered. (2) The signature on a check may appear to be different than on the signature card. (3) The amount written in words may be different from the amount in figures. (4) The check may be postdated. (5) The depositor's account may have insufficient funds to pay the check. A check that a bank refuses to pay is called a dishonored check.

Putt Around records checks received as cash. The checks are deposited in the bank. Putt Around records dishonored checks as cash payments.

On August 5, the bank notifies Putt Around that a customer's check has been dishonored.

> *August 5, 1982. Notice received from bank of a dishonored check, $5.00, plus bank fee, $1.00. Memorandum No. 2.*

A memorandum is prepared explaining the entry. The memorandum is the entry's source document. *(CONCEPT: Objective Evidence)* This entry is another cash payment not supported by a check stub as source document.

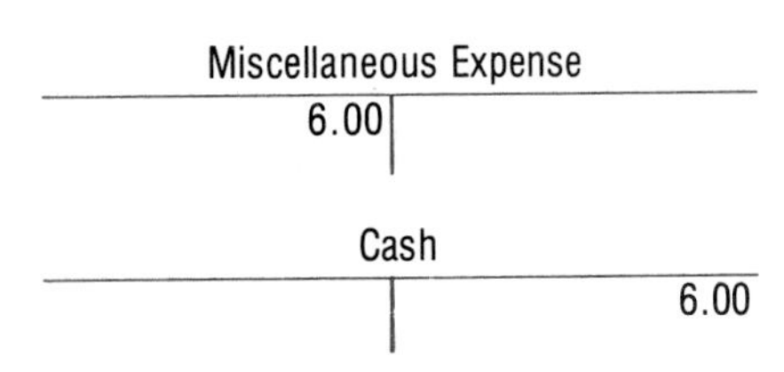

The entry affects Putt Around's accounts as shown in the T accounts at the left.

Dishonored checks are an expense. The total expense is the value of the dishonored check plus the bank fee. Miscellaneous Expense is debited for $6.00 to record the expense. The cash balance is decreased by this entry. Cash is credited for $6.00 to show this decrease.

The entry to record the dishonored check is below.

CASH JOURNAL — PAGE 3

	1 Cash Debit	2 Cash Credit	Date	Account Title	Doc. No.	Post. Ref.	3 General Debit	4 General Credit	5 Sales Credit	
14		6 00	5	Miscellaneous Expense	M2		6 00			14

Entry to record a dishonored check

The date, *5*, is written in the Date column. The debit to Miscellaneous Expense, *$6.00*, is recorded in the General Debit column. The credit to Cash, *$6.00*, is recorded in the Cash Credit column. The account title, *Miscellaneous Expense*, is written in the Account Title column. The source document, *M2*, is written in the Doc. No. column.

The decrease in cash is also recorded on a check stub. The check stub entry for the dishonored check is at the right.

> If a dishonored check *is* collected later, Cash is debited and Miscellaneous Expense is credited.

Issuing a check with insufficient money to pay it or altering a check is illegal in most states. Forging a check is also illegal in all states. When a check is dishonored, a question is raised about the maker's credit rating. A dishonored check is always a serious matter. Depositors must prepare checks with care to assure that all checks will be honored.

NO. 43 $

DATE 19

TO

FOR

BAL. BRO'T. FOR'D	1,590	00
Dishonored check AMT. DEPOSITED / DATE	— 6	00
TOTAL	1,584	00
AMT. THIS CHECK		
BAL. CAR'D. FOR'D.		

Dishonored check recorded on a check stub

ACCOUNTING TERMS

What is the meaning of each of the following?

1. making a deposit
2. depositor
3. checking account
4. savings account
5. signature card
6. deposit slip
7. ABA numbers
8. endorsement
9. blank endorsement
10. special endorsement
11. restrictive endorsement
12. qualified endorsement
13. drawer
14. payee
15. drawee
16. voiding a check
17. bank balance
18. bank statement
19. canceled checks
20. outstanding checks
21. outstanding deposits
22. bank service charge
23. reconciling a bank statement
24. memorandum
25. dishonored check

QUESTIONS FOR INDIVIDUAL STUDY

1. Why is cash less safe than most other assets?
2. Why is a depositor required to sign a signature card for a checking account?
3. How may checks be listed on a deposit slip?
4. What record does a depositor have that a deposit has been made in a checking account?
5. Why is a deposit not recorded in Putt Around's cash journal?
6. What are the three parts of an ABA number?
7. Why are magnetic ink characters printed along the bottom of a check?
8. What endorsements are often used by businesses to prepare checks for deposit?
9. What might a bank do if the amounts in figures and in words on a check differ?
10. Why is signing a check the last thing to do in preparing a check?
11. What should be done if a check is prepared incorrectly?
12. What should be done with a bank statement when received by a depositor?
13. Why will a bank statement balance often *not* agree with a checkbook balance?
14. When should a bank statement reconciliation be prepared?
15. Why does Putt Around use a memorandum as the source document for an entry for bank service charges?
16. What two accounts are affected by Putt Around's entry to record a bank service charge? How are they affected?
17. Why might a bank dishonor a check?
18. What accounts are affected by Putt Around's entry, page 174, to record a dishonored check? How are they affected?

CASES FOR MANAGEMENT DECISION

CASE 1 Melody Hall recently opened a checking account for her new business. She had all six of her employees sign the signature card. Is this a good practice? Explain your answer.

CASE 2 Michael O'Rielly owns a farm. He mails all deposits to the bank. In preparing checks for deposit, Mr. O'Rielly uses a blank endorsement. Is this a good practice? Explain your answer.

CASE 3 Jeff Watson often writes checks when he has insufficient money in his checking account. He dates the checks for the first of the next month. At the end of each month he deposits his paycheck to cover the checks he has already written. What are the dangers in this practice?

CASE 4 Peter Fischer accumulates his monthly bank statements. Once every four months he reconciles his checking account. Wanda Horowitz reconciles each monthly bank statement as it is received. Is Mr. Fischer or Ms. Horowitz using the better accounting practice? Explain your answer.

DRILLS FOR UNDERSTANDING

DRILL 10-D 1 Reconciling a bank statement

On June 30 of the current year, Wilma Phlong receives a bank statement dated June 25. The information below is obtained from the statement and her checkbook.

Bank balance, $639.45.
Service charge, $6.15.
Outstanding checks: No. 84, $32.40, and No. 102, $18.45.
Balance on Check Stub No. 103, $594.75.

Instructions: Reconcile Miss Phlong's bank statement.

DRILL 10-D 2 Reconciling a bank statement

On November 1 of the current year, Theodore Anderson receives a bank statement dated October 27. The information below is obtained from the statement and his checkbook.

Bank balance, $898.34.
Service charge, $3.40.
Outstanding deposit made on October 28, $128.94.
Outstanding checks: No. 1280, $12.99; No. 1296, $42.69; and No. 1299, $21.26.
Balance on Check Stub No. 1304, $953.74.

Instructions: Reconcile Mr. Anderson's bank statement.

DRILL 10-D 3 Reconciling a bank statement

On May 25 of the current year, JoAnn Wilson receives a bank statement dated May 20. The information on the next page is obtained from the statement and her checkbook.

Instructions: Reconcile Mrs. Wilson's bank statement.

Bank balance, $473.92.
Service charge, $1.84.
Outstanding check No. 47, $41.04.
Two outstanding deposits: May 21, $32.00 and May 24, $125.00.
Balance on Check Stub No. 50, $591.72.

APPLICATION PROBLEMS

PROBLEM 10-1 Preparing a deposit slip

On October 14 of the current year, Business Services makes a deposit. The business' checking account number is 74-34846-01. The items listed below are to be deposited.

Money on hand to be deposited	
Currency	$196.00
Coins	50.06
Checks on hand to be deposited	
Timothy Hedrick, drawn on First National Bank, Medford, OR (ABA No. 96-530)	65.00
Edna Falls, drawn on Farmers State Bank, Medford, OR (ABA No. 96-525)	21.42
Rodger Milley, drawn on the Citizens National Bank, Medford, OR (ABA No. 96-527)	52.02

Instructions: 1. Prepare a deposit slip for this deposit. Identify the checks by the ABA numbers.

2. Endorse the checks being deposited. Use a restrictive endorsement similar to the one on page 165. Sign your own name as part of the endorsement.

PROBLEM 10-2 Preparing check stubs and writing checks

You are authorized to sign checks for Key Car Wash. The first check is numbered 21. The balance brought forward from Check Stub No. 20 is $389.16. Use the current date on all checks.

Instructions: 1. Write the beginning balance on Check Stub No. 21.

2. Prepare check stubs and checks Nos. 21 and 22.

Check No. 21: $25.00; payee, Waters Supply Company; payment on account.
Check No. 22: $75.50; payee, Nichols Equipment Company; typewriter repairs.

3. Record a deposit of $126.70 on Check Stub No. 23.

4. Prepare check stubs and checks Nos. 23 and 24.

Check No. 23: $150.00; payee, Mercer Supply Company; for supplies.
Check No. 24: $100.00; payee, John Key (owner of Key Car Wash); for personal use.

PROBLEM 10-3 Reconciling a bank statement and recording a bank service charge

On November 30 of the current year, Bonnie Scott receives a bank statement for her business, Scotty's Plumbing Service. The bank statement is dated November 26. A comparison of the bank statement and the business' checkbook shows the information given on the next page.

The checkbook balance on Check Stub No. 201 is $203.60.
The bank statement balance is $200.53.
An outstanding deposit was made on November 29, $52.25.
The outstanding checks are: No. 196, $19.94.
No. 197, $8.91.
No. 201, $22.88.
The bank service charge is $2.55.

Instructions: 1. Prepare a bank reconciliation.
2. Record the bank service charge on page 8 of a cash journal. Memorandum No. 15.

ENRICHMENT PROBLEMS

MASTERY PROBLEM 10-M Reconciling a bank statement and recording a bank service charge

In the working papers accompanying this textbook are business papers related to a checking account for Lanes Service Company.

Instructions: 1. Check the canceled checks against the check stubs. Place a check mark next to the check stub number for each check returned by the bank.
2. Make a list of any checks not returned showing check number and amount. These are the outstanding checks.
3. Check the bank statement against the check stubs to determine if all the deposits are listed on the bank statement. List by date and amount any deposits shown on the check stubs and not shown on the bank statement. These are the outstanding deposits.
4. Prepare a bank reconciliation. Use the date October 4 of the current year.
5. Record the bank service charge on page 9 of a cash journal. Memorandum No. 22.
6. Record the bank service charge on Check Stub No. 805.

CHALLENGE PROBLEM 10-C Writing checks; reconciling a bank statement; recording a bank service charge and a dishonored check

You are authorized to sign checks for Kraddock's Service Company. On October 31 of the current year, there are three checks to be written. On November 1, the company receives a bank statement dated October 29.

Instructions: 1. Record the balance brought forward on Check Stub No. 53, $629.18.
2. Prepare check stubs and checks Nos. 53, 54, and 55.

Check No. 53. $62.50; Dave's Garage; automobile repairs.
Check No. 54. $10.00; Hazelburg's Cleaning Service; washing windows.
Check No. 55. $25.00; Midtown Supply Company; supplies.

3. Prepare a bank reconciliation. Use November 1 of the current year.

Bank service charge, $5.60.
Outstanding deposit made on October 30, $178.50.
Outstanding checks: Nos. 53, 54, and 55.
Bank statement balance, $445.08.

4. Record the bank service charge on page 10 of a cash journal. Memorandum No. 22.
5. Record a dishonored check on page 10 of a cash journal. Use November 5 of the current year. Amount of check, $5.00; bank fee, $1.00. Memorandum No. 23.

THE COURT YARD is a service business organized as a sole proprietorship. This reinforcement activity covers the transactions completed by a business that rents racquetball courts. A pictorial flowchart of the accounting cycle of THE COURT YARD is shown on the next two pages. This company uses a cash journal, general journal, and ledger. The books of account needed to complete this reinforcement activity are available from the publisher.

Flowchart of the
Accounting Cycle of
THE COURT YARD

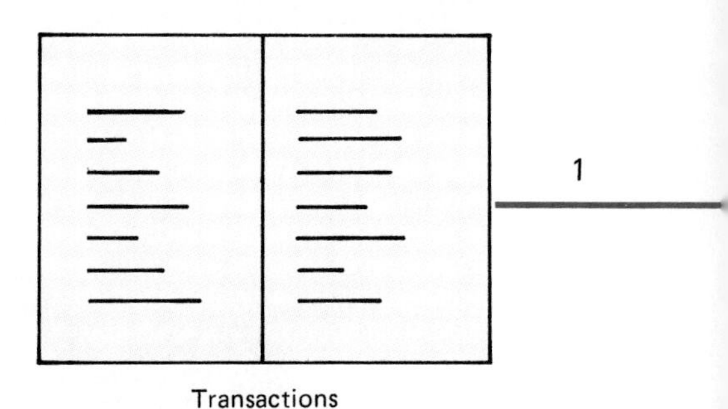

1 Record transactions in the cash journal.
2 Post items to be posted individually from the cash journal to the ledger.
3 Post cash journal column totals to the ledger.
4 Pencil foot ledger accounts and prepare the trial balance on the work sheet.
5 Complete the work sheet.
6 Prepare financial statements.
7 Record closing entries in the general journal.
8 Post closing entries to the ledger.
9 Prepare a post-closing trial balance.

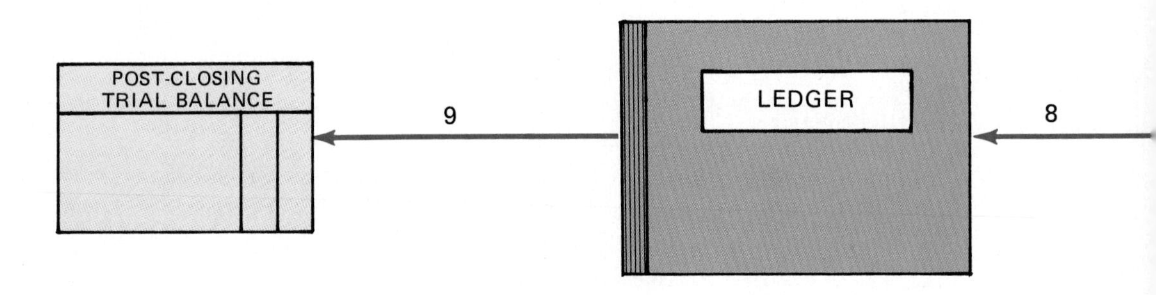

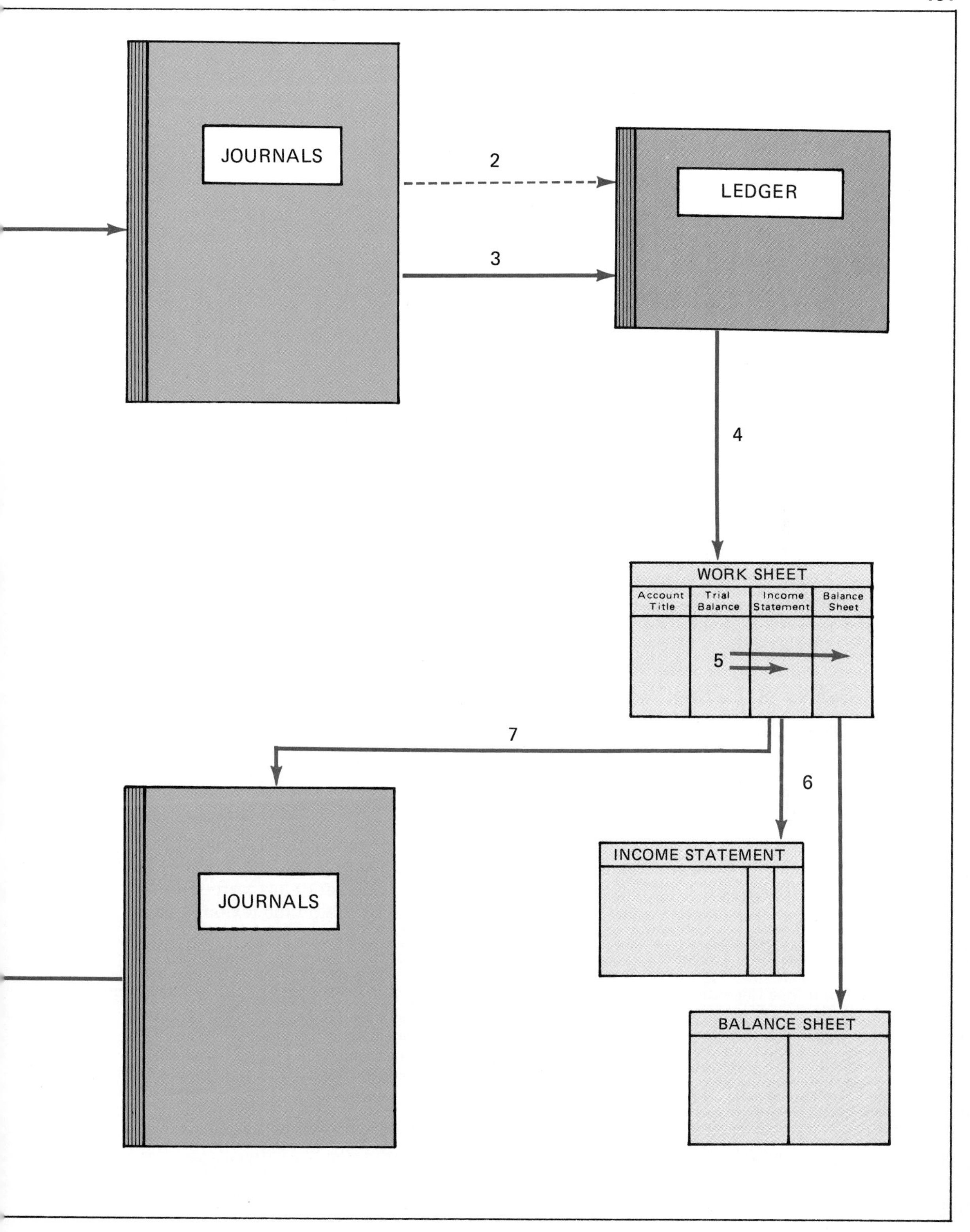
JOURNALS
2
3
LEDGER
4
WORK SHEET
Account Title
Trial Balance
Income Statement
Balance Sheet
5
7
6
JOURNALS
INCOME STATEMENT
BALANCE SHEET

Reinforcement Activity

The Court Yard

THE COURT YARD

A racquetball facility is located near a local shopping center. The building owner rents the facility to Judy Surito. Ms. Surito operates the business as a recreational center open to the general public. The business name chosen by Ms. Surito is *The Court Yard*.

Individual racquetball courts are rented for half hour intervals. Thus, the business' revenue comes from court rentals.

The Court Yard is open seven days a week from 9 a.m. to 10 p.m. Racquets and balls are provided by the business if customers do not have their own personal equipment. The court rentals include use of a locker.

On November 1 of the current year, The Court Yard begins a new accounting system.

Flowchart of The Court Yard's accounting cycle

This reinforcement activity illustrates a complete accounting cycle. The Court Yard uses a one-month fiscal period. The flowchart of the accounting cycle is on pages 180 and 181.

Required materials

Transactions are recorded in a cash journal and a general journal. Ledger accounts are kept using two-column ledger account forms. The business forms and records needed for the reinforcement activity may be obtained from the publisher of this textbook.

Model illustrations of the business forms and records are on the textbook pages listed below.

Business Forms and Records	Model Illustrations	Business Forms and Records	Model Illustrations
General journal	page 21	Income statement	page 132
Opening entry	page 22	Balance sheet	page 135
Cash journal	pages 82 and 83	Bank reconciliation	page 171
Ledger accounts	pages 115–117	Closing entries	pages 145–149
Work sheet	page 121	Post-closing trial balance	page 153

The Court Yard's cash journal is the same as the one on page 82 except for the title of column 5. The revenue amount column is headed *Court Rentals Credit*.

Source documents

The Court Yard uses four different source documents.

Source Documents	Abbreviations	Transactions Used For
1. Cash register tapes	T	Cash received from racquetball court rentals
2. Receipts	R	Cash received from other than court rentals
3. Checks/check stubs	C	Cash payments
4. Memorandums	M	Others not covered by items 1, 2, and 3 above

STARTING THE COURT YARD'S ACCOUNTING RECORDS

The Court Yard uses the chart of accounts below.

The Court Yard
Chart of Accounts

(1) ASSETS	Account Number	(4) REVENUE	Account Number
Cash	11	Court Rentals	41
Supplies	12		
Office Equipment	13	(5) EXPENSES	
Racquetball Equipment	14	Advertising Expense	51
(2) LIABILITIES		Maintenance Expense	52
Meyers Supply Company	21	Miscellaneous Expense	53
Racquetball, Inc.	22	Rent Expense	54
Sports Store	23	Utilities Expense	55
(3) CAPITAL			
Judy Surito, Capital	31		
Judy Surito, Drawing	32		
Income Summary	33		

On November 1 of the current year, Ms. Surito prepares the beginning balance sheet below.

The Court Yard
Balance Sheet
November 1, 19--

Assets		Liabilities	
Cash	4 000 00	Meyers Supply Company	600 00
Supplies	600 00	Racquetball, Inc.	500 00
Office Equipment	1 000 00	Sports Store	1 000 00
Racquetball Equipment	3 500 00	Total Liabilities	2 100 00
		Capital	
		Judy Surito, Capital	7 000 00
Total Assets	9 100 00	Total Liabilities and Capital	9 100 00

Instructions: 1. Record the opening entry on page 1 of the general journal. The source document is the November 1 balance sheet.

2. Open a ledger account for each account listed on the chart of accounts.

3. Post the opening entry to the ledger accounts.

RECORDING THE COURT YARD'S TRANSACTIONS

Instructions for recording transactions and doing other accounting tasks follow. Complete the tasks given in each instruction.

Instructions: 4. Analyze and record each of the following transactions. Begin on page 1 of the cash journal.

Trans. No.		
1	Nov. 1.	Record the cash on hand, $4,000.00.
2	1.	Paid cash for a new cash register, $500.00. C101.
3	1.	Paid cash for November rent, $1,500.00. C102.
4	1.	Paid cash for supplies, $25.00. C103.
5	1.	Received cash from court rentals, $250.00. T1.
6	2.	Paid cash for cleaning and maintenance, $100.00. C104.
7	2.	Paid cash for a new desk top calculator, $50.00. C105.
8	2.	Received cash from court rentals, $140.00. T2.
9	3.	Paid cash for new racquetball equipment, $500.00. C106.
10	3.	Paid cash for business license, $50.00. C107.
11	3.	Received cash from court rentals, $310.00. T3.
12	3.	Paid cash for telephone bill, $90.00. C108.

Instructions: 5. Post individual items from the cash journal's General Debit and Credit columns.

6. Analyze and record the transactions below.

Trans. No.		
13	Nov. 4.	Paid cash for advertising in local newspaper, $100.00. C109.
14	4.	Received cash from court rentals, $225.00. T4.
15	5.	Paid cash for a new electric typewriter, $500.00. C110.
16	5.	Paid cash for health department permit, $50.00. C111.
17	5.	Received cash from court rentals, $200.00. T5.
18	6.	Paid cash to owner for personal use, $200.00. C112.
19	6.	Received cash from court rentals, $480.00. T6.
20	7.	Received cash from court rentals, $120.00. T7.
21	8.	Paid cash for supplies, $25.00. C113.
22	8.	Paid cash for direct mail advertising, $150.00. C114.
23	8.	Paid cash for cleaning and maintenance, $100.00. C115.
24	8.	Received cash from court rentals, $335.00. T8.

Instructions: 7. Post individual items from the cash journal's General Debit and Credit columns.

8. Prove cash. The balance on the last used check stub is $2,120.00.

9. Total, prove, and rule page 1 of the cash journal.
10. Forward the column totals to page 2 of the cash journal.
11. Prepare a report of items as shown below. Give the report to your instructor.

Name ______________________

Column totals for page ___ of the cash journal.

Cash Debit	$______	Cash Credit	$______
General Debit	$______	General Credit	$______
		Court Rentals Credit	$______
Total Debits	$______	Total Credits	$______

Instructions: 12. Analyze and record the transactions below.

Trans. No.		
25	Nov. 9.	Received cash from court rentals, $120.00. T9.
26	10.	Paid cash to Racquetball, Inc., for part of amount owed, $200.00. C116.
27	10.	Received cash from court rentals, $450.00. T10.
28	11.	Paid cash for new racquetball equipment, $500.00. C117.
29	11.	Received cash from court rentals, $276.00. T11.
30	12.	Paid cash to Sports Store for part of amount owed, $500.00. C118.
31	12.	Received cash from court rentals, $296.00. T12.
32	13.	Paid cash for new business sign to be used as advertising, $400.00. C119.
33	13.	Paid cash to owner for personal use, $200.00. C120.
34	13.	Received cash from court rentals, $438.00. T13.
35	14.	Received cash from court rentals, $204.00. T14.

Instructions: 13. Post individual items from the cash journal's General Debit and Credit columns.

14. Analyze and record the transactions below.

Trans. No.		
36	Nov. 15.	Paid cash for advertising in local newspaper, $100.00. C121.
37	15.	Paid cash for cleaning and maintenance, $100.00. C122.
38	15.	Received cash from court rentals, $252.00. T15.
39	16.	Received cash from court rentals, $300.00. T16.
40	17.	Paid cash to Meyers Supply Company for part of amount owed, $300.00. C123.
41	17.	Received cash from court rentals, $249.00. T17.
42	18.	Received cash from sale of an old cash register, $50.00. R1.
43	18.	Received cash from court rentals, $204.00. T18.
44	19.	Paid cash for new racquetball equipment, $300.00. C124.
45	19.	Received cash from court rentals, $190.00. T19.
46	20.	Paid cash to owner for personal use, $200.00. C125.
47	20.	Received cash from court rentals, $350.00. T20.

Instructions: 15. Post individual items from the cash journal's General Debit and Credit columns.

16. Prove cash. The balance on the last used check stub is $2,699.00.
17. Total, prove, and rule page 2 of the cash journal.
18. Forward the column totals to page 3 of the cash journal.
19. Prepare a report similar to the one in Instruction 11.
20. Analyze and record the transactions below.

Trans. No.		
48	Nov. 21.	Received cash from court rentals, $156.00. T21.
49	22.	Paid membership in local Chamber of Commerce, $50.00. C126.
50	22.	Paid cash for direct mail advertising, $150.00. C127.
51	22.	Paid cash for cleaning and maintenance, $100.00. C128.
52	22.	Received cash from court rentals, $252.00. T22.
53	23.	Received cash from court rentals, $444.00. T23.
54	24.	Paid cash to Sports Store for part of amount owed, $250.00. C129.
55	24.	Received cash from court rentals, $380.00. T24.
56	25.	Paid cash for supplies, $20.00. C130.
57	25.	Received cash from court rentals, $156.00. T25.
58	26.	Paid cash for water bill, $150.00. C131.
59	26.	Received cash from court rentals, $210.00. T26.

Instructions: 21. Post individual items from the cash journal's General Debit and Credit columns.
22. Analyze and record the transactions below.

Trans. No.		
60	Nov. 27.	Paid cash to owner for personal use, $200.00. C132.
61	27.	Received cash from court rentals, $240.00. T27.
62	28.	Received cash from court rentals, $192.00. T28.
63	29.	Paid cash for a miscellaneous expense, $35.00. C133.
64	29.	Paid cash for electric bill, $300.00. C134.
65	29.	Paid cash for cleaning and maintenance, $100.00. C135.
66	29.	Received cash from court rentals, $216.00. T29.
67	30.	Paid cash for a new file cabinet, $200.00. C136.
68	30.	Paid cash for supplies, $30.00. C137.
69	30.	Received cash from court rentals, $264.00. T30.

Instructions: 23. Prepare a reconciliation of The Court Yard's bank statement received on November 30. The bank statement is dated November 28. A comparison of the bank statement and The Court Yard's checkbook shows the information below.

Bank statement balance, $3,763.00.
Checkbook balance on Check Stub No. 137, $3,624.00.
Outstanding deposits: November 28, $192.00.
November 29, $216.00.
November 30, $264.00.
Outstanding checks: Nos. 131, 133, 134, 135, 136, and 137.
Service charge listed on bank statement, $4.00.

24. Analyze and record the transaction given on the next page.

Trans. No.	
70	Nov. 30. Record the bank service charge, $4.00. M1.

Instructions: 25. Post the individual items from the cash journal's General Debit and Credit columns.

26. Prove cash. The balance on the last used check stub is $3,620.00.

27. Total, prove, and rule page 3 of the cash journal.

28. Post column totals from the cash journal to the ledger accounts.

29. Prepare a report similar to the one in Instruction 11.

COMPLETING THE END-OF-FISCAL-PERIOD WORK

The Court Yard uses a one-month fiscal period. Use the date November 30 of the current year.

Instructions: 30. Pencil foot the ledger accounts. Figure the account balances.

31. Prepare a trial balance on work sheet paper.

32. Complete the work sheet.

33. Prepare an income statement.

34. Prepare a balance sheet.

35. Record the closing entries in the general journal.

36. Post the closing entries.

37. Prepare a post-closing trial balance.

38. Assemble all business forms and records in the order given below.

Journals	Income statement	Post-closing trial balance
Ledger	Balance sheet	Bank reconciliation
Work sheet		

Be sure your name is on each item. Present all of your completed reinforcement activity to your instructor.

3 ACCOUNTING FOR A MERCHANDISING BUSINESS

GENERAL BEHAVIORAL GOALS

1. Know accounting terminology related to a merchandising business organized as a partnership.
2. Understand accounting principles and practices for a merchandising business organized as a partnership.
3. Demonstrate accounting procedures for a merchandising business organized as a partnership.

Denim Threads, the business for Part 3, sells casual wearing apparel.

DENIM THREADS
Chart of Accounts

(1) ASSETS	Account Number
Cash	11
Accounts Receivable	12
Merchandise Inventory	13
Supplies	14
Prepaid Insurance	15
(2) LIABILITIES	
Accounts Payable	21
Sales Tax Payable	22
(3) CAPITAL	
Eva Burgos, Capital	31
Eva Burgos, Drawing	32
Luis Perez, Capital	33
Luis Perez, Drawing	34
Income Summary	35

(4) REVENUE	Account Number
Sales	41
(5) COST OF MERCHANDISE	
Purchases	51
(6) EXPENSES	
Credit Card Fee Expense	61
Insurance Expense	62
Miscellaneous Expense	63
Rent Expense	64
Salary Expense	65
Supplies Expense	66

The chart of accounts for Denim Threads is illustrated above for ready reference as you study Part 3 of this textbook.

11

Journalizing Purchases and Cash Payments

ENABLING PERFORMANCE TASKS

After studying Chapter 11, you will be able to:

a. Define accounting terms related to purchases and cash payments.
b. Explain accounting principles and practices related to purchases and cash payments.
c. Classify accounts related to purchases and cash payments.
d. Analyze transactions related to purchases and cash payments into debit and credit parts.
e. Journalize purchases and cash payments in a combination journal.

Putt Around, described in Part 2, is owned by one person. A business owned by one person is known as a sole proprietorship. Putt Around is a service business. The service is providing facilities for people to play miniature golf.

Two or more persons may own a single business. A business may need more capital than one owner can provide. The type of business may also require the skills of more than one person. A business in which two or more persons combine their assets and abilities is called a partnership. Each member of a partnership is called a partner. Partners agree to share in the profit or loss of a business. As in sole proprietorships, financial records and reports of partnerships are kept separate from those of persons supplying the assets. *(CONCEPT: Business Entity)*

Partnerships are common in small businesses that purchase and sell goods. A business that purchases and sells goods is called a merchandising business. Goods that a merchandising business purchases to sell are called merchandise.

Denim Threads, the business described in Part 3, is a partnership owned by Eva Burgos and Luis Perez. The business purchases and sells casual wearing apparel such as blue jeans, sweaters, shirts, and belts.

Denim Threads expects to make money and to continue in business indefinitely. *(CONCEPT: Going Concern)*

USING A COMBINATION JOURNAL

A service business generally has a large number of cash transactions and a limited number of noncash transactions to record. Noncash transactions are those that do not involve either the receipt or payment of cash. Putt Around uses a five-column cash journal, described in Chapter 5, to record all cash transactions. A two-column general journal is used to record the small number of noncash transactions.

Denim Threads, a merchandising business, has many noncash transactions. Noncash transactions would take much time to enter in a general journal. Therefore, Denim Threads uses only one journal in which all transactions are recorded.

A multicolumn journal in which all transactions of a business are recorded is called a combination journal. A combination journal provides the additional special amount columns needed to record all cash and noncash transactions. The combination journal used by Denim Threads is below and on page 193.

Use of a combination journal is common in small merchandising businesses where only one person records transactions. Eva Burgos records all transactions for Denim Threads.

Form of combination journal

The combination journal for Denim Threads below has eleven amount columns. Special amount columns are provided for the recording of transactions related to the purchasing and selling of merchandise. The columns are arranged to make accurate recording and posting easier. Debit and credit columns for Cash, Accounts Receivable, and Accounts Payable are arranged in pairs. This arrangement helps avoid errors in recording amounts in the wrong columns. Since the Cash Debit and Credit columns are used often, they are placed at the left of the Account Title column. The remaining columns are placed at the right of the Account Title column. General Debit and Credit columns are placed first so that amounts in these columns will be close to the account titles.

Recording the beginning cash balance in a combination journal (left page)

PAGE 1 COMBINATION JOURNAL

	CASH 1		DATE	ACCOUNT TITLE	DOC. NO.	POST. REF.	GENERAL 3	4	
	DEBIT	CREDIT					DEBIT	CREDIT	
1			1982 Nov. 1	Balance on hand, $4,200.00		✓			1
2									2
3									3

Recording the beginning cash balance

An entry for the beginning cash balance is recorded at the beginning of each month. The entry is recorded in the journal so that the beginning cash balance is readily available for proving cash. The cash balance entry for Denim Threads on November 1, 1982, is on line 1 of the combination journal on page 192. This entry is similar to the one in the cash journal, Chapter 5.

PURCHASES OF MERCHANDISE

The price of merchandise a business purchases to sell is called cost of merchandise. For a business to make a profit, the selling price of merchandise must be greater than the cost of merchandise. The amount added to the cost of merchandise to establish the selling price is called markon. Revenue earned from the sale of merchandise includes both the cost of merchandise and the markon. All costs of merchandise are deducted from revenue because only the markon increases capital. Accounts showing the costs of merchandise are kept in a separate division of the ledger. This division is shown in the chart of accounts, page 190.

A merchandising business purchases merchandise to sell and buys supplies and equipment for use in the business. An account that shows the cost of merchandise purchased to sell is titled Purchases. This account is used only to record the value of merchandise purchased. Therefore, only purchases of merchandise are recorded in the Purchases Debit column of the combination journal. All other items bought, such as supplies, are recorded in the General Debit column of a combination journal. Purchases and other items bought are recorded and reported at the price agreed upon at the time the transaction occurs. *(CONCEPT: Historical Cost)*

Purchases of merchandise on account

A transaction in which the merchandise purchased is to be paid for later is called a purchase on account. A business to which payment is owed is called a creditor. Some businesses purchasing on account from only a few companies keep a separate ledger account for each creditor.

FOR MONTH OF *November* 19*82* PAGE */*

	5	6	7	8	9	10	11	
	ACCOUNTS RECEIVABLE		SALES CREDIT	SALES TAX PAYABLE CREDIT	ACCOUNTS PAYABLE		PURCHASES DEBIT	
	DEBIT	CREDIT			DEBIT	CREDIT		
1								1
2								2
3								3

Recording the beginning cash balance in a combination journal (right page)

Putt Around included separate accounts in its ledger, pages 150–152. However, a business that purchases on account from many firms will have many accounts with creditors. To avoid a bulky ledger, the total amount owed to all creditors can be summarized in a single ledger account. A liability account that summarizes the amounts owed to all creditors is titled Accounts Payable. Denim Threads uses the accounts payable account to summarize the amount owed to all creditors.

Source document for a purchase on account. When a seller sends merchandise to a buyer, the seller prepares a form showing what has been sent. A form describing the goods shipped, the quantity, and the price is called an invoice. An invoice used as a source document for recording a purchase on account transaction is called a purchase invoice. *(CONCEPT: Objective Evidence)* A purchase invoice received by Denim Threads is below.

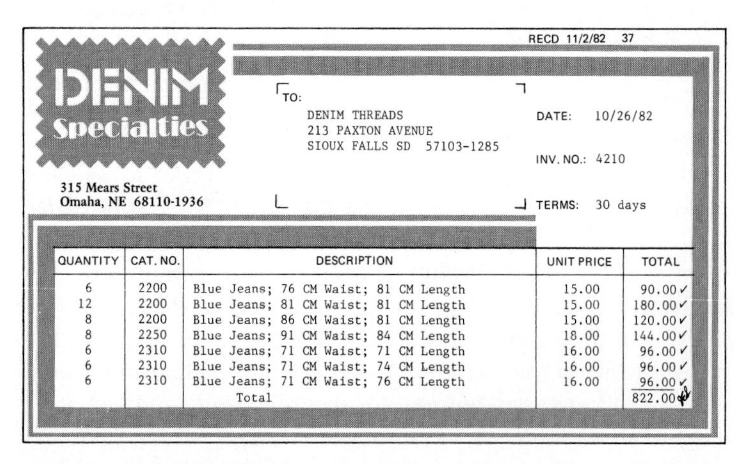
RECD 11/2/82 37

DENIM Specialties

315 Mears Street
Omaha, NE 68110-1936

TO:
DENIM THREADS
213 PAXTON AVENUE
SIOUX FALLS SD 57103-1285

DATE: 10/26/82

INV. NO.: 4210

TERMS: 30 days

QUANTITY	CAT. NO.	DESCRIPTION	UNIT PRICE	TOTAL
6	2200	Blue Jeans; 76 CM Waist; 81 CM Length	15.00	90.00✓
12	2200	Blue Jeans; 81 CM Waist; 81 CM Length	15.00	180.00✓
8	2200	Blue Jeans; 86 CM Waist; 81 CM Length	15.00	120.00✓
8	2250	Blue Jeans; 91 CM Waist; 84 CM Length	18.00	144.00✓
6	2310	Blue Jeans; 71 CM Waist; 71 CM Length	16.00	96.00✓
6	2310	Blue Jeans; 71 CM Waist; 74 CM Length	16.00	96.00✓
6	2310	Blue Jeans; 71 CM Waist; 76 CM Length	16.00	96.00✓
		Total		822.00

Purchase invoice

A purchase invoice lists the quantity, the description, the price of each item, and the total amount of the invoice. A purchase invoice provides the information needed for recording a purchase on account.

When Denim Threads receives a purchase invoice, a date and a number are stamped in the upper right-hand corner. Numbers are assigned in sequence to identify all purchase invoices. The *37* stamped on the invoice above is the number assigned by Denim Threads to that purchase invoice. This number should not be confused with the seller's invoice number which is 4210.

A buyer needs to know that all of the items ordered have been received at the correct prices. The check marks on the invoice show that the items and amounts have been checked and are correct. The initials near the total are those of the person at Denim Threads who checked the invoice.

An agreement between a buyer and a seller about payment for merchandise is called the terms of sale. The terms of sale on the invoice, page 194, are 30 days. These terms mean that payment is due within 30 days from the date of the invoice. The invoice is dated October 26. Therefore, payment must be made by November 25.

Analyzing a purchase on account. Denim Threads purchased merchandise on account.

November 2, 1982. Purchased merchandise on account from Denim Specialties, $822.00. Purchase Invoice No. 37.

A purchases account has a debit balance. Therefore, a purchases account is increased on its debit side. A purchases account is decreased on its credit side.

This transaction increases the balance of the purchases account. The cost account Purchases is debited for $822.00.

This transaction also increases the amount owed to creditors. The liability account Accounts Payable has a credit balance and is increased on its credit side. Accounts Payable, therefore, is credited for $822.00.

Purchases	
Debit Side Balance Increase	Credit Side Decrease

Purchases	
822.00	

Accounts Payable	
	822.00

Recording a purchase on account. The entry to record this purchase on account is on line 3 of the partial combination journal below.

COMBINATION JOURNAL 1982 PAGE 1

	DATE	ACCOUNT TITLE	DOC. NO.	POST. REF.	ACCOUNTS PAYABLE DEBIT (9)	ACCOUNTS PAYABLE CREDIT (10)	PURCHASES DEBIT (11)	
	2	Denim Specialties	P37			822 00	822 00	3
								4

Recording a purchase on account in a combination journal

The date, *2*, is written in the Date column. The debit amount, *$822.00*, is entered in the Purchases Debit column. The credit amount, *$822.00*, is written in the Accounts Payable Credit column. The name of the creditor, *Denim Specialties*, is entered in the Account Title column. The number of the purchase invoice, *P37*, is written in the Doc. No. column.

Both debit and credit amounts are recorded in special amount columns. Therefore, the writing of the names of either ledger account in the Account Title column is not necessary. However, the name of the creditor is written in the Account Title column to show to whom the amount is owed. The way Denim Threads keeps records of the amount owed to each creditor is described in Chapter 13.

Purchases of merchandise for cash

Denim Threads pays cash for some purchases. All payments are made by check.

Source document for a cash purchase. The source document for a cash purchase transaction is the check stub of the check issued in payment. *(CONCEPT: Objective Evidence)* The source document for the transaction below is the check stub for Check No. 326.

Analyzing a cash purchase. Denim Threads purchased merchandise for cash.

November 2, 1982. Purchased merchandise for cash, $425.00. Check No. 326.

This cash purchase transaction increases the balance of the purchases account. The cost account Purchases has a debit balance and is increased on its debit side. Thus, Purchases is debited for $425.00.

Purchases	
425.00	

Cash	
	425.00

This transaction also decreases the balance of the cash account. The asset account Cash has a debit balance and is decreased on its credit side. Cash is therefore credited for $425.00.

Recording a cash purchase. The entry to record this cash purchase is on line 4 of the partial combination journal below.

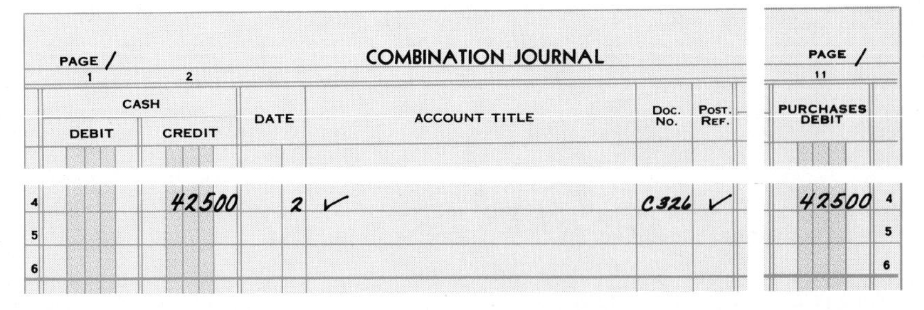

COMBINATION JOURNAL — PAGE 1

	CASH DEBIT (1)	CASH CREDIT (2)	DATE	ACCOUNT TITLE	DOC. NO.	POST. REF.	PURCHASES DEBIT (11)	
4		425 00	2	✓	C326	✓	425 00	4
5								5
6								6

Recording a cash purchase in a combination journal

The date of the transaction, 2, is entered in the Date column. The debit amount, *$425.00*, is written in the Purchases Debit column. The credit amount, *$425.00*, is entered in the Cash Credit column. A check mark is placed in the Account Title column. The check mark shows that no account title needs to be written. The check number, *C326*, is entered in the Doc. No. column. A check mark is placed in the Post. Ref. column. The check mark in this column shows that amounts on this line are not to be posted individually.

BUYING SUPPLIES

Denim Threads buys supplies for use in the business. Supplies are not recorded in the purchases account because supplies are not intended for sale to customers. Wrapping paper, cash register tapes, and office supplies are examples of supplies.

Buying supplies on account

Denim Threads usually buys supplies for cash. Recording a transaction for buying supplies for cash is described in Chapter 4. Occasionally some supplies are bought on account.

Source document for buying supplies on account. When Denim Threads buys supplies on account, an invoice is received from the seller. This invoice is similar to the purchase invoice received when merchandise is purchased. To show that this invoice is for supplies, a brief note is attached to the invoice. The note indicates that the invoice is for supplies and not for purchases. A form on which a brief interoffice message is written is known as a memorandum. Memorandum No. 47 is below. A memorandum with its attached invoice is the source document for a buying supplies on account transaction. *(CONCEPT: Objective Evidence)* After entries have been made, the memorandums are filed numerically.

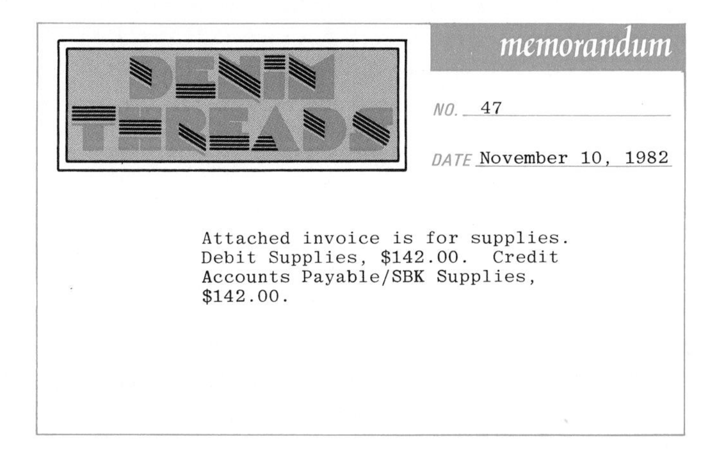

DENIM THREADS

memorandum

NO. 47

DATE November 10, 1982

Attached invoice is for supplies. Debit Supplies, $142.00. Credit Accounts Payable/SBK Supplies, $142.00.

Memorandum for buying supplies on account

Analyzing buying supplies on account. Denim Threads bought supplies on account.

November 10, 1982. Bought supplies on account from SBK Supplies, $142.00. Memorandum No. 47.

Buying supplies on account increases the balance of the supplies account. The asset account Supplies has a debit balance and is increased on its debit side. Supplies therefore is debited for $142.00. This transaction also increases the amount owed to creditors. The liability Accounts Payable has a credit balance and is increased on its credit side. Therefore, Accounts Payable is credited for $142.00.

Supplies	
142.00	

Accounts Payable	
	142.00

Recording buying supplies on account. This transaction is recorded in the partial combination journal on the next page.

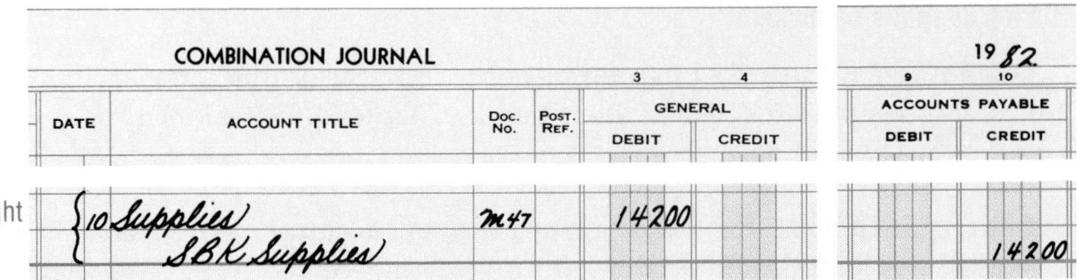

COMBINATION JOURNAL 1982

DATE	ACCOUNT TITLE	Doc. No.	Post. Ref.	GENERAL DEBIT (3)	GENERAL CREDIT (4)	ACCOUNTS PAYABLE DEBIT (9)	ACCOUNTS PAYABLE CREDIT (10)
10	Supplies	M47		14200			
	SBK Supplies						14200

Recording supplies bought on account in a combination journal

The date, *10*, is written in the Date column. No special amount column is provided for Supplies. Therefore, the debit amount for supplies, *$142.00*, is recorded in the General Debit column. The title, *Supplies*, is written in the Account Title column. Account titles are required for both the debit and the credit parts of the entry. Therefore, each amount and each account title is written on a separate line. The credit amount, *$142.00*, is entered in the Accounts Payable Credit column on the next line. The name of the creditor, *SBK Supplies*, is written in the Account Title column and is indented about 1 centimeter. A brace ({) is placed in the Date column to show that both entries on these two lines belong to the same transaction. The number of the memorandum, *M47*, is entered in the Doc. No. column.

Buying supplies for cash

Denim Threads buys most of its supplies for cash. Supplies are generally bought from local businesses.

Source document for buying supplies for cash. The source document for a supplies bought for cash transaction is the check stub issued in payment. *(CONCEPT: Objective Evidence)* The source document for the transaction below is the check stub for Check No. 328.

Analyzing buying supplies for cash. Denim Threads bought supplies for cash.

November 15, 1982. Bought supplies for cash, $86.00. Check No. 328.

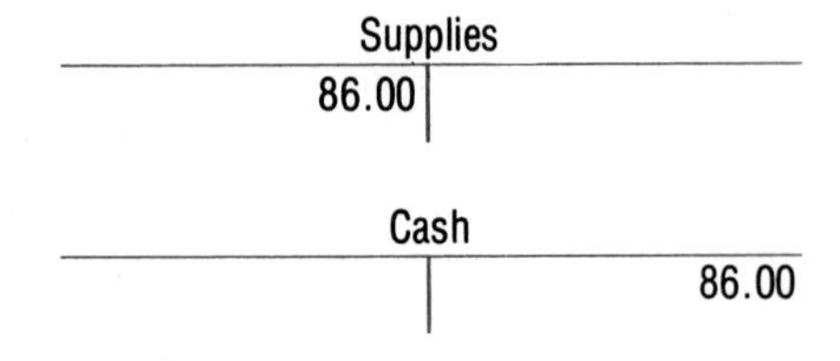

This transaction increases the balance of the supplies account. The asset account Supplies has a debit balance and is increased on its debit side. Therefore, Supplies is debited for $86.00. The asset account Cash has a debit balance and is decreased on its credit side. Thus, Cash is credited for $86.00.

Recording buying supplies for cash. The entry to record this transaction is on line 19 of the partial combination journal on the next page.

PAGE 1		COMBINATION JOURNAL					
1	2					3	4
CASH		DATE	ACCOUNT TITLE	DOC. NO.	POST. REF.	GENERAL	
DEBIT	CREDIT					DEBIT	CREDIT
	86 00	15	Supplies	C328		86 00	

Recording supplies bought for cash in a combination journal

A similar entry for Putt Around is described in Chapter 5.

The date, *15*, is written in the Date column. The debit amount for Supplies, *$86.00*, is recorded in the General Debit column. The title, *Supplies*, is entered in the Account Title column. The credit amount, *$86.00*, is written in the Cash Credit column. The check number, *C328*, is entered in the Doc. No. column.

CASH PAYMENTS

Payment to creditors is made according to the terms of sale on purchase invoices. Payment for an expense usually is made at the time the expense occurs.

Cash payment on account

Denim Threads pays by check for all cash purchases and for items bought on account.

Source document for a cash payment on account. The check stub for the check written to pay a creditor is the source document for a cash payment on account. *(CONCEPT: Objective Evidence)*

Analyzing a payment on account. Denim Threads made a cash payment on account.

November 15, 1982. Paid on account to Westwood, Inc., $580.00. Check No. 329.

This payment on account decreases the amount owed to creditors. The liability account Accounts Payable has a credit balance and is decreased on its debit side. Accounts Payable therefore is debited for $580.00. The balance of the asset account Cash is also decreased. Cash is credited for $580.00.

Accounts Payable	
580.00	

Cash	
	580.00

Recording a payment on account. The entry to record this payment on account is on line 20 of the partial combination journal on page 200.

The date, *15*, is written in the Date column. The amount debited to Accounts Payable, *$580.00*, is entered in the Accounts Payable Debit column. The amount credited to Cash, *$580.00*, is written in the Cash Credit col-

Recording a payment on account in a combination journal

PAGE 1			COMBINATION JOURNAL				19 82	
1	2						9	10
CASH		DATE	ACCOUNT TITLE	DOC. NO.	POST. REF.		ACCOUNTS PAYABLE	
DEBIT	CREDIT						DEBIT	CREDIT
20	580 00	15	Westwood, Inc.	C329			580 00	

umn. The name of the creditor, *Westwood, Inc.*, is entered in the Account Title column. The number of the check, *C329*, is entered in the Doc. No. column.

Cash payment of an expense

Denim Threads pays for an expense at the time the transaction occurs or within a few days.

Source document for payment of an expense. The check stub for the check written to pay an expense is the source document for the entry. *(CONCEPT: Objective Evidence)*

Analyzing a payment of an expense. Denim Threads made a payment of an expense.

November 15, 1982. Paid rent expense, $800.00. Check No. 330.

Rent Expense	
800.00	

Cash	
	800.00

Payment for the rent expense, *$800.00*, is due on the 15th day of each month. This payment increases the rent expense account. The expense account Rent Expense has a debit balance and is increased on its debit side. Rent Expense therefore is debited for $800.00. The balance of the asset account Cash is decreased. Cash therefore is credited for $800.00.

Recording a payment of an expense. This payment of an expense is on line 21 of the partial combination journal below.

Recording a payment of an expense in a combination journal

PAGE 1			COMBINATION JOURNAL					
1	2					3	4	
CASH		DATE	ACCOUNT TITLE	DOC. NO.	POST. REF.	GENERAL		
DEBIT	CREDIT					DEBIT	CREDIT	
21	800 00	15	Rent Expense	C330		800 00		21

A similar entry for Putt Around is in Chapter 5.

The date, *15*, is written in the Date column. The debit amount for rent expense, *$800.00*, is entered in the General Debit column. The name of the account, *Rent Expense*, is written in the Account Title column. The credit amount, *$800.00*, is entered in the Cash Credit column. The number of the check, *C330*, is written in the Doc. No. column.

OTHER TRANSACTIONS

Most transactions for a merchandising business relate to purchasing and selling merchandise. A merchandising business also has other transactions that must be recorded. A combination journal is also used to record these other transactions.

Changes in capital

The balances of capital accounts of a partnership are changed in three ways. (1) Partners may invest additional capital. (2) Partners may withdraw capital. (3) Net income or net loss is recorded.

An entry to record an additional cash investment for a sole proprietorship is described on page 78. The same procedure is followed to record additional investments by owners of a partnership. An entry to close net income or net loss into the capital account is described on pages 148 and 149. A similar closing entry in a combination journal is described in Chapter 16.

Assets taken out of a business for the personal use of the owner are known as withdrawals. Withdrawals reduce the amount of capital in the business. Since capital accounts have credit balances, decreases are recorded as debits. Withdrawals could be recorded as debits to the partners' capital accounts. However, withdrawals are normally recorded in separate accounts so that the total amounts are easily determined for each fiscal period. Denim Threads records withdrawals in accounts titled Eva Burgos, Drawing and Luis Perez, Drawing. Because drawing accounts show decreases in capital, drawing accounts have debit balances. An entry to record withdrawals for a sole proprietorship is described in Chapter 5.

Assets taken out of a business are generally of two types. (1) Owners withdraw cash. (2) Owners withdraw merchandise.

Source document for a cash withdrawal. When either Eva Burgos or Luis Perez withdraws cash from Denim Threads, a check is written for the payment. The check stub of the check is the source document for the transaction. *(CONCEPT: Objective Evidence)*

Analyzing a cash withdrawal. Eva Burgos withdrew cash.

November 15, 1982. Eva Burgos, partner, withdrew cash, $300.00. Check No. 331.

This cash withdrawal increases the balance of the drawing account. The capital account, Eva Burgos, Drawing has a debit balance and is increased

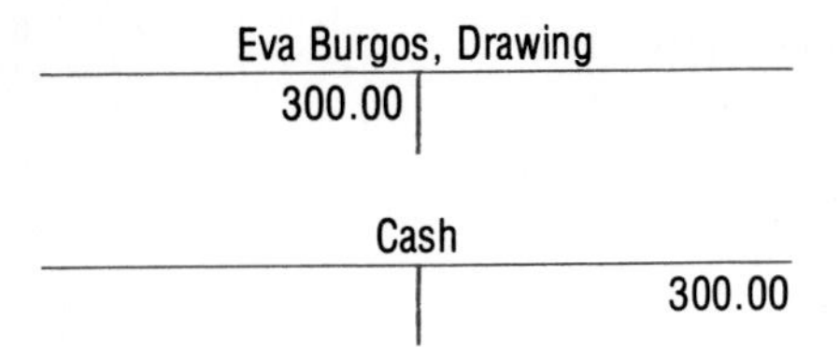

on its debit side. Eva Burgos, Drawing therefore is debited for $300.00. The transaction also decreases the asset account Cash. Therefore, Cash is credited for $300.00.

Recording a cash withdrawal. This cash withdrawal is on line 22 of the partial combination journal below.

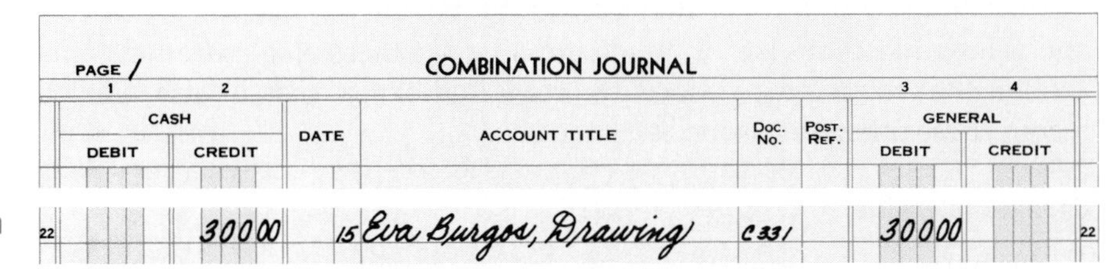

PAGE 1 — COMBINATION JOURNAL

	1 CASH DEBIT	2 CASH CREDIT	DATE	ACCOUNT TITLE	DOC. NO.	POST. REF.	3 GENERAL DEBIT	4 GENERAL CREDIT	
22		300 00	15	Eva Burgos, Drawing	C331		300 00		22

Recording a cash withdrawal by a partner in a combination journal

The date, *15*, is written in the Date column. The amount debited to the drawing account, *$300.00*, is entered in the General Debit column. The name of the capital account, *Eva Burgos, Drawing*, is written in the Account Title column. The amount credited to the cash account, *$300.00*, is entered in the Cash Credit column. The number of the check, *C331*, is written in the Doc. No. column.

Source document for a withdrawal of merchandise. A partner may take merchandise out of the business for personal use. The source document for this transaction is a memorandum prepared by the partner withdrawing the merchandise. *(CONCEPT: Objective Evidence)*

Analyzing a withdrawal of merchandise. Luis Perez, partner, withdrew merchandise.

November 16, 1982. Luis Perez, partner, withdrew merchandise, $45.00. Memorandum No. 48.

This transaction increases the balance of the drawing account. The capital account Luis Perez, Drawing has a debit balance and is increased on its debit side. Luis Perez, Drawing is therefore debited for $45.00.

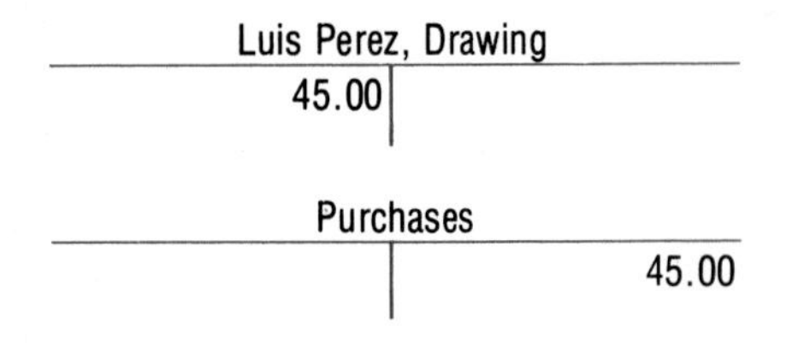

A withdrawal of merchandise decreases the amount of merchandise purchased for sale to customers. Therefore, the cost of merchandise withdrawn is deducted from the balance of the purchases account. The balance side of the purchases account is the debit side. This transaction decreases the balance of the purchases account. Purchases is therefore credited for $45.00.

Recording a withdrawal of merchandise. This withdrawal of merchandise is on lines 25 and 26 of the partial combination journal, page 203.

PAGE 1 COMBINATION JOURNAL

	Cash Debit (1)	Cash Credit (2)	Date	Account Title	Doc. No.	Post. Ref.	General Debit (3)	General Credit (4)	
25			16	Luis Perez, Drawing	M48		45 00		25
26				Purchases				45 00	26
27									27

Recording a withdrawal of merchandise in a combination journal

The date, *16*, is entered in the date column. The debit amount, *$45.00*, is written in the General Debit column. The title of the account, *Luis Perez, Drawing*, is entered in the Account Title column. Merchandise withdrawals do not occur frequently. Therefore, neither a Drawing Debit nor a Purchases Credit column is provided in the combination journal. The amount credited to the purchases account, *$45.00*, is written in the General Credit column on the next line. The name of the account, *Purchases*, is entered in the Account Title column, indented about 1 centimeter. The source document number, *M48*, is written in the Doc. No. column. A brace is drawn in the Date column to show that both lines belong to the same transaction.

Correcting entry

Errors may be made even though care is taken in recording transactions. Simple errors may be corrected by ruling through the incorrect item as described on page 86. However, a transaction may have been improperly recorded in the journal and posted to the ledger. Errors of this type should be corrected with a journal entry. A journal entry made to correct an error in the ledger is called a correcting entry.

Source document for a correcting entry. If an accounting error is discovered, a memorandum is prepared showing the correction to be made. A memorandum for a correcting entry is on page 204. The memorandum is the source document for the correcting entry. *(CONCEPT: Objective Evidence)*

Analyzing a correcting entry. Ms. Burgos discovered an accounting error that had been recorded in the journal and posted to the ledger.

November 17, 1982. Discovered that supplies bought on October 27 had been recorded and posted in error as a debit to Purchases instead of Supplies, $80.00. Memorandum No. 49.

To correct the error, an entry is made to remove $80.00 from the purchases account. The entry must also add $80.00 to the supplies account.

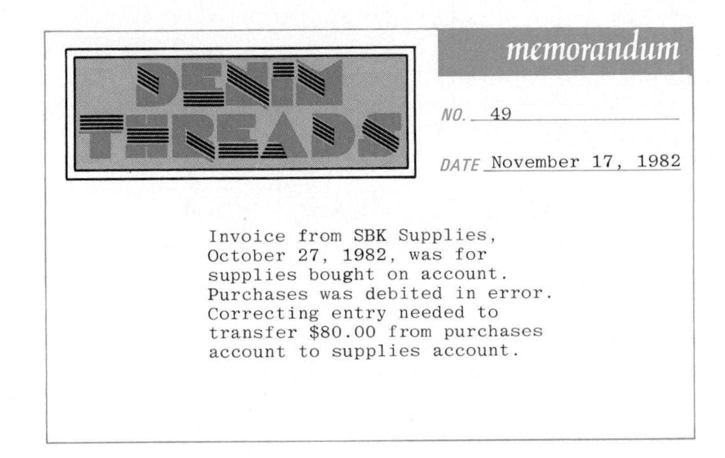

NO. 49

DATE November 17, 1982

Invoice from SBK Supplies, October 27, 1982, was for supplies bought on account. Purchases was debited in error. Correcting entry needed to transfer $80.00 from purchases account to supplies account.

Memorandum for a correcting entry

Supplies	
80.00	

Purchases	
	80.00

The asset account Supplies is increased by this entry. Supplies therefore is debited for $80.00.

Purchases is decreased by this correcting entry. The cost account Purchases has a debit balance and is decreased on its credit side. Therefore, Purchases is credited for $80.00.

Recording a correcting entry. The correcting entry is on lines 27 and 28 of the partial combination journal below.

COMBINATION JOURNAL — PAGE 1

	1 Cash Debit	2 Cash Credit	Date	Account Title	Doc. No.	Post. Ref.	3 General Debit	4 General Credit	
27			17	Supplies	M49		80 00		27
28				Purchases				80 00	28

Recording a correcting entry in a combination journal

The date, *17*, is written in the Date column. The debit amount for supplies, *$80.00*, is entered in the General Debit column. The title of the account, *Supplies*, is written in the Account Title column. The amount credited to the purchases account, *$80.00*, is entered in the General Credit column on the next line. The name of the account, *Purchases*, is written in the Account Title column. The name is indented about 1 centimeter. The source document number, *M49*, is entered in the Doc. No. column. A brace is drawn in the Date column to show that both lines belong to the same transaction.

SUMMARY

The chart on page 205 summarizes the entries for purchases, cash payments, and other transactions recorded in a combination journal.

	COMBINATION JOURNAL										
	1	2	3	4	5	6	7	8	9	10	11
	CASH		GENERAL		ACCOUNTS RECEIVABLE		SALES CREDIT	SALES TAX PAYABLE CREDIT	ACCOUNTS PAYABLE		PURCHASES DEBIT
	DEBIT	CREDIT	DEBIT	CREDIT	DEBIT	CREDIT			DEBIT	CREDIT	
Purchase on account										X	X
Purchase for cash		X									X
Buying supplies on account			X							X	
Buying supplies for cash		X	X								
Cash payment on account		X							X		
Cash payment of an expense		X	X								
Cash withdrawal		X	X								
Merchandise withdrawal			X	X							

Summary of entries in a combination journal

ACCOUNTING TERMS

What is the meaning of each of the following?

1. partnership
2. partner
3. merchandising business
4. merchandise
5. combination journal
6. cost of merchandise
7. markon
8. purchase on account
9. creditor
10. invoice
11. purchase invoice
12. terms of sale
13. correcting entry

QUESTIONS FOR INDIVIDUAL STUDY

1. Why would two or more persons want to own a single business?
2. What are noncash transactions?
3. Why doesn't Denim Threads use a cash journal like the one used by Putt Around?
4. Why are costs of merchandise deducted from revenue?
5. What is the name of the account that shows the cost of merchandise purchased for sale?
6. Why would a business use a single ledger account to summarize the amount owed to all creditors?
7. What accounts are affected by a purchase on account transaction? How are the accounts affected?
8. Which amount columns in the combination journal are used to record a purchase on account transaction?
9. What is the source document for a purchase on account journal entry?
10. Why are the names Purchases and Accounts Payable for a purchase on account entry not written in the Account Title column?
11. What accounts are affected by a cash purchase of merchandise? How are the accounts affected?
12. Which amount columns in the combination journal are used to record a cash purchase of merchandise?
13. Why is a check mark placed in the Account Title column of a combination

journal for a cash purchase transaction?

14. What is the source document for buying supplies on account transactions?

15. What accounts are affected by a buying supplies on account transaction? How are the accounts affected?

16. Why is the debit amount for Supplies recorded in the General Debit column for supplies bought transactions?

17. What is the source document for a cash payment on account transaction?

18. What accounts are affected by a cash payment on account transaction? How are the accounts affected?

19. Which amount columns in a combination journal are used to record a cash payment on account transaction?

20. What are the three kinds of entries that change the balances of capital accounts?

21. What accounts are affected by a withdrawal of merchandise transaction? How are the accounts affected?

22. What amount columns in a combination journal are used to record a withdrawal of merchandise?

23. When should a journal entry be made for errors in recording transactions?

CASES FOR MANAGEMENT DECISION

CASE 1 George Mason owns and operates the Sunnyside Gift Shop in a downtown shopping area. Business has been declining because of a shopping center that was started in one of the suburbs. Mr. Mason has an opportunity to close the business downtown and move the business to the shopping center. The future of the business is considered to be much better in the shopping center. Additional capital however is required to move and operate the business in the new location. The local bank has agreed to loan the money needed. The business hours would be extended in the new location. The business would be open seven days a week. Therefore, the extended hours plus the expected increase in business would require the hiring of one or two additional employees. Mr. Mason has been contacted by Mrs. Jan Perrigo, a person with similar experience who would like to become a partner. Mrs. Perrigo would provide the capital necessary to move the location of the business. For the capital provided, Mrs. Perrigo would share equally in the net income or loss of the business. Also, Mrs. Perrigo would share equally in the operation of the business. Which method of obtaining additional capital would be better? Should Mr. Mason (1) borrow the money from the bank, or (2) bring in a partner?

CASE 2 John Stewart, a high school student, works part-time in Rivera's Clothing Store. John observes several entries in the combination journal. He asks: "You use the purchase invoice as your source document for recording purchases of merchandise. You use a memorandum as your source document for recording the entry when supplies are bought. Why don't you use the invoice for both entries?" How will you answer him?

DRILLS FOR UNDERSTANDING

DRILL 11-D 1 Analyzing transactions into debit and credit parts

Instructions: Prepare two T accounts for each of the transactions on the next page. Show which account in the ledger is debited and which account is credited. The first transaction is given as an example.

Purchases	
800.00	

Accounts Payable	
	800.00

Transactions

1. Purchased merchandise on account from Smithfield Co., $800.00.
2. Bought supplies on account from Jack's Supply, $150.00.
3. Bought supplies for cash, $50.00.
4. Purchased merchandise for cash, $200.00.
5. Purchased merchandise on account from Komuro, Inc., $300.00.
6. Bought supplies for cash, $20.00.
7. Bought supplies on account from Watson Enterprises, $60.00.
8. Purchased merchandise for cash, $100.00.
9. Paid on account to Albert Grogan, $600.00.
10. Paid November rent, $500.00.
11. Paid for advertising, $50.00. (Miscellaneous Expense)
12. Mary McCormick, partner, withdrew cash, $400.00.
13. Jane Marsh, partner, withdrew cash, $400.00.
14. Paid on account to Southside Supply, $125.00.
15. Jane Marsh, partner, withdrew merchandise, $30.00.
16. Discovered that supplies bought last month had been recorded in error as a debit to Purchases instead of Supplies, $40.00.
17. Mary McCormick, partner, withdrew merchandise, $20.00.
18. Paid on account to Caldwell, Inc., $100.00.

The solution to Drill 11-D 1 is needed to complete Drill 11-D 2.

DRILL 11-D 2 Recording transactions using a combination journal

The solution to Drill 11-D 1 is needed to complete Drill 11-D 2.

Instructions: Use a form such as the one below. Based on the answers in Drill 11-D 1, show by a check mark which amount columns will be used to record the transactions. Transaction 1 is shown as an example.

Transaction	Cash		General		Accts. Pay.		Purch. Debit
	Debit	Credit	Debit	Credit	Debit	Credit	
1. Debit amount							✓
Credit amount						✓	

APPLICATION PROBLEM

PROBLEM 11-1 Journalizing transactions for purchases, supplies, and cash payments in a combination journal

Mary Boswell and Susan Turner, partners in a retail dress shop, completed the transactions, page 208, for November of the current year. The cash balance on November 1 was $4,750.00.

Instructions: 1. Record the cash balance on hand on page 12 of a combination journal like the one on pages 192 and 193.

2. Record the following transactions. Source documents are abbreviated as: purchase invoice, *P*; check, *C*; memorandum, *M*.

Nov. 1. Purchased merchandise on account from Baker Fashions, $900.00. P46.
2. Bought supplies for cash, $30.00. C220.
2. Bought supplies on account from Jansen Office Supply, $82.00. M23.
3. Purchased merchandise on account from Jason Co., $400.00. P47.
3. Purchased merchandise on account from Schmidt Co., $200.00. P48.
4. Bought supplies on account from Pacific Supply, $92.00. M24.
5. Purchased merchandise for cash, $120.00. C221.
5. Purchased merchandise for cash, $33.00. C222.
8. Bought supplies for cash, $25.00. C223.
9. Purchased merchandise for cash, $80.00. C224.
11. Bought supplies on account from Reese Supply, $42.00. M25.
13. Bought supplies for cash, $36.00. C225.
15. Mary Boswell, partner, withdrew cash, $500.00. C226.
15. Susan Turner, partner, withdrew cash, $500.00. C227.
16. Paid on account to Baker Fashions, $900.00. C228.
17. Paid on account to Jason Co., $400.00. C229.
19. Discovered that supplies bought last month had been recorded in error as a debit to Purchases instead of Supplies, $65.00. M26.
20. Paid telephone bill, $66.00. C230. (Miscellaneous Expense)
23. Paid on account to Jansen Office Supply, $82.00. C231.
24. Paid for advertising, $37.00. C232. (Miscellaneous Expense)
27. Susan Turner, partner, withdrew merchandise, $40.00. M27.
29. Paid on account to Schmidt Co., $400.00. C233.
30. Paid salaries, $1,200.00. C234.
30. Mary Boswell, partner, withdrew merchandise, $30.00. M28.

ENRICHMENT PROBLEMS

MASTERY PROBLEM 11-M Journalizing transactions for purchases, supplies, and cash payments in a combination journal

Judy Fields and William Hurley, partners, own and operate a gift shop. The transactions below were completed during December of the current year. The cash balance on December 1 was $3,800.00.

Instructions: 1. Record the cash balance on hand on page 13 of a combination journal like the one on pages 192 and 193.

2. Record the following transactions. Source documents are abbreviated as: check, *C*; purchase invoice, *P*; memorandum, *M*.

Dec. 1. Paid December rent, $700.00. C310.
1. Paid salaries, $1,500.00. C311.
2. Judy Fields, partner, withdrew cash, $700.00. C312.
2. William Hurley, partner, withdrew cash, $700.00. C313.
3. Purchased merchandise on account from Thompson Novelties, $330.00. P82.
3. Paid on account to Lakeside Supply, $77.00. C314.
4. Purchased merchandise on account from Mason Giftware, $220.00. P83.

Dec. 7. William Hurley, partner, withdrew merchandise, $22.00. M32.
8. Paid telephone bill, $48.00. C315. (Miscellaneous Expense)
9. Bought supplies on account from Lakeside Supply, $49.00. M33.
9. Purchased merchandise for cash, $150.00. C316.
11. Paid on account to Thompson Novelties, $160.00. C317.
13. Purchased merchandise on account from Streetman, Inc., $440.00. P84.
14. Purchased merchandise for cash, $210.00. C318.
15. Bought supplies for cash, $40.00. C319.
15. Paid on account to Streetman, Inc., $360.00. C320.
16. Judy Fields, partner, withdrew merchandise, $18.00. M34.
17. Purchased merchandise for cash, $130.00. C321.
20. Bought supplies on account from Drake Supply, $52.00. M35.
21. Purchased merchandise on account from Niehaus Co., $750.00. P85.
23. Bought supplies for cash, $15.00. C322.
25. Discovered that supplies bought in November had been recorded in error as a debit to Purchases instead of Supplies, $83.00. M36.
27. Bought supplies on account from Macon Supply, $26.00. M37.
29. Paid on account to Thompson Novelties, $330.00. C323.
30. Purchased merchandise for cash, $215.00. C324.
30. Paid on account to Mason Giftware, $220.00. C325.

CHALLENGE PROBLEM 11-C Journalizing correcting entries in a combination journal

The errors listed below were discovered in a combination journal.

Instructions: Record the needed correcting entries on page 8 of a combination journal like the one on pages 192 and 193. Use March 3 of the current year.

Mar. 3. Discovered that supplies bought had been recorded as a debit to Purchases, $225.00. M50.
3. Discovered that a payment for salaries had been recorded as a debit to Miscellaneous Expense, $500.00. M51.
3. Discovered that a withdrawal of merchandise by Christine Morgan, partner, had been recorded as a credit to Cash, $86.00. M52.
3. Discovered that a purchase of merchandise on account had been recorded as a debit to Supplies, $420.00. M53.
3. Discovered that a payment for rent had been recorded as a debit to Salary Expense, $650.00. M54.
3. Discovered that supplies bought on account had been recorded as a debit to Miscellaneous Expense, $46.00. M55.
3. Discovered that a withdrawal of cash for Cathy York, partner, had been recorded as a credit to Purchases, $300.00. M56.
3. Discovered that a payment for salaries had been recorded as a debit to Supplies, $500.00. M57.
3. Discovered that supplies bought had been recorded as a debit to Prepaid Insurance, $120.00. M58.

12

Journalizing Sales and Cash Receipts

ENABLING PERFORMANCE TASKS

After studying Chapter 12, you will be able to:

a. Define accounting terms related to sales and cash receipts.
b. Explain accounting principles and practices related to sales and cash receipts.
c. Classify accounts related to sales and cash receipts.
d. Analyze transactions related to sales and cash receipts into debit and credit parts.
e. Journalize sales and cash receipts in a combination journal.
f. Total, prove, and rule a combination journal.

A major activity of a merchandising business is the purchase of merchandise. Another major activity is the transfer of the merchandise to a person or firm. A person or firm to whom a business sells merchandise is called a customer. The transfer of merchandise to a customer in exchange for cash or a promise to pay is called a sale.

SALES TAX

A tax on a sale of goods is called a sales tax. Laws of most states and some cities require that a sales tax be collected from customers for each sale made. Sales tax rates are usually stated as a percentage of sales. Regardless of the tax rates used, the accounting procedures are the same.

Every business collecting a sales tax needs accurate records of the amount of tax collected. Businesses must file reports with the proper government unit and pay the amount of sales tax collected. Records need to show (1) total sales and (2) total sales tax.

Denim Threads operates in a state with a 4% sales tax rate. A customer must pay for the price of the goods plus the sales tax. Figuring the total amount of a sale for merchandise priced at $50.00 is on the next page.

Price of Goods	×	Sales Tax Rate	=	Sales Tax
$50.00	×	4%	=	$2.00
Price of Goods	+	**Sales Tax**	=	**Total Amount of Sale**
$50.00	+	$2.00	=	$52.00

A customer must pay $52.00 for the merchandise ($50.00 for the goods plus $2.00 for the sales tax). Denim Threads records the price of goods sold, the sales tax, and the total amount of a sale.

SALES AND CASH RECEIPTS FOR SALES

A sale of merchandise may be for (1) cash or (2) a promise to pay at a later date. A sale of merchandise increases the revenue of a business. Regardless of when payment is made, the increase in revenue should be recorded at the time of a sale. *(CONCEPT: Realization of Revenue)*

Cash sales

Denim Threads sells most of its merchandise for cash. A sale in which cash is received for the total amount of sale at the time of the transaction is called a cash sale.

Source document for cash sales. Denim Threads uses a cash register to list all cash sales. The cash register prints each transaction on a paper tape inside the machine. A printed receipt is also provided for each customer. Amounts on the cash register tape may be totaled daily or weekly.

Denim Threads records the total cash sales for each week. The cash register tape is used as the source document for the week's cash sales. *(CONCEPT: Objective Evidence)* The tape is marked with a symbol *T* and the day of the month it is removed from the cash register. Total sales for the week are then recorded as a single transaction.

Analyzing a week's cash sales. Total cash sales for the week ending November 6, 1982, are below.

November 6, 1982. Cash sales for the week, $1,850.00, plus sales tax, $74.00. Total, $1,924.00. Cash Register Tape No. T6.

This transaction increases the balance of the asset account Cash by a debit for the total amount of cash received, $1,924.00.

Denim Threads has one revenue account Sales in the revenue division of the ledger. The total price of goods sold, $1,850.00, is recorded in this account. This transaction increases the balance of the revenue account Sales. Sales has a credit balance and is increased on its credit side by $1,850.00.

Cash	
1,924.00	

Sales	
	1,850.00

Sales Tax Payable	
	74.00

The amount of sales tax collected is a liability. Denim Threads owes this amount to the state government. The liability account Sales Tax Payable is credited for the amount of sales tax collected, $74.00.

Recording cash sales. The entry for the week's cash sales is on line 8 of the partial combination journal below.

Cash sales recorded in a combination journal

PAGE 1 COMBINATION JOURNAL

	1	2					7	8
	CASH		DATE	ACCOUNT TITLE	DOC. NO.	POST. REF.	SALES CREDIT	SALES TAX PAYABLE CREDIT
	DEBIT	CREDIT						
8	192400		6	✓	T6	✓	185000	7400

The date, *6*, is written in the Date column. The amount debited to Cash, *$1,924.00*, is entered in the Cash Debit column. The amount credited to Sales, *$1,850.00*, is written in the Sales Credit column. The amount credited to Sales Tax Payable, *$74.00*, is entered in the Sales Tax Payable Credit column. A check mark is placed in the Account Title column. The check mark shows that no account title needs to be written for this transaction. The number of the cash register tape, *T6*, is entered in the Doc. No. column. A check mark is also placed in the Post. Ref. column. This check mark shows that amounts on this line do not need to be posted individually.

Sales on account

A sale for which payment will be made at a later date is called a sale on account. A sale on account is also known as a charge sale or a credit sale. A person or firm to whom a sale on account is made is called a charge customer.

Denim Threads summarizes in a ledger account, Accounts Receivable, the total amount due from all charge customers. Accounts Receivable is an asset account with a debit balance.

Source document for a sale on account. When a sale on account is made, the seller prepares a form showing what has been sold. A form issued to a charge customer describing the goods sold, the quantity, and the price is called a sales invoice. A sales invoice is also known as a sales ticket or a sales slip. The sales invoice used by Denim Threads is on page 213. Each sales invoice is prepared in duplicate. The original copy is used as the source document for recording the transaction. *(CONCEPT: Objective Evidence)* The carbon copy is given to the charge customer. Sales invoices are numbered in sequence. The number, *72*, is the number of the sales invoice for Ada Miranda.

DENIM THREADS

Sold to Ada Miranda
3340 Hampton Road
Mitchell, SD 57301-1037

No. 72
Date 11/4/82
Terms Net 30 days

Quantity	Description	Unit Price	Amount	
2	Blue Jeans	22.50	45	00
	Sales tax		1	80
		TOTAL	46	80

213 Paxton Avenue
Sioux Falls, SD 57103-1285

Ada Miranda — Customer's Signature
Mary Stevens — Sales Clerk

Sales invoice

The seller considers an invoice for a sale on account to be a sales invoice. The same invoice is considered by the buyer to be a purchase invoice.

Analyzing a sale on account. The transaction for the Denim Threads' sales invoice is below.

November 4, 1982. Sold merchandise on account to Ada Miranda, $45.00, plus sales tax, $1.80. Total, $46.80. Sales Invoice No. 72.

This sale on account increases the amount to be collected from customers. The asset account Accounts Receivable has a debit balance and is increased on its debit side. Accounts Receivable is debited for the total sale of goods on account, $46.80.

Accounts Receivable	
46.80	

How Denim Threads keeps records of amounts to be collected from each charge customer is described in Chapter 13.

Sales	
	45.00

Sales is credited for the price of goods, $45.00. Sales Tax Payable is increased by a credit for the amount of sales tax on the sale, $1.80.

Sales Tax Payable	
	1.80

Recording a sale on account. The entry for this sale on account is recorded in the partial combination journal below.

Sale on account recorded in a combination journal

COMBINATION JOURNAL

DATE	ACCOUNT TITLE	Doc. No.	Post. Ref.	5 ACCOUNTS RECEIVABLE DEBIT	6 ACCOUNTS RECEIVABLE CREDIT	7 SALES CREDIT	8 SALES TAX PAYABLE CREDIT
4	Ada Miranda	S72		46 80		45 00	1 80

The date, *4*, is entered in the Date column. The amount debited to Accounts Receivable, *$46.80*, is written in the Accounts Receivable Debit column. The amount credited to Sales, *$45.00*, is entered in the Sales Credit column. The amount of the sales tax, *$1.80*, is written in the Sales Tax Payable Credit column. The name of the charge customer, *Ada Miranda*, is entered in the Account Title column. The number of the sales invoice, *S72*, is written in the Doc. No. column.

Credit card sales

A special card is often used to identify approved charge customers. An embossed card used by a customer with an approved charge account is called a credit card. When a credit card is used, the card and a special sales invoice are placed in an imprinting device. This device records the customer's name and account number on all copies of the sales invoice.

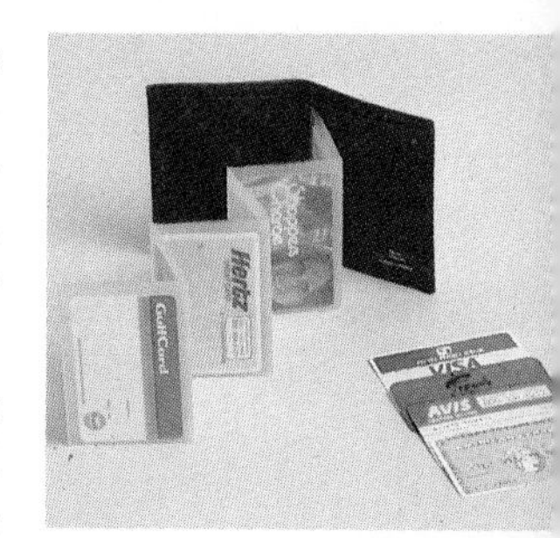

Major gasoline companies and many department store chains issue their own credit cards. When a business issues its own credit cards, the business bills each credit card holder for all credit card purchases. The card holder then pays the business. Because the business sends the bills and receives all payments, these credit card sales are recorded as regular charge sales.

Businesses may also subscribe to one or more of the regional credit card systems. The regional credit card system issues the credit card to a customer. The customer may then use the credit card at any business that has subscribed to the credit card system. In different regions of the United States, banks are designated to handle the credit card system.

When a regional credit card system is used, each credit card holder is billed through the credit card system. The card holder then pays the credit card system rather than the business from which the purchase was made. Because the credit card system handles billing and collection, the business records credit card sales as regular cash sales.

A business that subscribes to a regional credit card system periodically totals all credit card invoices. These invoices are then deposited at the bank designated to handle the credit card system. The bank credits the business' bank account for the total amount of the invoices. The bank charges the business a fee. The fee is usually based on a percentage of the credit card sales deposited by the business. At the end of the month, the bank includes the credit card fee on the bank statement.

Denim Threads subscribes to a regional credit card system. Both Visa and Master Card credit cards are accepted in payment for merchandise sold. Credit card sales are totaled and deposited with the bank at the end of each week.

Source document for credit card sales. At the end of each week, Denim Threads totals all credit card sales on an adding machine. Separate totals are figured for the price of goods sold, the sales tax charged, and the total amount of credit card sales. The symbol *CT* and the day of the month are written on the adding machine tape. The adding machine tape is used as the source document for the week's credit card sales. *(CONCEPT: Objective Evidence)*

Analyzing a week's credit card sales. Denim Threads gets credit for all credit card sales when the sales invoices are deposited at the bank. Therefore, the total weekly credit card sales are handled as cash sales rather than charge sales. Rather than recording each individual credit card sale, a weekly total of credit card sales is treated as one transaction. Total credit card sales for the week ending November 6, 1982, are below.

November 6, 1982. Credit card sales for the week, $1,300.00, plus sales tax, $52.00. Total, $1,352.00. Adding Machine Tape No. CT6.

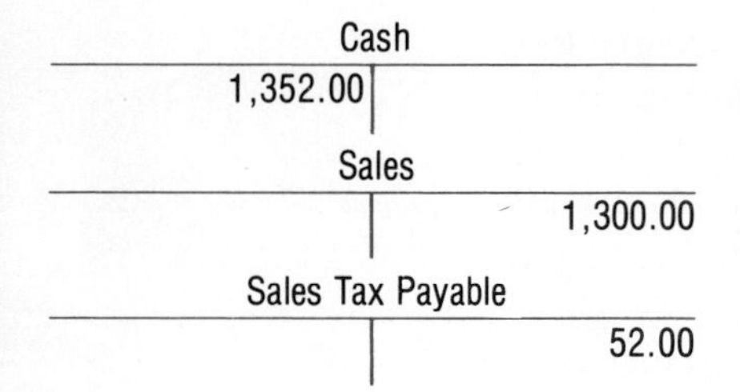

The balance of the asset account Cash is increased by a debit for the total credit card sales, $1,352.00.

The revenue account Sales is used for both cash sales and credit card sales. Sales is credited for the amount of credit card sales for the week, $1,300.00. Sales Tax Payable is credited for the amount of sales tax charged on the credit card sales, $52.00.

Recording credit card sales. The entry for the week's credit card sales is on line 9 of the partial combination journal below.

Recording credit card sales in a combination journal

PAGE 1 — COMBINATION JOURNAL

	1 Cash Debit	2 Cash Credit	Date	Account Title	Doc. No.	Post. Ref.	7 Sales Credit	8 Sales Tax Payable Credit
9	1352 00		6	✓	CT6	✓	1300 00	52 00

The date, *6*, is entered in the Date column. The amount debited to Cash, *$1,352.00*, is written in the Cash Debit column. The amount credited to Sales, *$1,300.00*, is entered in the Sales Credit column. The amount credited to Sales Tax Payable, *$52.00*, is written in the Sales Tax Payable Credit column. A check mark is placed in the Account Title column. The check mark shows that no account title needs to be written for this transaction. The number, *CT6*, is written in the Doc. No. column. A check mark is placed in the Post Ref. column. This check mark shows that amounts on this line do not need to be posted individually.

The entry for credit card sales is the same as for regular cash sales. This is shown in the illustration on page 212.

Cash received on account

Denim Threads prepares a receipt when cash is received on account from a customer. The receipts are prenumbered so all receipts can be accounted for. The original copy of the receipt is given to the charge customer.

Source document for cash received on account. The carbon copy of the receipt is used as the source document for the cash received on account transaction. *(CONCEPT: Objective Evidence)*

Analyzing cash received on account. Cash was received on account from a charge customer.

November 5, 1982. Received on account from Tien Yang, $78.00. Receipt No. 108.

The asset account Cash is increased by a debit for the amount of cash received, $78.00.

This transaction decreases the amount to be collected from charge customers. Therefore, the asset account Accounts Receivable is credited for $78.00.

Cash	
78.00	

Accounts Receivable	
	78.00

Recording cash received on account. The entry for this transaction is on line 7 of the partial combination journal below.

PAGE 1 COMBINATION JOURNAL

	1	2					5	6
	CASH		DATE	ACCOUNT TITLE	DOC. NO.	POST. REF.	ACCOUNTS RECEIVABLE	
	DEBIT	CREDIT					DEBIT	CREDIT
7	78 00		5	Tien Yang	R108			78 00

The date, *5*, is written in the Date column. The debit to Cash, *$78.00*, is entered in the Cash Debit column. The credit to Accounts Receivable, *$78.00*, is written in the Accounts Receivable Credit column. The name of the charge customer, *Tien Yang*, is entered in the Account Title column. The number of the receipt, *R108*, is written in the Doc. No. column.

Cash received on account recorded in a combination journal

SUMMARY OF SALES AND CASH RECEIPTS TRANSACTIONS

The chart below summarizes the entries in a combination journal for sales and cash receipts transactions.

COMBINATION JOURNAL

	1	2	3	4	5	6	7	8	9	10	11
	CASH		GENERAL		ACCOUNTS RECEIVABLE		SALES CREDIT	SALES TAX PAYABLE CREDIT	ACCOUNTS PAYABLE		PURCHASES DEBIT
	DEBIT	CREDIT	DEBIT	CREDIT	DEBIT	CREDIT			DEBIT	CREDIT	
Cash sales	X						X	X			
Sales on account					X		X	X			
Credit card sales	X						X	X			
Cash received on account	X					X					

Summary of sales and cash receipts transactions recorded in a combination journal

TOTALING AND PROVING A COMBINATION JOURNAL

A combination journal is totaled and proved when a page is filled and when a fiscal period ends. The steps are similar to those described for Putt Around's cash journal in Chapter 5.

PAGE 1 — COMBINATION JOURNAL

	1 CASH DEBIT	2 CASH CREDIT	DATE	ACCOUNT TITLE	DOC. NO.	POST. REF.	3 GENERAL DEBIT	4 GENERAL CREDIT	
1			1982 Nov. 1	Balance on hand, $4,200.00		✓			1
2		55000	1	Salary Expense	C325		55000		2
3			2	Denim Specialties	P37				3
4		42500	2	✓	C326	✓			4
5		5300	3	Miscellaneous Expense	C327		5300		5
6			4	Ada Miranda	S72				6
7	7800		5	Tien Yang	R108				7
8	192400		6	✓	J6	✓			8
9	135200		6	✓	CJ6	✓			9
10			8	Eastlake Clothiers	P38				10
11			9	Lisa Anderson	S73				11
12			10	Rick White	S74				12
13			10	Supplies	M47		14200		13
14				SBK Supplies					14
15			12	George Landon	S75				15
16			12	Gerando Manufacturing	P39				16
17	172120		13	✓	J13	✓			17
18	130000		13	✓	CJ13	✓			18
19		8600	15	Supplies	C328		8600		19
20		58000	15	Westwood, Inc.	C329				20
21		80000	15	Rent Expense	C330		80000		21
22		30000	15	Eva Burgos, Drawing	C331		30000		22
23		30000	15	Luis Perez, Drawing	C332		30000		23
24		55000	15	Salary Expense	C333		55000		24
25			16	Luis Perez, Drawing	M48		4500		25
26				Purchases				4500	26
27			17	Supplies	M49		8000		27
28				Purchases				8000	28
29	6240		17	Ada Miranda	R109				29
30	4160		18	Beth Ingram	R110				30
31		82200	19	Denim Specialties	C334				31
32	647920	446600	19	Carried Forward		✓	290600	12500	32
33									33

Combination journal totaled for forwarding (left page)

Forwarding the totals of a combination journal

Amount columns are totaled and proved when a combination journal page is filled. Line 32 of the illustration above and on page 219, shows the totals prepared for forwarding. The illustration, pages 220 and 221, shows how totals are brought forward to a new page. The procedures for forwarding totals are the same as those in Chapter 5.

FOR MONTH OF November 19 82 PAGE 1

	5	6	7	8	9	10	11	
	ACCOUNTS RECEIVABLE		SALES CREDIT	SALES TAX PAYABLE CREDIT	ACCOUNTS PAYABLE		PURCHASES DEBIT	
	DEBIT	CREDIT			DEBIT	CREDIT		
1								1
2								2
3						82200	82200	3
4							42500	4
5								5
6	4680		4500	180				6
7		7800						7
8			185000	7400				8
9			130000	5200				9
10						68000	68000	10
11	10920		10500	420				11
12	5200		5000	200				12
13								13
14						14200		14
15	1560		1500	60				15
16						41000	41000	16
17			165500	6620				17
18			125000	5000				18
19								19
20					58000			20
21								21
22								22
23								23
24								24
25								25
26								26
27								27
28								28
29		6240						29
30		4160						30
31					82200			31
32	22360	18200	627000	25080	140200	205400	233700	32
33								33

Combination journal totaled for forwarding (right page)

Proving a combination journal at the end of a month

Equality of debits and credits in a combination journal is proved at the end of each month. All columns are totaled on an adding machine or on paper. A journal is proved when the sum of the debit totals is equal to the sum of the credit totals. The proof for the combination journal, pages 218 and 219, is on the next page.

	1	2					3	4	
PAGE 2			COMBINATION JOURNAL						
	CASH		DATE	ACCOUNT TITLE	DOC. NO.	POST. REF.	GENERAL		
	DEBIT	CREDIT					DEBIT	CREDIT	
1	6479 20	4466 00	1982 Nov. 19	Brought Forward		✓	2906 00	125 00	1
27		300 00	30	Luis Perez, Drawing	C342		300 00		27
28	327 60		30	✓	J30	✓			28
29	67 60		30	✓	CJ30	✓			29
30	13551 20	6207 00	30	Totals			3705 00	125 00	30
31									31

Combination journal totaled and ruled (left page)

Col. No.	Column	Debit Totals	Credit Totals
1	Cash Debit	$13,551.20	
2	Cash Credit		$ 6,207.00
3	General Debit	3,705.00	
4	General Credit		125.00
5	Accounts Receivable Debit	639.60	
6	Accounts Receivable Credit		353.60
7	Sales Credit		13,305.00
8	Sales Tax Payable Credit		532.20
9	Accounts Payable Debit	2,164.00	
10	Accounts Payable Credit		3,614.00
11	Purchases Debit	4,077.00	
	Totals	$24,136.80	$24,136.80

These two totals are equal. Equality of debits and credits in the combination journal of Denim Threads for November is proved.

Proving cash with a combination journal

Denim Threads figures the cash proof at the end of November as shown below.

Beginning cash balance	$ 4,200.00
(Line 1, page 1, combination journal, page 218)	
Plus total cash received	13,551.20
(Total of Cash Debit column, line 30, page 2, above)	
Total	$17,751.20
Less total cash payments	6,207.00
(Total of Cash Credit column, line 30, page 2, above)	
Equals cash balance on hand at end of month	$11,544.20

The last check written in November, 1982, was Check No. 342. The checkbook balance after the last check had been written and after the last deposit was made is $11,544.20. Since the checkbook balance is the same as the balance on hand, cash is proved.

FOR MONTH OF *November* 19*82* PAGE *2*

	5	6	7	8	9	10	11	
	ACCOUNTS RECEIVABLE		SALES CREDIT	SALES TAX PAYABLE CREDIT	ACCOUNTS PAYABLE		PURCHASES DEBIT	
	DEBIT	CREDIT			DEBIT	CREDIT		
1	22360	18200	627000	25080	140200	205400	233700	1
27								27
28			31500	1260				28
29			6500	260				29
30	63960	35360	1330500	53220	216400	361400	407700	30
31								31

Combination journal totaled and ruled (right page)

Ruling a combination journal at the end of each month

Denim Threads' combination journal is ruled at the end of each month. The illustration above and on page 220 shows the ruling of the combination journal for November. Ruling procedures are the same as those used by Putt Around in Chapter 5.

A complete illustration of page 2 of Denim Threads' combination journal is on pages 242 and 243, Chapter 13.

ACCOUNTING TERMS

What is the meaning of each of the following?

1. customer
2. sale
3. sales tax
4. cash sale
5. sale on account
6. charge customer
7. sales invoice
8. credit card

QUESTIONS FOR INDIVIDUAL STUDY

1. What are the two major activities of a merchandising business?
2. How are sales tax rates usually stated?
3. Why must every business that collects a sales tax keep accurate records of the amount of tax collected?
4. What two amounts must sales tax records show?
5. What is the source document for a cash sales transaction?
6. What effect does a cash sales transaction have on the revenue account Sales?
7. Why is sales tax collected considered to be a liability to a business?
8. What is the name of the ledger account used to summarize the total amount due from all charge customers?
9. What is the source document for a sale on account transaction?
10. What accounts are affected by a sale on account transaction? How are the accounts affected?
11. Which amount columns in a combination journal are used to record a sale on account transaction?
12. How are credit card sales recorded by a business that issues its own credit cards?
13. How are credit card sales recorded by a business that subscribes to a regional credit card system?

14. What two accounts are affected when cash is received on account? How are the accounts affected?

15. At what two times is a combination journal totaled and proved?

CASES FOR MANAGEMENT DECISION

CASE 1 Judy Lawler operates an office supply store. A cash journal and a general journal similar to those described in Chapter 5 are used to record all transactions. The business sells merchandise for cash and also has a number of charge customers. The business also purchases most of its merchandise on account. Ms. Lawler asked an accountant to check the accounting system and recommend changes. The accountant suggests that a combination journal similar to the one described in Chapter 12 be used. Which would be better: (a) the cash journal and general journal, or (b) the combination journal? Why?

CASE 2 Andres Rios, accountant for a hardware store, has noted a major increase in the amounts due from charge customers. All sales are due within 30 days. The amounts due from charge customers have reduced the amount of cash available for the normal operation of the business. The accountant recommends that (1) all regular sales on account be stopped and (2) the business subscribe to a regional credit card system. The owner is reluctant to accept the recommendations. One concern is that the business might lose some reliable customers who do not have a credit card. Another concern is the increased expenses because of the credit card fee the business must pay. How do you respond to the concerns of the owner? What alternatives to the accountant's recommendations would you suggest?

DRILLS FOR UNDERSTANDING

DRILL 12-D 1 Analyzing transactions into debit and credit parts

Instructions: Prepare T accounts for each of the transactions below. Show which accounts in the ledger are debited and which accounts are credited. The first transaction is given as an example. Credit card sales are recorded as cash sales.

Cash		Sales		Sales Tax Payable	
1,680.00			1,600.00		80.00

Transactions

1. Cash sales for the week, $1,600.00, plus sales tax, $80.00. Total, $1,680.00.
2. Credit card sales for the week, $400.00, plus sales tax, $20.00. Total, $420.00.
3. Sold merchandise on account to Sally Sykes, $26.00, plus sales tax, $1.30. Total, $27.30.
4. Received on account from Harold Johnson, $37.80.
5. Received on account from Elaine Mitchell, $16.80.
6. Sold merchandise on account to Jeff Walker, $55.00, plus sales tax, $2.75. Total, $57.75.
7. Cash sales for the week, $1,800.00, plus sales tax, $90.00. Total, $1,890.00.
8. Credit card sales for the week, $600.00, plus sales tax, $30.00. Total, $630.00.

The solution to Drill 12-D 1 is needed to complete Drill 12-D 3.

DRILL 12-D 2 Analyzing the effect of sales transactions on accounts

Instructions: 1. Prepare T accounts for the ledger accounts Cash, Accounts Receivable, Sales, Sales Tax Payable. Label the debit and credit parts of each transaction as shown in the T accounts at the right. Transaction 1 is given as an example.

2. Using the T accounts show which accounts are debited and credited for the following transactions. Add a 5% sales tax to each sale.

Cash

(1) 2,100.00	

Accounts Receivable

Sales

	(1) 2,000.00

Sales Tax Payable

	(1) 100.00

Transactions

1. Cash sales for the week, $2,000.00.
2. Sold merchandise on account to Steven Durand, $35.00.
3. Received on account from Sharon Jewel, $39.90.
4. Cash sales for the week, $2,200.00.
5. Received on account from Justin Lane, $18.90.
6. Sold on account to Jim McCoy, $15.00.

DRILL 12-D 3 Recording transactions using a combination journal

The solution to Drill 12-D 1 is needed to complete Drill 12-D 3.

Instructions: Use a form such as the one below. Based on the answers in Drill 12-D 1, show by a check mark which amount columns will be used to record the transactions. Transaction 1 is shown as an example.

Transaction	Cash		Accts. Rec.		Sales Credit	Sales Tax Pay. Credit
	Debit	Credit	Debit	Credit		
1. Debit amount	√					
Credit amount					√	
Credit amount						√

APPLICATION PROBLEM

PROBLEM 12-1 Journalizing sales and cash receipts in a combination journal

Mark Dalton and Don James, partners in an office supply store, completed the transactions, page 224, for November of the current year. The cash balance on November 1 was $4,300.00.

Instructions: 1. Record the cash balance on page 16 of a combination journal like the one on pages 218 and 219.

2. Record the following transactions. Credit card sales are recorded as cash sales. Source documents are abbreviated as: sales invoice, *S*; receipt, *R*; cash register tape, *T*; adding machine tape, *CT*.

Nov. 1. Sold merchandise on account to Wallace Janes, $22.00, plus sales tax, $1.10. Total, $23.10. S62.
2. Sold merchandise on account to Beverly Winters, $30.00, plus sales tax, $1.50. Total, $31.50. S63.
3. Received on account from Timothy Jester, $29.40. R110.
6. Cash sales for the week, $2,200.00, plus sales tax, $110.00. Total, $2,310.00. T6.
6. Credit card sales for the week, $700.00, plus sales tax, $35.00. Total, $735.00. CT6.
8. Sold merchandise on account to Carol Munson, $35.00, plus sales tax, $1.75. Total, $36.75. S64.
9. Received on account from Cathy Curtis, $26.25. R111.
9. Received on account from Dan Mendenhall, $42.00. R112.
13. Cash sales for the week, $2,160.00, plus sales tax, $108.00. Total, $2,268.00. T13.
13. Credit card sales for the week, $555.00, plus sales tax, $27.75. Total, $582.75. CT13.
15. Sold merchandise on account to Bradley Mondale, $60.00, plus sales tax, $3.00. Total, $63.00. S65.
16. Sold merchandise on account to Carol Munson, $45.00, plus sales tax, $2.25. Total, $47.25. S66.
17. Received on account from Baker Co., $126.00. R113.
20. Cash sales for the week, $2,240.00, plus sales tax, $112.00. Total, $2,352.00. T20.
20. Credit card sales for the week, $560.00, plus sales tax, $28.00. Total, $588.00. CT20.
22. Received on account from Wallace Janes, $23.10. R114.
23. Received on account from Westside Grocery, $47.25. R115.
24. Sold merchandise on account to Carol Munson, $15.00, plus sales tax, $.75. Total, $15.75. S67.
27. Cash sales for the week, $1,950.00, plus sales tax, $97.50. Total, $2,047.50. T27.
27. Credit card sales for the week, $345.00, plus sales tax, $17.25. Total, $362.25. CT27.
27. Received on account from Beverly Winters, $31.50. R116.
29. Sold merchandise on account to Cathy Curtis, $60.00, plus sales tax, $3.00. Total, $63.00. S68.
30. Cash sales for the week, $720.00, plus sales tax, $36.00. Total, $756.00. T30.
30. Credit card sales for the week, $105.00, plus sales tax, $5.25. Total, $110.25. CT30.

Instructions: 3. Total the amount columns on the combination journal. Prove the equality of debits and credits.

4. Rule the combination journal. Use the illustration on pages 220 and 221 as a guide.

ENRICHMENT PROBLEMS

MASTERY PROBLEM 12-M Journalizing transactions in a combination journal

Gloria Jackson and John Lyons, partners, operate a hardware store. The transactions on the next page were completed during December of the current year. The cash balance on December 1 was $5,300.00.

Instructions: 1. Record the cash balance on page 14 of a combination journal like the one on pages 218 and 219.

2. Record the following transactions. Credit card sales are recorded as cash sales. A 5% sales tax is to be added to all sales. Source documents are abbreviated as: check, *C*; memorandum, *M*; purchase invoice, *P*; receipt, *R*; sales invoice, *S*; cash register tape, *T*; adding machine tape, *CT*.

Dec. 1. Paid salaries, $3,800.00. C218.
1. Paid December rent, $850.00. C219.
1. Paid telephone bill, $64.00. C220. (Miscellaneous Expense)
2. Purchased merchandise on account from Dannon, Inc., $670.00. P62.
3. Paid on account to Silva Co., $980.00. C221.
4. Cash sales for the week, $1,600.00. T4.
4. Credit card sales for the week, $230.00. CT4.
6. Sold merchandise on account to Donald Pearson, $84.00. S85.
6. Paid on account to Jefferson Hardware, $835.00. C222.
7. Received on account from Lois Arnold, $26.25. R240.
8. Discovered that a purchase of merchandise on account had been recorded as a debit to Supplies instead of Purchases, $142.00. M52.
9. Purchased merchandise for cash, $980.00. C223.
10. Bought supplies on account from Navarro Supply, $86.00. M53.
10. Sold merchandise on account to Benjamin Preston, $125.00. S86.
11. Received on account from Marsha Rankin, $86.10. R241.
11. Cash sales for the week, $2,450.00. T11.
11. Credit card sales for the week, $530.00. CT11.
13. Purchased merchandise on account from Higgins Hardware, $920.00. P63.
13. Bought supplies for cash, $22.00. C224.
15. Gloria Jackson, partner, withdrew cash, $650.00. C225.
15. John Lyons, partner, withdrew cash, $650.00. C226.
16. Paid on account to Dannon, Inc., $930.00. C227.
18. Cash sales for the week, $2,260.00. T18.
18. Credit card sales for the week, $486.00. CT18.
20. Purchased merchandise for cash, $710.00. C228.
20. Bought supplies on account from Navarro Supply, $45.00. M54.
21. Gloria Jackson, partner, withdrew merchandise, $56.00. M55.

Instructions: 3. Prepare page 14 of the combination journal for forwarding. Total the amount columns. Prove the equality of debits and credits and record on line 32 the totals to be carried forward.

4. Record the totals brought forward on line 1 of page 15 of the combination journal. Prove the equality of debits and credits again.

5. Record on page 15 the transactions listed below.

Dec. 22. Received on account from Donald Pearson, $57.80. R242.
24. Sold merchandise on account to Charles Tyler, $16.00. S87.
24. Discovered that a withdrawal of supplies for John Lyons, partner, had been recorded as a credit to Purchases instead of Supplies, $12.00. M56.
24. Cash sales for the week, $2,540.00. T24.
24. Credit card sales for the week, $720.00. CT24.
27. John Lyons, partner, withdrew merchandise, $42.00. M57.
29. Purchased merchandise on account from Mason, Inc., $330.00. P64.
30. Purchased merchandise for cash, $920.00. C229.
31. Cash sales for the week, $1,820.00. T31.
31. Credit card sales for the week, $280.00. CT31.

Instructions: 6. Total all amount columns of page 15 of the combination journal. Prove the equality of debits and credits.

7. Prove cash. The balance on Check Stub No. 230 is $7,640.95.

8. Rule page 15 of the combination journal.

The combination journal prepared in Mastery Problem 12-M is needed to complete Mastery Problem 13-M in Chapter 13.

CHALLENGE PROBLEM 12-C Journalizing transactions in a combination journal

A combination journal may be ruled in different ways. For example, the combination journal on pages 218 and 219 is referred to as a divided-column form. The amount columns are divided by the Account Title column. Some of the amount columns are to the left and some are to the right of the Account Title column. Another common arrangement is to have all amount columns to the right of the Account Title column.

Instructions: 1. Use a combination journal ruled as shown below.

Date	Account Title	Doc. No.	Post. Ref.	General		Cash		Accounts Payable		Accounts Receivable		Purchases Dr.	Sales Cr.	Sales Tax Pay. Cr.
				Dr.	Cr.	Dr.	Cr.	Dr.	Cr.	Dr.	Cr.			

2. Use the transactions and instructions for Mastery Problem 12-M. Complete all of the instructions using the combination journal above.

The combination journal prepared in Challenge Problem 12-C is needed to complete Challenge Problem 13-C in Chapter 13.

13 Posting to Ledgers

ENABLING PERFORMANCE TASKS

After studying Chapter 13, you will be able to:

a. Define accounting terms related to posting to ledgers.
b. Explain accounting principles and practices related to posting to ledgers.
c. Open accounts in subsidiary ledgers.
d. Post to ledgers from a combination journal.
e. Prepare subsidiary schedules.
f. Prove equality of debits and credits in the general ledger.

Business activities entered in a journal are sorted and summarized in ledger accounts. Transferring information from journals to ledger accounts is known as posting. Posting information from a journal to ledger accounts brings together in one place all activities affecting each single account.

LEDGERS AND CONTROLLING ACCOUNTS

The type and size of a business determine the number of ledgers used in the accounting system.

General ledger

A business with transactions involving mostly the receipt and payment of cash will generally use a single ledger. In Part 2, Putt Around uses only a single ledger. This single ledger sorts and summarizes all of the information affecting income statement and balance sheet accounts. A ledger that contains all accounts needed to prepare an income statement and a balance sheet is called a general ledger. Denim Threads uses a general ledger. The chart of accounts is on page 190. Because of the nature of the business, Denim Threads also uses additional ledgers in its accounting system.

Subsidiary ledgers

Accounts that are similar in nature are placed in a separate ledger. Besides the receipt and payment of cash, Denim Threads purchases merchandise on account and sells merchandise on account. A business must keep an individual account for each creditor and charge customer. A business needs to know the amount owed each creditor as well as the amount due from each charge customer.

A general ledger could contain an account for each creditor and for each charge customer. However, a business with many creditors and charge customers would have a bulky general ledger and a long trial balance. Denim Threads eliminates these problems by keeping separate ledgers for individual accounts of creditors and charge customers.

The total amount owed to all creditors is summarized in a single general ledger account, Accounts Payable. Likewise, the total amount due from all charge customers is summarized in a single general ledger account, Accounts Receivable. A ledger that is summarized in a single account in a general ledger is called a subsidiary ledger.

Controlling accounts

An account in a general ledger that summarizes all the accounts in a subsidiary ledger is called a controlling account. The separate ledger kept by Denim Threads for creditors is a subsidiary ledger. The general ledger account Accounts Payable is the controlling account. Denim Threads also keeps a subsidiary ledger for charge customers. The general ledger account Accounts Receivable is the controlling account. The balance of a controlling account equals the total of all the account balances in its related subsidiary ledger.

POSTING TO AN ACCOUNTS PAYABLE LEDGER

When the balance of a creditor's account is changed, the balance of the controlling account Accounts Payable is also changed. A subsidiary ledger that contains only accounts with creditors is called an accounts payable ledger. The relationship between the accounts payable ledger and the general ledger account Accounts Payable is on page 229.

Accounts payable ledger form

Denim Threads uses a three-column account form in the accounts payable ledger. The ledger form is on page 229.

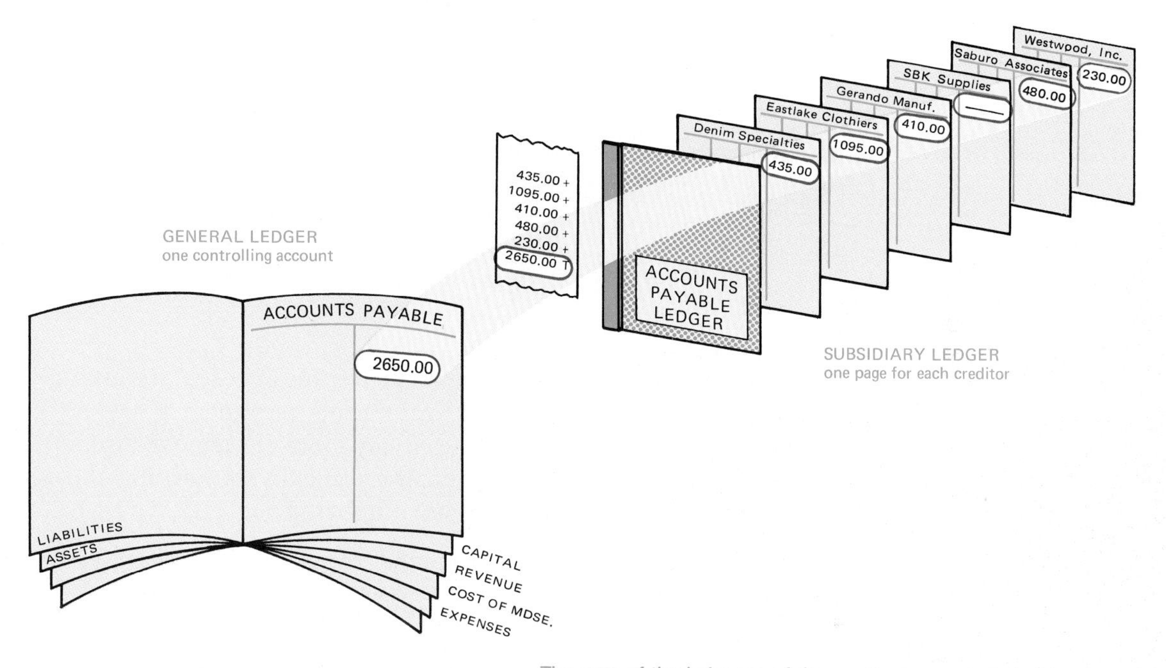

The sum of the balances of the creditor's accounts in the accounts payable ledger is summarized in Accounts Payable.

Each creditor's account has three amount columns. One column is for debit amounts, one column is for credit amounts, and one column is for the balance. Since accounts payable are liabilities and liabilities have credit balances, the last column is titled Credit Balance. With this third column, the balance of the account can be updated after each posting. After posting is completed, an accounts payable ledger shows how much is owed to each creditor.

NAME

ADDRESS

DATE	ITEM	POST. REF.	DEBIT	CREDIT	CREDIT BALANCE

Three-column account form used in an accounts payable ledger

Opening creditor accounts

Each new account is opened by writing the creditor's name and address on the first two lines of the ledger form. The account opened for

Denim Specialties is below. The name and address are obtained from the first purchase invoice received from a creditor.

NAME *Denim Specialties*
ADDRESS *315 Mears Street, Omaha, NE 68110-1936*

DATE		ITEM	POST. REF.	DEBIT	CREDIT	CREDIT BALANCE

Opening a creditor's account in the accounts payable ledger

Individual accounts for the creditors of Denim Threads are arranged alphabetically in a loose-leaf binder. Periodically accounts for new creditors are added and old accounts not used any more are removed from the subsidiary ledger. Therefore, to avoid the difficulty of keeping the accounts in order, the ledger pages are not numbered.

If a business has many accounts in the accounts payable ledger, each account may be given a number. The accounts then may be arranged in numerical order. A separate alphabetic card file is used to help locate a creditor's account number.

Posting from a combination journal to an accounts payable ledger

Each entry in the accounts payable columns of a combination journal affects the creditor named in the Account Title column. Each amount listed in these two columns is posted daily to a creditor's account in the accounts payable ledger. Posting daily keeps each creditor's account balance up to date. Totals of these special amount columns are posted at the end of the month.

Posting a credit to an accounts payable ledger. Posting a purchase on account from a combination journal to an accounts payable ledger is on page 231.

Steps to post the entry on line 3 are below.

1 Write the amount, *$822.00*, in the Credit column of the account.

2 Add the amount in the Credit column to the previous balance in the Credit Balance column. (Denim Specialties has no previous balance; therefore, 0 + $822.00 = $822.00.) Write the new balance, *$822.00*, in the Credit Balance column.

3 Write the date, *1982, Nov. 2*, in the Date column.

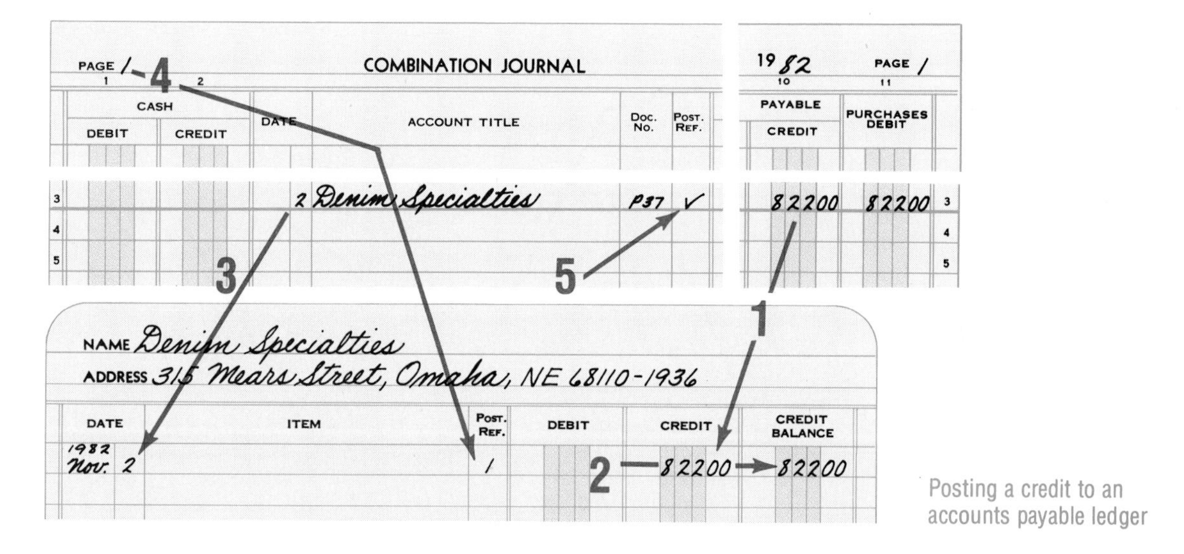

Posting a credit to an accounts payable ledger

4 Write the page number of the combination journal, *1*, in the Post. Ref. column of the account.

In Part 2 Putt Around used two journals. The posting reference was written as *C1* to show posting from the cash journal. G1 showed posting from the general journal. Denim Threads uses only one journal. Therefore, there is no need to put a letter code on the page number of the journal.

5 Place a check mark in the Post. Ref. column of the combination journal. The check mark shows that the posting for this entry is completed.

Individual accounts in the accounts payable ledger do not have page numbers. Therefore, a check mark is used to show that posting is completed. If individual accounts were numbered, the account number would be written in the Post. Ref. column of the combination journal.

Accounts Payable, the controlling account in the general ledger, is also increased because of this entry. At the end of a month, the Accounts Payable Credit column total is posted to the controlling account Accounts Payable. Posting of column totals is described on page 241.

Posting a debit to an accounts payable ledger. The same steps are followed to post a debit to a creditor's account as are used to post a credit. The difference is that the amount is entered in the Debit column of the account. The debit amount is then subtracted from the previous credit balance. Posting a payment on account, line 17 of the combination journal, to the subsidiary ledger is on the next page.

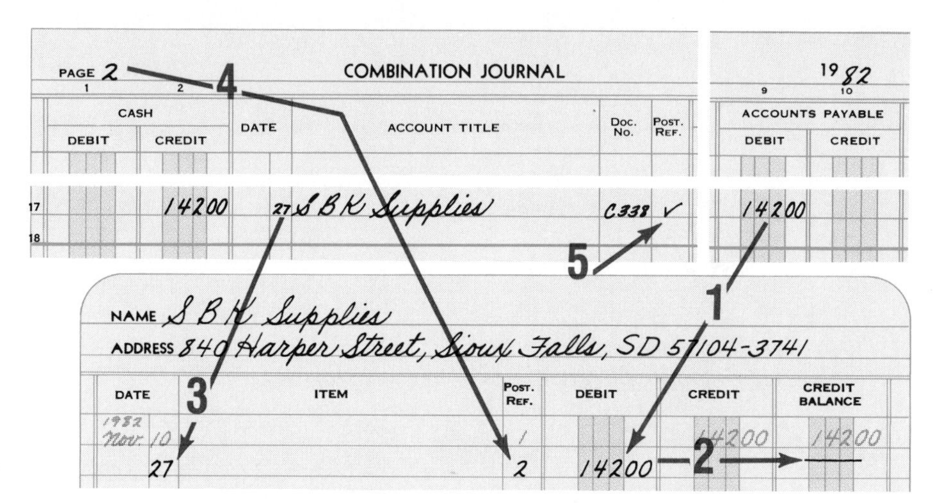

PAGE 2 — COMBINATION JOURNAL — 19 82

CASH DEBIT (1)	CASH CREDIT (2)	DATE	ACCOUNT TITLE	DOC. NO.	POST. REF.	ACCOUNTS PAYABLE DEBIT (9)	ACCOUNTS PAYABLE CREDIT (10)
17	14200	27	SBK Supplies	C338	✓	14200	
18							

NAME SBK Supplies
ADDRESS 840 Harper Street, Sioux Falls, SD 57104-3741

DATE		ITEM	POST. REF.	DEBIT	CREDIT	CREDIT BALANCE
1982 Nov.	10		1		14200	14200
	27		2	14200		—

Posting a debit to an accounts payable ledger

Opening a new page for a creditor in an accounts payable ledger

The number of entries that may be recorded on each ledger form depends on the number of lines provided. When all lines have been used, a new page is prepared. The name and address plus the account balance are recorded on the new page.

On November 1, 1982, Denim Threads prepared a new page for Gerando Manufacturing in the accounts payable ledger. On that day, the account balance was $360.00. The account is below.

NAME Gerando Manufacturing
ADDRESS 366 Mason Street, Sioux City, IA 51101-1129

DATE		ITEM	POST. REF.	DEBIT	CREDIT	CREDIT BALANCE
1982 Nov.	1	Balance	✓			36000

Opening a new page for a creditor in the accounts payable ledger

The name and address of the creditor are written at the top of the account page. The account balance, *$360.00*, is written in the Credit Balance column. The date, *1982, Nov. 1*, is entered in the Date column. The word *Balance* is written in the Item column. A check mark is placed in the Post. Ref. column. The check mark shows that the entry was not posted from the combination journal.

Completed accounts payable ledger

The accounts payable ledger for Denim Threads after all posting has been completed is on pages 233 and 234. Denim Threads posts daily each line from the Accounts Payable columns of the combination journal. This procedure keeps all accounts with creditors up to date. Accounts Payable column totals in the combination journal are posted at the end of each month.

Accounts payable ledger

NAME Denim Specialties
ADDRESS 315 Mears Street, Omaha, NE 68110-1936

DATE		ITEM	POST. REF.	DEBIT	CREDIT	CREDIT BALANCE
1982 Nov.	2		1		822 00	822 00
	19		1	822 00		—
	24		2		435 00	435 00

NAME Eastlake Clothiers
ADDRESS 735 Huron Avenue, Brookings, SD 57006-2183

DATE		ITEM	POST. REF.	DEBIT	CREDIT	CREDIT BALANCE
1982 Nov.	8		1		680 00	680 00
	28		2		415 00	1 095 00

NAME Gerando Manufacturing
ADDRESS 366 Mason Street, Sioux City, IA 51101-1129

DATE		ITEM	POST. REF.	DEBIT	CREDIT	CREDIT BALANCE
1982 Nov.	1	Balance	✓			360 00
	12		1		410 00	770 00
	28		2	360 00		410 00

NAME S B K Supplies
ADDRESS 840 Harper Street, Sioux Falls, SD 57104-3741

DATE		ITEM	POST. REF.	DEBIT	CREDIT	CREDIT BALANCE
1982 Nov.	10		1		142 00	142 00
	27		2	142 00		—

NAME Saburo Associates
ADDRESS 3840 Curtiss Avenue, Huron, SD 57350-9641

DATE		ITEM	POST. REF.	DEBIT	CREDIT	CREDIT BALANCE
1982 Nov.	1	Balance	✓			260 00
	22		2	260 00		—
	24		2		480 00	480 00

NAME Westwood, Inc.

ADDRESS 622 Cody Road, Watertown, SD 57201-1522

DATE		ITEM	POST. REF.	DEBIT	CREDIT	CREDIT BALANCE
1982 Nov.	1	Balance	✓			580 00
	15		1	580 00		—
	25		2		230 00	230 00

Accounts payable ledger (concluded)

POSTING TO AN ACCOUNTS RECEIVABLE LEDGER

When a charge customer's account is changed, the controlling account Accounts Receivable is also changed. A subsidiary ledger that contains only accounts with charge customers is called an accounts receivable ledger. The relationship between the accounts receivable ledger and the general ledger account Accounts Receivable is below.

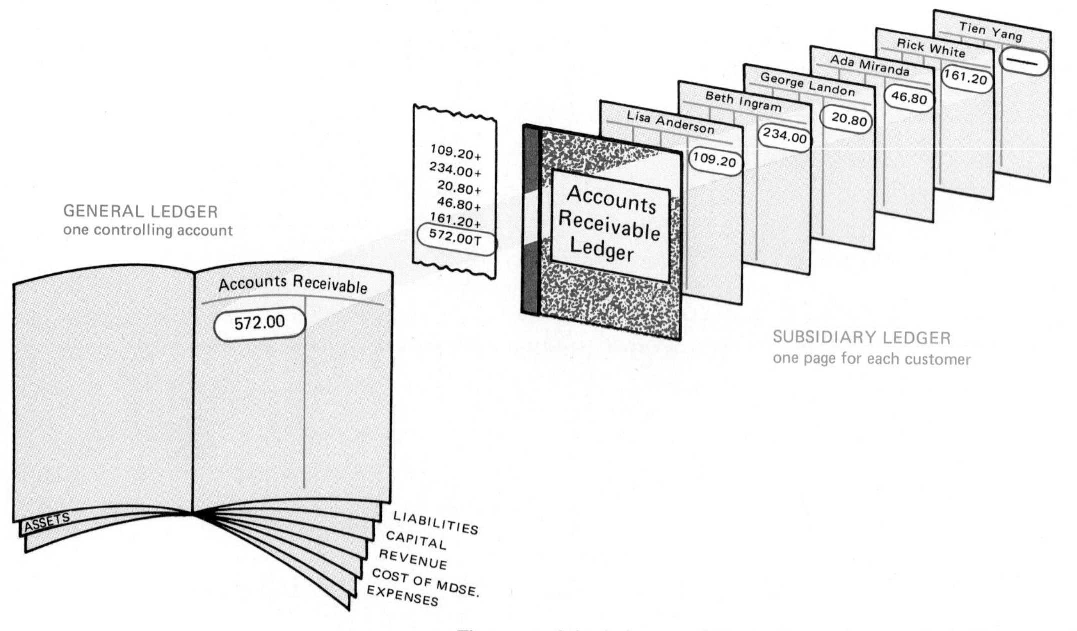

The sum of the balances of the customers' accounts in the accounts receivable ledger is summarized in Accounts Receivable.

Accounts receivable ledger form

Denim Threads uses a three-column account form in the accounts receivable ledger.

NAME Lisa Anderson

ADDRESS 1902 Cherry Street, Madison, SD 57042-8572

DATE	ITEM	POST. REF.	DEBIT	CREDIT	DEBIT BALANCE

Three-column account form used in an accounts receivable ledger

The form for the accounts receivable ledger is similar to the one used for the accounts payable ledger. Accounts receivable are assets and assets have debit balances. Therefore, the form used in the accounts receivable ledger has a Debit Balance column instead of a Credit Balance column.

Opening customers' accounts

Procedures for opening customers' accounts are similar to those used for opening creditors' accounts. The account opened for Lisa Anderson is above. For each customer's account the name and address are taken from the first sales invoice issued. Accounts are arranged in alphabetical order.

Posting from a combination journal to an accounts receivable ledger

Each entry in the accounts receivable columns of a combination journal affects the customer named in the Account Title column. Each amount listed in these two columns is posted daily to a customer's account in an accounts receivable ledger. Posting daily keeps each customer's account balance up to date. Totals of accounts receivable special amount columns are posted at the end of the month.

Posting a debit to an accounts receivable ledger. Posting a charge sale from a combination journal to an accounts receivable ledger is below.

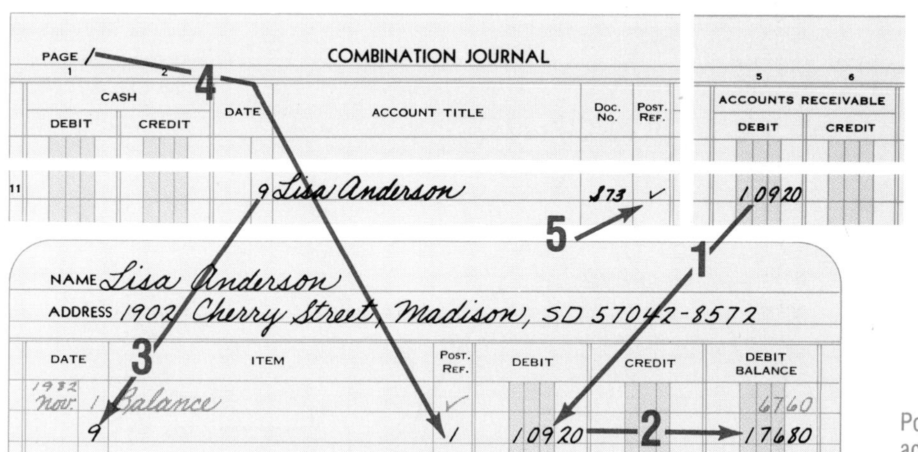

COMBINATION JOURNAL PAGE 1

	CASH DEBIT (1)	CASH CREDIT (2)	DATE	ACCOUNT TITLE	DOC. NO.	POST. REF.	ACCOUNTS RECEIVABLE DEBIT (5)	ACCOUNTS RECEIVABLE CREDIT (6)
11			9	Lisa Anderson	S73	✓	109 20	

NAME Lisa Anderson

ADDRESS 1902 Cherry Street, Madison, SD 57042-8572

DATE	ITEM	POST. REF.	DEBIT	CREDIT	DEBIT BALANCE
1982 Nov. 1	Balance	✓			67 60
9		1	109 20		176 80

Posting a debit to an accounts receivable ledger.

Steps to post this entry to the accounts receivable ledger are below.

1 Write the amount of the sale, *$109.20*, in the Debit column of the account for Lisa Anderson.

2 Add the amount in the Debit column to the previous balance in the Debit Balance column ($67.60 + $109.20 = $176.80). Write the new balance, *$176.80*, in the Debit Balance column.

3 Write the date, *9*, in the Date column.

4 Write the page number of the combination journal, *1*, in the Post. Ref. column of the account.

5 Place a check mark in the Post. Ref. column of the combination journal. The check mark shows that the item on line 11 is posted.

Accounts Receivable, the controlling account in the general ledger, is also increased by this entry. The total of the Accounts Receivable Debit column is posted to the controlling account Accounts Receivable. Posting column totals is described on page 241.

Posting a credit to an accounts receivable ledger. The same steps are followed to post a credit to a customer's account as are used to post a debit. However, the credit amount is written in the Credit column of the customer's account. The credit amount is then subtracted from the previous debit balance. Posting cash received on account, line 7 of the combination journal, to the subsidiary ledger is below.

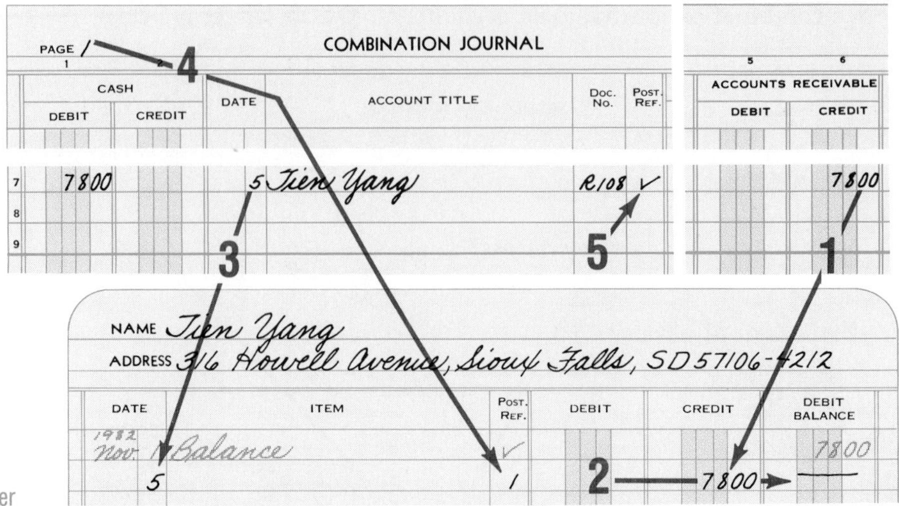

Posting a credit to an accounts receivable ledger

Accounts Receivable, the controlling account in the general ledger, is decreased by this entry. The Accounts Receivable Credit column total is posted to the controlling account Accounts Receivable at the end of the month.

Opening a new page for a customer in an accounts receivable ledger

Procedures for opening a new page in an accounts receivable ledger are similar to those for an accounts payable ledger. When all lines on a page have been used, a new page is prepared. The name and address of the customer are written at the top of the account page. The account balance however is recorded in the Debit Balance column rather than the Credit Balance column.

Completed accounts receivable ledger

The accounts receivable ledger for Denim Threads after all posting has been completed is below and on the next page. Denim Threads posts daily each line from the Accounts Receivable columns of the combination journal. This procedure keeps all customers' accounts up to date. The Accounts Receivable column totals in the combination journal are posted at the end of the month.

Accounts receivable ledger

NAME Lisa Anderson
ADDRESS 1902 Cherry Street, Madison, SD 57042-8572

DATE		ITEM	POST. REF.	DEBIT	CREDIT	DEBIT BALANCE
1982 Nov.	1	Balance	✓			67 60
	9		1	109 20		176 80
	27		2		67 60	109 20

NAME Beth Ingram
ADDRESS 1640 Pickard Lane, Sioux Falls, SD 57105-2583

DATE		ITEM	POST. REF.	DEBIT	CREDIT	DEBIT BALANCE
1982 Nov.	1	Balance	✓			78 00
	18		1		41 60	36 40
	25		2		36 40	—
	28		2	62 40		62 40
	30		2	171 60		234 00

NAME George Landon
ADDRESS 2205 Jackson Drive, Sioux Falls, SD 57107-3403

DATE		ITEM	POST. REF.	DEBIT	CREDIT	DEBIT BALANCE
1982 Nov.	12		1	1560		1560
	23		2	2080		3640
	26		2		1560	2080

NAME Ada Miranda
ADDRESS 3340 Hampton Road, Mitchell, SD 57301-1037

DATE		ITEM	POST. REF.	DEBIT	CREDIT	DEBIT BALANCE
1982 Nov.	1	Balance	✓			6240
	4		1	4680		10920
	17		1		6240	4680

NAME Rick White
ADDRESS 1520 Chandler Place, Yankton, SD 57078-6823

DATE		ITEM	POST. REF.	DEBIT	CREDIT	DEBIT BALANCE
1982 Nov.	10		1	5200		5200
	23		2	16120		21320
	29		2		5200	16120

NAME Tien Yang
ADDRESS 316 Howell Avenue, Sioux Falls, SD 57106-4212

DATE		ITEM	POST. REF.	DEBIT	CREDIT	DEBIT BALANCE
1982 Nov.	1	Balance	✓			7800
	5		1		7800	—

Accounts receivable ledger (concluded)

POSTING TO A GENERAL LEDGER

Daily account balances are usually not necessary for general ledger accounts. Balances of general ledger accounts are needed only when financial statements are prepared. Therefore, posting from a combination journal to a general ledger is done periodically throughout a month. The number of transactions determines how often to post to a general ledger. A business with many transactions would normally post more often than a business with few transactions. Posting must be done at least once a month.

General ledger account form

Many businesses, such as Putt Around, described in Part 2, use a two-column general ledger account form. Putt Around needs to know the up-to-date account balances once a month to prepare financial reports. If a business needs account balances infrequently, the two-column account form is satisfactory to use.

Some businesses prefer using ledger account forms that show an up-to-date account balance after each entry is posted. An example is the account forms used by Denim Threads for subsidiary ledgers. The need to pencil foot accounts is eliminated. Denim Threads also uses a balance-ruled form of account for its general ledger. The form has four amount columns: Debit, Credit, Debit Balance, and Credit Balance. The form is below.

ACCOUNT　　　　ACCOUNT NO.

DATE	ITEM	POST. REF.	DEBIT	CREDIT	BALANCE	
					DEBIT	CREDIT

Four-column account form used in a general ledger

The four-column account form shows the amount of each debit and each credit posted to the account. The amount of the new balance after an entry is posted is recorded in the appropriate Balance column. Asset, cost, and expense accounts normally have debit balances. Whereas, liability, capital, and revenue accounts normally have credit balances. Therefore, both Debit Balance and Credit Balance columns are needed for general ledger accounts.

> Some businesses using the four-column ledger form determine account balances only after all monthly postings have been completed. Then only the end-of-month balance is recorded in the proper balance column.

Posting from the General columns in a combination journal

Each amount in the General Debit and General Credit columns of a combination journal is posted individually. The amount is posted to the account shown in the Account Title column.

Posting a debit to a general ledger account. Posting a salary expense transaction from a combination journal to a general ledger is below.

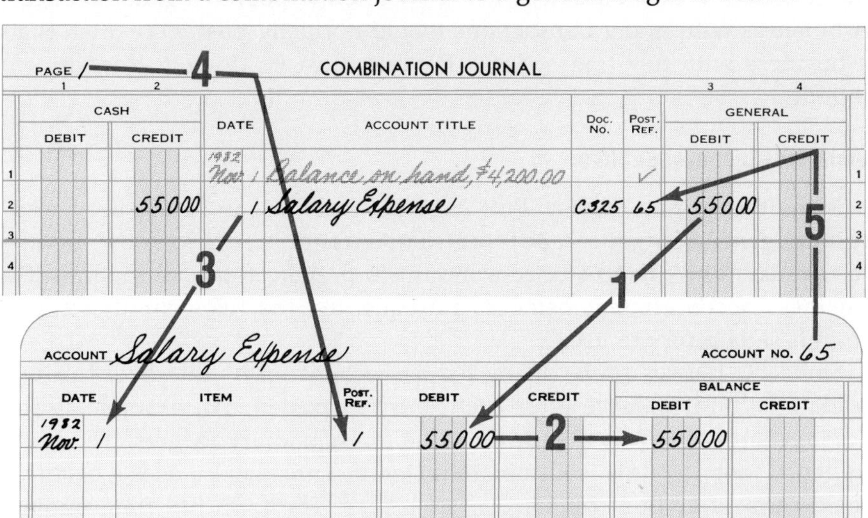

Posting a debit to a general ledger

Steps to post the General Debit amount on line 2 of the combination journal to the general ledger are below.

1 Write the amount, *$550.00*, in the Debit column of the general ledger account Salary Expense.

2 Add the amount in the Debit column to the amount of the previous balance in the Debit Balance column. (There is no previous balance; therefore, 0 + $550.00 = $550.00.) Write the new balance, *$550.00*, in the Debit Balance column.

3 Write the date, *1982, Nov. 1*, in the Date column.

4 Write the page number of the combination journal, *1*, in the Post. Ref. column of the account.

5 Write the number of the salary expense account, *65*, in the Post. Ref. column of the combination journal. Writing the account number in the Post. Ref. column shows that posting this line in the journal is completed.

Posting a credit to a general ledger account. A credit is posted by entering the amount in the Credit column of the general ledger account shown in the Account Title column. The new balance is figured by deducting the credit from the previous debit balance. If the previous balance is a credit, add the credit to the balance. The purchases account is shown below after the entry on line 28 of the combination journal is posted.

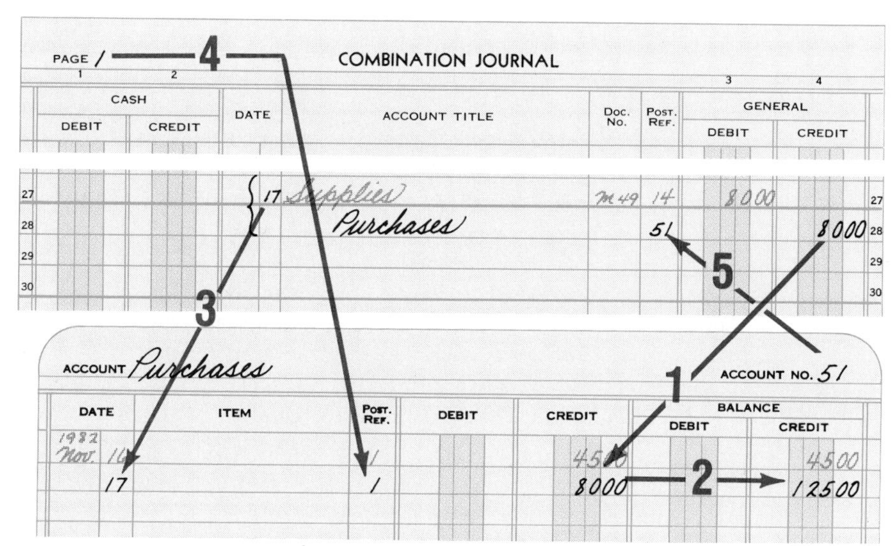

Posting a credit to a general ledger

Posting totals of the special columns in a combination journal

The total of each special column of a combination journal is posted to the account named in the column heading. After each column total is posted, the number of the account is written in parentheses below the column total. Totals of the General columns are not posted because each amount in these columns is posted individually. When totals are not to be posted, a check mark is placed in parentheses below the column total.

Illustrations on pages 242 and 243 show page 2 of the combination journal for November, 1982. All individual items in the General, the Accounts Receivable, and the Accounts Payable columns have been posted. Totals of all special columns also have been posted.

The cash account in the general ledger is shown below. Totals of the Cash Debit and Cash Credit columns of the combination journal for November have been posted.

ACCOUNT *Cash* ACCOUNT NO. 11

DATE		ITEM	POST. REF.	DEBIT	CREDIT	BALANCE DEBIT	BALANCE CREDIT
1982 Nov.	1	Balance	✓			4200 00	
	30		2	13551 20		17751 20	
	30		2		6207 00	11544 20	

Cash account after totals have been posted from a combination journal

PAGE 2 COMBINATION JOURNAL

	1	2					3	4	
	CASH						GENERAL		
	DEBIT	CREDIT	DATE	ACCOUNT TITLE	DOC. NO.	POST. REF.	DEBIT	CREDIT	
1	6479 20	4466 00	1982 Nov. 19	Brought Forward		✓	2906 00	125 00	1
2	1976 00		20	✓	J20	✓			2
3	1388 40		20	✓	CJ20	✓			3
4		29 00	22	Miscellaneous Expense	C335	63	29 00		4
5		260 00	22	Saburo Associates	C336	✓			5
6			23	Rick White	S76	✓			6
7			23	George Landon	S77	✓			7
8			24	Saburo Associates	P40	✓			8
9			24	Denim Specialties	P41	✓			9
10		180 00	25	✓	C337	✓			10
11			25	Westwood, Inc.	P42	✓			11
12	36 40		25	Beth Ingram	R111	✓			12
13	15 60		26	George Landon	R112	✓			13
14	1825 20		27	✓	J27	✓			14
15	1315 60		27	✓	CJ27	✓			15
16	67 60		27	Lisa Anderson	R113	✓			16
17		142 00	27	SBK Supplies	C338	✓			17
18			28	Beth Ingram	S78	✓			18
19			28	Eastlake Clothiers	P43	✓			19
20		360 00	28	Gerando Manufacturing	C339	✓			20
21		2 00	28	Miscellaneous Expense	M49	63	2 00		21
22		135 00	28	Credit Card Fee Expense	M50	61	135 00		22
23		33 00	28	Supplies	C340	14	33 00		23
24	52 00		29	Rick White	R114	✓			24
25			30	Beth Ingram	S79	✓			25
26		300 00	30	Eva Burgos, Drawing	C341	32	300 00		26
27		300 00	30	Luis Perez, Drawing	C342	34	300 00		27
28	327 60		30	✓	J30	✓			28
29	67 60		30	✓	CJ30	✓			29
30	13551 20	6207 00	30	Totals			3705 00	125 00	30
31	(11)	(11)					(✓)	(✓)	31
32									32
33									33
34									34

Combination journal after posting has been completed (left page)

Completed general ledger

The general ledger for Denim Threads is on pages 244–246. All entries in the combination journal for the month of November have been posted.

No postings appear in the following accounts: Income Summary, Insurance Expense, and Supplies Expense. Transactions for November did

FOR MONTH OF *November* 19*82* PAGE *2*

	5	6	7	8	9	10	11	
	ACCOUNTS RECEIVABLE		SALES CREDIT	SALES TAX PAYABLE CREDIT	ACCOUNTS PAYABLE		PURCHASES DEBIT	
	DEBIT	CREDIT			DEBIT	CREDIT		
1	22360	18200	627000	25080	140200	205400	233700	1
2			190000	7600				2
3			133500	5340				3
4								4
5					26000			5
6	16120		15500	620				6
7	2080		2000	80				7
8						48000	48000	8
9						43500	43500	9
10							18000	10
11						23000	23000	11
12		3640						12
13		1560						13
14			175500	7020				14
15			126500	5060				15
16		6760						16
17					14200			17
18	6240		6000	240				18
19						41500	41500	19
20					36000			20
21								21
22								22
23								23
24		5200						24
25	17160		16500	660				25
26								26
27								27
28			31500	1260				28
29			6500	260				29
30	63960	35360	1330500	53220	216400	361400	407700	30
31	(12)	(12)	(41)	(22)	(21)	(21)	(51)	31
32								32
33								33
34								34

Combination journal after posting has been completed (right page)

not affect these accounts. The use of these three accounts is described in Chapters 14 and 16.

Putt Around pencil footed the general ledger accounts, page 114, on the last day of the month. The balance was then determined for each account. Since general ledger accounts used by Denim Threads have balance columns, the accounts do not need to be pencil footed. The account balance for each account is updated each time an entry is posted.

ACCOUNT Cash ACCOUNT NO. 11

DATE		ITEM	POST. REF.	DEBIT	CREDIT	BALANCE DEBIT	BALANCE CREDIT
1982 Nov.	1	Balance	✓			4200 00	
	30		2	13551 20		17751 20	
	30		2		6207 00	11544 20	

ACCOUNT Accounts Receivable ACCOUNT NO. 12

DATE		ITEM	POST. REF.	DEBIT	CREDIT	BALANCE DEBIT	BALANCE CREDIT
1982 Nov.	1	Balance	✓			286 00	
	30		2	639 60		925 60	
	30		2		353 60	572 00	

ACCOUNT Merchandise Inventory ACCOUNT NO. 13

DATE		ITEM	POST. REF.	DEBIT	CREDIT	BALANCE DEBIT	BALANCE CREDIT
1982 Nov.	1	Balance	✓			68000 00	

ACCOUNT Supplies ACCOUNT NO. 14

DATE		ITEM	POST. REF.	DEBIT	CREDIT	BALANCE DEBIT	BALANCE CREDIT
1982 Nov.	1	Balance	✓			160 00	
	10		1	142 00		302 00	
	15		1	86 00		388 00	
	17		1	80 00		468 00	
	29		2	33 00		501 00	

ACCOUNT Prepaid Insurance ACCOUNT NO. 15

DATE		ITEM	POST. REF.	DEBIT	CREDIT	BALANCE DEBIT	BALANCE CREDIT
1982 Nov.	1	Balance	✓			430 00	

ACCOUNT Accounts Payable ACCOUNT NO. 21

DATE		ITEM	POST. REF.	DEBIT	CREDIT	BALANCE DEBIT	BALANCE CREDIT
1982 Nov.	1	Balance	✓				1200 00
	30		2	2164 00		964 00	
	30		2		3614 00		2650 00

General ledger after combination journal is posted

ACCOUNT *Sales Tax Payable* ACCOUNT NO. 22

DATE		ITEM	POST. REF.	DEBIT	CREDIT	BALANCE DEBIT	BALANCE CREDIT
1982 Nov.	1	Balance	✓				35680
	30		2		53220		88900

ACCOUNT *Eva Burgos, Capital* ACCOUNT NO. 31

DATE		ITEM	POST. REF.	DEBIT	CREDIT	BALANCE DEBIT	BALANCE CREDIT
1982 Nov.	1	Balance	✓				3575960

ACCOUNT *Eva Burgos, Drawing* ACCOUNT NO. 32

DATE		ITEM	POST. REF.	DEBIT	CREDIT	BALANCE DEBIT	BALANCE CREDIT
1982 Nov.	15		1	30000		30000	
	30		2	30000		60000	

ACCOUNT *Luis Perez, Capital* ACCOUNT NO. 33

DATE		ITEM	POST. REF.	DEBIT	CREDIT	BALANCE DEBIT	BALANCE CREDIT
1982 Nov.	1	Balance	✓				3575960

ACCOUNT *Luis Perez, Drawing* ACCOUNT NO. 34

DATE		ITEM	POST. REF.	DEBIT	CREDIT	BALANCE DEBIT	BALANCE CREDIT
1982 Nov.	15		1	30000		30000	
	16		1	4500		34500	
	30		2	30000		64500	

ACCOUNT *Income Summary* ACCOUNT NO. 35

DATE		ITEM	POST. REF.	DEBIT	CREDIT	BALANCE DEBIT	BALANCE CREDIT

ACCOUNT *Sales* ACCOUNT NO. 41

DATE		ITEM	POST. REF.	DEBIT	CREDIT	BALANCE DEBIT	BALANCE CREDIT
1982 Nov.	30		2		1330500		1330500

General ledger after combination journal is posted (continued)

ACCOUNT Purchases ACCOUNT NO. 51

DATE		ITEM	POST. REF.	DEBIT	CREDIT	BALANCE DEBIT	BALANCE CREDIT
1982 Nov.	16		1		4500		4500
	17		1		8000		12500
	30		2	407700		395200	

ACCOUNT Credit Card Fee Expense ACCOUNT NO. 61

DATE		ITEM	POST. REF.	DEBIT	CREDIT	BALANCE DEBIT	BALANCE CREDIT
1982 Nov.	28		2	13500		13500	

ACCOUNT Insurance Expense ACCOUNT NO. 62

DATE		ITEM	POST. REF.	DEBIT	CREDIT	BALANCE DEBIT	BALANCE CREDIT

ACCOUNT Miscellaneous Expense ACCOUNT NO. 63

DATE		ITEM	POST. REF.	DEBIT	CREDIT	BALANCE DEBIT	BALANCE CREDIT
1982 Nov.	3		1	5300		5300	
	22		2	2900		8200	
	28		2	200		8400	

ACCOUNT Rent Expense ACCOUNT NO. 64

DATE		ITEM	POST. REF.	DEBIT	CREDIT	BALANCE DEBIT	BALANCE CREDIT
1982 Nov.	15		1	80000		80000	

ACCOUNT Salary Expense ACCOUNT NO. 65

DATE		ITEM	POST. REF.	DEBIT	CREDIT	BALANCE DEBIT	BALANCE CREDIT
1982 Nov.	1		1	55000		55000	
	15		1	55000		110000	

ACCOUNT Supplies Expense ACCOUNT NO. 66

DATE		ITEM	POST. REF.	DEBIT	CREDIT	BALANCE DEBIT	BALANCE CREDIT

General ledger after combination journal is posted (concluded)

ELECTRONIC POSTING TO A GENERAL LEDGER

General-purpose accounting machine

Machines can be used to help process accounts receivable and accounts payable transactions. These machines print needed information on business forms. The machines also are able to add, subtract, multiply, or divide. A general-purpose accounting machine is at the right.

The principles of accounting used with an accounting machine are the same as those used when recording the information manually. The business forms may differ slightly because of the method used to record the information. For example, in manual accounting the accounts receivable account for Denim Threads appears as below.

ACCOUNT *Accounts Receivable* ACCOUNT NO. *12*

DATE		ITEM	POST. REF.	DEBIT	CREDIT	BALANCE	
						DEBIT	CREDIT
1982 *Nov.*	*1*	*Balance*	*✓*			*286 00*	
	30		*2*	*639 60*		*925 60*	
	30		*2*		*353 60*	*572 00*	

General ledger account used for processing information manually

The same information recorded by using a general-purpose accounting machine would appear as shown below.

LEDGER

ACCOUNT TITLE ACCOUNTS RECEIVABLE ACCOUNT NO. 12

DATE	REFERENCE	DEBITS	CREDITS	BALANCE
NOV 1 '82			BALANCE FWD. →	286.00
NOV 30 '82	2	639.60		925.60
NOV 30 '82	2		353.60	572.00

General ledger card used for processing information on a general-purpose accounting machine

Using a general-purpose accounting machine has several advantages over recording information manually.

1. The machine figures the new balance for each customer's account.
2. The machine prints more readable copy than when information is written manually.
3. The machine does the arithmetic more accurately than when done manually.
4. The machine makes more legible copies than can be done manually.

SUMMARY OF POSTING STEPS FROM A COMBINATION JOURNAL

A summary of the posting steps from a cash journal is on pages 102 and 103. The steps described for Putt Around, Part 2, also apply to posting from a combination journal. Special amount columns and controlling accounts, however, require an additional set of posting steps.

Posting from general columns

As shown below, individual amounts in General columns *are* posted separately. Totals of General columns are *not* posted.

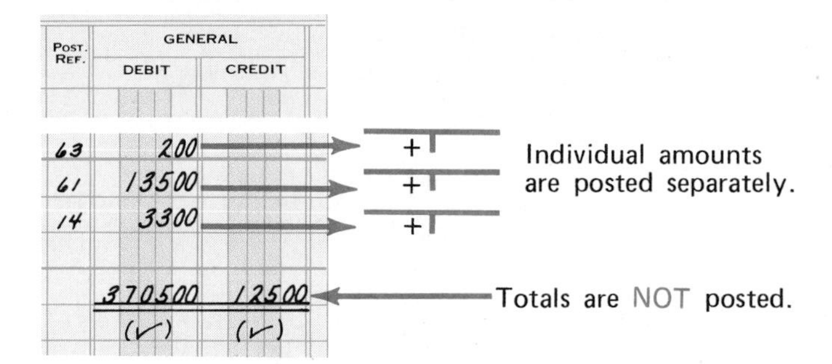

Posting from special columns

As shown below, totals of special columns *are* posted to the account named in the column heading. The total of the column shown is posted as a credit to the sales account. Individual amounts in special columns are *not* posted separately unless the columns are for a controlling account.

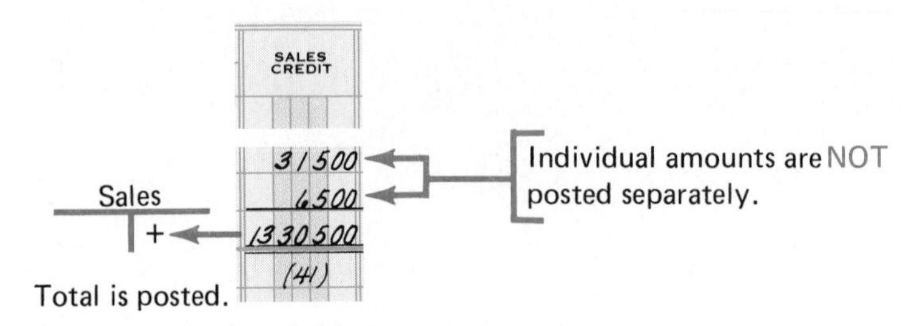

Posting from special columns for controlling accounts

As shown on page 249, individual amounts *and* total amounts are posted from special columns for controlling accounts. Individual amounts in the Accounts Receivable Debit and Credit columns *are* posted separately to charge customers' accounts. These accounts are found in an accounts receivable ledger. A check mark is placed in the

Post. Ref. column of the journal. The check mark shows that an individual amount has been posted to a customer's account.

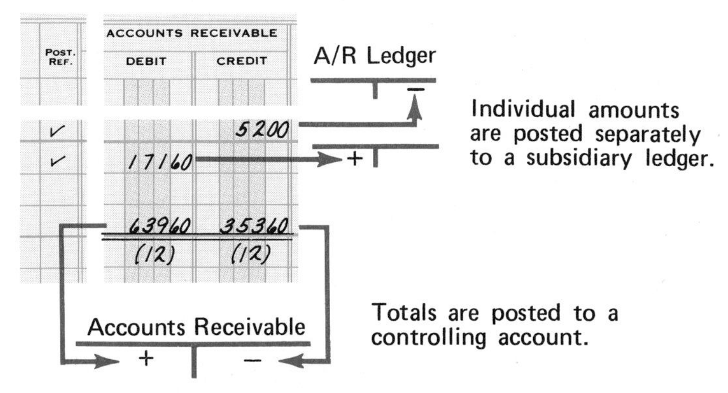

Totals of special columns *are* posted to the controlling accounts named in the column heading. The total of an Accounts Receivable Debit column is posted as a debit to Accounts Receivable in a general ledger. The total of an Accounts Receivable Credit column is posted as a credit to Accounts Receivable in a general ledger. An account number is placed in parentheses under the total of a special column. The number shows the general ledger account to which the total was posted.

The same principles used for Accounts Receivable columns also apply to Accounts Payable columns in a combination journal.

PROVING THE ACCURACY OF POSTING

A single error in posting to a ledger account may cause the balance sheet to be out of balance. An error in posting may also cause the profit to be understated or overstated on the income statement. An error in posting may also cause a business to overpay or underpay its creditors. Consequently, posting must be accurate to assure correct account balances in the ledgers.

Proving cash

The way to prove cash is described in Chapter 12. After posting is completed the balance of the general ledger cash account is compared with the cash proof. The cash proof total is also compared with the balance on the last completed check stub in the checkbook. The balance of the cash account on November 30, page 244, is $11,544.20. The same amount was found when cash was proved following the procedures on page 220. The checkbook balance also showed the same amount.

The cash proof is important. Because so many transactions affect the cash account, there are many chances to make an error in *Cash*.

Proving the subsidiary ledgers

A controlling account balance in a general ledger must equal the sum of all account balances in a subsidiary ledger.

Proving accounts payable. A listing of creditors' accounts, account balances, and total amount due all creditors is called a schedule of accounts payable. A schedule of accounts payable is prepared after all current entries in a journal are posted. The schedule prepared on November 30, 1982, for Denim Threads is below.

Denim Threads
Schedule of Accounts Payable
November 30, 1982

Denim Specialties	435 00
Eastlake Clothiers	1095 00
Gerando Manufacturing	410 00
Saburo Associates	480 00
Westwood, Inc.	230 00
Total Accounts Payable	2650 00

Schedule of accounts payable

The balance of the accounts payable account in the general ledger, page 244, is $2,650.00. The total of the schedule of accounts payable is the same, $2,650.00. The accounts payable ledger has been proved.

Proving accounts receivable. A listing of customers' accounts, account balances, and total amount due from all customers is called a schedule of accounts receivable. A schedule of accounts receivable is prepared after all current entries in a journal are posted. The schedule prepared on November 30, 1982, for Denim Threads is below.

Denim Threads
Schedule of Accounts Receivable
November 30, 1982

Lisa Anderson	109 20
Beth Ingram	234 00
George Landon	20 80
Ada Miranda	46 80
Rick White	161 20
Total Accounts Receivable	572 00

Schedule of accounts receivable

The balance of the accounts receivable account in the general ledger, page 244, is $572.00. The total of the schedule of accounts receivable is the same, $572.00. The accounts receivable ledger has been proved.

Proving equality of debits and credits in a general ledger

Debits and credits recorded in a journal must be equal. Debits and credits in the general ledger must also be equal. Therefore, balances of all accounts with debit balances are added. Then balances of all accounts with credit balances are added. The total of debit balances must equal the total of credit balances. The illustration at the right shows that both debit and credit balances in Denim Threads' general ledger total $88,363.20. Therefore, equality of debits and credits in the general ledger is proved. If the totals do not agree, one or more errors have been made. These errors must be found and corrected before work is continued.

DEBIT BALANCES	CREDIT BALANCES
11,544.20	
572.00	
68,000.00	
501.00	
430.00	
600.00	
645.00	
3,952.00	2,650.00
135.00	889.00
84.00	35,759.60
800.00	35,759.60
1,100.00	13,305.00
88,363.20T	88,363.20T

Adding machine tapes used to prove equality of debits and credits in the general ledger after posting is completed

ACCOUNTING TERMS

What is the meaning of each of the following?

1. general ledger
2. subsidiary ledger
3. controlling account
4. accounts payable ledger
5. accounts receivable ledger
6. schedule of accounts payable
7. schedule of accounts receivable

QUESTIONS FOR INDIVIDUAL STUDY

1. What determines the number and kinds of ledgers used in an accounting system?
2. What ledger contains all the accounts needed to prepare an income statement and a balance sheet?
3. Why must a business keep an individual account for each creditor and charge customer?
4. What kind of ledger is summarized in a single account in a general ledger?
5. What is the name of the general ledger controlling account for creditors?
6. Why does the three-column account form used in an accounts payable ledger have a Credit Balance column?
7. How are the name and address obtained for opening a new creditor's account in an accounts payable subsidiary ledger?
8. Why is a check mark placed in the Post. Ref. column when a new page for a creditor is opened?
9. Why is each amount listed in the accounts payable columns of a combination journal posted daily?
10. Why is a credit entry to an accounts payable account added to the previous balance?
11. Why does the three-column account form used in an accounts receivable ledger have a Debit Balance column?
12. How are the name and address obtained for opening a new customer's account in an accounts receivable subsidiary ledger?

13. Why is each amount listed in the accounts receivable columns of a combination journal posted daily?
14. Why is posting to a general ledger done only periodically throughout the month?
15. Why does the general ledger account form have both a Debit balance column and Credit balance column?
16. Why are the totals of the General Debit and Credit columns not posted at the end of the month?
17. Why is the cash proof important?
18. How are subsidiary ledgers proved at the end of the month?
19. How is a general ledger proved at the end of the month?

CASES FOR MANAGEMENT DECISION

CASE 1 Melinda Stevens is asked to evaluate the accounting system of Jefferson Supply Company. The general ledger of Jefferson Supply Company includes individual accounts for each creditor and charge customer. When checking the records and accounting procedures, Mrs. Stevens notes the bulky general ledger and long trial balance. Jefferson Supply Company uses a combination journal to record all transactions. A general ledger is used to maintain all income statement, balance sheet, creditor, and charge customer accounts. Transactions affecting creditor or charge customer accounts are recorded in the General Debit or General Credit columns of the combination journal. Creditor and charge customer entries are then posted individually to accounts in the general ledger. What recommendations should Mrs. Stevens make concerning the handling of creditor and charge customer accounts?

CASE 2 Jose Ramos observes his accountant at work and says, "You post each individual accounts receivable entry in the combination journal. Then you post the totals of the accounts receivable columns. You are posting these entries twice, which will make the records wrong." The accountant disagrees that the posting procedure is incorrect. Is Mr. Ramos or his accountant correct? Why?

CASE 3 Ruben's Gift Shop received a call from a customer, Beth Evans. Miss Evans stated she had purchased $50.00 worth of merchandise on account five weeks ago. She sent a check for $50.00 two weeks ago in payment of the account. Although no additional purchases had been made, she recently received a bill that listed her balance due as $100.00. What probably caused this error? When would the error probably be discovered?

DRILLS FOR UNDERSTANDING

DRILL 13-D 1 Analyzing transactions of a merchandising business

Instructions: Prepare T accounts for each of the transactions below. Show which general ledger accounts are to be debited and credited. A 5% sales tax is to be added to all sales transactions. The first transaction is shown as an example.

Accounts Receivable		Sales		Sales Tax Payable	
84.00			80.00		4.00

1. Sold merchandise on account to Lois Sailer, $80.00.
2. Cash sales for the week, $2,000.00.
3. Purchased merchandise on account from Marcourt Enterprises, $350.00.
4. Purchased merchandise for cash, $250.00.
5. Paid December rent, $750.00.
6. Bought supplies for cash, $40.00.
7. Received on account from Ed Gilbert, $62.25.
8. Ralph Manson, partner, withdrew merchandise, $38.00.
9. Paid on account to Bennington Supply, $200.00.
10. Discovered that a payment for rent had been recorded as a debit to Salary Expense instead of Rent Expense, $900.00.
11. Bought supplies on account from Northland Supply, $85.00.
12. Carol Benson, partner, withdrew cash, $300.00.

The solution to Drill 13-D 1 is needed to complete Drill 13-D 2.

DRILL 13-D 2 Recording and posting transactions of a merchandising business

The solution to Drill 13-D 1 is needed to complete Drill 13-D 2.

Instructions: 1. Use a form like the one below. Use the answers to Drill 13-D 1. Show by a check mark which amount columns in the combination journal will be used to record the transactions. Transaction 1 is shown as an example.

Transaction	Amount columns in the combination journal										
	Cash		General		Accts. Rec.		Sales	Sales Tax Pay.	Accts. Pay.		Purch.
	Debit	Credit	Debit	Credit	Debit	Credit	Credit	Credit	Debit	Credit	Debit
1. Debit amount					√						
Credit amount							√				
Credit amount								√			

Instructions: 2. Use a form such as the one below. Use the answers to Instruction 1. Show by a check mark whether the amount will or will not be posted separately to the ledgers. Transaction 1 is shown as an example.

Transaction	Posted separately to			Not posted separately to any ledger
	General Ledger	Accts. Rec. Ledger	Accts. Pay. Ledger	
1. Debit amount		√		
Credit amount				√
Credit amount				√

APPLICATION PROBLEM

PROBLEM 13-1 Posting to ledgers from a combination journal

The combination journal for Webster's Variety Store is given in the working papers.

Instructions: 1. Open the following creditors' accounts in the accounts payable ledger. Record the balances as of November 1 of the current year.

Creditor	Address	Account Balance
Harrison Supplies	1627 Madison Street, Beacon, NY 12508-1743	——
Miranda Specialties	2220 Park Avenue, Fanwood, NJ 07023-3355	$670.00
Mission Supply	8310 Mission Road, Bloomfield, NJ 07003-4005	——
Smith Supply	3860 Harrison Street, Milford, NH 03055-2727	430.00

2. Open the following customers' accounts in the accounts receivable ledger. Record the balances as of November 1 of the current year.

Customer	Address	Account Balance
Helen Fields	1316 Fancher Street, Bloomfield, NJ 07003-3520	$157.50
Marsha Harris	1610 Waverly, Bloomfield, NJ 07003-3916	——
Adrian Leon	840 West Elm Street, Bloomfield, NJ 07003-3743	262.50
Carlos Mendez	616 Grand Avenue, Bloomfield, NJ 07003-3820	210.00

3. Open the following accounts in the general ledger of Webster's Variety Store. Record the balances as of November 1 of the current year.

Account Title	Acct. No.	Account Balance
Cash	11	$ 4,600.00
Accounts Receivable	12	630.00
Merchandise Inventory	13	83,211.00
Supplies	14	360.00
Prepaid Insurance	15	900.00
Accounts Payable	21	1,100.00
Sales Tax Payable	22	526.40
Sherry Marshall, Capital	31	44,037.30
Sherry Marshall, Drawing	32	——
Harold Stark, Capital	33	44,037.30
Harold Stark, Drawing	34	——
Income Summary	35	——
Sales	41	——
Purchases	51	——
Credit Card Fee Expense	61	——
Insurance Expense	62	——
Miscellaneous Expense	63	——
Rent Expense	64	——
Salary Expense	65	——
Supplies Expense	66	——

Instructions: 4. Post the individual items recorded in the following columns of the combination journal. (a) General Debit and Credit. (b) Accounts Receivable Debit and Credit. (c) Accounts Payable Debit and Credit.

5. Post the totals of the special columns of the combination journal.

6. Prove cash. The balance on Check Stub No. 126 is $13,170.00.

7. Prepare a schedule of accounts payable similar to the one on page 250. Compare the total of the schedule with the balance of the controlling account Accounts Payable in the general ledger. If the totals are not the same, find and correct the errors.

8. Prepare a schedule of accounts receivable similar to the one on page 250. Compare the total of the schedule with the balance of the controlling account Accounts Receivable in the general ledger. If the totals are not the same, find and correct the errors.

9. Prove the equality of debits and credits in the general ledger. On an adding machine or on a sheet of paper, add the balances of all accounts with debit balances. Then add the balances of all the accounts with credit balances. If the two totals are not the same, find and correct the errors.

ENRICHMENT PROBLEMS

MASTERY PROBLEM 13-M Posting to ledgers from a combination journal

The combination journal prepared in Mastery Problem 12-M is needed to complete Mastery Problem 13-M.

The ledgers of J & L Hardware are given in the working papers.

Instructions: 1. Post the individual items recorded in the following columns of the combination journal prepared in Mastery Problem 12-M. (a) General Debit and Credit. (b) Accounts Receivable Debit and Credit. (c) Accounts Payable Debit and Credit.

2. Post the totals of the special columns of the combination journal.

3. Prove cash. The balance on Check Stub No. 230 is $7,640.95.

4. Prepare a schedule of accounts payable and a schedule of accounts receivable. Prove the accuracy of the subsidiary ledgers. Compare the schedule totals with the balances of the controlling accounts in the general ledger. If the totals are not the same, find and correct the errors.

5. Prove the equality of debits and credits in the general ledger. On an adding machine or sheet of paper, add the balances of all accounts with debit balances. Then add the balances of all accounts with credit balances. If the two totals are not the same, find and correct the errors.

CHALLENGE PROBLEM 13-C Posting to ledgers from a combination journal

The combination journal prepared in Challenge Problem 12-C is needed to complete Challenge Problem 13-C.

Instructions: Follow the instructions for Mastery Problem 13-M above. However, use the combination journal prepared for Challenge Problem 12-C in Chapter 12.

Reinforcement Activity 2

PART A

An Accounting Cycle for a Partnership Using a Combination Journal

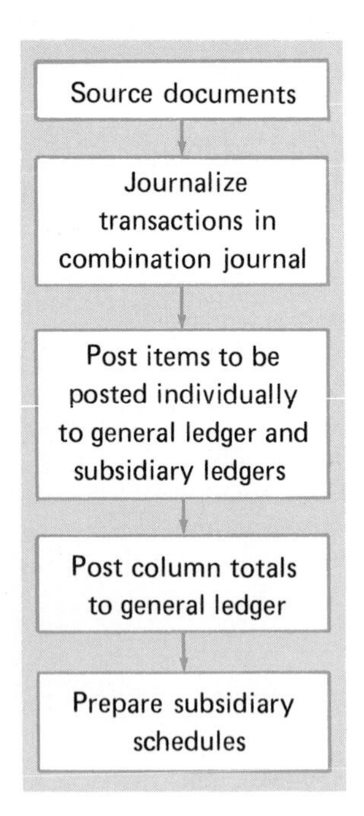

Reinforcement Activity 2 is designed to strengthen learnings from Part 3, Chapters 11–16. The activity covers a complete accounting cycle for a merchandising business organized as a partnership. Reinforcement Activity 2 is divided into two parts. Part A includes learnings from Chapters 11–13. Part B, page 320, includes learnings from Chapters 14–16.

Accounting work for a one-month fiscal period is included for a single merchandising business. However, the records kept and reports prepared illustrate the application of accounting concepts for all merchandising businesses. The business uses a credit card service in addition to its own company charge for sales transactions. The flowchart at the left shows that part of the accounting cycle covered in Reinforcement Activity 2, Part A.

INFOCUS

Ruth Dunn and Frank Gallagher, partners, own and operate a merchandising business called Infocus. The business sells cameras and related supplies and equipment. The business is located in a downtown shopping area and is open for business Monday through Saturday. A monthly rent is paid for the building, equipment, and furniture.

Infocus' chart of accounts

Infocus uses the chart of accounts shown on the next page.

Infocus' journal and ledgers

The journal and ledgers used by Infocus are listed below. Pages of this textbook on which the journal and ledgers are illustrated are also given.

Journal and Ledgers	Illustrated
Combination Journal	pages 242–243
General Ledger	pages 244–246
Accounts Receivable Ledger	pages 237–238
Accounts Payable Ledger	pages 233–234

INFOCUS
Chart of Accounts

	Account Number		Account Number
(1) ASSETS		**(4) REVENUE**	
Cash	11	Sales	41
Accounts Receivable	12	**(5) COST OF MERCHANDISE**	
Merchandise Inventory	13	Purchases	51
Supplies	14	**(6) EXPENSES**	
Prepaid Insurance	15	Credit Card Fee Expense	61
(2) LIABILITIES		Insurance Expense	62
Accounts Payable	21	Miscellaneous Expense	63
Sales Tax Payable	22	Rent Expense	64
(3) CAPITAL		Salary Expense	65
Ruth Dunn, Capital	31	Supplies Expense	66
Ruth Dunn, Drawing	32		
Frank Gallagher, Capital	33		
Frank Gallagher, Drawing	34		
Income Summary	35		

Opening Infocus' set of books

The required forms for the journal and ledgers are given in the working papers.

Instructions: 1. Begin numbering the combination journal with page 22.

2. Open all general ledger accounts that appear in the chart of accounts for Infocus, above. Open the accounts in the order in which they are listed. Record the beginning account balances given below as of December 1 of the current year.

Balance Sheet Accounts	Account Balances Debit	Credit
Cash	$ 8,340.00	—
Accounts Receivable	932.00	—
Merchandise Inventory	74,500.00	—
Supplies	430.00	—
Prepaid Insurance	640.00	—
Accounts Payable	—	$ 4,160.00
Sales Tax Payable	—	1,235.00
Ruth Dunn, Capital	—	40,790.00
Frank Gallagher, Capital	—	38,657.00

3. Open an account in the accounts receivable ledger for each customer listed below. Record each customer's beginning balance as of December 1 of the current year.

Customers' Names and Addresses	Account Balances
Iris Adams, 325 Pinemeadow Lane, Stockton, CA 95207-2531	$260.50
Olivia Espino, 4250 North Drive, Stockton, CA 95207-2640	—
James Fitzgerald, 946 Lark Lane, Stockton, CA 95205-2089	136.25
Eva Lawson, 2268 Heritage Road, Stockton, CA 95206-2476	345.15
Ralph Moya, 3840 Glade Drive, Stockton, CA 95207-2791	190.10
Steven Reynolds, 4320 Sutton Place, Stockton, CA 95206-2403	—

4. Open an account in the accounts payable ledger for each creditor listed below. Record the balances as of December 1 of the current year.

Creditors' Names and Addresses	Account Balances
A & M Photo, 540 Winding Way, Riverside, CA 92503-1581	$1,860.00
Beach Camera Company, 328 Horizon Drive, Seattle, WA 98122-3407	830.50
Fisher Office Supply, 845 West 14th Street, Stockton, CA 95204-1392	—
Garland Photo Products, 582 Harrison Road, Los Angeles, CA 90058-7018	—
Mori Photo Equipment, 258 Burkhardt Street, Stockton, CA 95207-2131	1,469.50
Newberry Office Supply, 236 Nieman Drive, Stockton, CA 95207-2285	—

5. Record the cash on hand, *$8,340.00*, on line 1 of the combination journal.

Recording Infocus' transactions

Instructions: 6. Record the following transactions. Credit card sales are recorded as cash sales. Source documents are abbreviated as: check, *C*; memorandum, *M*; purchase invoice, *P*; receipt, *R*; sales invoice, *S*; cash register tape, *T*; adding machine tape, *CT*.

Dec. 1. Paid December rent, $850.00. C320.
1. Paid salaries, $800.00. C321.
1. Ruth Dunn, partner, withdrew cash, $800.00. C322.
1. Frank Gallagher, partner, withdrew cash, $800.00. C323.
2. Sold merchandise on account to Olivia Espino, $125.00, plus sales tax, $5.94. Total, $130.94. S83.
2. Paid on account to Beach Camera Company, $830.50. C324.
3. Paid on account to Mori Photo Equipment, $1,469.50. C325.
4. Cash sales for the week, $1,570.00, plus sales tax, $74.58. Total, $1,644.58. T4.
4. Credit card sales for the week, $625.00, plus sales tax, $29.69. Total, $654.69. CT4.

   Posting: Post the items that are to be posted individually.
6. Bought supplies on account from Newberry Office Supply, $135.00. M42.
6. Purchased merchandise on account from A & M Photo, $960.00. P74.
6. Paid telephone bill, $62.00. C326. (Miscellaneous Expense)
7. Frank Gallagher, partner, withdrew merchandise, $38.00. M43.
8. Sold merchandise on account to Steven Reynolds, $350.00, plus sales tax, $16.63. Total, $366.63. S84.
8. Sold merchandise on account to Iris Adams, $83.25, plus sales tax, $3.95. Total, $87.20. S85.
9. Received on account from James Fitzgerald, $136.25. R90.
9. Received on account from Ralph Moya, $190.10. R91.
10. Discovered that supplies bought in November had been recorded in error as a debit to Prepaid Insurance, $65.00. M44.
11. Cash sales for the week, $2,430.00, plus sales tax, $115.43. Total, $2,545.43. T11.
11. Credit card sales for the week, $910.00, plus sales tax, $43.23. Total, $953.23. CT11.
11. Ruth Dunn, partner, withdrew merchandise, $28.00. M45.

    Posting: Post the items that are to be posted individually.
13. Bought supplies for cash, $46.00. C327.
13. Paid utility bill, $83.00. C328. (Miscellaneous Expense)
14. Paid on account to A & M Photo, $1,860.00. C329.
15. Sold merchandise on account to James Fitzgerald, $48.50, plus sales tax, $2.30. Total, $50.80. S86.

Dec. 15. Paid salaries, $800.00. C330.

Posting: Post the items that are to be posted individually.

Forwarding: Total the amount columns. Prove the equality of debits and credits and record on line 32 the totals to be carried forward. Record the totals brought forward on line 1 of page 23 of the combination journal.

16. Purchased merchandise on account from Garland Photo Products, $645.00. P75.
16. Purchased merchandise for cash, $430.00. C331.
17. Received on account from Eva Lawson, $238.62. R92.
18. Cash sales for the week, $2,560.00, plus sales tax, $121.60. Total, $2,681.60. T18.
18. Credit card sales for the week, $820.00, plus sales tax, $38.95. Total, $858.95. CT18.
18. Purchased merchandise on account from Mori Photo Equipment, $950.00. P76.

Posting: Post the items that are to be posted individually.

20. Paid for advertising, $65.00. C332. (Miscellaneous Expense)
20. Purchased merchandise on account from Beach Camera Company, $348.00. P77.
21. Received on account from Iris Adams, $260.50. R93.
22. Sold merchandise on account to Steven Reynolds, $34.95, plus sales tax, $1.66. Total, $36.61. S87.
22. Sold merchandise on account to Ralph Moya, $73.50, plus sales tax, $3.49. Total, $76.99. S88.
23. Purchased merchandise for cash, $220.00. C333.
23. Bought supplies on account from Newberry Office Supply, $74.00. M46.
24. Cash sales for the week, $2,310.00, plus sales tax, $109.73. Total, $2,419.73. T24.
24. Credit card sales for the week, $420.00, plus sales tax, $19.95. Total, $439.95. CT24.
24. Received on account from Eva Lawson, $106.53. R94.

Posting: Post the items that are to be posted individually.

27. Purchased merchandise on account from Garland Photo Products, $720.00. P78.
27. Bought supplies on account from Fisher Office Supply, $93.00. M47.
28. Purchased merchandise for cash, $247.00. C334.
28. Ruth Dunn, partner, withdrew merchandise, $65.00. M48.

Reconciling a bank statement: Prepare a reconciliation of Infocus' bank statement. Use illustration, page 171, as a guide. Information from the bank statement dated December 27 is below.

Balance shown on bank statement, $9,551.05.
Balance shown on Check Stub No. 334, $12,107.16.
Outstanding deposit made on December 24, $2,966.21.
Outstanding checks are Nos. C332, C333, C334.
Service charge shown on bank statement, $4.10.
Credit Card Fee Expense shown on bank statement, $117.80.

Infocus' bank charges a fee for handling the collection of credit card sales. The fee is based on a percentage of the credit card sales deposited during the month. The credit card fee is deducted from Infocus' bank account. The amount is then shown on the bank statement. The credit card fee is recorded in the combination journal as a reduction in cash. The entry is similar to the one for a checking account bank service charge, page 173.

28. Record the bank service charge, $4.10. M49. (Miscellaneous Expense)
28. Record the credit card fee, $117.80. M50. (Debit Credit Card Fee Expense; credit Cash.)
29. Purchased merchandise on account from Mori Photo Equipment, $840.00. P79.
30. Bought supplies for cash, $22.50. C335.

Dec. 30. Paid on account to A & M Photo, $960.00. C336.
31. Cash sales for the week, $2,240.00, plus sales tax, $106.40. Total, $2,346.40. T31.
31. Credit card sales for the week, $440.00, plus sales tax, $20.90. Total, $460.90. CT31.

Posting: Post the items that are to be posted individually.

Proving Infocus' combination journal at the end of the month

Instructions: 7. Total all amount columns of page 23 of the combination journal. Prove the equality of debits and credits.

8. Prove cash. Check Stub No. 337 shows a balance on hand of $13,810.06.

9. Rule page 23 of the combination journal.

Posting totals of the special columns of Infocus' combination journal

Instructions: 10. Post the totals of the special columns of the combination journal.

Proving Infocus' general ledger

Instructions: 11. On a piece of paper or adding machine, total all general ledger accounts with debit balances. Then total all general ledger accounts with credit balances. If the two totals are not the same, find and correct the errors.

Proving Infocus' subsidiary ledgers

Instructions: 12. Prepare a schedule of accounts payable and a schedule of accounts receivable. Compare the schedule totals with the balances of the controlling accounts in the general ledger. If the two totals are not the same, find and correct the errors.

The ledgers used in Reinforcement Activity 2, Part A, will be needed to complete Part B.

14

Eight-Column Work Sheet

ENABLING PERFORMANCE TASKS

After studying Chapter 14, you will be able to:

a. Define accounting terms related to an eight-column work sheet.
b. Explain accounting principles and practices related to the use of an eight-column work sheet.
c. Record a trial balance on an eight-column work sheet.
d. Plan adjustments on an eight-column work sheet.
e. Complete an eight-column work sheet.

Information about how well a business is doing is needed to make management decisions about future plans of operation. An owner or manager of a business must know if a profit is being made or if money is being lost. This profit or loss information helps an owner or manager make decisions that may increase profits. Profit and loss information is also needed to prepare required tax reports.

To figure profit or loss of a business, a work sheet is prepared at the end of each fiscal period. A work sheet may be prepared at the end of each month, each three months, each six months, or each year. *(CONCEPT: Accounting Period Cycle)* Denim Threads prepares a work sheet monthly.

Putt Around uses a six-column work sheet as described in Chapter 7. Denim Threads uses an eight-column work sheet. An eight-column work sheet is used because some accounts must be brought up to date before the profit or loss is figured. Two additional columns headed Adjustments Debit and Credit provide the space to plan how to bring accounts up to date. The completed eight-column work sheet used by Denim Threads is on page 272.

RECORDING A TRIAL BALANCE ON A WORK SHEET

At the end of a fiscal period, accuracy of posting is proved as described in Chapter 13. A trial balance is then entered in the Trial Balance columns of a work sheet. General ledger accounts are listed in the same order in which they appear in a general ledger. All accounts are listed regardless of whether there is a balance or not. Listing all accounts reduces the possibility of overlooking an account needing to be brought up to date.

Denim Threads' trial balance on November 30, 1982, is on the partial work sheet below. The following accounts do not show a balance in the Trial Balance columns: Income Summary, Insurance Expense, and Supplies Expense.

Denim Threads
Work Sheet
For Month Ended November 30, 1982

	ACCOUNT TITLE	TRIAL BALANCE 1 DEBIT	TRIAL BALANCE 2 CREDIT
1	Cash	1154420	
2	Accounts Receivable	57200	
3	Merchandise Inventory	6800000	
4	Supplies	50100	
5	Prepaid Insurance	43000	
6	Accounts Payable		265000
7	Sales Tax Payable		88900
8	Eva Burgos, Capital		3575960
9	Eva Burgos, Drawing	60000	
10	Luis Perez, Capital		3575960
11	Luis Perez, Drawing	64500	
12	Income Summary		
13	Sales		1330500
14	Purchases	395200	
15	Credit Card Fee Expense	13500	
16	Insurance Expense		
17	Miscellaneous Expense	8400	
18	Rent Expense	80000	
19	Salary Expense	110000	
20	Supplies Expense		
21		8831320	8831320
22			
23			
24			
25			
26			
27			

Recording a trial balance on a work sheet

GENERAL LEDGER ACCOUNTS NEEDING TO BE BROUGHT UP TO DATE

Some general ledger accounts do not show a true, up-to-date balance at the end of a fiscal period. These general ledger accounts do not have an up-to-date balance though all transactions have been journalized and posted. For example, Denim Threads debits the asset account Supplies each time supplies are bought. To credit Supplies each time an item of supplies is used however would not be practical. The balance of the supplies account therefore needs to be brought up to date at the end of a fiscal period.

Changes recorded to update ledger account balances at the end of a fiscal period are called adjustments. Denim Threads' general ledger accounts needing adjustments are Merchandise Inventory, Supplies, and Prepaid Insurance.

Adjustments for the general ledger accounts are first planned in the Adjustments columns of a work sheet. Every adjustment has a debit and a credit. Therefore, at least two accounts must be used in each adjustment. An adjustment transfers part or all of the balance of one account to another account. This transfer is planned by writing the debit part in the Adjustments Debit column. The credit part is entered in the Adjustments Credit column.

Adjustments recorded on a work sheet are for planning purposes only. All changes in general ledger accounts result only from posting journal entries. Journal entries made to bring general ledger accounts up to date are called adjusting entries. The accuracy of the adjusting entries can be checked on a work sheet before they are actually recorded in a journal.

Recording adjusting entries in a combination journal is described in Chapter 16.

ADJUSTMENTS FOR MERCHANDISE INVENTORY

An itemized list showing the value of goods on hand is called an inventory. An itemized list showing the value of goods on hand for sale to customers is called merchandise inventory. The general ledger account in which merchandise inventory is recorded is Merchandise Inventory.

Procedures for taking an inventory are described in Chapter 30.

Adjusting a merchandise inventory account affects two financial statements. The correct value of merchandise inventory will be shown on a balance sheet. The cost of merchandise sold will be shown on an income statement. Denim Threads prepares financial statements at the end of each month. The merchandise inventory account therefore is adjusted at the end of each month.

Some businesses prepare financial statements only at the end of a year. For these businesses an inventory adjustment is needed only at the end of a year.

Need for adjusting a merchandise inventory account

Denim Threads' merchandise inventory account on November 1, 1982, has a debit balance of $68,000.00. The balance of the merchandise inventory account on the November 30, 1982, trial balance is the same amount, *$68,000.00*. The account has the same beginning and ending balance because no entries have been made during the fiscal period. The changes in inventory resulting from purchases and sales transactions have not been recorded.

Merchandise Inventory	
Nov. 1 Bal. 68,000.00	

Each purchase transaction increases the amount of merchandise on hand. All purchases however are recorded in the purchases account. Each sale transaction decreases the amount of merchandise on hand. However, all sales are recorded in the sales account. This procedure makes it easier to determine quickly the total purchases and sales during a fiscal period. The merchandise inventory account balance is adjusted to reflect the changes resulting from purchases and sales during a fiscal period.

Merchandise inventory and cost of merchandise sold

The total original purchase price of all merchandise sold during a fiscal period is called the cost of merchandise sold. *(CONCEPT: Historical Cost)* Cost of merchandise sold is sometimes known as cost of goods sold or cost of sales. Cost of merchandise sold is figured as shown below.

	Beginning Merchandise Inventory
Plus	Purchases
Equals	Total Merchandise Available for Sale
Minus	Ending Merchandise Inventory
Equals	Cost of Merchandise Sold

The cost of merchandise sold makes up a large part of the total costs of operating most merchandising businesses.

Analyzing an adjustment for a beginning merchandise inventory. The two accounts used to adjust the beginning merchandise inventory are Merchandise Inventory and Income Summary. The T accounts at the left and on page 265 show the merchandise inventory account and the income summary account. The accounts are shown before and after the adjustment for a beginning merchandise inventory is made.

BEFORE ADJUSTMENT

Merchandise Inventory	
Nov. 1 Bal. 68,000.00	

Income Summary	

The beginning merchandise inventory, as shown in the merchandise inventory account, is *$68,000.00*. The mer-

AFTER ADJUSTMENT

Merchandise Inventory	
Nov. 1 Bal. 68,000.00	Nov. 30 (a) 68,000.00

Income Summary	
Nov. 30 (a) 68,000.00	

chandise inventory account however is not up to date. The actual count of merchandise on November 30 shows that the inventory is valued at *$64,000.00*.

The first step in updating the inventory account is to transfer the beginning inventory to the income summary account. The beginning merchandise inventory, *$68,000.00*, is credited to Merchandise Inventory and debited to Income Summary.

After the beginning merchandise inventory adjustment is journalized and posted, Merchandise Inventory has a zero balance. The value of the beginning inventory appears as a debit in the income summary account.

Recording a beginning merchandise inventory adjustment on a work sheet. The adjustment for the beginning merchandise inventory is shown in the Adjustments columns of the partial work sheet below.

Denim Threads
Work Sheet
For Month Ended November 30, 1982

	ACCOUNT TITLE	TRIAL BALANCE DEBIT (1)	TRIAL BALANCE CREDIT (2)	ADJUSTMENTS DEBIT (3)	ADJUSTMENTS CREDIT (4)
1	Cash	11544 20			
2	Accounts Receivable	572 00			
3	Merchandise Inventory	68000 00			(a) 68000 00
12	Income Summary			(a) 68000 00	
13					

Recording an adjustment for a beginning merchandise inventory on a work sheet

Steps in recording Denim Threads' adjustment for beginning merchandise inventory on a work sheet are given below.

1 Write the amount, *$68,000.00*, in the Adjustments Debit column on the line with the account title Income Summary. (Line 12)

2 Write the amount, *$68,000.00*, in the Adjustments Credit column on the line with the account title Merchandise Inventory. (Line 3)

3 Write the small letter "a" in parentheses, *(a)*, before the amounts in the Adjustments columns.

> A small letter is assigned according to the order in which adjustments are entered on a work sheet. This labeling helps locate the two parts of an adjustment when the adjusting entries are journalized.

Analyzing an adjustment for an ending merchandise inventory. The T accounts on the next page show the merchandise inventory and income

BEFORE ADJUSTMENT

Merchandise Inventory	
Nov. 1 Bal. 68,000.00	Nov. 30 (a) 68,000.00

Income Summary	
Nov. 30 (a) 68,000.00	

AFTER ADJUSTMENT

Merchandise Inventory	
Nov. 1 Bal. 68,000.00	Nov. 30 (a) 68,000.00
Nov. 30 (b) 64,000.00	

Income Summary	
Nov. 30 (a) 68,000.00	Nov. 30 (b) 64,000.00

summary accounts. The accounts are shown before and after the adjustment for an ending merchandise inventory is made.

The merchandise inventory account is debited for *$64,000.00*, the value of the ending inventory. The same amount, *$64,000.00*, is credited to the income summary account.

The merchandise inventory account is brought up to date. The balance of the merchandise inventory account after the adjustment is the value of the ending inventory, *$64,000.00*.

Recording an ending merchandise inventory adjustment on a work sheet. The adjustment for the ending merchandise inventory is shown in the Adjustments columns of the partial work sheet below.

Denim Threads
Work Sheet
For Month Ended November 30, 1982

	Account Title	Trial Balance Debit (1)	Trial Balance Credit (2)	Adjustments Debit (3)	Adjustments Credit (4)
1	Cash	11 544 20			
2	Accounts Receivable	572 00			
3	Merchandise Inventory	68 000 00		(b) 64 000 00	(a) 68 000 00
12	Income Summary			(a) 68 000 00	(b) 64 000 00
13					

Recording an adjustment for an ending merchandise inventory on a work sheet

Steps in recording Denim Threads' adjustment for ending merchandise inventory on a work sheet are given below.

1. Write the amount, *$64,000.00*, in the Adjustments Debit column on the line with the account title Merchandise Inventory. (Line 3)
2. Write the amount, *$64,000.00*, in the Adjustments Credit column on the line with the account title Income Summary. (Line 12)
3. Write the small letter "b" in parentheses, *(b)*, before the amounts in the Adjustments columns.

ADJUSTMENTS FOR PREPAID EXPENSES

Amounts paid in advance for supplies to be used later and for services to be received are called prepaid expenses. For example, supplies are recorded in an asset account when bought. However, a portion of the supplies becomes an expense when used. Recording the expense each time supplies are used is not practical.

Need for adjusting a supplies account

The balance of a supplies account may be partly an asset and an expense. All expenses must be recorded for the fiscal period in which they occur. *(CONCEPT: Matching Expenses with Revenue)* Therefore, an adjustment is made at the end of the fiscal period to update the supplies account.

Analyzing an adjustment for supplies. The asset account Supplies needs to be brought up to date at the end of a fiscal period. The supplies account balance will then be the same as the ending inventory of supplies on hand at that time.

The T account at the right shows Denim Threads' supplies account on November 30, 1982. Denim Threads had a beginning supplies balance of $160.00. Supplies valued at $341.00 were bought during the month. Supplies has a debit balance of $501.00 at the end of the fiscal period.

Supplies	
Nov. 1 Bal. 160.00	
10 142.00	
15 86.00	
17 80.00	
29 33.00	
501.00	

Supplies used during the fiscal period are an expense of a business. The two accounts used in the adjustment for supplies are Supplies and Supplies Expense.

Denim Threads' supplies and supplies expense accounts are shown in T accounts at the right. Accounts are shown before and after the adjustment for supplies.

Four questions are asked in analyzing the adjustment for supplies.

1. What is the balance of the supplies account?........ $501.00
2. What should the balance be for this account?....... $241.00
3. What must be done to correct the account balance? ....Subtract $260.00
4. What adjusting entry is made?
   ....Debit Supplies Expense $260.00
   Credit Supplies $260.00

BEFORE ADJUSTMENT

Supplies	
Nov. 1 Bal. 160.00	
10 142.00	
15 86.00	
17 80.00	
29 33.00	
501.00	

Supplies Expense	

AFTER ADJUSTMENT

Supplies	
Nov. 1 Bal. 160.00	Nov. 30 (c) 260.00
10 142.00	
15 86.00	
17 80.00	
29 33.00	
501.00	

Supplies Expense	
Nov. 30 (c) 260.00	

The cost of supplies used is recorded as a credit to Supplies to show a decrease in this asset account. The total of the debit side, *$501.00*, less the credit side, *$260.00*, equals the ending inventory of supplies, *$241.00*.

The balance of the supplies expense account, *$260.00*, is the cost of supplies used during the fiscal period. The supplies account balance, *$241.00*, is the value of supplies on hand at the end of the fiscal period.

Recording a supplies adjustment on a work sheet. The supplies adjustment is shown in the Adjustments columns of the partial work sheet below.

Denim Threads
Work Sheet
For Month Ended November 30, 1982

	ACCOUNT TITLE	TRIAL BALANCE DEBIT (1)	TRIAL BALANCE CREDIT (2)	ADJUSTMENTS DEBIT (3)	ADJUSTMENTS CREDIT (4)
1	Cash	11 544 20			
2	Accounts Receivable	572 00			
3	Merchandise Inventory	68 000 00		(b) 64 000 00	(a) 68 000 00
4	Supplies	501 00			(c) 260 00
12	Income Summary			(a) 68 000 00	(b) 64 000 00
20	Supplies Expense			(c) 260 00	

Recording an adjustment for supplies on a work sheet

Steps in recording Denim Threads' adjustment for supplies on a work sheet are given below.

1 Write the amount, *$260.00*, in the Adjustments Debit column on the line with the account title Supplies Expense. (Line 20)

2 Write the amount, *$260.00*, in the Adjustments Credit column on the line with the account title Supplies. (Line 4)

3 Label the two parts of this adjustment with the small letter "c" in parentheses, *(c)*.

Need for adjusting a prepaid insurance account

Insurance premiums paid in advance are a prepaid expense. The portion of the prepaid insurance premiums not used up during the fiscal period is an asset. The portion of the insurance premiums that has been used up (expired) during the fiscal period is an expense.

Analyzing an adjustment for prepaid insurance. Denim Threads' prepaid insurance account has a debit balance of $430.00 on November 1, 1982. For every day that passed since that date, the business is entitled to insurance coverage for one less day. Thus, the value of this asset is being reduced constantly. Keeping this account up to date by making daily entries to record the value of insurance used is not practical. Instead, the prepaid insurance account is brought up to date at the end of a fiscal period.

Prepaid Insurance	
Nov. 1 Bal. 430.00	

The two accounts used in an adjustment for prepaid insurance are Prepaid Insurance and Insurance Expense.

Denim Threads' prepaid insurance and insurance expense accounts are shown in T accounts at the right. The accounts are shown before and after the adjustment for prepaid insurance.

Before the adjustment, the prepaid insurance account has a debit balance of *$430.00*. A review of the insurance policies showed that as of November 30, *$75.00* of the prepaid insurance had expired. Thus, the value of the prepaid insurance at the end of the fiscal period is *$355.00*. The prepaid insurance account therefore must be adjusted to show its true value. At the same time, the insurance expense must be recorded for the fiscal period.

Four questions are asked in analyzing the adjustment for prepaid insurance.

BEFORE ADJUSTMENT

Prepaid Insurance	
Nov. 1 Bal. 430.00	

Insurance Expense	

AFTER ADJUSTMENT

Prepaid Insurance	
Nov. 1 Bal. 430.00	Nov. 30 (d) 75.00

Insurance Expense	
Nov. 30 (d) 75.00	

1. What is the balance of the prepaid insurance account? $430.00
2. What should the balance be for this account? $355.00
3. What must be done to correct the account balance? ....Subtract $ 75.00
4. What adjusting entry is made? ....Debit Insurance Expense $ 75.00
   Credit Prepaid Insurance $ 75.00

The prepaid insurance account balance, *$355.00*, is the value of Prepaid Insurance at the end of the fiscal period. The insurance expense account balance, *$75.00*, is the value of the insurance premiums expired during the fiscal period.

Recording a prepaid insurance adjustment on a work sheet. Denim Threads' prepaid insurance adjustment is shown in the Adjustments columns of the partial work sheet below.

Denim Threads
Work Sheet
For Month Ended November 30, 1982

	ACCOUNT TITLE	1 TRIAL BALANCE DEBIT	2 TRIAL BALANCE CREDIT	3 ADJUSTMENTS DEBIT	4 ADJUSTMENTS CREDIT
1	Cash	11544 20			
2	Accounts Receivable	572 00			
3	Merchandise Inventory	68000 00		(b) 64000 00	(a) 68000 00
4	Supplies	501 00			(c) 260 00
5	Prepaid Insurance	430 00			(d) 75 00 ← 2
12	Income Summary			(a) 68000 00	(b) 64000 00
16	Insurance Expense			(d) 75 00 ← 1	
20	Supplies Expense			(c) 260 00	
21					

(Callout 3 points from the credit entry on line 5 to the debit entry on line 16.)

Recording an adjustment for prepaid insurance on a work sheet

Steps in recording Denim Threads' adjustment for prepaid insurance on a work sheet are given below.

1 Write the amount, *$75.00*, in the Adjustments Debit column on the line with the account title Insurance Expense. (Line 16)

2 Write the amount, *$75.00*, in the Adjustments Credit column on the line with the account title Prepaid Insurance. (Line 5)

3 Label the two parts of this adjustment with the small letter "d" in parentheses, *(d)*.

PROVING THE EQUALITY OF DEBITS AND CREDITS IN THE ADJUSTMENTS COLUMNS OF A WORK SHEET

After all adjustments have been recorded on a work sheet, a single line is ruled across the Adjustments columns. The two columns are totaled. Columns are totaled to prove the equality of debits and credits. The first four columns of Denim Threads' work sheet below are totaled, proved, and ruled.

Denim Threads
Work Sheet
For Month Ended November 30, 1982

	ACCOUNT TITLE	TRIAL BALANCE (1) DEBIT	TRIAL BALANCE (2) CREDIT	ADJUSTMENTS (3) DEBIT	ADJUSTMENTS (4) CREDIT
1	Cash	11544 20			
2	Accounts Receivable	572 00			
3	Merchandise Inventory	68000 00		(b) 64000 00	(a) 68000 00
4	Supplies	501 00			(c) 260 00
5	Prepaid Insurance	430 00			(d) 75 00
6	Accounts Payable		2650 00		
7	Sales Tax Payable		889 00		
8	Eva Burgos, Capital		35759 60		
9	Eva Burgos, Drawing	600 00			
10	Luis Perez, Capital		35759 60		
11	Luis Perez, Drawing	645 00			
12	Income Summary			(a) 68000 00	(b) 64000 00
13	Sales		13305 00		
14	Purchases	3952 00			
15	Credit Card Fee Expense	135 00			
16	Insurance Expense			(d) 75 00	
17	Miscellaneous Expense	84 00			
18	Rent Expense	800 00			
19	Salary Expense	1100 00			
20	Supplies Expense			(c) 260 00	
21		88363 20	88363 20	132335 00	132335 00

Adjustments columns on a work sheet totaled and ruled

The total of the Adjustments Debit column, *$132,335.00*, is the same as the total of the Adjustments Credit column, *$132,335.00*. Debits and Credits in the Adjustments columns are proved because the column totals are the same. Double lines are ruled across the Adjustments columns.

COMPLETING AN EIGHT-COLUMN WORK SHEET

Denim Threads' eight-column work sheet, page 272, is completed as described below.

1 Extend the balance sheet items to the Balance Sheet columns.

- Extend balance sheet items *not* affected by adjustments. Extend balances from Trial Balance columns (Columns 1 or 2) to appropriate Balance Sheet columns (Columns 7 or 8).
- Extend balance sheet items affected by adjustments. Extend *adjusted* balances to appropriate Balance Sheet columns.

Adjusted balance sheet items on Denim Threads' work sheet are given below.

Line 3, Merchandise Inventory.

Trial Balance Debit column	$ 68,000.00
Plus Adjustments Debit column	64,000.00
	$132,000.00
Less Adjustments Credit column	68,000.00
Balance Sheet Debit column	$ 64,000.00

Line 4, Supplies.

Trial Balance Debit column	$501.00
Less Adjustments Credit column	260.00
Balance Sheet Debit column	$241.00

Line 5, Prepaid Insurance.

Trial Balance Debit column	$430.00
Less Adjustments Credit column	75.00
Balance Sheet Debit column	$355.00

2 Extend the revenue, cost, and expense items to the Income Statement columns.

- Extend income statement items *not* affected by adjustments. Extend balances from Trial Balance columns (Columns 1 or 2) to appropriate Income Statement columns (Columns 5 or 6).

Denim Threads
Work Sheet
For Month Ended November 30, 1982

	Account Title	Trial Balance Debit (1)	Trial Balance Credit (2)	Adjustments Debit (3)	Adjustments Credit (4)	Income Statement Debit (5)	Income Statement Credit (6)	Balance Sheet Debit (7)	Balance Sheet Credit (8)	
1	Cash	11544 20						11544 20		1
2	Accounts Receivable	572 00						572 00		2
3	Merchandise Inventory	68000 00		(b) 64000 00	(a) 68000 00			64000 00		3
4	Supplies	501 00			(c) 260 00			241 00		4
5	Prepaid Insurance	430 00			(d) 75 00			355 00		5
6	Accounts Payable		2650 00						2650 00	6
7	Sales Tax Payable		889 00						889 00	7
8	Eva Burgos, Capital		35759 60						35759 60	8
9	Eva Burgos, Drawing	600 00						600 00		9
10	Luis Perez, Capital		35759 60						35759 60	10
11	Luis Perez, Drawing	645 00						645 00		11
12	Income Summary			(a) 68000 00	(b) 64000 00	68000 00	64000 00			12
13	Sales		13305 00				13305 00			13
14	Purchases	3952 00				3952 00				14
15	Credit Card Fee Expense	135 00				135 00				15
16	Insurance Expense			(d) 75 00		75 00				16
17	Miscellaneous Expense	84 00				84 00				17
18	Rent Expense	800 00				800 00				18
19	Salary Expense	1100 00				1100 00				19
20	Supplies Expense			(c) 260 00		260 00				20
21		88363 20	88363 20	132335 00	132335 00	74406 00	77305 00	77957 20	75058 20	21
22	Net Income					2899 00			2899 00	22
23						77305 00	77305 00	77957 20	77957 20	23
24										24
25										25

Completed eight-column work sheet

- Extend income statement items *affected* by adjustments. Extend *adjusted* balances to appropriate Income Statement columns.

  Extension of Income Summary is an exception to this procedure. Income Summary, line 12, has no balance in the Trial Balance columns. The Adjustments Debit column amount, *$68,000.00*, the beginning inventory, is extended to the Income Statement Debit column. The Adjustments Credit column amount, *$64,000.00*, the ending inventory, is extended to the Income Statement Credit column. Both these amounts are extended because they will be used in preparing the income statement.

  Adjusted income statement items on Denim Threads' work sheet are given below.

  Line 16, Insurance Expense.

Trial Balance Debit column	–0–
Plus Adjustments Debit column	$ 75.00
Income Statement Debit column	$ 75.00

  Line 20, Supplies Expense.

Trial Balance Debit column	–0–
Plus Adjustments Debit column	$260.00
Income Statement Debit column	$260.00

3 Figure the net income on the work sheet.

- Rule a single line across the Income Statement columns and the Balance Sheet columns to indicate addition.
- Add each column and write the totals on the same line as the Trial Balance totals. (Line 21)
- Subtract the smaller total from the larger total in the Income Statement columns.

Total of Income Statement Credit column	$77,305.00
Less Total of Income Statement Debit column	74,406.00
Equals Net Income	$ 2,899.00

4 Balance the Income Statement columns.

- Write the amount of the net income, *$2,899.00*, immediately below the smaller total in the Income Statement columns. (Line 22)
- Write the words *Net Income* in the Account Title column on the same line as the amount of the net income.

- Total the Income Statement columns. (Line 23)

5 Balance the Balance Sheet columns.

- Extend the net income, *$2,899.00*, to the Balance Sheet Credit column on the same line with the words *Net Income*.
- Total the Balance Sheet columns. (Line 23) Figures on the work sheet are considered to be correct since the Balance Sheet Debit and Credit columns are equal.

6 Rule double lines below the proving totals of the Income Statement and Balance Sheet columns.

FIGURING A NET LOSS ON A WORK SHEET

When the Income Statement Debit column total exceeds the Credit column total, there is a net loss. An example of a net loss is shown on the partial work sheet below.

	ACCOUNT TITLE	5 INCOME STATEMENT DEBIT	6 INCOME STATEMENT CREDIT	7 BALANCE SHEET DEBIT	8 BALANCE SHEET CREDIT	
19		82540 00	81320 00	86140 00	87360 00	19
20	Net Loss		1220 00	1220 00		20
21		82540 00	82540 00	87360 00	87360 00	21
22						22
23						23
24						24
25						25
26						26
27						27
28						28

Showing a net loss on a work sheet

The total of the Income Statement Debit column is larger than the total of the Income Statement Credit column. (Line 19) The costs and expenses are greater than the revenues. Therefore, the net loss amount, *$1,220.00*, is written in the Income Statement Credit column. (Line 20) The net loss amount, *$1,220.00*, is then extended to the Balance Sheet Debit column. The words *Net Loss* are written on the same line.

CENTURY 21 TRANS-VISION® PRESENTATION OF AN EIGHT-COLUMN WORK SHEET

The following Century 21 Trans-Vision® insert provides a visual review of an eight-column work sheet. Follow the directions below in using the insert.

1. Before beginning your study, be sure the pages and transparent overlays are arranged correctly. The correct arrangement is shown below.

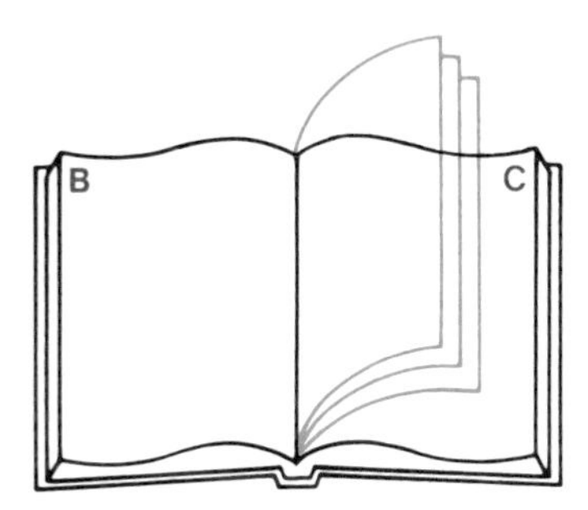

2. Place your book in a horizontal position. Study the steps on page C in preparing the eight-column work sheet. You will be able to read the text through the transparent overlays. When directed, carefully lift the transparent overlays and apply them over the work sheet as shown below.

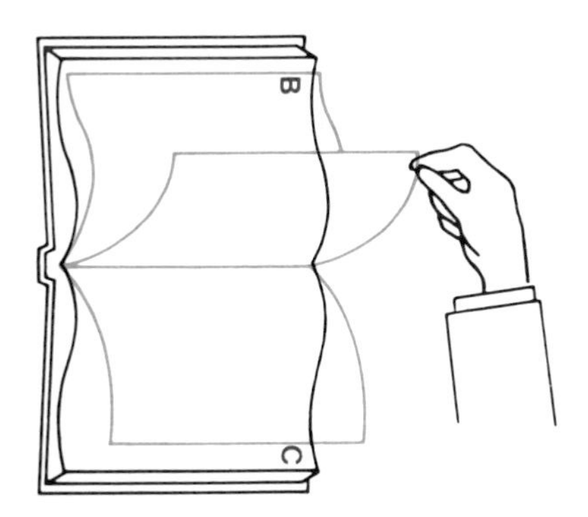

PREPARING AN EIGHT-COLUMN WORK SHEET

To correctly use the Century 21 Trans-Vision® insert, read the steps below. Apply the transparent overlays when directed to do so in the steps.

B

1

Denim Threads
Work Sheet
For Month Ended November 30, 1982

2

	ACCOUNT TITLE	TRIAL BALANCE DEBIT (1)	TRIAL BALANCE CREDIT (2)	ADJUSTMENTS DEBIT (3)	ADJUSTMENTS CREDIT (4)	INCOME STATEMENT DEBIT (5)	INCOME STATEMENT CREDIT (6)	BALANCE SHEET DEBIT (7)	BALANCE SHEET CREDIT (8)
1	Cash	1154420							
2	Accounts Receivable	57200							
3	Merchandise Inventory	6800000			(a) 6800000				
4	Supplies	50100							
5	Prepaid Insurance	43000							
6	Accounts Payable		265000						
7	Sales Tax Payable		88900						
8	Eva Burgos, Capital		3575960						
9	Eva Burgos, Drawing	60000							
10	Luis Perez, Capital		3575960						
11	Luis Perez, Drawing	64500							
12	Income Summary			(a) 6800000					
13	Sales		1330500						
14	Purchases	395200							
15	Credit Card Fee Expense	13500							
16	Insurance Expense								
17	Miscellaneous Expense	8400							
18	Rent Expense	80000							
19	Salary Expense	110000							
20	Supplies Expense								
21		8836320	8836320						
22									
23									
24									
25									

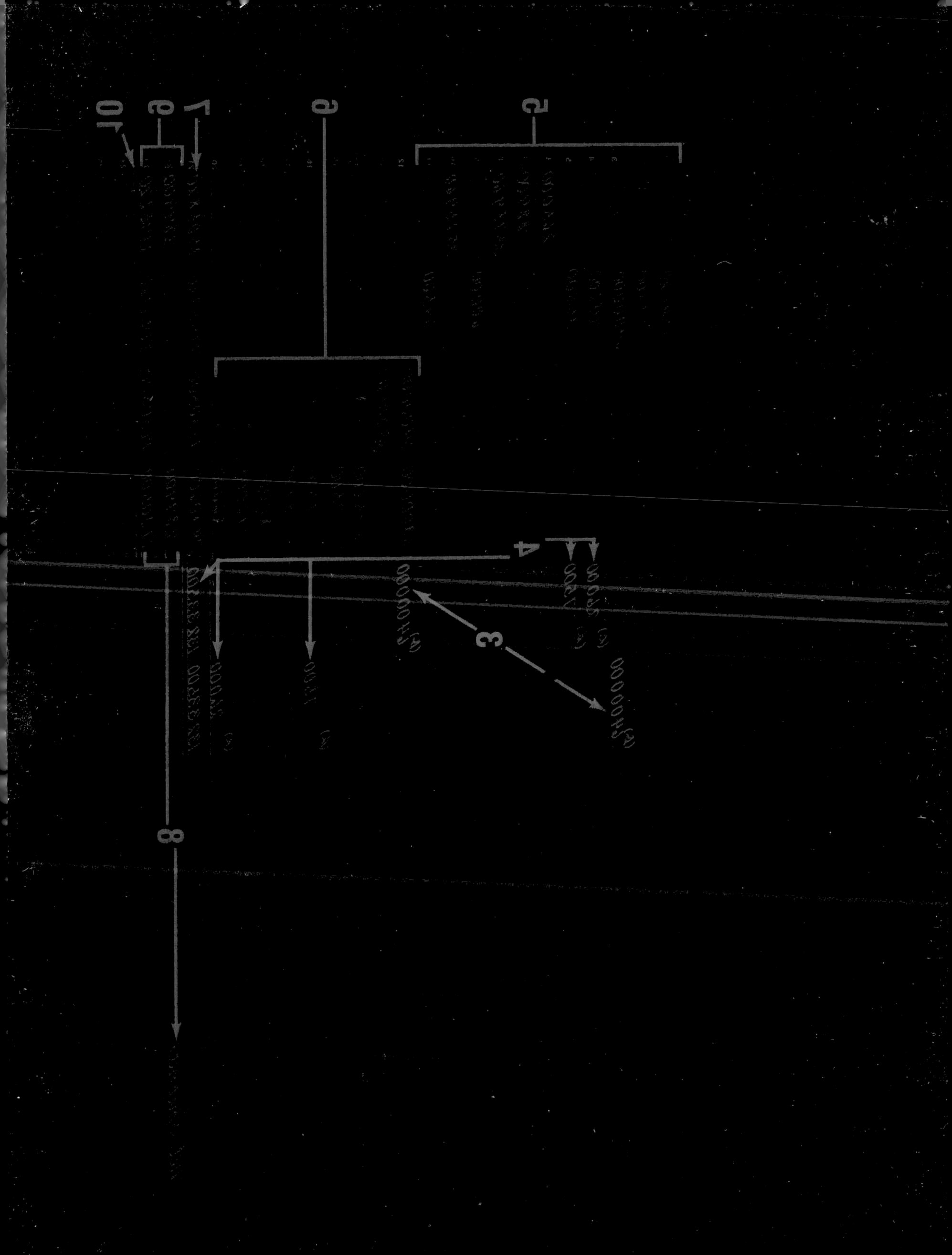

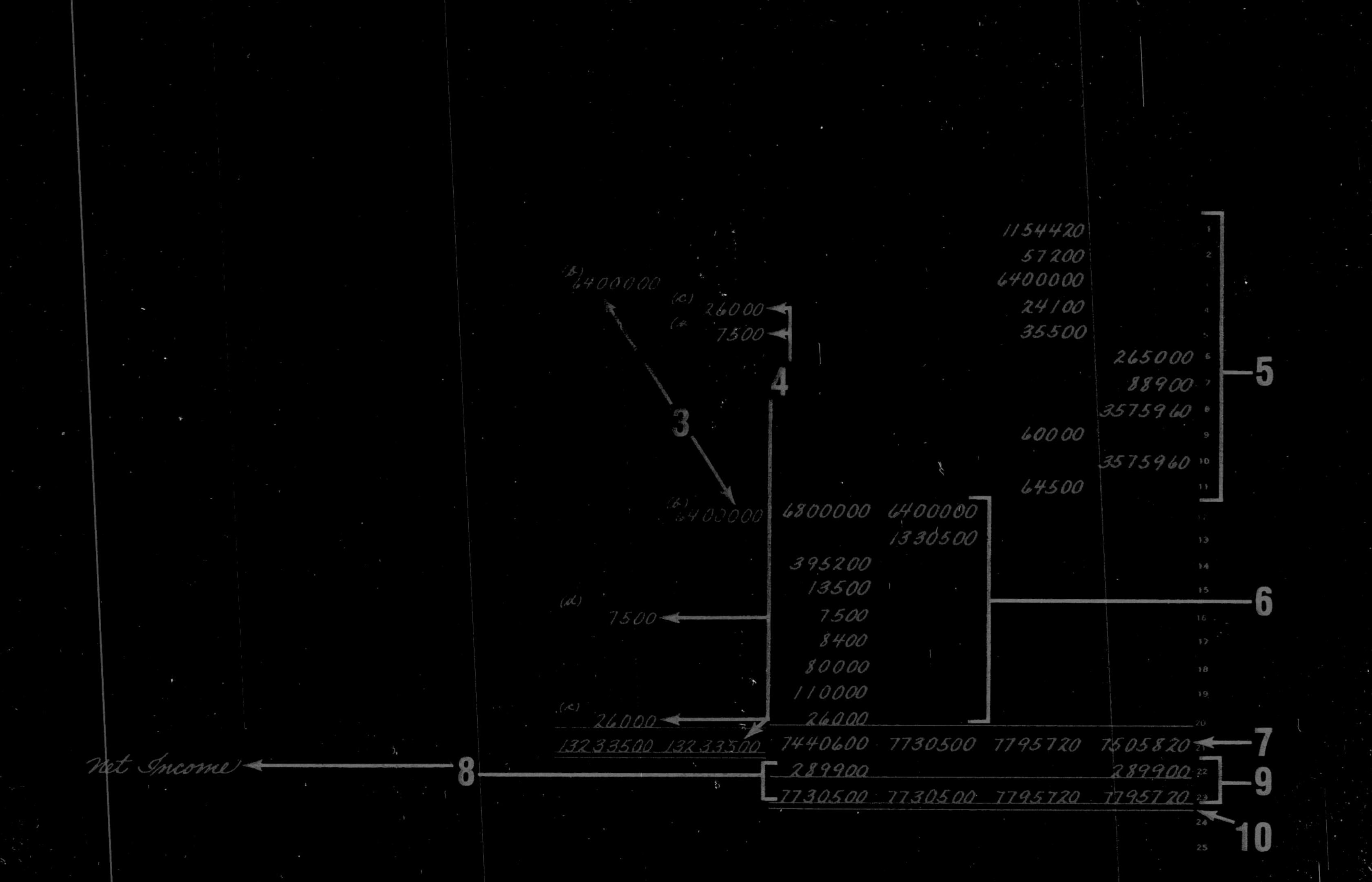

Net Income
3
4
5
6
7
8
9
10

STEPS IN PREPARING AN EIGHT-COLUMN WORK SHEET

1 Write the heading and record the trial balance.

2 Record the beginning merchandise inventory in the Adjustments columns — adjustment (a).
- Write the amount in the Adjustments Debit column on the line with the account title Income Summary.
- Write the amount in the Adjustments Credit column on the line with the account title Merchandise Inventory. *Carefully apply the first overlay.*

3 Record the ending merchandise inventory in the Adjustments columns — adjustment (b).
- Write the amount in the Adjustments Debit column on the line with the account title Merchandise Inventory.
- Write the amount in the Adjustments Credit column on the line with the account title Income Summary. *Carefully apply the second overlay.*

4 Record the remaining adjustments in the Adjustments columns — adjustments (c) and (d).
- Write the amount of the supplies adjustment debiting Supplies Expense and crediting Supplies.
- Write the amount of the insurance adjustment debiting Insurance Expense and crediting Prepaid Insurance.
- Rule a single line across both Adjustments columns under the last amount listed.
- Add each Adjustments column and compare the totals.
- Rule double lines below the proving totals of the Adjustments columns. *Carefully apply the third overlay.*

5 Extend all of the balance sheet items after adjustments into the Balance Sheet columns.
- Extend the amount of each asset after adjustments into the Balance Sheet Debit column (Column 7).
- Extend the amount of each liability, capital, and drawing account into the appropriate Balance Sheet column (Column 7 or 8).

6 Extend all of the income statement items after adjustments into the Income Statement columns.
- Extend both adjustments to Income Summary for merchandise inventory to the respective Income Statement columns (Columns 5 and 6).
- Extend the amount of revenue into the Income Statement Credit column (Column 6).
- Extend the amount of purchases and each expense after adjustments into the Income Statement Debit column (Column 5).

7 Total the Income Statement columns and the Balance Sheet columns.
- Rule a single line across the Income Statement columns and the Balance Sheet columns.
- Add each column and write the totals on the same line as the Trial Balance totals.

8 Figure and record the net income (or the net loss).
- Subtract the smaller total in the Income Statement columns from the larger total.
- Write the amount of the net income (or the net loss) immediately below the smaller of the two totals.
- Write the words *Net Income* (or *Net Loss*) in the Account Title column.
- Rule a single line across the Income Statement columns. Add and write the proving totals on the next line.

9 Extend the net income (or the net loss) to the Balance Sheet columns.
- Extend the net income into the Balance Sheet Credit column (or net loss into the Balance Sheet Debit column).
- Rule a single line across the Balance Sheet columns. Add and write the proving totals on the next line.

10 Rule double lines below the proving totals of the Income Statement columns and the Balance Sheet columns.

ACCOUNTING TERMS

What is the meaning of each of the following?

1. adjustments
2. adjusting entries
3. inventory
4. merchandise inventory
5. cost of merchandise sold
6. prepaid expenses

QUESTIONS FOR INDIVIDUAL STUDY

1. Why does the owner of a business need to know the amount of profit or loss made by the business?
2. How often does Denim Threads prepare a work sheet?
3. Why does Denim Threads use an eight-column work sheet?
4. What are the headings for the columns used to provide the space necessary for planning the adjustments?
5. Why are all general ledger accounts listed on the Trial Balance columns of a work sheet?
6. Which Denim Threads' general ledger accounts need to be adjusted?
7. Why are the adjustments planned on a work sheet before they are recorded in a journal?
8. What two financial statements are affected by the merchandise inventory adjustment?
9. What are the two accounts used to adjust the beginning merchandise inventory? How are the accounts adjusted?
10. What are the two accounts used to adjust the ending merchandise inventory? How are the accounts adjusted?
11. Why are the two parts of an adjustment labeled on a work sheet?
12. Why is the supplies account adjusted at the end of a fiscal period?
13. What are the two accounts used in the adjustment for supplies?
14. Why is it necessary to adjust the prepaid insurance account at the end of a fiscal period?
15. What are the two accounts used in the adjustment for prepaid insurance?
16. Why are the Adjustments columns on a work sheet totaled?

CASES FOR MANAGEMENT DECISION

CASE 1 Mary Dextor prepared her business' work sheet at the end of the fiscal period. The proper adjustment for the beginning merchandise inventory was made. However, Ms. Dextor forgot to make the adjustment for the ending inventory. What effect will this omission have on the net income shown on the work sheet?

CASE 2 After completing a work sheet, Marsha Delfield finds an error was made in preparing the supplies inventory. Three large boxes of typewriter ribbons were counted twice. The value of the supplies counted twice was $100.00. How does this error effect the amount of net income as figured on the work sheet for the fiscal period?

CASE 3 Crandon Company paid $648.00 for a one-year fire insurance policy. The company prepares income statements and balance sheets every three months. However, the accountant prepares an adjusting entry only at the end of the year. Mr. Crandon, the owner, thinks the prepaid insurance should be adjusted every three months. Who is correct? Why?

DRILLS FOR UNDERSTANDING

DRILL 14-D 1 Adjusting the merchandise inventory, supplies, and prepaid insurance accounts

The chart below contains adjustment information related to the preparation of work sheets for three businesses.

Business	Trial Balance Debit Column		End-of-Period Information	
A	Merchandise Inventory...	$48,500.00	Inventory on hand...........	$45,000.00
	Supplies..........................	520.00	Supplies on hand............	380.00
	Prepaid Insurance...........	560.00	Insurance remaining.......	480.00
B	Merchandise Inventory...	$52,600.00	Inventory on hand...........	$54,200.00
	Supplies..........................	450.00	Supplies on hand............	380.00
	Prepaid Insurance...........	720.00	Insurance remaining.......	610.00
C	Merchandise Inventory...	$62,000.00	Inventory on hand...........	$59,000.00
	Supplies..........................	640.00	Supplies on hand............	520.00
	Prepaid Insurance...........	180.00	Insurance remaining.......	None

Use a form similar to the one below.

1	2	3	4	5
Business	Adjustment Number	Accounts Affected	Adjustment Column	
			Debit	Credit
A	1.	*Income Summary*	*$48,500.00*	
		Merchandise Inventory		*$48,500.00*

Instructions: For each business list the accounts affected and the amounts for each adjustment given below. List the names of the accounts in Column 3 and the amounts in either Column 4 or 5. Adjustment Number 1 for Business A is given as an example.

1. Adjustment for beginning merchandise inventory.
2. Adjustment for ending merchandise inventory.
3. Adjustment for supplies.
4. Adjustment for prepaid insurance.

DRILL 14-D 2 Extending balance sheet and income statement items

Jacobs and Nelson Company's partial work sheet showing the completed Trial Balance and Adjustments columns is on the next page.

Instructions: **1.** Extend the balance sheet items to the Balance Sheet columns of the work sheet.

2. Extend the income statement items to the Income Statement columns of the work sheet.

Jacobs and Nelson Company
Work Sheet
For Month Ended November 30, 19--

		1	2	3	4
	Account Title	Trial Balance		Adjustments	
		Debit	Credit	Debit	Credit
1	Cash	9 640 00			
2	Accounts Receivable	820 00			
3	Merchandise Inventory	82 000 00		(b) 80 000 00	(a) 82 000 00
4	Supplies	610 00			(c) 180 00
5	Prepaid Insurance	980 00			(d) 85 00
6	Accounts Payable		3 120 00		
7	Sales Tax Payable		720 00		
8	J. B. Jacobs, Capital		41 690 00		
9	J. B. Jacobs, Drawing	500 00			
10	S. K. Nelson, Capital		41 690 00		
11	S. K. Nelson, Drawing	500 00			
12	Income Summary			(a) 82 000 00	(b) 80 000 00
13	Sales		14 200 00		
14	Purchases	4 100 00			
15	Credit Card Fee Expense	160 00			
16	Insurance Expense			(d) 85 00	
17	Miscellaneous Expense	110 00			
18	Rent Expense	700 00			
19	Salary Expense	1 300 00			
20	Supplies Expense			(c) 180 00	
21		101 420 00	101 420 00	162 265 00	162 265 00

3. Complete the work sheet.
   a. Add the Income Statement columns and the Balance Sheet columns.
   b. Figure and record the net income or net loss.
   c. Total and rule the Income Statement and Balance Sheet columns.

APPLICATION PROBLEMS

PROBLEM 14-1 Preparing a work sheet

The accounts and their balances in Downtown Sporting Goods' general ledger appear on page 277. Ending inventories and the value of insurance policies are also given.

Instructions: 1. Prepare a trial balance on a work sheet for the monthly fiscal period ending December 31 of the current year. Use as a guide the partial work sheet, page 262.

2. Enter the adjustment for beginning merchandise inventory on the work sheet. Use as a guide the partial work sheet, page 265.

3. Enter the adjustment for ending merchandise inventory on the work sheet. Use as a guide the partial work sheet, page 266.

Account Title	Balance
Cash	$ 8,820.00
Accounts Receivable	740.00
Merchandise Inventory	92,600.00
Supplies	530.00
Prepaid Insurance	760.00
Accounts Payable	4,610.00
Sales Tax Payable	622.00
Eileen Brandon, Capital	45,600.00
Eileen Brandon, Drawing	700.00
Diane Baxter, Capital	44,800.00
Diane Baxter, Drawing	650.00
Income Summary	—
Sales	15,560.00
Purchases	3,820.00
Credit Card Fee Expense	280.00
Insurance Expense	—
Miscellaneous Expense	92.00
Rent Expense	950.00
Salary Expense	1,250.00
Supplies Expense	—

Adjustment Information, December 31	
Merchandise inventory	$87,500.00
Supplies inventory	250.00
Value of insurance policies	670.00

4. Enter the adjustment for supplies on the work sheet. Use as a guide the partial work sheet, page 268.

5. Enter the adjustment for prepaid insurance on the work sheet. Use as a guide the partial work sheet, page 269.

6. Figure and record net income or loss. Use as a guide the work sheets, pages 272 and 274.

7. Complete the work sheet for the monthly fiscal period ending December 31 of the current year. Use as a guide the completed work sheet, page 272.

The solution to Problem 14-1 is needed to complete Problem 15-1 and Problem 16-1 in Chapters 15 and 16.

PROBLEM 14-2 Preparing a work sheet

The accounts and their balances in Quality Office Supply's general ledger appear below and on the next page. Ending inventories and the value of insurance policies are also given.

Account Title	Balance
Cash	$ 9,350.00
Accounts Receivable	960.00
Merchandise Inventory	86,300.00
Supplies	670.00
Prepaid Insurance	840.00
Accounts Payable	6,400.00
Sales Tax Payable	865.00
Alice Brown, Capital	43,025.00
Alice Brown, Drawing	750.00
Harold Brown, Capital	39,600.00
Harold Brown, Drawing	700.00
Income Summary	—

Account Title	Balance
Sales	$17,300.00
Purchases	4,320.00
Credit Card Fee Expense	380.00
Insurance Expense	—
Miscellaneous Expense	130.00
Rent Expense	1,250.00
Salary Expense	1,540.00
Supplies Expense	—
Adjustment Information, December 31	
Merchandise inventory	$84,600.00
Supplies inventory	420.00
Value of insurance policies	560.00

Instructions: Prepare Quality Office Supply's eight-column work sheet for the monthly fiscal period ending December 31 of the current year. Use as a guide the eight-column work sheet, page 272.

ENRICHMENT PROBLEMS

MASTERY PROBLEM 14-M Preparing a work sheet

The accounts and their balances in Value Appliances' general ledger appear below. Ending inventories and the value of insurance policies are also given.

Instructions: Prepare Value Appliances' eight-column work sheet for the monthly fiscal period ending October 31 of the current year. Use as a guide the eight-column work sheet, page 272.

Account Title	Account Balance
Cash	$ 10,400.00
Accounts Receivable	1,920.00
Merchandise Inventory	120,000.00
Supplies	860.00
Prepaid Insurance	520.00
Accounts Payable	6,230.00
Sales Tax Payable	915.00
C. K. Fields, Capital	63,800.00
C. K. Fields, Drawing	1,000.00
John Miller, Capital	65,650.00
John Miller, Drawing	900.00
Income Summary	—
Sales	18,300.00
Purchases	16,200.00
Credit Card Fee Expense	340.00
Delivery Expense	190.00
Insurance Expense	—
Miscellaneous Expense	65.00
Rent Expense	1,000.00
Salary Expense	1,500.00
Supplies Expense	—
Adjustment Information, October 31	
Merchandise inventory	$126,000.00
Supplies inventory	685.00
Value of insurance policies	410.00

CHALLENGE PROBLEM 14-C Preparing a work sheet

The accounts and their balances in C & B Hardware's general ledger appear below. Ending inventories and the value of insurance policies are also given.

Instructions: Prepare C & B Hardware's eight-column work sheet for the monthly fiscal period ending January 31 of the current year. Use as a guide the eight-column work sheet, page 272.

Account Title	Account Balance
Cash	$ 8,830.00
Accounts Receivable	960.00
Merchandise Inventory	93,500.00
Supplies	480.00
Prepaid Insurance	930.00
Accounts Payable	4,120.00
Sales Tax Payable	560.00
Carmen Lopez, Capital	49,700.00
Carmen Lopez, Drawing	800.00
Janet Carter, Capital	48,610.00
Janet Carter, Drawing	850.00
Income Summary	—
Sales	10,200.00
Purchases	2,800.00
Credit Card Fee Expense	230.00
Insurance Expense	—
Miscellaneous Expense	60.00
Rent Expense	950.00
Salary Expense	2,800.00
Supplies Expense	—
Adjustment Information, January 31	
Merchandise inventory	$89,800.00
Supplies inventory	360.00
Value of insurance policies	850.00

15

Financial Statements of a Partnership

ENABLING PERFORMANCE TASKS

After studying Chapter 15, you will be able to:

a. Define accounting terms related to financial statements.
b. Explain accounting principles and practices related to financial statements.
c. Prepare an income statement with a cost of merchandise sold section.
d. Prepare a distribution of net income statement.
e. Prepare a capital statement.
f. Prepare a balance sheet.

Journals and ledgers are used during a fiscal period to classify and record information about a business' financial activities. A work sheet is used at the end of a fiscal period to organize and summarize this financial information. All of these activities are done so that the financial progress and condition of a business can be reported. The financial progress and condition of a business are reported on financial statements. Financial statements should contain all information necessary to understand a business' financial progress and condition. *(CONCEPT: Adequate Disclosure)* In the preparation of financial statements, accounting principles are applied the same way from one fiscal period to the next. *(CONCEPT: Consistent Reporting)*

FINANCIAL STATEMENTS OF A PARTNERSHIP

Businesses organized as partnerships report their financial progress and condition by preparing four financial statements. (1) Income statement. (2) Distribution of net income statement. (3) Capital statement. (4) Balance sheet. Financial statements of a partnership are similar to those prepared by a sole proprietorship. However, for a partnership, the distribution of net income or net loss is reported separately for each partner.

Also, the equity of each partner is reported separately on the financial statements.

INCOME STATEMENT

An income statement reports the financial progress of a business. Revenue, cost of merchandise sold, gross profit on sales, expenses, and net income or loss are reported for merchandising businesses. Current and previous income statements can be compared to determine the reasons for increases or decreases in net income.

Preparing an income statement

The Account Title and Income Statement columns of a completed work sheet are used to prepare the income statement. Denim Threads' partial work sheet for the month ended November 30, 1982, is on the next page.

The complete work sheet for Denim Threads is on page 272.

Denim Threads' income statement, page 283, has three main sections. (1) Revenue section. (2) Cost of merchandise sold section. (3) Expenses section.

Steps in preparing Denim Threads' income statement are given below.

1 Write the heading of the income statement on three lines.

2 Prepare the revenue section. Use the information from the Income Statement Credit column of the work sheet.

- Write the name of this section, *Revenue*, at the extreme left of the wide column on the first line.
- Write the title of the revenue account, *Sales*, on the next line, indented about 1 centimeter.
- Write the balance of the sales account, *$13,305.00*, in the second amount column. This amount is also the total of the revenue section for Denim Threads.

If there is more than one source of revenue, each revenue account title is listed in the wide column. The balance of each account is written in the first amount column. The words *Total Revenue* are written in the wide column on the next line below the last revenue account title. The total amount of revenue is written in the second amount column.

3 Prepare the cost of merchandise sold section. Use the information from the Income Statement columns of the work sheet.

Denim Threads
Work Sheet
For Month Ended November 30, 1982

	Account Title	Income Statement Debit (5)	Income Statement Credit (6)
12	Income Summary	6800000	6400000
13	Sales		1330500
14	Purchases	395200	
15	Credit Card Fee Expense	13500	
16	Insurance Expense	7500	
17	Miscellaneous Expense	8400	
18	Rent Expense	80000	
19	Salary Expense	110000	
20	Supplies Expense	26000	
21		7440600	7730500
22	Net Income	289900	
23		7730500	7730500
24			
25			
26			
27			
28			
29			
30			

Partial work sheet showing income statement columns

The cost of merchandise sold is determined as described below.

Beginning merchandise inventory, November 1, 1982...... (This amount is shown as a debit to Income Summary in the Income Statement Debit column of the work sheet.)	$68,000.00
Plus purchases made during the fiscal period................. (This amount is shown as a debit to Purchases in the Income Statement Debit column of the work sheet.)	3,952.00
Equals total cost of merchandise available for sale during the fiscal period	$71,952.00
Less ending merchandise inventory, November 30, 1982... (This amount is shown as a credit to Income Summary in the Income Statement Credit column of the work sheet.)	64,000.00
Equals cost of merchandise sold during the fiscal period ...	$ 7,952.00

The cost of merchandise sold section is entered on the income statement.

- Write the name of this section, *Cost of Merchandise Sold*, at the extreme left of the wide column.

Denim Threads Income Statement For Month Ended November 30, 1982		
Revenue:		
Sales		13305 00
Cost of Merchandise Sold:		
Merchandise Inventory, Nov. 1, 1982	68000 00	
Purchases	3952 00	
Total Cost of Mdse. Available for Sale	71952 00	
Less Mdse. Inventory, Nov. 30, 1982	64000 00	
Cost of Merchandise Sold		7952 00
Gross Profit on Sales		5353 00
Expenses:		
Credit Card Fee Expense	135 00	
Insurance Expense	75 00	
Miscellaneous Expense	84 00	
Rent Expense	800 00	
Salary Expense	1100 00	
Supplies Expense	260 00	
Total Expenses		2454 00
Net Income		2899 00

Income statement for a merchandising business

- Indent 1 centimeter and write in the wide column items needed to figure cost of merchandise sold. Write the amount of each item in the first amount column.
- Write the amount of the cost of merchandise sold, *$7,952.00*, in the second amount column.

4 Figure the gross profit on sales. The revenue remaining after cost of merchandise sold has been deducted is called gross profit on sales.

- Write the words *Gross Profit on Sales* on the next line at the extreme left of the wide column.
- Subtract cost of merchandise sold, *$7,952.00*, from total revenue, *$13,305.00*, to find gross profit on sales, *$5,353.00*. Write the amount of the gross profit on sales, *$5,353.00*, in the second amount column.

5 Prepare the expenses section. Use the information from the Income Statement Debit column on the work sheet.

- Write the name of this section, *Expenses*, at the extreme left of the wide column.
- Indent 1 centimeter and list the expense account titles in the order in which they appear on the work sheet. Write the amount of each expense account balance in the first amount column.
- Write the words *Total Expenses* in the wide column on the next line below the last expense account title. Total the individual expenses and write the total, *$2,454.00*, in the second amount column on the total line.

6 Figure the net income.

- Write the words *Net Income* on the next line at the extreme left of the wide column.
- Subtract total expenses, *$2,454.00*, from gross profit on sales, *$5,353.00*, to find net income, *$2,899.00*. Write this amount in the second amount column on the net income line.

  Compare the amount of net income figured on the income statement, *$2,899.00*, with the amount on the work sheet, *$2,899.00*. The two amounts must be the same.

- Rule double lines across both amount columns on the income statement to show that the statement has been completed.

Income statement showing a net loss

When the expenses of a business are greater than the gross profit on sales, the difference is known as a net loss. For example, the partial income statement below shows a loss of $1,220.00 for the fiscal period.

Gross Profit on Sales		2983 00
Expenses:		
Delivery Expense	493 00	
Miscellaneous Expense	205 00	
Rent Expense	1250 00	
Salary Expense	1750 00	
Supplies Expense	505 00	
Total Expenses		4203 00
Net Loss		1220 00

Partial income statement showing a net loss

The net loss is found by subtracting the gross profit on sales, *$2,983.00*, from the total expenses, *$4,203.00*. The difference, *$1,220.00*, is written in the second amount column on the line with the words *Net Loss*.

DISTRIBUTION OF NET INCOME STATEMENT

The net income or net loss of a partnership may be divided in any way agreed upon by the partners. For example, partners may agree to share the net income or net loss (1) equally or (2) unequally. Eva Burgos and Luis Perez, partners in Denim Threads, agreed to share net income or net loss equally.

The distribution of net income or net loss of a partnership is usually shown in a separate financial statement. A partnership financial statement showing net income or loss distribution to partners is called a distribution of net income statement.

Preparing a distribution of net income statement

The net income, *$2,899.00*, from the income statement, page 283, is used to prepare the distribution of net income statement. The distribution of net income statement for Denim Threads is below.

Denim Threads Distribution of Net Income Statement For Month Ended November 30, 1982	
Eva Burgos	
50% of Net Income	1449 50
Luis Perez	
50% of Net Income	1449 50
Net Income	2899 00

Distribution of net income statement of a partnership

Steps in preparing Denim Threads' distribution of net income statement are described below.

1 Write the heading of the distribution of net income statement on three lines.

2 Write the name *Eva Burgos* on the first line at the extreme left of the wide column.

3 Indent 1 centimeter and write on the next line Eva Burgos' share of net income, *50% of Net Income*. Write Ms. Burgos' share of net income, *$1,449.50* (50% × $2,899.00) in the amount column on the same line.

4 Write the name *Luis Perez* on the next line at the extreme left of the wide column.

5 Indent 1 centimeter and write on the next line Luis Perez's share of net income, *50% of Net Income*. Write Mr. Perez' share of net income, *$1,449.50* (50% × $2,899.00), in the amount column on the same line.

6 Write the words *Net Income* on the next line at the extreme left of the wide column. Add the distribution of net income for Eva Burgos, *$1,449.50*, and for Luis Perez, *$1,449.50*. Write the total amount, *$2,899.00*, in the amount column.

Compare the total amount, *$2,899.00*, with the net income reported on the income statement, *$2,899.00*. The two amounts must be the same.

7 Rule double lines across the amount column on the distribution of net income statement. The ruling shows that the statement has been completed.

Distribution of net income statement with unequal distribution of earnings

The steps in preparing a distribution of net income statement are the same regardless of how earnings are shared. The only difference is the description of how the earnings are to be shared by the partners. A partial distribution of net income statement with unequal shares of earnings is below.

Harriett Crandon	
60% of Net Income	2400 00
Susan Fulton	
40% of Net Income	1600 00
Net Income	4000 00

Distribution of net income statement with unequal distribution of earnings

Harriett Crandon and Susan Fulton, partners, agree to share net income or loss unequally. Harriett Crandon gets 60% of net income or loss. Susan Fulton gets 40% of net income or loss. With a net income of $4,000.00, Harriett Crandon receives 60% or $2,400.00. Susan Fulton receives 40% or $1,600.00.

CAPITAL STATEMENT

The amount of net income earned by a business is important to the owners. Owners are also interested in changes that occur in the capital during a fiscal period. A financial statement that summarizes the changes in capital during a fiscal period is called a capital statement. Owners of a business can review a capital statement to determine if and why the capital is increasing or decreasing. There are three reasons why changes in the amount of capital occur.

1. Additional investments are made.
2. Cash, merchandise, or other assets are withdrawn.
3. Net income or net loss occurs from business operations.

Preparing a capital statement

Information about changes in the capital of each partner during a fiscal period is shown in a partnership capital statement. Information needed to prepare a capital statement is obtained from the capital accounts in the general ledger. Information is also obtained from the Balance Sheet columns of the work sheet and the distribution of net income statement. Information from the general ledger includes the beginning balance of each capital account and any additional investments. Information from the work sheet includes the withdrawals for the fiscal period. The distribution of net income statement provides the amount of each partner's share of net income.

The general ledger capital accounts for Eva Burgos and Luis Perez, partners, are below.

ACCOUNT Eva Burgos, Capital — ACCOUNT NO. 31

DATE		ITEM	POST. REF.	DEBIT	CREDIT	BALANCE DEBIT	BALANCE CREDIT
1982 Nov.	1	Balance	✓				35 759 60

ACCOUNT Luis Perez, Capital — ACCOUNT NO. 33

DATE		ITEM	POST. REF.	DEBIT	CREDIT	BALANCE DEBIT	BALANCE CREDIT
1982 Nov.	1	Balance	✓				35 759 60

Partners' capital accounts

Neither Eva Burgos nor Luis Perez invested any additional capital during November, 1982. Therefore, the beginning and ending capital balances are the same as recorded in the trial balance on the work sheet. If additional investments had been made, the ending balance on November 30 would be greater than the beginning balance.

The portions of the work sheet needed to prepare the capital statement are on the next page. The distribution of net income statement is on page 285.

Denim Threads
Work Sheet
For Month Ended November 30, 1982

	ACCOUNT TITLE	BALANCE SHEET DEBIT (7)	BALANCE SHEET CREDIT (8)	
8	Eva Burgos, Capital		35759 60	8
9	Eva Burgos, Drawing	600 00		9
10	Luis Perez, Capital		35759 60	10
11	Luis Perez, Drawing	645 00		11

Partial work sheet showing balance sheet columns

Denim Threads' capital statement prepared on November 30, 1982, is below.

Denim Threads
Capital Statement
For Month Ended November 30, 1982

Eva Burgos			
Capital, November 1, 1982		35759 60	
Share of Net Income	1449 50		
Less Withdrawals	600 00		
Net Increase in Capital		849 50	
Capital, November 30, 1982			36609 10
Luis Perez			
Capital, November 1, 1982		35759 60	
Share of Net Income	1449 50		
Less Withdrawals	645 00		
Net Increase in Capital		804 50	
Capital, November 30, 1982			36564 10
Total Capital, November 30, 1982			73173 20

Capital statement

Steps in preparing Denim Threads' capital statement are described below.

1 Write the heading of the capital statement on three lines.

2 Write the name *Eva Burgos* on the first line at the extreme left of the wide column.

3 Figure the net increase in capital for Eva Burgos.

- Indent 1 centimeter and write on the next line the words *Capital, November 1, 1982*. Write the beginning capital amount, *$35,759.60*, in the second amount column on the same line. (This amount is obtained from Ms. Burgos' capital account.)

- Indent 1 centimeter and write on the next line the words *Share of Net Income*. On the same line write the share of net income amount, *$1,449.50*, in the first amount column. (This amount is obtained from the Distribution of Net Income Statement.)
- Indent 1 centimeter and write on the next line the words *Less Withdrawals*. On the same line write the withdrawals amount, *$600.00*, in the first amount column. (This amount is obtained from the work sheet.)
- Indent 1 centimeter and write on the next line the words *Net Increase in Capital*. Subtract the withdrawals, *$600.00*, from the share of net income, *$1,449.50*. On the same line write the difference, *$849.50*, in the second amount column.
- Indent 1 centimeter and write on the next line the words *Capital, November 30, 1982*. Add the November 1 capital, *$35,759.60*, and the net increase in capital, *$849.50*, to obtain the November 30 capital, *$36,609.10*. On the same line write the November 30 capital amount, *$36,609.10*, in the third amount column.

4 Write the name *Luis Perez* on the next line at the extreme left of the wide column.

5 Figure the net increase in capital for Luis Perez.

- Indent 1 centimeter and write on the next line the words *Capital, November 1, 1982*. On the same line write the beginning capital amount, *$35,759.60*, in the second amount column.
- Indent 1 centimeter and write on the next line the words *Share of Net Income*. On the same line write the share of net income amount, *$1,449.50*, in the first amount column.
- Indent 1 centimeter and write on the next line the words *Less Withdrawals*. On the same line write the withdrawals amount, *$645.00*, in the first amount column.
- Indent 1 centimeter and write on the next line the words *Net Increase in Capital*. On the same line write the difference, *$804.50*, in the second amount column.
- Indent 1 centimeter and write on the next line the words *Capital, November 30, 1982*. On the same line write the November 30 capital amount, *$36,564.10*, in the third amount column.

6 Write the words *Total Capital, November 30, 1982*, on the next line at the extreme left of the wide column. On the same line write the total capital amount, $73,173.20, in the third amount column.

7 Rule double lines across the three amount columns on the capital statement. The ruling shows that the statement has been completed.

In some businesses the information on the capital statement may be included as part of the balance sheet. An example of this method of reporting changes in capital is on page 137.

Preparing a capital statement with an additional investment and with a net loss

On December 31, 1982, the capital accounts of Alice Jefferson and William Richards showed additional investments of $3,000.00 each. Also, the work sheet, page 274, showed a net loss of $1,220.00. The net loss of $1,220.00 was also shown on the income statement, page 284. The partners agreed to share net income or net loss equally. The capital statement for J & R Clothiers is below.

J & R Clothiers
Capital Statement
For Month Ended December 31, 1982

Alice Jefferson			
Capital, December 1, 1982	42500 00		
Plus Additional Investment	3000 00		
Total		45500 00	
Share of Net Loss	610 00		
Plus Withdrawals	800 00		
Net Decrease in Capital		1410 00	
Capital, December 31, 1982			44090 00
William Richards			
Capital, December 1, 1982	43200 00		
Plus Additional Investment	3000 00		
Total		46200 00	
Share of Net Loss	610 00		
Plus Withdrawals	650 00		
Net Decrease in Capital		1260 00	
Capital, December 31, 1982			44940 00
Total Capital, December 31, 1982			89030 00

Capital statement showing an additional investment and a net loss

BALANCE SHEET

Owners make many management decisions about the business. Some of these decisions can best be made after owners have determined the amount of assets, liabilities, and capital. Owners obtain some of the information needed by inspecting general ledger accounts. The information needed may also be found on a work sheet. However, the information is easier to use when organized and reported on financial statements. A balance sheet reports the financial condition of a business: assets and equities.

Two forms of balance sheet

A balance sheet may be prepared in one of two forms: (1) account form or (2) report form. A balance sheet listing assets on the left and equities on the right is called an account form of balance sheet. The account form of balance sheet, used by Putt Around, is described in Chapter 8.

A balance sheet listing the assets, liabilities, and capital vertically is called a report form of balance sheet. Denim Threads uses the report form of balance sheet.

Report form of balance sheet

The portion of the work sheet used in preparing Denim Threads' balance sheet is below.

Denim Threads
Work Sheet
For Month Ended November 30, 1982

	ACCOUNT TITLE	BALANCE SHEET 7 DEBIT	8 CREDIT	
1	Cash	11544 20		1
2	Accounts Receivable	572 00		2
3	Merchandise Inventory	64000 00		3
4	Supplies	241 00		4
5	Prepaid Insurance	355 00		5
6	Accounts Payable		2650 00	6
7	Sales Tax Payable		889 00	7

Partial work sheet showing balance sheet columns

Denim Threads' report form of balance sheet prepared on November 30, 1982, is on the next page.

Steps in preparing Denim Threads' balance sheet are described below.

1 Write the heading of the balance sheet on three lines.

2 Prepare the assets section of the balance sheet. Use the information in the Balance Sheet Debit column of the work sheet above.

- Write the section title, *Assets*, in the middle of the wide column.
- Write the titles of asset accounts on separate lines at the extreme left of the wide column. Write the balance of each asset account in the first amount column.

Denim Threads Balance Sheet November 30, 1982		
Assets		
Cash	11544 20	
Accounts Receivable	572 00	
Merchandise Inventory	64000 00	
Supplies	241 00	
Prepaid Insurance	355 00	
Total Assets		76712 20
Liabilities		
Accounts Payable	2650 00	
Sales Tax Payable	889 00	
Total Liabilities		3539 00
Capital		
Eva Burgos, Capital	36609 10	
Luis Perez, Capital	36564 10	
Total Capital		73173 20
Total Liabilities and Capital		76712 20

Balance sheet

- Write the words *Total Assets* below the last asset account title at the extreme left of the wide column. Total the individual assets and write the total, *$76,712.20*, in the second amount column on the total line.
- Rule double lines across both amount columns.

3 Prepare the liabilities section of the balance sheet. Use the information in the Balance Sheet Credit column of the work sheet, page 291.

- Write the title of the section, *Liabilities*, in the middle of the wide column.
- Write the titles of liability accounts on separate lines at the extreme left of the wide column. Write the balance of each liability account in the first amount column.
- Write the words *Total Liabilities* below the last liability account title. Write the words on the next line at the extreme left of the wide column. Add the individual liabilities and write the total, *$3,539.00*, in the second amount column on the total line.

4 Prepare the capital section of the balance sheet. Use the information in the capital statement, page 288.

- Write the title of the section, *Capital*, in the middle of the wide column.
- On the next line write the account title, *Eva Burgos, Capital*, at the extreme left of the wide column. On the same line write the amount of current capital for Eva Burgos, *$36,609.10*, in the first amount column.
- On the next line write the account title, *Luis Perez, Capital*, at the extreme left of the wide column. On the same line write the amount of current capital for Luis Perez, *$36,564.10*, in the first amount column.
- Write the words *Total Capital* on the next line at the extreme left of the wide column. Total the two capital accounts and write the total, *$73,173.20*, in the second amount column on the total line.

5 Total the liabilities and capital section of the balance sheet.

- Write the words *Total Liabilities and Capital* on the next line at the extreme left of the wide column. Add the amounts in the second amount column. Write the total, *$76,712.20*, in the second amount column on the total line.

  Compare the total amount of assets and the total amount of liabilities and capital. These two amounts must be the same. The two amounts, *$76,712.20*, are the same. The balance sheet is assumed to be correct.

- Rule double lines across both amount columns to show that the balance sheet has been completed.

Supporting schedules for a balance sheet

A report prepared to give details about an item on a principal financial statement is called a supporting schedule. A supporting schedule is sometimes known as a supplementary report or an exhibit.

Two supporting schedules are prepared by Denim Threads to accompany the balance sheet. The supporting schedules are a schedule of accounts payable and a schedule of accounts receivable. A balance sheet shows only the total amount of accounts payable. An account balance of each creditor is not shown. When this detailed information is needed, a supporting schedule of accounts payable is usually prepared. When information about the account balance of each charge customer is needed, a supporting schedule of accounts receivable is prepared. These supporting schedules for Denim Threads on November 30, 1982, are in Chapter 13, page 250.

STATEMENT OF ACCOUNT

A business usually sends to each charge customer a monthly statement showing the amount owed by the customer. The statement may include only the total balance owed. Many businesses, however, include all information about sales to and cash received from the customer. A business form showing the charges, receipts, and balance of a customer's account is called a statement of account.

Denim Threads sends statements of account to charge customers at the end of each month. An example of the statement of account used by Denim Threads is below.

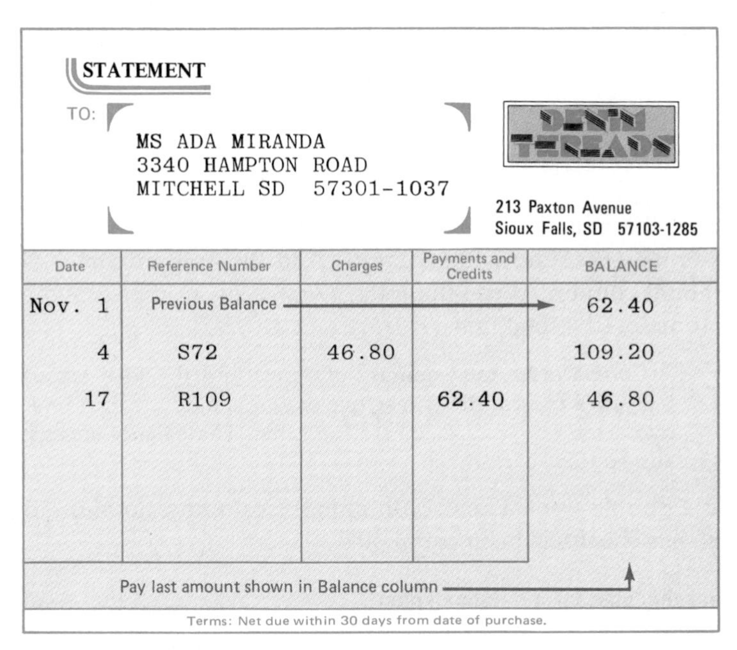
STATEMENT

TO:
MS ADA MIRANDA
3340 HAMPTON ROAD
MITCHELL SD 57301-1037

DENIM THREADS
213 Paxton Avenue
Sioux Falls, SD 57103-1285

Date	Reference Number	Charges	Payments and Credits	BALANCE
Nov. 1	Previous Balance			62.40
4	S72	46.80		109.20
17	R109		62.40	46.80

Pay last amount shown in Balance column

Terms: Net due within 30 days from date of purchase.

Statement of account

Customers should compare statements of account with their records. If an error is found on the statement, the business from whom the statement is received should be notified.

Many businesses mail statements of account to a portion of their charge customers on different days of a month. This procedure spreads out the work of preparing the statements over the month. Preparing and mailing statements of account to customers on different days of each month is called cycle billing. A cycle billing schedule is at the left. For example, on the 4th of each month, statements are mailed to customers whose names begin with A to D.

Initial of customers' last names	Date on which statement of account is prepared and mailed
A to D	4th
E to K	10th
L to P	16th
Q to S	22d
T to Z	28th

Cycle billing schedule

When mailing dates fall on Sundays or holidays, statements are mailed on the next regular business day.

Businesses with a small number of accounts receivable seldom use cycle billing. All statements of account are prepared and mailed once each month. Denim Threads, with few accounts receivable, mails statements once a month.

ACCOUNTING TERMS

What is the meaning of each of the following?

1. gross profit on sales
2. distribution of net income statement
3. capital statement
4. account form of balance sheet
5. report form of balance sheet
6. supporting schedule
7. statement of account
8. cycle billing

QUESTIONS FOR INDIVIDUAL STUDY

1. Why does a business prepare financial statements at the end of a fiscal period?
2. What four financial statements are prepared by a partnership?
3. What are the major differences in reporting owners' equity for a partnership and for a sole proprietorship?
4. Which financial statement reports the financial progress of a business?
5. Where does a business find the information needed to prepare an income statement?
6. What are the three main sections of Denim Threads' income statement?
7. How is the cost of merchandise sold figured?
8. How is the gross profit on sales figured?
9. How is the net income figured?
10. What are two ways that partners may agree to share the net income or net loss of a partnership?
11. Why does a partnership prepare a distribution of net income statement?
12. Why does a partnership prepare a capital statement?
13. What three factors change the amount of capital during a fiscal period?
14. Where is information obtained to use in preparing a capital statement?
15. Which financial statement reports the financial condition of the business?
16. What are the two forms in which a balance sheet may be prepared? Which form is used by Denim Threads?
17. What are the two supporting schedules prepared by Denim Threads?
18. Why do some businesses use cycle billing?

CASES FOR MANAGEMENT DECISION

CASE 1 Jack Gruber and Andy Sweeney, partners, compared their current income statement with their income statement of a year ago. They noted that sales this year are 15% higher than a year ago. They also have noted that expenses have increased nearly 20%. What points should be considered in deciding whether the increase in expenses is justified?

CASE 2 Curtis Danfield and Bradley Marshall own a sporting goods store. The store is on a yearly fiscal period. At the end of each year, a public accountant is employed to prepare financial statements. At the end of each month during the year, Mr. Marshall prepares a work sheet. The work sheet is prepared to determine if the business is making or losing money for that month. The public accountant suggests that monthly financial statements also be prepared. Mr. Marshall believes, however, that the monthly work sheet is sufficient to determine how the business is doing. Do you agree with Mr. Marshall or with the public accountant? Why?

CASE 3 Alice Abernathy and Steven Clemmons differ as to which financial statement is most important to them. Miss Abernathy believes the income statement is most important; Mr. Clemmons believes the balance sheet is most important. Who is correct? Explain.

DRILLS FOR UNDERSTANDING

DRILL 15-D 1 Figuring the cost of merchandise sold

Information from the work sheets of three businesses appears below.

Business	Account Title	Income Statement Debit	Income Statement Credit
1	Purchases	$ 4,600.00	
	Income Summary	62,000.00	$64,000.00
2	Purchases	$ 3,980.00	
	Income Summary	74,000.00	$72,000.00
3	Purchases	$ 4,350.00	
	Income Summary	68,000.00	$66,350.00

Instructions: Figure the cost of merchandise sold for each business.

DRILL 15-D 2 Figuring the net income or loss

Information from the work sheets of three businesses appears below.

Business	Account Title	Income Statement Debit	Income Statement Credit
1	Income Summary	$54,000.00	$52,500.00
	Sales		14,100.00
	Purchases	3,600.00	
	Total Expenses	1,800.00	
2	Income Summary	$36,200.00	$33,900.00
	Sales		10,200.00
	Purchases	9,850.00	
	Total Expenses	4,730.00	
3	Income Summary	$44,200.00	$46,400.00
	Sales		12,400.00
	Purchases	3,200.00	
	Total Expenses	1,400.00	

Instructions: Figure the net income or loss for each business.

DRILL 15-D 3 Figuring the distribution of net income or loss

Instructions: 1. Assume that each business shown at the right earned a net income of $15,000.00. What is the amount of income to be distributed to each partner in each business?

2. Assume that each business shown at the right had a loss of $8,000.00. What is the amount of loss to be distributed to each partner in each business?

Business	Partner	Agreement on sharing of income or loss
1	A B	50% of income or loss 50% of income or loss
2	A B	60% of income or loss 40% of income or loss
3	A B C	40% of income or loss 30% of income or loss 30% of income or loss

APPLICATION PROBLEMS

PROBLEM 15-1 Preparing financial statements

The work sheet completed in Problem 14-1 is needed to complete Problem 15-1.

Instructions: 1. Prepare an income statement similar to the one on page 283.

2. Prepare a distribution of net income statement similar to the one on page 285. The net income is to be shared equally.

3. Prepare a capital statement similar to the one on page 288. No additional investments were made.

4. Prepare a balance sheet in report form similar to the one on page 292.

The solution to Problem 15-1 is needed to complete Problem 16-1 in Chapter 16.

PROBLEM 15-2 Preparing a distribution of net income statement and capital statement

Mary Clancy and Karen Jordon are partners in a merchandising business. The following information was taken from the records on December 31 of the current year, the end of a monthly fiscal period.

Partner	Balance of capital account	Balance of drawing account	Distribution of net income
Clancy	$63,000.00	$840.00	70%
Jordon	$27,000.00	$620.00	30%

Instructions: 1. Assume that on December 31 the partnership had a net income of $9,400.00 as shown on the income statement. Prepare a distribution of net income statement for the partnership of Clancy & Jordon Sales.

2. Prepare a capital statement. No additional investments were made.

3. Assume that on December 31 the partnership had a loss of $5,600.00 instead of a net income. Prepare a distribution of net income statement showing the loss.

4. Prepare a capital statement showing the loss.

ENRICHMENT PROBLEMS

MASTERY PROBLEM 15-M Preparing a work sheet and financial statements

The accounts and their balances in Household Furniture's general ledger appear below. Ending inventories and the value of insurance policies are also given.

Account Title	Account Balance
Cash	$ 9,800.00
Accounts Receivable	1,100.00
Merchandise Inventory	115,000.00
Supplies	460.00
Prepaid Insurance	730.00
Accounts Payable	6,120.00
Sales Tax Payable	748.00
Frank Garcia, Capital	56,800.00
Frank Garcia, Drawing	950.00
James Allen, Capital	57,403.00
James Allen, Drawing	875.00
Income Summary	—
Sales	18,700.00
Purchases	7,200.00
Credit Card Fee Expense	420.00
Delivery Expense	250.00
Insurance Expense	—
Miscellaneous Expense	86.00
Rent Expense	1,100.00
Salary Expense	1,800.00
Supplies Expense	—

Adjustment Information, December 31	
Merchandise inventory	$113,000.00
Supplies inventory	280.00
Value of insurance policies	635.00

Instructions: 1. Prepare Household Furniture's eight-column work sheet for the monthly fiscal period ending December 31 of the current year.

2. Prepare an income statement.

3. Prepare a distribution of net income statement. Net income is to be shared equally.

4. Prepare a capital statement. No additional investments were made.

5. Prepare a balance sheet in report form.

The work sheet prepared for Mastery Problem 15-M is needed to complete Challenge Problem 15-C.

CHALLENGE PROBLEM 15-C Preparing financial statements (unequal distribution of net income; additional investment)

The work sheet completed for Mastery Problem 15-M is needed to complete Challenge Problem 15-C.

Instructions: 1. Prepare a distribution of net income statement. The net income is to be shared as follows: Frank Garcia, 60%; James Allen, 40%. Use the net income from the work sheet completed in Mastery Problem 15-M.

2. Prepare a capital statement. Mr. Allen made an additional investment of $5,000.00 during the month. He had a beginning capital of $52,403.00.

16

Adjusting and Closing Entries

ENABLING PERFORMANCE TASKS

After studying Chapter 16, you will be able to:

a. Explain accounting principles and practices related to adjusting and closing entries.
b. Journalize adjusting entries.
c. Journalize closing entries.
d. Post adjusting and closing entries.
e. Prepare a post-closing trial balance.

A merchandising business uses an eight-column work sheet at the end of a fiscal period for three reasons. (1) To plan adjustments of general ledger accounts. (2) To assemble information needed for preparing financial statements. (3) To assemble information needed for making closing entries.

Accounts in a general ledger are changed only by posting journal entries. Information needed for journalizing adjusting entries is taken from the work sheet's Adjustments columns. Information needed for journalizing closing entries is taken from two places. (1) Work sheet Income Statement and Balance Sheet columns. (2) Distribution of net income statement.

ADJUSTING ENTRIES

Each adjustment in a work sheet's Adjustments columns is journalized and posted to general ledger accounts. Four adjustments are shown in Denim Threads' work sheet, page 272.

Adjusting entry for beginning merchandise inventory

Denim Threads' adjustment for beginning merchandise inventory on November 30, 1982, is shown in the partial work sheet on the next page.

The debit and credit parts of this adjustment are identified by the letter *(a)*.

Partial work sheet showing adjustment for beginning merchandise inventory

	Account Title	Trial Balance Debit (1)	Trial Balance Credit (2)	Adjustments Debit (3)	Adjustments Credit (4)
3	Merchandise Inventory	68000 00			(a) 68000 00
12	Income Summary			(a) 68000 00	

Denim Threads' adjusting entry for beginning merchandise inventory is shown in the combination journal below. The general ledger accounts affected by this entry are also shown.

Journal entry to adjust beginning merchandise inventory

COMBINATION JOURNAL — PAGE 3

	Cash Debit (1)	Cash Credit (2)	Date	Account Title	Doc. No.	Post. Ref.	General Debit (3)	General Credit (4)	
1				Adjusting Entries					1
2			1982 Nov. 30	Income Summary		35	68000 00		2
3				Mdse. Inventory		13		68000 00	3
4									4

General ledger accounts after posting adjusting entry for beginning merchandise inventory

ACCOUNT Income Summary — ACCOUNT NO. 35

Date	Item	Post. Ref.	Debit	Credit	Balance Debit	Balance Credit
1982 Nov. 30		3	68000 00		68000 00	

ACCOUNT Merchandise Inventory — ACCOUNT NO. 13

Date	Item	Post. Ref.	Debit	Credit	Balance Debit	Balance Credit
1982 Nov. 1	Balance	✓			68000 00	
30		3		68000 00	—	—

The words *Adjusting Entries* are written in the middle of the journal's Account Title column. This heading explains all of the adjusting entries that follow. Therefore, indicating a source document is unnecessary.

The first adjusting entry is recorded on the next line below the heading. The adjusting entry for beginning merchandise inventory debits Income Summary and credits Merchandise Inventory for $68,000.00. The debit transfers the beginning balance of the merchandise inventory account to the income summary account. The credit cancels the debit balance in the merchandise inventory account. The merchandise inventory account has a zero balance after the adjusting entry for beginning merchandise inventory is posted.

Adjusting entry for ending merchandise inventory

Denim Threads' adjustment for ending merchandise inventory is shown in the partial work sheet below. The debit and credit parts of this adjustment are identified by the letter *(b)*.

	Account Title	1 Trial Balance Debit	2 Trial Balance Credit	3 Adjustments Debit	4 Adjustments Credit
3	Merchandise Inventory	68000 00		(b) 64000 00	(a) 68000 00
12	Income Summary			(a) 68000 00	(b) 64000 00

Partial work sheet showing adjustment for ending merchandise inventory

Denim Threads' adjusting entry for the ending merchandise inventory is shown in the partial combination journal below. The general ledger accounts affected by this entry are also shown.

COMBINATION JOURNAL — PAGE 3

	1 Cash Debit	2 Cash Credit	Date	Account Title	Doc. No.	Post. Ref.	3 General Debit	4 General Credit	
4			30	Merchandise Inventory		13	64000 00		4
5				Income Summary		35		64000 00	5

Journal entry to adjust ending merchandise inventory

ACCOUNT Merchandise Inventory — ACCOUNT NO. 13

Date		Item	Post. Ref.	Debit	Credit	Balance Debit	Balance Credit
1982 Nov.	1	Balance	✓			68000 00	
	30		3		68000 00	—	—
	30		3	64000 00		64000 00	

ACCOUNT Income Summary — ACCOUNT NO. 35

Date		Item	Post. Ref.	Debit	Credit	Balance Debit	Balance Credit
1982 Nov.	30		3	68000 00		68000 00	
	30		3		64000 00	4000 00	

General ledger accounts after posting adjusting entry for ending merchandise inventory

The adjusting entry for ending merchandise inventory debits Merchandise Inventory and credits Income Summary for $64,000.00. This adjusting entry brings the asset account Merchandise Inventory up to date. The ending merchandise inventory, $64,000.00, is now recorded as a debit to the merchandise inventory account. This adjusting entry also records the ending merchandise inventory as a credit to the income summary account.

Adjusting entry for supplies

Denim Threads' adjustment for supplies on November 30, 1982, is shown on the partial work sheet below. The debit and credit parts of the adjustment are identified by the letter (*c*).

	Account Title	Trial Balance Debit (1)	Trial Balance Credit (2)	Adjustments Debit (3)	Adjustments Credit (4)
4	Supplies	501 00			(c) 260 00
20	Supplies Expense			(c) 260 00	

Partial work sheet showing adjustment for supplies

Denim Threads' entry to record the supplies adjustment is below. The general ledger accounts affected by this entry are also shown.

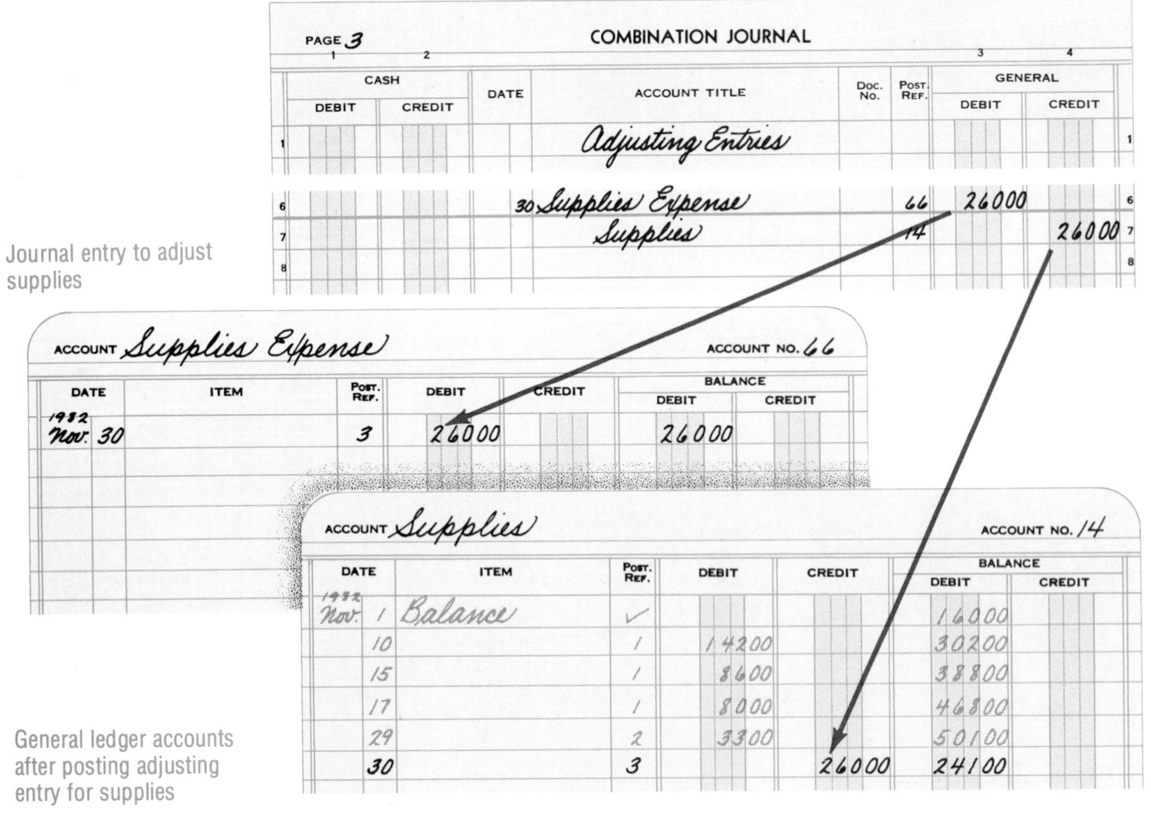

COMBINATION JOURNAL — PAGE 3

	Cash Debit (1)	Cash Credit (2)	Date	Account Title	Doc. No.	Post. Ref.	General Debit (3)	General Credit (4)	
1				Adjusting Entries					1
6			30	Supplies Expense		66	260 00		6
7				Supplies		14		260 00	7
8									8

Journal entry to adjust supplies

ACCOUNT Supplies Expense — ACCOUNT NO. 66

Date	Item	Post. Ref.	Debit	Credit	Balance Debit	Balance Credit
1982 Nov. 30		3	260 00		260 00	

ACCOUNT Supplies — ACCOUNT NO. 14

Date	Item	Post. Ref.	Debit	Credit	Balance Debit	Balance Credit
1982 Nov. 1	Balance	✓			160 00	
10		1	142 00		302 00	
15		1	86 00		388 00	
17		1	80 00		468 00	
29		2	33 00		501 00	
30		3		260 00	241 00	

General ledger accounts after posting adjusting entry for supplies

After the adjusting entry for supplies is posted, the supplies expense account has a debit balance of $260.00. The $260.00 debit to Supplies Expense is the expense resulting from the use of supplies during the fiscal period. The supplies account has a debit balance of $241.00. The $260.00 credit to Supplies is the decrease in the balance of this asset account.

Adjusting entry for prepaid insurance

Denim Threads' adjustment for prepaid insurance on November 30, 1982, is shown on the partial work sheet below. The debit and credit parts of the adjustment are identified by the letter *(d)*.

	ACCOUNT TITLE	TRIAL BALANCE DEBIT (1)	TRIAL BALANCE CREDIT (2)	ADJUSTMENTS DEBIT (3)	ADJUSTMENTS CREDIT (4)
5	Prepaid Insurance	43000			(d) 7500
16	Insurance Expense			(d) 7500	

Partial work sheet showing adjustment for prepaid insurance

The entry to record the prepaid insurance adjustment is below. The general ledger accounts affected by this entry are also shown.

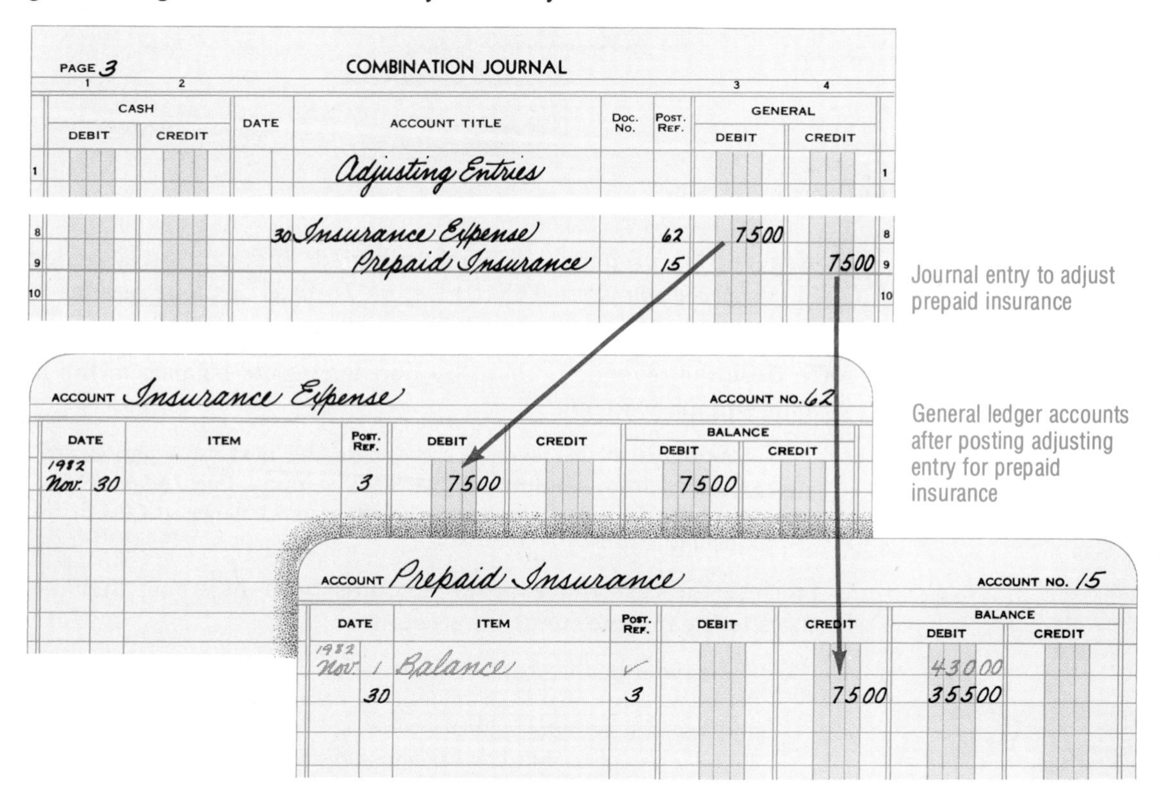

PAGE 3 COMBINATION JOURNAL

	CASH DEBIT (1)	CASH CREDIT (2)	DATE	ACCOUNT TITLE	DOC. NO.	POST. REF.	GENERAL DEBIT (3)	GENERAL CREDIT (4)	
1				Adjusting Entries					1
8			30	Insurance Expense		62	7500		8
9				Prepaid Insurance		15		7500	9
10									10

Journal entry to adjust prepaid insurance

ACCOUNT Insurance Expense ACCOUNT NO. 62

DATE	ITEM	POST. REF.	DEBIT	CREDIT	BALANCE DEBIT	BALANCE CREDIT
1982 Nov. 30		3	7500		7500	

ACCOUNT Prepaid Insurance ACCOUNT NO. 15

DATE	ITEM	POST. REF.	DEBIT	CREDIT	BALANCE DEBIT	BALANCE CREDIT
1982 Nov. 1	Balance	✓			43000	
30		3		7500	35500	

General ledger accounts after posting adjusting entry for prepaid insurance

When the adjusting entry for prepaid insurance is posted, the insurance expense account has a debit balance of $75.00. The $75.00 debit to Insurance Expense is the expense resulting from the insurance expired during the fiscal period. The prepaid insurance account has a debit balance of $355.00. The $75.00 credit to Prepaid Insurance is the decrease in the balance of this asset account.

Summary of adjusting entries

Denim Threads' four adjusting entries recorded on November 30, 1982, are below.

PAGE 3 COMBINATION JOURNAL

Cash Debit (1)	Cash Credit (2)	Date	Account Title	Doc. No.	Post. Ref.	General Debit (3)	General Credit (4)	
			Adjusting Entries					1
		1982 Nov. 30	Income Summary		35	6800000		2
			Mdse. Inventory		13		6800000	3
		30	Merchandise Inventory		13	6400000		4
			Income Summary		35		6400000	5
		30	Supplies Expense		66	26000		6
			Supplies		14		26000	7
		30	Insurance Expense		62	7500		8
			Prepaid Insurance		15		7500	9
								10

Adjusting entries

CLOSING ENTRIES

Closing entries prepare a general ledger for the next fiscal period. *(CONCEPT: Accounting Period Cycle)* Denim Threads has four reasons for recording closing entries.

1. To close the revenue account by transferring its balance to the income summary account.

   Amounts in the revenue account for the next fiscal period are separated from amounts of past fiscal periods. Each revenue account begins a new fiscal period with a zero balance. *(CONCEPT: Matching Expenses with Revenue)*

2. To close the cost and expense accounts by transferring their balances to the income summary account.

   Amounts in the cost and expense accounts for the next fiscal period are separated from amounts of past fiscal periods. Each cost and expense account begins a new fiscal period with a zero balance. *(CONCEPT: Matching Expenses with Revenue)*

3. To close Income Summary and record the net income or net loss.

   A closing entry is made to record the net income (or net loss) in the partners' capital accounts. The balance of the income summary account is equal to the net income (or net loss) for a fiscal period. *(CONCEPT: Accounting Period Cycle)*

4. To close the partners' drawing accounts by transferring their balances to the partners' capital accounts.

A closing entry is made to transfer the balances of the partners' drawing accounts to the capital accounts. After these drawing accounts are closed, amounts for the next fiscal period are separated from amounts of past fiscal periods. Each drawing account begins a new fiscal period with a zero balance.

Information needed for the closing entries is obtained from two places. (1) Work sheet Income Statement and Balance Sheet columns. (2) Distribution of net income statement.

Closing entry for revenue account

The part of Denim Threads' work sheet needed to close the revenue, cost, and expense accounts is below.

	ACCOUNT TITLE	INCOME STATEMENT DEBIT (5)	INCOME STATEMENT CREDIT (6)
13	Sales		13305 00
14	Purchases	3952 00	
15	Credit Card Fee Expense	135 00	
16	Insurance Expense	75 00	
17	Miscellaneous Expense	84 00	
18	Rent Expense	800 00	
19	Salary Expense	1100 00	
20	Supplies Expense	260 00	
21		74406 00	77305 00
22	Net Income	2899 00	
23		77305 00	77305 00
24			

Partial work sheet showing revenue, cost, and expense accounts balances

Information needed for closing the revenue account is taken from line 13 of the Income Statement Credit column. Sales is Denim Threads' only revenue account. Denim Threads' entry to close the revenue account Sales is below.

PAGE 3 COMBINATION JOURNAL

	CASH DEBIT (1)	CASH CREDIT (2)	DATE	ACCOUNT TITLE	DOC. NO.	POST. REF.	GENERAL DEBIT (3)	GENERAL CREDIT (4)	
10				Closing Entries					10
11			30	Sales		41	13305 00		11
12				Income Summary		35		13305 00	12

Sales

Debit		Credit	
Closing	13,305.00	Balance	13,305.00

Income Summary

Debit		Credit	
Beg. Inv.	68,000.00	End. Inv.	64,000.00
		Revenue	13,305.00

Journal entry to close the revenue account

The words *Closing Entries* are written in the middle of the journal's Account Title column. This heading is the explanation for all closing entries that follow. A source document is not indicated when journalizing closing entries.

The first closing entry is recorded on the next line below the heading. After Denim Threads' closing entry for revenue is posted, the sales account has a zero balance. The balance of the sales account, *$13,305.00*, is transferred as a credit to the income summary account.

Closing entry for cost and expense accounts

Information needed for closing the cost and expense accounts is taken from Denim Threads' work sheet, page 305. The information is in the Income Statement Debit column, lines 14–20. All account balances in the Income Statement Debit column of the work sheet are closed with one combined journal entry. Cost and expense accounts are closed with credit entries. One combined journal entry eliminates separate debit entries in Income Summary for each cost and expense account. The journal entry to close the cost and expense accounts is below.

PAGE 3 COMBINATION JOURNAL

	1	2					3	4	
	CASH		DATE	ACCOUNT TITLE	DOC. NO.	POST. REF.	GENERAL		
	DEBIT	CREDIT					DEBIT	CREDIT	
10				Closing Entries					10
13			30	Income Summary		35	6406 00		13
14				Purchases		51		3952 00	14
15				Credit Card Fee Exp.		61		135 00	15
16				Insurance Expense		62		75 00	16
17				Miscellaneous Exp.		63		84 00	17
18				Rent Expense		64		800 00	18
19				Salary Expense		65		1100 00	19
20				Supplies Expense		66		260 00	20

Journal entry to close the cost and expense accounts

Income Summary

Beg. Inv. 68,000.00	End. Inv. 64,000.00
Cost & Exp. 6,406.00	Revenue 13,305.00

Purchases

Balance 3,952.00	Closing 3,952.00

Credit Card Fee Expense

Balance 135.00	Closing 135.00

Insurance Expense

Balance 75.00	Closing 75.00

Miscellaneous Expense

Balance 84.00	Closing 84.00

Rent Expense

Balance 800.00	Closing 800.00

Salary Expense

Balance 1,100.00	Closing 1,100.00

Supplies Expense

Balance 260.00	Closing 260.00

The income summary account is debited for the total of these account balances, $6,406.00. Each account in the Income Statement Debit column is credited for the amount of its balance. After the closing entry for cost and expense accounts is posted, the accounts have zero balances.

When closing entries for revenue, cost, and expenses are posted, the income summary account has a credit balance of $2,899.00. This credit balance, *$2,899.00*, is the amount of net income. This amount is the same as on line 22 of the work sheet, page 305. When net income (or net loss) is the same in both places, closing entries are assumed to be correct.

Closing entry for recording net income (or net loss) in the partners' capital accounts

The net income is recorded in the partners' capital accounts. Information needed for this entry is obtained from the distribution of net income statement, page 285. This entry is recorded as shown below.

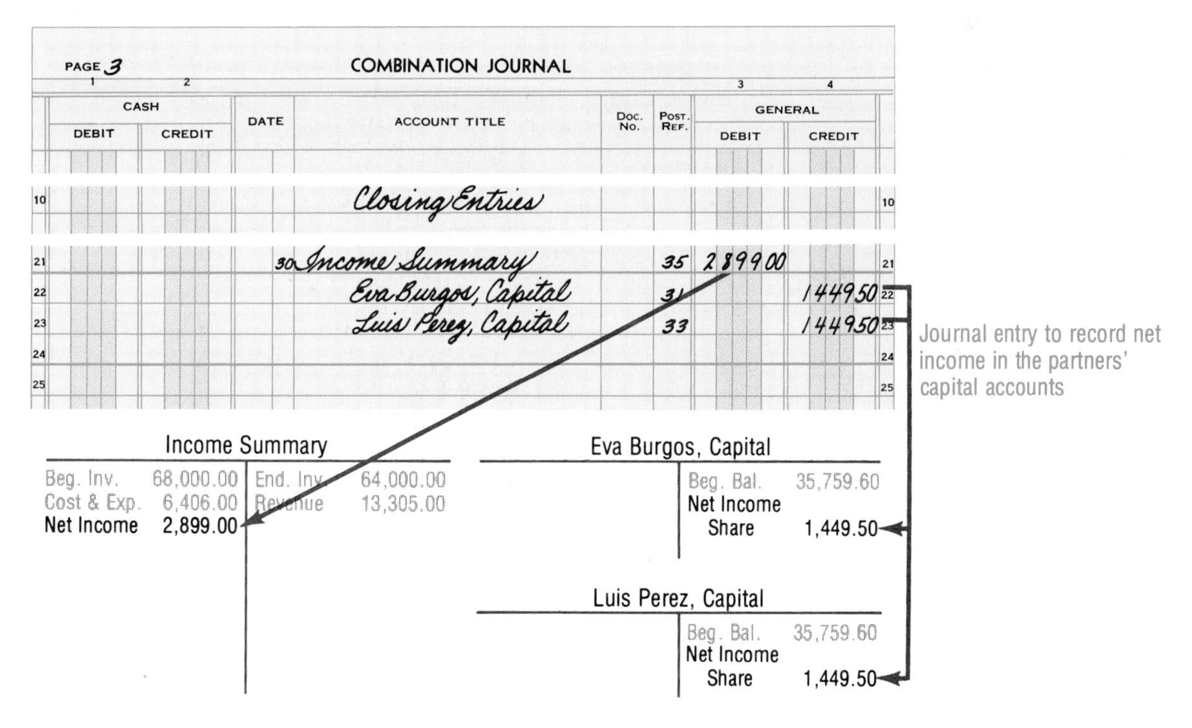

Journal entry to record net income in the partners' capital accounts

When the entry to record the net income is posted, Income Summary has a zero balance. An equal amount, *$1,449.50*, is recorded as a credit in each partner's capital account. The two amounts recorded in the partners' capital accounts total the net income, *$2,899.00*.

If a business has a net loss, the income summary account has a debit balance. The partners' capital accounts would then be debited and the income summary account credited for the net loss.

Closing entries for partners' drawing accounts

Withdrawals by partners decrease capital. The drawing accounts are closed into the partners' respective capital accounts at the end of a fiscal period. *(CONCEPT: Accounting Period Cycle)* Information needed for closing partners' drawing accounts is obtained from the work sheet's Balance Sheet Debit column. The portion of Denim Threads' work sheet showing partners' drawing account balances is below.

	ACCOUNT TITLE	7 BALANCE SHEET DEBIT	8 BALANCE SHEET CREDIT	
8	Eva Burgos, Capital		35759 60	8
9	Eva Burgos, Drawing	600 00		9
10	Luis Perez, Capital		35759 60	10
11	Luis Perez, Drawing	645 00		11
12				12

Partial work sheet showing partners' drawing accounts

Line 9 of the partial work sheet above shows the balance of Eva Burgos' drawing account, $600.00. Line 11 shows the balance of Luis Perez' drawing account, $645.00. The closing entries to close each drawing account are below.

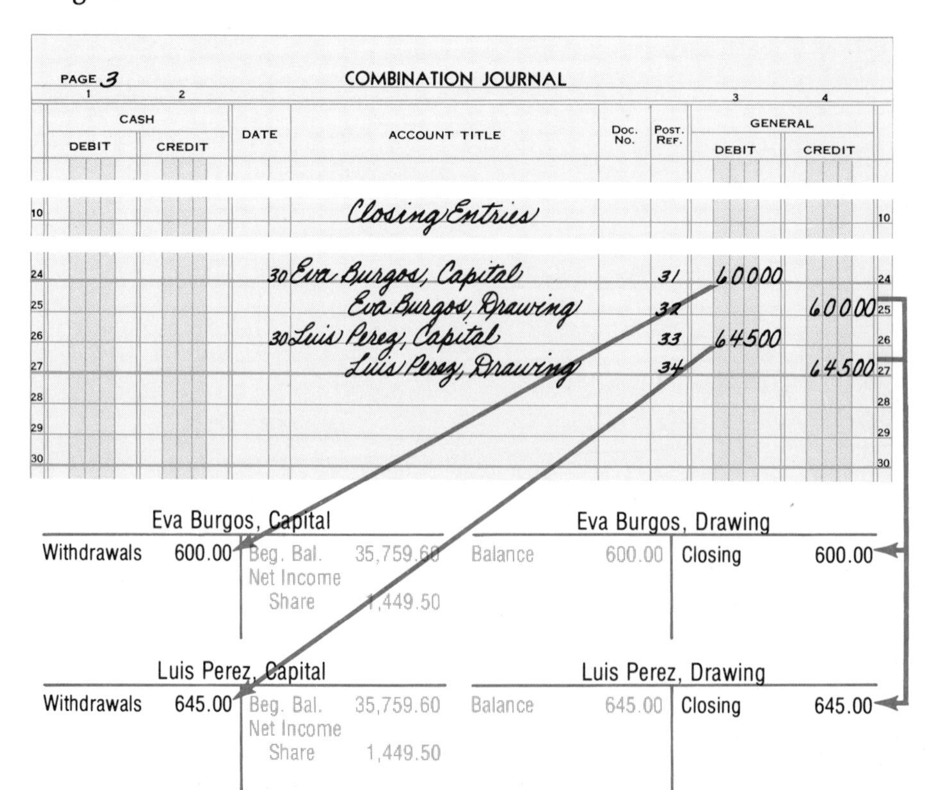
PAGE 3 COMBINATION JOURNAL

	1 CASH DEBIT	2 CASH CREDIT	DATE	ACCOUNT TITLE	DOC. NO.	POST. REF.	3 GENERAL DEBIT	4 GENERAL CREDIT	
10				Closing Entries					10
24			30	Eva Burgos, Capital		31	600 00		24
25				Eva Burgos, Drawing		32		600 00	25
26			30	Luis Perez, Capital		33	645 00		26
27				Luis Perez, Drawing		34		645 00	27
28									28
29									29
30									30

Journal entries to close the drawing accounts

When the closing entries for the partners' drawing accounts are posted, these accounts have zero balances. Also, the capital accounts of Eva Burgos and Luis Perez show the decrease in capital because of withdrawals.

Summary of closing entries

Denim Threads' closing entries on November 30, 1982, are below.

PAGE 3 COMBINATION JOURNAL

	1	2					3	4	
	CASH		DATE	ACCOUNT TITLE	DOC. NO.	POST. REF.	GENERAL		
	DEBIT	CREDIT					DEBIT	CREDIT	
10				Closing Entries					10
11			30	Sales		41	13305 00		11
12				Income Summary		35		13305 00	12
13			30	Income Summary		35	6406 00		13
14				Purchases		51		3952 00	14
15				Credit Card Fee Exp.		61		135 00	15
16				Insurance Expense		62		75 00	16
17				Miscellaneous Exp.		63		84 00	17
18				Rent Expense		64		800 00	18
19				Salary Expense		65		1100 00	19
20				Supplies Expense		66		260 00	20
21			30	Income Summary		35	2899 00		21
22				Eva Burgos, Capital		31		1449 50	22
23				Luis Perez, Capital		33		1449 50	23
24			30	Eva Burgos, Capital		31	600 00		24
25				Eva Burgos, Drawing		32		600 00	25
26			30	Luis Perez, Capital		33	645 00		26
27				Luis Perez, Drawing		34		645 00	27
28									28

Closing entries

CHECKING THE ACCURACY OF A GENERAL LEDGER AFTER ADJUSTING AND CLOSING ENTRIES HAVE BEEN POSTED

Denim Threads uses a four-column general ledger account form. The form has separate columns for Debit Balance and Credit Balance. Each time an entry is posted to a general ledger account, the account balance is figured. The balance is then recorded in the appropriate balance column. When an account is closed, a short line is drawn in both the Debit and Credit Balance columns. Each general ledger account shows its current balance at all times. The ending balance for one fiscal period is the beginning balance for the next fiscal period.

Completed general ledger

Denim Threads' general ledger appears as shown below and on pages 311 to 313 after adjusting and closing entries are posted.

ACCOUNT Cash — ACCOUNT NO. 11

DATE		ITEM	POST. REF.	DEBIT	CREDIT	BALANCE DEBIT	BALANCE CREDIT
1982 Nov.	1	Balance	✓			4200 00	
	30		2	13551 20		17751 20	
	30		2		6207 00	11544 20	

ACCOUNT Accounts Receivable — ACCOUNT NO. 12

DATE		ITEM	POST. REF.	DEBIT	CREDIT	BALANCE DEBIT	BALANCE CREDIT
1982 Nov.	1	Balance	✓			286 00	
	30		2	639 60		925 60	
	30		2		353 60	572 00	

ACCOUNT Merchandise Inventory — ACCOUNT NO. 13

DATE		ITEM	POST. REF.	DEBIT	CREDIT	BALANCE DEBIT	BALANCE CREDIT
1982 Nov.	1	Balance	✓			68000 00	
	30		3		68000 00	—	—
	30		3	64000 00		64000 00	

ACCOUNT Supplies — ACCOUNT NO. 14

DATE		ITEM	POST. REF.	DEBIT	CREDIT	BALANCE DEBIT	BALANCE CREDIT
1982 Nov.	1	Balance	✓			160 00	
	10		1	142 00		302 00	
	15		1	86 00		388 00	
	17		1	80 00		468 00	
	29		2	33 00		501 00	
	30		3		260 00	241 00	

ACCOUNT Prepaid Insurance — ACCOUNT NO. 15

DATE		ITEM	POST. REF.	DEBIT	CREDIT	BALANCE DEBIT	BALANCE CREDIT
1982 Nov.	1	Balance	✓			430 00	
	30		3		75 00	355 00	

General ledger after adjusting and closing entries are posted

General ledger after adjusting and closing entries are posted (continued)

ACCOUNT *Accounts Payable* ACCOUNT NO. 21

DATE		ITEM	POST. REF.	DEBIT	CREDIT	BALANCE DEBIT	BALANCE CREDIT
1982 Nov.	1	Balance	✓				1 200 00
	30		2	2 164 00		964 00	
	30		2		3 614 00		2 650 00

ACCOUNT *Sales Tax Payable* ACCOUNT NO. 22

DATE		ITEM	POST. REF.	DEBIT	CREDIT	BALANCE DEBIT	BALANCE CREDIT
1982 Nov.	1	Balance	✓				356 80
	30		2		532 20		889 00

ACCOUNT *Eva Burgos, Capital* ACCOUNT NO. 31

DATE		ITEM	POST. REF.	DEBIT	CREDIT	BALANCE DEBIT	BALANCE CREDIT
1982 Nov.	1	Balance	✓				35 759 60
	30		3		1 449 50		37 209 10
	30		3	600 00			36 609 10

ACCOUNT *Eva Burgos, Drawing* ACCOUNT NO. 32

DATE		ITEM	POST. REF.	DEBIT	CREDIT	BALANCE DEBIT	BALANCE CREDIT
1982 Nov.	15		1	300 00		300 00	
	30		2	300 00		600 00	
	30		3		600 00	—	—

ACCOUNT *Luis Perez, Capital* ACCOUNT NO. 33

DATE		ITEM	POST. REF.	DEBIT	CREDIT	BALANCE DEBIT	BALANCE CREDIT
1982 Nov.	1	Balance	✓				35 759 60
	30		3		1 449 50		37 209 10
	30		3	645 00			36 564 10

ACCOUNT *Luis Perez, Drawing* ACCOUNT NO. 34

DATE		ITEM	POST. REF.	DEBIT	CREDIT	BALANCE DEBIT	BALANCE CREDIT
1982 Nov.	15		1	300 00		300 00	
	16		1	45 00		345 00	
	30		2	300 00		645 00	
	30		3		645 00	—	—

ACCOUNT *Income Summary* ACCOUNT NO. 35

DATE		ITEM	POST. REF.	DEBIT	CREDIT	BALANCE DEBIT	BALANCE CREDIT
1982 Nov.	30		3	6800000		6800000	
	30		3		6400000	400000	
	30		3		1330500		930500
	30		3	640600			289900
	30		3	289900		—	—

ACCOUNT *Sales* ACCOUNT NO. 41

DATE		ITEM	POST. REF.	DEBIT	CREDIT	BALANCE DEBIT	BALANCE CREDIT
1982 Nov.	30		2		1330500		1330500
	30		3	1330500		—	—

ACCOUNT *Purchases* ACCOUNT NO. 51

DATE		ITEM	POST. REF.	DEBIT	CREDIT	BALANCE DEBIT	BALANCE CREDIT
1982 Nov.	16		1		4500		4500
	17		1		8000		12500
	30		2	407700		395200	
	30		3		395200	—	—

ACCOUNT *Credit Card Fee Expense* ACCOUNT NO. 61

DATE		ITEM	POST. REF.	DEBIT	CREDIT	BALANCE DEBIT	BALANCE CREDIT
1982 Nov.	28		2	13500		13500	
	30		3		13500	—	—

ACCOUNT *Insurance Expense* ACCOUNT NO. 62

DATE		ITEM	POST. REF.	DEBIT	CREDIT	BALANCE DEBIT	BALANCE CREDIT
1982 Nov.	30		3	7500		7500	
	30		3		7500	—	—

ACCOUNT *Miscellaneous Expense* ACCOUNT NO. 63

DATE		ITEM	POST. REF.	DEBIT	CREDIT	BALANCE DEBIT	BALANCE CREDIT
1982 Nov.	3		1	5300		5300	
	22		2	2900		8200	
	28		2	200		8400	
	30		3		8400	—	—

General ledger after adjusting and closing entries are posted (continued)

General ledger after adjusting and closing entries are posted (concluded)

ACCOUNT Rent Expense ACCOUNT NO. 64

DATE		ITEM	POST. REF.	DEBIT	CREDIT	BALANCE DEBIT	BALANCE CREDIT
1982 Nov.	15		1	80000		80000	
	30		3		80000	—	—

ACCOUNT Salary Expense ACCOUNT NO. 65

DATE		ITEM	POST. REF.	DEBIT	CREDIT	BALANCE DEBIT	BALANCE CREDIT
1982 Nov.	1		1	55000		55000	
	15		1	55000		110000	
	30		3		110000	—	—

ACCOUNT Supplies Expense ACCOUNT NO. 66

DATE		ITEM	POST. REF.	DEBIT	CREDIT	BALANCE DEBIT	BALANCE CREDIT
1982 Nov.	30		3	26000		26000	
	30		3		26000	—	—

Balance sheet accounts (asset, liability, and capital accounts) all have up-to-date balances on November 30, 1982. Balances in the balance sheet accounts agree with the amounts on the balance sheet, page 292. General ledger account balances on November 30, 1982, are the beginning balances for December 1, 1982.

Income statement accounts (revenue, cost, and expense accounts) all have zero balances to begin the new fiscal period.

Post-closing trial balance

A post-closing trial balance is prepared after adjusting and closing entries have been posted. The post-closing trial balance is prepared to prove the equality of debits and credits in the general ledger. Denim Threads' post-closing trial balance, prepared on November 30, 1982, is on the next page.

General ledger accounts that have balances are listed on a post-closing trial balance. Accounts are listed in the same order as they appear in the general ledger. Accounts with zero balances are not listed on a post-closing trial balance.

Denim Threads Post-Closing Trial Balance November 30, 1982		
ACCOUNT TITLE	DEBIT	CREDIT
Cash	11544 20	
Accounts Receivable	572 00	
Merchandise Inventory	64000 00	
Supplies	241 00	
Prepaid Insurance	355 00	
Accounts Payable		2650 00
Sales Tax Payable		889 00
Eva Burgos, Capital		36609 10
Luis Perez, Capital		36564 10
	76712 20	76712 20

Post-closing trial balance

Account balances on the post-closing trial balance above agree with the balances on the balance sheet, page 292. Also, on the post-closing trial balance, the debit and credit balance totals are the same, $76,712.20. The equality of debits and credits in the general ledger is proved. The general ledger is ready for the next fiscal period. *(CONCEPT: Accounting Period Cycle)*

SUMMARIZING AN ACCOUNTING CYCLE FOR A MERCHANDISING BUSINESS

An accounting cycle contains the same basic steps for a merchandising business as for a service business. Also, the accounting cycle is similar for a sole proprietorship and a partnership. Minor variations occur when subsidiary ledgers are used. Variations also occur in preparing financial statements. The steps in Putt Around's accounting cycle are shown in the flowchart on page 154. The flowchart, page 315, shows the steps in Denim Threads' accounting cycle.

QUESTIONS FOR INDIVIDUAL STUDY

1. Why are the adjustments, as planned on a work sheet, recorded as entries in a journal?
2. Where is the information obtained for journalizing the adjusting entries?
3. Where is the information obtained for journalizing closing entries?
4. Where is the explanation for the adjusting entries written in a combination journal?
5. Why does the merchandise inventory account have a zero balance after posting the adjusting entry for beginning merchandise inventory?

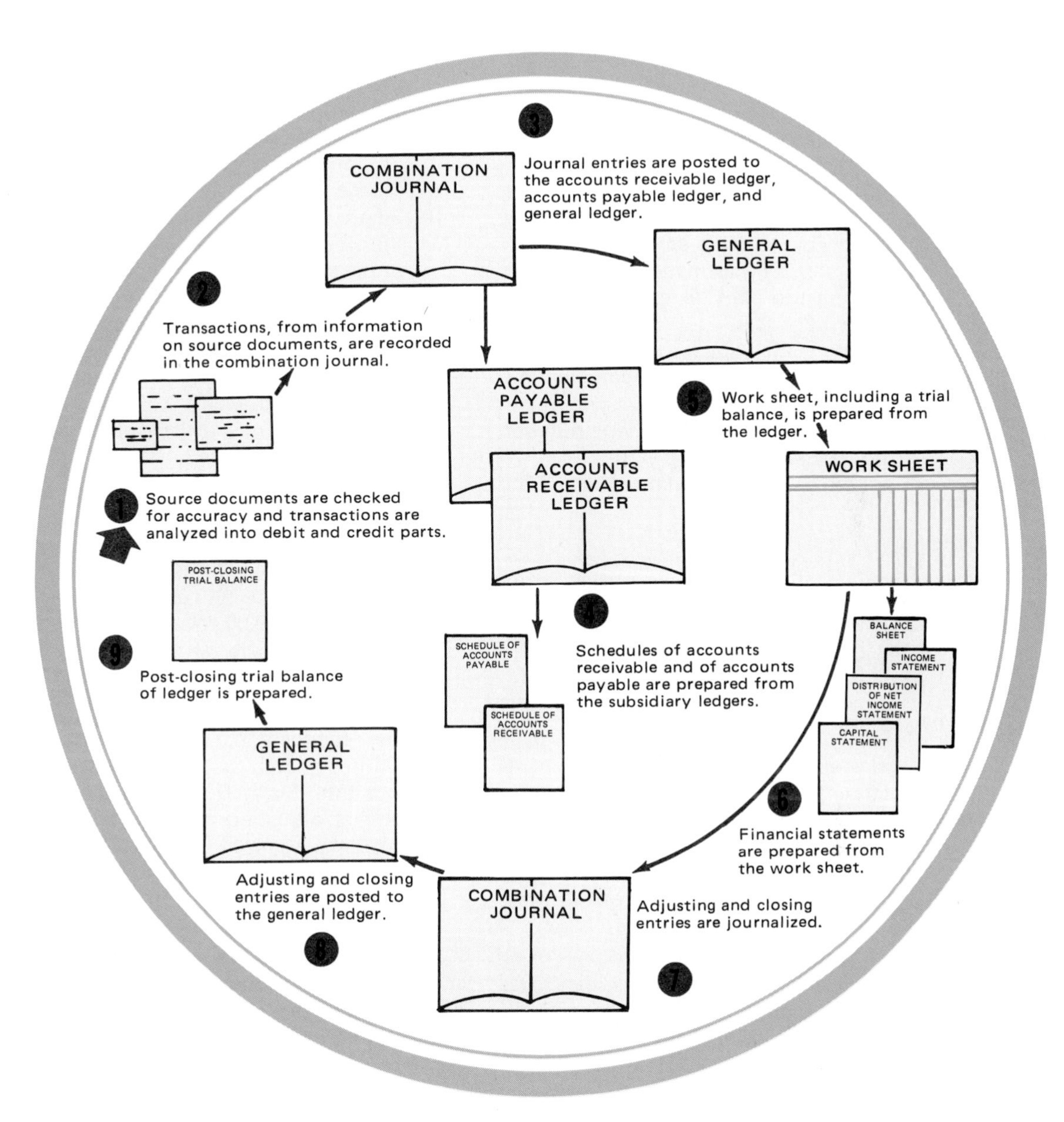

Flowchart of the steps in the accounting cycle

6. Why does the adjustment for ending inventory bring the asset account Merchandise Inventory up to date?
7. Why does the adjustment for supplies debit Supplies Expense and credit Supplies?
8. Why does the adjustment for prepaid insurance debit Insurance Expense and credit Prepaid Insurance?
9. Why are closing entries needed at the end of a fiscal period?
10. Why is the revenue account closed at the end of a fiscal period?
11. Why do cost and expense accounts

begin a new fiscal period with a zero balance?

12. Why is the balance of the income summary account transferred to the partners' capital accounts?
13. Why are the partners' drawing accounts transferred to the capital accounts by a closing entry?
14. Where is the information obtained for making the entry to close a revenue account?
15. Where is the explanation for the closing entries written in a combination journal?
16. Why is a source document number not written for closing entries?
17. Where is the information obtained for making the entry to close cost and expense accounts?
18. Why are the account balances in the work sheet's Income Statement Debit column closed with one combined journal entry?
19. Where is the information obtained for the closing entry to record net income or net loss in the capital accounts?
20. Where is the information obtained for the entry to close the drawing accounts?
21. What is the reason for preparing a post-closing trial balance?
22. What accounts are listed on a post-closing trial balance?

CASES FOR MANAGEMENT DECISION

CASE 1 Crestline Furniture had a debit balance of $580.00 in the prepaid insurance account on January 1. On January 31, an adjusting entry was made. Debit Prepaid Insurance $40.00; credit Insurance Expense $40.00. What effect will this adjusting entry have on the net income? On Capital?

CASE 2 Donley's, a merchandising business, prepares a work sheet and financial statements at the end of each month. However, the business uses a yearly fiscal period ending December 31. No adjusting or closing journal entries are made at the end of each month. Steven Donley, partner, suggests that adjusting and closing entries should be made at the end of each month. Marie Donley, partner, suggests that adjusting and closing entries need be made only at the end of the fiscal year. Do you agree with Marie Donley or Steven Donley?

CASE 3 Two businesses have been using different accounting practices. One business first closes the drawing accounts and then records the net income in the capital accounts. The other business records the net income first and then closes the drawing accounts. Which practice is correct? Explain.

DRILLS FOR UNDERSTANDING

DRILL 16-D 1 Recording adjusting entries

A partial work sheet of Anderson Supply is on the next page.

Instructions: 1. Prepare T accounts for each account on the partial work sheet. For those accounts that have a balance, record the balance on the proper side of the T account.

2. Record the adjustments for merchandise inventory, supplies, and prepaid insurance in the appropriate T accounts.

Account Title	Trial Balance Debit	Trial Balance Credit	Adjustments Debit	Adjustments Credit
Merchandise Inventory	42 900 00		(b) 44 600 00	(a) 42 900 00
Supplies	390 00			(c) 60 00
Prepaid Insurance	260 00			(d) 110 00
Income Summary			(a) 42 900 00	(b) 44 600 00
Insurance Expense			(d) 110 00	
Supplies Expense			(c) 60 00	

DRILL 16-D 2 Recording adjusting entries

Information for three businesses is below. This information is related to adjustments needed at the end of a fiscal period.

Business	Account Title	Account Balance in General Ledger	Adjustment Information: Ending Inventories	Adjustment Information: Ending Value
1	Merchandise Inventory	$39,500.00	$41,000.00	
	Supplies	430.00	320.00	
	Prepaid Insurance	720.00		$580.00
2	Merchandise Inventory	$62,300.00	$58,800.00	
	Supplies	530.00	460.00	
	Prepaid Insurance	480.00		$320.00
3	Merchandise Inventory	$47,600.00	$45,800.00	
	Supplies	490.00	370.00	
	Prepaid Insurance	650.00		$560.00

Instructions: 1. Prepare six T accounts for each of the three businesses. (1) Merchandise Inventory. (2) Supplies. (3) Prepaid Insurance. (4) Income Summary. (5) Insurance Expense. (6) Supplies Expense. Record the account balance on the proper side of each T account.

2. Record the adjustments for merchandise inventory, supplies, and prepaid insurance in the appropriate T accounts for each business.

DRILL 16-D 3 Recording closing entries

A partial work sheet for Smithfield Plumbing is below.

Account Title	Income Statement Debit	Income Statement Credit
Income Summary	42 650 00	45 300 00
Sales		12 510 00
Purchases	3 180 00	
Credit Card Fee Expense	270 00	
Insurance Expense	120 00	
Miscellaneous Expense	60 00	
Rent Expense	900 00	
Salary Expense	1 300 00	
Supplies Expense	160 00	

Instructions: 1. Prepare a T account for each account on the partial work sheet. In each T account, record the amount that is shown in the Income Statement columns.

2. Record the debit and credit amounts to close the revenue, cost, and expense accounts.

APPLICATION PROBLEMS

PROBLEM 16-1 Completing the work at the end of a fiscal period

The solutions to Problems 14-1 and 15-1 are needed to complete Problem 16-1.

Instructions: 1. On page 3 of a combination journal record the adjusting entries shown in the Adjustments columns of the work sheet. Use the adjusting entries, page 304, as a guide.

2. Record in the combination journal the closing entries from information on the work sheet and distribution of net income statement. Use the closing entries, page 309, as a guide.

3. Post the adjusting and closing entries to the general ledger.

4. Prepare a post-closing trial balance. Use the post-closing trial balance, page 314, as a guide.

PROBLEM 16-2 Completing a work sheet; recording adjusting and closing entries

The ledger accounts of Melbourne Supply as of November 30 are given in the working papers.

Instructions: 1. Prepare a trial balance in the Trial Balance columns of a work sheet.

2. Complete the work sheet. The information about inventories and value of insurance policies on November 30 is below.

Merchandise inventory, November 30	$47,600.00
Supplies inventory, November 30	392.00
Value of insurance policies, November 30	530.00

3. Prepare an income statement from the information on the work sheet.

4. Prepare a distribution of net income statement. Net income or loss is to be distributed equally.

5. Prepare a capital statement.

6. Prepare a balance sheet.

7. On page 6 of a combination journal record the adjusting entries shown in the Adjustments columns of the work sheet.

8. Record in the combination journal the closing entries from information on the work sheet and distribution of net income statement.

9. Post the adjusting and closing entries to the general ledger.

10. Prepare a post-closing trial balance.

ENRICHMENT PROBLEMS

MASTERY PROBLEM 16-M Completing the work at the end of a fiscal period

The ledger accounts of Dubolt Associates as of October 31 are given in the working papers.

Instructions: **1.** Prepare a trial balance in the Trial Balance columns of a work sheet.

2. Complete the work sheet. The information about inventories and value of insurance policies on October 31 is below.

Merchandise inventory, October 31	$53,250.00
Supplies inventory, October 31	435.00
Value of insurance policies, October 31	620.00

3. Prepare an income statement from the information on the work sheet.

4. Prepare a distribution of net income statement. Net income or loss is to be distributed equally.

5. Prepare a capital statement.

6. Prepare a balance sheet.

7. On page 4 of a combination journal record the adjusting entries shown in the Adjustments columns of the work sheet.

8. Record in the combination journal the closing entries from information on the work sheet and distribution of net income statement.

9. Post the adjusting and closing entries to the general ledger.

10. Prepare a post-closing trial balance.

CHALLENGE PROBLEM 16-C Locating and correcting errors on a completed work sheet

Mayberry Electronics' work sheet for the month ended January 31, 1983, is given in the working papers. The information about inventories and value of insurance policies is below.

Ending merchandise inventory, January 31	$35,200.00
Supplies used during January	120.00
Insurance expired during January	90.00

The totals of the Balance Sheet Debit and Credit columns do not balance after net income is added.

Instructions: Locate the errors made in preparing the work sheet and prepare a new work sheet. The trial balance on the work sheet has been checked and is correct.

Reinforcement Activity 2
PART B

An Accounting Cycle for a Partnership Using a Combination Journal

Complete trial balance on work sheet
↓
Enter adjustments and complete work sheet
↓
Prepare financial statements
↓
Journalize adjusting and closing entries
↓
Post adjusting and closing entries to general ledger
↓
Prepare post-closing trial balance

The ledgers used in Part A are needed to complete Part B.

Reinforcement Activity 2, Part B, covers those accounting activities needed to complete Infocus' accounting cycle. The flowchart at the left shows that part of the accounting cycle covered in Reinforcement Activity 2, Part B.

Completing Infocus' end-of-fiscal-period work

Instructions: 1. Prepare a trial balance on an eight-column work sheet. Use December 31 of the current year as the date.

2. Complete the work sheet using the adjustment information below.

Adjustment Information, December 31	
Merchandise inventory	$72,300.00
Supplies inventory	520.50
Value of insurance policies	506.00

3. Prepare an income statement from the information on the work sheet.

4. Prepare a distribution of net income statement. Net income or loss is to be distributed equally.

5. Prepare a capital statement.

6. Prepare a balance sheet.

7. On page 24 of a combination journal record the adjusting entries shown in the Adjustments columns of the work sheet.

8. Record in the combination journal the closing entries from the information on the work sheet and distribution of net income statement.

9. Post the adjusting and closing entries to the general ledger.

10. Prepare a post-closing trial balance.

CYCLE CENTER is a merchandising business organized as a partnership. This business simulation covers the realistic transactions completed by a partnership that sells bicycles, mopeds, motorcycles, and dirt bikes. Transactions are recorded in a combination journal from source documents. In addition, a general ledger, an accounts receivable ledger, and an accounts payable ledger are used. A pictorial flowchart of the accounting cycle of CYCLE CENTER is shown on the next two pages. This business simulation is available from the publisher.

Flowchart of the
Accounting Cycle of
CYCLE CENTER

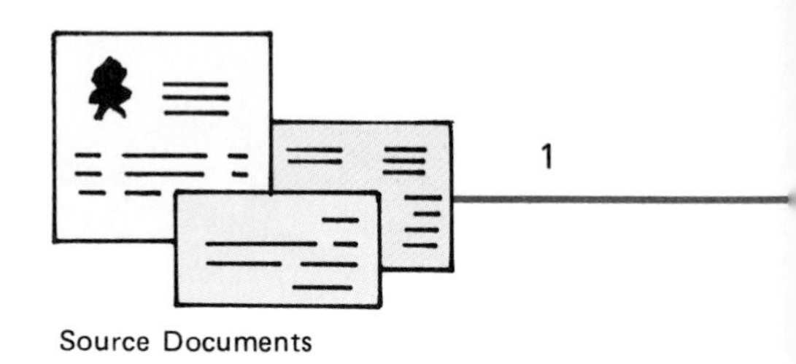

1 Record transactions in the combination journal from source documents.
1a File source documents.
2 Post items to be posted individually to the general ledger and subsidiary ledgers.
3 Post column totals to the general ledger.
4 Prepare schedules of accounts receivable and accounts payable from subsidiary ledgers.
5 Prepare the trial balance on the work sheet.
6 Plan adjustments and complete the work sheet.
7 Prepare financial statements.
8 Record adjusting and closing entries from the work sheet.
9 Post adjusting and closing entries to the general ledger.
10 Prepare a post-closing trial balance from the general ledger.

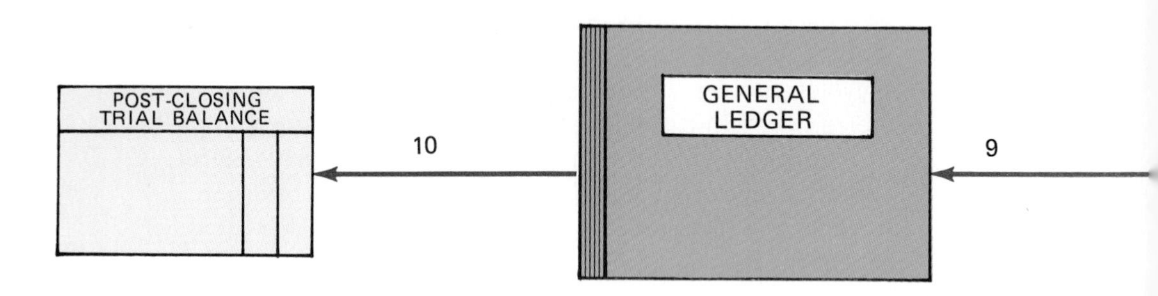

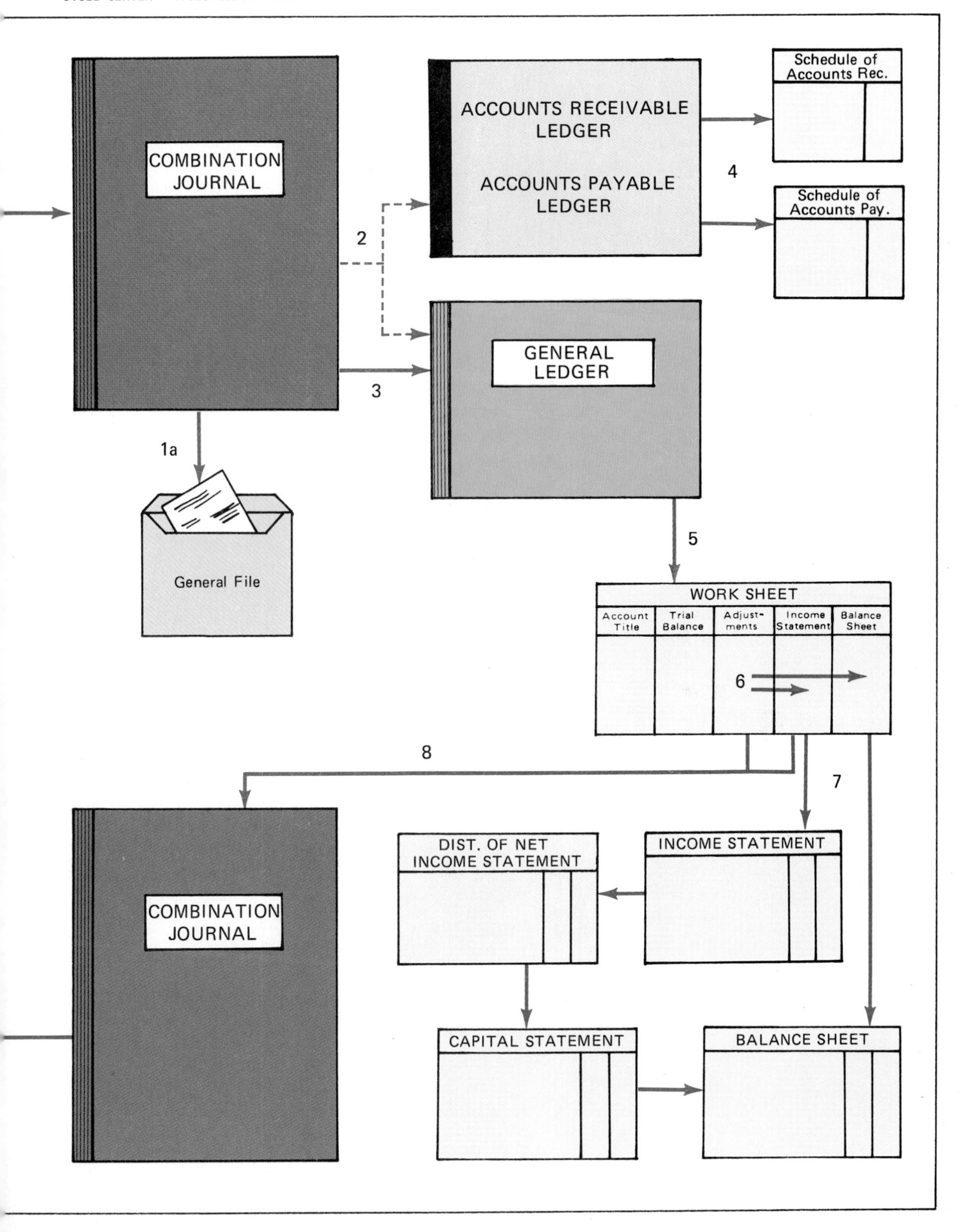
COMBINATION JOURNAL
ACCOUNTS RECEIVABLE LEDGER
ACCOUNTS PAYABLE LEDGER
Schedule of Accounts Rec.
Schedule of Accounts Pay.
4
2
GENERAL LEDGER
3
1a
General File
5
WORK SHEET
Account Title
Trial Balance
Adjust-ments
Income Statement
Balance Sheet
6
8
7
COMBINATION JOURNAL
DIST. OF NET INCOME STATEMENT
INCOME STATEMENT
CAPITAL STATEMENT
BALANCE SHEET

4 AN AUTOMATED ACCOUNTING SYSTEM

GENERAL BEHAVIORAL GOALS

1. Know terminology related to automated accounting for a merchandising business organized as a partnership.
2. Understand automated accounting principles and practices for a merchandising business organized as a partnership.
3. Demonstrate automated accounting procedures for a merchandising business organized as a partnership.

Allsports, the business for Part 4, sells sporting goods.

RAWHIDE LACING

ALLSPORTS
Chart of Accounts

Account Number	(1) ASSETS
11000	Cash
11500	Accounts Receivable
12000	Merchandise Inventory
12500	Office Supplies
13000	Store Supplies
13500	Prepaid Insurance
14000	Delivery Equipment
14500	Office Equipment
15000	Store Equipment
	(2) LIABILITIES
21000	Accounts Payable
	(3) CAPITAL
31000	Helen Lewis, Capital
31500	Helen Lewis, Drawing
32000	Samuel Sullivan, Capital
32500	Samuel Sullivan, Drawing
33000	Income Summary

Account Number	(4) REVENUE
41000	Sales
	(5) COST OF MERCHANDISE
51000	Purchases
	(6) EXPENSES
61000	Advertising Expense
61500	Credit Card Fee Expense
62000	Delivery Expense
62500	Insurance Expense
63000	Miscellaneous Expense
63500	Office Supplies Expense
64000	Rent Expense
64500	Salary Expense
65000	Store Supplies Expense

The chart of accounts for Allsports is illustrated above for ready reference as you study Part 4 of this textbook.

17

Data Processing Systems

ENABLING PERFORMANCE TASKS

After studying Chapter 17, you will be able to:

a. Define terminology related to automated general ledger accounting for a merchandising business.
b. Explain automated general ledger accounting principles and practices.
c. Assign account numbers to accounts in a general ledger.
d. Prepare a chart of accounts setup form.
e. Prepare financial statement setup forms.

Procedures for recording and reporting a business' financial activities are described in earlier chapters. Recording and reporting procedures vary according to business size and type. The accounting cycle for Putt Around, a small service business, is described in Part 2. The accounting cycle for Denim Threads, a small merchandising business, is described in Part 3. Effective business decisions can be made only when the information is current, accurate, and complete. As a business becomes larger, the volume of information to be recorded and reported also increases. When the volume of information increases, a business generally needs faster recording and reporting procedures. The use of machines is one way to speed the recording and reporting processes.

DATA PROCESSING

Detailed or factual information is called data. Many different kinds of data are used in business. One important kind of data in any business is financial data. To be useful data must be recorded, organized, and reported. A series of operations performed upon data is called data processing. A combination of procedures, forms, and machines converting data into useful information is called a data processing system.

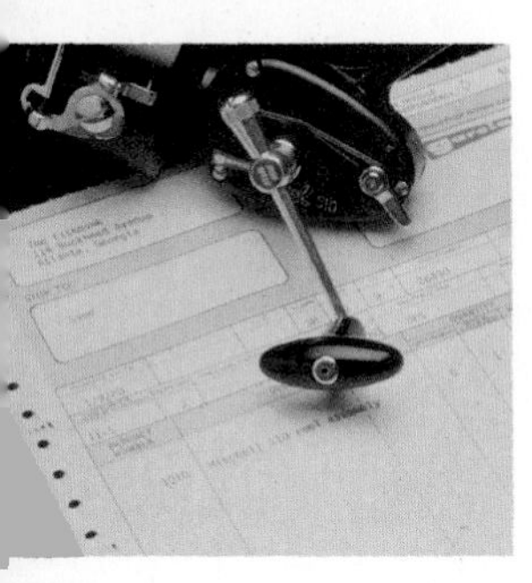

Helen Lewis and Samuel Sullivan, partners, operate a retail store known as Allsports. *(CONCEPT: Business Entity)* The store sells a complete sporting goods line. Sales are made to individuals as well as to school systems. A monthly rent is paid for the use of building and fixtures. Helen and Samuel want to improve their data processing system. They want the work done faster and less expensively.

Types of data processing systems

Data processing systems are classified in many ways. One way to classify these systems is according to the procedures and equipment used. Two common types of data processing systems are used. (1) Manual data processing. (2) Automated data processing.

A system in which data are processed mostly by hand is called manual data processing. The financial data in previous chapters was processed through manual data processing procedures. A manual system may not be adequate to complete all the accounting work. The total amount of data in the system may be too large or efficiency may need improvement. Ms. Lewis found both to be true for Allsports. The amount of data had increased. More efficient procedures were needed.

A process by which work is done mostly by machines is called automation. A system using automated machines to process data is called automated data processing (ADP). Even in automated data processing some procedures are done manually.

Planning for automated data processing

Planning for automated data processing is similar to planning for manual data processing. Planning any data processing system consists of two steps. (1) Setting goals — deciding what is to be processed and reported. (2) Establishing procedures and determining the equipment needed to process the data. Allsports had such goals when the current manual data processing system was planned.

Accuracy in every detail is equally important in both automated and manual data processing. Results in any data processing system can only be as accurate as the information put into the system. For example, if an accountant records an amount as $15.80 rather than $18.50, information on financial statements will be incorrect.

Phases of a data processing system

A data processing system consists of four phases. (1) Input. (2) Processing. (3) Storage. (4) Output. These four phases are illustrated on page 329.

Data put into a system are called input. Input may be data on sales invoices, purchase invoices, and other business forms. Working with data according to precise instructions is called processing. Filing or hold-

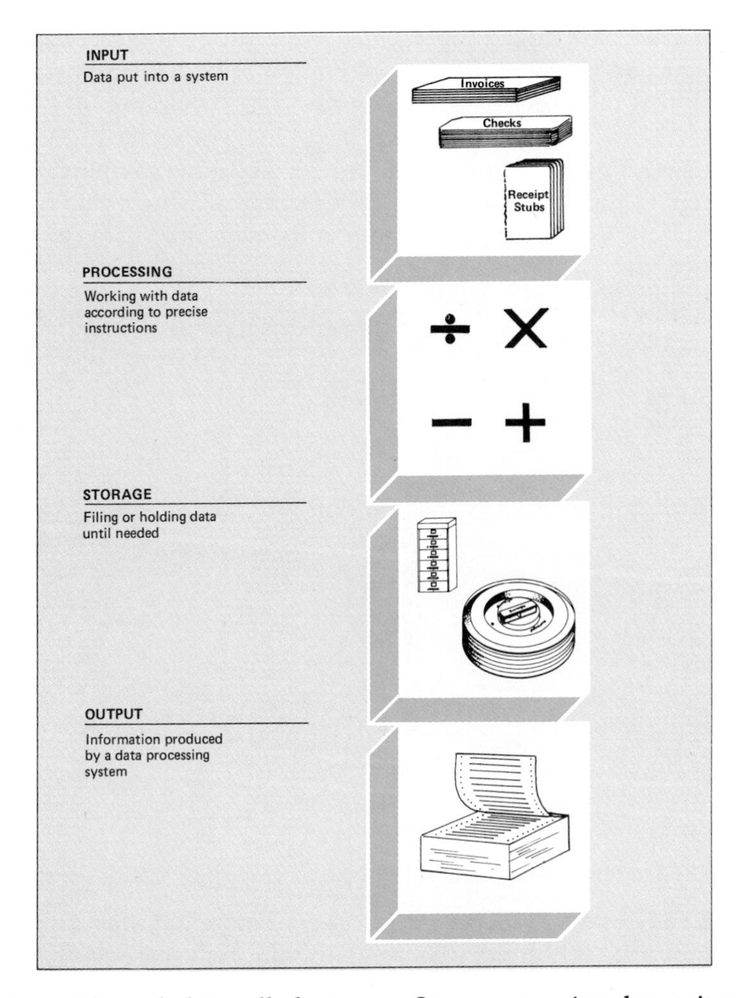

Phases of a data processing system

ing data until needed is called storage. Storage may involve using filing cabinets or other devices. Information produced by a data processing system is called output. Examples of output are facts about assets, liabilities, capital, revenue, and expenses reported on financial statements. Output can also be printed on forms such as checks and invoices. Output may be facts that will be further processed.

ELECTRONIC DATA PROCESSING

A group of interconnected machines that process data according to stored instructions is called a computer. Automated data processing using a computer is called electronic data processing (EDP). Electronic data processing is the most common automated data processing system.

A computer handles data in all four data processing phases: input, processing, storage, and output. Separate machines, often referred to as computer units, are linked together by electrical cables. Electrical cables allow data to be transferred from one computer unit to another. A computer unit that processes data and controls other computer units is called a central processing unit (CPU).

A diagram showing data flow through an electronic computer is below. The arrows in the diagram show the direction in which data move in a computer. Arrows with points at both ends mean that data can move in either direction.

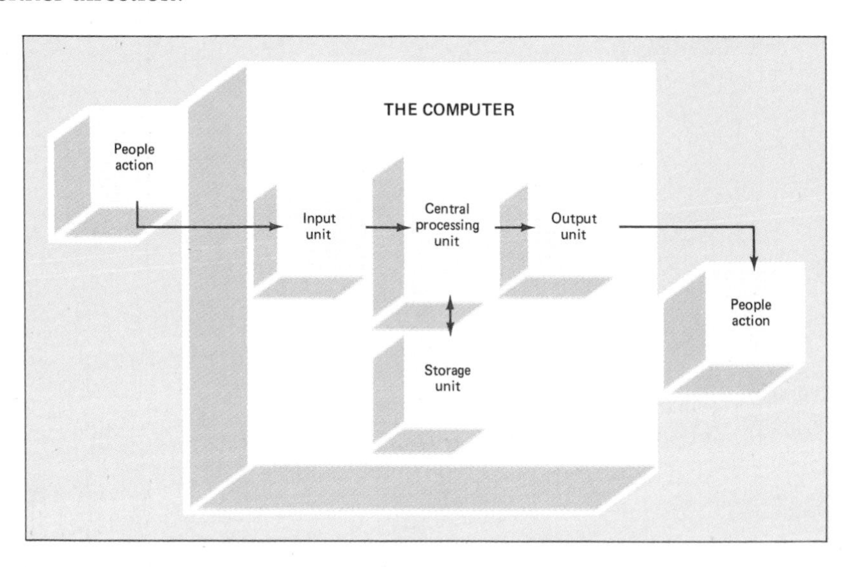

Data flow in a computer

People action in electronic data processing

Five types of people action are necessary before data can be processed by a computer. (1) Output type and form are fully described. (2) Flowcharts are prepared showing the sequence for each job to be processed. (3) Instructions are written for the computer. (4) Data (input) to be processed are arranged according to set procedures and checked for accuracy. (5) Input is entered into the computer.

Two types of people action are necessary after data have been processed by a computer. (1) Output is inspected. (2) Output is given to people who can interpret and use it.

Planning instructions for a computer

Step-by-step instructions for doing each job must be prepared before data can be processed by a computer. A set of instructions followed by a computer to process data is called a computer program. The term "program" may also describe a set of step-by-step instructions for processing data by manual means. For example, on page 20 is a program for manually preparing a balance sheet. A person who prepares a computer program is called a computer programmer.

Computer programmers need special training in electronic data processing. Understanding accounting principles is helpful to a computer programmer. However, such understanding is not essential to program a computer. Understanding the basic concepts of a computer system is important to an accountant using computer services. Steps of the accounting cycle that are computer processed and steps that require manual processing must be understood. Using a computer does not change basic accounting principles. Only the equipment changes.

COMPUTER SERVICE CENTER

For many years automated data processing was used only by larger businesses. The high cost of computers made it impossible for smaller businesses to go beyond manual systems. Today, however, small businesses use automated data processing. The cost of computer services is based on the amount and type of data processed. A business established to sell computer services is called a computer service center. A computer service center is also known as a computer service bureau or a business service bureau.

After gathering facts about data processing systems, Ms. Lewis decides that Allsports will benefit by using automated data processing (ADP). More complete accounting information can be obtained by using an automated system. Allsports does not have the amount of data needed to justify owning the automated equipment. Therefore, Ms. Lewis decides that Allsports will use the services of a computer service center.

Services provided for small businesses

Processing accounting data for small businesses is one of the most important services provided by a computer service center. Accounting services are also provided for professional people such as doctors, dentists, and lawyers. Five major services are provided. (1) Assist in training personnel who will prepare data to be processed by a computer. (2) Assist in designing procedures for a business' data processing system. (3) Assist in designing a business' output reports. (4) Enter input data into a computer. (5) Process data to produce output reports.

Services provided for large businesses

Businesses that own computers often use a computer service center. Most businesses have peak periods of business activity. Using a computer service center during these peak periods avoids installing additional costly, new and larger automated machines.

Using a computer service center does not eliminate an accountant's need to master basic accounting principles. A computer performs routine and repetitive operations based on accounting principles and concepts.

AUTOMATED GENERAL LEDGER ACCOUNTING

Many computer service centers provide training sessions for clients. The training sessions help acquaint clients with the automated services available. Various approaches can be taken in designing an automated accounting system. Two major items need to be considered when deciding on the automated accounting procedures to use. (1) Immediate and future data processing needs of a business. (2) Cost.

Based on immediate and future needs plus cost, Ms. Lewis decides that an automated general ledger accounting system will be used. Allsports operates primarily on a cash basis with credit card privileges available to customers. Regular charge privileges are available only to area school systems. Allsports has a small number of suppliers from whom to buy merchandise and supplies. Ms. Lewis determines that the cost of automating the subsidiary ledgers is not justified when compared with benefits received. Therefore, the decision is made to continue to maintain manually the subsidiary ledgers. Only entries to the general ledger controlling accounts will be entered into the computer system.

Coding the chart of accounts

A computer service center first asks a client to submit a list of ledger accounts. Each account title has meaning for a client. However, automated machines work more efficiently with numbers. Account titles therefore are assigned numbers with which machines can work.

A chart of accounts coding system for an automated accounting system provides for three items. (1) A numeric sequence within each division. (2) A proper order within each division. (3) Enough digits to provide for addition of new accounts. Businesses using EDP will normally need at least a five-digit account number. Less than five digits will not allow enough digits to sequentially add new accounts within each division. Each business numbers its accounts according to its particular needs. A partial chart of accounts with five-digit account numbers is below.

Partial chart of accounts for a general ledger

CHART OF ACCOUNTS GENERAL LEDGER			
Account Number	(1) ASSETS	Account Number	(2) LIABILITIES
11000	Cash	21000	Accounts Payable
11500	Accounts Receivable		
12000	Merchandise Inventory		
12500	Supplies		
13000	Prepaid Insurance		

A breakdown of the five-digit coding system is on the next page.

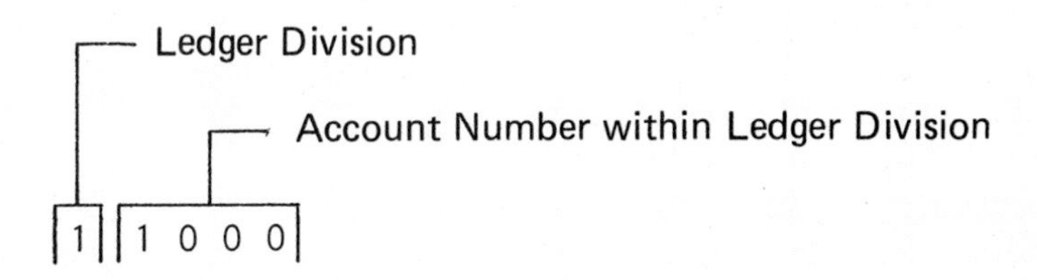

Account number for cash

The first digit of the chart of accounts coding system identifies the ledger division. The second through the fifth digits provide identification of accounts within each division. For the account Cash, the *1* indicates the account is an asset. The number *1000* indicates that the asset account Cash is the first account in the asset division. For Accounts Payable, page 332, the *2* indicates the account is a liability. The number *1000* indicates that Accounts Payable is the first account in the liability division. Remaining accounts within each division are assigned numbers by five hundreds. For example, Accounts Receivable, page 332, is assigned the asset number 11500.

New accounts added at the end of a division are assigned the next five-hundred number. For example, a new account *Store Equipment* is added to the assets division on page 332 following Prepaid Insurance. The Prepaid Insurance number is 13000. Therefore, the Store Equipment number is 13500.

New accounts added between two existing accounts are assigned the unused middle number. For example, a new account Office Equipment is inserted between Prepaid Insurance (13000) and Store Equipment (13500). The Office Equipment number is 13250. Assigning new numbers between two existing accounts is below.

Existing Account Numbers	Assignment of One New Account Number	Additional Account Numbers Available
13000		13001–13249
←	13250	
13500		13251–13499

Coding procedures for new accounts, described above, keep the chart of accounts in numeric sequence. The unused middle number is always assigned to new accounts inserted between two existing accounts. Also, the illustration above shows that the numbers 13001–13249 and 13251–13499 are still available. If Delivery Equipment is added between Prepaid Insurance and Office Equipment, the number 13125 is assigned.

Prepaid Insurance	13000
DELIVERY EQUIPMENT	13125
Office Equipment	13250

If no exact middle number is available, either of the two numbers closest to the middle is used. For example, the middle number between

13000 and 13125 is 13062.5. The number 13062.5 contains six digits and cannot be assigned in a five-digit coding system. Therefore, either 13062 or 13063 is used.

Prepaid Insurance	13000
NEW ACCOUNT	13062
Delivery Equipment	13125

Allsports uses a five-digit coding system for its chart of accounts as described above. Allsports' chart of accounts is on page 326.

Chart of accounts setup

The chart of accounts, page 326, shows all balance sheet and income statement sections. The chart further lists all accounts within each section. The accounts are listed in the same order as they will appear on the balance sheet and income statement.

Before data from a chart of accounts are entered into a computer, a special form is prepared. The form shows the account numbers, account classifications, account titles, and normal balances. An EDP form used to describe chart of accounts data is called a chart of accounts setup form.

Setup for Allsports' general ledger chart of accounts. General ledger chart of accounts data are recorded by Ms. Lewis on the chart of accounts setup form, page 335. This printed form is supplied by the computer service center.

Steps in preparing the chart of accounts setup form. Allsports' chart of accounts setup form is prepared as described below.

1 Enter the business' name in the space provided.

2 Enter the client number, *320*, in the space provided. The client number is assigned by the computer service center and is used for all data transmitted to the center.

3 Enter the account number obtained from the chart of accounts, page 326. All account titles are identified by numbers in numeric sequence.

4 Enter the account classification code. Code *AS* is used for an asset account. Code *LI* is used for a liability account. Code *CA* is used for a capital account. Code *RE* is used for a revenue account. Code *CO* is used for a cost account. Code *EX* is used for an expense account.

5 Enter the account title just as it will appear on the output.

6 Enter the account normal balance code. Code *Dr* is used for debit. Code *Cr* is used for credit.

CHART OF ACCOUNTS SETUP

CLIENT NO. 320 NAME OF BUSINESS Allsports

	ACCOUNT NUMBER	ACCT. CLASS.	ACCOUNT TITLE	NORM. BAL.	
1	11000	AS	CASH	DR	1
2	11500	AS	ACCOUNTS RECEIVABLE	DR	2
3	12000	AS	MERCHANDISE INVENTORY	DR	3
4	12500	AS	OFFICE SUPPLIES	DR	4
5	13000	AS	STORE SUPPLIES	DR	5
6	13500	AS	PREPAID INSURANCE	DR	6
7	14000	AS	DELIVERY EQUIPMENT	DR	7
8	14500	AS	OFFICE EQUIPMENT	DR	8
9	15000	AS	STORE EQUIPMENT	DR	9
10	21000	LI	ACCOUNTS PAYABLE	CR	10
11	31000	CA	HELEN LEWIS, CAPITAL	CR	11
12	31500	CA	HELEN LEWIS, DRAWING	DR	12
13	32000	CA	SAMUEL SULLIVAN, CAPITAL	CR	13
14	32500	CA	SAMUEL SULLIVAN, DRAWING	DR	14
15	33000	CA	INCOME SUMMARY	CR	15
16	41000	RE	SALES	CR	16
17	51000	CO	PURCHASES	DR	17
18	61000	EX	ADVERTISING EXPENSE	DR	18
19	61500	EX	CREDIT CARD FEE EXPENSE	DR	19
20	62000	EX	DELIVERY EXPENSE	DR	20
21	62500	EX	INSURANCE EXPENSE	DR	21
22	63000	EX	MISCELLANEOUS EXPENSE	DR	22
23	63500	EX	OFFICE SUPPLIES EXPENSE	DR	23
24	64000	EX	RENT EXPENSE	DR	24
25	64500	EX	SALARY EXPENSE	DR	25
26	65000	EX	STORE SUPPLIES EXPENSE	DR	26

ACCOUNT CLASSIFICATION:
AS = ASSET CA = CAPITAL CO = COST
LI = LIABILITY EX = EXPENSE RE = REVENUE

PREPARED BY Helen Lewis
DATE 2/10/83

Chart of accounts setup form for general ledger chart of accounts

Adding new general ledger accounts. A chart of accounts setup form is also used to describe new accounts that are added to a general ledger. For example, a new account Utilities Expense would be included on a chart of accounts setup form as shown below.

CHART OF ACCOUNTS SETUP

CLIENT NO. 320 NAME OF BUSINESS Allsports

	ACCOUNT NUMBER	ACCT. CLASS.	ACCOUNT TITLE	NORM. BAL.	
1	65500	EX	UTILITIES EXPENSE	DR	1

Chart of accounts setup form adding a new general ledger account

The account number is determined using procedures described on page 333.

Financial statements setup

Formats for financial statements to be prepared by a computer service center are described on setup forms. An EDP form used to describe output format of financial statements is called a financial statement setup form.

Setup forms for Allsports' financial statements. Allsports' four financial statements are prepared by the computer service center at the end of each month. *(CONCEPT: Accounting Period Cycle)* Allsports' financial statements are similar to those used by Denim Threads in Chapter 15. (1) Income statement — similar to form on page 283. (2) Distribution of net income statement — similar to form on page 285. (3) Capital statement — similar to form on page 288. (4) Balance sheet — similar to form on page 292. Each statement is described on a financial statement setup form. The printed setup form is supplied by the computer service center. Completed financial statement setup forms are on pages 337–339. Each statement heading (business name, statement name, and date) prints as a result of computer program instructions.

Steps in preparing the setup form. Each of Allsports' financial statement setup forms is prepared as described below.

1 Enter client number, *320*, in space provided.

2 Enter account number from chart of accounts, page 326. The Account Number column is left blank for all headings that appear on the forms. For example, the heading Revenue appears on line 1 of the setup form for the income statement, page 337. Therefore, the Account Number column is left blank.

3 Enter financial statement code. Code *1* is used for Income Statement. Code *2* is used for Distribution of Net Income Statement. Code *3* is used for Capital Statement. Code *4* is used for Balance Sheet.

4 Enter column code. Code *0* is used when only the description is to print. Code *1* is used when both description and amount are to print. Code *2* is used when both description and total amount are to print.

For codes *1* and *2* a line will print only when an account or heading has a balance. For example, line 22, income statement setup form, page 337, would not print when there is a net income. Likewise, line 21 would not print when there is a net loss.

FINANCIAL STATEMENT SETUP

CLIENT NO. 320

	ACCOUNT NUMBER	STMT. CODE	COL. CODE	DESCRIPTION	
1		1	0	REVENUE:	1
2	41000	1	1	SALES	2
3		1	0	COST OF MERCHANDISE SOLD:	3
4	12000	1	1	BEGINNING MDSE. INVENTORY	4
5	51000	1	1	PURCHASES	5
6		1	2	TOTAL COST OF MDSE. AVAILABLE	6
7	12000	1	1	ENDING MERCHANDISE INVENTORY	7
8		1	2	COST OF MERCHANDISE SOLD	8
9		1	2	GROSS PROFIT ON SALES	9
10		1	0	EXPENSES:	10
11	61000	1	1	ADVERTISING EXPENSE	11
12	61500	1	1	CREDIT CARD FEE EXPENSE	12
13	62000	1	1	DELIVERY EXPENSE	13
14	62500	1	1	INSURANCE EXPENSE	14
15	63000	1	1	MISCELLANEOUS EXPENSE	15
16	63500	1	1	OFFICE SUPPLIES EXPENSE	16
17	64000	1	1	RENT EXPENSE	17
18	64500	1	1	SALARY EXPENSE	18
19	65000	1	1	STORE SUPPLIES EXPENSE	19
20		1	2	TOTAL EXPENSES	20
21		1	2	NET INCOME	21
22		1	2	NET LOSS	22

STATEMENT CODE:
1 = INCOME STATEMENT
2 = DISTRIBUTION OF NET INCOME STATEMENT
3 = CAPITAL STATEMENT
4 = BALANCE SHEET

COLUMN CODE:
0 = ONLY DESCRIPTION PRINTS
1 = DESCRIPTION AND AMOUNT PRINT
2 = DESCRIPTION AND TOTAL AMOUNT PRINT

PREPARED BY Helen Lewis

DATE 2/16/83

Setup form for income statement

5 Enter headings and account titles for the body of each financial statement as they will appear on output. An account title or heading must be entered for all possible lines of required output. For example, lines 3 and 4, capital statement setup form, page 338, may not print each time. These lines would print only when an additional investment is made. Likewise, lines 5 or 6, not both, will print. Line 5 will print if there is a net income. Line 6 will print if there is a net loss.

On all financial statements other than the balance sheet, the description is either aligned at the left or indented. When the description is indented, the first letter of the description starts in space 3. On the setup form for the income statement above, line 1, the heading Revenue is left aligned. The account title Sales, line 2, is indented starting in space 3.

FINANCIAL STATEMENT SETUP

CLIENT NO. 320

	ACCOUNT NUMBER	STMT. CODE	COL. CODE	DESCRIPTION	
1		2	0	HELEN LEWIS	1
2		2	1	60% OF NET INCOME	2
3		2	1	60% OF NET LOSS	3
4		2	0	SAMUEL SULLIVAN	4
5		2	1	40% OF NET INCOME	5
6		2	1	40% OF NET LOSS	6
7		2	2	NET INCOME	7
8		2	2	NET LOSS	8

Setup form for distribution of net income statement

FINANCIAL STATEMENT SETUP

CLIENT NO. 320

	ACCOUNT NUMBER	STMT. CODE	COL. CODE	DESCRIPTION	
1		3	0	HELEN LEWIS	1
2	31000	3	1	BEGINNING CAPITAL	2
3	31000	3	1	PLUS ADDITIONAL INVESTMENT	3
4		3	2	TOTAL	4
5		3	1	SHARE OF NET INCOME	5
6		3	1	SHARE OF NET LOSS	6
7	31500	3	1	LESS WITHDRAWALS	7
8	31500	3	1	PLUS WITHDRAWALS	8
9		3	2	NET INCREASE IN CAPITAL	9
10		3	2	NET DECREASE IN CAPITAL	10
11		3	2	ENDING CAPITAL	11
12		3	0	SAMUEL SULLIVAN	12
13	32000	3	1	BEGINNING CAPITAL	13
14	32000	3	1	PLUS ADDITIONAL INVESTMENT	14
15		3	2	TOTAL	15
16		3	1	SHARE OF NET INCOME	16
17		3	1	SHARE OF NET LOSS	17
18	32500	3	1	LESS WITHDRAWALS	18
19	32500	3	1	PLUS WITHDRAWALS	19
20		3	2	NET INCREASE IN CAPITAL	20
21		3	2	NET DECREASE IN CAPITAL	21
22		3	2	ENDING CAPITAL	22
23		3	2	TOTAL ENDING CAPITAL	23

STATEMENT CODE:
1 = INCOME STATEMENT
2 = DISTRIBUTION OF NET INCOME STATEMENT
3 = CAPITAL STATEMENT
4 = BALANCE SHEET

COLUMN CODE:
0 = ONLY DESCRIPTION PRINTS
1 = DESCRIPTION AND AMOUNT PRINT
2 = DESCRIPTION AND TOTAL AMOUNT PRINT

PREPARED BY Helen Lewis

DATE 2/16/83

Setup form for capital statement

FINANCIAL STATEMENT SETUP

CLIENT NO. 320

	ACCOUNT NUMBER	STMT. CODE	COL. CODE	DESCRIPTION	
1		4	0	ASSETS	1
2	11000	4	1	CASH	2
3	11500	4	1	ACCOUNTS RECEIVABLE	3
4	12000	4	1	MERCHANDISE INVENTORY	4
5	12500	4	1	OFFICE SUPPLIES	5
6	13000	4	1	STORE SUPPLIES	6
7	13500	4	1	PREPAID INSURANCE	7
8	14000	4	1	DELIVERY EQUIPMENT	8
9	14500	4	1	OFFICE EQUIPMENT	9
10	15000	4	1	STORE EQUIPMENT	10
11		4	2	TOTAL ASSETS	11
12		4	0	LIABILITIES	12
13	21000	4	1	ACCOUNTS PAYABLE	13
14		4	0	CAPITAL	14
15	31000	4	1	HELEN LEWIS, CAPITAL	15
16	32000	4	1	SAMUEL SULLIVAN, CAPITAL	16
17		4	2	TOTAL CAPITAL	17
18		4	2	TOTAL LIABILITIES AND CAPITAL	18
19					19
20					20
21					21

STATEMENT CODE:
1 = INCOME STATEMENT
2 = DISTRIBUTION OF NET INCOME STATEMENT
3 = CAPITAL STATEMENT
4 = BALANCE SHEET

COLUMN CODE:
0 = ONLY DESCRIPTION PRINTS
1 = DESCRIPTION AND AMOUNT PRINT
2 = DESCRIPTION AND TOTAL AMOUNT PRINT

PREPARED BY Helen Lewis

DATE 2/16/83

Setup form for balance sheet

Allsports' report form of balance sheet has section names centered over the account titles. The computer program provides for a maximum of 32 spaces (characters and spaces) per line. The location of the section name ASSETS is figured below.

a.	Number of positions available on line	32
b.	*Less* number of letters in the section name (Assets)	6
	Remainder	26
c.	*Divide* remainder by 2	13
d.	This position is the space on the line for writing the first letter of the name	13

On line 1 of the setup form above the word *Assets* is centered starting in space 13. If division by 2 (c. above) results in a fraction, round answer to next nearest whole number. For example, the location of the section name LIABILITIES is figured on the next page.

a. Number of positions available on line	32
b. *Less* number of letters in section name (Liabilities)	11
Remainder	21
c. *Divide* remainder by 2	10.5
d. *Round* to the next nearest whole number. This number is the position on the line for writing the first letter of the name	11

On line 12 of the setup form, page 339, the word *Liabilities* is centered starting in space 11.

Processing the chart of accounts and financial statement setup forms

Allsports' completed chart of accounts and financial statement setup forms are sent to the computer service center. At the computer service center the data from the forms are entered into the computer. This procedure is described in Chapter 18.

ACCOUNTING TERMS

What is the meaning of each of the following?

1. data
2. data processing
3. data processing system
4. manual data processing
5. automation
6. automated data processing (ADP)
7. input
8. processing
9. storage
10. output
11. computer
12. electronic data processing (EDP)
13. central processing unit (CPU)
14. computer program
15. computer programmer
16. computer service center
17. chart of accounts setup form
18. financial statement setup form

QUESTIONS FOR INDIVIDUAL STUDY

1. Why is current, accurate, and complete information important to a business?
2. When would a business find a need for faster recording and reporting procedures?
3. What is one way to speed up the recording and reporting procedures?
4. What is one of the most important kinds of data in any business?
5. What must be done to make data useful?
6. What are the two most common types of data processing systems?
7. What are the two steps involved in planning for any data processing system?
8. What are the four data processing phases?
9. Give one example of input.
10. What is the most common type of automated data processing system?
11. What five types of people action are necessary before a computer can process data?
12. What two types of people action are necessary after data have been processed by a computer?
13. Does using a computer change basic accounting principles? Why?
14. Why did Allsports decide to use a computer service center?

15. What is one of the most important services provided by a computer service center?
16. What are the five services provided by a computer service center?
17. What are the two major items a business must consider when deciding on the automated accounting procedures to use?
18. Why did Allsports decide not to automate the subsidiary ledger?
19. What three items must the chart of accounts coding system provide?
20. What is normally the least number of digits used for a business' account number when using EDP?
21. Assume that a new account is to be added following account number 17000. What account number would be assigned to the new account?
22. Assume that a new account is to be added between two existing accounts — 14000 and 14500. What account number would be assigned to the new account?
23. What four types of data are entered on the chart of accounts setup form?
24. What are the four financial statements that Allsports will have the computer service center prepare?
25. When is column code *0* used on a financial statement setup form?
26. Why must all possible lines of output be entered on a financial statement setup form?

CASES FOR MANAGEMENT DECISION

CASE 1 James King and Ellen Frazer, partners, own and operate a home improvement business called J and E Supply. The business uses a manual accounting system. Ms. Frazer does all the accounting herself. Other business activities have been taking more and more of her time. Consequently, she has been having difficulty finding time to run an efficient accounting system. Ms. Frazer has also considered hiring an accountant. What factors should be considered in making the decision to either automate the accounting system or hire an accountant?

CASE 2 Jason Imports uses a manual accounting system with two-digit, general ledger account numbers. Plans are being made to change to an automated accounting system. The business plans to continue using a two-digit account number. What problems, if any, will a two-digit account number create in an automated accounting system?

DRILLS FOR UNDERSTANDING

DRILL 17-D 1 Adding new general ledger accounts

This drill provides practice in assigning account numbers to new accounts being added to general ledger chart of accounts.

Instructions: A partial chart of accounts is on the next page. New accounts to be added to this chart of accounts are also given. Use the form given in your working papers and assign account numbers to the new accounts. Use the "unused middle number" method of assigning new accounts as explained on page 333.

Account Number	Account Title	New Accounts to be Added
12000	Merchandise Inventory	Office Supplies
12500	Store Supplies	Office Equipment
13000	Delivery Equipment	Credit Card Fee Expense
13250	Store Equipment	Insurance Expense
61000	Advertising Expense	Office Supplies Expense
61250	Delivery Expense	Store Supplies Expense
61500	Miscellaneous Expense	
62000	Rent Expense	
62500	Salary Expense	

DRILL 17-D 2 Analyzing a chart of accounts setup form

Instructions: Refer to the completed chart of accounts setup form, page 335, and answer the following questions.

1. Who assigns the client number?
2. What is Allsports' client number?
3. What is the maximum number of digits that may be recorded in the Account Number column?
4. How many account classification codes may be entered?
5. What account classification code is entered in the Acct. Class. column for an asset account?
6. What account classification code is entered in the Acct. Class. column for a liability account?
7. What account classification code is entered in the Acct. Class. column for a capital account?
8. What normal balance code is entered in the Norm. Bal. column for an asset account?
9. What normal balance code is entered in the Norm. Bal. column for a liability account?
10. What normal balance code is entered in the Norm. Bal. column for an owner's capital account?

DRILL 17-D 3 Analyzing a financial statement setup form

Instructions: Refer to the completed financial statement setup forms, pages 337–339, and answer the following questions.

1. When is the Account Number column left blank?
2. What financial statement code is entered in the Stmt. Code column for an income statement?
3. What financial statement code is entered in the Stmt. Code column for a capital statement?
4. What financial statement code is entered in the Stmt. Code column for a distribution of net income statement?
5. What financial statement code is entered in the Stmt. Code column for a balance sheet?
6. What column code is entered in the Col. Code column when both description and

amount are to print?

7. What column code is entered in the Col. Code column when only the description is to print?
8. What column code is entered in the Col. Code column when both description and total amount are to print?
9. When a description is to be indented, in which space of the Description column is the first letter entered?
10. For Allsports' financial statements, which statement is to have section names centered over account titles?

APPLICATION PROBLEMS

PROBLEM 17-1 Preparing a general ledger chart of accounts setup form

The general ledger chart of accounts for Soto Auto Supply is below.

Account Number	ASSETS	Account Number	REVENUE
11000	Cash	41000	Sales
11500	Accounts Receivable		
12000	Merchandise Inventory		COST OF MERCHANDISE SOLD
12500	Office Supplies	51000	Purchases
13000	Store Supplies		
13500	Prepaid Insurance		EXPENSES
14000	Office Equipment		
14500	Store Equipment	61000	Advertising Expense
		61500	Credit Card Fee Expense
	LIABILITIES	62000	Insurance Expense
		62500	Miscellaneous Expense
21000	Accounts Payable	63000	Office Supplies Expense
		63500	Rent Expense
	CAPITAL	64000	Salary Expense
31000	Alice Soto, Capital	64500	Store Supplies Expense
31500	Alice Soto, Drawing		
32000	Frank Soto, Capital		
32500	Frank Soto, Drawing		
33000	Income Summary		

Instructions: Prepare a general ledger chart of accounts setup form dated February 22 of the current year. Soto Auto Supply's client number is 183. Use chart of accounts setup form, page 335, as a guide.

The chart of accounts prepared in Problem 17-1 is needed to complete Problems 18-1, 19-1, and 19-2, Chapters 18 and 19.

PROBLEM 17-2 Preparing financial statement setup forms

Instructions: Prepare the following financial statement setup forms dated February 23 of the current year for Soto Auto Supply. (1) Income statement. (2) Distribution of net income statement. (3) Capital statement. (4) Balance sheet. Use financial statement setup forms, pages 337–339, as a guide. Use the chart of accounts given in Problem 17-1. The client number is 183. Net income is to be shared equally.

ENRICHMENT PROBLEMS

MASTERY PROBLEM 17-M Adding new accounts to general ledger chart of accounts

The general ledger chart of accounts for the Appliance Center is given in the working papers. New accounts that are being added appear in their proper order within each division.

Instructions: 1. Assign account numbers to the new accounts. Use the "unused middle number" method described on page 333.

2. Prepare a chart of accounts setup form dated March 16 of the current year for the new accounts. Appliance Center's client number is 274. Follow procedures given on page 334.

The chart of accounts prepared in Mastery Problem 17-M is needed to complete Mastery Problems 18-M and 19-M, Chapters 18 and 19.

CHALLENGE PROBLEM 17-C Adding new accounts to general ledger chart of accounts

The general ledger chart of accounts for Adkins Leather Goods is given in the working papers. New accounts that are being added appear in their proper order within each division.

Instructions: 1. Assign account numbers to the new accounts. Use the "unused middle number" method described on page 333.

2. Prepare a chart of accounts setup form dated April 19 of the current year for the new accounts. Adkins Leather Goods' client number is 422. Follow procedures given on page 334.

3. Prepare a distribution of net income statement setup form dated April 20 of the current year. Net income is to be distributed as follows: Susan Adkins, 40%; Marsha Gilbert, 25%; Patricia Mason, 35%. Use distribution of net income statement setup form, page 338, as a guide.

The chart of accounts prepared in Challenge Problem 17-C is needed to complete Challenge Problems 18-C and 19-C, Chapters 18 and 19.

18

Automated General Ledger Accounting: Processing the Chart of Accounts, Setup Forms, and Opening Entry

ENABLING PERFORMANCE TASKS

After studying Chapter 18, you will be able to:

a. Define terminology related to automated general ledger accounting for a merchandising business.
b. Explain automated general ledger accounting principles and practices for processing chart of accounts and financial statement setup data and an opening entry.
c. Analyze a systems flowchart.
d. Prepare a journal entry transmittal for an opening entry.

A business must consider all possible approaches before deciding to change accounting procedures. Immediate and future needs plus the cost of a change must be considered. Chapter 17 described methods followed by Allsports to decide whether or not to change accounting procedures. First, Ms. Lewis learned about the two data processing systems. Based on her study of data processing systems, a number of decisions and preparations were made. Allsports decided to automate the accounting procedures and to use a computer service center. Also, Allsports decided to automate only the general ledger accounting procedures. New general ledger account numbers were assigned and a general ledger chart of accounts setup form was prepared. Lastly, a financial statement setup form for each financial statement was prepared. The data on the setup forms are processed by computer at the computer service center.

ELECTRONIC DATA PROCESSING (EDP)

Data moves through a data processing system following a set of procedures. A system using a computer to process data is known as electronic data processing (EDP). In EDP, data are processed with a minimum of human effort. The computer service center processing accounting data for Allsports uses EDP.

COMPUTER UNITS

Each EDP phase uses a different computer unit. Computer units are machines linked together by electrical cables. Data move from unit to unit through the electrical cables. A computer is divided into four separate units. (1) Central processing unit (CPU). (2) Input unit. (3) Output unit. (4) External storage unit. Each unit serves a special function. The four computer units are shown in the block diagram, below.

The four EDP units are combined to form a computer. However, the central processing unit (CPU) is often referred to as the "computer."

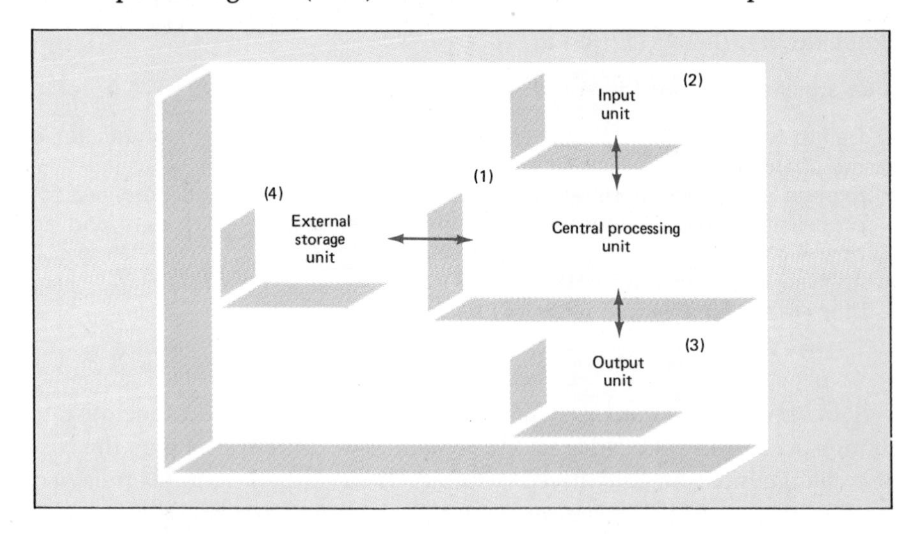

Computer units

Central processing unit (CPU)

A central processing unit (CPU) performs three distinct functions. (1) Controls (directs) all units of a computer. (2) Stores (files) computer instructions and data to be processed. (3) Processes data that have been stored.

Central processing unit

Input unit

Before data are processed by a computer, data must be converted to machine-readable form. A computer unit that converts data from human-readable to machine-readable form is called an input unit. Input units are linked to and controlled by a CPU. A CPU uses program instructions to direct an input unit. Many different kinds of input units may be used by modern day computers.

Direct-entry terminal. A common input unit is a direct-entry terminal. A direct-entry terminal converts data into machine-readable form. A direct-entry terminal looks much like a small television set equipped with a type-writer-type keyboard. Operation of a direct-entry terminal is similar to operation of a regular typewriter. Copy however is displayed on the screen of a terminal. Data entered on a direct-entry terminal are sent to a CPU based on instructions in a computer program. The computer service center processing Allsports' accounting data uses direct-entry terminals as input units.

Direct-entry terminal

Card punch machine. Some input units read punched cards. Holes are punched in a card in special places. Placement of holes forms a code. The complete code for punching numbers, the alphabet, and special characters in a card is below.

0123456789 ABCDEFGHIJKLMNOPQRSTUVWXYZ &#,$./@%*¤

Numbers — The alphabet — Special characters

Punched card

A machine used to make holes in a card representing data is known as a card punch machine. This machine is also known as a keypunch machine. A card punch machine is not linked to a computer and is not considered an input unit. A card punch machine is used only for preparing punched cards.

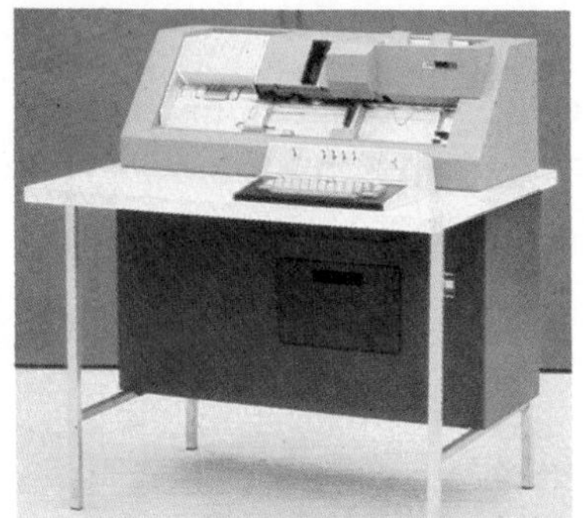
Card punch

Card reader

Card reader. Punched cards are read by an input unit known as a card reader. A card reader is linked to a CPU. Data on punched cards are read and sent to a CPU by a card reader. Data on punched cards are sent to a CPU as a result of instructions in a computer program.

Output unit

The end result of processing data by a computer is the computer output. A computer unit that converts data from machine-readable to human-readable form is called an output unit. An output unit is linked to and controlled by a CPU. Many different kinds of output units may be used by computers.

Direct-entry terminal. A direct-entry terminal used as an input unit, page 347, may also function as an output unit. Processing results not requiring a printed copy may be displayed as output on a direct-entry terminal screen.

Printer. An output unit producing a printed, human-readable copy of processed data is known as a printer. A printer is the most common computer output unit. Computer output in printed, human-readable form is called a printout.

Printer

A printer, linked to a CPU, can produce a wide variety of forms and paper sizes. Printers produce output data at high speeds because an entire line is printed at one time.

External storage unit

A CPU has limited space for the internal storage of data. A computer's capacity can be expanded by linking external storage units to a CPU. External storage units attached to and under control of a CPU are sometimes known as auxiliary or secondary storage. Data are transferred from external storage to a CPU as needed during processing. A CPU uses a computer program to direct an external storage unit. Computers may use many different kinds of external storage units.

The computer service center processing Allsports' accounting data uses a magnetic disk drive as external storage. Data are recorded on removable magnetic disk packs. Disk packs come in different sizes. Each of the disks in a pack looks something like a record for a stereo system. Amount of data that can be stored on a disk pack depends on the size of a pack. Most packs will store several million characters. Disk packs can be removed from a disk drive. Therefore, amount of data that can be stored on magnetic disk packs is unlimited. More external storage can be made available simply by adding new packs.

A magnetic disk drive is the storage unit used for placing data on or reading data from disk packs. A magnetic disk drive is linked to and directed by a CPU.

Disk pack and disk drive

AUTOMATED GENERAL LEDGER ACCOUNTING

Allsports' automated general ledger accounting system requires the same basic accounting principles as a manual system. Only equipment and procedures are different.

Flowcharting procedures

A chart made of symbols showing steps required in EDP is called a systems flowchart. A systems flowchart shows a plan for computer processing of data. After consulting with Ms. Lewis, the computer service center prepared a systems flowchart for each general ledger accounting job. Common, standard flowchart symbols are on the next page.

A computer program provides instructions to a CPU. Several computer programs may be needed for different parts of an EDP general ledger accounting cycle. Allsports' computer programs are stored on external magnetic disk storage.

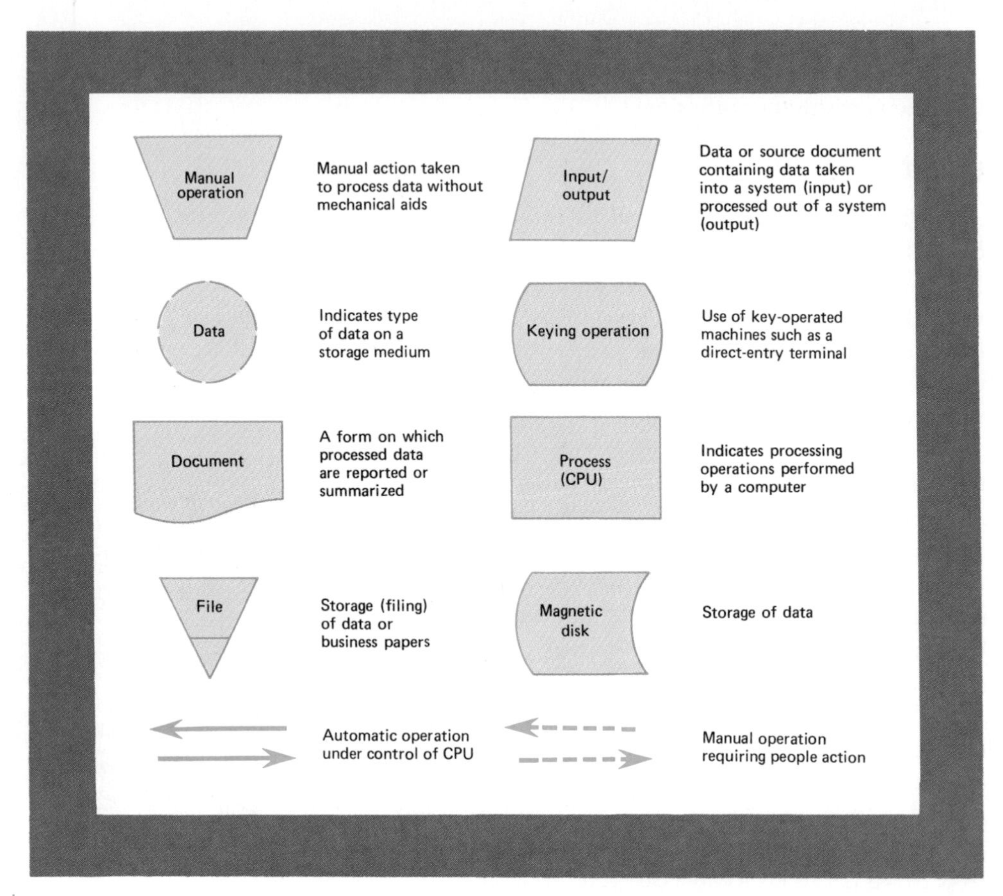

Flowchart symbols

The computer service center uses computer programs to complete each of the following accounting activities. (1) Recording general ledger chart of accounts on magnetic disk. (2) Recording each financial statement setup form on magnetic disk. (3) Posting an opening entry to general ledger stored on magnetic disk. (4) Posting daily transactions to general ledger stored on magnetic disk. (5) Printing each set of transactions processed. A computer printout of transaction data entered into a computer is called an entry register. An entry register is also known as a transaction register. (6) Preparing work sheet printout with trial balance. (7) Posting adjusting entries to general ledger stored on magnetic disk. (8) Preparing financial statements. (9) Posting closing entries to general ledger stored on magnetic disk. (10) Preparing post-closing trial balance. Processing the chart of accounts setup, financial statement setups, and opening entry is described later in this chapter. The processing of daily transactions and end-of-fiscal-period work is described in Chapter 19.

The systems flowchart, page 351, shows Allsports' complete EDP general ledger accounting cycle. Eight steps are required to process each

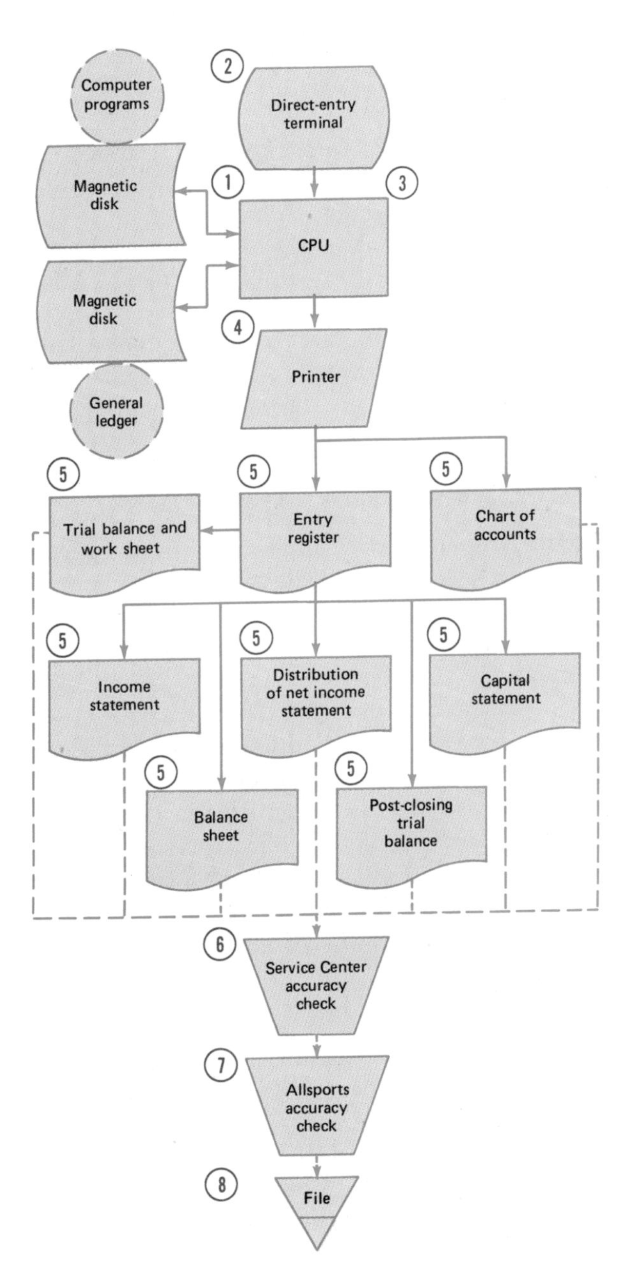

Systems flowchart of EDP general ledger accounting cycle

computer program. The eight steps are completed in the order given below.

1 CPU reads computer program instructions and directs terminal input unit to accept data from terminal keyboard.

2 Data are entered on terminal keyboard and transmitted to CPU.

3 CPU directs data processing based on computer program instructions.

4 CPU transfers processed data to printer output unit.

5 Printer prepares processed data printout.

6 Printout is inspected for accuracy and forwarded to Allsports.

7 Allsports checks printout for accuracy and makes decisions about business progress and condition.

8 Allsports files printout for future reference.

Processing chart of accounts setup data

In manual accounting an account for each account title is opened on a separate ledger page. A ledger is usually a loose-leaf book or sheets in a file. A ledger is a storage phase of manual data processing. In Allsports' EDP general ledger accounting cycle, each account title is stored on magnetic disk. The magnetic disk represents the EDP storage phase.

The computer service center uses the chart of accounts setup form prepared by Ms. Lewis. The chart of accounts data are entered on the direct-entry terminal keyboard and transferred to the CPU. The CPU, based on computer program instructions, transmits the data to magnetic disk storage. A computer printout of the chart of accounts is prepared and forwarded to Allsports. Ms. Lewis checks the printout for accuracy and then files the chart of accounts printout for future reference. The computer printout of Allsports' chart of accounts is on page 353.

Processing financial statement setup data

The computer service center uses the financial statement setup forms prepared by Ms. Lewis. Data for each financial statement setup are entered on the direct-entry terminal and sent to the CPU. The CPU, based on computer program instructions, stores the financial statement setup data on magnetic disk. Data are stored on magnetic disk in the same format as described on financial statement setup forms. At the end of a fiscal period, the amounts needed to complete each financial statement are figured by the CPU. These amounts plus the financial statement setup data on magnetic disk provide the information needed to prepare a financial statement.

Setup form data are used by the computer service center to prepare Allsports' end-of-fiscal-period reports. Computer printouts of the financial statements described on the setup forms are prepared at the end of the fiscal period. *(CONCEPT: Accounting Period Cycle)* Any future

ALLSPORTS
CHART OF ACCOUNTS
GENERAL LEDGER
FEBRUARY 10, 1983

CLIENT NO. 320

ACCOUNT NUMBER	ACCOUNT CLASSIFICATION	ACCOUNT TITLE	NORMAL BALANCE
11000	AS	CASH	DR
11500	AS	ACCOUNTS RECEIVABLE	DR
12000	AS	MERCHANDISE INVENTORY	DR
12500	AS	OFFICE SUPPLIES	DR
13000	AS	STORE SUPPLIES	DR
13500	AS	PREPAID INSURANCE	DR
14000	AS	DELIVERY EQUIPMENT	DR
14500	AS	OFFICE EQUIPMENT	DR
15000	AS	STORE EQUIPMENT	DR
21000	LI	ACCOUNTS PAYABLE	CR
31000	CA	HELEN LEWIS, CAPITAL	CR
31500	CA	HELEN LEWIS, DRAWING	DR
32000	CA	SAMUEL SULLIVAN, CAPITAL	CR
32500	CA	SAMUEL SULLIVAN, DRAWING	DR
33000	CA	INCOME SUMMARY	CR
41000	RE	SALES	CR
51000	CO	PURCHASES	DR
61000	EX	ADVERTISING EXPENSE	DR
61500	EX	CREDIT CARD FEE EXPENSE	DR
62000	EX	DELIVERY EXPENSE	DR
62500	EX	INSURANCE EXPENSE	DR
63000	EX	MISCELLANEOUS EXPENSE	DR
63500	EX	OFFICE SUPPLIES EXPENSE	DR
64000	EX	RENT EXPENSE	DR
64500	EX	SALARY EXPENSE	DR
65000	EX	STORE SUPPLIES EXPENSE	DR

Computer printout of general ledger chart of accounts

changes in a financial statement format require that a new financial statement setup form be prepared.

Processing opening entry

Ms. Lewis closes the books for Allsports' manual accounting system on February 28, 1983. She changes to EDP general ledger accounting on March 1, 1983.

Source document for the opening entry. Allsports' February 28, 1983, balance sheet, page 354, is the source document for the opening entry. *(CONCEPT: Objective Evidence)*

Recording the opening entry. When Ms. Lewis started Allsports' manual accounting system, the opening entry was recorded in a general journal. The computer service center could process the opening entry data directly from a balance sheet. However, the center prefers that all original documents be retained in a client's accounting office. Ms. Lewis is

Allsports
Balance Sheet
February 28, 1983

Assets		
Cash	940000	
Accounts Receivable	38500	
Merchandise Inventory	23746000	
Office Supplies	18000	
Store Supplies	11500	
Prepaid Insurance	27000	
Delivery Equipment	720000	
Office Equipment	94000	
Store Equipment	340000	
Total Assets		25935000
Liabilities		
Accounts Payable		463000
Capital		
Helen Lewis, Capital	13356000	
Samuel Sullivan, Capital	12116000	
Total Capital		25472000
Total Liabilities and Capital		25935000

Balance sheet

instructed to write the opening entry data on a special form supplied by the computer service center. All future entries and transactions will be written on this special form. A special EDP form used for recording accounting transactions is called a journal entry transmittal (JET). A journal entry transmittal (JET) is also known as a transaction transmittal.

A JET form resembles the general journal presently used by Allsports. The arrangement of columns on a JET form has special meaning. Data are recorded on a JET form in the same order as data are entered on direct-entry terminals. The advantages of using a JET form are below.

1. All source documents are kept in the client's accounting department. This method reduces the possibility of documents being lost.
2. Entering data on direct-entry terminal keyboards is faster. Terminal operators read from single sheets the data arranged in the same order as data are entered into a terminal.

Allsports' completed JET form for the opening entry is on page 355. Steps followed by Ms. Lewis in recording Allsports' opening entry on the JET form are below.

1 Enter client number, *320*.

2 Enter date, *3/1/83*.

JOURNAL ENTRY TRANSMITTAL

CLIENT NO. 320 DATE 3/1/83 PAGE 1 OF 1 PAGES

	1 BCH. NO.	2 REF. NUMBER	3 ACCOUNT NUMBER	4 EXPLANATION	5 DEBIT	6 CREDIT	
1			11000	Opening Entry	940000		1
2			11500		38500		2
3			12000		23746000		3
4			12500		18000		4
5			13000		11500		5
6			13500		27000		6
7			14000		720000		7
8			14500		94000		8
9			15000		340000		9
10			21000			463000	10
11			31000			13356000	11
12			32000			12116000	12

PREPARED BY Helen Lewis PAGE TOTALS 25935000 25935000

Journal entry transmittal for opening entry

3 Enter page number, *1*. (Delay filling in number of pages until total number of pages needed for opening entry has been determined.)

4 Leave Bch. No. column, *Column 1*, blank for opening entry. The opening entry does not require the use of this column. (Use of the Bch. No. column is described in Chapter 19.)

5 Leave Ref. Number column, *Column 2*, blank for opening entry. The opening entry does not require the use of this column. (Use of the Ref. Number column is described in Chapter 19.)

6 Enter account number in Account Number column, *Column 3*, for each general ledger account with a balance. These accounts are listed on the balance sheet, page 354. The account numbers are listed on the chart of accounts, page 326.

7 Enter explanation for entries in Explanation column, *Column 4*. The explanation written for the completed JET form above is *Opening Entry*. Account titles were stored on magnetic disk during the processing of the chart of accounts. Therefore, account titles need not be entered again. Accounts are identified and processed by account number.

8 Enter Debit or Credit amount in appropriate column, *Column 5 or 6*.

9 Add debit entries, *Column 5*, and record sum in space provided for Page Totals.

10 Add credit entries, *Column 6*, and record sum in space provided for Page Totals.

11 Compare the two totals to be sure that debits and credits are equal.

12 Enter number of pages being submitted, *1*, in space provided at top of form.

If two pages are required for an opening entry, the first page is numbered page 1 of 2 pages. The second page is numbered page 2 of 2 pages. This numbering system helps keep all pages together and assures that all pages have been accounted for.

The complete opening entry JET form is sent to the computer service center. Opening entry data on the JET form are entered on the direct-entry terminal and sent to the CPU. The CPU, based on computer program instructions, transmits the data to the general ledger stored on magnetic disk. An entry register of the opening entry is then prepared by the printer output unit. Allsports' entry register for the opening entry is below.

ALLSPORTS
ENTRY REGISTER
OPENING ENTRY
MARCH 1, 1983

CLIENT NO. 320 PAGE 1 OF 1 PAGES

ACCOUNT NUMBER	EXPLANATION	DEBIT	CREDIT
11000	CASH	$ 9,400.00	
11500	ACCOUNTS RECEIVABLE	385.00	
12000	MERCHANDISE INVENTORY	237,460.00	
12500	OFFICE SUPPLIES	180.00	
13000	STORE SUPPLIES	115.00	
13500	PREPAID INSURANCE	270.00	
14000	DELIVERY EQUIPMENT	7,200.00	
14500	OFFICE EQUIPMENT	940.00	
15000	STORE EQUIPMENT	3,400.00	
21000	ACCOUNTS PAYABLE		$ 4,630.00
31000	HELEN LEWIS, CAPITAL		133,560.00
32000	SAMUEL SULLIVAN, CAPITAL		121,160.00
	TOTALS	$259,350.00*	$259,350.00*

Entry register for opening entry

The entry register is sent to Allsports. Ms. Lewis checks the accuracy of the entry register. The JET form and entry register are then filed for future reference.

In EDP where a card reader is used as an input unit, punched cards are first prepared on a card punch machine. A similar chart of accounts setup form, financial statement setup form, and JET form are used. Completed punched cards are placed in a card reader and data are read into the CPU. CPU processing of data is the same regardless of input unit used.

ACCOUNTING TERMS

What is the meaning of each of the following?

1. input unit
2. output unit
3. printout
4. systems flowchart
5. entry register
6. journal entry transmittal (JET)

QUESTIONS FOR INDIVIDUAL STUDY

1. What are the four computer units?
2. What computer unit is often referred to as the "computer"?
3. What are the three distinct functions of a CPU?
4. What is the major difference between a direct-entry terminal and a regular typewriter?
5. What machine makes holes in a card to represent data?
6. What input unit reads punched cards?
7. What is the end result of processing data by a computer?
8. What is the most common computer output unit?
9. What external storage unit is used by the computer service center that processes Allsports' data?
10. Why is there no limit to the amount of data stored on magnetic disk packs?
11. What type of chart shows the data flow among EDP machines?
12. What is Allsports' opening entry source document for the general ledger accounts?
13. What form commonly used in manual accounting resembles the JET form used in EDP?
14. What are the advantages of using a JET form?

CASES FOR MANAGEMENT DECISION

CASE 1 Oakwood Gift Center's accounting data are processed by a computer service center. Source documents for transactions are sent directly to the computer service center for processing. Recently, one set of source documents got lost in the mail and was never recovered. The loss of these source documents created serious problems in accounting for the data that were lost. How could the method of sending transactions to the computer service center be improved?

CASE 2 Ferguson Supply uses a computer service center to process its accounting data. Ferguson Supply prepares a JET form for data to be processed by the computer service center. A direct-entry terminal is used at the computer service center to key in the transaction data for computer processing. Ferguson Supply is considering installing a card punch machine to prepare data for computer processing. Ferguson Supply feels time could be saved because data could be keyed directly from source documents. Also, they would not have to pay the computer service center for preparing the input data. The punched cards could be mailed to the computer service center for processing directly on the computer. What factors should Ferguson Supply consider before deciding whether or not to install a card punch machine?

DRILL FOR UNDERSTANDING

DRILL 18-D 1 Analyzing a systems flowchart

Instructions: Refer to Allsports' systems flowchart, page 351, and answer the following questions.

1. How many total steps are required to complete Allsports' EDP general ledger accounting system?
2. In which step does the processing take place?
3. How many output reports are prepared?
4. Which steps indicate manual operations?
5. What external storage is used for computer program storage?
6. What external storage is used for general ledger storage?
7. In which step are output reports prepared?
8. In which step does Allsports receive processed data output?
9. Why is the line broken between steps 6 and 7?
10. In which step are data entered into the computer?

APPLICATION PROBLEM

PROBLEM 18-1 Recording an opening entry in an EDP general ledger accounting system

The chart of accounts prepared in Problem 17-1, Chapter 17, is needed to complete Problem 18-1.

Soto Auto Supply's balance sheet for February 28 of the current year is below.

Soto Auto Supply Balance Sheet February 28, 19--		
Assets		
Cash	9 850 00	
Accounts Receivable	840 00	
Merchandise Inventory	225 420 00	
Office Supplies	670 00	
Store Supplies	410 00	
Prepaid Insurance	930 00	
Office Equipment	1 100 00	
Store Equipment	1 840 00	
Total Assets		241 060 00
Liabilities		
Accounts Payable		4 680 00
Capital		
Alice Soto, Capital	119 840 00	
Frank Soto, Capital	116 540 00	
Total Capital		236 380 00
Total Liabilities and Capital		241 060 00

Instructions: Record the opening entry for Soto Auto Supply, Client No. 183, on a journal entry transmittal. Use March 1 of the current year as the date of the opening entry. Use account numbers from the chart of accounts prepared in Problem 17-1. Use the journal entry transmittal, page 355, as a model.

ENRICHMENT PROBLEMS

MASTERY PROBLEM 18-M Recording an opening entry in an EDP general ledger accounting system

The chart of accounts prepared in Mastery Problem 17-M, Chapter 17, is needed to complete Mastery Problem 18-M.

Appliance Center's balance sheet for March 31 of the current year is below.

Appliance Center Balance Sheet March 31, 19--		
Assets		
Cash	8,760.00	
Accounts Receivable	690.00	
Merchandise Inventory	190,520.00	
Office Supplies	530.00	
Store Supplies	315.00	
Prepaid Insurance	640.00	
Delivery Equipment	7,620.00	
Office Equipment	955.00	
Store Equipment	730.00	
Total Assets		210,760.00
Liabilities		
Accounts Payable		3,480.00
Capital		
Carol Bennett, Capital	104,510.00	
Steve Franklin, Capital	102,770.00	
Total Capital		207,280.00
Total Liabilities and Capital		210,760.00

Instructions: Record the opening entry for the Appliance Center, Client No. 274, on a journal entry transmittal. Use April 1, of the current year as the date of the opening entry. Use account numbers from the chart of accounts prepared in Mastery Problem 17-M.

CHALLENGE PROBLEM 18-C Recording an opening entry in an EDP general ledger accounting system

The chart of accounts prepared in Challenge Problem 17-C, Chapter 17, is needed to complete Challenge Problem 18-C.

Adkins Leather Goods' balance sheet for April 30 of the current year is on the next page.

Adkins Leather Goods Balance Sheet April 30, 19--		
Assets		
Cash	9 100 00	
Accounts Receivable	735 00	
Merchandise Inventory	205 200 00	
Office Supplies	675 00	
Store Supplies	460 00	
Prepaid Insurance	740 00	
Office Equipment	1 240 00	
Store Equipment	830 00	
Total Assets		218 980 00
Liabilities		
Accounts Payable		3 860 00
Capital		
Susan Adkins, Capital	90 120 00	
Marsha Gilbert, Capital	50 000 00	
Patricia Mason, Capital	75 000 00	
Total Capital		215 120 00
Total Liabilities and Capital		218 980 00

Instructions: Record the opening entry for Adkins Leather Goods, Client No. 422, on a journal entry transmittal. Use May 1 of the current year as the date of the opening entry. Use account numbers from the chart of accounts prepared in Challenge Problem 17-C.

19

Automated General Ledger Accounting: Processing Transactions and End-of-Fiscal-Period Reports

ENABLING PERFORMANCE TASKS

After studying Chapter 19, you will be able to:

a. Define terminology related to automated general ledger accounting for a merchandising business.
b. Explain automated general ledger accounting principles and practices for processing transactions and end-of-fiscal-period reports.
c. Analyze a completed journal entry transmittal.
d. Prepare a journal entry transmittal with batched transactions.
e. Plan adjusting entries on a work sheet printout and complete the work sheet printout.
f. Record adjusting and closing entries on a journal entry transmittal.

Chapter 18 described electronic data processing (EDP) procedures used by a computer service center to process Allsports' data. Allsports prepared and submitted three types of forms. (1) Chart of accounts setup form. (2) Financial statement setup forms. (3) Journal entry transmittal (JET) form for opening entry. Data submitted on these forms was processed by the computer service center. Allsports verified the printouts received from the computer center. Now, Ms. Lewis submits JET forms describing accounting transactions to the computer service center. Also, Ms. Lewis submits data needed by the computer center to prepare Allsports' end-of-fiscal-period financial statements.

PROCESSING TRANSACTIONS

All accounting transactions are submitted on JET forms weekly to the computer service center for processing.

Arranging transaction data for EDP processing

Source documents are required as objective evidence for each transaction processed through EDP procedures. *(CONCEPT: Objective Evidence)* Manual and automated accounting transactions use the same types of source documents. Methods of arranging transactions for EDP vary depending on the business involved. Allsports uses the following methods.

Batching transactions. Ms. Lewis records all transactions on a JET form. Transactions are manually arranged by groups before the entries are made. For example, accounts payable transactions are in one group and cash payments transactions are in another group. Arranging similar transaction documents in one group is called batching. Batching reduces the number of journal entries to be made. For example, five accounts payable transactions would require five accounts payable credit entries. By batching, the five accounts payable transactions are combined into one entry with only one accounts payable credit entry.

Allsports arranges daily transactions into five batches. (1) Accounts payable. (2) Cash payments. (3) Accounts receivable. (4) Cash receipts. (5) General.

Assigning reference numbers to batched transactions. Allsports combines all daily transactions on a weekly JET form. As transactions are completed during a week, Ms. Lewis files each transaction source document according to one of the five batches. On the next business day following the close of a week's business, Ms. Lewis prepares a weekly JET form. Transactions are entered on the weekly JET forms in batches according to the order given on page 363. Some source documents may affect the same general ledger account. For example, on March 6, 1983, Ms. Lewis has six source documents in the accounts payable batch. (a) Three source documents for office supplies bought on account. (b) One source document for store supplies bought on account. (c) Two source documents for merchandise purchased on account. Data from the six source documents are combined and recorded as one entry. When data are combined into one entry, some reference must be made to individual source documents. Using individual source document numbers becomes cumbersome when many source documents affect a single general ledger account in a single week.

Allsports uses a number to identify a single or a group of source documents for a week's batched transactions. A number used to identify a single or a group of source documents is called a reference number. The reference number is written on the source documents and on the JET form. For example, the following are the total data for the accounts payable batch on March 6, 1983.

Bought office supplies on account....	$140.00.	M14.	Ref. No. 1000
Bought office supplies on account....	$ 40.00.	M15.	
Bought office supplies on account....	$ 60.00.	M16.	
Bought store supplies on account	$130.00.	M17.	Ref. No. 1001
Purchased merchandise on account .	$460.00.	P21.	Ref. No. 1002
Purchased merchandise on account .	$165.00.	P22.	
Total accounts payable...............	$995.00.		

Thus, all like kinds of source documents in the same batch have the same reference number written on them. Three memorandums for office supplies bought on account (M14, M15, and M16) have reference number 1000 written on them. The single memorandum for store supplies bought on account (M17) has reference number 1001 written on it. The two purchase invoices (P21 and P22) have reference number 1002 written on them. The accounts payable batch entry is entered on the JET form, page 365, lines 1–4. Source documents may be traced by locating the source documents with reference numbers 1000, 1001, and 1002 written on them.

Allsports assigns reference numbers sequentially in the order given below.

Batches	Reference Numbers
Accounts Payable	1000–1999
Cash Payments	2000–2999
Accounts Receivable	3000–3999
Cash Receipts	4000–4999
General	5000–5999

Reference numbers 1000, 1001, 1002 were used for the accounts payable batch on March 6, 1983, JET form. On the JET form for the next week, the accounts payable reference numbers will start with 1003.

Recording accounts payable transactions

All supplies and equipment bought on account and all purchases of merchandise on account are included in the accounts payable batch. Total accounts payable transactions are recorded in general ledger accounts. Allsports' accounts payable transactions for week ended March 6, 1983, are above. The accounts payable transactions showing only total amounts affecting general ledger accounts are below.

Bought office supplies on account....................	*$240.00.*	*Ref. No. 1000.*
Bought store supplies on account......................	*$130.00.*	*Ref. No. 1001.*
Purchased merchandise on account................	*$625.00.*	*Ref. No. 1002.*
Total accounts payable...................................	*$995.00.*	

ACCOUNTS PAYABLE BATCH

Office Supplies	
240.00	

Store Supplies	
130.00	

Purchases	
625.00	

Accounts Payable	
	995.00

Analyzing batched accounts payable transactions. Office Supplies is debited for the total office supplies bought on account, *$240.00*. Store Supplies is debited for the total store supplies bought on account, *$130.00*. Purchases is debited for the total purchases of merchandise on account, *$625.00*. Accounts Payable is credited for the total supplies bought and merchandise purchased on account, *$995.00*.

Recording batched accounts payable transactions on a JET form. The accounts payable batch for week ended March 6, 1983, is on lines 1–4, JET form, page 365.

Steps in recording the accounts payable batch on a JET form are below.

1 Enter client number, *320*.

2 Enter date, *3/6/83*. Enter the date of the last business day for the week's transactions.

3 Enter page number, *1*.

4 Enter batch number, *1*, in Bch. No. column, *Column 1*. The batch number is entered just once for each batch. Lines 1–4 contain data for the first batch.

5 Enter reference numbers in Ref. Number column, *Column 2*. Each reference number refers to a single or a group of source documents. The source documents for batch 1 are memorandums and purchase invoices. On line 4, since there is no related source document, no reference number is entered in the Ref. Number column. Reference numbers are entered on the same line as the general ledger account to which the reference number applies. For example, *1000* is entered on line 1 for Office Supplies.

6 Enter account number in *Column 3*. Use account numbers from the chart of accounts, page 326. For example, on line 1, enter *12500*, the account number for Office Supplies. As data are recorded on remaining lines, enter the numbers of the accounts affected.

7 Enter explanation of transactions included in batch in *Column 4* on first line of batch. For example, the batch 1 explanation written in Column 4, line 1, is Accounts Payable. Account titles were stored on magnetic disk during the processing of the chart of accounts. There-

fore, the account titles need not be entered again. Accounts are identified and processed by account number.

8 Enter Debit or Credit amounts in appropriate column, *Column 5 or 6.*

JOURNAL ENTRY TRANSMITTAL

CLIENT NO. 320 DATE 3/6/83 PAGE 1 OF 1 PAGES

	1 BCH. NO.	2 REF. NUMBER	3 ACCOUNT NUMBER	4 EXPLANATION	5 DEBIT	6 CREDIT	
1	1	1000	12500	Accounts Payable	240 00		1
2		1001	13000		130 00		2
3		1002	51000		625 00		3
4			21000			995 00	4
5	2	2000	12500	Cash Payments	160 00		5
6		2001	13000		105 00		6
7		2002	13500		680 00		7
8		2003	21000		540 00		8
9		2004	31500		600 00		9
10		2005	32500		600 00		10
11		2006	51000		430 00		11
12		2007	63000		18 00		12
13		2008	64000		800 00		13
14		2009	64500		1000 00		14
15			11000			4933 00	15
16	3	3000	11500	Accounts Receivable	92 00		16
17			41000			92 00	17
18	4		11000	Cash Receipts	3805 00		18
19		4000	11500			385 00	19
20		4001	41000			3420 00	20
21	5	5000	31500	General	42 00		21
22		5001	32500		78 00		22
23			51000			120 00	23
24							24
25							25
26							26

PREPARED BY Helen Lewis PAGE TOTALS 9945 00 9945 00

Journal entry transmittal for batched transactions

Recording cash payments transactions

The cash payments batch includes payments for expenses, withdrawals, and payments on account. Allsports had the following cash payments transactions for week ended March 6, 1983.

Bought office supplies for cash	*$ 160.00. Ref. No. 2000.*
Bought store supplies for cash	*$ 105.00. Ref. No. 2001.*
Paid for insurance policy	*$ 680.00. Ref. No. 2002.*
Paid on account	*$ 540.00. Ref. No. 2003.*
Helen Lewis, partner, withdrew cash	*$ 600.00. Ref. No. 2004.*
Samuel Sullivan, partner, withdrew cash	*$ 600.00. Ref. No. 2005.*
Purchased merchandise for cash	*$ 430.00. Ref. No. 2006.*
Paid miscellaneous expense	*$ 18.00. Ref. No. 2007.*
Paid March rent	*$ 800.00. Ref. No. 2008.*
Paid salaries	*$1,000.00. Ref. No. 2009.*
Total cash payments	*$4,933.00.*

CASH PAYMENTS BATCH

Account	Debit	Credit
Office Supplies	160.00	
Store Supplies	105.00	
Prepaid Insurance	680.00	
Accounts Payable	540.00	
Helen Lewis, Drawing	600.00	
Samuel Sullivan, Drawing	600.00	
Purchases	430.00	
Miscellaneous Expense	18.00	
Rent Expense	800.00	
Salary Expense	1,000.00	
Cash		4,933.00

Analyzing batched cash payments transactions. Office Supplies is debited for total office supplies bought for cash, *$160.00*. Store Supplies is debited for total store supplies bought for cash, *$105.00*. Prepaid Insurance is debited for total cash paid for insurance policy, *$680.00*. Accounts Payable is debited for total cash paid on account, *$540.00*. Helen Lewis, Drawing, and Samuel Sullivan, Drawing, are debited for cash withdrawals, *$600.00* each. Purchases is debited for total merchandise purchased for cash, *$430.00*. Miscellaneous Expense is debited for total cash paid for miscellaneous items, *$18.00*. Rent Expense is debited, *$800.00*. Salary Expense is debited, *$1,000.00*. Cash is credited, *$4,933.00*, for total cash payments for week ended March 6, 1983.

Recording batched cash payments on a JET form. The batched cash payments for week ended March 6, 1983, are on lines 5–15, JET form, page 365. Data are recorded in each column in the same way as data recorded for batch 1. The cash payments batch is the second one recorded. Therefore, the number 2 is entered in the Bch. No. column, *Column 1*, line 5. The words *Cash Payments* are written in the Explanation column, *Column 4*, line 5, to explain the transactions included in batch 2. The single credit to Cash, *$4,933.00*, line 15, has no related source document. Therefore, the Ref. Number column, *Column 2*, line 15, is left blank.

Recording accounts receivable transactions

All sales of merchandise on account transactions are included in the accounts receivable batch. Allsports had the following accounts receivable transactions for week ended March 6, 1983.

Sold merchandise on account	*$92.00. Ref. No. 3000.*
Total accounts receivable	*$92.00.*

Analyzing batched accounts receivable transactions. Accounts Receivable is debited and Sales is credited for the total sales of merchandise on account, *$92.00*.

ACCOUNTS RECEIVABLE BATCH

Accounts Receivable	
92.00	

Sales	
	92.00

Recording batched accounts receivable on a JET form. The accounts receivable batch for week ended March 6, 1983, is on lines 16–17, JET form, page 365. The accounts receivable batch is the third one recorded. Therefore, the number *3* is entered in the Bch. No. column, *Column 1*, line 16. The words *Accounts Receivable* are written in the Explanation column, *Column 4*, line 16, to explain the transactions included in batch 3. The single credit to Sales, *$92.00*, has no related source document. Therefore, the Ref. Number column, *Column 2*, line 17, is left blank.

Recording cash receipts transactions

The cash receipts batch includes total cash received on account and total cash received from sales. Allsports had the following cash receipts transactions for week ended March 6, 1983.

Cash received on account	*$ 385.00. Ref. No. 4000.*
Cash received from sales	*$3,420.00. Ref. No. 4001.*
Total cash receipts	*$3,805.00.*

Analyzing batched cash receipts transactions. Cash is debited for total cash received, *$3,805.00*. Accounts Receivable is credited for total cash received on account, *$385.00*. Sales is credited for total cash received from sales, *$3,420.00*.

CASH RECEIPTS BATCH

Cash	
3,805.00	

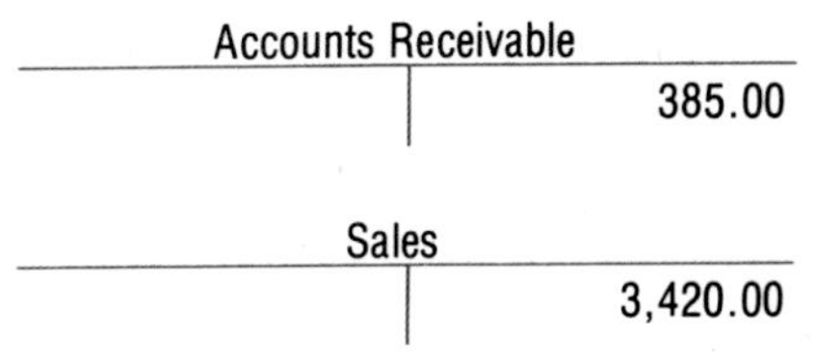

Recording batched cash receipts on a JET form. The cash receipts batch for week ended March 6, 1983, is on lines 18–20, JET form, page 365. The cash receipts batch is the fourth one recorded. Therefore, the number *4* is entered in the Bch. No. column, *Column 1*, line 18. The single debit to Cash, *$3,805.00*, has no related source document. Therefore, the Ref. Number column, *Column 2*, line 18, is left blank. The words *Cash Receipts* are written in the Explanation column, *Column 4*, line 18, to explain the transactions included in batch 4.

Recording general transactions

The general batch includes all transactions that cannot be included in any of the other four batches. One example is the withdrawal of merchandise. Allsports had the following general transactions for week ended March 6, 1983.

Helen Lewis, partner, withdrew merchandise...	*$ 42.00. Ref. No. 5000.*
Samuel Sullivan, partner, withdrew merchandise...	*$ 78.00. Ref. No. 5001.*
Total withdrawals of merchandise...	*$120.00.*

GENERAL TRANSACTIONS BATCH

Helen Lewis, Drawing	
42.00	

Samuel Sullivan, Drawing	
78.00	

Purchases	
	120.00

Analyzing batched general transactions. Helen Lewis, Drawing, is debited for her withdrawal of merchandise, *$42.00*. Samuel Sullivan, Drawing, is debited for his withdrawal of merchandise, *$78.00*. Purchases is credited for the total withdrawal of merchandise by the partners, *$120.00*.

Recording batched general transactions on a JET form. The general batch for week ended March 6, 1983, is on lines 21–23, JET form, page 365. The general transactions batch is the fifth one recorded. Therefore, the number *5* is entered in the Bch. No. column, *Column 1*, line 21. The word *General* is written in the Explanation column, *Column 4*, line 21, to explain the transactions included in batch 5. The single credit to Purchases, *$120.00*, has no related source document. Therefore, the Ref. Number column, *Column 2*, line 23, is left blank.

When a JET form page is full, Ms. Lewis does the following to complete the page.

1 Add debit entries and record sum in space provided for Page Totals, *Column 5*.

2 Add credit entries and record sum in space provided for Page Totals, *Column 6*.

3 Compare the two totals to be sure debits equal credits.

4 Enter number of pages being submitted, *1*, in the space provided at top of form.

If two pages had been required for these five batches, the first page is numbered page 1 of 2 pages. The second page is numbered page 2 of 2 pages. This numbering system helps keep all pages together and assures that all pages have been accounted for.

Allsports' completed JET form is sent to the computer service center. Data on the JET form are entered on a direct-entry terminal and sent to the CPU. The CPU, based on computer program, posts transaction data to general ledger accounts stored on magnetic disk.

After posting general ledger transaction data, the computer prints an entry register. Total debits and total credits are figured by the computer and printed on the entry register. Totals on an entry register are identified with an asterisk (*) next to each total. The computer operator compares entry register totals with totals on the JET form prepared by Ms. Lewis. This comparison is made to prove accuracy of data entered and processed by the computer. A copy of Allsports' entry register based on the JET form, page 365, is below. Total debits and total credits on the entry register below and JET form, page 365, are the same. Therefore, the entry register data are assumed to be correct.

Entry register for batched transactions

ALLSPORTS
ENTRY REGISTER
FOR WEEK ENDED MARCH 6, 1983

CLIENT NO. 320 PAGE 1 OF 1 PAGES

LINE NO.	BATCH NO.	REFERENCE NO.	ACCOUNT NO.	EXPLANATION	DEBIT	CREDIT
1	1	1000	12500	OFFICE SUPPLIES	$ 240.00	
2		1001	13000	STORE SUPPLIES	130.00	
3		1002	51000	PURCHASES	625.00	
4			21000	ACCOUNTS PAYABLE		$ 995.00
5	2	2000	12500	OFFICE SUPPLIES	160.00	
6		2001	13000	STORE SUPPLIES	105.00	
7		2002	13500	PREPAID INSURANCE	680.00	
8		2003	21000	ACCOUNTS PAYABLE	540.00	
9		2004	31500	HELEN LEWIS, DRAWING	600.00	
10		2005	32500	SAMUEL SULLIVAN, DRAWING	600.00	
11		2006	51000	PURCHASES	430.00	
12		2007	63000	MISCELLANEOUS EXPENSE	18.00	
13		2008	64000	RENT EXPENSE	800.00	
14		2009	64500	SALARY EXPENSE	1,000.00	
15			11000	CASH		4,933.00
16	3	3000	11500	ACCOUNTS RECEIVABLE	92.00	
17			41000	SALES		92.00
18	4		11000	CASH	3,805.00	
19		4000	11500	ACCOUNTS RECEIVABLE		385.00
20		4001	41000	SALES		3,420.00
21	5	5000	31500	HELEN LEWIS, DRAWING	42.00	
22		5001	32500	SAMUEL SULLIVAN, DRAWING	78.00	
23			51000	PURCHASES		120.00
				TOTALS	$9,945.00*	$9,945.00*

PROCESSING END-OF-FISCAL-PERIOD WORK

Financial statements are prepared by the computer service center at the end of each monthly fiscal period. *(CONCEPT: Accounting Period Cycle)*

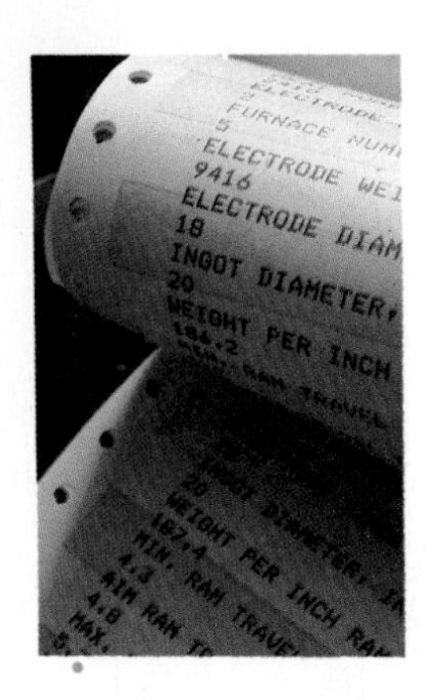

Four financial statements are prepared. (1) Income statement. (2) Distribution of net income statement. (3) Capital statement. (4) Balance sheet. Financial statement printouts follow the format indicated on financial statement setup forms prepared by Ms. Lewis, pages 337–339. All possible headings and account titles for the body of each financial statement are stored on magnetic disk. *(CONCEPT: Adequate Disclosure)* These data were stored when setup forms were processed as described in Chapter 17. The computer determines the amount for each printout line. Before preparing financial statement printouts, two things are done. (1) The computer service center prepares a trial balance and work sheet printout. The trial balance is printed on the work sheet to prove equality of general ledger debits and credits. (2) Ms. Lewis plans adjustments to general ledger accounts on the trial balance and work sheet printout.

Preparing a work sheet

The computer service center prepares a trial balance and a work sheet printout at the end of each fiscal period. The computer, based on a computer program, figures and arranges the general ledger data for the trial balance. The work sheet printout with completed trial balance is sent to Allsports. The work sheet printout provides spaces for planning adjusting entries and extending amounts to income statement and balance sheet columns.

Planning adjusting entries

At the end of a fiscal period, certain general ledger accounts need to be brought up to date. Adjustments to these general ledger accounts are planned and entered in the Adjustments columns of the work sheet printout. The data needed for Allsports' adjustments are below.

Ending merchandise inventory	$232,500.00
Ending office supplies inventory	455.00
Ending store supplies inventory	235.00
Ending value of insurance policies	804.00

Allsports follows the same procedures as Denim Threads, Chapter 14, for completing the work sheet. Allsports' completed work sheet is on page 371.

Recording adjusting entries

Each adjustment must be processed by computer and posted to general ledger accounts stored on magnetic disk. Allsports' five adjusting entries are shown in the completed work sheet printout, page 371. Ms. Lewis records the adjusting entries on a JET form. The completed JET form for the adjusting entries is on page 372.

ALLSPORTS
WORK SHEET
FOR MONTH ENDED MARCH 31, 1983

	TRIAL BALANCE		ADJUSTMENTS		INCOME STATEMENT		BALANCE SHEET	
	DEBIT	CREDIT	DEBIT	CREDIT	DEBIT	CREDIT	DEBIT	CREDIT
CASH	$ 16,420.00						16,420.00	
ACCOUNTS RECEIVABLE	580.00						580.00	
MERCHANDISE INVENTORY	237,460.00		(b) 232,500.00	(a) 237,460.00			232,500.00	
OFFICE SUPPLIES	580.00			(c) 125.00			455.00	
STORE SUPPLIES	350.00			(d) 115.00			235.00	
PREPAID INSURANCE	950.00			(e) 146.00			804.00	
DELIVERY EQUIPMENT	7,200.00						7,200.00	
OFFICE EQUIPMENT	940.00						940.00	
STORE EQUIPMENT	3,400.00						3,400.00	
ACCOUNTS PAYABLE		$ 4,256.00						4,256.00
HELEN LEWIS, CAPITAL		133,560.00						133,560.00
HELEN LEWIS, DRAWING	672.00						672.00	
SAMUEL SULLIVAN, CAPITAL		121,160.00						121,160.00
SAMUEL SULLIVAN, DRAWING	690.00						690.00	
INCOME SUMMARY			(a) 237,460.00	(b) 232,500.00	237,460.00	232,500.00		
SALES		16,840.00				16,840.00		
PURCHASES	3,240.00				3,240.00			
ADVERTISING EXPENSE	66.00				66.00			
CREDIT CARD FEE EXPENSE	252.00				252.00			
DELIVERY EXPENSE	86.00				86.00			
INSURANCE EXPENSE			(e) 146.00		146.00			
MISCELLANEOUS EXPENSE	130.00				130.00			
OFFICE SUPPLIES EXPENSE			(c) 125.00		125.00			
RENT EXPENSE	800.00				800.00			
SALARY EXPENSE	2,000.00				2,000.00			
STORE SUPPLIES EXPENSE			(d) 115.00		115.00			
	$275,816.00	$275,816.00	470,346.00	470,346.00	244,420.00	249,340.00	263,896.00	258,976.00
Net Income					4,920.00			4,920.00
					249,340.00	249,340.00	263,896.00	263,896.00

Completed work sheet printout

JOURNAL ENTRY TRANSMITTAL

CLIENT NO. 320 DATE 3/31/83 PAGE 1 OF 1 PAGES

	BCH. NO.	REF. NUMBER	ACCOUNT NUMBER	EXPLANATION	DEBIT	CREDIT	
1	1		33000	Adjusting Entries	23746000		1
2			12000			23746000	2
3			12000		23250000		3
4			33000			23250000	4
5			63500		12500		5
6			12500			12500	6
7			65000		11500		7
8			13000			11500	8
9			62500		14600		9
10			13500			14600	10

PREPARED BY Helen Lewis PAGE TOTALS 47034600 47034600

Journal entry transmittal for adjusting entries

The completed JET form is sent to the computer service center. Data are entered on a direct-entry terminal. The computer posts the adjusting entries to general ledger accounts stored on magnetic disk. The computer also prepares an entry register for adjustments. Allsports' entry register for adjustments is below. Total debits and total credits on the entry register below and JET form above are the same. Therefore, the entry register data for adjustments are assumed to be correct.

ALLSPORTS
ENTRY REGISTER
ADJUSTING ENTRIES
MARCH 31, 1983

CLIENT NO. 320 PAGE 1 OF 1 PAGES

LINE NO.	BATCH NO.	REFERENCE NO.	ACCOUNT NO.	EXPLANATION	DEBIT	CREDIT
1	1		33000	INCOME SUMMARY	$237,460.00	
2			12000	MERCHANDISE INVENTORY		$237,460.00
3			12000	MERCHANDISE INVENTORY	232,500.00	
4			33000	INCOME SUMMARY		232,500.00
5			63500	OFFICE SUPPLIES EXPENSE	125.00	
6			12500	OFFICE SUPPLIES		125.00
7			65000	STORE SUPPLIES EXPENSE	115.00	
8			13000	STORE SUPPLIES		115.00
9			62500	INSURANCE EXPENSE	146.00	
10			13500	PREPAID INSURANCE		146.00
				TOTALS	$470,346.00*	$470,346.00*

Entry register for adjustments

Preparing financial statements

In manual accounting the financial statements are prepared from a completed work sheet. In automated accounting the financial statements are prepared by a computer from data stored on magnetic disk. Allsports' financial statements are below and on page 374.

The entry register and financial statements prepared by the computer are forwarded to Allsports. Ms. Lewis inspects the financial statements to make business decisions. These decisions are based on the financial progress and condition at the end of the fiscal period. The entry register and financial statements are filed for future reference.

ALLSPORTS
INCOME STATEMENT
FOR MONTH ENDED MARCH 31, 1983

REVENUE:		
SALES		$16,840.00
COST OF MERCHANDISE SOLD:		
BEGINNING MERCHANDISE INVENTORY	$237,460.00	
PURCHASES	3,240.00	
TOTAL COST OF MERCHANDISE AVAILABLE	$240,700.00	
ENDING MERCHANDISE INVENTORY	232,500.00	
COST OF MERCHANDISE SOLD		8,200.00
GROSS PROFIT ON SALES		$ 8,640.00
EXPENSES:		
ADVERTISING EXPENSE	$ 66.00	
CREDIT CARD FEE EXPENSE	252.00	
DELIVERY EXPENSE	86.00	
INSURANCE EXPENSE	146.00	
MISCELLANEOUS EXPENSE	130.00	
OFFICE SUPPLIES EXPENSE	125.00	
RENT EXPENSE	800.00	
SALARY EXPENSE	2,000.00	
STORE SUPPLIES EXPENSE	115.00	
TOTAL EXPENSES		3,720.00
NET INCOME		$ 4,920.00

Income statement printout

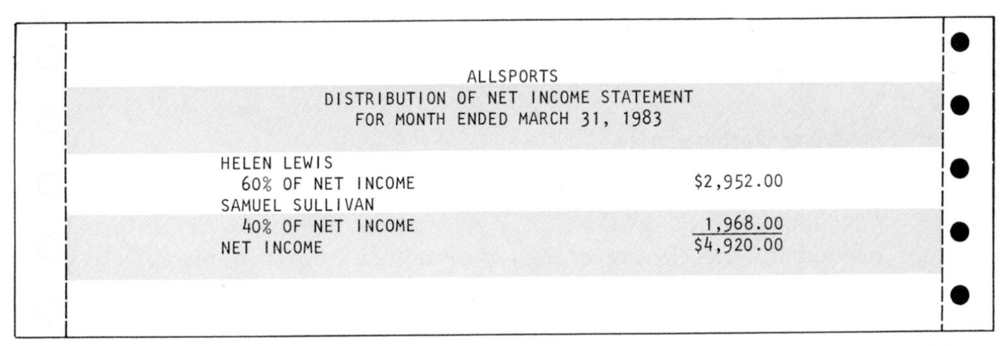

ALLSPORTS
DISTRIBUTION OF NET INCOME STATEMENT
FOR MONTH ENDED MARCH 31, 1983

HELEN LEWIS	
60% OF NET INCOME	$2,952.00
SAMUEL SULLIVAN	
40% OF NET INCOME	1,968.00
NET INCOME	$4,920.00

Distribution of net income statement printout

ALLSPORTS
CAPITAL STATEMENT
FOR MONTH ENDED MARCH 31, 1983

HELEN LEWIS			
BEGINNING CAPITAL		$133,560.00	
SHARE OF NET INCOME	$2,952.00		
LESS WITHDRAWALS	672.00		
NET INCREASE IN CAPITAL		2,280.00	
ENDING CAPITAL			$135,840.00
SAMUEL SULLIVAN			
BEGINNING CAPITAL		121,160.00	
SHARE OF NET INCOME	$1,968.00		
LESS WITHDRAWALS	690.00		
NET INCREASE IN CAPITAL		1,278.00	
ENDING CAPITAL			122,438.00
TOTAL ENDING CAPITAL			$258,278.00

Capital statement printout

ALLSPORTS
BALANCE SHEET
MARCH 31, 1983

ASSETS		
CASH	$ 16,420.00	
ACCOUNTS RECEIVABLE	580.00	
MERCHANDISE INVENTORY	232,500.00	
OFFICE SUPPLIES	455.00	
STORE SUPPLIES	235.00	
PREPAID INSURANCE	804.00	
DELIVERY EQUIPMENT	7,200.00	
OFFICE EQUIPMENT	940.00	
STORE EQUIPMENT	3,400.00	
TOTAL ASSETS		$262,534.00
LIABILITIES		
ACCOUNTS PAYABLE		$ 4,256.00
CAPITAL		
HELEN LEWIS, CAPITAL	$135,840.00	
SAMUEL SULLIVAN, CAPITAL	122,438.00	
TOTAL CAPITAL		258,278.00
TOTAL LIABILITIES AND CAPITAL		$262,534.00

Balance sheet printout

Recording closing entries

Closing entries are needed to prepare Allsports' general ledger for the next fiscal period. *(CONCEPT: Accounting Period Cycle)* Information needed for the closing entries is obtained from two places. (1) Work sheet Income Statement and Balance Sheet columns. (2) Distribution of net income statement. Ms. Lewis records Allsports' closing entries on a JET form, page 375.

JOURNAL ENTRY TRANSMITTAL

CLIENT NO. 320 DATE 3/31/83 PAGE 1 OF 1 PAGES

	BCH. NO.	REF. NUMBER	ACCOUNT NUMBER	EXPLANATION	DEBIT	CREDIT	
1	1		41000	Closing Entries	16840 00		1
2			33000			16840 00	2
3			33000		6960 00		3
4			51000			3240 00	4
5			61000			66 00	5
6			61500			252 00	6
7			62000			86 00	7
8			62500			146 00	8
9			63000			130 00	9
10			63500			125 00	10
11			64000			800 00	11
12			64500			2000 00	12
13			65000			115 00	13
14			33000		4920 00		14
15			31000			2952 00	15
16			32000			1968 00	16
17			31000		672 00		17
18			31500			672 00	18
19			32000		690 00		19
20			32500			690 00	20

PREPARED BY Helen Lewis PAGE TOTALS 30082 00 30082 00

Journal entry transmittal for closing entries

Allsports' JET form for closing entries is sent to the computer service center. Data are entered on a direct-entry terminal. The computer posts the closing entries to general ledger accounts stored on magnetic disk. The computer also prepares an entry register for the closing entries. Allsports' entry register for closing entries is on page 376.

The totals on the entry register, page 376, and JET form above are the same. Therefore, the entry register for closing entries is assumed to be correct. The entry register for closing entries is sent to Allsports. At Allsports, Ms. Lewis files the entry register for future reference.

Preparing a post-closing trial balance

In Allsports' previous manual accounting system, the post-closing trial balance was prepared from general ledger accounts. In Allsports' new EDP accounting system, the post-closing trial balance is prepared by the computer from data stored on magnetic disk. Allsports' EDP post-closing trial balance is on page 376.

ALLSPORTS
ENTRY REGISTER
CLOSING ENTRIES
CLIENT NO. 320 MARCH 31, 1983 PAGE 1 OF 1 PAGES

LINE NO.	BATCH NO.	REFERENCE NO.	ACCOUNT NO.	EXPLANATION	DEBIT	CREDIT
1	1		41000	SALES	$16,840.00	
2			33000	INCOME SUMMARY		$16,840.00
3			33000	INCOME SUMMARY	6,960.00	
4			51000	PURCHASES		3,240.00
5			61000	ADVERTISING EXPENSE		66.00
6			61500	CREDIT CARD FEE EXPENSE		252.00
7			62000	DELIVERY EXPENSE		86.00
8			62500	INSURANCE EXPENSE		146.00
9			63000	MISCELLANEOUS EXPENSE		130.00
10			63500	OFFICE SUPPLIES EXPENSE		125.00
11			64000	RENT EXPENSE		800.00
12			64500	SALARY EXPENSE		2,000.00
13			65000	STORE SUPPLIES EXPENSE		115.00
14			33000	INCOME SUMMARY	4,920.00	
15			31000	HELEN LEWIS, CAPITAL		2,952.00
16			32000	SAMUEL SULLIVAN, CAPITAL		1,968.00
17			31000	HELEN LEWIS, CAPITAL	672.00	
18			31500	HELEN LEWIS, DRAWING		672.00
19			32000	SAMUEL SULLIVAN, CAPITAL	690.00	
20			32500	SAMUEL SULLIVAN, DRAWING		690.00
				TOTALS	$30,082.00*	$30,082.00*

Entry register for closing entries

ALLSPORTS
POST-CLOSING TRIAL BALANCE
MARCH 31, 1983

Account	Debit	Credit
CASH	$ 16,420.00	
ACCOUNTS RECEIVABLE	580.00	
MERCHANDISE INVENTORY	232,500.00	
OFFICE SUPPLIES	455.00	
STORE SUPPLIES	235.00	
PREPAID INSURANCE	804.00	
DELIVERY EQUIPMENT	7,200.00	
OFFICE EQUIPMENT	940.00	
STORE EQUIPMENT	3,400.00	
ACCOUNTS PAYABLE		$ 4,256.00
HELEN LEWIS, CAPITAL		135,840.00
SAMUEL SULLIVAN, CAPITAL		122,438.00
TOTALS	$262,534.00	$262,534.00

Post-closing trial balance printout

SUMMARY OF AUTOMATED GENERAL LEDGER ACCOUNTING SYSTEM

The flowchart, page 377, outlines Allsports' automated general ledger accounting system. Steps 1 and 2 are described in Chapter 17. Steps 3–6 are presented in Chapter 18. Steps 7–15 are described in Chapter 19 to complete the accounting cycle.

Flowchart of steps for automated general ledger accounting

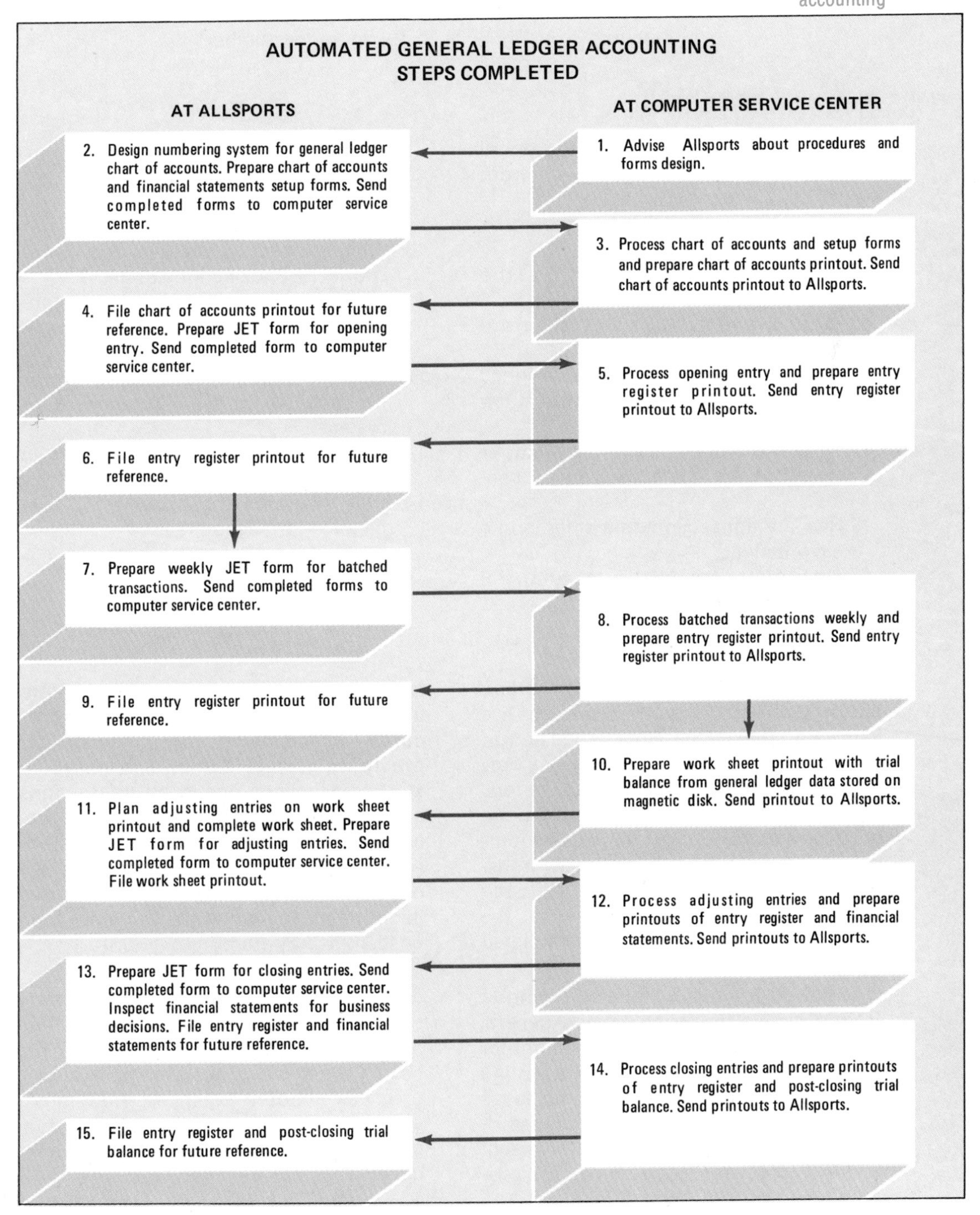

ACCOUNTING TERMS

What is the meaning of each of the following?

1. batching
2. reference number

QUESTIONS FOR INDIVIDUAL STUDY

1. What EDP form is used to record transaction data obtained from source documents?
2. How often does Allsports submit its daily transactions?
3. Why does batching reduce the number of journal entries?
4. What five transaction batches are used by Allsports?
5. Why are reference numbers assigned to source documents within each batch?
6. Where is Allsports' general ledger stored at the computer service center?
7. How are transaction data entered into a computer?
8. How often are Allsports' financial statements prepared?
9. What four financial statements are prepared for Allsports by the computer service center?
10. Why is a trial balance needed in Allsports' EDP accounting system?
11. How are adjustments planned and recorded in Allsports' EDP accounting system?
12. How are financial statements prepared in Allsports' EDP accounting system?
13. How are closing entries recorded in Allsports' EDP accounting system?
14. Who prepares the post-closing trial balance for Allsports?

CASES FOR MANAGEMENT DECISION

CASE 1 Steven Parker and Todd Brent, partners, own and operate a chain of five hardware stores. One store is located in the downtown shopping area. Four stores are located in suburban shopping centers. A computer system is installed in the downtown store. All five stores use a journal entry transmittal to record daily transactions for computer processing. Each morning a JET form is prepared for the previous day's business. The completed forms are delivered to the downtown store to be processed by computer. The procedures for automated accounting do not provide a way to distinguish in which store transactions occur. All transactions are batched together. The data are processed as if only one store were involved. A need exists to be able to analyze business activity by store. What changes might be made so that transactions could be identified by store?

CASE 2 A lumber company changed from a manual to an automated general ledger accounting system. A computer service center processes the accounting data. Source documents are batched as they occur and recorded weekly on a journal entry transmittal. The JET form is sent to the computer service center for processing. A filing system is used for storing source documents in five batches. The owner has expressed a concern over not having a manual general ledger available to check account balances. How might you provide the owner with individual general ledger account balances when requested?

DRILLS FOR UNDERSTANDING

DRILL 19-D 1 Batching transactions

This drill provides practice in arranging transactions in groups. Use a form similar to the one below.

Trans. No.	Accounts Payable Batch	Cash Payments Batch	Accounts Receivable Batch	Cash Receipts Batch	General Batch
1.	✓				

Instructions: For each transaction below, indicate the batch in which the transaction would be entered by checking the appropriate column. Transaction No. 1 is given as an example.

Transactions

1. Bought office supplies on account.
2. Received cash on account.
3. Purchased merchandise for cash.
4. Paid salaries.
5. Purchased merchandise on account.
6. Partner withdrew cash.
7. Sold merchandise on account.
8. Bought store supplies on account.
9. Partner withdrew merchandise.
10. Paid on account.

DRILL 19-D 2 Analyzing a journal entry transmittal

Instructions: Refer to the completed journal entry transmittal, page 365, and answer the following questions.

1. How many batches are recorded?
2. In batch 1, line 1, which account is affected? How?
3. How many reference numbers were assigned to batch 1?
4. In batch 1, line 4, why is the Ref. Number column left blank?
5. Why are account titles not recorded on a journal entry transmittal?
6. Why is there only one entry to Cash for batch 2 on lines 5–15?
7. Did the accounts payable account increase or decrease as a result of the transactions? How much?
8. Did the accounts receivable account increase or decrease as a result of the transactions? How much?
9. Did the purchases account increase or decrease as a result of the transactions? How much?
10. Did the cash account increase or decrease as a result of the transactions? How much?

APPLICATION PROBLEMS

PROBLEM 19-1 Recording weekly batched transactions for EDP using a journal entry transmittal

The chart of accounts prepared in Problem 17-1, Chapter 17, is needed to complete Problem 19-1.

Soto Auto Supply arranges transaction source documents into five batches. (1) Accounts payable. (2) Cash payments. (3) Accounts receivable. (4) Cash receipts. (5) General. Reference numbers are assigned to transaction source documents within each batch. The batched transactions are recorded as combined entries weekly. Batched transactions for week ended March 5 of current year are below.

Accounts payable		
Bought office supplies on account	$ 141.00.	Ref. No. 1000.
Bought store supplies on account	$ 74.00.	Ref. No. 1001.
Purchased merchandise on account	$2,100.00.	Ref. No. 1002.
Total accounts payable	$2,315.00.	
Cash payments		
Bought store supplies for cash	$ 36.00.	Ref. No. 2000.
Paid for insurance policy	$ 320.00.	Ref. No. 2001.
Paid on account	$2,160.00.	Ref. No. 2002.
Alice Soto, partner, withdrew cash	$ 750.00.	Ref. No. 2003.
Frank Soto, partner, withdrew cash	$ 750.00.	Ref. No. 2004.
Purchased merchandise for cash	$ 380.00.	Ref. No. 2005.
Paid March rent	$ 850.00.	Ref. No. 2006.
Paid salaries	$1,200.00.	Ref. No. 2007.
Total cash payments	$6,446.00.	
Accounts receivable		
Sold merchandise on account	$ 370.00.	Ref. No. 3000.
Total accounts receivable	$ 370.00.	
Cash receipts		
Cash received on account	$ 344.00.	Ref. No. 4000.
Cash received from sales	$3,680.00.	Ref. No. 4001.
Total cash receipts	$4,024.00.	
General		
Alice Soto, partner, withdrew merchandise	$ 42.00.	Ref. No. 5000.
Frank Soto, partner, withdrew merchandise	$ 28.00.	Ref. No. 5001.
Total withdrawals of merchandise by partners	$ 70.00.	

Instructions: Record the batched transactions for Soto Auto Supply, Client No. 183, on a journal entry transmittal. Use March 5 of the current year as the date of the last business day for the week's business. Use account numbers from the chart of accounts prepared in Problem 17-1. Use the journal entry transmittal, page 365, as your model.

PROBLEM 19-2 Recording adjusting and closing entries for EDP using a journal entry transmittal

The chart of accounts prepared in Problem 17-1, Chapter 17, is needed to complete Problem 19-2.

Soto Auto Supply's trial balance is shown in the partial work sheet printout on the next page. Ending inventories and the value of insurance policies are also given.

SOTO AUTO SUPPLY
WORK SHEET
FOR MONTH ENDED MARCH 31, 19--

	TRIAL BALANCE	
	DEBIT	CREDIT
CASH	$ 14,086.00	
ACCOUNTS RECEIVABLE	760.00	
MERCHANDISE INVENTORY	225,420.00	
OFFICE SUPPLIES	811.00	
STORE SUPPLIES	520.00	
PREPAID INSURANCE	1,250.00	
OFFICE EQUIPMENT	1,100.00	
STORE EQUIPMENT	1,840.00	
ACCOUNTS PAYABLE		$ 4,330.00
ALICE SOTO, CAPITAL		119,840.00
ALICE SOTO, DRAWING	1,542.00	
FRANK SOTO, CAPITAL		116,540.00
FRANK SOTO, DRAWING	1,528.00	
INCOME SUMMARY		
SALES		15,580.00
PURCHASES	3,820.00	
ADVERTISING EXPENSE	68.00	
CREDIT CARD FEE EXPENSE	215.00	
INSURANCE EXPENSE		
MISCELLANEOUS EXPENSE	80.00	
OFFICE SUPPLIES EXPENSE		
RENT EXPENSE	850.00	
SALARY EXPENSE	2,400.00	
STORE SUPPLIES EXPENSE		
	$256,290.00	$256,290.00

Adjustment Information, March 31

Merchandise inventory	$221,860.00
Office supplies inventory	671.00
Store supplies inventory	410.00
Value of insurance policies	1,125.00

Instructions: 1. Enter adjustments and complete work sheet printout for month ended March 31 of the current year. Use as a guide the work sheet printout, page 371.

2. Record adjusting entries for Soto Auto Supply, Client No. 183, on a journal entry transmittal. Use account numbers from the chart of accounts prepared in Problem 17-1. Use the journal entry transmittal, page 372, as your model.

3. Record closing entries for Soto Auto Supply on a journal entry transmittal. Distribution of net income statement printout shows net income shared equally: Alice Soto, $2,106.00; Frank Soto, $2,106.00.

ENRICHMENT PROBLEMS

MASTERY PROBLEM 19-M Recording weekly batched transactions for EDP using a journal entry transmittal

The chart of accounts prepared in Mastery Problem 17-M, Chapter 17, is needed to complete Mastery Problem 19-M.

The Appliance Center arranges source documents into five batches. (1) Accounts payable. (2) Cash payments. (3) Accounts receivable. (4) Cash receipts. (5) General. Reference numbers are assigned to transaction source documents within each batch. The batched transactions are recorded as combined entries weekly. Batched transactions for week ended April 16 of the current year are below.

Transaction	Amount	Reference
Accounts payable		
Bought office supplies on account	$ 110.00.	Ref. No. 1016.
Bought store supplies on account	$ 120.00.	Ref. No. 1017.
Purchased merchandise on account	$ 640.00.	Ref. No. 1018.
Total accounts payable	$ 870.00.	
Cash payments		
Paid on account	$ 520.00.	Ref. No. 2021.
Carol Bennett, partner, withdrew cash	$ 600.00.	Ref. No. 2022.
Steve Franklin, partner, withdrew cash	$ 600.00.	Ref. No. 2023.
Purchased merchandise for cash	$ 320.00.	Ref. No. 2024.
Paid salaries	$1,350.00.	Ref. No. 2025.
Total cash payments	$3,390.00.	
Accounts receivable		
Sold merchandise on account	$ 500.00.	Ref. No. 3011.
Total accounts receivable	$ 500.00.	
Cash receipts		
Cash received on account	$ 120.00.	Ref. No. 4013.
Cash received from sales	$2,850.00.	Ref. No. 4014.
Total cash receipts	$2,970.00.	

Instructions: Record the batched transactions for the Appliance Center, Client No. 274, on a journal entry transmittal. Use April 16 of the current year as the date of the last business day for the week's transactions. Use account numbers from the chart of accounts prepared in Mastery Problem 17-M. Use the journal entry transmittal, page 365, as your model.

CHALLENGE PROBLEM 19-C Recording weekly batched transactions for EDP using a journal entry transmittal

The chart of accounts prepared in Challenge Problem 17-C, Chapter 17, is needed to complete Challenge Problem 19-C.

Adkins Leather Goods arranges source documents into four batches. (1) Accounts payable. (2) Cash payments. (3) Cash receipts. (4) General. On May 15 the business stopped issuing credit other than on credit card purchases. Therefore, Adkins Leather Goods no longer has any accounts receivable. Reference numbers are assigned to transaction source documents within each batch. The batched transactions are recorded as combined entries weekly. Batched transactions for week ended May 21 of the current year are on the next page.

Accounts payable

Purchased merchandise on account	$1,010.00.	Ref. No. 1123.
Total accounts payable	$1,010.00.	

Cash payments

Paid advertising expense	$ 75.00.	Ref. No. 2330.
Paid on account	$ 900.00.	Ref. No. 2331.
Purchased merchandise for cash	$ 180.00.	Ref. No. 2332.
Paid miscellaneous expense	$ 25.00.	Ref. No. 2333.
Total cash payments	$1,180.00.	

Cash receipts

Cash received from sales	$2,450.00.	Ref. No. 4021.
Total cash receipts	$2,450.00.	

General

Susan Adkins, partner, withdrew merchandise	$ 30.00.	Ref. No. 5008.
Total withdrawals of merchandise by partners	$ 30.00.	

Instructions: Record the batched transactions for Adkins Leather Goods, Client No. 422, on a journal entry transmittal. Use May 21 of the current year as the date of the last business day for the week's transactions. Use account numbers from the chart of accounts prepared in Challenge Problem 17-C. Use the journal entry transmittal, page 365, as your model.

Reinforcement Activity 3

An Accounting Cycle for a Partnership Using Automated Data Processing

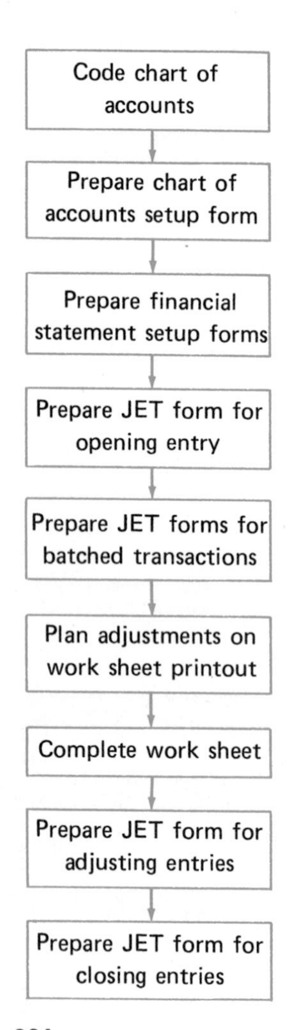

Reinforcement Activity 3 is designed to strengthen learnings from Part 4, Chapters 17–19. Accounting activities necessary to convert from a manual to an automated general ledger accounting system are covered. Accounting work is then included for a one-month fiscal period for a merchandising business organized as a partnership. The business uses a credit card service in addition to its own limited company charge accounts. The activities illustrate the application of automated general ledger accounting concepts to merchandising businesses. The flowchart at the left shows the activities covered in Reinforcement Activity 3.

BACKPACKERS

Anne and Martha Palmer, partners, own and operate a merchandising business called Backpackers. The business sells backpacks, camping supplies, hiking footwear, outdoor clothing, and sleeping bags. A monthly rent is paid for the store space.

A decision is made to convert from a manual to an automated general ledger accounting system beginning June 1 of the current year. Backpackers will use a computer service center for automated processing of general ledger accounting data. Transactions will be batched and submitted weekly to the computer service center on journal entry transmittal (JET) forms for processing. Backpackers will arrange daily transactions into five batches. (1) Accounts payable. (2) Cash payments. (3) Accounts receivable. (4) Cash receipts. (5) General.

Backpackers' setup and JET forms

Pages on which setup and JET forms are illustrated are below.

Setup and JET forms	Illustrated
Chart of accounts setup form	page 335
Financial statement setup forms	pages 337–339
JET form for opening entry	page 355
JET form for batched transactions	page 365
JET form for adjusting entries	page 372
JET form for closing entries	page 375

Blank forms needed to complete Reinforcement Activity 3 are given in the working papers.

Backpackers' chart of accounts coding system

Backpackers will use a five-digit coding system for its chart of accounts. The general ledger chart of accounts with five-digit account numbers assigned is below.

BACKPACKERS
Chart of Accounts

Account Number	(1) ASSETS	Account Number	(4) REVENUE
11000	Cash	41000	Sales
11500	Accounts Receivable		(5) COST OF MERCHANDISE SOLD
12000	Merchandise Inventory	51000	Purchases
12500	Office Supplies		(6) EXPENSES
13000	Store Supplies	61000	Advertising Expense
13500	Prepaid Insurance	61500	Credit Card Fee Expense
14000	Office Equipment	62000	Insurance Expense
14500	Store Equipment	62500	Miscellaneous Expense
	(2) LIABILITIES	63000	Office Supplies Expense
21000	Accounts Payable	63500	Rent Expense
	(3) CAPITAL	64000	Salary Expense
31000	Anne Palmer, Capital	64500	Store Supplies Expense
31500	Anne Palmer, Drawing		
32000	Martha Palmer, Capital		
32500	Martha Palmer, Drawing		
33000	Income Summary		

Preparing Backpackers' chart of accounts setup

Instructions: 1. Prepare a general ledger chart of accounts setup form, Client Number 286, dated May 19 of the current year. Use Backpackers' general ledger chart of accounts given above.

Preparing Backpackers' financial statement setups

Instructions: 2. Prepare the following financial statement setup forms, Client Number 286, dated May 23 of the current year. (1) Income statement. (2) Distribution of net income statement. Net income is to be shared equally. (3) Capital statement. (4) Balance sheet. Computer printouts of the financial statements are prepared by the computer service center at the end of the monthly fiscal period.

Recording Backpackers' opening entry

Backpackers' balance sheet for May 31 of the current year is on the next page.

Instructions: 3. Record Backpackers' opening entry, Client Number 286, on a JET form. Use June 1 of the current year as the date of the opening entry. Use the account numbers from the chart of accounts above.

Backpackers
Balance Sheet
May 31, 19--

Assets		
Cash	920000	
Accounts Receivable	74000	
Merchandise Inventory	12350000	
Office Supplies	28000	
Store Supplies	16000	
Prepaid Insurance	72000	
Office Equipment	116000	
Store Equipment	282000	
Total Assets		13858000
Liabilities		
Accounts Payable		318000
Capital		
Anne Palmer, Capital	6860000	
Martha Palmer, Capital	6680000	
Total Capital		13540000
Total Liabilities and Capital		13858000

Recording Backpackers' batched transactions

Instructions: 4. Record the following batched transactions, Client Number 286, on a JET form. Reference numbers are assigned to single and groups of transactions. Use June 5 of the current year as the date of the last business day for the week's business. Use the account numbers from the chart of accounts, page 385.

Accounts Payable

Bought office supplies on account	$ 112.00.	Ref. No. 1000.
Bought store supplies on account	$ 93.00.	Ref. No. 1001.
Purchased merchandise on account	$1,840.00.	Ref. No. 1002.
Total accounts payable	$2,045.00.	

Cash Payments

Bought store supplies for cash	$ 62.00.	Ref. No. 2000.
Paid on account	$1,840.00.	Ref. No. 2001.
Anne Palmer, partner, withdrew cash	$ 800.00.	Ref. No. 2002.
Martha Palmer, partner, withdrew cash	$ 800.00.	Ref. No. 2003.
Paid June rent	$1,200.00.	Ref. No. 2004.
Paid salaries	$ 900.00.	Ref. No. 2005.
Total cash payments	$5,602.00.	

Accounts Receivable

Sold merchandise on account	$ 84.00.	Ref. No. 3000.
Total accounts receivable	$ 84.00.	

Cash Receipts

Cash received on account	$ 340.00.	Ref. No. 4000.
Cash received from sales	$2,620.00.	Ref. No. 4001.
Total cash receipts	$2,960.00.	

General

Anne Palmer, partner, withdrew merchandise	$ 103.00.	Ref. No. 5000.
Total withdrawal of merchandise by partners	$ 103.00.	

Instructions: 5. Record the following batched transactions, Client Number 286, on a JET form. Use June 12 of the current year as the date of the last business day for the week's business. Use the account numbers from the chart of accounts, page 385.

Accounts Payable

Bought store supplies on account	$ 48.00.	Ref. No. 1003.
Purchased merchandise on account	$1,350.00.	Ref. No. 1004.
Total accounts payable	$1,398.00.	

Cash Payments

Paid on account	$ 675.00.	Ref. No. 2006.
Purchased merchandise for cash	$ 380.00.	Ref. No. 2007.
Paid advertising expense	$ 83.00.	Ref. No. 2008.
Paid miscellaneous expense	$ 48.00.	Ref. No. 2009.
Total cash payments	$1,186.00.	

Accounts Receivable

Sold merchandise on account	$ 116.00.	Ref. No. 3001.
Total accounts receivable	$ 116.00.	

Cash Receipts

Cash received on account	$ 88.00.	Ref. No. 4002.
Cash received from sales	$3,610.00.	Ref. No. 4003.
Total cash receipts	$3,698.00.	

Instructions: 6. Record the following batched transactions, Client Number 286, on a JET form. Use June 19 of the current year as the date of the last business day for the week's business. Use the account numbers from the chart of accounts, page 385.

Accounts Payable

Bought office supplies on account	$ 38.00.	Ref. No. 1005.
Purchased merchandise on account	$1,960.00.	Ref. No. 1006.
Total accounts payable	$1,998.00.	

Cash Payments

Paid on account	$ 230.00.	Ref. No. 2010.
Purchased merchandise for cash	$ 161.00.	Ref. No. 2011.
Paid miscellaneous expense	$ 36.00.	Ref. No. 2012.
Paid salaries	$ 900.00.	Ref. No. 2013.
Total cash payments	$1,327.00.	

Accounts Receivable

Sold merchandise on account	$ 320.00.	Ref. No. 3002.
Total accounts receivable	$ 320.00.	

Cash Receipts

Cash received on account	$ 260.00.	Ref. No. 4004.
Cash received from sales	$3,730.00.	Ref. No. 4005.
Total cash receipts	$3,990.00.	

General

Martha Palmer, partner, withdrew merchandise	$ 96.00.	Ref. No. 5001.
Total withdrawal of merchandise by partners	$ 96.00.	

Instructions: 7. Record the following batched transactions, Client Number 286, on a JET form. Use June 26 of the current year as the date of the last business day for the week's business. Use the account numbers from the chart of accounts, page 385.

Accounts Payable

Bought office supplies on account	$ 41.00.	Ref. No. 1007.
Bought store supplies on account	$ 62.00.	Ref. No. 1008.
Purchased merchandise on account	$ 240.00.	Ref. No. 1009.
Total accounts payable	$ 343.00.	

Cash Payments

Paid on account	$ 435.00.	Ref. No. 2014.
Paid advertising expense	$ 96.00.	Ref. No. 2015.
Paid credit card fee expense	$ 240.00.	Ref. No. 2016.
Paid miscellaneous expense	$ 41.00.	Ref. No. 2017.
Total cash payments	$ 812.00.	

Accounts Receivable

Sold merchandise on account	$ 162.00.	Ref. No. 3003.
Total accounts receivable	$ 162.00.	

Cash Receipts

Cash received from sales	$3,460.00.	Ref. No. 4006.
Total cash receipts	$3,460.00.	

Instructions: 8. Record the following batched transactions, Client Number 286, on a JET form. Use June 30 of the current year as the date of the last business day for the monthly fiscal period. Use the account numbers from the chart of accounts, page 385.

Accounts Payable

Bought store supplies on account	$ 32.00.	Ref. No. 1010.
Purchased merchandise on account	$ 470.00.	Ref. No. 1011.
Total accounts payable	$ 502.00.	

Cash Payments

Bought office supplies for cash	$ 16.00.	Ref. No. 2018.
Bought store supplies for cash	$ 34.00.	Ref. No. 2019.
Purchased merchandise for cash	$ 160.00.	Ref. No. 2020.
Paid advertising expense	$ 46.00.	Ref. No. 2021.
Total cash payments	$ 256.00.	

Cash Receipts

Cash received on account	$ 24.00.	Ref. No. 4007.
Cash received from sales	$2,180.00.	Ref. No. 4008.
Total cash receipts	$2,204.00.	

General

Anne Palmer, partner, withdrew merchandise	$ 26.00.	Ref. No. 5002.
Martha Palmer, partner, withdrew merchandise	$ 96.00.	Ref. No. 5003.
Total withdrawal of merchandise by partners	$ 122.00.	

Recording Backpackers' adjusting and closing entries

Backpackers' trial balance is in the partial work sheet printout on page 389. Ending inventories and the value of insurance policies are also given.

BACKPACKERS
WORK SHEET
FOR MONTH ENDED JUNE 30, 19--

	TRIAL BALANCE	
	DEBIT	CREDIT
CASH....................	$ 16,329.00	
ACCOUNTS RECEIVABLE......	710.00	
MERCHANDISE INVENTORY....	123,500.00	
OFFICE SUPPLIES..........	487.00	
STORE SUPPLIES...........	491.00	
PREPAID INSURANCE........	720.00	
OFFICE EQUIPMENT.........	1,160.00	
STORE EQUIPMENT..........	2,820.00	
ACCOUNTS PAYABLE.........		$ 6,286.00
ANNE PALMER, CAPITAL.....		68,600.00
ANNE PALMER, DRAWING.....	929.00	
MARTHA PALMER, CAPITAL...		66,800.00
MARTHA PALMER, DRAWING...	992.00	
INCOME SUMMARY...........		
SALES....................		16,282.00
PURCHASES................	6,240.00	
ADVERTISING EXPENSE......	225.00	
CREDIT CARD FEE EXPENSE..	240.00	
INSURANCE EXPENSE........		
MISCELLANEOUS EXPENSE....	125.00	
OFFICE SUPPLIES EXPENSE..		
RENT EXPENSE.............	1,200.00	
SALARY EXPENSE...........	1,800.00	
STORE SUPPLIES EXPENSE...		
	$157,968.00	$157,968.00

Adjustment Information, June 30

Merchandise inventory	$121,790.00
Office supplies inventory	427.00
Store supplies inventory	401.00
Value of insurance polices	660.00

Instructions: 9. Enter adjustments and complete work sheet printout for month ended June 30 of the current year.

10. Record Backpackers' adjusting entries, Client Number 286, on a JET form. Use the account numbers from the chart of accounts, page 385.

11. Record Backpackers' closing entries, Client Number 286, on a JET form. Use the account numbers from the chart of accounts, page 385. Net income is shared equally by the two partners.

5 AN ACCOUNTING SYSTEM WITH SPECIAL JOURNALS

GENERAL BEHAVIORAL GOALS

1. Know accounting terminology related to a merchandising business organized as a corporation.
2. Understand accounting principles and practices for a merchandising business organized as a corporation.
3. Demonstrate accounting procedures for a merchandising business organized as a corporation.

Lin's Music Center, the business for Part 5, sells musical instruments, records, and tapes.

LIN'S MUSIC CENTER
Chart of Accounts

Balance Sheet Accounts

(1) ASSETS	Account Number
11 Current Assets	
Cash	1101
Notes Receivable	1102
Accounts Receivable	1103
Allowance for Uncollectible Accounts	1103.1
Merchandise Inventory	1104
Supplies	1105
Prepaid Insurance	1106
12 Plant Assets	
Delivery Equipment	1201
Accumulated Depreciation — Delivery Equipment	1201.1
Office Equipment	1202
Accumulated Depreciation — Office Equipment	1202.1
Store Equipment	1203
Accumulated Depreciation — Store Equipment	1203.1
(2) LIABILITIES	
21 Current Liabilities	
Notes Payable	2101
Accounts Payable	2102
Employees Income Tax Payable	2103
Federal Income Tax Payable	2104
FICA Tax Payable	2105
Sales Tax Payable	2106
Unemployment Tax Payable — Federal	2107
Unemployment Tax Payable — State	2108
Hospital Insurance Premiums Payable	2109
U.S. Savings Bonds Payable	2110
United Way Donations Payable	2111
Dividends Payable	2112
(3) STOCKHOLDERS' EQUITY	
Capital Stock	3101
Retained Earnings	3201
Income Summary	3301

Income Statement Accounts

(4) OPERATING REVENUE	Account Number
Sales	4101
Sales Returns and Allowances	4101.1
(5) COST OF MERCHANDISE	
Purchases	5101
Purchases Returns and Allowances	5101.1
Purchases Discount	5101.2
(6) OPERATING EXPENSES	
Advertising Expense	6101
Bad Debts Expense	6102
Credit Card Fee Expense	6103
Delivery Expense	6104
Depreciation Expense — Delivery Equipment	6105
Depreciation Expense — Office Equipment	6106
Depreciation Expense — Store Equipment	6107
Insurance Expense	6108
Miscellaneous Expense	6109
Payroll Taxes Expense	6110
Rent Expense	6111
Salary Expense	6112
Supplies Expense	6113
(7) OTHER REVENUE	
Interest Income	7101
(8) OTHER EXPENSES	
Interest Expense	8101
(9) INCOME TAX	
Federal Income Tax	9101

The chart of accounts for Lin's Music Center is illustrated above for ready reference as you study Part 5 of this textbook.

20

Recording Transactions with Special Journals: Purchases and Cash Payments

ENABLING PERFORMANCE TASKS

After studying Chapter 20, you will be able to:

a. Define accounting terms related to purchases and cash payments.
b. Explain accounting principles and practices related to purchases and cash payments.
c. Analyze transactions affecting purchases and cash payments.
d. Journalize purchases on account transactions in a purchases journal.
e. Post from a purchases journal.
f. Journalize cash payments transactions in a cash payments journal.
g. Post from a cash payments journal.
h. Journalize purchases returns and allowances and buying of supplies on account transactions in a general journal.
i. Post from a general journal.

A business should use an accounting system that provides the desired financial information with the least amount of effort. Most businesses expect to remain in business for an indefinite time. Therefore, accounting records should be kept with the assumption that the business will continue indefinitely. *(CONCEPT: Going Concern)*

The preferred type of accounting system may vary with the size and kind of business. A business with few transactions may need only one bookkeeper or accounting clerk to record all the transactions. When one person records all the transactions, a business may prefer the convenience of recording all entries in one journal. In Part 3, Denim Threads uses a combination journal to record all transactions. However, a business with many daily transactions may need several accounting clerks to record the transactions. Normally these larger businesses use several journals. Using several journals permits the accounting clerks to specialize in the kind of transactions recorded. This specialization generally helps improve the efficiency of recording transactions. A journal in which only one kind of business transaction is recorded is known as a special journal.

Lin's Music Center is a corporation that sells musical instruments, stereo equipment, records, tapes, and music. Lin's uses five journals to record its transactions.

1. Purchases journal — for all purchases on account
2. Cash payments journal — for all cash payments
3. Sales journal — for all sales on account
4. Cash receipts journal — for all cash receipts
5. General journal — for all other transactions

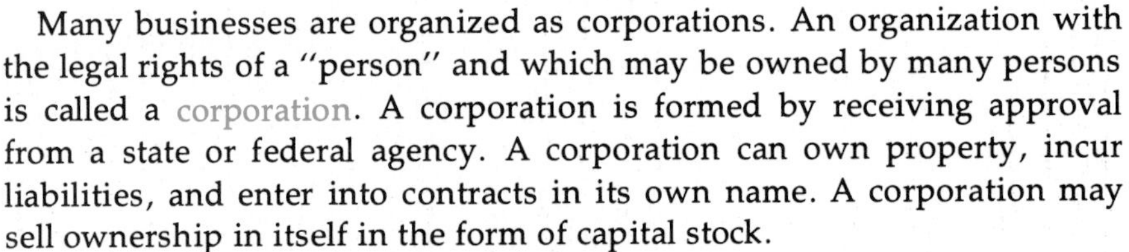

Many businesses are organized as corporations. An organization with the legal rights of a "person" and which may be owned by many persons is called a corporation. A corporation is formed by receiving approval from a state or federal agency. A corporation can own property, incur liabilities, and enter into contracts in its own name. A corporation may sell ownership in itself in the form of capital stock.

Lin's was formed as a corporation because several owners can provide larger amounts of capital than one owner. The principal difference between the accounting records of sole proprietorships, partnerships, and corporations is in the capital accounts. A corporation has a separate capital account for the stock issued and for the earnings kept in the business. The different capital accounts will be explained in Chapter 27. As in sole proprietorships and partnerships, information in a corporation accounting system relates to a specific business entity. *(CONCEPT: Business Entity)*

RECORDING PURCHASES ON ACCOUNT IN A PURCHASES JOURNAL

A special journal used to record only purchases on account is called a purchases journal.

The purchases journal used by Lin's Music Center is on page 395. A purchase on account can be recorded on one line in the purchases journal. Each entry in the single amount column is both a debit to Purchases and a credit to Accounts Payable. Since the debit and credit entries are always to the same accounts, recording time is shortened by using one column. The names of both general ledger accounts are listed in the column heading.

Journalizing purchases on account in a purchases journal

The source document for recording a purchase on account is a purchase invoice received from a creditor. *(CONCEPT: Objective Evidence)*

Lin's dates, numbers, and checks its purchase invoices as shown on page 194 for Denim Threads. Lin's purchased merchandise on account.

February 1, 1983. Purchased merchandise on account from Slater Company, $2,648.00. Purchase Invoice No. 33.

In this entry, Purchases is debited for $2,648.00 and Accounts Payable is credited for $2,648.00. Purchases are recorded at their cost. *(CONCEPT: Historical Cost)* The entry to record this transaction in a purchases journal is below.

PURCHASES JOURNAL PAGE 2

	DATE		ACCOUNT CREDITED	PURCH. NO.	POST. REF.	PURCHASES, DR. ACCTS. PAY. CR.	
1	1983 Feb.	1	Slater Company	33		2648 00	1
2							2
3							3

Purchases on account recorded in a purchases journal

The date, *1983, Feb. 1*, is written in the Date column. The amount of the invoice, *$2,648.00*, is written in the amount column. The name of the creditor, *Slater Company*, is written in the Account Credited column. The number stamped on the invoice, *33*, is written in the Purch. No. column.

Each purchase on account is recorded in the purchases journal in the same way.

Posting a purchases journal to an accounts payable ledger

Each amount in a purchases journal is posted as a credit to the named creditor's account in the accounts payable ledger.

Lin's posts daily to the accounts payable ledger. In this way, each creditor's account always shows an up-to-date daily balance. The illustration on the next page shows the posting of the entry on line 1 of the purchases journal.

Write the amount, *$2,648.00*, in the Credit column of the creditor's account. Add the amount in the Credit column to the previous balance in the Credit Balance column ($963.00 + $2,648.00 = $3,611.00). Write the new balance, *$3,611.00*, in the Credit Balance column. Write the date, *1*, in the Date column. Write the abbreviation for the purchases journal, *P2*, in the Post. Ref. column of the account. Place a check mark in the Post. Ref. column of the purchases journal to show completion of the posting of this line.

When several journals are used, an abbreviation is used to show the journal from which the posting is made. *P* is the abbreviation used for the purchases journal. The abbreviation *P2* means page 2 of the purchases journal.

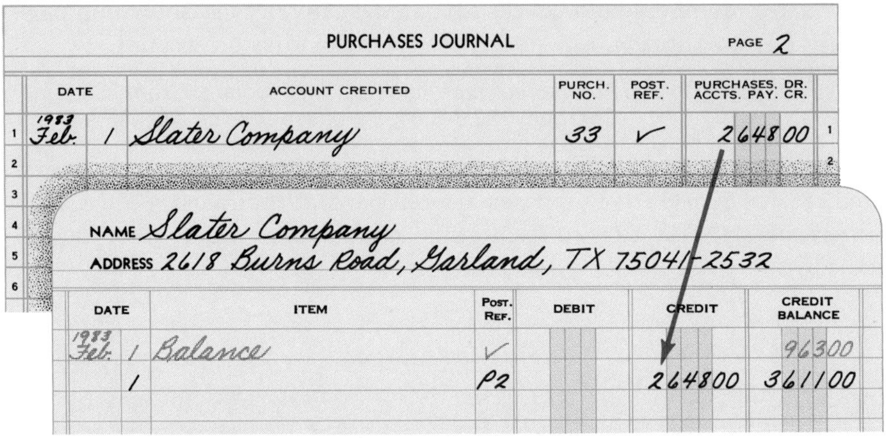

PURCHASES JOURNAL — PAGE 2

	DATE		ACCOUNT CREDITED	PURCH. NO.	POST. REF.	PURCHASES, DR. ACCTS. PAY. CR.	
1	1983 Feb.	1	Slater Company	33	✓	2 648 00	1

NAME Slater Company
ADDRESS 2618 Burns Road, Garland, TX 75041-2532

DATE		ITEM	POST. REF.	DEBIT	CREDIT	CREDIT BALANCE
1983 Feb.	1	Balance	✓			963 00
	1		P2		2 648 00	3 611 00

Posting from a purchases journal to an accounts payable ledger

This procedure is the same as posting from an Accounts Payable Credit column of a combination journal. Posting from a combination journal is described in Chapter 13.

Posting the totals of a purchases journal to a general ledger

At the end of each month, a purchases journal is totaled and ruled. A single line is drawn across the amount column under the last amount recorded, and the column is added. The total is written directly below the single line as illustrated on page 397. The date of the last day of the month, *28*, is written in the Date column. The word *Total* is written in the Account Credited column. Double lines are ruled across the amount column under the total amount.

The purchases journal total is posted to two general ledger accounts. The total is posted once to Purchases as a debit. The total is also posted once to Accounts Payable as a credit. The same total amount is posted as both a debit and a credit. This maintains the equality of debits and credits in the general ledger. The illustration, page 397, shows the posting of the purchases journal to the general ledger accounts.

The total amount of the purchases journal is posted to two general ledger accounts. The total amount, *$42,870.00*, is posted to Purchases as a debit and to Accounts Payable as a credit. After the total is posted to Purchases, the account number, *5101*, is written under the total in the purchases journal. After this same total is posted to Accounts Payable, the account number, *2102*, is written under the purchases journal total. Both account numbers are written within parentheses.

Summary of journalizing and posting from a purchases journal

(1) Lin's Music Center records all purchases on account in a one-column purchases journal. (2) Items in the amount column are posted daily to creditors' accounts in the accounts payable ledger. (3) At the end of the

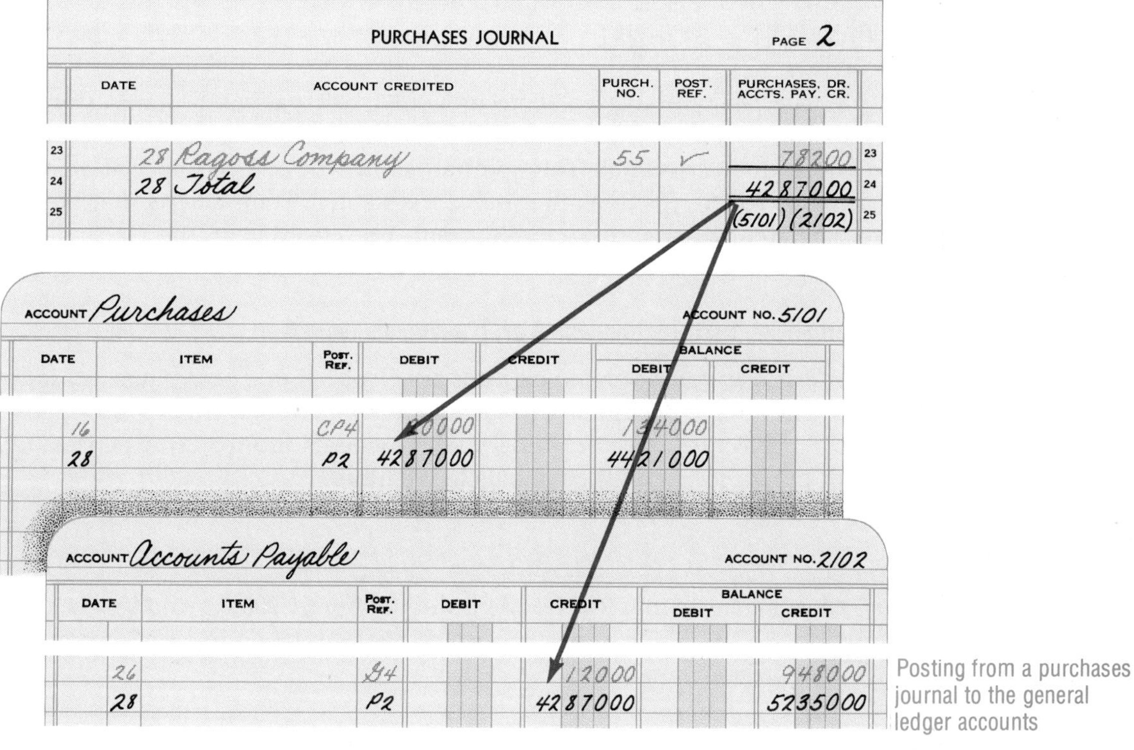

PURCHASES JOURNAL PAGE 2

	DATE	ACCOUNT CREDITED	PURCH. NO.	POST. REF.	PURCHASES, DR. ACCTS. PAY. CR.	
23	28	Ragoss Company	55	✓	78200	23
24	28	Total			4287000	24
25					(5101) (2102)	25

ACCOUNT Purchases ACCOUNT NO. 5101

DATE	ITEM	POST. REF.	DEBIT	CREDIT	BALANCE DEBIT	BALANCE CREDIT
16		CP4	[illegible]0000		134000	
28		P2	4287000		4421000	

ACCOUNT Accounts Payable ACCOUNT NO. 2102

DATE	ITEM	POST. REF.	DEBIT	CREDIT	BALANCE DEBIT	BALANCE CREDIT
26		G4		12000		948000
28		P2		4287000		5235000

Posting from a purchases journal to the general ledger accounts

month, the purchases journal total is posted to two general ledger accounts. Purchases is debited; Accounts Payable is credited. The flowchart below shows this procedure.

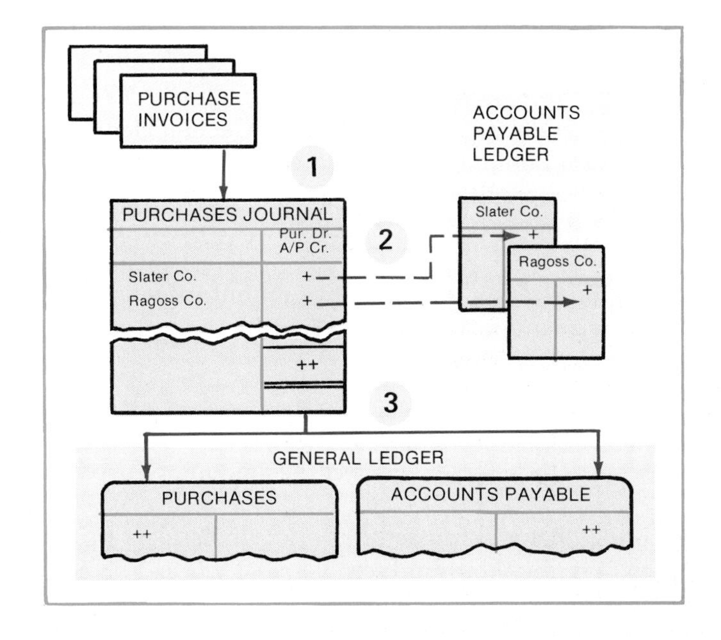

Flowchart showing journalizing and posting purchases on account using a purchases journal

RECORDING CASH PAYMENTS IN A CASH PAYMENTS JOURNAL

A special journal used to record only cash payments transactions is called a cash payments journal. Lin's Music Center uses a five-column cash payments journal. This journal, shown below, has special amount columns for transactions that occur frequently. Transactions that do not occur often, such as the monthly rent, are recorded in the General columns.

Journalizing cash payments in a cash payments journal

All cash payments made by Lin's are recorded in a cash payments journal. The source document for each cash payment is a check stub. *(CONCEPT: Objective Evidence)* Most cash payments are for (1) expenses, (2) cash purchases, and (3) payments to creditors.

Lin's paid an expense.

February 1, 1983. Paid rent expense, $1,200.00. Check No. 98.

In this transaction, Rent Expense is debited for $1,200.00, and Cash is credited for $1,200.00. The entry to record this transaction in a cash payments journal is below on line 1.

CASH PAYMENTS JOURNAL — PAGE 4

	Date		Account Title	Check No.	Post. Ref.	1 General Debit	2 General Credit	3 Accounts Payable Debit	4 Purchases Discount Credit	5 Cash Credit	
1	1983 Feb.	1	Rent Expense	98		1200 00				1200 00	1
2		1	Purchases	99		180 00				180 00	2
3		2	Kuhns Paint Company	100				644 00		644 00	3

Cash payments recorded in a cash payments journal

The date, *1983, Feb. 1*, is written in the Date column. The amount debited to Rent Expense, *$1,200.00*, is written in the General Debit column. The name of the account debited, *Rent Expense*, is written in the Account Title column. The amount credited to Cash, *$1,200.00*, is written in the Cash Credit column. The number of the check, *98*, is written in the Check No. column.

Line 2 of the illustration above shows an entry for a cash purchase. Line 3 shows a payment on account to a creditor.

Figuring discounts

The total amount shown on an invoice is not always the amount that the buyer will pay. Discounts may affect the amount to be paid.

Trade discount. Many manufacturers and wholesalers print price lists and catalogs to describe their products. Generally prices listed in catalogs

are the manufacturers' suggested retail prices. A business' printed or catalog price is called a list price. When a merchandising business purchases a number of products from a manufacturer, the price frequently is quoted as "list price less a trade discount." A reduction in the list price granted to customers is called a trade discount. Trade discounts are used to quote different prices for different quantities purchased without changing catalog or list prices.

When a trade discount is granted, the seller's invoice shows the actual amount charged. This is the net amount after the trade discount has been deducted from the list price. Only the net amount of the invoice is used in a journal entry. The invoice is recorded by both the seller and buyer at the same amount. No journal entry is made to show the amount of a trade discount.

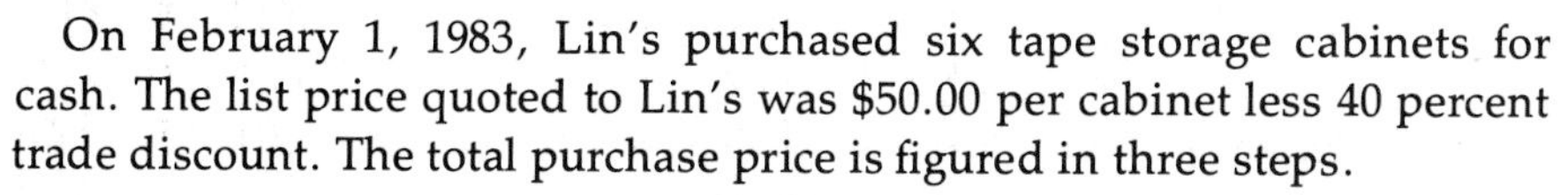

On February 1, 1983, Lin's purchased six tape storage cabinets for cash. The list price quoted to Lin's was $50.00 per cabinet less 40 percent trade discount. The total purchase price is figured in three steps.

Step 1:	List price	*times*	Trade discount rate	*equals*	Trade discount
	$50.00	×	40%	=	$20.00
Step 2:	List price	*less*	Trade discount	*equals*	Net amount
	$50.00	–	$20.00	=	$30.00
Step 3:	Net amount	*times*	Number of cabinets	*equals*	Total purchase price
	$30.00	×	6	=	$180.00

The journal entry for this purchase is a debit to Purchases, $180.00, and a credit to Cash, $180.00. This journal entry is on line 2 of the cash payments journal, page 398.

Cash discount. A buyer is expected to pay the seller for a credit sale within the credit period agreed upon. To encourage earlier payment, a seller may allow a deduction from the amount of the invoice. A deduction that a seller allows on the amount of an invoice to encourage prompt payment is called a cash discount.

A cash discount is usually stated as a percentage that can be deducted from the amount of the invoice. For example, the terms of sale on an invoice may be written as *2/10, n/30*. These terms are commonly read *two ten, net thirty*. The term *two ten* means 2% of the invoice amount may be deducted if paid within 10 days from invoice date. The term *net thirty* means that the total amount of the invoice *must* be paid within 30 days. A business also may indicate the date for full payment of an invoice as *EOM*. This means that full payment is expected not later than the *end of the month*.

Purchases discount. A cash discount on purchases taken by a buyer is called a purchases discount. When a purchases discount is taken, the buyer pays less cash than the purchase price recorded on the books. Therefore, purchases discounts are deducted from purchases when net purchases are figured. Purchases discounts are recorded in a general ledger account titled Purchases Discount.

In Lin's general ledger, the account Purchases Discount is numbered 5101.2. The purchases discount account is in the cost of merchandise division of the general ledger, as shown on page 392. An account that reduces a related account on financial statements is called a contra account.

The decimal in the account number of Purchases Discount, *5101.2*, indicates the account is a contra or minus account. Thus on the income statement, this account is deducted from the balance of the account with the number 5101, *Purchases*. The balance of any account with a decimal account number is deducted from the balance of the account having the same whole number.

Journalizing cash payments on account with purchases discounts

Lin's tries to pay all creditors on or before the last date to take the purchases discount. This policy reduces the cost of merchandise purchased by Lin's.

Lin's paid on account.

February 9, 1983. Paid on account to Slater Company, $2,621.52, for Purchase Invoice No. 33, for $2,648.00 less 1% discount of $26.48. Check No. 115.

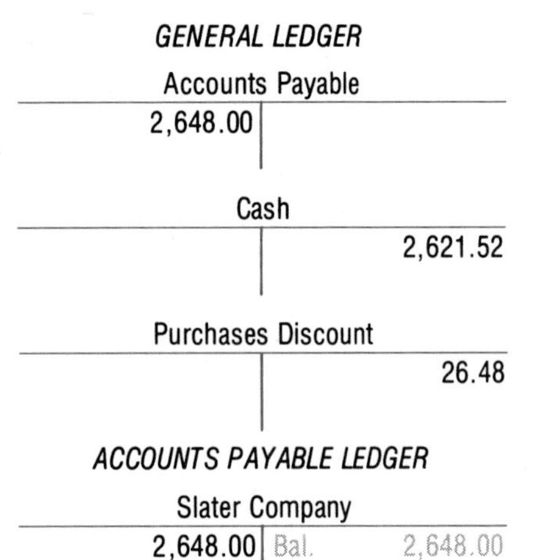

Accounts Payable is debited for the amount of the purchase invoice, $2,648.00. This debit decreases the amount owed to creditors. This same amount, $2,648.00, also is debited to the account of Slater Company in the accounts payable ledger.

Cash is credited for the amount of the check, $2,621.52.

Purchases Discount is credited for the amount of the purchases discount, $26.48. The discount is figured by multiplying the amount of the purchase invoice, $2,648.00, by the discount rate, 1% ($2,648.00 × .01 = $26.48). On an income statement, the balance of a purchases discount account is deducted from the balance of a purchases account. A purchases account has a debit balance. Therefore, to show a deduction from Purchases a purchases discount account has a credit balance.

The entry for this payment on account with a purchases discount is shown in the cash payments journal on the next page.

The amount of the purchase invoice, *$2,648.00*, is written in the Accounts Payable Debit column. The amount of the purchases discount, *$26.48*, is written in the Purchases Discount Credit column. The amount of cash paid, *$2,621.52*, is written in the Cash Credit column. The name

CASH PAYMENTS JOURNAL — PAGE 4

	DATE	ACCOUNT TITLE	CHECK No.	POST. REF.	GENERAL DEBIT (1)	GENERAL CREDIT (2)	ACCOUNTS PAYABLE DEBIT (3)	PURCHASES DISCOUNT CREDIT (4)	CASH CREDIT (5)	
18	9	Slater Company	115				264800	2648	262152	18
19										19
20										20

of the creditor, *Slater Company*, is written in the Account Title column. The total of the two credits ($26.48 + $2,621.52) is $2,648.00 and is equal to the one debit of $2,648.00.

Payment on account with purchases discount recorded in cash payments journal

Purchases discounts are recorded frequently by Lin's. Therefore, a special amount column for Purchases Discount Credit is provided in the cash payments journal.

Posting a cash payments journal to an accounts payable ledger

Each entry in the accounts payable column of a cash payments journal affects the creditor named in the Account Title column. Each amount listed in this column is posted daily to the proper creditor's account in the accounts payable ledger. In this way, each creditor's account always shows an up-to-date balance. The illustration below shows the posting of a cash payments journal entry to a creditor's account.

CASH PAYMENTS JOURNAL — PAGE 4

	DATE	ACCOUNT TITLE	CHECK No.	POST. REF.	GENERAL DEBIT (1)	GENERAL CREDIT (2)	ACCOUNTS PAYABLE DEBIT (3)	PURCHASES DISCOUNT CREDIT (4)	CASH CREDIT (5)	
3	2	Kuhns Paint Company	100	✓			64400		64400	3

NAME Kuhns Paint Company
ADDRESS 1820 Linden Road, Richardson, TX 75081-9368

DATE		ITEM	POST. REF.	DEBIT	CREDIT	CREDIT BALANCE
1983 Feb.	1	Balance	✓			95900
	2		CP4	64400		31500

Posting from a cash payments journal to an accounts payable ledger

The amount in the Accounts Payable Debit column, *$644.00*, is posted to the Debit column of the creditor's account. After the amount is posted, *CP4* is written in the Post. Ref. column of the creditor's account. The abbreviation CP4 means page 4 of the cash payments journal. As a last step, place a check mark in the Post. Ref. column of the cash payments journal. This check mark shows that the posting for this entry is complete.

Posting a cash payments journal to a general ledger

Each amount in the General columns of a cash payments journal is posted to a general ledger account. However, only the monthly total of each special column is posted to a general ledger account.

Posting from the General columns of a cash payments journal. Each amount in the General columns is posted individually to the general ledger account named in the Account Title column. The illustration below shows the posting from a General column of a cash payments journal to a general ledger account.

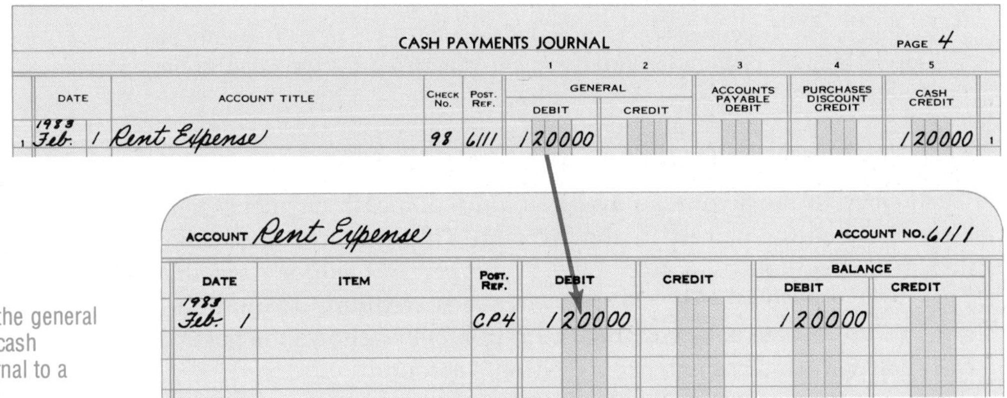

CASH PAYMENTS JOURNAL PAGE 4

	DATE		ACCOUNT TITLE	CHECK NO.	POST. REF.	1 GENERAL DEBIT	2 GENERAL CREDIT	3 ACCOUNTS PAYABLE DEBIT	4 PURCHASES DISCOUNT CREDIT	5 CASH CREDIT	
1	1983 Feb.	1	Rent Expense	98	6111	1200 00				1200 00	1

ACCOUNT Rent Expense ACCOUNT NO. 6111

DATE		ITEM	POST. REF.	DEBIT	CREDIT	BALANCE DEBIT	BALANCE CREDIT
1983 Feb.	1		CP4	1200 00		1200 00	

Posting from the general columns of a cash payments journal to a general ledger

The amount in the General Debit column, *$1,200.00*, is posted to the Debit column of the general ledger account Rent Expense. After the amount is posted, *CP4* is written in the Post. Ref. column of the account Rent Expense. The abbreviation *CP4* means page 4 of the cash payments journal. Last, the number of the rent expense account, *6111*, is written in the Post. Ref. column of the cash payments journal. This account number shows that posting of the General amount on this line in the journal is complete.

Posting totals of the special columns in a cash payments journal. At the end of each month, equality of debits and credits is proved for a cash payments journal. The cash payments journal is then ruled as shown on the next page. Next the total for each special column is posted to the account named in the cash payments journal column headings. The illustration on the next page shows the posting of cash payments journal special column totals to the general ledger accounts.

After a special column total is posted, *CP6* is written in the Post. Ref. column of the posted account. Last, the account number of the posted account is written under the related cash payments journal special column total. The account number is written within parentheses.

The totals of the General columns are not posted. Each amount in these columns was posted individually to a general ledger account. To indicate that these totals are not to be posted, a check mark is placed in parentheses below each column total.

CASH PAYMENTS JOURNAL — PAGE 6

	DATE	ACCOUNT TITLE	CHECK No.	POST. REF.	1 GENERAL DEBIT	2 GENERAL CREDIT	3 ACCOUNTS PAYABLE DEBIT	4 PURCHASES DISCOUNT CREDIT	5 CASH CREDIT	
1	1983 Feb. 21	Brought Forward		✓	1371800	152700	3026500	35400	4210200	1
26	28	Delivery Expense	183	6104	8400				8400	26
27	28	Totals			1959700	218200	4323600	50500	6014600	27
28					(✓)	(✓)	(2102)	(5101.2)	(1101)	28

ACCOUNT Accounts Payable — ACCOUNT NO. 2102

DATE	ITEM	POST. REF.	DEBIT	CREDIT	BALANCE DEBIT	BALANCE CREDIT
28		P2		4287000		5235000
28		CP6	4323600			911400

ACCOUNT Purchases Discount — ACCOUNT NO. 5101.2

DATE	ITEM	POST. REF.	DEBIT	CREDIT	BALANCE DEBIT	BALANCE CREDIT
1983 Feb. 28		CP6		50500		50500

ACCOUNT Cash — ACCOUNT NO. 1101

DATE	ITEM	POST. REF.	DEBIT	CREDIT	BALANCE DEBIT	BALANCE CREDIT
1983 Feb. 1	Balance	✓			6826800	
28		CR10	7041530		13868330	
28		CP6		6014600	7853730	

Posting totals of the special columns in a cash payments journal to a general ledger

Posting from a cash receipts journal to the cash account, shown on line 2, is described in Chapter 21.

Summary of journalizing and posting cash payments using a cash payments journal

(1) Lin's Music Center records all cash payments in a five-column cash payments journal. (2) Amounts in the Accounts Payable Debit column are posted daily to the named creditor's account in the accounts payable ledger. (3) Individual items in the General Debit and Credit columns are posted often during the month to the general ledger. (4) At the end of the month, the totals of the special columns are posted to the general ledger.

The flowchart below shows the procedure for journalizing and posting cash payments using a cash payments journal.

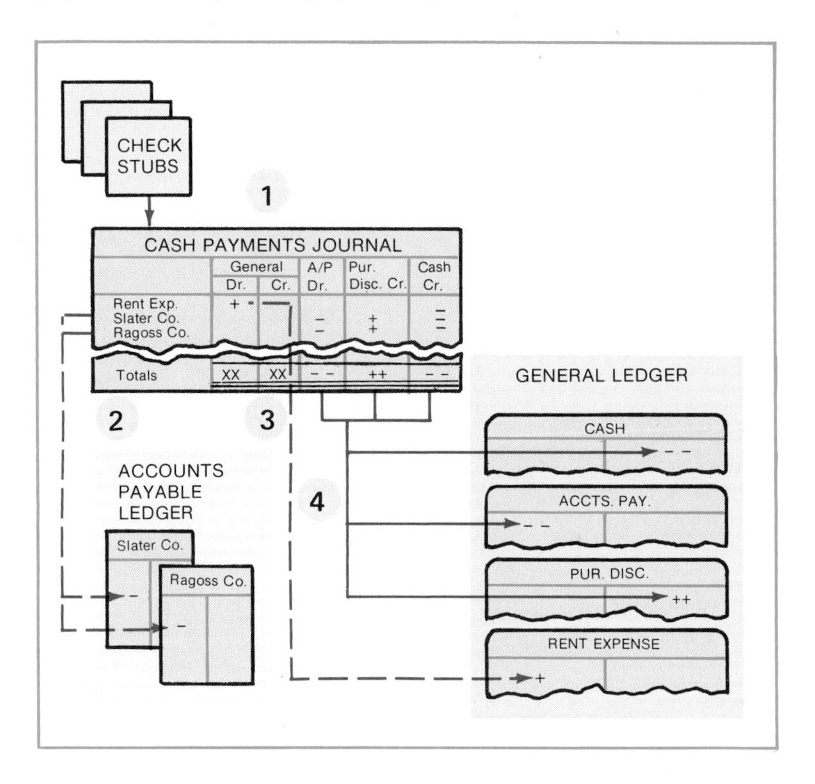

Flowchart showing journalizing and posting of cash payments using a cash payments journal

RECORDING TRANSACTIONS IN A GENERAL JOURNAL

Lin's Music Center uses a general journal, page 406, to record transactions that cannot be recorded in the special journals. Two merchandise and supplies transactions that are not recorded in a special journal are described below.

Purchases returns and allowances

A buyer may not want to keep merchandise that is inferior in quality or is damaged when received. A buyer may be allowed to return part or all of the merchandise purchased. Merchandise returned by a buyer for credit is called a purchases return. Sometimes the seller lets the buyer keep the merchandise at a reduced price. Credit allowed for part of the price of merchandise that is not returned is called a purchases allowance.

A purchases return or allowance should be confirmed in writing. The details may be stated in a letter or on a form. A form prepared by the buyer showing the price deduction taken by the buyer for returns and allowances is called a debit memorandum. The form is called a debit memorandum because the amount is a deduction (debit) from the liability account Accounts Payable.

The buyer may use a copy of the debit memorandum as the source document for journalizing purchases returns and allowances. However, the buyer may wait for written confirmation from the seller and use that confirmation as the source document. Lin's issues a debit memorandum for each purchases return or allowance. This debit memorandum is used as the source document for purchases returns and allowances transactions. *(CONCEPT: Objective Evidence)* The transaction then can be recorded immediately without waiting for written confirmation from the seller. The original of the debit memorandum is sent to the creditor. The carbon copy is kept by Lin's. The debit memorandum form used by Lin's is below.

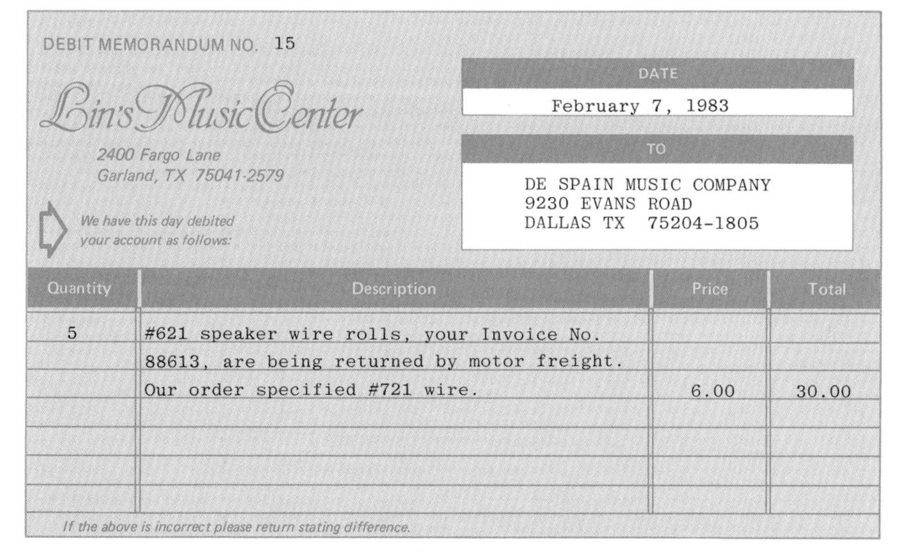

DEBIT MEMORANDUM NO. 15

Lin's Music Center
2400 Fargo Lane
Garland, TX 75041-2579

DATE: February 7, 1983

TO: DE SPAIN MUSIC COMPANY
9230 EVANS ROAD
DALLAS TX 75204-1805

We have this day debited your account as follows:

Quantity	Description	Price	Total
5	#621 speaker wire rolls, your Invoice No. 88613, are being returned by motor freight. Our order specified #721 wire.	6.00	30.00

If the above is incorrect please return stating difference.

Debit memorandum for purchases returns and allowances

Purchases returns and allowances decrease the amount of purchases. Some businesses credit the purchases account for the amount of the purchases return or allowance. However, better information is provided if these amounts are credited to a separate account Purchases Returns and Allowances. A business then can see how large its purchases returns and allowances are. Also, the business can see if purchases returns and allowances are increasing or decreasing from year to year. If the amounts are large, one account may be kept for purchases returns and another account for purchases allowances. Usually a single, combined account is satisfactory.

Lin's uses a single account Purchases Returns and Allowances. The account is in the cost of merchandise division of the general ledger as shown on page 392. The account number, 5101.1, shows that this contra purchases account is a deduction from the balance of account number 5101, Purchases.

Journalizing purchases returns and allowances

Lin's recorded a purchases returns and allowances transaction.

February 7, 1983. Returned merchandise to DeSpain Music Company, $30.00. Debit Memorandum No. 15.

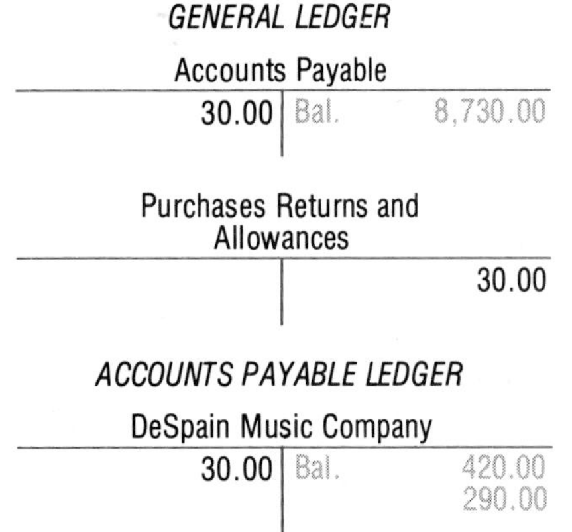

The source document for this purchases return is a debit memorandum. *(CONCEPT: Objective Evidence)*

The amount owed to a creditor is decreased by this transaction. Accounts Payable is debited for the amount of the return, $30.00. The same amount is also debited to the account of DeSpain Music Company in the accounts payable ledger. Because Purchases has a debit balance, the contra purchases account, Purchases Returns and Allowances, has a credit balance. Therefore, the purchases returns and allowances account is increased on the credit side. Since this transaction increases the purchases returns and allowances account, Purchases Returns and Allowances is credited for $30.00.

The entry to record this purchases returns and allowances transaction in a general journal is below.

GENERAL JOURNAL PAGE 2

	DATE		ACCOUNT TITLE	POST. REF.	DEBIT	CREDIT	
1	1983 Feb.	7	Accts. Pay./DeSpain Music Co.	/	30 00		1
2			Purchases Ret. & Allow.			30 00	2
3			Debit Memo. No. 15.				3
4							4

Purchases returns and allowances recorded in a general journal

The date, *1983, Feb. 7,* is written in the Date column. The amount of the debit, *$30.00,* is written in the Debit column. The accounts to be debited, *Accounts Payable/DeSpain Music Company,* are written in the Account Title column. The amount of the credit, *$30.00,* is written on the next line in the Credit column. The account to be credited, *Purchases Returns and Allowances,* is written in the Account Title column. This account title is indented about 1 centimeter. The source document for the entry, *Debit Memo. No. 15,* is written on the next line and is indented another centimeter.

Both the controlling account, Accounts Payable, and the creditor's name, DeSpain Music Company, are written in the Account Title column. The single debit amount is posted both to the general ledger account and the accounts payable ledger account. A diagonal line is placed between the two account titles to separate them clearly. A diagonal line also is placed in the Post. Ref. column to show that the debit is posted to two accounts.

Journalizing buying of supplies on account

Lin's generally buys supplies on account. Supplies are not merchandise. Only merchandise purchased on account is recorded in the purchases journal. Therefore, buying on account any item that is not merchandise is recorded in the general journal.

Lin's received an invoice for supplies bought on account.

> *February 8, 1983. Bought supplies on account from Ruhl Office Supplies, $146.00. Memorandum No. 31.*

The source document for this transaction is a memorandum. *(CONCEPT: Objective Evidence)* A memorandum is used as the source document so the supplies will not accidentally be recorded as merchandise. The invoice received from Ruhl Office Supplies is attached to the memorandum to confirm the price paid.

This transaction increases the balance of the supplies account. Supplies is debited for $146.00.

The amount owed to a creditor is increased by this transaction. Therefore, Accounts Payable is credited for $146.00. The same amount also is credited to the account of Ruhl Office Supplies in the accounts payable ledger.

The entry to record this transaction in a general journal is below.

GENERAL LEDGER

Supplies

	Debit		Credit
Bal.	480.00		
	146.00		

Accounts Payable

	Debit		Credit
		Bal.	8,700.00
			146.00

ACCOUNTS PAYABLE LEDGER

Ruhl Office Supplies

Debit	Credit
	146.00

GENERAL JOURNAL — PAGE 2

	DATE		ACCOUNT TITLE	POST. REF.	DEBIT	CREDIT	
4		8	Supplies		146 00		4
5			Accts. Pay./Ruhl Office Supplies			146 00	5
6			Memorandum No. 31.				6
7							7
8							8
9							9

Buying of supplies on account recorded in a general journal

The date, *8*, is written in the Date column. The amount of the debit, *$146.00*, is written in the Debit column. The account to be debited, *Supplies*, is written in the Account Title column. The amount of the credit, *$146.00*, is written on the next line in the Credit column. The accounts to be credited, *Accounts Payable/Ruhl Office Supplies*, are written in the Account Title column. These accounts are indented about 1 centimeter. The source document, *Memorandum No. 31*, is written on the next line and is indented another centimeter.

Posting from a general journal

Each amount in the general journal Debit and Credit columns is posted to a general ledger account. The posting of an entry for supplies bought on account from a general journal is below.

GENERAL JOURNAL PAGE 2

	DATE	ACCOUNT TITLE	POST. REF.	DEBIT	CREDIT	
4	8	Supplies	1105	14600		4
5		Accts. Pay./Ruhl Office Supplies	2102/✓		14600	5
6		Memorandum No. 31.				6

ACCOUNT Supplies ACCOUNT NO. 1105

DATE		ITEM	POST. REF.	DEBIT	CREDIT	BALANCE DEBIT	BALANCE CREDIT
1983 Feb.	1	Balance	✓			48000	
	8		G2	14600		62600	

ACCOUNT Accounts Payable ACCOUNT NO. 2102

DATE	ITEM	POST. REF.	DEBIT	CREDIT	BALANCE DEBIT	BALANCE CREDIT
7		G2	3000			870000
8		G2		14600		884600

NAME Ruhl Office Supplies

ADDRESS 1742 Live Oak Street, Greenville, TX 75401-1023

DATE		ITEM	POST. REF.	DEBIT	CREDIT	CREDIT BALANCE
1983 Feb.	8		G2		14600	14600

Posting a buying supplies on account entry from a general journal

The amount in the Debit column, *$146.00*, is posted to the Debit column of the general ledger account Supplies. After the amount is posted, *G2* is written in the Post. Ref. column of the account Supplies. Then the supplies account number, *1105*, is written in the Post. Ref. column of the general journal.

The amount in the Credit column, *$146.00*, is posted twice. The amount is posted as a credit to the general ledger account Accounts Payable. The amount also is posted as a credit to the Ruhl Office Supplies account in the accounts payable ledger. After the amount is posted, *G2* is written in the Post. Ref. column of both Accounts Payable and Ruhl Office Supplies.

Last, the account number of Accounts Payable, *2102*, is written in the Post. Ref. column of the general journal. The number is written at the left of the diagonal line. A check mark, placed at the right of the diagonal line, shows the completion of posting to the subsidiary ledger.

ACCOUNTING TERMS

What is the meaning of each of the following?

1. corporation
2. purchases journal
3. cash payments journal
4. list price
5. trade discount
6. cash discount
7. purchases discount
8. contra account
9. purchases return
10. purchases allowance
11. debit memorandum

QUESTIONS FOR INDIVIDUAL STUDY

1. What kind of accounting system should a business use?
2. How can an equality of debits and credits be maintained when only one amount is recorded in a purchases journal?
3. What is a common source document for recording a purchase on account?
4. Purchases journal entries are posted to what two ledgers?
5. What should be the last step in posting a purchases journal to a general ledger that shows the posting is complete?
6. Which cash payments made by Lin's Music Center are recorded in a cash payments journal?
7. How is a trade discount recorded on a purchaser's books?
8. What is meant by terms of sale 2/10, n/30?
9. Why is the purchases discount account given an account number with a decimal, as 5101.2?
10. When Lin's Music Center issues a check on account for a purchase with a purchases discount, what accounts are debited and credited?
11. Why are the column totals from the General Debit and Credit columns of a cash payments journal *not* posted?
12. If purchases returns and allowances are a decrease in purchases, why are returns and allowances credited to a separate account?
13. What accounts are debited and credited by a buyer to record a purchases returns and allowances transaction?
14. When supplies are bought on account, why is the entry made in a general journal instead of a purchases journal?
15. What is meant by the posting reference P2? CP6? G2?

CASES FOR MANAGEMENT DECISION

CASE 1 Alice Simpson manages a sports equipment store. The store has been using a combination journal. The company's accountant has suggested that because the store is increasing its total amount of sales, special journals be used. What should Mrs. Simpson consider in making a decision either to stay with the combination journal or to change to special journals?

CASE 2 O'Brien Lumber Company has employed an accounting firm to install a new accounting system using special journals. You and two others are designing the special journals. John, one of the accountants, recommends a cash payments journal with one special column, Cash Credit. Mary, another accountant, recommends a cash payments journal with three special columns, Purchases Debit, Purchases Discount Credit, and Cash Credit. You have been asked to make the decision as to the cash payments journal to be used. Give your decision and the reason for that decision.

CASE 3 Fred Arvin, accounting clerk for Zaloudek Company, has been recording supplies bought on account in a purchases journal. When the manager questioned him, Fred said, "It won't affect the net income, and recording in a purchases journal is much quicker than recording in a general journal." Is Fred right or wrong? Explain.

DRILLS FOR UNDERSTANDING

DRILL 20-D 1 Analyzing transactions affecting purchases and cash payments

Use a form similar to the one below.

Trans. No.	(a) Account Debited	(b) Account Credited	(c) Journal in Which Recorded	(d) Name of Amount Column Used in Journal	(e)
				For Amount Debited	For Amount Credited
1.	*Purchases*	*Cash*	*Cash Payments*	*General Debit*	*Cash Credit*

Instructions: Do each of the following for the transactions listed below. Write in Column a the name of the account(s) debited. Write in Column b the name of the account(s) credited. Write in Column c the name of the journal in which the transaction is recorded. Write in Columns d and e the names of the journal amount column(s) in which debit and credit amounts are recorded. Transaction 1 is given as an example in the form above.

1. Paid cash for purchases of merchandise.
2. Purchased merchandise on account from Cannon Music Company.
3. Paid cash on account to Cannon Music Company; no discount.
4. Paid cash for supplies.
5. Issued a debit memorandum and returned merchandise to Cannon Music Company.
6. Paid cash on account to Nichols Company for a purchase invoice less the amount of purchases discount.
7. Bought supplies on account from Plouff Company.
8. Purchased merchandise on account from Winston Music Shop.
9. Paid cash for February rent.
10. Issued a debit memorandum to Winston Music Shop for faulty merchandise returned.

DRILL 20-D 2 Posting transactions from special journals

Use a form similar to the one on the next page.

Instructions: 1. Write in Column a the account titles affected by each transaction in Drill 20-D 1. These account titles are taken from Columns a and b of the completed Drill 20-D 1.

Trans. No.	(a) Accounts affected	(b) Amounts posted separately to General Ledger	(c) Amounts posted separately to Accounts Payable Ledger	(d) Amounts not posted separately to any ledger
1.	*Purchases*	✓		
	Cash			✓

2. Place a check mark in Column b if the amount is posted separately to the general ledger. Place a check mark in Column c if the amount is posted separately to the accounts payable ledger. Place a check mark in Column d if the amount is not posted separately to any ledger. Transaction 1 is given above as an example.

APPLICATION PROBLEMS

PROBLEM 20-1 Journalizing and posting transactions affecting purchases

The accounts payable ledger and general ledger accounts of Karl's Florist are given in the working papers. The balances are recorded as of February 1 of the current year.

ACCOUNTS PAYABLE LEDGER

Creditor	Account Balance
Brozek Company, 141 Indigo Avenue, Tulsa, OK 74101-4983	$ 245.00
Eagle Company, 233 Adamson Drive, Broken Arrow, OK 74012-4119	896.00
Franz Supplies, 2047 Fulton Drive, Claremore, OK 74017-2882	—
Kinlaw Company, 1997 Mapleridge Road, Tulsa, OK 74102-7985	1,215.00
Ortiz Company, 431 Hunting Creek, Muskogee, OK 74401-7323	87.00

PARTIAL GENERAL LEDGER

Account Title	Account No.	Account Balance
Accounts Payable	2102	$2,443.00
Purchases	5101	—

Instructions: 1. The following purchases on account were made by Karl's Florist during February of the current year. Record these transactions on page 4 of a purchases journal similar to the one illustrated in this chapter. The abbreviation for purchase invoice is *P*.

Feb. 1. Purchased merchandise on account from Kinlaw Company, $135.00. P37.
2. Purchased merchandise on account from Ortiz Company, $74.00. P38.
7. Purchased merchandise on account from Franz Supplies, $489.00. P39.
9. Purchased merchandise on account from Brozek Company, $932.00. P40.
11. Purchased merchandise on account from Kinlaw Company, $1,578.00. P41.
14. Purchased merchandise on account from Eagle Company, $2,403.00. P42.
15. Purchased merchandise on account from Brozek Company, $386.00. P43.
22. Purchased merchandise on account from Ortiz Company, $198.00. P44.
24. Purchased merchandise on account from Eagle Company, $898.00. P45.
28. Purchased merchandise on account from Kinlaw Company, $579.00. P46.

Instructions: 2. Post each amount in the purchases journal to the accounts payable ledger.

3. Total and rule the purchases journal. Post the total.

4. Prepare a schedule of accounts payable similar to the one on page 250. Compare the schedule total with the balance of the accounts payable account in the general ledger. The total and the balance should be the same.

PROBLEM 20-2 Journalizing and posting transactions affecting cash payments

The accounts payable ledger and general ledger accounts of Superior Company are given in the working papers. The balances are recorded as of February 1 of the current year.

ACCOUNTS PAYABLE LEDGER

Creditor	Account Balance
Ayala Company, 731 Riddle Road, Phoenix, AZ 85002-4822	$1,258.00
Clark's Furnishings, 3401 Brookline Drive, Scottsdale, AZ 85251-1984	2,903.00
Irvine Company, 637 Devil's Backbone Drive, Glendale, AZ 85301-3247	830.00
Ragland Company, 4993 Quail Run Road, Tempe, AZ 85281-5780	1,793.00

PARTIAL GENERAL LEDGER

Account Title	Account No.	Account Balance
Cash	1101	$22,375.00
Supplies	1105	745.00
Accounts Payable	2102	6,784.00
Purchases	5101	—
Purchases Discount	5101.2	—
Delivery Expense	6103	—
Rent Expense	6110	—

Instructions: 1. The following cash payments were made by Superior Company during February of the current year. Record these cash payments in a cash payments journal similar to the one illustrated in this chapter. Use page 6 for the cash payments journal. The abbreviation for check is *C*.

Feb. 1. Paid February rent, $600.00. C102.
2. Paid on account to Clark's Furnishings, $1,440.60, covering invoice for $1,470.00 less a 2% cash discount of $29.40. C103.
4. Bought supplies for cash, $126.00. C104.
7. Paid on account to Ragland Company, $1,267.20, covering invoice for $1,280.00 less a 1% cash discount of $12.80. C105.
9. Paid delivery expense, $48.00. C106.
10. Purchased merchandise for cash, $385.00. C107.
15. Paid on account to Ayala Company, $1,258.00. No discount. C108.
22. Bought supplies for cash, $93.00. C109.
25. Paid on account to Irvine Company, $830.00. No discount. C110.
28. Paid delivery expense, $26.00. C111.

Instructions: 2. Post accounts payable amounts to the appropriate accounts in the accounts payable ledger.

3. Post the amounts in the General columns to the appropriate general ledger accounts.

4. Total, prove, and rule the cash payments journal. Post the special column totals to the appropriate general ledger accounts.

PROBLEM 20-3 Journalizing and posting transactions affecting purchases and cash payments

The accounts payable ledger and general ledger accounts of Jacob's Cycle Shop are given in the working papers. The balances are recorded as of February 1 of the current year.

ACCOUNTS PAYABLE LEDGER

Creditor	Account Balance
Barton Company, 743 Epworth Avenue, Davenport, IA 52801-2973	$ 348.00
Cycle Enterprises, 3405 Clifton Avenue, Davenport, IA 52802-8953	—
Gear Shop Supplies, 3811 Dogwood Drive, Moline, IL 61265-7986	3,312.00
Jessup Company, 3779 Westmont Circle, Des Moines, IA 50302-4227	1,290.00
Sumiyo Motorcycles, 578 Abilene Trail, Des Moines, IA 50302-8443	—

PARTIAL GENERAL LEDGER

Account Title	Acct. No.	Account Balance
Cash	1101	$26,880.00
Supplies	1105	1,061.30
Accounts Payable	2102	4,950.00
Purchases	5101	—
Purchases Returns and Allowances	5101.1	—
Purchases Discount	5101.2	—
Delivery Expense	6103	—
Miscellaneous Expense	6108	—
Rent Expense	6110	—

Instructions: 1. The following transactions affecting purchases and cash payments were completed by Jacob's Cycle Shop during February of the current year. Record these transactions in a purchases journal, a general journal, and a cash payments journal similar to those in this chapter. Use page 4 for each journal. Source documents are abbreviated as: check, C; memorandum, M; purchase invoice, P; debit memorandum, DM.

Feb. 1. Purchased merchandise on account from Gear Shop Supplies, $2,304.00. P43.
1. Paid February rent, $900.00. C92.
3. Returned merchandise to Gear Shop Supplies, $144.00. DM8.
4. Purchased merchandise on account from Cycle Enterprises, $2,246.00. P44.
Posting. Post the items that are to be posted individually. Post from the journals in this order: purchases journal, general journal, and cash payments journal.
7. Bought supplies on account from Barton Company, $302.00. M10.
9. Paid on account to Jessup Company, $1,277.10, covering P39 for $1,290.00 less a 1% cash discount of $12.90. C93.
Posting. Post the items that are to be posted individually.
14. Purchased merchandise for cash, $504.00. C94.
15. Paid on account to Cycle Enterprises, $2,223.54, covering P44 for $2,246.00 less a 1% discount of $22.46. C95.
16. Purchased merchandise on account from Sumiyo Motorcycles, $3,916.00. P45.
19. Purchased merchandise on account from Cycle Enterprises, $2,720.00. P46.
Posting. Post the items that are to be posted individually.

Feb. 21. Paid on account to Gear Shop Supplies for February 1 beginning balance of $3,312.00; no discount. C96.
22. Paid miscellaneous expense, $43.00. C97.
22. Paid on account to Barton Company, $348.00; no discount. C98.
22. Paid delivery expense, $86.00. C99.
23. Purchased merchandise on account from Jessup Company, $1,440.00. P47.
25. Paid on account to Sumiyo Motorcycles, $3,837.68, covering P45 for $3,916.00 less a 2% discount of $78.32. C100.
25. Purchased merchandise on account from Gear Shop Supplies, $948.00. P48.
Posting. Post the items that are to be posted individually.
28. Paid on account to Barton Company, $302.00; no discount. C101.
28. Purchased merchandise on account from Sumiyo Motorcycles, $1,132.00. P49.
28. Paid on account to Cycle Enterprises, $2,692.80, covering P46 for $2,720.00 less a 1% discount of $27.20. C102.
28. Purchased merchandise on account from Cycle Enterprises, $1,036.00. P50.
28. Paid on account to Gear Shop Supplies, $2,160.00, covering P43 for $2,304.00 less DM8 for $144.00; no discount. C103.
28. Paid miscellaneous expense, $118.00. C104.
28. Returned merchandise to Cycle Enterprises, $346.00. DM9.
Posting. Post the items that are to be posted individually.

Instructions: 2. Total and rule the purchases journal. Post the total.

3. Total, prove, and rule the cash payments journal. Post the totals of the special columns.

4. Prepare a schedule of accounts payable similar to the one shown on page 250. Compare the schedule total with the balance of the accounts payable account in the general ledger. The total and the balance should be the same.

ENRICHMENT PROBLEMS

MASTERY PROBLEM 20-M Journalizing and posting transactions affecting purchases and cash payments

The accounts payable ledger and general ledger accounts of Travis Paint Center are given in the working papers. The balances are recorded as of May 1 of the current year.

ACCOUNTS PAYABLE LEDGER

Creditor	Account Balance
Ajax Paint Company, 2312 Ravine Street, Santa Rosa, CA 95401-7686	$ 317.00
Drake Supply Company, 1771 Northbend Drive, Santa Rosa, CA 95401-6109	—
Keminiski Company, 900 Terrace Drive, Eureka, CA 95501-7510	616.00
Leidy Paint Supply, 1026 West Front Street, Richmond, CA 94801-3813	—
Patterson Company, 209 Betz Road, Eureka, CA 95501-2214	1,294.00

PARTIAL GENERAL LEDGER

Account Title	Account No.	Account Balance
Cash	1101	$16,170.00
Supplies	1105	326.30
Accounts Payable	2102	2,227.00
Purchases	5101	—
Purchases Returns and Allowances	5101.1	—
Purchases Discount	5101.2	—

Account Title	Account No.	Account Balance
Delivery Expense	6103	—
Miscellaneous Expense	6108	—
Rent Expense	6110	—

Instructions: 1. The following transactions affecting purchases and cash payments were completed by Travis Paint Center during May of the current year. Record these transactions in a purchases journal, general journal, and cash payments journal similar to those in this chapter. Use page 10 for the purchases and cash payments journals. Use page 6 for the general journal.

Source documents are abbreviated as: check, C; memorandum, M; purchase invoice, P; debit memorandum, DM.

May 2. Paid May rent, $950.00. C121.

2. Returned merchandise to Keminiski Company, $132.00. DM16.
3. Paid on account to Ajax Paint Company, $313.83, covering P110 for $317.00 less a 1% cash discount of $3.17. C122.
4. Purchased merchandise on account from Patterson Company, $554.00. P112.
5. Purchased merchandise on account from Ajax Paint Company, $436.00. P113.
6. Paid on account to Patterson Company, $1,268.12, covering P111 for $1,294.00 less a 2% discount of $25.88. C123.

   Posting. Post the items that are to be posted individually. Post from the journals in this order: purchases journal, general journal, and cash payments journal.
9. Paid on account to Keminiski Company, $484.00, covering P109 for $616.00 less DM16 for $132.00; no discount. C124.
9. Paid cash for delivery expense, $40.00. C125.
10. Bought supplies on account from Leidy Paint Supply, $198.00. M30.
12. Purchased merchandise on account from Keminiski Company, $653.00. P114.
13. Paid on account to Patterson Company, $542.92, covering P112 for $554.00 less a 2% discount of $11.08. C126.
13. Paid on account to Ajax Paint Company, $431.64, covering P113 for $436.00 less a 1% discount of $4.36. C127.

    Posting. Post the items that are to be posted individually.
16. Returned merchandise to Keminiski Company, $84.00. DM17.
16. Discovered that supplies bought for cash in April had been recorded in error as a debit to Purchases, $150.00. M31.
17. Purchased merchandise on account from Patterson Company, $625.00. P115.
18. Purchased merchandise on account from Ajax Paint Company, $578.00. P116.
20. Paid on account to Leidy Paint Supply, $198.00; no discount. C128.
20. Paid on account to Keminiski Company, $569.00, covering P114 for $653.00 less DM17 for $84.00; no discount. C129.

    Posting. Post the items that are to be posted individually.
23. Bought supplies on account from Leidy Paint Supply, $308.00. M32.
24. Paid miscellaneous expenses, $125.00. C130.
24. Discovered that supplies bought on account from Drake Supply Co. in April had been recorded as a credit to Cash instead of Accounts Payable, $225.00. M33.
25. Purchased merchandise on account from Keminiski Company, $250.00. P117.
27. Paid on account to Ajax Paint Company, $572.22, covering P116 for $578.00 less a 1% discount of $5.78. C131.

    Posting. Post the items that are to be posted individually.

Instructions: 2. Total and rule the purchases journal. Post the total.

3. Total, prove, and rule the cash payments journal. Post the totals of the special columns.

4. Prepare a schedule of accounts payable similar to the one on page 250. Compare the schedule total with the balance of the accounts payable account in the general ledger. The total and the balance should be the same.

CHALLENGE PROBLEM 20-C Journalizing transactions in a combined purchases-cash payments journal

The accountant for Travis Paint Center has suggested that time could be saved if the purchases journal and the cash payments journal were combined into one journal. She suggests using a journal such as the one below.

PURCHASES — CASH PAYMENTS JOURNAL

				1	2	3	4	5	6	7
Date	Account Title	Doc. No.	Post. Ref.	General		Purchases Debit	Accounts Payable		Purchases Discount Credit	Cash Credit
				Debit	Credit		Debit	Credit		

Carlos Valdez, manager, has asked the accountant to show him how the journal would appear after transactions have been recorded.

Instructions: 1. Use page 10 of a journal like the one above. Use page 6 of a general journal like the one on page 406. Journalize the transactions given in Mastery Problem 20-M, page 414.

2. Total, prove, and rule the combined purchases-cash payments journal.

3. Do you agree with the accountant that the combined purchases-cash payments journal used in this problem saves time in journalizing and posting? Why?

21

Recording Transactions with Special Journals: Sales and Cash Receipts

ENABLING PERFORMANCE TASKS

After studying Chapter 21, you will be able to:

a. Define accounting terms related to sales and cash receipts.
b. Explain accounting principles and practices related to sales and cash receipts.
c. Analyze transactions affecting sales and cash receipts.
d. Journalize sales on account transactions in a sales journal.
e. Post from a sales journal.
f. Journalize cash receipts transactions in a cash receipts journal.
g. Post from a cash receipts journal.
h. Journalize sales returns and allowances and correcting entries in a general journal.
i. Post from a general journal.

Lin's Music Center uses a system of special journals to record accounting transactions. Five journals are used. A sales journal, cash receipts journal, and general journal are described in this chapter. A purchases journal and cash payments journal were described in Chapter 20.

RECORDING SALES ON ACCOUNT IN A SALES JOURNAL

A special journal used to record only sales on account is called a sales journal. Regardless of when cash is received, revenue should be recorded when merchandise is sold. *(CONCEPT: Realization of Revenue)* Lin's Music Center uses a sales journal, page 418, to record only sales on account transactions. A sale on account can be recorded on one line in a sales journal. Lin's uses a sales journal with three amount columns: Accounts Receivable Debit, Sales Credit, and Sales Tax Payable Credit. The state where Lin's is located has a sales tax on many items sold at retail. A retail business must collect the sales tax from customers and periodically send the sales tax collected to the state. Customers must pay a sales tax on items sold by Lin's. Therefore, Lin's uses a sales journal that includes a special column for Sales Tax Payable Credit. This column permits the company to keep a record of sales tax separate from sales.

Journalizing sales on account in a sales journal

Lin's prepares a sales invoice in duplicate for each sale on account. The original copy is given to the charge customer. The carbon copy is the source document for recording sales on account transactions. *(CONCEPT: Objective Evidence)* The sales invoice used by Lin's is similar to the one on page 213.

GENERAL LEDGER

Accounts Receivable	
472.50	

Sales	
	450.00

Sales Tax Payable	
	22.50

ACCOUNTS RECEIVABLE LEDGER

Yolanda Bergdahl	
472.50	

Lin's sold merchandise on account.

> *February 1, 1983. Sold merchandise on account to Yolanda Bergdahl, $450.00, plus sales tax, $22.50. Sales Invoice No. 86.*

In this entry, Accounts Receivable is debited for $472.50, the amount of the sale plus the sales tax. Sales is credited for $450.00, the amount of the sale. Sales Tax Payable is credited for $22.50, the amount of the tax on this sale. Lin's owes the tax to the state government. Therefore, the amount of sales tax charged each customer is a liability.

Yolanda Bergdahl's account in the accounts receivable ledger is also debited for $472.50.

The entry to record this transaction in a sales journal is below.

SALES JOURNAL PAGE 6

	DATE		ACCOUNT DEBITED	SALE NO.	POST. REF.	1 ACCOUNTS RECEIVABLE DEBIT	2 SALES CREDIT	3 SALES TAX PAYABLE CREDIT	
1	1983 Feb.	1	Yolanda Bergdahl	86		472 50	450 00	22 50	1
2									2

Sale on account recorded in a sales journal

The date, *1983, Feb. 1*, is written in the Date column. The amount of the sale plus the sales tax, *$472.50*, is written in the Accounts Receivable Debit column. The amount of the sale, *$450.00*, is written in the Sales Credit column. The amount of sales tax, *$22.50*, is written in the Sales Tax Payable Credit column. The name of the charge customer, *Yolanda Bergdahl*, is written in the Account Debited column. The sales invoice number, *86*, is written in the Sale No. column. Each sale on account is recorded in the sales journal in this same way.

Posting a sales journal to an accounts receivable ledger

Each amount in the Accounts Receivable Debit column of a sales journal is posted to an accounts receivable ledger. Each amount is posted as a debit to the charge customer's account listed in the account title column. Lin's posts daily to the accounts receivable ledger. With daily posting, each customer's account always shows an up-to-date daily balance. The illustration below shows the posting of the entry on line 1 of the sales journal.

SALES JOURNAL PAGE 6

	Date		Account Debited	Sale No.	Post. Ref.	1 Accounts Receivable Debit	2 Sales Credit	3 Sales Tax Payable Credit	
1	1983 Feb.	1	Yolanda Bergdahl	86	✓	472 50	450 00	22 50	1
2									2

NAME Yolanda Bergdahl

ADDRESS 1810 Valley Drive, Garland, TX 75041-2682

Date		Item	Post. Ref.	Debit	Credit	Debit Balance
1983 Feb.	1	Balance	✓			127 00
	1		S6	472 50		599 50

Posting from a sales journal to an accounts receivable ledger

Write the amount, *$472.50*, in the Debit column of the customer's account. Add the amount in the Debit column to the previous balance in the Debit Balance column ($127.00 + $472.50 = $599.50). Write the new balance, *$599.50*, in the Debit Balance column. Write the date, *1*, in the Date column. Write the abbreviation for the sales journal, *S6*, in the Post. Ref. column of the account. Place a check mark in the Post. Ref. column of the sales journal to show completion of posting of this line.

This procedure is the same as posting from an Accounts Receivable Debit column of a combination journal. Posting from a combination journal is described in Chapter 13.

Posting the totals of a sales journal to a general ledger

At the end of each month, equality of debits and credits is proved for a sales journal. The sales journal then is ruled as shown on page 420. A single line is drawn across the amount columns under the last amounts. The column totals are written below the single line as shown on page 420. The last day of the month, *28*, is placed in the Date column. The word *Totals* is written in the Account Debited column. Double lines are ruled across the amount columns under the totals. Next, each amount column total is posted to the general ledger account named in the sales journal column headings.

The illustration on the next page shows the posting of sales journal amount column totals.

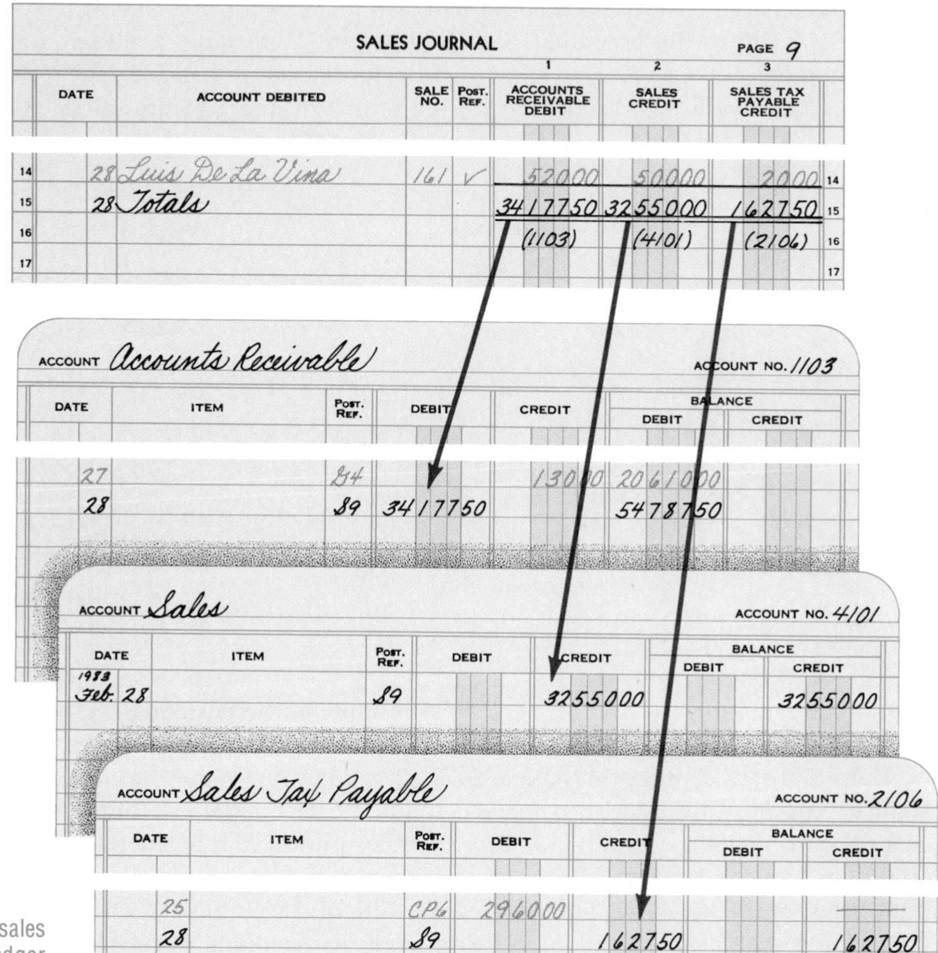

Posting totals of the special columns in a sales journal to a general ledger

When each sales journal amount column total is posted, *S9* is written in the Post. Ref. column of the accounts. The accounts receivable account number, *1103*, is written under the column total in the sales journal. The sales account number, *4101*, is written under the total of the Sales Credit column. The sales tax payable account number, *2106*, is written under the total of the Sales Tax Payable Credit column. All three account numbers are written within parentheses.

Summary of journalizing and posting from a sales journal

(1) Lin's Music Center records all sales on account in a three-column sales journal. (2) Individual items in the sales journal are posted daily. The items are posted to the individual accounts for charge customers in the accounts receivable ledger. (3) At the end of each month, each amount column total is posted. The Accounts Receivable Debit column

total is posted to Accounts Receivable as a debit. The Sales Credit column total is posted to Sales as a credit. The Sales Tax Payable Credit column total is posted to Sales Tax Payable as a credit. The flowchart below shows this procedure.

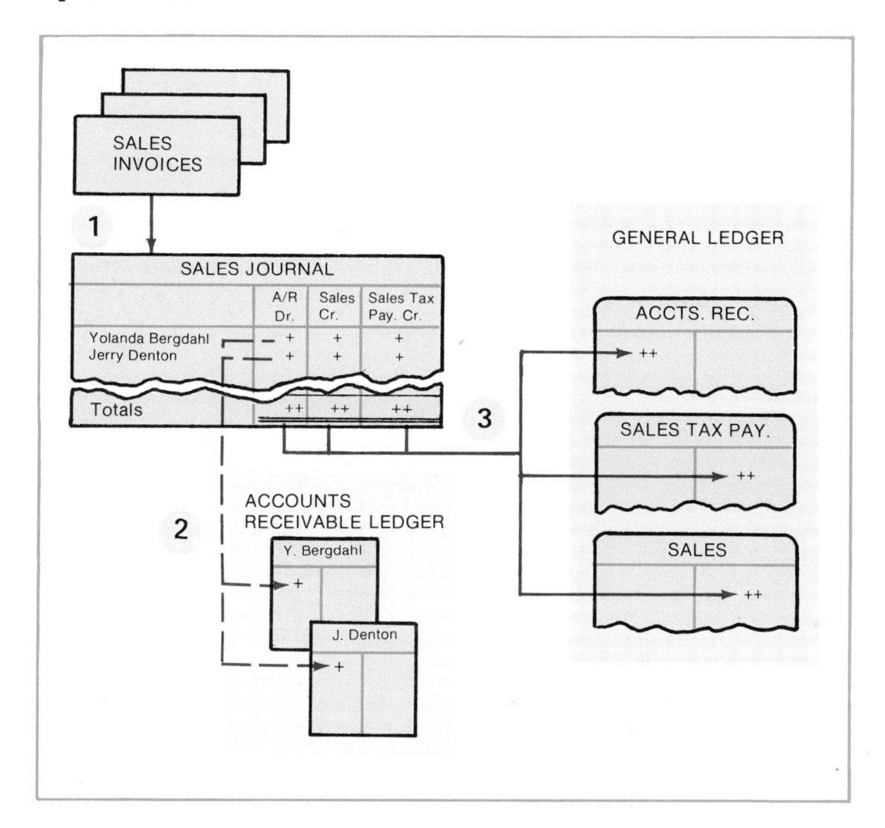

Flowchart showing journalizing and posting of sales on account using a sales journal

RECORDING CASH RECEIPTS IN A CASH RECEIPTS JOURNAL

A special journal in which only cash receipts transactions are recorded is called a cash receipts journal. The cash receipts journal used by Lin's Music Center is on page 422. The cash receipts journal has special amount columns for those kinds of cash receipts transactions that occur most often. For example, Lin's has many cash sales transactions. *(CONCEPT: Realization of Revenue)* Special amount columns are provided for Cash Debit, Sales Credit, and Sales Tax Payable Credit entries.

Journalizing cash receipts in a cash receipts journal

All cash receipts are recorded in a cash receipts journal. Most cash receipts are for (1) cash received from customers on account, (2) cash sales, and (3) credit card sales. The source document for cash sales is a cash register tape. The source document for credit card sales is an adding machine tape for the day's credit card sales. A common source document for other cash receipts is the stub of a receipt. *(CONCEPT: Objective Evidence)*

At the beginning of each month, an entry is made to record the cash balance on hand in the cash receipts journal. This entry makes the beginning cash balance readily available for proving cash. This entry in a cash receipts journal is below on line 1.

Lin's received cash on account.

February 1, 1983. Received cash on account from Luis Garcez, $504.00. Receipt No. 202.

In this transaction, Cash is debited for $504.00 and Accounts Receivable is credited for $504.00. The entry to record this transaction in a cash receipts journal is below on line 2.

CASH RECEIPTS JOURNAL — PAGE 6

	DATE		ACCOUNT TITLE	DOC. NO.	POST. REF.	GENERAL DEBIT (1)	GENERAL CREDIT (2)	ACCOUNTS RECEIVABLE CREDIT (3)	SALES CREDIT (4)	SALES TAX PAYABLE CREDIT (5)	CASH DEBIT (6)	
1	1983 Feb.	1	Balance on hand, $68,268.00		✓							1
2		1	Luis Garcez	R202				504 00			504 00	2
3		1	✓	T1	✓				455 60	22 78	478 38	3
4		1	✓	CT1	✓				683 40	34 17	717 57	4

Cash receipts transactions recorded in a cash receipts journal

The date, *1*, is written in the Date column. The amount credited to Accounts Receivable, *$504.00*, is written in the Accounts Receivable Credit column. The amount of cash received, *$504.00*, is written in the Cash Debit column. The name of the charge customer, *Luis Garcez*, is written in the Account Title column. The number of the receipt, *R202*, is written in the Doc. No. column.

Line 3 above shows cash sales for the day. Line 4 above shows credit card sales for the day.

Posting a cash receipts journal to an accounts receivable ledger

Each entry in the Accounts Receivable Credit column affects the charge customer named in the Account Title column. Each amount listed in this column is posted daily to the proper customer's account in the accounts receivable ledger. Posting of a cash receipts journal entry to a customer's account is on the next page.

The amount in the Accounts Receivable Credit column, *$504.00*, is posted to the Credit column of the customer's account. After the amount is posted, *CR6* is written in the Post. Ref. column of the customer's account. The abbreviation CR6 means page 6 of the cash receipts journal. As a last step, place a check mark in the Post. Ref. column of the cash receipts journal.

CASH RECEIPTS JOURNAL PAGE 6

	DATE		ACCOUNT TITLE	DOC. NO.	POST. REF.	1 GENERAL DEBIT	2 GENERAL CREDIT	3 ACCOUNTS RECEIVABLE CREDIT	4 SALES CREDIT	5 SALES TAX PAYABLE CREDIT	6 CASH DEBIT	
1	1983 Feb.	1	Balance on hand, $68,268.00		✓							1
2		1	Luis Garcez	R202	✓			504 00			504 00	2

NAME Luis Garcez

ADDRESS 2733 Alms Avenue, Garland, TX 75041-2891

DATE		ITEM	POST. REF.	DEBIT	CREDIT	DEBIT BALANCE
1983 Feb.	1	Balance	✓			504 00
	1		CR6		504 00	—

Posting from a cash receipts journal to an accounts receivable ledger

Posting a cash receipts journal to a general ledger

Each amount in the General columns of a cash receipts journal is posted to a general ledger account. However, only the monthly total of each special column is posted to a general ledger account.

Posting from the General columns of a cash receipts journal. Each amount in the General columns is posted individually to the general ledger account named in the Account Title column. Transactions involving entries in the General Debit and Credit columns are described in Chapter 26.

Posting totals of the special columns in a cash receipts journal. At the end of each month, equality of debits and credits is proved for a cash receipts journal. Cash is then proved. The cash proof for Lin's at the end of February is below.

Beginning cash balance, February 1, 1983 .... (Line 1 of cash receipts journal, page 422)	$ 68,268.00
Plus total cash received .... (Total of Cash Debit column, cash receipts journal, page 424)	70,415.30
Total...	$138,683.30
Less total cash payments .... (Total of Cash Credit column, cash payments journal, page 403)	60,146.00
Equals cash balance, February 28, 1983	$ 78,537.30

The balance after the last check (Check Stub No. 183) was written is $78,537.30. The balance on the check stub agrees with the balance figured above. Therefore, cash is proved.

After cash is proved, the cash receipts journal is ruled as shown on page 424. Next the total for each special column is posted to the account named in the cash receipts journal column headings. Posting of cash receipts journal special column totals to the general ledger accounts is below.

CASH RECEIPTS JOURNAL — PAGE 10

	DATE	ACCOUNT TITLE	Doc. No.	Post. Ref.	1 GENERAL DEBIT	2 GENERAL CREDIT	3 ACCOUNTS RECEIVABLE CREDIT	4 SALES CREDIT	5 SALES TAX PAYABLE CREDIT	6 CASH DEBIT	
16	28	✓	T28	✓				1128 00	56 40	1184 40	16
17	28	Totals				4224 50	32017 50	32546 00	1627 30	70415 30	17
18						(✓)	(1103)	(4101)	(2106)	(1101)	18

ACCOUNT Accounts Receivable — ACCOUNT NO. 1103

DATE	ITEM	Post. Ref.	DEBIT	CREDIT	BALANCE DEBIT	BALANCE CREDIT
28		S9	34177 50		54787 50	
28		CR10		32017 50	22770 00	

ACCOUNT Sales — ACCOUNT NO. 4101

DATE	ITEM	Post. Ref.	DEBIT	CREDIT	BALANCE DEBIT	BALANCE CREDIT
1983 Feb. 28		S9		32550 00		32550 00
28		CR10		32546 00		65096 00

ACCOUNT Sales Tax Payable — ACCOUNT NO. 2106

DATE	ITEM	Post. Ref.	DEBIT	CREDIT	BALANCE DEBIT	BALANCE CREDIT
28		S9		1627 50		1627 50
28		CR10		1627 30		3254 80

ACCOUNT Cash — ACCOUNT NO. 1101

DATE	ITEM	Post. Ref.	DEBIT	CREDIT	BALANCE DEBIT	BALANCE CREDIT
1983 Feb. 1	Balance	✓			68268 00	
28		CR10	70415 30		138683 30	
28		CP6		60146 00	78537 30	

Posting totals of the special columns in a cash receipts journal to a general ledger

Posting from a cash payments journal to the cash account was described in Chapter 20.

When each special column total is posted, *CR10* is written in the Post. Ref. column of the accounts. The general ledger account number is written under the related cash receipts journal special column total. The account numbers, written within parentheses, show that posting of a column total is complete.

The totals of the General columns are not posted. Each amount in these columns was posted individually to a general ledger account. To indicate that these totals are not to be posted, a check mark is placed in parentheses below each column total.

Summary of journalizing and posting cash receipts using a cash receipts journal

(1) Lin's Music Center records all cash receipts in a six-column cash receipts journal. (2) Amounts in the Accounts Receivable Credit column are posted daily to the customer's account in the accounts receivable ledger. (3) At the end of the month, the totals of the special columns are posted to the general ledger. This procedure is shown in the flowchart below.

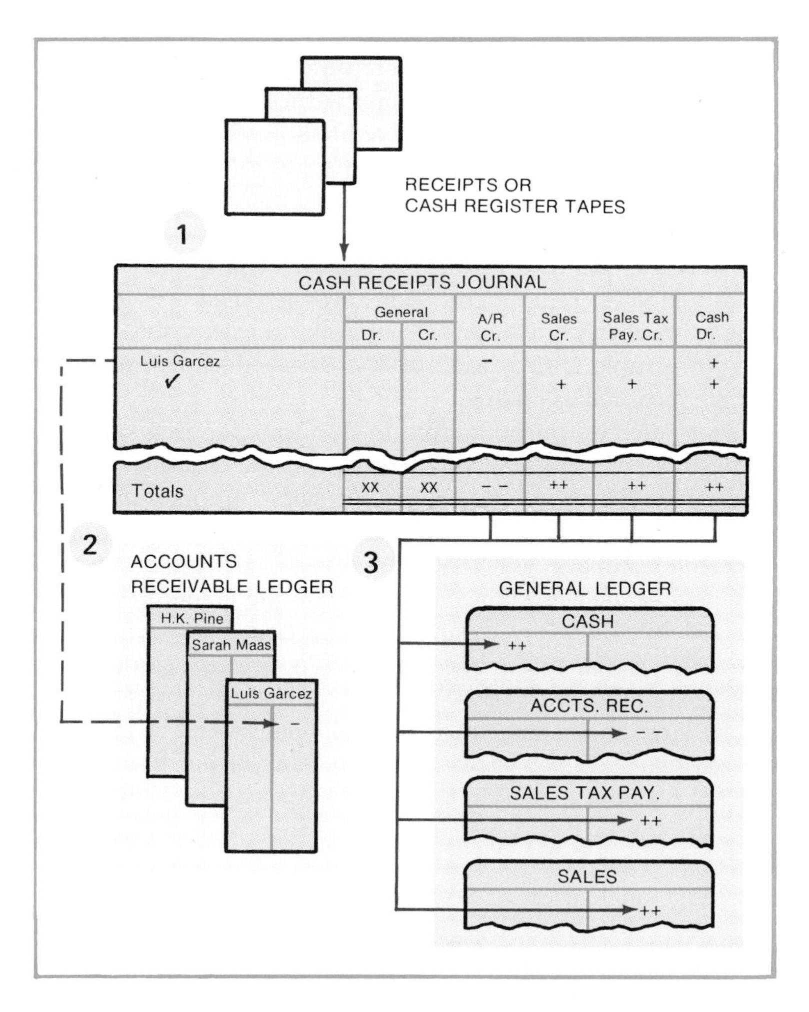

Flowchart showing journalizing and posting of cash receipts using a cash receipts journal

RECORDING OTHER TRANSACTIONS IN A GENERAL JOURNAL

Some purchases-related transactions recorded in a general journal were described in Chapter 20. Lin's Music Center also records two sales-related transactions in a general journal.

1. Sales returns and allowances.
2. Correcting entries affecting charge customers' accounts but not the controlling account.

Sales returns and allowances

Most merchandising businesses expect to have some merchandise returned because a customer may decide not to keep the merchandise. A customer may have received the wrong style, the wrong size, or damaged goods. A customer may return merchandise to the seller and ask for a credit on account or a cash refund. Merchandise returned from a customer for a credit on account or a cash refund is called a sales return.

A seller may grant credit to a customer without asking for the return of damaged or imperfect merchandise. Credit allowed a customer for part of the sales price of merchandise not returned is called a sales allowance. An allowance also may be given because of a shortage in a shipment.

A seller usually informs a buyer in writing when a sales return or a sales allowance is granted. A form prepared by the seller showing the amount deducted for returns and allowances is called a credit memorandum. The form is called a *credit* memorandum because the asset account Accounts Receivable is decreased by the transaction. Decreases in asset accounts are recorded as credits.

Lin's issues a credit memorandum in duplicate for each sales return or sales allowance. The original copy is given to the customer. The carbon copy is used as the source document for sales returns and allowances. *(CONCEPT: Objective Evidence)* The credit memorandum form used by Lin's is on the next page.

Sales returns and sales allowances decrease the amount of sales. Some businesses debit the sales account for the amount of a return or allowance. However, better information is provided if these amounts are debited to a separate account *Sales Returns and Allowances*. A separate account shows how large the sales returns and allowances are. Also, a business can see if returns and allowances are increasing or decreasing from year to year. If the amounts are large, one account may be kept for sales returns and another account for sales allowances. Usually a single, combined account is used.

Lin's uses a single account Sales Returns and Allowances. The account is in the revenue division of the general ledger, page 392. The account number, 4101.1, shows that this contra sales account is a deduction from

CREDIT MEMORANDUM NO. 36

Lin's Music Center
2400 Fargo Lane
Garland, TX 75041-2579

We have this day credited your account as follows:

DATE: February 11, 1983

TO:
CALVIN RONEY
4816 OAKHAM STREET
GARLAND TX 75402-3068

Quantity	Description	Price	Total
1	Speaker, Model SR1032	200.00	
	Sales Tax	10.00	210.00

If the above is incorrect please return stating difference.

Credit memorandum

the balance of account 4101, Sales. A customer is entitled to credit for the amount of a sales return or allowance. The credit must include the sales tax on the return or allowance.

Journalizing sales returns and allowances

On February 7, Lin's sold merchandise on account to Calvin Roney for $400.00. Mr. Roney's account was debited for $420.00, $400.00 sales and $20.00 sales tax. On February 11, Mr. Roney returned part of the merchandise.

February 11, 1983. Granted credit to Calvin Roney for merchandise returned, $200.00, plus sales tax, $10.00. Credit Memorandum No. 36.

The source document for this sales return is a credit memorandum. *(CONCEPT: Objective Evidence)* Because Sales has a credit balance, the contra sales account, Sales Returns and Allowances, has a debit balance. Therefore, the sales returns and allowances account is increased on the debit side. Since this transaction increases the balance of the account, Sales Returns and Allowances is debited for $200.00.

The sales tax payable account, a liability account, has a credit balance. Therefore, the sales tax payable account is increased on the credit side. Since this transaction decreases the balance of the account, Sales Tax Payable is debited for $10.00. The debit to Sales Tax Payable is for the amount of tax on the returned merchandise.

The amount to be collected from the charge customer is decreased. Mr. Roney is entitled to a $200.00 credit for the

GENERAL LEDGER

Sales Returns and Allowances

Debit	Credit
200.00	

Sales Tax Payable

Debit	Credit
10.00	

Accounts Receivable

Debit	Credit
	210.00

ACCOUNTS RECEIVABLE LEDGER

Calvin Roney

	Debit	Credit
Bal.	420.00	210.00

merchandise returned and a $10.00 credit for sales tax. Therefore, Accounts Receivable is credited for the total amount, $210.00. The same amount also is credited to Calvin Roney's account in the accounts receivable ledger.

The entry to record this sales returns and allowances transaction in a general journal is below.

GENERAL JOURNAL PAGE 2

	DATE		ACCOUNT TITLE	POST. REF.	DEBIT	CREDIT	
13		11	Sales Returns and Allowances		200 00		13
14			Sales Tax Payable		10 00		14
15			Accts. Rec./Calvin Roney	/		210 00	15
16			Credit Memo. No. 36.				16
17							17

Sales returns and allowances recorded in a general journal

The date, *11*, is written in the Date column. The amount of the debit, *$200.00*, is written in the Debit column. *Sales Returns and Allowances* is written in the Account Title column. The amount of the debit, *$10.00*, is written on the next line in the Debit column. *Sales Tax Payable* is written in the Account Title column. The amount of the credit, *$210.00*, is written on the next line in the Credit column. The accounts credited, *Accounts Receivable/Calvin Roney*, are written in the Account Title column. These account titles are indented about 1 centimeter. The source document, *Credit Memo. No. 36*, is written on the next line indented about 2 centimeters.

Both the controlling account, *Accounts Receivable*, and the customer's name, Calvin Roney, are written in the Account Title column. The single credit amount is posted both to the general ledger account and the accounts receivable ledger account. A diagonal line is placed between the two account titles to separate them. A diagonal line is placed in the Post. Ref. column to show that the credit is posted to two accounts.

Journalizing a correcting entry affecting charge customers' accounts

Errors may be made in recording amounts in subsidiary ledgers that do not affect the general ledger controlling account. For example, a sale on account may be recorded for the wrong charge customer in the sales journal. The column total posted from the sales journal to the general ledger is correct. The accounts receivable account shows the correct balance. However, two of the charge customers' accounts in the accounts receivable ledger show incorrect balances. To correct this error, only the subsidiary ledger accounts need to be corrected.

Lin's discovered and corrected an error.

February 12, 1983. Discovered that a sale on account to Ann Bryan on January 26 was incorrectly charged to Anna Bryant, $126.00. Memorandum No. 35.

The source document for this correcting entry is a memorandum. *(CONCEPT: Objective Evidence)*

The total of the Accounts Receivable Credit column in the sales journal, posted January 31, is correct. Accounts Receivable was debited $126.00; Sales was credited $120.00; Sales Tax Payable was credited $6.00. No correction is needed for these amounts. The correcting entry involves only subsidiary ledger accounts. The account of Anna Bryant was debited for $126.00 when the account of Ann Bryan should have been debited. The Ann Bryan account is debited for $126.00 to record the charge sale in the correct account. The Anna Bryant account is credited for $126.00 to cancel the incorrect entry. No entry is made for the sales tax of $6.00. The sales tax was correctly recorded and posted at the time of sale.

ACCOUNTS RECEIVABLE LEDGER

Ann Bryan

	Debit		Credit
Feb. 12	126.00		

Anna Bryant

	Debit		Credit
Jan. 26	126.00	Feb. 12	126.00

The entry to record this correcting entry in a general journal is below.

GENERAL JOURNAL PAGE 2

	DATE	ACCOUNT TITLE	POST. REF.	DEBIT	CREDIT	
17	12	Ann Bryan		126 00		17
18		Anna Bryant			126 00	18
19		Memorandum No. 35.				19
20						20

Correcting entry recorded in a general journal

The date, *12*, is written in the Date column. The amount of the debit, *$126.00*, is written in the Debit column. The name of the correct charge customer, *Ann Bryan*, is written in the Account Title column. On the next line, the amount of the credit, *$126.00*, is written in the Credit column. The name of the incorrectly charged customer, *Anna Bryant*, is written in the Account Title column. This account name is indented about 1 centimeter. The source document, *Memorandum No. 35*, is written on the next line indented about 2 centimeters.

Posting from a general journal

Each amount in the Debit and Credit columns is posted to the account or accounts named in the Account Title column. The posting of a general journal is described in Chapter 20, pages 408–409. The two general journal entries described in this chapter are posted in the same way.

ORDER OF POSTING FROM SPECIAL JOURNALS

Items affecting customers' or creditors' accounts are posted often during the month. Some businesses post daily so that the balances of the subsidiary ledger accounts will be up to date daily. Items affecting general ledger accounts are posted less often during the month because daily balances are not needed. All items, including the totals of special columns, must be posted before a trial balance is prepared.

The best order in which to post the journals is listed below.

1. Sales journal.
2. Purchases journal.
3. General journal.
4. Cash receipts journal.
5. Cash payments journal.

This order of posting usually puts the debits and credits in the accounts in the order the transactions occurred.

ACCOUNTING TERMS

What is the meaning of each of the following?

1. sales journal
2. cash receipts journal
3. sales return
4. sales allowance
5. credit memorandum

QUESTIONS FOR INDIVIDUAL STUDY

1. Why does Lin's Music Center use a three-column sales journal?
2. What source document does Lin's use for a sale on account?
3. How can a journal entry be found that supports an amount posted to a general ledger account?
4. What should determine whether a special column, such as Accounts Receivable Credit, is needed in a cash receipts journal?
5. What source document does Lin's use for a cash received on account transaction?
6. What source document does Lin's use for a cash sales transaction?
7. Why does Lin's enter the cash balance on hand on the first line of the cash receipts journal?
8. What general ledger accounts are affected by a cash receipt from a customer on account transaction? In what way?
9. Which amounts in a cash receipts journal are posted individually to general ledger accounts?
10. What source document does Lin's use for a sales returns and allowances transaction?
11. Why does the account number for Sales Returns and Allowances, 4101.1, have a decimal number?
12. What accounts in the general ledger are affected by a sales returns and allowances transaction? How are the accounts affected?
13. In what order should special journals be posted? Why?

CASES FOR MANAGEMENT DECISION

CASE 1 Crowell Appliances uses a three-column sales journal with special columns similar to the one on page 418. The company records sales tax payable at the time a sale on account is made. David Suarez, the office manager, questions this practice. He suggests that sales tax payable not be recorded until cash is actually collected for this sale. Which procedure is preferable? Why?

CASE 2 Crosby Restaurant Supply Company uses a six-column cash receipts journal similar to the one on page 422. The company records only cash receipts transactions in this journal. Vanessa Evers, an accounting clerk, suggested that since the cash receipts journal has General Debit and Credit columns, noncash receipt transactions could be recorded also. This change would eliminate the necessity for a general journal. Who is correct? Why?

CASE 3 Oaks Musical Instruments uses a general journal similar to the one on page 428. Fred Scales, the company accountant, suggested a special column titled Sales Returns and Allowances Debit be added to the general journal. Under what circumstances would this special column be acceptable in a general journal?

DRILLS FOR UNDERSTANDING

DRILL 21-D 1 Analyzing transactions affecting sales and cash receipts

Use a form similar to the one below.

Trans. No.	(a) Account Debited	(b) Account Credited	(c) Journal in Which Recorded	(d) Name of Amount Column Used in Journal — For Amount Debited	(e) Name of Amount Column Used in Journal — For Amount Credited
1.	*Cash*	*Sales* *Sales Tax Pay.*	*Cash Receipts*	*Cash Debit*	*Sales Credit* *Sales Tax Pay. Credit*

Instructions: Do each of the following for the transactions listed below. Write in Column a the name of the account(s) debited. Write in Column b the name of the account(s) credited. Write in Column c the name of the journal in which the transaction is recorded. Write in Columns d and e the names of the journal amount column(s) in which debit and credit amounts are recorded. Transaction 1 is given as an example in the form above.

1. Recorded cash sales plus sales tax for the day.
2. Sold merchandise on account with sales tax to Mary Olcott.
3. Recorded credit card sales plus sales tax.
4. Received cash on account from Dale Haley.
5. Granted credit to Betty Cleland for merchandise she returned plus sales tax on merchandise.
6. Discovered that a sale on account to Ralph Brock was incorrectly charged to Ralf Brook.
7. Granted credit to Darold Cole as an allowance for damaged merchandise delivered to him plus sales tax on merchandise.

DRILL 21-D 2 Posting transactions from special journals

Use a form similar to the one on the next page.

Instructions: 1. Write in Column a the account titles affected by each transaction in Drill 21-D 1. Use account titles from Columns a and b of the completed Drill 21-D 1.

2. Place a check mark in Column b if the amount is posted separately to the general ledger. Place a check mark in Column c if the amount is posted separately to the accounts

Trans. No.	(a) Accounts affected	(b) Amounts posted separately to General Ledger	(c) Amounts posted separately to Accounts Receivable Ledger	(d) Amounts not posted separately to any ledger
1.	*Cash*			✓
	Sales			✓
	Sales Tax Pay.			✓

receivable ledger. Place a check mark in Column d if the amount is not posted separately to any ledger. Transaction 1 is given above as an example.

APPLICATION PROBLEMS

PROBLEM 21-1 Journalizing and posting sales on account transactions

The accounts receivable ledger and general ledger accounts of Simpson Company are given in the working papers. The balances are recorded as of March 1 of the current year.

ACCOUNTS RECEIVABLE LEDGER

Charge Customer	Account Balance
Cara Adamson, 590 Plum Drive, Mesa, AZ 85201-1203	$421.00
Sara Adkinson, 4389 Thompson Road, Phoenix, AZ 85002-1587	144.00
Martha James, 657 Hampton Street, Gila Bend, AZ 85337-4921	360.00
Sherman Kook, 435 Yuma Avenue, Holbrook, AZ 86025-3274	334.50
Samual Sammons, 3467 Mohave Avenue, Mesa, AZ 85201-1239	248.00
Roger Watkins, 6722 Hubbard Street, Phoenix, AZ 85002-1522	255.00

PARTIAL GENERAL LEDGER

Account Title	Acct. No.	Account Balance
Accounts Receivable.......	1103	$1,762.50
Sales Tax Payable............	2106	——
Sales..............................	4101	——

Instructions 1. The following sales on account were made by Simpson Company during March of the current year. Record these transactions on page 10 of a sales journal similar to the one illustrated in this chapter. The abbreviation for sales invoice is *S*.

Mar. 1. Sold merchandise on account to Sara Adkinson, $150.00, plus sales tax, $7.50. S76.

2. Sold merchandise on account to Sherman Kook, $123.00, plus sales tax, $6.15. S77.

7. Sold merchandise on account to Samual Sammons, $75.00, plus sales tax, $3.75. S78.

11. Sold merchandise on account to Cara Adamson, $89.00, plus sales tax, $4.45. S79.

14. Sold merchandise on account to Martha James, $145.00, plus sales tax, $7.25. S80.

Mar. 17. Sold merchandise on account to Roger Watkins, $133.00, plus sales tax, $6.65. S81.
22. Sold merchandise on account to Sara Adkinson, $85.00, plus sales tax, $4.25. S82.
25. Sold merchandise on account to Samual Sammons, $113.00, plus sales tax, $5.65. S83.
28. Sold merchandise on account to Martha James, $83.50, plus sales tax, $4.18. S84.
31. Sold merchandise on account to Sherman Kook, $160.00, plus sales tax, $8.00. S85.

Instructions: 2. Post each amount in the Accounts Receivable Debit column of the sales journal to the accounts receivable ledger.

3. Total, prove, and rule the sales journal. Post the totals of the special columns.

4. Prepare a schedule of accounts receivable similar to the one on page 250. Compare the schedule total with the balance of the accounts receivable account in the general ledger. The total and the balance should be the same.

PROBLEM 21-2 Journalizing and posting cash receipts transactions

The accounts receivable ledger and general ledger accounts of Annie Claire Toys are given in the working papers. The balances are recorded as of March 1 of the current year.

ACCOUNTS RECEIVABLE LEDGER

Charge Customer	Account Balance
Martin Chambers, 145 Ocean Drive, Camden, NJ 08108-2031	$150.00
Nancy Fitzgerald, 3634 Ferris Street, Camden, NJ 08101-1334	450.00
Paul Gionet, 611 Sailfish Avenue, Elizabeth, NJ 07201-1238	189.00
Terri Johnston, 4323 Maria Place, Camden, NJ 08110-2576	115.00
Carrie Sciotto, 7524 Beekman Boulevard, Elizabeth, NJ 07202-1133	253.00

PARTIAL GENERAL LEDGER

Account Title	Acct. No.	Account Balance
Cash	1101	$7,752.50
Accounts Receivable	1103	1,157.00
Sales Tax Payable	2106	—
Sales	4101	—

Instructions: 1. The following cash receipts were received by Annie Claire Toys during March of the current year. Record these cash receipts in a cash receipts journal similar to the one illustrated in this chapter. Use page 12 for the cash receipts journal. Source documents are abbreviated as: receipt, R; cash register tape, T; credit card sales adding machine tape, CT.

Mar. 1. Recorded the cash balance on hand in the cash receipts journal, $7,752.50.
2. Received cash on account from Paul Gionet, $189.00. R39.
5. Received cash on account from Nancy Fitzgerald, $175.00. R40.
10. Received cash on account from Terri Johnston, $115.00. R41.
12. Recorded cash sales, $2,979.00, plus sales tax, $148.95. T12.
12. Recorded credit card sales, $2,588.00, plus sales tax, $129.40. CT12.
14. Received cash on account from Martin Chambers, $150.00. R42.

Mar. 18. Received cash on account from Carrie Sciotto, $190.00. R43.
25. Received cash on account from Nancy Fitzgerald, $160.00. R44.
31. Recorded cash sales, $2,686.00, plus sales tax, $134.30. T31.
31. Recorded credit card sales, $2,534.00, plus sales tax, $126.70. CT31.

Instructions: 2. Post each amount in the Accounts Receivable Credit column of the cash receipts journal to the accounts receivable ledger.

3. Prove the equality of debits and credits for the cash receipts journal.

4. Prove cash. The total of the Cash Credit column of the cash payments journal for Annie Claire Toys is $10,890.40. The balance on the last check stub on March 31 is $9,167.45.

5. Rule the cash receipts journal. Post the special column totals.

PROBLEM 21-3 Journalizing and posting sales and cash receipts transactions

The accounts receivable ledger and general ledger accounts of Kahler Ceramics are given in the working papers. The balances are recorded as of February 1 of the current year.

ACCOUNTS RECEIVABLE LEDGER

Charge Customer	Account Balance
Kevin Hoffman, 352 Patrick Avenue, Duluth, MN 55802-1342	$179.00
Stephen Norstrand, 8234 Swan River Drive, Duluth, MN 55810-2189	495.00
Sara Norwood, 642 Pinecreek Drive, Duluth, MN 55803-1567	435.00
Doris Schultz, 456 Charlton Drive, Duluth, MN 55811-2591	335.00
Lucy Stacy, 798 Rosemont Avenue, Duluth, MN 55803-1589	580.00
Samuel Wilton, 579 South Rushmore, Duluth, MN 55813-2705	549.00
Karl Zimmerman, 1925 Lytle Drive, Duluth, MN 55810-2330	267.00

PARTIAL GENERAL LEDGER

Account Title	Acct. No.	Account Balance
Cash	1101	$5,593.40
Accounts Receivable	1103	2,840.00
Sales Tax Payable	2106	—
Sales	4101	—
Sales Returns and Allowances	4101.1	—

Instructions: 1. The following transactions affecting sales and cash receipts were completed by Kahler Ceramics during February of the current year. Record these transactions in a sales journal, general journal, and cash receipts journal similar to those illustrated in this chapter. Use page 6 of each journal. Source documents are abbreviated: sales invoice, S; receipt, R; cash register tape, T; credit card sales adding machine tape, CT; credit memorandum, CM; memorandum, M.

Feb. 1. Recorded the cash balance on hand in the cash receipts journal, $5,593.40.
1. Sold merchandise on account to Sara Norwood, $175.00, plus sales tax, $8.75. S78.
2. Received cash on account from Kevin Hoffman, $179.00. R26.
3. Received cash on account from Stephen Norstrand, $225.00. R27.
3. Sold merchandise on account to Karl Zimmerman, $135.00, plus sales tax, $6.75. S79.
3. Received cash on account from Lucy Stacy, $189.00. R28.

Feb. 4. Found that on January 19 a sale on account to Sara Norwood (S64) was incorrectly charged to Stephen Norstrand, $135.00. M57.
5. Recorded cash sales for the week, $889.00, plus sales tax, $44.45. T5.
5. Recorded credit card sales for the week, $572.00, plus sales tax, $28.60. CT5.
Posting. Post the items that are to be posted individually. Post from the journals in this order: sales journal, general journal, and cash receipts journal.
7. Credited Samuel Wilton's account for merchandise returned, $35.00, plus sales tax, $1.75. CM22.
7. Received cash on account from Karl Zimmerman, $235.00. R29.
7. Received cash on account from Doris Schultz, $135.00. R30.
8. Sold merchandise on account to Kevin Hoffman, $256.00, plus sales tax, $12.80. S80.
9. Sold merchandise on account to Stephen Norstrand, $117.00, plus sales tax, $5.85. S81.
10. Received cash on account from Samuel Wilton, $195.00. R31.
11. Sold merchandise on account to Doris Schultz, $182.00, plus sales tax, $9.10. S82.
12. Recorded cash sales for the week, $1,702.00, plus sales tax, $85.10. T12.
12. Recorded credit card sales for the week, $888.00, plus sales tax, $44.40. CT12.
Posting. Post the items that are to be posted individually.
14. Received cash on account from Sara Norwood, $435.00. R32.
15. Received cash on account from Lucy Stacy, $391.00. R33.
17. Received cash on account from Sara Norwood, $183.75. R34.
18. Received cash on account from Samuel Wilton, $317.25. R35.
19. Recorded cash sales for the week, $1,127.00, plus sales tax, $56.35. T19.
19. Recorded credit card sales for the week, $709.00, plus sales tax, $35.45. CT19.
Posting. Post the items that are to be posted individually.
22. Sold merchandise on account to Stephen Norstrand, $225.00, plus sales tax, $11.25. S83.
24. Sold merchandise on account to Lucy Stacy, $167.00, plus sales tax, $8.35. S84.
25. Received cash on account from Karl Zimmerman, $32.00. R36.
26. Recorded cash sales for the week, $978.00, plus sales tax, $48.90. T26.
26. Recorded credit card sales for the week, $610.00, plus sales tax, $30.50. CT26.
Posting. Post the items that are to be posted individually.
28. Received cash on account from Doris Schultz, $200.00. R37.
28. Sold merchandise on account to Samuel Wilton, $245.00, plus sales tax, $12.25. S85.
28. Recorded cash sales for the week, $304.00, plus sales tax, $15.20. T28.
28. Recorded credit card sales for the week, $189.00, plus sales tax, $9.45. CT28.
Posting. Post the items that are to be posted individually.

Instructions: 2. Total, prove, and rule the sales journal. Post the totals of the special columns.

3. Prove the equality of debits and credits for the cash receipts journal.

4. Prove cash. The total of the Cash Credit column of the cash payments journal for Kahler Ceramics is $10,729.50. The balance on the last check stub on February 28 is $5,947.30.

5. Rule the cash receipts journal. Post the special column totals.

6. Prepare a schedule of accounts receivable similar to the one on page 250. Compare the schedule total with the balance of the accounts receivable account in the general ledger. The total and the balance should be the same.

ENRICHMENT PROBLEMS

MASTERY PROBLEM 21-M Journalizing and posting sales and cash receipts transactions

The accounts receivable ledger and general ledger accounts of Klondike Company are given in the working papers. The balances are recorded as of April 1 of the current year.

ACCOUNTS RECEIVABLE LEDGER

Charge Customer	Account Balance
Grady Graham, 755 Random Drive, Jackson, MS 39208-1764	$275.00
Melinda Grant, 563 Glen Allen Drive, Jackson, MS 39212-2347	187.00
David Hill, 452 Elsinore Avenue, Jackson, MS 39204-1591	435.00
Preston Miles, 75 Renfro Avenue, Jackson, MS 39201-1043	198.00
Ralph Needham, 7054 West Masonwood, Battlefield, MS 39221-4982	342.00
Titus Newton, 179 Ottawa Drive, Jackson, MS 39203-1460	245.00
Melvin Peterson, 4891 Poppington Drive, Myrtle, MS 38650-9181	525.00

PARTIAL GENERAL LEDGER

Account Title	Acct. No.	Account Balance
Cash	1101	$5,872.51
Accounts Receivable	1103	2,207.00
Sales Tax Payable	2106	—
Sales	4101	—
Sales Returns and Allowances	4101.1	—

Instructions: 1. The following transactions affecting sales and cash receipts were completed by Klondike Company during April of the current year. Record these transactions in a sales journal, general journal, and cash receipts journal similar to those illustrated in this chapter. Use page 9 of each journal. Source documents are abbreviated: sales invoice, S; receipt, R; cash register tape, T; credit card sales adding machine tape, CT; credit memorandum, CM; memorandum, M.

Apr. 1. Recorded the cash balance on hand in the cash receipts journal, $5,872.51.
2. Recorded cash sales for the week, $256.00, plus sales tax, $12.80. T2.
2. Recorded credit card sales for the week, $176.00, plus sales tax, $8.80. CT2.
5. Credited Ralph Needham's account for merchandise returned $40.00, plus sales tax, $2.00. CM31.
5. Received cash on account from Ralph Needham, $100.00. R92.
6. Sold merchandise on account to Melinda Grant, $226.00, plus sales tax, $11.30. S69.
8. Received cash on account from Titus Newton, $245.00. R93.
9. Recorded cash sales for the week, $782.50, plus sales tax, $39.13. T9.
9. Recorded credit card sales for the week, $345.00, plus sales tax, $17.25. CT9.

Posting. Post the items that are to be posted individually. Post from the journals in this order: sales journal, general journal, and cash receipts journal.

11. Received cash on account from Melvin Peterson, $300.00. R94.
12. Sold merchandise on account to Ralph Needham, $125.00, plus sales tax, $6.25. S70.
12. Received cash on account from Melinda Grant, $187.00. R95.
13. Credited David Hill's account for merchandise returned $125.00, plus sales tax, $6.25. CM32.
15. Received cash on account from Preston Miles, $198.00. R96.

Apr. 16. Recorded cash sales for the week, $992.00, plus sales tax, $49.60. T16.
16. Recorded credit card sales for the week, $567.00, plus sales tax, $28.35. CT16.
Posting. Post the items that are to be posted individually.
18. Received cash on account from Grady Graham, $275.00. R97.
19. Received cash on account from Melinda Grant, $237.30. R98.
21. Sold merchandise on account to Titus Newton $139.00, plus sales tax, $6.95. S71.
22. Found that on March 12 a sale on account to Titus Newton (S55) was incorrectly charged to the account of Ralph Needham, $200.00. M66.
22. Received cash on account from Melvin Peterson, $225.00. R99.
22. Sold merchandise on account to Preston Miles, $336.00, plus sales tax, $16.80. S72.
23. Received cash on account from David Hill, $303.75. R100.
23. Recorded cash sales for the week, $1,253.00, plus sales tax, $62.65. T23.
23. Recorded credit card sales for the week, $567.00, plus sales tax, $28.35. CT23.
Posting. Post the items that are to be posted individually.
25. Sold merchandise on account to Grady Graham, $337.00, plus sales tax, $16.85. S73.
26. Received cash on account from Titus Newton, $145.95. R101.
26. Received cash on account from Ralph Needham, $131.25. R102.
27. Sold merchandise on account to David Hill, $289.00, plus sales tax, $14.45. S74.
28. Received cash on account from Titus Newton, $200.00. R103.
29. Received cash on account from Preston Miles, $352.80. R104.
30. Recorded cash sales for the week, $1,575.00, plus sales tax, $78.75. T30.
30. Recorded credit card sales for the week, $753.00, plus sales tax, $37.65. CT30.
Posting. Post the items that are to be posted individually.

Instructions: 2. Total, prove, and rule the sales journal. Post the totals of the special columns.

3. Prove the equality of debits and credits for the cash receipts journal.

4. Prove cash. The total of the Cash Credit column of the cash payments journal for Klondike Equipment Company is $11,846.20. The balance on the last check stub on April 30 is $4,557.19.

5. Rule the cash receipts journal. Post the special column totals.

6. Prepare a schedule of accounts receivable similar to the one on page 250. Compare the schedule total with the balance of the accounts receivable account in the general ledger. The total and the balance should be the same.

CHALLENGE PROBLEM 21-C Journalizing and posting sales, purchases, cash receipts, and cash payments transactions

The accounts receivable, accounts payable, and general ledger accounts of Kohnke Company are given in the working papers. The balances are recorded as of March 1 of the current year.

ACCOUNTS RECEIVABLE LEDGER

Charge Customer	Account Balance
Earl Butler, 4230 Casco Street, Dallas, TX 75235-4126	$367.00
Chelsea Eastman, 905 Cato Avenue, Dallas, TX 75220-3705	178.00
Franklin Fox, 741 Dannon Drive, Dallas, TX 75213-2881	299.00
Loretta Linwood, 593 West Gilman, Dallas, TX 75222-3940	115.00
Jennifer Wellman, 5421 Moorman Avenue, Dallas, TX 75208-1960	456.00

ACCOUNTS PAYABLE LEDGER

Creditor	Account Balance
Foster Company, 122 Vignette Avenue, Dallas, TX 75236-4583	$1,298.00
Newton Paint Company, 244 Ingram Avenue, Dallas, TX 75221-3817	1,500.00
Shell Supply Company, 54 Three Mile Road, Dallas, TX 75218-3542	153.00
Tomah Company, 760 Wesley Drive, Dallas, TX 75215-3002	2,345.00

PARTIAL GENERAL LEDGER

Account Title	Acct. No.	Account Balance
Cash	1101	$5,700.00
Accounts Receivable	1103	1,415.00
Supplies	1105	267.00
Accounts Payable	2102	5,296.00
Sales Tax Payable	2106	—
Sales	4101	—
Sales Returns and Allowances	4101.1	—
Purchases	5101	—
Purchases Returns and Allowances	5101.1	—
Purchases Discount	5101.2	—
Delivery Expense	6103	—
Miscellaneous Expense	6108	—
Rent Expense	6110	—

Instructions: 1. The following transactions affecting sales, purchases, cash receipts, and cash payments were completed during March of the current year. Kohnke Company must collect a 5% sales tax on all sales. Figure and record Sales Tax Payable on all sales as described on page 418. Record the transactions in a sales journal, purchases journal, general journal, cash receipts journal, and cash payments journal. Use page 11 of each journal. Source documents are abbreviated: check, C; sales invoice, S; receipt, R; cash register tape, T; credit card sales adding machine tape, CT; credit memorandum, CM; memorandum, M; purchase invoice, P; debit memorandum, DM.

Mar. 1. Recorded the cash balance on hand in the cash receipts journal, $5,700.00.
2. Paid March rent, $585.00. C89.
2. Received cash on account from Loretta Linwood, $115.00. R35.
3. Returned merchandise to Tomah Company, $205.00. DM16.
3. Paid on account to Shell Supply Company, $151.47, covering P83 for $153.00 less a 1% cash discount of $1.53. C90.
5. Recorded cash sales for the week, $680.00, plus sales tax. T5.
5. Recorded credit card sales for the week, $578.00, plus sales tax. CT5.

Posting. Post the items that are to be posted individually. Post from the journals in this order: sales journal, purchases journal, general journal, cash receipts journal, and cash payments journal.

7. Paid on account to Newton Paint Company, $1,500.00, no discount. C91.
7. Received cash on account from Jennifer Wellman, $206.00. R36.
8. Sold merchandise on account to Chelsea Eastman, $145.00, plus sales tax. S72.
8. Purchased merchandise on account from Newton Paint Company, $1,354.00. P101.
9. Paid on account to Tomah Company, $2,097.20, covering P78 for $2,345.00 less DM16 for $205.00, and less a 2% discount of $42.80. C92.

Mar. 10. Received cash on account from Earl Butler, $367.00. R37.
10. Sold merchandise on account to Jennifer Wellman, $376.00, plus sales tax. S73.
11. Bought supplies on account from Foster Company, $368.00. M27.
12. Recorded cash sales for the week, $720.00, plus sales tax. T12.
12. Recorded credit card sales for the week, $677.00, plus sales tax. CT12.
Posting. Post the items that are to be posted individually.
14. Paid on account to Foster Company, $1,298.00, no discount. C93.
14. Paid cash for delivery expense, $35.00. C94.
14. Purchased merchandise on account from Newton Paint Company, $1,678.00. P102.
14. Sold merchandise on account to Loretta Linwood, $545.00, plus sales tax. S74.
15. Credited Chelsea Eastman's account for merchandise returned, $78.00, plus sales tax. CM56.
15. Sold merchandise on account to Earl Butler, $490.00, plus sales tax. S75.
16. Sold merchandise on account to Chelsea Eastman, $682.00, plus sales tax. S76.
17. Received cash on account from Franklin Fox, $299.00. R38.
18. Bought supplies on account from Shell Supply Company, $135.00. M28.
19. Recorded cash sales for the week, $648.00, plus sales tax. T19.
19. Recorded credit card sales for the week, $669.00, plus sales tax. CT19.
Posting. Post the items that are to be posted individually.
21. Paid on account to Newton Paint Company, $1,354.00, no discount. C95.
22. Paid miscellaneous expenses, $125.00. C96.
23. Received cash on account from Jennifer Wellman, $250.00. R39.
24. Purchased merchandise on account from Tomah Company, $750.00. P103.
26. Recorded cash sales for the week, $650.00, plus sales tax. T26.
26. Recorded credit card sales for the week, $690.00, plus sales tax. CT26.
Posting. Post the items that are to be posted individually.
28. Paid on account to Shell Supply Company, $133.65, covering M28 for $135.00 less 1% discount of $1.35. C97.
31. Recorded cash sales for the week, $680.00, plus sales tax. T31.
31. Recorded credit card sales for the week, $643.00, plus sales tax. CT31.
Posting. Post the items that are to be posted individually.

Instructions: 2. Total, prove, and rule the sales journal. Post the totals of the special columns.

3. Total and rule the purchases journal. Post the total.

4. Prove the equality of debits and credits for the cash receipts and cash payments journals.

5. Prove cash. The balance on the last check stub on March 31 is $6,624.43.

6. Rule the cash receipts journal. Post the special column totals.

7. Rule the cash payments journal. Post the totals of the special columns.

8. Prepare a schedule of accounts receivable similar to the one on page 250. Prepare a schedule of accounts payable similar to the one on page 250. Compare the schedules' totals with the balances of the accounts in the general ledger. The total and the balance of accounts receivable should be the same. The total and the balance of accounts payable should be the same.

22

Payroll Records

ENABLING PERFORMANCE TASKS

After studying Chapter 22, you will be able to:

a. Define accounting terms related to payroll records.
b. Explain accounting principles and practices related to payroll records.
c. Figure an employee's earnings from a time card.
d. Determine payroll income tax withholdings.
e. Apply for a social security account number.
f. Complete payroll time cards.
g. Prepare a semimonthly payroll.
h. Prepare a payroll register.
i. Prepare an employee's earnings record.
j. Write a payroll check.

A business periodically pays employees for their services. The money paid for an employee's services is known as a salary. The period covered by a salary payment is called a pay period. Not all businesses base their salary payments on the same length of time. A pay period may be weekly, biweekly, semimonthly, or monthly. The same procedure is used for figuring a salary regardless of the length of the pay period.

A list of employees that shows the payments due them for a pay period is called a payroll. Various methods of recording payroll are used by different companies. The method used depends on the number of employees and the type of office equipment available. To speed the preparation of payroll, many businesses use automated data processing equipment. The basic accounting principles are the same regardless of whether manual or automated methods are used.

PAYROLL TAXES

Taxes based on the payroll of a business are called payroll taxes. A business is required by law to withhold certain payroll taxes from salaries earned by employees. A business also is required to pay certain payroll taxes. All payroll taxes are based on employees' earnings. Accurate and detailed payroll records therefore are important. Errors in payroll records could cause incorrect payroll tax payments. A business may have to pay a penalty for failure to pay taxes on time.

Employees' income tax

A business must withhold federal income tax based on its employees' salaries. The business also must forward the tax withheld to the federal government. Each person supported by an employee reduces the employee's income tax. For example, a married person supporting a spouse pays less income tax than a single person with the same earnings. One withholding allowance can be claimed for each person supported by the employee. One withholding allowance also can be claimed by the employee.

The withholding allowances and marital status of an employee affect the amount of federal income tax withheld each pay period. All new employees must report the withholding allowances and marital status to the employer. Employees do this by filling out and signing Form W-4, Employee's Withholding Allowance Certificate. Form W-4 for Joann D. Boyd, shown below, indicates that she is married and claims one allowance for herself.

Form **W-4**

Department of the Treasury—Internal Revenue Service

Employee's Withholding Allowance Certificate

Print your full name ▶ JOANN D. BOYD | Your social security number ▶ 450 59 8679

Address (including ZIP code) ▶ 2586 SHADY BROOK DRIVE, GARLAND, TX 75041-2787

Marital status: ☐ Single ☒ Married ☐ Married, but withhold at higher Single rate

Note: *If married, but legally separated, or spouse is a nonresident alien, check the single block.*

1 Total number of allowances you are claiming 1

2 Additional amount, if any, you want deducted from each pay (if your employer agrees) . . . . . $ NONE

3 I claim exemption from withholding because (see instructions and check boxes below that apply):

a ☐ Last year I did not owe any Federal income tax and had a right to a full refund of **ALL** income tax withheld, **AND**

b ☐ This year I do not expect to owe any Federal income tax and expect to have a right to a full refund of **ALL** income tax withheld. If both a and b apply, enter "EXEMPT" here . . . . . ▶

c If you entered "EXEMPT" on line 3b, are you a full-time student? . . . . . ☐ Yes ☐ No

Under the penalties of perjury, I certify that I am entitled to the number of withholding allowances claimed on this certificate, or if claiming exemption from withholding, that I am entitled to claim the exempt status.

Employee's signature ▶ Joann D. Boyd Date ▶ January 3, 19 83

Employer's name and address (including ZIP code) (FOR EMPLOYER'S USE ONLY) | Employer identification number

Form W-4, Employee's Withholding Allowance Certificate

Federal law requires that each employer have on file a properly completed Form W-4 for each employee. An employee should file a revised form if the withholding allowances or marital status changes. Information from the completed Form W-4 is used when a business figures the federal income tax to be withheld.

Federal income tax is withheld from employees' earnings in all 50 states. Employers in many states also are required to withhold state, city, or county income taxes from employees' pay. State and local tax rates vary. Therefore, an employer must be familiar with local tax regulations.

Payroll taxes withheld represent a liability for an employer until payment is made. Federal payroll taxes may be paid to a Federal Reserve Bank. The taxes also may be paid to a bank authorized to receive such funds for the government.

Some employees are exempt from having federal taxes withheld from their salaries. For example, a student employed part time may be exempt. An employee must certify that no income tax was paid in the prior year. Also, an employee must certify that no income tax is expected to be paid for the current year. An exemption is certified by filling in "EXEMPT" on line 3 of a withholding allowance certificate as shown below.

Form **W-4** | Department of the Treasury—Internal Revenue Service
Employee's Withholding Allowance Certificate

Print your full name ▶ Paul E. Walsh | Your social security number ▶ 450 65 8647
Address (including ZIP code) ▶ 3135 Bonneville Drive Garland, TX 75041-2830
Marital status: ☒ Single ☐ Married ☐ Married, but withhold at higher Single rate
Note: *If married, but legally separated, or spouse is a nonresident alien, check the single block.*

1 Total number of allowances you are claiming
2 Additional amount, if any, you want deducted from each pay (if your employer agrees) $
3 I claim exemption from withholding because (see instructions and check boxes below that apply):
a ☒ Last year I did not owe any Federal income tax and had a right to a full refund of **ALL** income tax withheld, **AND**
b ☒ This year I do not expect to owe any Federal income tax and expect to have a right to a full refund of **ALL** income tax withheld. If both a and b apply, enter "EXEMPT" here ▶ Exempt
c If you entered "EXEMPT" on line 3b, are you a full-time student? ☒ Yes ☐ No

Under the penalties of perjury, I certify that I am entitled to the number of withholding allowances claimed on this certificate, or if claiming exemption from withholding, that I am entitled to claim the exempt status.

Employee's signature ▶ Paul E. Walsh Date ▶ February 1, 1983
Employer's name and address (including ZIP code) (FOR EMPLOYER'S USE ONLY) | Employer identification number

Form W-4, showing Exemption from Withholding

An employer is not required to withhold federal income tax for employees who have claimed exemption on a Form W-4. However, other payroll taxes must still be withheld.

Employees' and employers' social security taxes

The federal social security law includes three programs.

1. Old-age, survivors, and disability insurance benefits for qualified employees and their spouses, widows or widowers, dependent children, and parents.
2. Grants to states that provide benefits for persons temporarily unemployed and for certain relief and welfare purposes.

3. Payments to the aged for the cost of certain hospital and related services. The federal health insurance program, designed for people who have reached age 65, is called medicare.

FICA tax. A federal tax paid by employees and employers for old-age, survivors, disability, and hospitalization insurance is called FICA tax. FICA is the abbreviation for the Federal Insurance Contributions Act. The FICA tax is based on the amount of salaries paid to employees. Employers are required to withhold FICA tax from a specified amount of each employee's salary paid in a calendar year. Employers must pay the same amount of FICA tax as withheld from employees' wages.

The regulations for social security taxes are set by Congress. Changes are made frequently. Regardless of changes in tax regulations, the accounting principles involved are the same. Therefore, for illustration, a rate of 6% on a maximum annual salary of $20,000.00 is used in this textbook.

Federal unemployment tax. A federal tax used for state and federal administrative expenses of the unemployment program is called federal unemployment tax. This tax is paid entirely by the employer.

State unemployment tax. A state tax used to pay benefits to unemployed workers is called state unemployment tax. This tax is usually paid by the employer although employee payroll deductions are made in certain states. The Social Security Act specifies certain standards for unemployment compensation laws. Therefore, there is a high degree of uniformity in the state unemployment laws and their requirements. However, the details of state unemployment laws do differ. Because of these differences, employers should learn the requirements of the states in which they operate.

Retention of records. An employer is required to keep all payroll records showing payments and deductions. Some records must be kept longer than others. Records pertaining to social security tax payments and deductions should be retained for four years. The length of time state unemployment tax payment records must be kept varies from state to state.

Obtaining a social security card and an account number

Every employee in an occupation covered by the social security law must have a social security number. A new employee without a social security number must obtain one. An application for a new social security number is on the next page.

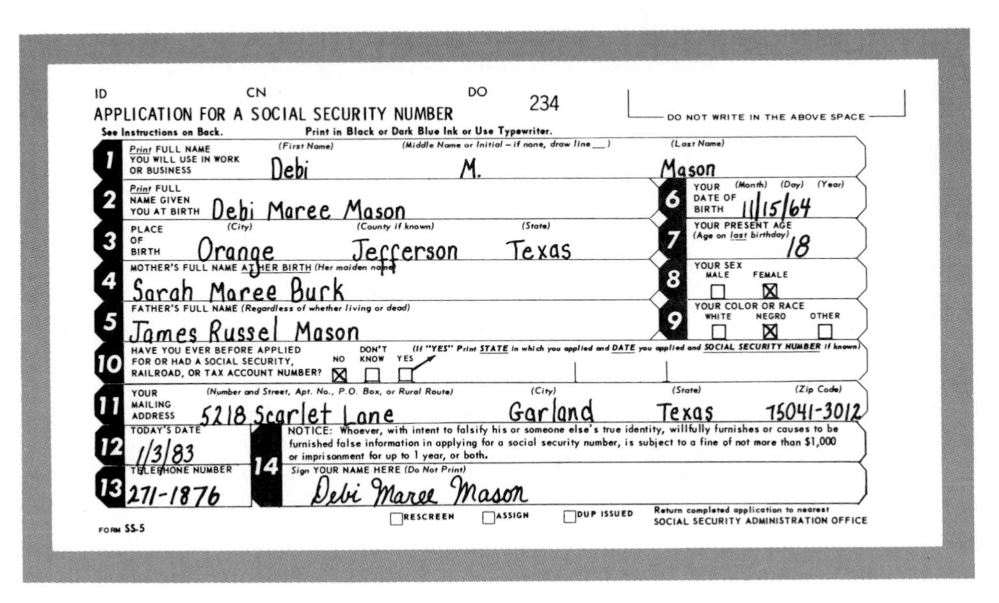

ID CN DO 234
DO NOT WRITE IN THE ABOVE SPACE

APPLICATION FOR A SOCIAL SECURITY NUMBER
See Instructions on Back. Print in Black or Dark Blue Ink or Use Typewriter.

1 Print FULL NAME YOU WILL USE IN WORK OR BUSINESS (First Name) Debi (Middle Name or Initial – if none, draw line ___) M. (Last Name) Mason

2 Print FULL NAME GIVEN YOU AT BIRTH Debi Maree Mason

6 YOUR DATE OF BIRTH (Month) (Day) (Year) 11/15/64

3 PLACE OF BIRTH (City) Orange (County if known) Jefferson (State) Texas

7 YOUR PRESENT AGE (Age on last birthday) 18

4 MOTHER'S FULL NAME AT HER BIRTH (Her maiden name) Sarah Maree Burk

8 YOUR SEX MALE ☐ FEMALE ☒

5 FATHER'S FULL NAME (Regardless of whether living or dead) James Russel Mason

9 YOUR COLOR OR RACE WHITE ☐ NEGRO ☒ OTHER ☐

10 HAVE YOU EVER BEFORE APPLIED FOR OR HAD A SOCIAL SECURITY, RAILROAD, OR TAX ACCOUNT NUMBER? NO ☒ DON'T KNOW ☐ YES ☐ (If "YES" Print STATE in which you applied and DATE you applied and SOCIAL SECURITY NUMBER if known)

11 YOUR MAILING ADDRESS (Number and Street, Apt. No., P.O. Box, or Rural Route) 5218 Scarlet Lane (City) Garland (State) Texas (Zip Code) 75041-3012

12 TODAY'S DATE 1/3/83

NOTICE: Whoever, with intent to falsify his or someone else's true identity, willfully furnishes or causes to be furnished false information in applying for a social security number, is subject to a fine of not more than $1,000 or imprisonment for up to 1 year, or both.

13 TELEPHONE NUMBER 271-1876

14 Sign YOUR NAME HERE (Do Not Print) Debi Maree Mason

☐ RESCREEN ☐ ASSIGN ☐ DUP ISSUED

Return completed application to nearest SOCIAL SECURITY ADMINISTRATION OFFICE

FORM SS-5

Form SS-5, Application for a Social Security Number

An application form may be obtained from any Social Security Administration or Internal Revenue Service office and most post offices. The form should be sent to the nearest field office of the Social Security Administration. A social security card is issued to anyone upon request and without charge. Every person seeking a job should obtain a social security card in advance. Having a card simplifies making application for employment. A social security card is at the left.

Social security card

A person who loses a social security card may apply for a new card. A new card is issued with the same account number. Each person should have only one account number. An employee with more than one account number may not receive all the earned social security benefits.

If an employee's name is changed, the Social Security Administration should be notified of the change. The account number will not be changed. A form for reporting a change in name may be obtained from a social security administration office.

Need for social security account number

Each employee must have a social security account number. The employee's social security account number is placed on state and federal tax reports. An employer also is required to place each employee's social security number on reports of payroll taxes.

Banks must furnish the federal government with a list of persons receiving interest payments of $10.00 or more. The social security number must be reported for each person on the list. Social security numbers are shown on drivers' licenses in some states and on both personal and business income tax returns. Social security numbers are used as student identification numbers at some colleges and universities. Social security numbers also are used as serial numbers for members of the armed forces.

PAYROLL TIME CARDS

Time clock

A payroll system must include an accurate record of the time each employee has worked. Several means are available for keeping time records. Employee time records most frequently are kept on time cards. Time cards provide the information required by law about the hours worked by each employee. Time cards are used as the basic source of data to prepare a payroll. The time worked by each employee may be recorded on a time card by hand or by a time clock.

A time card showing hours worked may be recorded by a supervisor who knows when employees arrive and leave work. Some businesses record only the total hours worked each day. Other firms record the exact time employees arrive and leave.

Many companies have a time clock which their employees use to record times of arrival and departure. These times are imprinted by the time clock on a time card. Each employee has a time card in a rack beside the time clock. The employee uses the time clock to register arrival and departure times. Executives usually are not required to use a time clock. Their pay is not affected by brief absences from the office.

Lin's Music Center uses a time clock to record arrival and departure times of each employee each day. The time card for Joann D. Boyd, stock clerk, for the semimonthly period ending February 15 is below.

Analyzing a payroll time card

At the top of the card is Ms. Boyd's employee number. Below the employee number are her name, her social security number, and the date of the payroll period.

Lin's time cards have three sections, Morning, Afternoon, and Overtime, with In and Out columns under each section. When Ms. Boyd reported for work on February 1, she inserted the card in the time clock. The clock recorded her time of arrival as 7:56. The other entries on this line indicate that she left for lunch at 12:00. She returned at 12:55 and left for the day at 5:02. On February 2 she worked 2½ hours overtime, as shown on the line for February 2.

Lin's figures overtime pay for each employee who works over 8 hours in any one day.

EMPLOYEE NO. 3
NAME Joann D. Boyd
SOC. SEC. NO. 450-59-8679
PERIOD ENDING Feb. 15, 1983
Lin's

	MORNING		AFTERNOON		OVERTIME		HOURS	
	IN	OUT	IN	OUT	IN	OUT	REG	OT
1	7^{56}	12^{00}	12^{55}	5^{02}			8	
2	7^{50}	12^{00}	12^{59}	5^{01}	6^{00}	8^{31}	8	2½
14	7^{51}	12^{01}	12^{50}	5^{04}			8	
15	8^{00}	12^{05}	1^{01}	5^{03}			8	

	HOURS	RATE	AMOUNT
REGULAR	88	5.50	484.00
OVERTIME	2½	8.25	20.63
TOTAL HOURS	90½	TOTAL EARNINGS	504.63

Payroll time card

Figuring each employee's total earnings from a time card

Each employee's hours of work and earnings are figured.

1 Examine the time card for tardiness and early departure.

Ms. Boyd's working day is from 8:00 a.m. to 5:00 p.m. with a one-hour lunch period from 12:00 noon until 1:00 p.m. She reported to work one minute late on the afternoon of February 15. Lin's does not deduct for tardiness periods of ten or fewer minutes.

2 Extend the regular hours into the Hours Reg. column.

The regular hours for Ms. Boyd are 8 hours each day.

3 Figure the number of hours of overtime for each day and enter the amount in the Hours OT column.

Ms. Boyd worked from 6:00 p.m. to 8:31 p.m. on February 2. Therefore, 2½ hours are recorded in the OT column (6:00 p.m. to 8:31 p.m. equals 2½ hours).

4 Add the Regular Hours column and enter the total in the space provided at the bottom of the card.

Ms. Boyd worked 88 regular hours (8 hours × 11 days). Therefore, 88 is recorded in the Regular Hours space at the bottom of the card.

5 Enter the rate for regular time. Figure the regular earnings by multiplying hours times rate.

Ms. Boyd's regular rate is $5.50 per hour. Enter $5.50 in the Regular Rate space. Regular earnings are $484.00 (88 hours × $5.50 rate). Regular earnings, $484.00, are entered in the appropriate amount space.

6 Add the Overtime Hours column and enter the total in the space provided at the bottom of the card.

Ms. Boyd worked 2½ overtime hours during the semimonthly pay period. Therefore, 2½ is recorded in the Overtime Hours space at the bottom of the card.

7 Enter the rate for overtime. Figure the overtime earnings by multiplying hours times rate.

Ms. Boyd is paid one and one-half times her regular rate for overtime work. Thus her overtime rate is $8.25 per hour ($5.50 × 1½). Enter $8.25 in the Overtime Rate space. Overtime earnings are $20.63 (2½ hours × $8.25 rate). Overtime earnings, $20.63, are entered in the appropriate amount space.

8 Add the Hours column to find the total hours. Add the Amount column to find the total earnings.

Ms. Boyd earned $504.63 for the semimonthly period. Total hours, 90½, (88 regular plus 2½ overtime hours) are entered in the Total Hours space. Total earnings, $504.63, ($484.00 regular plus $20.63 overtime earnings) are entered in the Total Earnings space.

The total pay due for a pay period before deductions is called total earnings. Total earnings are sometimes known as gross pay or gross earnings.

PAYROLL REGISTER

A business form on which all payroll information is recorded is called a payroll register. Lin's payroll register for the semimonthly period ended February 15 is below. All information about a payroll is recorded on a payroll register. Regular, overtime, and total earnings are recorded from time cards. Amounts deducted for taxes, hospital insurance, savings bonds, and United Way contributions are figured and recorded on a payroll register. Also total deductions, net pay, and check number of each payroll check are recorded on a payroll register.

PAYROLL REGISTER

SEMIMONTHLY PERIOD ENDED *February 15, 1983* — DATE OF PAYMENT *February 15, 1983*

	EMPL. NO.	EMPLOYEE'S NAME	MARITAL STATUS	NO. OF ALLOWANCES	EARNINGS			DEDUCTIONS					NET PAY	CK. NO.	
					REGULAR	OVERTIME	TOTAL	FEDERAL INCOME TAX	FICA TAX	HOSP. INS.	OTHER	TOTAL			
1	6	Allen, Don T.	M	3	484.00		484.00	42.50	29.04	35.00	UW 3.00	109.54	374.46	323	1
2	3	Boyd, Joann D.	M	1	484.00	20.63	504.63	61.50	30.28	12.00	B 5.00	108.78	395.85	324	2
3	4	Danner, Tommy J.	S	1	374.00	12.75	386.75	51.70	23.21	12.00		86.91	299.84	325	3
4	10	DeLozier, Irene G.	S	1	82.50		82.50	Exempt	4.95			4.95	77.55	326	4
5	2	Flores, Charles A.	M	3	506.00		506.00	46.10	30.36	35.00	B 5.00	116.46	389.54	327	5
6	8	Kurtz, Richard L.	S	1	176.00		176.00	11.60	10.56			22.16	153.84	328	6
7	9	Mason, Debi M.	S	1	165.00		165.00	9.80	9.90			19.70	145.30	329	7
8	1	Roark, Carl H.	M	4	850.00		850.00	108.40	51.00	35.00	B 10.00	204.40	645.60	330	8
9	7	Schweitzer, Gail L.	M	2	462.00		462.00	46.40	27.72	35.00	UW 2.00	111.12	350.88	331	9
10	5	Spears, Phyllis R.	M	2	528.00		528.00	57.20	31.68	35.00	UW 3.00	126.88	401.12	332	10
11	11	Walsh, Paul E.	S	1	82.50		82.50	Exempt	4.95			4.95	77.55	333	11
12		Totals			4,194.00	33.38	4,227.38	435.20	253.65	199.00	B 20.00 UW 8.00	915.85	3,311.53		12

Recording earnings on a payroll register

Payroll register

Each employee's number, name, marital status, and withholding allowances are listed in a payroll register. Each employee's earnings for a pay period are written in the appropriate columns of a payroll register.

Recorded on line 2 of a payroll register are Ms. Boyd's employee number, *3*, and name, *Boyd, Joann D.* Also recorded are marital status, *M*, married; withholding allowances, *1*; regular earnings, *$484.00*; overtime earnings, *$20.63*; and total earnings, *$504.63*. Earnings information is recorded from Ms. Boyd's time card for the period February 1–15.

Figuring the deductions section of a payroll register

The deductions section of a payroll register is used to record the various amounts deducted from employees' earnings. Certain payroll taxes must be deducted from each employee's total earnings. Also some companies deduct amounts for hospitalization and retirement plans. These deductions will vary from one company to another depending on policies established by management and employees.

1 The Federal Income Tax column is used to record the amount of federal income tax withheld from each employee's earnings. This amount is determined from tables furnished by the federal government. Portions of semimonthly earnings tables showing the tax to be withheld are below and on page 449.

SEMIMONTHLY Payroll Period—Employee NOT MARRIED

And the wages are—		And the number of withholding allowances claimed is—										
At least	But less than	0	1	2	3	4	5	6	7	8	9	10 or more
		The amount of income tax to be withheld shall be—										
156	160	15.40	8.60	2.30	0	0	0	0	0	0	0	0
160	164	16.20	9.20	2.90	0	0	0	0	0	0	0	0
164	168	16.90	9.80	3.50	0	0	0	0	0	0	0	0
168	172	17.60	10.40	4.10	0	0	0	0	0	0	0	0
172	176	18.30	11.00	4.70	0	0	0	0	0	0	0	0
176	180	19.00	11.60	5.30	0	0	0	0	0	0	0	0
180	184	19.80	12.30	5.90	0	0	0	0	0	0	0	0
184	188	20.50	13.00	6.50	.30	0	0	0	0	0	0	0
188	192	21.20	13.70	7.10	.90	0	0	0	0	0	0	0
192	196	21.90	14.40	7.70	1.50	0	0	0	0	0	0	0
196	200	22.60	15.10	8.30	2.10	0	0	0	0	0	0	0
200	210	23.90	16.40	9.40	3.10	0	0	0	0	0	0	0
210	220	25.70	18.20	10.90	4.60	0	0	0	0	0	0	0
220	230	27.50	20.00	12.50	6.10	0	0	0	0	0	0	0
230	240	29.30	21.80	14.30	7.60	1.40	0	0	0	0	0	0
240	250	31.10	23.60	16.10	9.10	2.90	0	0	0	0	0	0
250	260	32.90	25.40	17.90	10.60	4.40	0	0	0	0	0	0
260	270	34.70	27.20	19.70	12.20	5.90	0	0	0	0	0	0
270	280	36.50	29.00	21.50	14.00	7.40	1.10	0	0	0	0	0
280	290	38.40	30.80	23.30	15.80	8.90	2.60	0	0	0	0	0
290	300	40.50	32.60	25.10	17.60	10.40	4.10	0	0	0	0	0
300	320	43.60	35.30	27.80	20.30	12.80	6.40	.10	0	0	0	0
320	340	47.80	39.10	31.40	23.90	16.40	9.40	3.10	0	0	0	0
340	360	52.00	43.30	35.00	27.50	20.00	12.50	6.10	0	0	0	0
360	380	56.20	47.50	38.70	31.10	23.60	16.10	9.10	2.90	0	0	0
380	400	60.40	51.70	42.90	34.70	27.20	19.70	12.20	5.90	0	0	0
400	420	64.60	55.90	47.10	38.40	30.80	23.30	15.80	8.90	2.60	0	0
420	440	69.10	60.10	51.30	42.60	34.40	26.90	19.40	11.90	5.60	0	0
440	460	74.30	64.30	55.50	46.80	38.00	30.50	23.00	15.50	8.60	2.40	0
460	480	79.50	68.60	59.70	51.00	42.20	34.10	26.60	19.10	11.60	5.40	0
480	500	84.70	73.80	63.90	55.20	46.40	37.70	30.20	22.70	15.20	8.40	2.10
500	520	89.90	79.00	68.20	59.40	50.60	41.90	33.80	26.30	18.80	11.40	5.10
520	540	95.10	84.20	73.40	63.60	54.80	46.10	37.40	29.90	22.40	14.90	8.10
540	560	100.30	89.40	78.60	67.80	59.00	50.30	41.50	33.50	26.00	18.50	11.10
560	580	105.50	94.60	83.80	73.00	63.20	54.50	45.70	37.10	29.60	22.10	14.60
580	600	110.70	99.80	89.00	78.20	67.40	58.70	49.90	41.20	33.20	25.70	18.20
600	620	116.60	105.00	94.20	83.40	72.50	62.90	54.10	45.40	36.80	29.30	21.80
620	640	122.60	110.20	99.40	88.60	77.70	67.10	58.30	49.60	40.80	32.90	25.40
640	660	128.60	116.10	104.60	93.80	82.90	72.10	62.50	53.80	45.00	36.50	29.00
660	680	134.60	122.10	109.80	99.00	88.10	77.30	66.70	58.00	49.20	40.50	32.60
680	700	140.60	128.10	115.60	104.20	93.30	82.50	71.70	62.20	53.40	44.70	36.20
700	720	146.60	134.10	121.60	109.40	98.50	87.70	76.90	66.40	57.60	48.90	40.10
720	740	153.10	140.10	127.60	115.10	103.70	92.90	82.10	71.20	61.80	53.10	44.30
740	760	159.90	146.10	133.60	121.10	108.90	98.10	87.30	76.40	66.00	57.30	48.50
760	780	166.70	152.60	139.60	127.10	114.60	103.30	92.50	81.60	70.80	61.50	52.70
780	800	173.50	159.40	145.60	133.10	120.60	108.50	97.70	86.80	76.00	65.70	56.90
800	820	180.30	166.20	152.00	139.10	126.60	114.10	102.90	92.00	81.20	70.40	61.10
820	840	187.10	173.00	158.80	145.10	132.60	120.10	108.10	97.20	86.40	75.60	65.30
840	860	193.90	179.80	165.60	151.40	138.60	126.10	113.60	102.40	91.60	80.80	69.90
860	880	200.70	186.60	172.40	158.20	144.60	132.10	119.60	107.60	96.80	86.00	75.10

Section of income tax withholding tables for semimonthly pay period

Ms. Boyd's federal income tax on $504.63 is found in the table, below, for married persons. The proper wage bracket is from $500.00 to $520.00. The income tax to be withheld is the amount shown on this line under the column for one allowance, $61.50.

The income tax withholding tables, below and on page 448, are those available when materials for this textbook were prepared. Federal income tax tables are also available for daily, weekly, biweekly, and monthly pay periods.

2 The FICA Tax column is used to record the amount deducted for social security tax. This amount may be figured two ways. Tax tables supplied by the federal government may be used. Also total earnings may be multiplied by the tax rate. FICA tax rates change periodically.

SEMIMONTHLY Payroll Period—Employee MARRIED

And the wages are-		And the number of withholding allowances claimed is—										
At least	But less than	0	1	2	3	4	5	6	7	8	9	10 or more
		The amount of income tax to be withheld shall be—										
156	160	8.70	2.50	0	0	0	0	0	0	0	0	0
160	164	9.30	3.10	0	0	0	0	0	0	0	0	0
164	168	9.90	3.70	0	0	0	0	0	0	0	0	0
168	172	10.50	4.30	0	0	0	0	0	0	0	0	0
172	176	11.10	4.90	0	0	0	0	0	0	0	0	0
176	180	11.70	5.50	0	0	0	0	0	0	0	0	0
180	184	12.30	6.10	0	0	0	0	0	0	0	0	0
184	188	12.90	6.70	.40	0	0	0	0	0	0	0	0
188	192	13.50	7.30	1.00	0	0	0	0	0	0	0	0
192	196	14.10	7.90	1.60	0	0	0	0	0	0	0	0
196	200	14.70	8.50	2.20	0	0	0	0	0	0	0	0
200	210	15.80	9.50	3.30	0	0	0	0	0	0	0	0
210	220	17.30	11.00	4.80	0	0	0	0	0	0	0	0
220	230	18.80	12.50	6.30	0	0	0	0	0	0	0	0
230	240	20.30	14.00	7.80	1.50	0	0	0	0	0	0	0
240	250	21.80	15.50	9.30	3.00	0	0	0	0	0	0	0
250	260	23.30	17.00	10.80	4.50	0	0	0	0	0	0	0
260	270	24.80	18.50	12.30	6.00	0	0	0	0	0	0	0
270	280	26.30	20.00	13.80	7.50	1.30	0	0	0	0	0	0
280	290	28.10	21.50	15.30	9.00	2.80	0	0	0	0	0	0
290	300	29.90	23.00	16.80	10.50	4.30	0	0	0	0	0	0
300	320	32.60	25.30	19.00	12.80	6.50	.30	0	0	0	0	0
320	340	36.20	28.70	22.00	15.80	9.50	3.30	0	0	0	0	0
340	360	39.80	32.30	25.00	18.80	12.50	6.30	0	0	0	0	0
360	380	43.40	35.90	28.40	21.80	15.50	9.30	3.00	0	0	0	0
380	400	47.00	39.50	32.00	24.80	18.50	12.30	6.00	0	0	0	0
400	420	50.60	43.10	35.60	28.10	21.50	15.30	9.00	2.80	0	0	0
420	440	54.20	46.70	39.20	31.70	24.50	18.30	12.00	5.80	0	0	0
440	460	57.80	50.30	42.80	35.30	27.80	21.30	15.00	8.80	2.50	0	0
460	480	61.80	53.90	46.40	38.90	31.40	24.30	18.00	11.80	5.50	0	0
480	500	66.00	57.50	50.00	42.50	35.00	27.50	21.00	14.80	8.50	2.30	0
500	520	70.20	61.50	53.60	46.10	38.60	31.10	24.00	17.80	11.50	5.30	0
520	540	74.40	65.70	57.20	49.70	42.20	34.70	27.20	20.80	14.50	8.30	2.00
540	560	78.60	69.90	61.10	53.30	45.80	38.30	30.80	23.80	17.50	11.30	5.00
560	580	82.80	74.10	65.30	56.90	49.40	41.90	34.40	26.90	20.50	14.30	8.00
580	600	87.00	78.30	69.50	60.80	53.00	45.50	38.00	30.50	23.50	17.30	11.00
600	620	91.20	82.50	73.70	65.00	56.60	49.10	41.60	34.10	26.60	20.30	14.00
620	640	95.60	86.70	77.90	69.20	60.40	52.70	45.20	37.70	30.20	23.30	17.00
640	660	100.40	90.90	82.10	73.40	64.60	56.30	48.80	41.30	33.80	26.30	20.00
660	680	105.20	95.20	86.30	77.60	68.80	60.10	52.40	44.90	37.40	29.90	23.00
680	700	110.00	100.00	90.50	81.80	73.00	64.30	56.00	48.50	41.00	33.50	26.00
700	720	114.80	104.80	94.80	86.00	77.20	68.50	59.70	52.10	44.60	37.10	29.60
720	740	119.60	109.60	99.60	90.20	81.40	72.70	63.90	55.70	48.20	40.70	33.20
740	760	124.40	114.40	104.40	94.40	85.60	76.90	68.10	59.40	51.80	44.30	36.80
760	780	129.20	119.20	109.20	99.20	89.80	81.10	72.30	63.60	55.40	47.90	40.40
780	800	134.00	124.00	114.00	104.00	94.00	85.30	76.50	67.80	59.00	51.50	44.00
800	820	139.20	128.80	118.80	108.80	98.80	89.50	80.70	72.00	63.20	55.10	47.60
820	840	144.80	133.60	123.60	113.60	103.60	93.70	84.90	76.20	67.40	58.70	51.20
840	860	150.40	138.70	128.40	118.40	108.40	98.40	89.10	80.40	71.60	62.90	54.80
860	880	156.00	144.30	133.20	123.20	113.20	103.20	93.30	84.60	75.80	67.10	58.40

Section of income tax withholding tables for semimonthly pay period

In this textbook, a rate of 6% on a maximum earnings of $20,000.00 is used. The procedure is the same regardless of the rate or maximum earnings established by Congress.

Ms. Boyd's FICA tax is figured by multiplying her total earnings by the FICA tax rate ($504.63 × 6% = $30.28).

3 The Hosp. Ins. column is used to record hospital insurance premiums. Most employees of Lin's subscribe to the company's hospitalization insurance to take advantage of a lower group rate. A special column is used for these deductions.

Ms. Boyd's semimonthly hospital insurance premium is $12.00. This premium is the rate set by the insurance company for an employee.

4 The Other column is used to list amounts withheld for which no special column is provided. These withholdings are voluntary deductions requested by an employee. The entries in this column are identified by code letters. Lin's uses the letter *B* to identify amounts withheld for buying U.S. Savings Bonds. *UW* is used to identify amounts withheld for contributions to the United Way. A separate total is shown for each different type of deduction.

Ms. Boyd has authorized Lin's to withhold $5.00 each pay period to buy U.S. Savings Bonds for her.

5 The Total column is used to record total deductions. All deductions on a line for each employee are added. The total deductions are recorded in the Total column.

Total deductions for Ms. Boyd are $108.78 ($61.50, $30.28, $12.00, and $5.00).

Figuring the net pay column of a payroll register

The Net Pay column is used to record the amount due each employee. Net pay is figured by subtracting the amount of each employee's total deductions from the employee's total earnings.

Ms. Boyd's net pay is $395.85 (total earnings, $504.63, less total deductions, $108.78). Payroll check number 324 was issued to Ms. Boyd.

Completing a payroll register

After the net pay has been recorded for each employee, each amount column is totaled. The accuracy of these additions is verified by subtracting the Total Deductions column total from the Total Earnings column total. The result should equal the total of the Net Pay column. If the totals do not agree, the errors must be found and corrected. After the totals are proved, a double rule is drawn below the totals across all amount columns.

Total earnings on line 12 of Lin's payroll register, page 447, are $4,227.38. Total deductions, on line 12, are $915.85. Total net pay for February 15, 1983, is $3,311.53 (total earnings, $4,227.38, less total deductions, $915.85).

Before a check is written for each employee's net pay, the payroll computations are checked for accuracy. The manager approves the payroll after the accuracy is verified. After each check is written, the check number is recorded in the Ck. No. column.

PAYROLL CHECKS

Lin's pays its employees by check. A special payroll check form is used that has a detachable stub on which are recorded earnings and amounts deducted. Employees detach the stubs for a record of deductions and cash received.

The information used to prepare payroll checks is taken from a payroll register. A payroll check for the pay period ending February 15 is below.

Lin's Music Center
2400 Fargo Lane
Garland, TX 75041-2579

324

February 15 19 83 — 88-593/1119

PAY TO THE ORDER OF Joann D. Boyd $ 395.85

Three hundred ninety-five and 85/100 DOLLARS

AMERICAN NATIONAL BANK
Garland, TX 75041-2579

Carl H. Loark

:1119059391: 66349" 0243" 324

STATEMENT OF EMPLOYEE EARNINGS AND PAYROLL DEDUCTIONS

Lin's Music Center

PERIOD ENDING	HOURS	EARNINGS		TOTAL EARNINGS	FEDERAL INCOME TAX	FICA TAX	HOSP. INS.	OTHER	TOTAL DEDUCTIONS	NET PAY
		REGULAR	OVERTIME							
2/15/83	90½	484.00	20.63	504.63	61.50	30.28	12.00	5.00	108.78	395.85
YEAR-TO-DATE TOTALS		1,408.00	20.63	1,428.63	169.30	85.72	36.00	15.00	306.02	1,122.61

Payroll check with detachable stub

A check for the total amount of the payroll is written on Lin's regular checking account. This check is deposited in a separate bank account for payroll checks only. A separate bank account for payroll checks provides additional protection and control. Amounts on checks could be increased or unauthorized payroll checks could be prepared. The payroll account would then have insufficient funds to pay the checks. Also, the payroll account equals the payroll register total net amount and can be reconciled easily against the payroll records. Only the check drawn for the total payroll is recorded in the cash payments journal. Detailed data about employees' payroll checks are obtained from a payroll register.

Some businesses will deposit pay directly to an employee's bank account. The payroll must still be figured. But individual checks are not written and do not have to be distributed. Under this system the payroll department prepares the payroll register and a statement of earnings and deductions for each employee. The employees' statements are given to them on payday to compare with the amount of the payroll deposit.

EMPLOYEES' EARNINGS RECORDS

A business form showing details of all items affecting payments made to an employee is called an employee's earnings record. This information is recorded each pay period. The record includes earnings, deductions, net pay, and accumulated earnings for the calendar year.

Recording information on an employee's earnings record

Lin's keeps all employee's earnings records on cards. One card is used for each calendar quarter of the year. Quarterly totals are used in the preparation of reports required by the government. Each quarter the last amount in the Accumulated Earnings column is carried forward to the Accumulated Earnings section for the following quarter. Therefore, the Accumulated Earnings column always reflects total earnings of an employee from the beginning of the year.

After a payroll register has been prepared, the payroll data for each employee are recorded on the employee's earnings record. The February 15 payroll register data for Joann D. Boyd, page 447, is recorded on her first quarter earnings record below.

EARNINGS RECORD FOR QUARTER ENDING *March 31, 1983*

Boyd, (LAST NAME) *Joann* (FIRST) *D.* (MIDDLE INITIAL) EMPLOYEE NO. *3* MARITAL STATUS *M* WITHHOLDING ALLOWANCES *1*

SOCIAL SECURITY NO. *450-59-8679*

RATE OF PAY *$5.50* PER HR. POSITION *Stock Clerk*

PAY PERIOD		EARNINGS			DEDUCTIONS						NET PAY	ACCUMULATED EARNINGS
NO.	ENDED	REGULAR	OVERTIME	TOTAL	FEDERAL INCOME TAX	FICA TAX	HOSP. INS.	OTHER		TOTAL		-0-
1	1/15	440 00		440 00	50 30	26 40	12 00	B	5 00	93 70	346 30	440 00
2	1/31	484 00		484 00	57 50	29 04	12 00	B	5 00	103 54	380 46	924 00
3	2/15	484 00	20 63	504 63	61 50	30 28	12 00	B	5 00	108 78	395 85	1428 63
4	2/28	396 00		396 00	39 50	23 76	12 00	B	5 00	80 26	315 74	1824 63
5	3/15	484 00	33 00	517 00	61 50	31 02	12 00	B	5 00	109 52	407 48	2341 63
6	3/31	528 00		528 00	65 70	31 68	12 00	B	5 00	114 38	413 62	2869 63
QUARTERLY TOTALS		2816 00	53 63	2869 63	336 00	172 18	72 00	B	30 00	610 18	2259 45	

OTHER DEDUCTIONS: B — U.S. SAVINGS BONDS; UW — UNITED WAY

Employee's earnings record

Analyzing an employee's earnings record

Ms. Boyd's earnings record for the first quarter is on page 452. Her name, employee number, social security number, and other payroll data are entered at the top of her earnings record.

Amount columns of an employee's earnings record are the same as amount columns of a payroll register. In addition the earnings record has an Accumulated Earnings column. Amounts opposite an employee's name on a payroll register are recorded in the corresponding columns of the employee's earnings record. The pay period ending February 15 is the third pay period in the first quarter. Ms. Boyd's earnings and deductions for that week are therefore entered on line 3 of her earnings record. Total earnings are added to the accumulated earnings on line 2 to get the new total earnings to date. Accumulated earnings are sometimes known as year-to-date earnings.

The Accumulated Earnings column shows the earnings for Ms. Boyd since the first of the year. The first entry in this column is zero since this is the beginning of the fiscal year. The last entry in this column, $2,869.63, will be carried forward to Ms. Boyd's earnings record for the second quarter. The amounts in the Accumulated Earnings column supply an up-to-date reference for an employee's year-to-date earnings. When an employee's earnings reach a specified amount, certain payroll taxes do not apply. For example, employers pay state and federal unemployment taxes only on a specified amount of each employee's earnings. Also, the maximum amount on which FICA taxes are paid is determined by law.

The Quarterly Totals line provides space for the totals for the quarter. These totals are needed to prepare required government reports.

OTHER METHODS OF PROCESSING A PAYROLL

Preparing a payroll requires computing, recording, and reporting payroll information. Each business selects a system of preparing the payroll resulting in adequate control for the least amount of cost.

Pegboard processing of a payroll

A special device used to write the same information at one time on several forms is called a pegboard. The pegboard is also known as an account board. One form of a pegboard is on the next page.

The name, pegboard, comes from pegs along one side of the board. The forms used with this device have holes punched along one side. Each of the forms is placed on the pegs. Thus, the line on each form on which data are to be written is aligned one below the other.

When a payroll is recorded, a page of the payroll register is attached to the pegboard. Next, the employee's earnings record is properly posi-

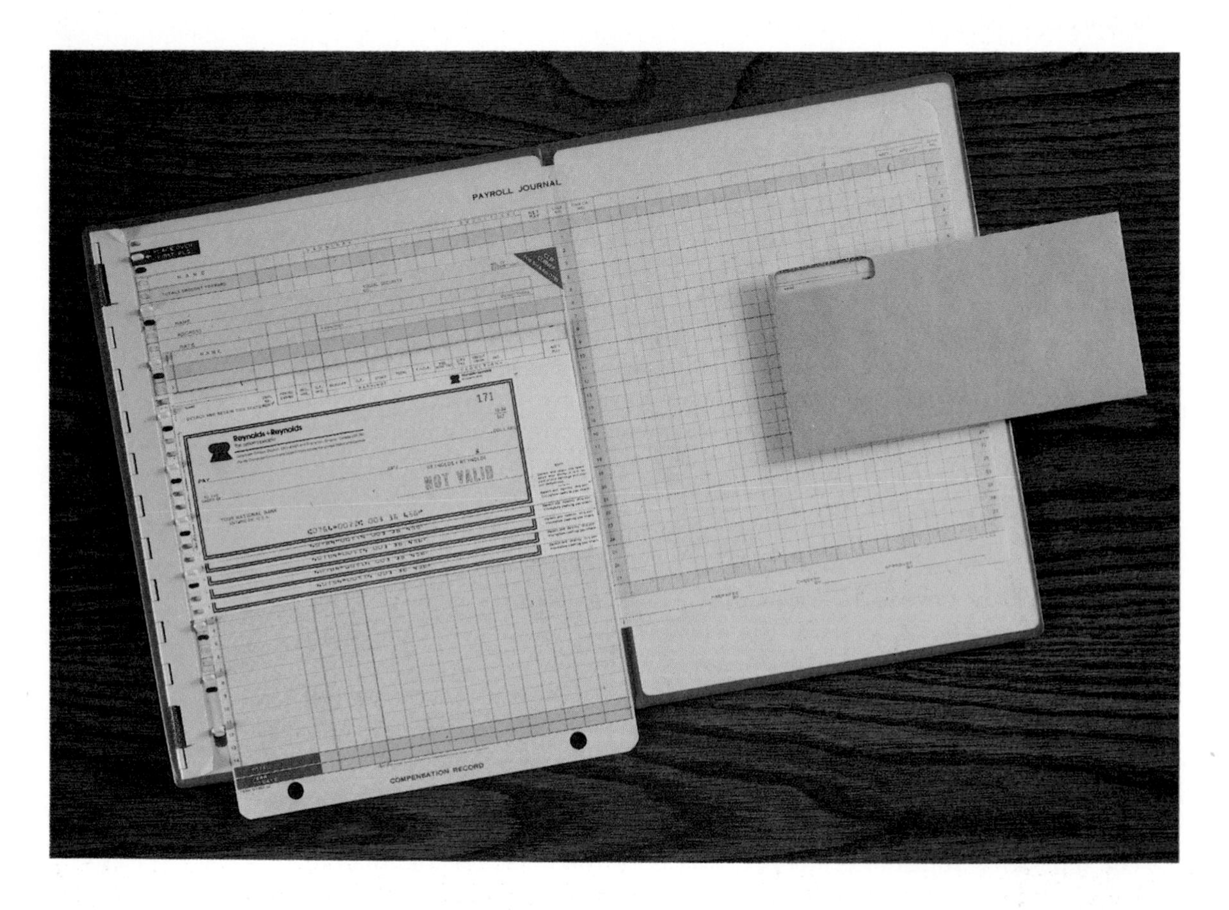

A pegboard

tioned on top of the payroll register page. Then, the check is positioned on top of both of these sheets. As the check stub is written, the same data are recorded on the employee's earnings record and the payroll register. The data are written only once. However, the data are recorded on three different records at the same time. Recording data on several forms with one writing is called the write-it-once principle.

The pegboard has two major purposes. First, the pegboard provides a solid writing base for writing on the forms by hand. Second, data are recorded on several forms with one writing.

ACCOUNTING TERMS

What is the meaning of each of the following?

1. pay period
2. payroll
3. payroll taxes
4. medicare
5. FICA tax
6. federal unemployment tax
7. state unemployment tax
8. total earnings
9. payroll register
10. employee's earnings record
11. pegboard
12. write-it-once principle

QUESTIONS FOR INDIVIDUAL STUDY

1. How frequently do businesses pay employee salaries?
2. What determines the method used for recording payroll?
3. What determines the amount of payroll taxes a business must pay?
4. How does an employer know how many withholding allowances each employee is entitled to?
5. Do any states have state income taxes? If so, how are these taxes collected?
6. How long must records pertaining to social security tax payments and deductions be retained?
7. How may a person obtain a social security card?
8. How is the amount of income tax withheld from an employee's salary determined?
9. Which column of the payroll register shows the amount of money due each employee?
10. Where is the information obtained to prepare a payroll check?
11. What is the major purpose of the Accumulated Earnings column on an employee's earnings record?
12. What are the purposes for using a pegboard device for preparing a payroll?

CASES FOR MANAGEMENT DECISION

CASE 1 Murchinson Home Supplies has 9 employees. A hand written time card currently is being used to record arrival and departure times for each employee. The accounting clerk suggests that a time clock be installed to record the arrival and departure times. The manager believes that the present system is satisfactory. Do you agree with the accounting clerk or the manager? Give your reasons.

CASE 2 Porter's Auto Repair prepares as part of its payroll procedure, a payroll register for each payroll and an earnings record for each employee. After reviewing both forms, the manager suggests that since both forms contain the same information, the company prepare only the payroll register. The manager states that omitting the earnings record will save considerable time and cost without affecting the payroll preparation. The accountant recommends that the present payroll procedure be retained. Do you agree with the accountant or the manager? Give your reasons.

DRILLS FOR UNDERSTANDING

DRILL 22-D 1 Figuring employees' earnings

The information below is taken from the time cards for each employee.

Employee Number	Hours Worked		Pay Rate	Amount of Pay		Total Earnings
	Regular	Overtime		Regular	Overtime	
1	40	1	$4.20	$168.00	$6.30	$174.30
2	40	5	6.00			
3	30	0	4.00			
4	40	4	5.50			
5	40	3	6.20			
6	40	2	5.80			

Instructions: For each employee, figure the amount of regular pay, overtime pay, and total earnings. The amounts for Employee No. 1 are given as an example. Overtime hours are paid at one and one-half times the regular pay rate.

DRILL 22-D 2 Determining payroll income tax withholdings

The information below is from a semimonthly payroll register.

1	2	3	4
Employee's Name	Marital Status	Number of Withholding Allowances	Total Earnings
1. Byers, Virgil	S	1	$425.00
2. Dario, Carmen	S	1	510.00
3. Espino, Luis	M	2	490.00
4. Frese, Margaret	S	1	575.00
5. Groom, Harold	M	3	590.00
6. Kouri, Margaret	M	4	675.00

Instructions: Determine the federal income tax that must be withheld for each of the six employees. Use the tax withholding tables on pages 448 and 449.

APPLICATION PROBLEMS

PROBLEM 22-1 Applying for a social security account number

Instructions: Complete an application for a social security account number. Use your own personal data. Compare your application with the illustration, page 444.

PROBLEM 22-2 Completing payroll time cards

Employees' time cards are given in the working papers accompanying this textbook.

Instructions: 1. Figure the regular, overtime, and total hours worked by each of the employees. Any hours over the regular 8-hour day are considered overtime.

2. Determine each employee's regular, overtime, and total earnings.

PROBLEM 22-3 Preparing a semimonthly payroll

Information from employee time cards for the semimonthly pay period April 1–15 of the current year is on the next page.

Instructions: 1. Prepare a payroll register similar to the illustration on page 447. The date of payment is April 16. Use the income tax withholding tables, pages 448 and 449, to find the income tax deduction for each employee. Deduct 6% of each employee's total earnings for FICA taxes.

2. Prepare a check for the total amount of the net pay. Make the check payable to *Payroll Account* and sign your name as treasurer of the company. The beginning check stub balance is $12,089.26.

3. Prepare payroll checks for Theresa Norwood, Check No. 411, and Sherri Rowe, Check No. 415. Sign your name as treasurer of the company. Record the payroll check numbers in the payroll register.

Quitman Equipment Company

Employee		Marital Status	No. of Allow-ances	Time card amounts for period April 1–15		Deductions	
No.	Name			Regular	Overtime	Hospital Insurance	U.S. Savings Bonds
3	Alpine, Mark	M	1	$372.00	$ 6.75		
2	Clark, Karl	M	4	585.20		$28.00	
9	Kelley, Garrett	M	4	672.00	26.25	28.00	$20.00
10	Kirby, Kay	M	1	550.00	28.14		
5	Norwood, Theresa	M	1	564.00			15.00
4	Oatman, Sara	S	1	431.50	15.30	12.00	
1	Parker, Ralph	M	3	526.50	48.75	28.00	15.00
6	Randolph, Gary	M	2	506.00	12.95	20.00	
7	Rowe, Sherri	S	1	479.60	18.36		6.00
8	Thatcher, Grace	M	4	662.40	20.70	28.00	
12	Warren, Lila	M	2	421.95	7.28	20.00	
11	Webb, Lester	S	1	435.75			

PROBLEM 22-4 Preparing an employee's earnings record

Jim Perry's earnings for six semimonthly pay periods for April through June of the current year are below.

Pay Period Ended	Earnings		
	Regular	Overtime	Total
4/15	$572.00	$19.50	$591.50
4/30	520.00	9.75	529.75
5/15	572.00	29.25	601.25
5/31	572.00	48.75	620.75
6/15	572.00	—	572.00
6/30	572.00	39.00	611.00

Other data about Jim Perry needed to complete the record are below.

(1) Employee number: 22
(2) Marital status: married
(3) Rate of pay: regular, $6.50; overtime, $9.75
(4) Social security number: 444-03-4236
(5) Position: nurse
(6) Accumulated earnings for first quarter: $3,640.00
(7) Deductions from total earnings are below.
Hospitalization insurance: $11.75 each semimonthly pay period
U.S. savings bonds: $10.00 each semimonthly pay period
Federal income tax: appropriate amount withheld each pay period; withholding tables, pages 448 and 449
Withholding allowances: 3
FICA taxes: 6% of total earnings each pay period

Instructions: 1. Prepare an employee's earnings record for Jim Perry similar to the one on page 452. Prepare the earnings record for the second quarter of the current year.

2. Verify the accuracy of the completed employee's earnings record. The Quarter Total for Regular and Overtime Earnings should equal the Quarter Total for Total Earnings. The Quarter Total for Total Earnings should equal the Quarter Total for Net Pay plus Total Deductions. The Quarter Total for Total Earnings should equal the end-of-quarter Accumulated Earnings minus beginning-of-quarter Accumulated Earnings.

ENRICHMENT PROBLEMS

MASTERY PROBLEM 22-M Preparing a semimonthly payroll

Information from employee time cards for the semimonthly pay period May 16–31 of the current year is below.

Gowans Company

Employee		Marital Status	No. of Allow-ances	Time card amounts for period May 16–31		Deductions	
No.	Names			Regular	Overtime	Hospital Insurance	U.S. Savings Bonds
5	Bryant, Michael	M	1	$600.00	$18.76		
8	Chapman, Avis	M	1	624.00	24.38	$16.00	
7	Gordon, Clay	S	1	437.00			
1	Horton, Joe	M	3	540.50	25.89	25.00	$20.00
2	Humes, Jerry	M	2	657.60			20.00
9	Jones, Diane	M	1	514.15	42.40		
10	Keystone, Alberta	M	3	644.00		25.00	10.00
3	Marriott, Barbara	M	4	672.00	21.00	28.50	
4	Sanders, Roberta	M	2	601.60	19.20		10.00
6	Sutton, Victor	S	1	432.00		16.00	

Instructions: 1. Prepare a payroll register similar to the illustration on page 447. The date of payment is June 1. Use the income tax withholding tables, pages 448 and 449. Deduct 6% of each employee's total earnings for FICA taxes.

2. Prepare a check for the total amount of the net pay. Make the check payable to *Payroll Account* and sign your name as treasurer of the company. The beginning check stub balance is $10,629.23.

3. Prepare payroll checks for Jerry Humes, Check No. 345, and Alberta Keystone, Check No. 347. Sign your name as treasurer of the company. Record the payroll check numbers in the payroll register.

CHALLENGE PROBLEM 22-C Figuring piecework wages

Introductory remarks. Production workers in factories are frequently paid on the basis of the number of units they produce. This is known as the piecework incentive wage plan. Most piecework wage plans include a guaranteed hourly rate to employees regardless of the number of units they produce. This guaranteed hourly rate is known as the base rate.

Time and motion study engineers usually determine the standard time required for producing a single unit. Assume, for example, time studies determine that one-fourth hour is the standard time required to produce a unit. Then the standard rate for an 8-hour day would be 32 units (8 hours ÷ ¼ hour = 32 units per day). If a worker's daily base pay is $44.80, the incentive rate per unit is $1.40 ($44.80 ÷ 32 units = $1.40 per unit). Therefore, the worker who produces 32 or fewer units per day is paid the base pay, $44.80 per day. However, each worker is paid an additional $1.40 for each unit over 32 produced each day.

Rivera Cabinet Company has nine employees. The employees work in three departments: Cutting, Assembly, and Finishing. Standard rates and incentive rates are as follows.

Department	Standard Rate Per Employee	Incentive Rate Per Unit
Cutting	32 units per day	$1.40
Assembly	24 units per day	2.10
Finishing	16 units per day	4.50

Each employee worked eight hours a day during the semimonthly pay period, May 1–15. Payroll records for May 1–15 show the data below.

Rivera Cabinet Company

Employee No.	Employee Name	Marital Status	No. of Allowances	Guaranteed Daily Rate	Units Produced Per Day, Pay Period May 1–15: 2	3	4	5	6	9	10	11	12	13
	Cutting Department													
C6	Baker, Deanna	S	1	$44.80	29	30	30	32	30	31	32	30	33	29
C2	Chiang, Lu	M	2	44.80	33	34	33	36	32	34	38	33	31	35
	Assembly Department													
A3	Coker, Harvey	M	3	50.40	24	24	25	23	23	26	25	24	24	23
A5	Fouracre, Louis	S	1	50.40	22	23	24	24	22	23	25	23	22	23
A1	Valdez, Maria	M	2	50.40	25	26	27	25	24	26	28	26	26	25
	Finishing Department													
F5	Hayes, Michael	M	4	72.00	16	16	15	18	16	17	15	16	17	16
F1	Lewis, Roy	M	2	72.00	17	18	17	20	16	16	17	17	18	16
F4	Rehl, Barbara	M	3	72.00	15	17	16	18	15	16	16	17	15	16
F7	Young, Steven	M	2	72.00	14	15	15	16	14	15	16	15	16	15

Instructions: Prepare a payroll register similar to the illustration, page 447. The Earnings column heading Incentive is used instead of Overtime. The date of payment is May 15. Use the income tax withholding tables, pages 448 and 449. Deduct 6% of each employee's total earnings for FICA taxes. None of the employees had Hospital Insurance or Other deductions.

23

Payroll Accounts, Taxes, and Reports

ENABLING PERFORMANCE TASKS

After studying Chapter 23, you will be able to:

a. Explain accounting principles and practices related to payroll accounts, tax reports, and payments.
b. Analyze payroll transactions.
c. Journalize a payroll in a cash payments journal.
d. Post a payroll entry from a cash payments journal.
e. Figure an employer's payroll taxes.
f. Journalize an employer's payroll taxes in a general journal.
g. Post an employer's payroll taxes entry from a general journal.
h. Prepare an Employer's Quarterly Federal Tax Return, Form 941.
i. Journalize payment of liabilities for withholding and payroll taxes in a cash payments journal.

Payroll information for each employee is recorded in a payroll register at the end of each pay period. A separate employee's earnings record is kept for each employee to record payroll information for all pay periods. These two business forms provide all the payroll information needed about individual employees. Therefore, separate payroll accounts for each employee are not kept in the general ledger. Accounts are kept in the general ledger to summarize total earnings and deductions for all employees. A summary of this payroll information is recorded in the accounting records by a journal entry.

RECORDING A PAYROLL IN A JOURNAL

A portion of the payroll register for Lin's Music Center for the semimonthly period ended February 15, is on the next page. The complete payroll register is in Chapter 22, page 447.

PAYROLL REGISTER

SEMIMONTHLY PERIOD ENDED *February 15, 1983* DATE OF PAYMENT *February 15, 1983*

	EMPL. NO.	EMPLOYEE'S NAME	MARITAL STATUS	NO. OF ALLOWANCES	EARNINGS			DEDUCTIONS					NET PAY	CK. NO.	
					REGULAR	OVERTIME	TOTAL	FEDERAL INCOME TAX	FICA TAX	HOSP. INS.	OTHER	TOTAL			
1	6	Allen, Don T.	M	3	484 00		484 00	42 50	29 04	35 00	UW 3 00	109 54	374 46	323	1
11	11	Walsh, Paul E.	S	1	82 50		82 50	Exempt	4 95			4 95	77 55	333	11
12		Totals			4194 00	33 38	4227 38	435 20	253 65	199 00	B 20 00 UW 8 00	915 85	3311 53		12
13															13

Payroll register

Analyzing payroll debits and credits

Column totals of a payroll register provide the debit and credit amounts needed to journalize a payroll. Lin's February 15 payroll is summarized in the T accounts below.

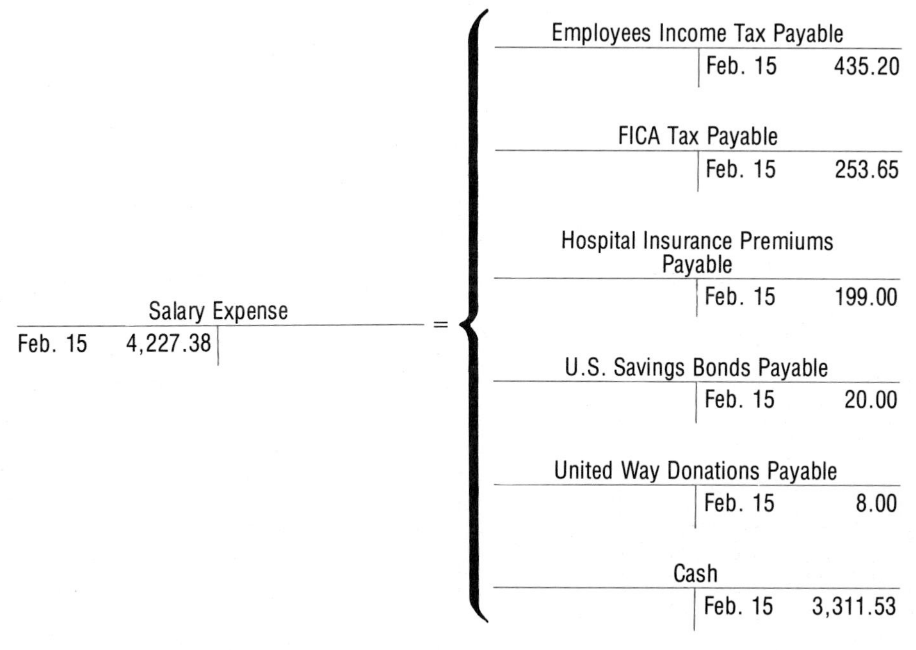

The total of the Total Earnings column, *$4,227.38*, is the salary expense for the period. Salary Expense is debited for this amount.

The total of the Federal Income Tax column, *$435.20*, is the amount withheld from employees' salaries for federal income tax. The amount withheld is a liability of the business until the tax is paid to the government. Employees Income Tax Payable is credited for $435.20 to record this liability.

The total of the FICA Tax column, *$253.65*, is the amount withheld from salaries of employees for FICA tax. The amount withheld is a liability of the business until the tax is paid to the government. FICA Tax Payable is credited for $253.65.

The total of the Hosp. Ins. column, *$199.00*, is the amount withheld from salaries for hospitalization insurance premiums. The amount withheld is a liability of the business until the premiums are paid to the insurance company. Hospital Insurance Premiums Payable is credited for $199.00 to record this liability.

The Other column of the deductions section may contain more than one total. In the payroll register, page 461, there are two types of other deductions. The $20.00 Other column total identified with the letter *B* is withheld to buy savings bonds for employees. The $8.00 total identified with the letters *UW* is withheld for employees' United Way pledges. Until these amounts have been paid by the employer, they are liabilities of the business. U.S. Savings Bonds Payable is credited for $20.00. United Way Donations Payable is credited for $8.00.

The total of the Net Pay column, *$3,311.53*, the net amount paid to employees, is credited to Cash.

Journalizing a payroll entry

A check for the amount of the total net pay is written on Lin's regular checking account. This amount is deposited in a special bank account for employee payroll checks. Only the check written for the total payroll is recorded in the cash payments journal. The entry made in the cash payments journal to record Lin's February 15 payroll is below.

CASH PAYMENTS JOURNAL PAGE 5

	DATE		ACCOUNT TITLE	CHECK NO.	POST. REF.	1 GENERAL DEBIT	2 GENERAL CREDIT	3 ACCOUNTS PAYABLE DEBIT	4 PURCHASES DISCOUNT CREDIT	5 CASH CREDIT	
1	1983 Feb.	15	Salary Expense	123		4227 38				3311 53	1
2			Employees Income Tax Pay.				435 20				2
3			FICA Tax Payable				253 65				3
4			Hospital Insur. Prem. Pay.				199 00				4
5			U.S. Savings Bonds Payable				20 00				5
6			United Way Donations Pay.				8 00				6
7											7
8											8
9											9
10											10

Entry to record a payroll

The source document for a payroll journal entry is the check stub. *(CONCEPT: Objective Evidence)* Salary Expense is debited for the total amount of the payroll, *$4,227.38*. *(CONCEPT: Historical Cost)* Cash is credited for the net amount paid to employees, *$3,311.53*. Five liability accounts are credited for the amounts deducted from employees' salaries. Two liability accounts are withheld taxes: Employees Income Tax Payable, *$435.20*, and FICA Tax Payable, *$253.65*. Three liabilities are other deductions: Hospital Insurance Premiums Payable, *$199.00*; U.S. Savings Bonds Payable, *$20.00*; and United Way Donations Payable, *$8.00*.

Posting a payroll entry

Amounts recorded in the General columns of a cash payments journal are posted individually to general ledger accounts. After the February 15 payroll entry is posted, the liability accounts and salary expense account appear as shown below.

General ledger accounts after payroll entry is posted

ACCOUNT Employees Income Tax Payable — ACCOUNT NO. 2103

DATE		ITEM	POST. REF.	DEBIT	CREDIT	BALANCE DEBIT	BALANCE CREDIT
	15		CP5		435 20		435 20

ACCOUNT FICA Tax Payable — ACCOUNT NO. 2105

DATE		ITEM	POST. REF.	DEBIT	CREDIT	BALANCE DEBIT	BALANCE CREDIT
	15		CP5		253 65		253 65

ACCOUNT Hospital Insurance Premiums Payable — ACCOUNT NO. 2109

DATE		ITEM	POST. REF.	DEBIT	CREDIT	BALANCE DEBIT	BALANCE CREDIT
	15		CP5		199 00		199 00

ACCOUNT U. S. Savings Bonds Payable — ACCOUNT NO. 2110

DATE		ITEM	POST. REF.	DEBIT	CREDIT	BALANCE DEBIT	BALANCE CREDIT
	15		CP5		20 00		60 00

ACCOUNT United Way Donations Payable — ACCOUNT NO. 2111

DATE		ITEM	POST. REF.	DEBIT	CREDIT	BALANCE DEBIT	BALANCE CREDIT
	15		CP5		8 00		16 00

ACCOUNT Salary Expense — ACCOUNT NO. 6112

DATE		ITEM	POST. REF.	DEBIT	CREDIT	BALANCE DEBIT	BALANCE CREDIT
1983 Feb.	15		CP5	4227 38		4227 38	

The credit to Cash, *$3,311.53*, is not posted separately to the cash account. The amount is included in the journal's Cash Credit column total that is posted at the end of the month.

RECORDING AN EMPLOYER'S PAYROLL TAXES

Employers must pay to the government the taxes withheld from employees' wages. In addition, employers must pay several payroll taxes of their own. An employer's payroll taxes are expenses of the business.

Figuring an employer's payroll taxes

There are three separate payroll taxes for most employers. These taxes are: (1) employer's FICA tax, (2) federal unemployment tax, and (3) state unemployment tax. An employer's payroll tax expenses are based on a percentage of employees' earnings.

Employer's FICA tax. An employer's FICA tax is based on the same rate and earnings as employees' FICA tax. (The rate used in this textbook is 6% on the first $20,000.00.)

Lin's withheld $253.65 in FICA tax from employees' wages for the pay period ended February 15, 1983. In effect, the employer pays the same FICA taxes as all employees. Therefore, Lin's FICA tax for the pay period ended February 15, 1983, is $253.65.

Federal unemployment tax. Federal unemployment insurance laws require that employers pay taxes for unemployment compensation. These tax funds are used to pay workers benefits for limited periods of unemployment and to administer the program.

The federal unemployment tax is 3.4% of wages paid. The tax applies to the first $6,000.00 paid each employee as wages during a calendar year. An employer generally can deduct from federal unemployment payments amounts paid into state unemployment funds. This deduction cannot be more than 2.7% of taxable wages. The effective federal unemployment tax rate in most states therefore is 0.7% on the first $6,000.00 earned by each employee. (Federal 3.4% — deductible for state 2.7% = 0.7%) All of the unemployment tax (3.4% on first $6,000.00) is paid by the employer.

In a few states however employees' earnings also are taxed for additional state unemployment programs.

No employee on Lin's payroll of February 15 had yet earned $6,000.00 in 1983. Thus, Lin's federal unemployment tax on total wages of $4,227.38 is 0.7% of this amount, or $29.59.

Tax rates for federal and state unemployment taxes at the time this textbook was written are used.

State unemployment tax. Most states require that employers pay unemployment tax of 2.7% on the first $6,000.00 earned by each employee. No employee on Lin's payroll of February 15 had yet earned $6,000.00. Thus, the state unemployment tax to be paid by Lin's is $114.14 (2.7% of $4,227.38 total wages).

Journalizing an employer's payroll taxes entry

Payroll taxes expense for each payroll is recorded when the payroll is recorded. Since the payroll taxes expense is recorded but not paid until later, the expenses are recorded in a general journal.

Lin's recorded the following payroll taxes expense on February 15, 1983.

February 15, 1983. Recorded payroll taxes expense for the semimonthly period ended February 15, 1983, $397.38. Memorandum No. 35.

The source document for an employer's payroll taxes journal entry is a memorandum. *(CONCEPT: Objective Evidence)* The entry to record employer's payroll taxes is analyzed in the T accounts at the right.

Payroll Taxes Expense is debited for $397.38 to show the increase in the balance of this expense account. Three liability accounts are credited to show the increase in these liability accounts. FICA Tax Payable is credited for $253.65. Unemployment Tax Payable — Federal is credited for $29.59. Unemployment Tax Payable — State is credited for $114.14.

GENERAL LEDGER

Payroll Taxes Expense	
397.38	

FICA Tax Payable	
	253.65

Unemployment Tax Payable — Federal	
	29.59

Unemployment Tax Payable — State	
	114.14

Lin's three payroll tax expenses are recorded in the combined entry below.

GENERAL JOURNAL — PAGE 3

	DATE		ACCOUNT TITLE	POST. REF.	DEBIT	CREDIT	
1	1983 Feb.	15	Payroll Taxes Expense		397 38		1
2			FICA Tax Payable			253 65	2
3			Unemploy. Tax Pay. - Fed.			29 59	3
4			Unemploy. Tax Pay. - State			114 14	4
5			Memorandum No. 35.				5
6							6
7							7

Combined entry for employer's payroll taxes

Payroll Taxes Expense is debited for $397.38 in the Debit column. FICA Tax Payable is credited for $253.65 in the Credit column. Unemployment Tax Payable — Federal is credited for $29.59 in the Credit column. Unemployment Tax Payable — State is credited for $114.14 in the Credit column.

Posting an employer's payroll taxes entry

After the entry for the employer's payroll taxes is posted, the four accounts involved appear as shown below.

ACCOUNT *FICA Tax Payable* ACCOUNT NO. *2105*

DATE		ITEM	POST. REF.	DEBIT	CREDIT	BALANCE DEBIT	BALANCE CREDIT
	15		CP5		253 65		253 65
	15		G3		253 65		507 30

ACCOUNT *Unemployment Tax Payable—Federal* ACCOUNT NO. *2107*

DATE		ITEM	POST. REF.	DEBIT	CREDIT	BALANCE DEBIT	BALANCE CREDIT
	15		G3		29 59		86 70

ACCOUNT *Unemployment Tax Payable—State* ACCOUNT NO. *2108*

DATE		ITEM	POST. REF.	DEBIT	CREDIT	BALANCE DEBIT	BALANCE CREDIT
	15		G3		114 14		334 43

ACCOUNT *Payroll Taxes Expense* ACCOUNT NO. *6110*

DATE		ITEM	POST. REF.	DEBIT	CREDIT	BALANCE DEBIT	BALANCE CREDIT
1983 Feb.	15		G3	397 38		397 38	

The $397.38 debit to Payroll Taxes Expense is the employer's total payroll taxes expense. FICA Tax Payable is credited for $253.65. Unemployment Tax Payable — Federal is credited for $29.59. Unemployment Tax Payable — State is credited for $114.14.

The FICA tax payable account has two credits. The first credit, $253.65, is the FICA tax withheld from *employees'* wages for the semimonthly period ended February 15. This amount was posted from the entry that recorded the payroll, page 462. The second credit, $253.65, is the *employer's* liability for FICA tax. This amount was posted from the entry that recorded the employer's share of liability for FICA tax, page 465.

REPORTING WITHHOLDING AND PAYROLL TAXES

Each employer is required by law to report periodically on withholding taxes and payroll taxes. Some reports are submitted quarterly and others are submitted annually.

Employer's quarterly federal tax return

Each employer must file a quarterly federal tax return, Form 941, on employee withholding taxes with the Internal Revenue Service. Lin's Form 941 for the calendar quarter ended March 31, 1983, is below. Data needed to prepare Form 941 are obtained from employees' earnings records.

Form 941, Employer's Quarterly Federal Tax Return

Form **941** — Department of the Treasury, Internal Revenue Service

Employer's Quarterly Federal Tax Return

Your name, address, employer identification number, and calendar quarter of return. (If not correct, please change)

Name (as distinguished from trade name): Lin's Music Center — Date quarter ended: March 31, 1983
Trade name, if any — Employer identification number: 31-0318521
Address and ZIP code: 2400 Fargo Lane, Garland, Texas 75041-2579

T / FF / FD / FP / I / T

If address is different from prior return, check here ▶ ☐

Line	Item	Amount
1	Number of employees (except household) employed in the pay period that includes March 12th (complete for first quarter only)	11
2	Total wages and tips subject to withholding, plus other compensation	24,853 00
3	Total income tax withheld from wages, tips, annuities, gambling, etc.	2,559 07
4	Adjustment of withheld income tax for preceding quarters of calendar year	
5	Adjusted total of income tax withheld	2,559 07
6	Taxable FICA wages paid $24,853.00 multiplied by 12.0% = TAX	2,982 36
7	Taxable tips reported $ multiplied by 6.0% = TAX	none
8	Total FICA taxes (add lines 6 and 7)	2,982 36
9	Adjustment of FICA taxes (see instructions)	none
10	Adjusted total of FICA taxes	2,982 36
11	Total taxes (add lines 5 and 10)	5,541 43
12	Advance earned income credit (EIC) payments, if any (see instructions)	none
13	Net taxes (subtract line 12 from line 11)	5,541 43

Record of Federal Tax Deposits (See instructions on page 4)

Deposit period ending:	I. Tax liability for period	II. Date of deposit	III. Amount deposited
Overpayment from previous quarter			
First month of quarter — 1st through 7th day			
8th through 15th day			
16th through 22d day			
23d through last day			
A First month total	1,819.46	2-15-83	1,819.46
Second month of quarter — 1st through 7th day			
8th through 15th day			
16th through 22d day			
23d through last day			
B Second month total	1,746.64	3-15-83	1,746.64
Third month of quarter — 1st through 7th day			
8th through 15th day			
16th through 22d day			
23d through last day			
C Third month total	1,975.33	4-15-83	1,975.33
D Total for quarter (add items A, B, and C)	5,541.43		5,541.43
E Final deposit made for quarter. (Enter zero if the final deposit made for the quarter is included in item D)			0.00

14 Total deposits for quarter (including final deposit made for quarter) and overpayment from previous quarter. (See instructions for deposit requirements on page 4.) — 5,541 43

Note: *If undeposited taxes at the end of the quarter are $200 or more, deposit the full amount with an authorized financial institution or a Federal Reserve bank according to the instructions on the back of the Federal Tax Deposit Form 501. Enter this deposit in the Record of Federal Tax Deposits and include it on line 14.*

15 Undeposited taxes due (subtract line 14 from line 13—this should be less than $200). Pay to Internal Revenue Service and enter here — none

16 If line 14 is more than line 13, enter overpayment here ▶ $ and check if to be: ☐ Applied to next return, or ☐ Refunded.

17 Number of Forms W-4 enclosed. Do not send originals. (See General and Specific Instructions.)

18 If you are not liable for returns in the future, write "FINAL" (see instructions) ▶ Date final wages paid ▶

Under penalties of perjury, I declare that I have examined this return, including accompanying schedules and statements, and to the best of my knowledge and belief it is true, correct, and complete.

Date ▶ April 30, 1983 Signature ▶ Carl H. Poark Title ▶ Manager

Form 941 must be filed by the last day of the month following the end of a calendar quarter. If a company owes less than $200.00 for a quarter, payment may be sent with the report. If a company owes $200.00 or more in any month, periodic deposits of the amount due must be made.

Employer's annual report to employees of taxes withheld

Each employer who withholds income tax and FICA tax from employees' wages must furnish each employee with an annual statement. This statement shows an employee's total year's earnings and the amounts withheld for taxes. This report is prepared on the Internal Revenue Service's Form W-2.

Employers are required to furnish Form W-2 to each employee for the previous calendar year's earnings by January 31. If an employee ends employment before December 31, Form W-2 must be furnished within 30 days of employment termination.

Form W-2 prepared by Lin's for Joann D. Boyd for the year 1983 is below.

1 Control number: 222

2 Employer's name, address, and ZIP code
Lin's Music Center
2400 Fargo Lane
Garland, TX 75041-2579

3 Employer's identification number: 31-0318521

4 Employer's State number

5 Stat. employee ☐ Deceased ☐ Pension plan ☐ Legal rep. ☐ 942 emp. ☐ Subtotal ☐ Correction ☐ Void ☐

6

7 Advance EIC payment

8 Employee's social security number: 450-59-8679

9 Federal income tax withheld: 1,690.65

10 Wages, tips, other compensation: 12,265.00

11 FICA tax withheld: 735.90

12 Employee's name, address, and ZIP code
Joann D. Boyd
2586 Shady Brook Drive
Garland, TX 75041-2787

13 FICA wages: 12,265.00

14 FICA tips

16 Employer's use

Form **W-2 Wage and Tax Statement 1983** Copy B To be filed with employee's FEDERAL tax return. This information is being furnished to the Internal Revenue Service. Department of the Treasury Internal Revenue Service

Form W-2, Wage and Tax Statement

Four copies (A to D) of Form W-2 are prepared for each employee. Copies B and C are given to the employee. The employee attaches Copy B to a personal federal income tax return and keeps Copy C for a personal record. The employer sends Copy A to the federal government and keeps Copy D for the business' records.

Businesses in states with state income tax also must prepare Copies 1 and 2 of Form W-2. Copy 2 is given to the employee. The employee attaches Copy 2 to a personal state income tax return. The employer sends Copy 1 to the state government.

Employer's annual transmittal of income and tax statements

Form W-3, Transmittal of Income and Tax Statements, is sent to the Internal Revenue Service by February 28 each year. Attached to Form W-3 is Copy A of the W-2 form for each employee.

Employers may report withholding tax information on magnetic tape rather than send the actual W-3 and W-2 forms.

The Form W-3 prepared by Lin's is below.

1 Control number: 333

Kind of Tax Statements Transmitted ☐

2 941/941E ☐ | Military ☐ | 943 ☐ | 3 W-2 ☒ | 4 Original ☒ | 5 With TIN ☒

CT-1 ☐ | 942 ☐ | Section 218 ☐ | W-2P ☐ | Corrected ☐ | Without TIN ☐

6 State SSA number

7 Advance EIC payments

8 Number of statements attached: 11

9 Federal income tax: 12,107.86

10 Wages, tips, and other compensation: 117,552.00

11 FICA tax withheld: 7,029.12

12 Employer's State number

13 FICA wages: 117,152.00

14 FICA tips

15 Employer's identification number: 31-0318521

16 Establishment number

17 Employer's name: Lin's Music Center

18 Gross annuity, pension, retired pay, or IRA payment

2400 Fargo Lane
Garland, TX 75041-2579

20 Taxable amount

19 Employer's address and ZIP code (If available, place label over boxes 15, 17, and 19.)

Under penalties of perjury, I declare that I have examined this return, including accompanying documents, and to the best of my knowledge and belief, it is true, correct, and complete. In the case of documents without recipients' identifying numbers, I have complied with the requirements of the law by requesting such numbers from the recipients, but did not receive them.

Signature ► Carl H. Roark Title ► Manager Date ► 2/14/84

Form **W-3 Transmittal of Income and Tax Statements 1983** Department of the Treasury Internal Revenue Service

Form W-3, Transmittal of Income and Tax Statements

Employer's federal and state unemployment tax returns

Each employer must file unemployment tax returns with the federal and state governments. Form 940, Employer's Annual Federal Unemployment Tax Return is filed annually. Form 940 must be filed by January 31 for the previous year's tax. State requirements vary for reporting state unemployment tax. In general, employers are required to file state unemployment tax returns quarterly.

PAYING WITHHOLDING AND PAYROLL TAXES

Employers must pay to the federal government at least quarterly, the income tax and FICA tax withheld from employees' wages. In addition, employer's payroll taxes generally must be paid at least quarterly.

Paying the liability for employees' income tax and for FICA tax

Employees' withheld income tax, employees' FICA tax, and employer's FICA tax are paid periodically in a combined payment. The frequency of payment is determined by the amount owed. If the amount is less than $200.00 a quarter, employers send payment with the quarterly federal tax return, Form 941. However, if an employer owes between $200.00 and $2,000.00 by the end of any month, monthly payments are required. The monthly payments are made by the 15th of the following month. Employers who owe $2,000.00 or more must make payments four times a month.

Tax payments are deposited in banks authorized to accept these payments or in a Federal Reserve bank. A deposit is recorded on Form 501 which is forwarded to a bank with the payment.

In February, Lin's withheld from its employees' salaries $806.32 for federal income taxes. The liability for FICA tax for February is $940.32. This amount includes both the employer's share and the amounts withheld from employees. The total FICA tax and income tax for February is $1,746.64. Lin's federal tax deposit is sent with Form 501 on March 15 as shown below.

Form 501, Federal Tax Deposit — Withheld Income and FICA Taxes

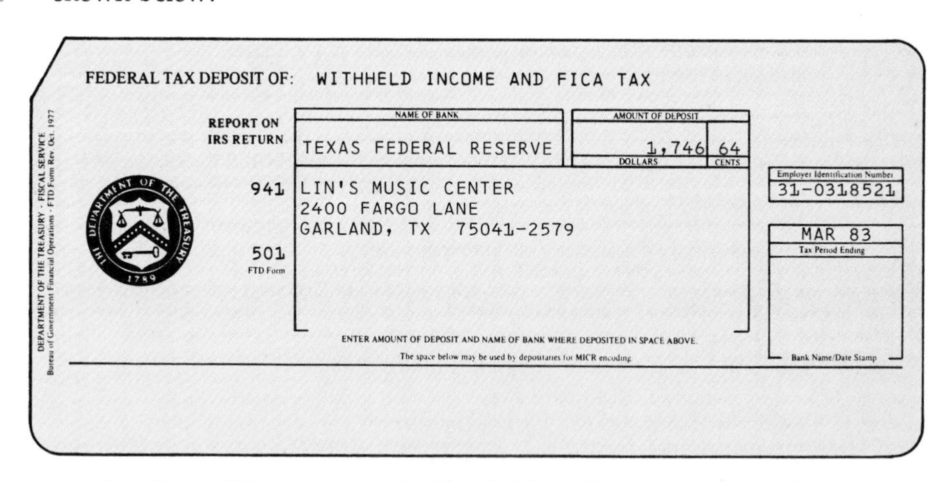
FEDERAL TAX DEPOSIT OF: WITHHELD INCOME AND FICA TAX

REPORT ON IRS RETURN

NAME OF BANK: TEXAS FEDERAL RESERVE

AMOUNT OF DEPOSIT: 1,746 DOLLARS 64 CENTS

941

LIN'S MUSIC CENTER
2400 FARGO LANE
GARLAND, TX 75041-2579

501 FTD Form

Employer Identification Number: 31-0318521

MAR 83 Tax Period Ending

ENTER AMOUNT OF DEPOSIT AND NAME OF BANK WHERE DEPOSITED IN SPACE ABOVE.

The space below may be used by depositaries for MICR encoding

Bank Name/Date Stamp

DEPARTMENT OF THE TREASURY · FISCAL SERVICE · FTD Form Rev. Oct. 1977
Bureau of Government Financial Operations

After Form 501 is prepared, Check No. 223 is issued for the amount owed, $1,746.64.

GENERAL LEDGER

Employees Income Tax Payable	
806.32	

FICA Tax Payable	
940.32	

Cash	
	1,746.64

March 15, 1983. Paid liability for employees' income tax and for FICA tax, $1,746.64. Check No. 223.

The source document for this transaction is a check stub. *(CONCEPT: Objective Evidence)* The two liability accounts are reduced by this transaction. Therefore, Employees Income Tax Payable is debited for $806.32. FICA Tax Payable is debited for $940.32. The balance of the asset account Cash is decreased by a credit for the total payment, $1,746.64.

Payment of these liabilities is journalized in the cash payments journal below.

CASH PAYMENTS JOURNAL PAGE 8

	DATE	ACCOUNT TITLE	CHECK NO.	POST. REF.	1 GENERAL DEBIT	2 GENERAL CREDIT	3 ACCOUNTS PAYABLE DEBIT	4 PURCHASES DISCOUNT CREDIT	5 CASH CREDIT	
7	15	Employees Income Tax Pay.	223		806 32				1746 64	7
8		FICA Tax Payable			940 32					8
9										9
10										10
11										11
12										12

Employees Income Tax Payable is debited for $806.32 in the General Debit column. FICA Tax Payable is debited for $940.32 in the General Debit column. Cash is credited for the total amount paid, $1,746.64, in the Cash Credit column.

Entry to record payment of liability for employees' income tax and for FICA tax

Paying the liability for federal unemployment tax

Federal unemployment tax is payable annually by January 31 of the following year if the annual tax is $100.00 or less. If the annual tax is over $100.00, quarterly payments are required. No payment is required until the calendar quarter in which the accumulated tax exceeds $100.00.

Lin's federal unemployment tax at the end of March is $173.97. Therefore, a quarterly payment is required. A payment is made each quarter but no report is due until the end of the year. The payment for federal unemployment tax is deposited in designated banks. The deposit for federal unemployment tax is similar to the one required for income tax and FICA tax. Form 508 accompanies the unemployment tax deposit. Lin's Form 508 for the first quarter is below.

Form 508, Federal Tax Deposit — Unemployment Taxes

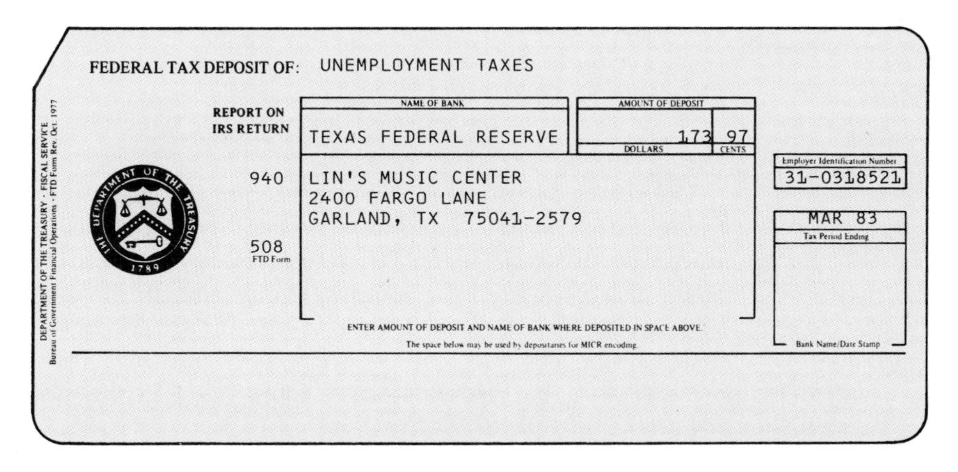

FEDERAL TAX DEPOSIT OF: UNEMPLOYMENT TAXES

REPORT ON IRS RETURN

NAME OF BANK: TEXAS FEDERAL RESERVE

AMOUNT OF DEPOSIT: 173 97 (DOLLARS / CENTS)

940

LIN'S MUSIC CENTER
2400 FARGO LANE
GARLAND, TX 75041-2579

508 FTD Form

Employer Identification Number: 31-0318521

MAR 83 — Tax Period Ending

ENTER AMOUNT OF DEPOSIT AND NAME OF BANK WHERE DEPOSITED IN SPACE ABOVE.
The space below may be used by depositaries for MICR encoding.

Bank Name/Date Stamp

DEPARTMENT OF THE TREASURY - FISCAL SERVICE
Bureau of Government Financial Operations - FTD Form Rev. Oct. 1977

THE DEPARTMENT OF THE TREASURY 1789

After Form 508 is prepared, Check No. 282 is issued for the amount of the payment, $173.97.

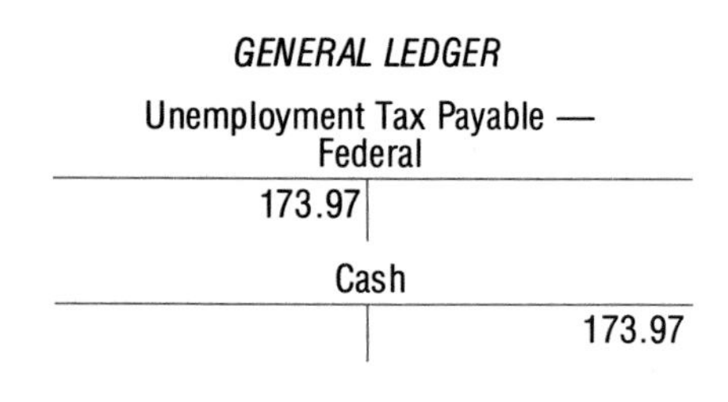

April 30, 1983. Paid liability for first quarter federal unemployment tax, $173.97. Check No. 282.

The source document for this transaction is a check stub. *(CONCEPT: Objective Evidence)* The liability account is reduced by this transaction. Therefore, Unemployment Tax Payable — Federal is debited for $173.97. The balance of the asset account Cash is decreased by a credit for the payment, $173.97.

Payment for Unemployment Tax Payable — Federal is journalized in the cash payments journal below.

CASH PAYMENTS JOURNAL — PAGE 12

	DATE	ACCOUNT TITLE	CHECK NO.	POST. REF.	1 GENERAL DEBIT	2 GENERAL CREDIT	3 ACCOUNTS PAYABLE DEBIT	4 PURCHASES DISCOUNT CREDIT	5 CASH CREDIT	
4	30	Unemployment Tax Pay. - Fed.	282		173 97				173 97	4
5										5

Entry to record payment of liability for federal unemployment tax

Unemployment Tax Payable — Federal is debited for $173.97 in the General Debit column. Cash is credited for $173.97 in the Cash Credit column.

Paying the liability for state unemployment tax

State requirements vary for reporting and paying state unemployment taxes. The forms used for reporting this tax also vary from state to state. In general, employers are required to pay the state unemployment tax during the month following each calendar quarter.

Lin's state unemployment tax based on the payrolls of the first quarter of 1983 is $671.03. On April 30, Check No. 283 is issued for the amount of the payment.

GENERAL LEDGER

Unemployment Tax Payable — State

Debit	Credit
671.03	

Cash

Debit	Credit
	671.03

April 30, 1983. Paid liability for first quarter state unemployment tax, $671.03. Check No. 283.

The source document for this transaction is a check stub. *(CONCEPT: Objective Evidence)* The liability account is reduced by this transaction. Therefore, Unemployment Tax Payable — State is debited for $671.03. The balance of the asset account Cash is decreased by a credit for the payment, $671.03.

Payment for Unemployment Tax Payable — State is journalized in the cash payments journal on the next page.

CASH PAYMENTS JOURNAL PAGE 12

	DATE	ACCOUNT TITLE	CHECK No.	POST. REF.	GENERAL DEBIT (1)	GENERAL CREDIT (2)	ACCOUNTS PAYABLE DEBIT (3)	PURCHASES DISCOUNT CREDIT (4)	CASH CREDIT (5)	
5	30	Unemployment Tax Pay. - State	283		671 03				671 03	5
6										6
7										7
8										8

Unemployment Tax Payable — State is debited for $671.03 in the General Debit column. Cash is credited for $671.03 in the Cash Credit column.

Entry to record payment of liability for state unemployment tax

QUESTIONS FOR INDIVIDUAL STUDY

1. Total earnings of Lin's employees, as illustrated in the payroll register on page 461, amounted to $4,227.38. However, the total amount actually paid to the employees was $3,311.53. Why is there a difference between these two amounts?
2. What is the source document for journalizing a payroll entry?
3. What accounts does Lin's debit and credit to record a payroll?
4. What are the three payroll taxes paid by most employers?
5. How does the employer's FICA tax compare in amount with the employees' FICA tax?
6. What accounts are debited and credited to record an employer's payroll taxes?
7. Where are the data obtained that are needed to prepare a quarterly federal tax return, Form 941?
8. When is the employer's quarterly federal tax return filed?
9. Who receives completed W-2 forms, Wage and Tax Statement?
10. What information is reported on a W-2 form?
11. What should an employee do with Copies B and C of Form W-2, Wage and Tax Statement, received from an employer?
12. An employer has the following income tax withholdings and FICA tax liabilities: January, $1,389.00; February, $1,234.00; and March, $1,478.00. When must these tax liabilities be paid?
13. Under what circumstances should Form 501 be used?
14. What accounts are debited and credited to record payment of an employer's liability for employees' income tax and for FICA tax?
15. Under what circumstances should a Form 508 be used?
16. What accounts are debited and credited to record payment of an employer's liability for federal unemployment tax?
17. What accounts are debited and credited to record payment of an employer's liability for state unemployment tax?

CASES FOR MANAGEMENT DECISION

CASE 1 Carsberg Corporation had a total payroll expense for the month of August of $12,000.00. Mr. Howard Daily, the accounting clerk, figured the August payroll taxes as $1,128.00. He figured the taxes as follows: FICA tax — $12,000.00 × 6% = $720.00; total unemployment taxes — $12,000.00 × 3.4% = $408.00. Miss Jane Horner, the accountant, stated that the company's total payroll taxes for

August were $796.00. What is the most likely reason for the difference between Mr. Daily's and Miss Horner's figures for payroll taxes? Explain.

CASE 2 A Woodlawn Company accounting clerk told the manager that the company should file Form 941 each quarter. The clerk also stated that payment for each quarter's income tax and FICA tax liability should accompany Form 501. Taxes withheld from employees and the employer's FICA tax for the first quarter amount to $1,416.00. To check the accuracy of the accounting clerk's information, the manager asks you when Form 941 should be filed. The manager also asks when the liability for employees' income tax and for FICA tax should be paid. Is the accounting clerk correct? Explain.

DRILL FOR UNDERSTANDING

DRILL 23-D 1 Analyzing payroll transactions

Instructions: 1. Open the following T accounts for each business. Cash, Employees Income Tax Payable, FICA Tax Payable, Unemployment Tax Payable — Federal, Unemployment Tax Payable — State, Payroll Taxes Expense, Salary Expense.

Business	Total Earnings	Federal Income Tax Withheld	Employees' FICA Tax	Employer's FICA Tax	Federal Unemployment Tax	State Unemployment Tax
A	$4,000.00	$ 440.00	$240.00	$240.00	$28.00	$108.00
B	2,860.00	314.00	171.60	171.60	20.02	77.22
C	7,400.00	962.00	444.00	444.00	51.80	199.80
D	8,600.00	1,118.00	(Figure from rates given in Chapter 23)			

2. Use T accounts to analyze the payroll entries for each business.
(a) Entry to record payroll.
(b) Entry to record employer's payroll taxes.

APPLICATION PROBLEMS

PROBLEM 23-1 Journalizing and posting semimonthly payrolls

McKnight's payroll register totals for two semimonthly pay periods, April 1–15 and April 16–30, are below.

Pay period April 1–15

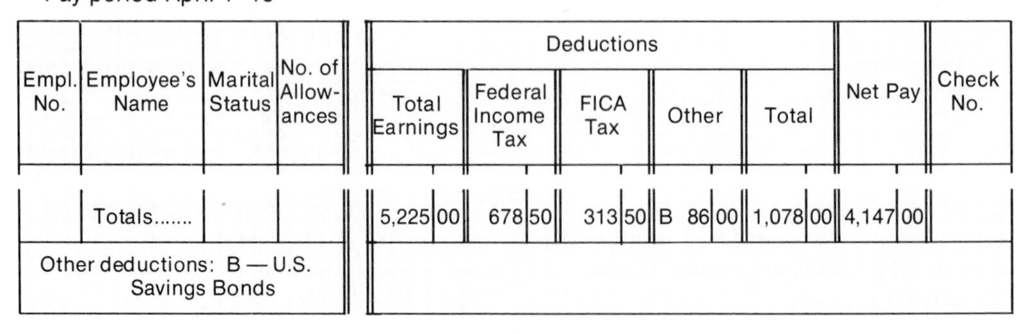

Empl. No.	Employee's Name	Marital Status	No. of Allowances	Total Earnings	Deductions: Federal Income Tax	Deductions: FICA Tax	Deductions: Other	Deductions: Total	Net Pay	Check No.
	Totals.......			5,225 00	678 50	313 50	B 86 00	1,078 00	4,147 00	

Other deductions: B — U.S. Savings Bonds

Pay period April 16–30

Empl. No.	Employee's Name	Marital Status	No. of Allow-ances	Deductions						Net Pay	Check No.
				Total Earnings	Federal Income Tax	FICA Tax	Other	Total			
	Totals.......			4,679 00	586 40	280 74	B 69 00	936 14		3,742 86	
Other deductions: B — U.S. Savings Bonds											

Instructions: 1. Record the two payrolls and withholdings on page 7 of a cash payments journal. The first payroll was paid by Check No. 536 on April 16 of the current year. The second payroll was paid by Check No. 583 on May 1 of the current year.

2. Post the individual items recorded in the cash payments journal's General Debit and Credit columns. The general ledger accounts are given in the working papers. On April 15, all account balances are zero.

Account Title	Acct. No.	Account Title	Acct. No.
Employees Income Tax Payable	2103	U.S. Savings Bonds Payable	2110
FICA Tax Payable	2105	Salary Expense	6111

The general ledger accounts prepared in Problem 23-1 are needed to complete Problem 23-2.

PROBLEM 23-2 Figuring, recording, and posting employer's payroll taxes

The general ledger accounts prepared in Problem 23-1 are needed to complete Problem 23-2.

McKnight's semimonthly payroll register totals are shown in Problem 23-1, pages 474 and 475. Employer tax rates are: FICA, 6%; federal unemployment, 0.7%; state unemployment, 2.7%.

Instructions: 1. Figure the employer's tax amounts for each pay period.

2. Record the employer's payroll taxes on page 3 of a general journal. Use the dates April 16 and May 1 of the current year. The source documents are Memorandum No. 83 and Memorandum No. 89.

3. Post the items recorded in the general journal. Use the accounts prepared in Problem 23-1 and the additional accounts given in the working papers. The additional accounts have zero balances on April 15.

Account Title	Acct. No.
Unemployment Tax Payable — Federal	2107
Unemployment Tax Payable — State	2108
Payroll Taxes Expense	6109

PROBLEM 23-3 Reporting employer's quarterly withholding and payroll taxes

Payroll data for Diaz Pipe Supply are shown on the next page for the first quarter of the current year.

Month	Total Wages	Federal Income Tax Withheld	Total FICA Tax Liability
January	$ 6,560.00	$ 675.60	$ 787.20
February	5,964.00	614.20	715.68
March	7,356.00	757.40	882.72
Total for Quarter	$19,880.00	$2,047.20	$2,385.60

Additional data are below.

a. Company address: 1540 Dawn Road, Tampa, Florida 33602-3950
b. Employer identification number: 38-0568292
c. Number of employees: 8
d. Federal tax deposits have been made on February 15, March 15, and April 15.

Instructions: Prepare a Form 941, Employer's Quarterly Federal Tax Return, for Diaz Pipe Supply. The return is for the first quarter of the current year. Use the date April 22. Sign your name as manager of the company.

PROBLEM 23-4 Figuring and recording withholding and payroll taxes

Payroll data for Wig Imports for the first quarter of the current year are below.

Period	Total Wages	Federal Income Tax Withheld
March	$ 7,052.00	$725.76
First Quarter	22,368.00	——

In addition, total wages are subject to 6% employee's and 6% employer's FICA tax. Federal unemployment tax rate is 0.7% and state unemployment tax rate is 2.7% on total wages. The appropriate withholding and payroll tax liabilities have been recorded in the accounts below.

Account Title	Acct. No.	Account Title	Acct. No.
Employees Income Tax Payable	2103	Unemployment Tax Payable — Federal	2107
FICA Tax Payable	2105	Unemployment Tax Payable — State	2108

Instructions: 1. Figure the appropriate liability amounts of employee federal income taxes withheld and FICA taxes for March. Record the payment of these two liabilities on page 8 of a cash payments journal. The taxes were paid by Check No. 423 on April 15 of the current year.

2. Figure the appropriate federal unemployment liability for the first quarter. Record payment of this liability on page 9 of a cash payments journal. The tax was paid by Check No. 458 on April 30 of the current year.

3. Figure the appropriate state unemployment liability for the first quarter. Record payment of this liability on page 9 of a cash payments journal. The tax was paid by Check No. 459 on April 30 of the current year.

ENRICHMENT PROBLEMS

MASTERY PROBLEM 23-M Recording and posting payroll transactions

A-1 Garden Supply completed the payroll transactions given below during the period January 1 to February 15. Payroll tax rates are: FICA, 6%; federal unemployment, 0.7%;

state unemployment, 2.7%. The company buys U.S. Savings Bonds for employees as accumulated withholdings reach the necessary amount for each employee.

The ledger accounts are given in the working papers. The balances are recorded as of January 1 of the current year.

Account Title	Acct. No.	January 1 Balance
Employees Income Tax Payable	2103	$779.00
FICA Tax Payable	2105	671.20
Unemployment Tax Payable — Federal	2107	117.40
Unemployment Tax Payable — State	2108	452.80
U.S. Savings Bonds Payable	2110	280.00
Payroll Taxes Expense	6109	—
Salary Expense	6111	—

Instructions: 1. Record the selected transactions given below. Use page 3 of a cash payments journal and page 2 of a general journal. Source documents are abbreviated as check, C, and memorandum, M.

Jan. 15. Paid semimonthly payroll, $3,120.00 (less deductions: employees' income tax, $343.20; FICA tax, $187.20; U.S. Savings Bonds, $84.00). C52.
15. Recorded the employer's payroll tax liabilities. M11.
15. Paid deposit for December payroll liabilities (employees' income tax and FICA tax), $1,450.20. C53.
15. Bought 10 U.S. Savings Bonds at $25.00 each for employees, $250.00. C54.
31. Paid semimonthly payroll, $3,100.00 (less deductions: employees' income tax, $341.00; FICA tax, $186.00; U.S. Savings Bonds, $96.00). C73.
31. Recorded the employer's payroll tax liabilities. M14.
31. Paid federal unemployment tax owed for the quarter ended December 31, $117.40. C74.
31. Paid state unemployment tax owed for the quarter ended December 31, $452.80. C75.

Posting. Post the items that are to be posted individually.

Feb. 15. Paid semimonthly payroll, $3,160.00 (less deductions: employees' income tax, $347.60; FICA tax, $189.60; U.S. Savings Bonds, $96.00). C96.
15. Recorded the employer's payroll tax liabilities. M17.
15. Bought 8 U.S. Savings Bonds at $25.00 each for employees, $200.00. C97.
15. Paid deposit for January payroll liabilities (employees' income tax and FICA tax), $1,430.60. C98.

Instructions: 2. Prove the cash payments journal.

3. Post the general journal entries. Post the individual items recorded in the General Debit and Credit columns of the cash payments journal.

CHALLENGE PROBLEM 23-C Recording and posting payroll transactions

Valley Sporting Goods completed the payroll transactions given below during the period January 1 to April 15. Payroll tax rates are: FICA, 6%; federal unemployment, 0.7%; and state unemployment, 2.7%. The company buys U.S. Savings Bonds for employees as accumulated withholdings for each employee reach the necessary amounts.

The ledger accounts are given in the working papers. The balances are recorded as of January 1 of the current year.

Account Title	Acct. No.	January 1 Balance
Employees Income Tax Payable	2103	$702.90
FICA Tax Payable	2105	766.80
Unemployment Tax Payable — Federal	2107	134.20
Unemployment Tax Payable — State	2108	517.60
U.S. Savings Bonds Payable	2110	375.00
Payroll Taxes Expense	6109	—
Salary Expense	6111	—

Instructions: 1. Record the selected transactions below. Use pages 4 and 5 of a cash payments journal and page 2 of a general journal. Source documents are abbreviated as check, C, and memorandum, M.

Jan. 2. Bought U.S Savings Bonds for employees (15 bonds at $25.00 each), $375.00. C58.
15. Paid deposit for December payroll liabilities (employees' income tax and FICA tax). C68.
15. Paid federal unemployment tax for the quarter ended December 31, $134.20. C69.
15. Paid state unemployment tax for the quarter ended December 31, $517.60. C70.
31. Paid monthly payroll, $7,180.00 (less deductions: employees' income tax, $789.80; FICA tax, $430.80; U.S. Savings Bonds, $375.00). C83.
31. Recorded the employer's payroll tax liabilities. M31.
Posting. Post the items that are to be posted individually.

Feb. 1. Bought U.S. Savings Bonds for employees, $375.00. C86.
15. Paid deposit for January payroll liabilities (employees' income tax and FICA tax). C93.
28. Paid monthly payroll, $7,120.00 (less deductions: employees' income tax, $783.20; FICA tax, $427.20; U.S. Savings Bonds, $375.00). C113.
28. Recorded the employer's payroll tax liabilities. M34.
Posting. Post the items that are to be posted individually.

Mar. 1. Bought U.S. Savings Bonds for employees, $375.00. C122.
15. Paid deposit for February payroll liabilities (employees' income tax and FICA tax). C132.
31. Paid monthly payroll, $7,280.00 (less deductions: employees' income tax, $800.80; FICA tax, $436.80; U.S. Savings Bonds, $375.00). C159.
31. Recorded the employer's payroll tax liabilities. M39.
Posting. Post the items that are to be posted individually.

Apr. 1. Bought U.S. Savings Bonds for employees, $375.00. C163.
15. Paid deposit for March payroll liabilities (employees' income tax and FICA tax). C178.
30. Paid federal unemployment tax owed for the quarter ended March 31. C228.
30. Paid state unemployment tax owed for the quarter ended March 31. C229.

Instructions: 2. Prove the cash payments journal.

3. Post the general journal items. Post the individual items recorded in the General Debit and Credit columns of the cash payments journal.

Reinforcement Activity 4

PART A

An Accounting Cycle for a Corporation Using Special Journals

This activity is planned to reinforce learnings from Part 5, Chapters 20 to 27. A complete accounting cycle is covered for a business organized as a corporation. The general ledger account balances of Electronic Emporium now include transactions from the first eleven months of the fiscal year ended December 31. Reinforcement Activity 4 is organized in two parts. Part A includes learnings from Chapters 20 to 23. Part B, page 562, includes learnings from Chapters 24 to 27.

ELECTRONIC EMPORIUM

Electronic Emporium is a corporation that sells stereophonic and high fidelity equipment and supplies. The business is located in a shopping center and is open Monday through Saturday. Space for the business is rented. However, the corporation owns the office and sales equipment in the store.

Chart of accounts

Electronic Emporium uses the chart of accounts on the next page.

Journals and ledgers

Electronic Emporium uses the journals and ledgers listed below. The journals and ledgers are similar to those illustrated on the textbook pages given.

Journals and Ledgers	Illustrated
Sales journal	page 418
Purchases journal	page 395
General journal	page 406
Cash receipts journal	page 422
Cash payments journal	page 398
Accounts receivable ledger	page 423
Accounts payable ledger	page 396
General ledger	page 397

ELECTRONIC EMPORIUM
Chart of Accounts

Balance Sheet Accounts

(1) ASSETS	Account Number
11 Current Assets	
Cash	1101
Notes Receivable	1102
Accounts Receivable	1103
Allowance for Uncollectible Accounts	1103.1
Merchandise Inventory	1104
Supplies	1105
Prepaid Insurance	1106
12 Plant Assets	
Office Equipment	1201
Accumulated Depreciation — Office Equipment	1201.1
Store Equipment	1202
Accumulated Depreciation — Store Equipment	1202.1
(2) LIABILITIES	
21 Current Liabilities	
Notes Payable	2101
Accounts Payable	2102
Employees Income Tax Payable	2103
Federal Income Tax Payable	2104
FICA Tax Payable	2105
Sales Tax Payable	2106
Unemployment Tax Payable — Federal	2107
Unemployment Tax Payable — State	2108
Dividends Payable	2109
(3) STOCKHOLDERS' EQUITY	
Capital Stock	3101
Retained Earnings	3201
Income Summary	3301

Income Statement Accounts

(4) OPERATING REVENUE	Account Number
Sales	4101
Sales Returns and Allowances	4101.1
(5) COST OF MERCHANDISE	
Purchases	5101
Purchases Returns and Allowances	5101.1
Purchases Discount	5101.2
(6) OPERATING EXPENSES	
Advertising Expense	6101
Bad Debts Expense	6102
Credit Card Fee Expense	6103
Depreciation Expense — Office Equipment	6104
Depreciation Expense — Store Equipment	6105
Insurance Expense	6106
Miscellaneous Expense	6107
Payroll Taxes Expense	6108
Rent Expense	6109
Salary Expense	6110
Supplies Expense	6111
(7) OTHER REVENUE	
Interest Income	7101
(8) OTHER EXPENSES	
Interest Expense	8101
(9) INCOME TAX	
Federal Income Tax	9101

Opening a corporation's set of books

The required journal and ledger forms are given in the working papers. If you are using the working papers, omit Instructions 1 to 6. These instructions have been completed for you. Turn to page 482 and begin with Instruction 7.

Instructions: 1. Begin numbering the journals as listed. Sales journal, page 13; purchases journal, page 12; general journal, page 8; cash receipts journal, page 15; and cash payments journal, page 16.

2. Open all general ledger accounts as shown in Electronic Emporium's chart of accounts above.

3. Record the general ledger account balances given on the next page as of December 1 of the current year.

Account Title	Account Balance Debit	Credit
Cash	$ 25,649.80	
Notes Receivable	3,300.00	
Accounts Receivable	15,053.10	
Allowance for Uncollectible Accounts		$ 25.50
Merchandise Inventory	83,370.20	
Supplies	1,417.90	
Prepaid Insurance	5,040.00	
Office Equipment	4,340.00	
Accumulated Depreciation — Office Equipment		1,520.00
Store Equipment	7,775.00	
Accumulated Depreciation — Store Equipment		2,955.00
Notes Payable		8,000.00
Accounts Payable		7,338.90
Employees Income Tax Payable		992.00
Federal Income Tax Payable	—	—
FICA Tax Payable		923.20
Sales Tax Payable		2,200.90
Unemployment Tax Payable — Federal		24.00
Unemployment Tax Payable — State		92.60
Dividends Payable	—	—
Capital Stock		60,000.00
Retained Earnings	—	15,622.00
Income Summary	—	—
Sales		475,238.40
Sales Returns and Allowances	3,577.60	
Purchases	321,312.20	
Purchases Returns and Allowances		1,164.50
Purchases Discount		2,341.60
Advertising Expense	6,115.00	
Bad Debts Expense	—	—
Credit Card Fee Expense	4,752.30	
Depreciation Expense — Office Equipment	—	—
Depreciation Expense — Store Equipment	—	—
Insurance Expense	—	—
Miscellaneous Expense	3,749.50	
Payroll Taxes Expense	4,768.90	
Rent Expense	13,750.00	
Salary Expense	68,127.10	
Supplies Expense	—	—
Interest Income		1,240.00
Interest Expense	1,580.00	
Federal Income Tax	6,000.00	

Instructions: 4. Open an account in the accounts receivable ledger for each customer listed below. Record the balances as of December 1 of the current year.

Customers	Account Balance
Arlinghouse, Ltd., 830 Wymore Road, Austin, TX 78751-8010	$2,408.50
Hampton's, Inc., 9216 Lane Boulevard, Austin, TX 78703-1287	2,709.60
Kaleidoscape Construction, 3715 Fowler Road, Austin, TX 78703-1436	3,311.70
Owatonna's, 5910 Rugged Trail, Austin, TX 78703-1408	1,806.30
Strickland Systems, 2434 Pitt Road, Austin, TX 78702-1042	3,913.80
E. J. Traver, 8532 West 59th Street, Austin, TX 78711-1803	903.20

Instructions: 5. Open an account in the accounts payable ledger for each creditor listed on the next page. Record the balances as of December 1 of the current year.

Creditors	Account Balance
DeChaines Electronics, 4350 Marvin Drive, Austin, TX 78751-8397	$1,761.00
Fidelity Sound Systems, 1635 Victory Expressway, Dallas, TX 75206-2347	1,468.00
Gulf Sound, Ltd., 6742 St. James Ave., Austin, TX 78703-1533	1,687.90
Stereo Systems, Inc., 10836 Camp Dixie Blvd., Ft. Worth, TX 76119-3462	1,321.00
Westside Communications, 5937 West 61st Street, Austin, TX 78711-2741	1,101.00

Instructions: 6. Record the cash on hand, *$25,649.80*, on line 1 of the cash receipts journal.

Journalizing a corporation's transactions

Instructions: 7. Record the following transactions for December of the current year. Electronic Emporium must collect a 5% sales tax on all sales. Source documents are abbreviated as: check, C; sales invoice, S; receipt, R; cash register tape, T; credit card sales adding machine tape, CT; credit memorandum, CM; memorandum, M; purchase invoice, P; debit memorandum, DM.

Dec. 1. Paid December rent, $1,250.00. C302.
1. Received cash on account from Arlinghouse, Ltd., $2,408.50. R61.
1. Purchased merchandise on account from Gulf Sound, Ltd., $8,425.30. P89.
2. Credited Hampton's, Inc.'s account for merchandise returned, $378.00, plus sales tax, $18.90. CM15.
2. Received cash on account from Hampton's, Inc., $2,312.70. R62.
3. Sold merchandise on account to Strickland Systems, $1,478.40, plus sales tax, $73.92. S182.
3. Paid on account to DeChaines Electronics, $1,725.78, covering P82 for $1,761.00 less a 2 percent cash discount of $35.22. C303.
3. Recorded cash sales for the week, $3,770.20, plus sales tax, $188.51. T3.
3. Recorded credit card sales for the week, $1,615.80, plus sales tax, $80.79. CT3.
   Posting. Post the items that are to be posted individually. Post the journals in the following order: Sales journal, purchases journal, general journal, cash receipts journal, and cash payments journal.
5. Returned merchandise to Gulf Sound, Ltd., $1,164.50. DM17.
6. Paid on account to Stereo Systems, Inc., $1,294.58, covering P83 for $1,321.00 less a 2 percent cash discount of $26.42. C304.
7. Received cash on account from Strickland Systems, $3,913.80. R63.
7. Purchased merchandise on account from Westside Communications, $4,116.00. P90.
8. Sold merchandise on account to Kaleidoscape Construction, $1,723.10, plus sales tax, $86.16. S183.
8. Paid on account to Westside Communications, $1,089.99, covering P84 for $1,101.00 less a 1 percent discount of $11.01. C305.
9. Received cash on account from Kaleidoscape Construction, $3,311.70. R64.
10. Recorded cash sales for the week, $8,361.80, plus sales tax, $418.09. T10.
10. Recorded credit card sales for the week, $3,756.70, plus sales tax, $187.84, CT10.
   Posting. Post the items that are to be posted individually.
12. Purchased merchandise on account from Stereo Systems, Inc., $8,370.50. P91.
13. Paid miscellaneous expense, $163.40. C306.
13. Bought supplies for cash, $126.50. C307.
13. Received cash on account from Strickland Systems, $1,552.32. R65.

Dec. 14. Sold merchandise on account to Owatonna's, $518.00, plus sales tax, $25.90. S184.

14. Paid advertising expense, $416.30. C308.
15. Paid semimonthly payroll, $4,536.90 (less deductions: employees' income tax, $544.43; FICA tax, $272.21). C309.
15. Recorded the employer's payroll tax liabilities, $294.90 (FICA tax, $272.21; federal unemployment tax, $4.67; state unemployment tax, $18.02). M23.
15. Paid deposit for November liabilities, $1,915.20 (employees' income tax, $992.00; FICA tax, $923.20). C310.
15. Paid quarterly estimated federal income tax, $2,000.00 (debit Federal Income Tax; credit Cash). C311.
16. Paid on account to Westside Communications, $4,074.84, covering P90 for $4,116.00 less a 1 percent discount of $41.16. C312.
16. Received cash on account from Owatonna's, $1,806.30. R66.
17. Received cash on account from Kaleidoscape Construction, $1,809.26. R67.
17. Purchased merchandise for cash, $338.20. C313.
17. Recorded cash sales for the week, $8,545.80, plus sales tax, $427.29. T17.
17. Recorded credit card sales for the week, $4,021.50, plus sales tax, $201.08. CT17.
    Posting. Post the items that are to be posted individually.
19. Paid miscellaneous expense, $89.50. C314.
19. Sold merchandise on account to Hampton's, Inc., $1,856.50, plus sales tax, $92.83. S185.
20. Paid on account to Gulf Sound, Ltd., $523.40, covering P85 for $1,687.90 less DM 17 for $1,164.50; no discount. C315.
21. Paid on account to Fidelity Sound Systems, $1,468.00, covering P86; no discount. C316.
21. Paid miscellaneous expense, $207.10. C317.
22. Purchased merchandise on account from DeChaines Electronics, $5,146.50. P92.
22. Paid on account to Stereo Systems, Inc., $8,203.09, covering P91 for $8,370.50 less a 2 percent cash discount of $167.41. C318.
23. Purchased merchandise for cash, $443.60. C319.
24. Sold merchandise on account to Kaleidoscape Construction, $449.20, plus sales tax, $22.46. S186.
24. Recorded cash sales for the week, $7,818.60, plus sales tax, $390.93. T24.
24. Recorded credit card sales for the week, $3,851.10, plus sales tax, $192.56. CT24.
    Posting. Post the items that are to be posted individually.
26. Bought supplies on account from Fidelity Sound Systems, $243.40. M24.
27. Sold merchandise on account to Arlinghouse, Ltd., $1,287.20, plus sales tax, $64.36. S187.
27. Paid advertising expense, $262.70. C320.
28. Purchased merchandise on account from Westside Communications, $8,243.00. P93.
29. Received on account from Hampton's, Inc., $1,949.33. R68.
29. Paid on account to Gulf Sound, Ltd., $8,425.30, covering P89; no discount. C321.
30. Sold merchandise on account to Strickland Systems, $608.20, plus sales tax, $30.41. S188.
30. Paid sales tax liability for November, $2,182.00. C322. (Debit Sales Tax Payable; credit Cash).
31. Paid semimonthly payroll, $3,024.60 (less deductions: employees' income tax, $362.95; FICA tax, $181.48). C323.

Dec. 31. Recorded the employer's payroll tax liabilities, $196.60 (FICA tax, $181.48; federal unemployment tax, $3.11; state unemployment tax, $12.01). M25.

31. Recorded cash sales for the week, $2,073.60, plus sales tax, $103.68. T31.

31. Recorded credit card sales for the week, $1,068.30, plus sales tax, $53.42. CT31.

31. Recorded the credit card fee for December, $528.00. M26.

Posting. Post the items that are to be posted individually.

Proving and posting a corporation's special journals

Instructions: 8. Total, prove, and rule the sales journal. Post the totals of the special columns.

9. Total and rule the purchases journal. Post the total.

10. Prove the equality of debits and credits for the cash receipts and cash payments journals.

11. Prove cash. The balance on the last check stub on December 31 is $48,913.39.

12. Rule the cash receipts journal. Post the special column totals to the appropriate general ledger accounts.

13. Rule the cash payments journal. Post the totals of the special columns.

14. Prepare a schedule of accounts receivable and a schedule of accounts payable. Compare the schedules' totals with the balances of the accounts in the general ledger.

The general ledger used in Reinforcement Activity 4, Part A, is needed to complete Part B. The general journal used in Part A is needed to complete Part B.

fish tank

PEGBOARD PAYROLL SYSTEM

A BUSINESS SIMULATION

FISH TANK Pegboard Payroll System provides experience in preparing records using a pegboard and no-carbon-required forms. When data are entered on the statement of earnings and deductions stub on the check, the employee's earnings record and the payroll register are simultaneously prepared. Posting is eliminated. A pictorial flowchart of this write-it-once system is on the next page. This business simulation is available from the publisher.

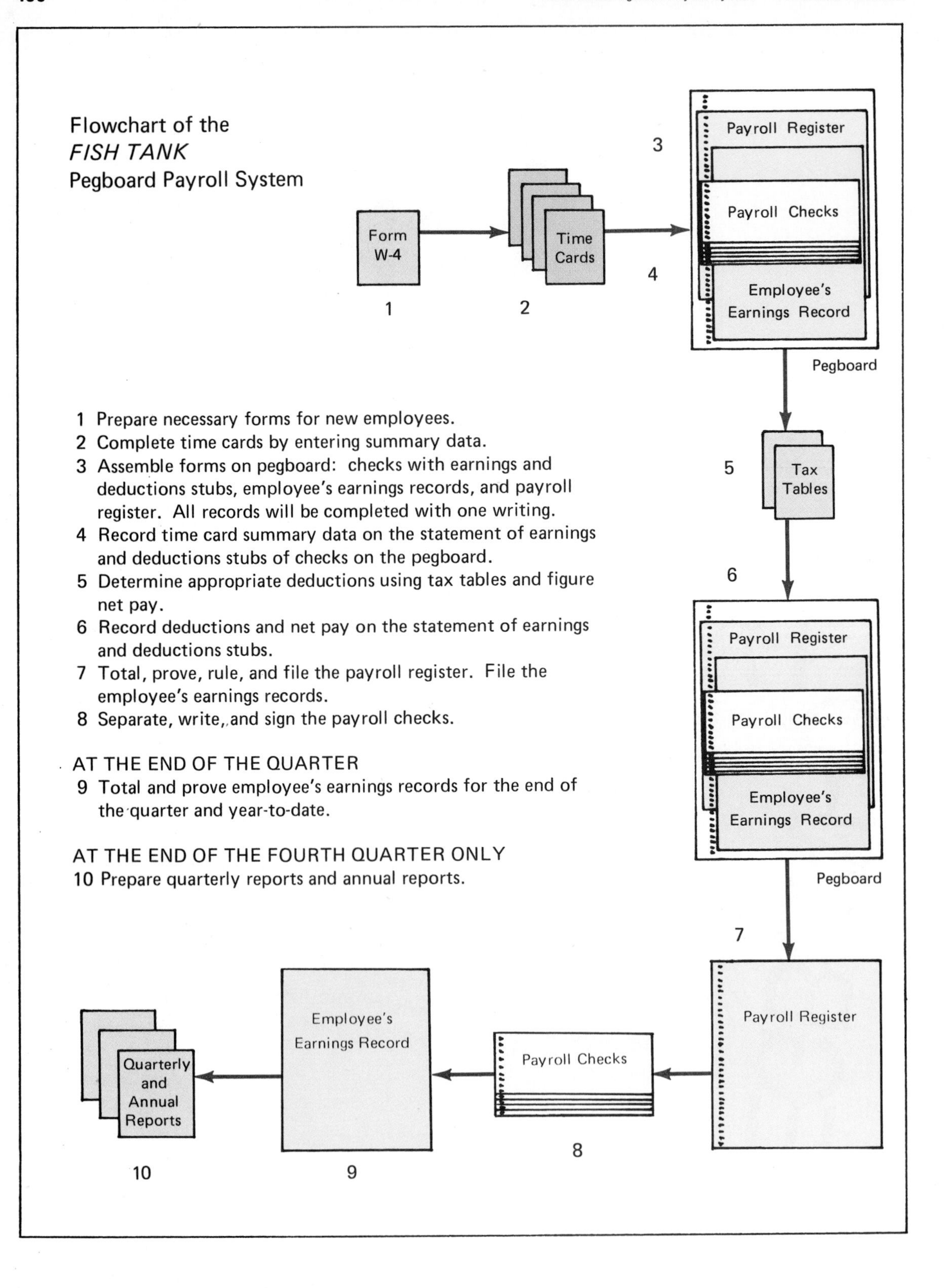
Flowchart of the
FISH TANK
Pegboard Payroll System
Form W-4
Time Cards
Payroll Register
Payroll Checks
Employee's Earnings Record
Pegboard
1
2
3
4
1 Prepare necessary forms for new employees.
2 Complete time cards by entering summary data.
3 Assemble forms on pegboard: checks with earnings and deductions stubs, employee's earnings records, and payroll register. All records will be completed with one writing.
4 Record time card summary data on the statement of earnings and deductions stubs of checks on the pegboard.
5 Determine appropriate deductions using tax tables and figure net pay.
6 Record deductions and net pay on the statement of earnings and deductions stubs.
7 Total, prove, rule, and file the payroll register. File the employee's earnings records.
8 Separate, write, and sign the payroll checks.
AT THE END OF THE QUARTER
9 Total and prove employee's earnings records for the end of the quarter and year-to-date.
AT THE END OF THE FOURTH QUARTER ONLY
10 Prepare quarterly reports and annual reports.
5
Tax Tables
6
Payroll Register
Payroll Checks
Employee's Earnings Record
Pegboard
7
Payroll Register
Payroll Checks
8
Employee's Earnings Record
9
Quarterly and Annual Reports
10

24 Accounting for Uncollectible Accounts

ENABLING PERFORMANCE TASKS

After studying Chapter 24, you will be able to:

a. Define accounting terms related to accounting for uncollectible accounts.
b. Explain accounting principles and practices related to accounting for uncollectible accounts.
c. Figure bad debts expense.
d. Journalize an entry to write off an uncollectible account.
e. Journalize an adjustment for bad debts expense.

Many businesses sell merchandise or service on account to customers. Selling on account frequently is more convenient to the business and the customer. Merchandise may be sold on one date but payment not received until a later date. Regardless of when payment is received, revenue should be recorded at the time of sale. *(CONCEPT: Realization of Revenue)*

Businesses try to insure that all of their accounts receivable will be collected. Before a business sells on account to a customer, the customer's credit rating is determined. A business may request a prospective charge customer's financial statement to evaluate the customer's ability to pay for merchandise. Also credit ratings may be obtained from local credit bureaus or national credit agencies.

Dun & Bradstreet, Inc., publishes a credit-rating book containing data about the financial condition of businesses throughout the United States.

DETERMINING UNCOLLECTIBLE ACCOUNTS RECEIVABLE

Even though a business is careful in selling on account, some accounts receivable cannot be collected. Accounts receivable that cannot be collected are called uncollectible accounts. Uncollectible accounts are sometimes known as bad debts. If a business fails to collect from a charge customer, the business loses part of the asset Accounts Receivable. To properly record this loss in the asset, two accounts must be adjusted. The uncollectible amount must be deducted from Accounts Receivable. The same amount must be added to an operating expense account. The expense caused by uncollectible accounts is called bad debts expense. Therefore, Lin's Music Center uses the expense account Bad Debts Expense.

An uncollectible amount does not decrease the amount from revenue. The loss is considered a regular expense of doing business. Therefore, the amount of the uncollectible account is recorded as an expense.

DIRECT WRITE-OFF OF AN UNCOLLECTIBLE ACCOUNT

Terms of sale for many charge sales is n/30 or n/EOM. The term *n/30* means the net invoice amount is due in 30 days. The term *n/EOM* means the net invoice amount is due by the end of the current month. Most businesses make a special effort to collect accounts not paid within the terms of sale. However, if special efforts fail and chances for collection are slight, the credit manager should declare the account uncollectible.

Some businesses assume that an account receivable is good until the account is proven uncollectible. When the account proves to be uncollectible, the amount becomes an expense. Recording bad debts expense only when a customer's account is known to be uncollectible is called the direct write-off of uncollectible accounts. The direct write-off method is used for two reasons. (a) Bad Debts Expense is increased only when an account is proven to be uncollectible. (b) The method is simple and convenient to use.

Analyzing an entry for direct write-off of an uncollectible account

Galinn Company uses the direct write-off of uncollectible accounts. After several months of collection effort, the company declared the account of J. B. Boles uncollectible.

March 15, 1983. Wrote off past-due account of J. B. Boles as uncollectible, $176.00. Memorandum No. 63.

GENERAL LEDGER

Bad Debts Expense

	Debit	Credit
	176.00	

Accounts Receivable

	Debit	Credit
Bal.	9,260.00	176.00

ACCOUNTS RECEIVABLE LEDGER

J. B. Boles

	Debit	Credit
Bal.	176.00	176.00

The entry to write off this uncollectible account is analyzed in the T accounts at the left.

Bad Debts Expense is debited for $176.00 to show the increase in the balance of this expense account. Accounts Receivable is credited for $176.00 to reduce the amount due from charge customers. The new balance of the accounts receivable account is $9,084.00 ($9,260.00 − $176.00). J. B.

Boles' account in the accounts receivable ledger is also credited for $176.00. This entry brings the balance of Boles' account to zero. Boles' account is written off. Canceling the balance of a customer's account because the customer does not pay is called writing off an account.

Journalizing an entry for direct write-off of an uncollectible account

The entry to write off the account of J. B. Boles is below.

GENERAL JOURNAL PAGE 5

	DATE		ACCOUNT TITLE	POST. REF.	DEBIT	CREDIT	
	1983						
1	Mar.	15	Bad Debts Expense		176 00		1
2			Accounts Rec./J. B. Boles	✓		176 00	2
3			Memorandum No. 63.				3
4							4
5							5
6							6

Entry to write off an uncollectible account when direct write-off method is used

Bad Debts Expense is debited for $176.00 in the Debit column. Accounts Receivable and J. B. Boles are both credited for $176.00.

Posting an entry for direct write-off of an uncollectible account

After the journal entry above is posted, the general ledger account Bad Debts Expense appears as shown below.

ACCOUNT Bad Debts Expense ACCOUNT NO. 6102

DATE		ITEM	POST. REF.	DEBIT	CREDIT	BALANCE DEBIT	BALANCE CREDIT
1983							
Mar.	15		G5	176 00		176 00	

Bad Debts Expense after entry writing off an uncollectible account is posted

After the credit entry is posted, Accounts Receivable in the general ledger appears as shown below.

ACCOUNT Accounts Receivable ACCOUNT NO. 1103

DATE		ITEM	POST. REF.	DEBIT	CREDIT	BALANCE DEBIT	BALANCE CREDIT
Feb.	28		CR9		5 350 00	9 260 00	
Mar.	15		G5		176 00	9 084 00	

Accounts Receivable after entry writing off an uncollectible account is posted

After the credit to J. B. Boles' account is posted, the account appears as shown below.

NAME J. B. Boles
ADDRESS 8962 Eastwood Avenue, Shreveport, LA 71102-1301

DATE		ITEM	POST. REF.	DEBIT	CREDIT	DEBIT BALANCE
1982 Sept.	10		S28	176 00		176 00
1983 Mar.	15	Written off	G5		176 00	—

Customer's account after entry writing off the account as uncollectible is posted

ESTIMATING BAD DEBTS EXPENSE

Risk of loss occurs when a business makes a sale on account. This possible loss is present even though several months may pass before the actual loss is determined. Accurate financial reporting requires that expenses be recorded in the accounting period in which the expenses contribute to earning revenue. *(CONCEPT: Matching Expenses with Revenue)*

A business does not know which charge sales will become bad debts at the time charge sales are made. Therefore, a business should estimate the amount of its bad debts expense. This estimate normally is made at the end of each fiscal period. The estimated amount of bad debts expense is recorded for two reasons. Recording the estimated bad debts expense prevents the overstatement of the value of accounts receivable on the balance sheet. Also bad debts expense is included on the income statement for the fiscal period in which the charge sale is made.

The net value of accounts receivable is reported on a balance sheet. This is shown by subtracting the estimated value of uncollectible accounts from the balance of accounts receivable. The difference between the balance of Accounts Receivable and the estimated uncollectible accounts is called the book value of accounts receivable.

Using a contra account

A business has no way of knowing for sure now which charge customers will fail to pay in the future. Since the company does not know which customers will not pay, specific customers' accounts cannot be credited as uncollectible. Neither can the accounts receivable account in the general ledger be credited. The balance of Accounts Receivable, a controlling account, must equal the sum of the customers' accounts in the subsidiary ledger. However, the company can record an *estimated* bad debts expense.

Lin's Music Center records estimated bad debts expense by making an adjusting entry. The estimated value of uncollectible accounts is credited to an account titled Allowance for Uncollectible Accounts. The same amount is debited to an expense account titled Bad Debts Expense.

Allowance for Bad Debts and Allowance for Doubtful Accounts are account titles sometimes used instead of Allowance for Uncollectible Accounts.

As discussed previously, an account that reduces a related account on the financial statements is known as a contra account. Allowance for Uncollectible Accounts is a contra account to its related account Accounts Receivable. The difference between these two accounts is the book value of accounts receivable. A contra asset account has a credit balance because it reduces the balance of an asset account.

A contra account is numbered the same as its related account, followed by a decimal point and a number. Lin's accounts receivable account is numbered 1103. Allowance for Uncollectible Accounts is numbered 1103.1. Crediting the estimated value of uncollectible accounts to a contra account is called the allowance method of recording losses from uncollectible accounts.

Estimating bad debts expense based on charge sales

Lin's has found it can best estimate bad debts expense by figuring a percentage of charge sales. A review of Lin's previous financial statements shows that actual bad debts expense has been about 1% (.01) of total charge sales. The company's total charge sales for the fiscal year is $474,000.00. Lin's *estimates* that $4,740.00 ($474,000.00 × .01) of its accounts receivable may be bad debts expense.

Analyzing an adjustment for bad debts expense

An adjusting entry is made to record estimated bad debts expense for a fiscal year. The T accounts at the right show the accounts Bad Debts Expense and Allowance for Uncollectible Accounts. The accounts are shown before the adjustment for bad debts expense is made.

BEFORE ADJUSTMENT

Bad Debts Expense	

Allowance for Uncollectible Accounts	
	Prev. Bal. 280.00

Four questions are asked in analyzing the adjustment for estimated bad debts expense.

1. What is the balance of the bad debts expense account? ..... zero
2. What should the balance be for this account? $4,740.00
3. What must be done to correct the account balance? ....Add $4,740.00
4. What adjusting entry is made? ......Debit Bad Debts Expense $4,740.00
   Credit Allowance for Uncollectible Accounts $4,740.00

The T accounts are shown on the next page after the adjustment for bad debts expense is made.

AFTER ADJUSTMENT

Bad Debts Expense	
Dec. 31 Adj. 4,740.00	

Allowance for Uncollectible Accounts	
	Prev. Bal. 280.00
	Dec. 31 Adj. 4,740.00
	Dec. 31 Bal. 5,020.00

Bad Debts Expense is debited for $4,740.00 to show the increase in the balance of this expense account. The balance of this account, *$4,740.00*, is the bad debts expense for the fiscal period.

Allowance for Uncollectible Accounts is credited for $4,740.00 to show the increase in the balance of this contra account. The previous balance, *$280.00*, plus the fiscal year increase, *$4,740.00*, equals the December 31 balance, *$5,020.00*.

Planning an adjustment on a work sheet for bad debts expense

At the end of the fiscal period, an adjustment for bad debts expense is planned on a work sheet. This adjustment for Lin's is shown in the Adjustments columns, lines 4 and 35, of the partial work sheet below.

Lin's Music Center
Work Sheet
For Year Ended December 31, 1983

	ACCOUNT TITLE	TRIAL BALANCE DEBIT (1)	TRIAL BALANCE CREDIT (2)	ADJUSTMENTS DEBIT (3)	ADJUSTMENTS CREDIT (4)
4	Allow. for Uncoll. Accts.		28000		(a) 474000
35	Bad Debts Expense			(a) 474000	
36					
37					
38					

Partial work sheet showing adjustment for bad debts expense

On line 35 above, Bad Debts Expense is debited for $4,740.00 in the Adjustments Debit column. On line 4, Allowance for Uncollectible Accounts is credited for $4,740.00 in the Adjustments Credit column.

The percent of charge sales method of estimating assumes a portion of every charge-sale dollar will become a bad debt. An Allowance for Uncollectible Accounts balance in the Trial Balance Credit column means previous period estimates are not yet identified as uncollectible. When the allowance account has a previous balance, the amount of the adjustment is added to the previous balance. The new balance is then extended to the Balance Sheet Credit column. This new balance of the allowance account is the estimated amount of accounts receivable that will be uncollectible.

Journalizing an adjustment for bad debts expense

Information used to journalize an adjustment for bad debts expense is obtained from the Adjustments columns of a work sheet. The adjusting entry is shown in the general journal on the next page.

GENERAL JOURNAL PAGE 27

	DATE		ACCOUNT TITLE	POST. REF.	DEBIT	CREDIT	
1			Adjusting Entries				1
2	1983 Dec.	31	Bad Debts Expense		474000		2
3			Allow. for Uncoll. Accts.			474000	3
4							4

Adjusting entry for estimated bad debts expense

Posting an adjustment for bad debts expense

After the adjustment is posted, Accounts Receivable, Allowance for Uncollectible Accounts, and Bad Debts Expense appear as shown below.

General ledger accounts after adjustment for estimated bad debts expense is posted

ACCOUNT Accounts Receivable ACCOUNT NO. 1103

DATE		ITEM	POST. REF.	DEBIT	CREDIT	BALANCE DEBIT	BALANCE CREDIT
Dec.	31		S48	4378000		6741500	
	31		CR37		2528000	4213500	

ACCOUNT Allowance for Uncollectible Accounts ACCOUNT NO. 1103.1

DATE		ITEM	POST. REF.	DEBIT	CREDIT	BALANCE DEBIT	BALANCE CREDIT
Dec.	16		G26	17500			28000
	31		G27		474000		502000

ACCOUNT Bad Debts Expense ACCOUNT NO. 6102

DATE		ITEM	POST. REF.	DEBIT	CREDIT	BALANCE DEBIT	BALANCE CREDIT
1983 Dec.	31		G27	474000		474000	

Accounts Receivable has a debit balance of $42,135.00, the total amount due from charge customers on December 31. Allowance for Uncollectible Accounts has a credit balance of $5,020.00 on December 31. The account number 1103.1 shows that this is a contra account. The balance of this contra account is to be subtracted from the balance of its related account, No. 1103, on the balance sheet. The balance of the bad debts expense account is $4,740.00. This is the estimated bad debts expense for the fiscal period ended December 31, 1983.

Lin's figures the book value of its accounts receivable on December 31, 1983, as shown below.

Balance of accounts receivable account	$42,135.00
Less allowance for uncollectible accounts	5,020.00
Equals book value of accounts receivable	$37,115.00

WRITING OFF ACTUAL UNCOLLECTIBLE ACCOUNTS THAT HAVE BEEN ESTIMATED

Lin's uses a planned collection procedure to collect customers' accounts. Most accounts are paid within the terms of sale. A few accounts, regardless of collection efforts, prove to be uncollectible. When a customer's account is determined to be uncollectible, a journal entry is made to write off the account.

Analyzing an entry to write off an uncollectible account using an estimated method

Lin's decides that the past-due account of David Ott is uncollectible.

January 3, 1984. Wrote off past-due account of David Ott as uncollectible, $123.00. Memorandum No. 11.

GENERAL LEDGER

Allowance for Uncollectible Accounts

Debit	Credit
123.00	Bal. 5,020.00

Accounts Receivable

Debit	Credit
Bal. 42,135.00	123.00

ACCOUNTS RECEIVABLE LEDGER

David Ott

Debit	Credit
Bal. 123.00	123.00

The entry to write off this uncollectible account is analyzed in the T accounts at the left.

Allowance for Uncollectible Accounts is debited for $123.00 to reduce the balance of this account. This specific amount of the allowance is no longer an *estimate*; it is an actual amount. Therefore, the amount of the uncollectible account is deducted from the allowance account.

Accounts Receivable is credited for $123.00 to reduce the balance due from charge customers. The new balance of the accounts receivable account is $42,012.00 ($42,135.00 less $123.00).

David Ott's account in the accounts receivable ledger is also credited for $123.00. This entry cancels the debit balance of his account. His account is written off.

The book value of accounts receivable is the same before and after writing off an uncollectible account. The book value of accounts receivable at Lin's before writing off David Ott's account is below.

Balance of accounts receivable	$42,135.00
Less allowance for uncollectible accounts	5,020.00
Book value of accounts receivable	$37,115.00

The book value of accounts receivable after writing off David Ott's account is below.

Balance of accounts receivable	$42,012.00
Less allowance for uncollectible accounts	4,897.00
Book value of accounts receivable	$37,115.00

The book value remains the same because the same amount is deducted from both the accounts receivable and the allowance account.

Journalizing an entry to write off an uncollectible account using an estimated method

The entry to write off the account of David Ott is shown in the general journal below.

GENERAL JOURNAL PAGE 1

	DATE		ACCOUNT TITLE	POST. REF.	DEBIT	CREDIT	
16		3	Allow. for Uncollectible Accts.		123 00		16
17			Accts. Rec./David Ott	✓		123 00	17
18			Memorandum No. 11.				18
19							19

Entry to write off an uncollectible account when estimated method is used

Allowance for Uncollectible Accounts is debited for $123.00 in the Debit column. Accounts Receivable and David Ott are both credited for $123.00 in the Credit column.

Posting an entry to write off an uncollectible account using an estimated method

The journal entry to write off an uncollectible account is above. After this entry is posted, Allowance for Uncollectible Accounts in the general ledger appears as shown below.

ACCOUNT Allowance for Uncollectible Accounts ACCOUNT NO. 1103.1

DATE		ITEM	POST. REF.	DEBIT	CREDIT	BALANCE DEBIT	BALANCE CREDIT
	31		G27		4,740 00		5,020 00
1984 Jan.	3		G1	123 00			4,897 00

Allowance for Uncollectible Accounts after entry writing off an uncollectible account is posted

After the credit entry is posted, Accounts Receivable in the general ledger appears as shown on the next page.

ACCOUNT Accounts Receivable ACCOUNT NO. 1103

DATE		ITEM	POST. REF.	DEBIT	CREDIT	BALANCE DEBIT	BALANCE CREDIT
	31		CR37		25280 00	42135 00	
1984 Jan.	3		G1		123 00	42012 00	

Accounts Receivable after entry writing off an uncollectible account is posted

After the credit to David Ott's account is posted, his account appears as shown below.

NAME David Ott

ADDRESS 3841 Cottingham Road, Mesquite, TX 75149-7320

DATE		ITEM	POST. REF.	DEBIT	CREDIT	DEBIT BALANCE
1983 Apr.	12		S14	123 00		123 00
1984 Jan.	3	Written off	G1		123 00	———

Customer's account after entry writing off the account as uncollectible is posted

USING AUTOMATED DATA PROCESSING FOR VALUATION OF ACCOUNTS RECEIVABLE

The best method of estimating bad debts expense often depends on the size and type of business. Lin's estimates its bad debts expense based on charge sales. This method is simple and permits Lin's to match revenue of a period with its related bad debts expense. *(CONCEPT: Matching Expenses with Revenue)*

Credit experiences show that the longer a customer's account is overdue, the more likely the account will be uncollectible. Some businesses prefer to estimate the amount of uncollectible accounts by analyzing the age of their past-due accounts. Analyzing accounts receivable according to when they are due is called aging accounts receivable. Aging accounts generally gives a less accurate estimate of uncollectible accounts for a period than using a percent of charge sales. However, many businesses find that aging accounts provides a more accurate estimate of the value of accounts that will be collected.

The calculations necessary to age accounts receivable usually make this method impractical for businesses using manual data processing systems. For businesses using automated data processing systems however aging accounts receivable is a commonly used method.

When an automated data processing system is used, a report is printed that shows the status of each customer's account. A list of charge customers that shows the balances due by age of account is called a schedule of accounts receivable by age. A computer printout of a schedule of accounts receivable by age for Sound City is below.

SOUND CITY
SCHEDULE OF ACCOUNTS RECEIVABLE BY AGE
MARCH 31, 1983

CUSTOMER NUMBER	CUSTOMER NAME	DATE OF LAST PAYMENT	BALANCE DUE	DUE FOR LESS THAN 30 DAYS	ACCOUNTS PAST DUE 30-59 DAYS	60-89 DAYS	90 DAYS AND OVER
10040	S.R. ABALOS	3-03-83	433.80	168.00	265.80		
10085	MARIE ARDIS	2-12-83	163.20		84.00	79.20	
10235	KATHY ZORN	3-15-83	344.78	92.40	252.38		
	TOTALS		63 445.85*	49 677.24*	7 724.23*	4 406.04*	1 638.34*

Computer printout of a schedule of accounts receivable by age

Sound City has learned from past experience the percent of past due accounts that will be uncollectible. (a) 30–59 days, 0.5%, (b) 60–89 days, 3%, (c) 90 days and over, 10%. The schedule above, can be used to estimate the amount of uncollectible accounts Sound City has on March 31, 1983. The amount Sound City should have as the balance of Allowance for Uncollectible Accounts is figured below.

Number of Days Past Due	Amount Past Due	Percentage	Estimated Uncollectible Amounts
30–59 days	$7,724.23	0.5%	$ 38.62
60–89 days	4,406.04	3.0%	132.18
90 + days	1,638.34	10.0%	163.83
Total			$334.63

When the percent of charge sales is used, the amount of bad debts expense is estimated. When the aging method is used, the amount of uncollectible accounts is estimated. As figured above, Sound City's estimated uncollectible amount on March 31 is $334.63. Therefore, Allowance for Uncollectible Accounts should have a credit balance of $334.63. Before adjustment, the balance of the allowance account is $48.50. To bring the allowance account balance to $334.63, the estimated bad debts expense is $286.13 ($334.63 − $48.50). The following adjustment is recorded on a journal entry transmittal. (a) Debit Bad Debts Expense for $286.13. (b) Credit Allowance for Uncollectible Accounts for $286.13. After the adjustment is journalized and posted, the balance of Allowance for Uncollectible Accounts is $334.63 ($48.50 + $286.13).

ACCOUNTING TERMS

What is the meaning of each of the following?

1. uncollectible accounts
2. bad debts expense
3. direct write-off of uncollectible accounts
4. writing off an account
5. book value of accounts receivable
6. allowance method of recording losses from uncollectible accounts
7. aging accounts receivable
8. schedule of accounts receivable by age

QUESTIONS FOR INDIVIDUAL STUDY

1. When should revenue from sales be recorded?
2. If a business fails to collect from a charge customer, how should this loss be properly recorded in the accounts?
3. What does "terms of sale" mean that is stated n/EOM?
4. What are two reasons why a company may use the direct method to write-off uncollectible accounts?
5. When the direct write-off of uncollectible accounts method is used, what entry is made to record bad debts expense?
6. Why is recording estimated bad debts generally considered better than recording bad debts expense only when specific accounts are proven uncollectible?
7. How is the book value of accounts receivable figured?
8. Why is Allowance for Uncollectible Accounts called a contra account?
9. What is the procedure for estimating bad debts based on charge sales?
10. What journal entry is made to record bad debts expense?
11. What kind of situation would cause the account Allowance for Uncollectible Accounts to have a credit balance in the trial balance?
12. Why is the Allowance for Uncollectible Accounts debited when a customer's account is written off?
13. How does the book value of accounts receivable differ before and after writing off an account? Why?
14. Why do some businesses prefer to estimate the amount of uncollectible accounts by analyzing the age of past-due accounts?

CASES FOR MANAGEMENT DECISION

CASE 1 McKenzie Corporation has always assumed an account receivable is good until the account is proven bad. When an account proves to be uncollectible, the credit manager notifies the general accounting clerk to write off the account. The accounting clerk then debits Bad Debts Expense and credits Accounts Receivable. Recently the company's auditor, Nita Barnes, suggested the method be changed for recording bad debts expense. Ms. Barnes recommended the company change to the estimating method, percent of charge sales. Ms. Barnes stated the change would provide more accurate information in the income statement and balance sheet. Which method provides the most accurate financial statements? Why?

CASE 2 Plastics Unlimited credits Accounts Receivable for the amount of estimated bad debts expense at the end of each fiscal period. Ivory Imports credits Allowance for Uncollectible Accounts for the amount of estimated bad debts expense at the end of each fiscal period. Is Plastics Unlimited or Ivory Imports using the better method? Why?

DRILLS FOR UNDERSTANDING

DRILL 24-D 1 Journalizing uncollectible accounts

Instructions: Use a form similar to the one below. For each transaction, place a check mark for each general ledger account that is either debited or credited. Place a check mark in the Accounts Not Affected column if no journal entry should be made.

Transaction	General Ledger Accounts			Accounts Not Affected
	Accounts Receivable	Allowance for Uncollectible Accounts	Bad Debts Expense	
Direct Write-Off Method Used: a. Estimated amount of uncollectible accounts				
b. Wrote off an uncollectible account......................................				
Estimated Method Used: c. Estimated amount of uncollectible accounts at end of fiscal period				
d. Wrote off an uncollectible account......................................				

DRILL 24-D 2 Figuring bad debts expense

Accounting records of three stores show the following summary information for the fiscal period ending December 31 of the current year.

Store	Total Charge Sales	Balance in Accounts Receivable Account				Actual Accounts Written off
		Current	Past Due			
			30–59 days	60–89 days	90 days & over	
1	$47,560	$ 7,168	$1,103	$ 643	$276	$415
2	98,300	19,169	2,949	1,720	737	620
3	84,550	14,509	2,232	1,302	558	425

Instructions: Figure the *bad debts expense* for each of these stores using the methods on the next page.

a. Direct write-off method.
b. Percent of charge sales method. Percent of accounts uncollectible is estimated at .005 of charge sales.
c. Aging method. Percent of accounts uncollectible is estimated as follows:

Past Due Accounts	Percent Uncollectible
30–59 days	5%
60–89 days	15%
90 days and over	30%

End-of-fiscal-period balances in the account Allowance for Uncollectible Accounts are below.

Store 1	$ 36.00 Credit Balance
Store 2	$ 89.00 Debit Balance
Store 3	$104.00 Credit Balance

APPLICATION PROBLEMS

PROBLEM 24-1 Recording entries for bad debts expense

Keltner Corporation used the direct write-off method to record uncollectible accounts and bad debts expense. Selected entries affecting uncollectible accounts are given below.

Instructions: Record all the necessary entries for the following. Use page 15 of a general journal similar to the one on page 489.

Jan. 25. Wrote off past-due account of Joyce Maloney as uncollectible, $86.00. M138.
Mar. 10. Wrote off past-due account of J. E. Prafka as uncollectible, $43.50. M161.
Apr. 27. Wrote off past-due account of Albert Chisum as uncollectible, $72.60. M183.
July 7. Wrote off past-due account of Paul Gastineau as uncollectible, $21.75. M227.
Sept. 12. Wrote off past-due account of Celia Masters as uncollectible, $37.65. M249.
Dec. 8. Wrote off past-due account of Royal Walenta as uncollectible, $97.50. M301.

PROBLEM 24-2 Recording entries for bad debts expense

Syntron Company has general ledger accounts for Allowance for Uncollectible Accounts and Bad Debts Expense. At the beginning of the current year, the credit balance of Allowance for Uncollectible Accounts was $1,023.20.
Selected entries affecting bad debts are given below.

Instructions: Record the following selected entries on page 24 of a general journal like the one on page 493.

Mar. 8. Wrote off past-due account of Joseph Merz as uncollectible, $185.40. M117.
Mar. 31. *End of first quarterly fiscal period.* Make adjusting entry for estimated bad debts expense. Bad debts expense is estimated as 0.5% of total charge sales. Total charge sales for the first quarterly fiscal period were $52,118.00.
Apr. 10. Wrote off past-due account of Ruth Hatch as uncollectible, $356.40. M152.
June 14. Wrote off past-due account of Roy Pilant, $417.30. M216.
June 30. *End of second quarterly fiscal period.* Make adjusting entry for estimated bad debts expense. Total charge sales for the second quarterly fiscal period were $45,282.10.
Aug. 24. Wrote off past-due account of Ruby Olendorff as uncollectible, $255.02. M283.

Sept. 30. *End of third quarterly fiscal period.* Make adjusting entry for estimated bad debts expense. Total charge sales for the third quarterly fiscal period were $49,690.30.
Nov. 30. Wrote off past-due account of E. L. Semones as uncollectible, $269.91. M326.
Dec. 31. *End of fourth quarterly fiscal period.* Make adjusting entry for estimated bad debts expense. Total charge sales for the fourth quarterly fiscal period were $51,269.90.

ENRICHMENT PROBLEMS

MASTERY PROBLEM 24-M Recording entries for bad debts expense

Gardiner Appliances has general ledger accounts for Allowance for Uncollectible Accounts and Bad Debts Expense. At the beginning of the current year, the credit balance of Allowance for Uncollectible Accounts was $854.19. Selected entries affecting uncollectible accounts are given below.

Instructions: Record all the necessary entries for the following on page 16 of a general journal like the one on page 493.

Jan. 17. Wrote off past-due account of Kay Taylor as uncollectible, $537.84. M26.
Mar. 31. *End of first quarterly fiscal period.* Make adjusting entry for estimated bad debts expense. Bad debts expense is estimated as 1% of the total charge sales. Total charge sales for the first quarterly fiscal period were $59,174.40.
Apr. 14. Wrote off past-due account of Margaret Ryan as uncollectible, $378.00. M48.
June 30. *End of second quarterly fiscal period.* Make adjusting entry for estimated bad debts expense. Total charge sales for the second quarterly fiscal period were $49,572.90.
July 13. Wrote off past-due account of Billy Franks as uncollectible, $398.70. M78.
Sept. 30. *End of third quarterly fiscal period.* Make adjusting entry for estimated bad debts expense. Total charge sales for the third quarterly fiscal period were $50,581.20.
Dec. 30. Wrote off past-due account of J. E. Byrd as uncollectible, $789.00. M129.
Dec. 31. *End of fourth quarterly fiscal period.* Make adjusting entry for estimated bad debts expense. Total charge sales for the fourth quarterly fiscal period were $65,895.00.

CHALLENGE PROBLEM 24-C Recording entries for bad debts expense

LaFiesta Corporation has general ledger accounts for Allowance for Uncollectible Accounts and Bad Debts Expense. The corporation ages its accounts to estimate uncollectible accounts. At the beginning of the current year, the credit balance of Allowance for Uncollectible Accounts was $1,470.00.

Selected entries affecting bad debts are given below.

Instructions: 1. Record the following selected entries on page 12 of a general journal like the one on page 495.

Mar. 18. Wrote off past-due account of Virda McGhee as uncollectible, $223.50. M38.
May 11. Wrote off past-due account of Jake Browning as uncollectible, $194.60. M69.
Aug. 22. Wrote off past-due account of Robert Palmer as uncollectible, $224.20. M116.
Dec. 20. Wrote off past-due account of Dean Molitar as uncollectible, $150.30. M158.

Instructions: 2. The totals from the Schedule of Accounts Receivable by Age for La-Fiesta Corporation on December 31 are below.

	Balance Due	Due for Less than 30 days	Accounts Past Due 30–59 Days	60–89 Days	90 Days And Over
Totals	$28,250.00	$22,035.00	$3,390.00	$1,978.00	$847.00

The percent of past due accounts are estimated uncollectible as shown below.

Number Days Past Due	Percentage Uncollectible
30–59 days	5%
60–89 days	10%
90 + days	50%

Figure and record the adjusting journal entry for Bad Debts Expense for the fiscal period ended December 31.

25

Accounting for Plant Assets and Depreciation

ENABLING PERFORMANCE TASKS

After studying Chapter 25, you will be able to:

a. Define accounting terms related to accounting for plant assets and depreciation.
b. Explain accounting principles and practices related to accounting for plant assets and depreciation.
c. Figure depreciation expense.
d. Figure book value of a plant asset.
e. Journalize the buying of a plant asset in a cash payments journal.
f. Prepare a plant asset record.
g. Journalize work sheet adjustments for depreciation expense in a general journal.
h. Journalize the sale of a plant asset in a cash receipts journal.

Some business assets such as cash, accounts receivable, and merchandise inventory usually are turned into cash within a year. Another group of assets are used for a long period to operate a business. Assets that will be used for a number of years in the operation of a business are called plant assets. Some examples of plant assets are delivery equipment, store equipment, office equipment, buildings, and land. Plant assets can be used repeatedly and are expected to last more than a year. Also, plant assets are not bought for purposes of resale to customers in the normal course of business. Thus, land on which a business is located is classified as a plant asset. However, land bought with the intention of renting or reselling at a profit is not classified as a plant asset.

Some businesses use the term "fixed assets." However, the American Institute of Certified Public Accountants recommends that "plant" rather than "fixed" be used in the account title.

Plant assets such as delivery trucks, machinery, display cases, tables, typewriters, and desks are called equipment. Some businesses record the cost of all equipment in one asset account titled Equipment. Other businesses record various kinds of equipment in separate plant asset accounts such as Delivery Equipment and Office Equipment. Lin's Music Center uses three plant asset accounts: Delivery Equipment, Store Equipment, and Office Equipment.

BUYING AND RECORDING PLANT ASSETS

A plant asset is recorded at its cost. *(CONCEPT: Historical Cost)* On April 1, 1983, Lin's Music Center bought a new delivery truck for $7,000.00 cash. The entry to record this transaction is shown in the cash payments journal below.

CASH PAYMENTS JOURNAL PAGE 10

	DATE	ACCOUNT TITLE	CHECK NO.	POST. REF.	GENERAL DEBIT (1)	GENERAL CREDIT (2)	ACCOUNTS PAYABLE DEBIT (3)	PURCHASES DISCOUNT CREDIT (4)	CASH CREDIT (5)	
4	1	Delivery Equipment	248		700000				700000	4

Entry to record the buying of a plant asset

Lin's has a separate plant asset account for delivery equipment. Delivery Equipment is debited for the cost of the delivery truck, *$7,000.00*, and Cash is credited for the same amount. After the entry is posted, Delivery Equipment in the general ledger appears as shown below.

ACCOUNT Delivery Equipment ACCOUNT NO. 1201

DATE		ITEM	POST. REF.	DEBIT	CREDIT	BALANCE DEBIT	BALANCE CREDIT
1983 Jan.	1	Balance	✓			1088000	
Apr.	1		CP10	700000		1788000	

A plant asset account in the general ledger

The $10,880.00 balance of Delivery Equipment is the original cost of equipment owned on January 1, 1983. The $17,880.00 balance of Delivery Equipment is the original cost of equipment owned on April 1. The debit balance of Delivery Equipment always shows the original cost of all delivery equipment owned. *(CONCEPT: Historical Cost)*

DESCRIBING THE EFFECT OF DEPRECIATION ON PLANT ASSETS

A typewriter bought for $800.00 in January is not worth $800.00 twelve months later. Similarly, a plant asset of any kind bought in July for $1,000.00 is not worth $1,000.00 in December. Plant assets such as store equipment decrease in value because of use. Plant assets also decrease in value with passage of time as they become older and new models become available. A decrease in value of a plant asset because of use and passage of time is called depreciation. Land, because of its permanent nature, generally is not subject to depreciation.

An amount by which a plant asset depreciates is an expense of a business. A plant asset is used to operate a business and earn revenue. Therefore, depreciation expense should be recorded in each fiscal period that a plant asset is used to earn revenue. *(CONCEPT: Matching Expenses with Revenue)* If depreciation expense is not recorded, an income statement will not report all expenses of a business. Therefore, net income will be overstated.

Federal income tax laws allow a business to deduct depreciation expense in figuring net income. If depreciation expenses are not included on income tax reports, a business will pay more income tax than required.

FIGURING DEPRECIATION EXPENSE

A business normally expects to use a plant asset for several years. Depreciation expense is recorded for each fiscal period a plant asset is used.

Factors affecting depreciation expense

Three factors affect the amount of plant asset depreciation expense for a fiscal period.

1. The original cost of a plant asset.
2. The amount a business estimates will be received when disposing of a plant asset.
3. The estimated useful life of a plant asset.

Original cost. The original cost of a plant asset is obtained from the seller's invoice. The cost of the new delivery truck bought by Lin's is $7,000.00.

Estimated salvage value. The amount an owner expects to receive when a plant asset is removed from use is called estimated salvage value. Estimated salvage value also is known as scrap value.

Lin's estimates a salvage value of $1,000.00 for the new delivery truck at the end of its useful life.

Estimated useful life. The total amount of depreciation expense is distributed over the estimated useful life of a plant asset. When a plant asset is bought, the exact length of useful life is impossible to predict. Therefore, the number of years of useful life must be estimated.

Lin's estimates that the useful life of a delivery truck is 5 years. An estimate of useful life should be based on prior experience with similar assets and available guidelines. The Internal Revenue Service issues guidelines for the estimated life of many common plant assets. Trade associations also may publish similar guidelines for specialized plant assets.

Figuring depreciation expense for a fiscal period

Lin's figures the total amount of estimated depreciation for the delivery truck as shown below.

Original cost	*minus*	Estimated salvage value	*equals*	Amount of estimated depreciation
$7,000.00	–	$1,000.00	=	$6,000.00

The annual depreciation expense for the delivery truck is figured as shown below.

Total amount of estimated depreciation	*divided by*	Years of estimated useful life	*equals*	Estimated amount of annual depreciation expense
$6,000.00	÷	5	=	$1,200.00

Monthly depreciation is figured by dividing annual depreciation by twelve ($1,200.00 ÷ 12 = $100.00). Lin's bought the delivery truck on April 1, 1983. Nine months passed from April 1, 1983, to the end of the fiscal year, December 31, 1983. Therefore, nine months depreciation, *$900.00*, is charged as an expense for the year 1983 ($100.00 × 9 = $900.00).

Charging an *equal* amount of annual depreciation expense for a plant asset is called the straight-line method of depreciation. Lin's uses the straight-line method to figure depreciation.

There are other methods of figuring depreciation expense. However, the straight-line method is widely used because it is simple.

PREPARING PLANT ASSET RECORDS

A separate record for each plant asset is kept. An accounting form on which a business records data about each plant asset is called a plant asset record.

When Lin's bought a delivery truck on April 1, 1983, a plant asset record was prepared. The plant asset record for the delivery truck is on page 507.

A plant asset record includes a complete description of an asset, including the serial number. A record also includes the date the asset was bought, the cost, and the estimated useful life. Other items of information on the record are the estimated salvage value and the annual amount of depreciation expense.

PLANT ASSET RECORD

Lin's Music Center — Account No. 1201

Item: Delivery Truck — General Ledger Account: Delivery Equipment
Serial No.: 8735M96025 — Description: Model C20
From Whom Purchased: Star Motors, Dallas, TX — Cost: $7,000.00
Estimated Life: 5 years — Estimated Salvage or Trade-in Value: $1,000.00 — Depreciation per year: $1,200.00
Disposal date: — Disposal amount:

Date Mo. Day Yr.	Annual Depreciation Expense	Accumulated Depreciation	Book Value
4 1 83			7,000.00
12 31 83	900.00	900.00	6,100.00

Plant asset record showing first-year depreciation

On December 31, 1983, Lin's has owned the delivery truck for three fourths of a year. Therefore, the depreciation expense for 1983, *$900.00*, is recorded in the Accumulated Depreciation column. The original cost of a plant asset minus the accumulated depreciation is called the book value of a plant asset. Since the delivery truck had no previous depreciation, the amount, *$900.00*, is deducted from the original cost, *$7,000.00*. The new book value at the end of the fiscal period, *$6,100.00*, is recorded in the Book Value column.

At the close of each fiscal period, each plant asset record is brought up to date. The depreciation expense for that period is recorded and the new book value of the asset is figured. The book value of Lin's delivery truck at the end of 1988, shown below, is $1,000.00. This amount, *$1,000.00*, is

PLANT ASSET RECORD

Lin's Music Center — Account No. 1201

Item: Delivery Truck — General Ledger Account: Delivery Equipment
Serial No.: 8735M96025 — Description: Model C20
From Whom Purchased: Star Motors, Dallas, TX — Cost: $7,000.00
Estimated Life: 5 years — Estimated Salvage or Trade-in Value: $1,000.00 — Depreciation per year: $1,200.00
Disposal date: — Disposal amount:

Date Mo. Day Yr.	Annual Depreciation Expense	Accumulated Depreciation	Book Value
4 1 83			7,000.00
12 31 83	900.00	900.00	6,100.00
12 31 87	1,200.00	5,700.00	1,300.00
12 31 88	300.00	6,000.00	1,000.00

Plant asset record brought up to date the last fiscal period of a plant asset's life the salvage value Lin's estimates the truck is worth after 5 years. When a plant asset's book value equals its estimated salvage value, no further depreciation expense is recorded. Therefore, on December 31, 1988, only $300.00 depreciation expense is recorded on the plant asset record.

ACCOUNTS AFFECTING THE VALUATION OF PLANT ASSETS

Three general ledger accounts are used to record data about each kind of plant asset. (1) An asset account, such as Delivery Equipment, is used to record the original cost of the asset. (2) A contra asset account, such as Accumulated Depreciation — Delivery Equipment, is used to record the total amount of depreciation to date. (3) An expense account, such as Depreciation Expense — Delivery Equipment, is used to record the annual amount of depreciation expense.

Plant asset accounts

Lin's uses three plant asset accounts: Delivery Equipment, Office Equipment, and Store Equipment. The appropriate plant asset account is debited for the cost when equipment is bought. The account is credited for the cost when equipment is disposed of. Therefore, the balance of a plant asset account always shows the cost of all equipment in current use.

Accumulated depreciation accounts

Depreciation is credited to a contra asset account titled Accumulated Depreciation. The name of the related equipment account is added to the title, such as Accumulated Depreciation — Delivery Equipment. Lin's uses three accumulated depreciation accounts. The three accounts are Accumulated Depreciation — Delivery Equipment, Accumulated Depreciation — Office Equipment, and Accumulated Depreciation — Store Equipment.

The location of these contra accounts in the general ledger is shown in the chart of accounts, page 392.

The account title Allowance for Depreciation sometimes is used instead of Accumulated Depreciation.

The debit balance of each plant asset account shows the original cost of the assets in use. The credit balance of the accumulated depreciation account shows the estimated decrease in value of the assets because of depreciation. The difference between the balances of the two accounts is the book value of the plant assets.

Depreciation expense accounts

Depreciation expense is an expense of a business. Lin's uses three depreciation expense accounts. The three depreciation accounts are, Depreciation Expense — Delivery Equipment, Depreciation Expense — Office Equipment, and Depreciation Expense — Store Equipment.

DETERMINING ADJUSTMENTS FOR DEPRECIATION

At the end of the fiscal period, December 31, 1983, Lin's figures the depreciation expense for each asset. Next, the total depreciation expense is figured for all plant assets of the same kind. For example, in 1983 the depreciation expense for the new delivery truck is $900.00. The depreciation expense for other delivery equipment is $1,000.00. Thus, the total delivery equipment depreciation expense for 1983 is $1,900.00. Lin's total depreciation expense for each kind of plant asset on December 31, 1983, is below.

Kind of equipment	Estimated depreciation expense this year	Previous balance of accumulated depreciation	New balance of accumulated depreciation
Delivery equipment	$1,900.00	$5,250.00	$7,150.00
Office equipment	950.00	1,950.00	2,900.00
Store equipment	2,840.00	5,400.00	8,240.00

Analyzing an adjustment for estimated depreciation

An adjusting entry is made to record estimated depreciation expense for a fiscal year. The T accounts at the right show the delivery equipment account, accumulated depreciation account, and depreciation expense account. The accounts are shown before the adjustment for depreciation expense is made.

BEFORE ADJUSTMENT

Delivery Equipment

Debit	Credit
Jan. 1 Bal. 10,880.00	
Apr. 1 7,000.00	
Dec. 31 Bal. 17,880.00	

Depreciation Expense — Delivery Equipment

Debit	Credit

Accumulated Depreciation — Delivery Equipment

Debit	Credit
	Jan. 1 Bal. 5,250.00

Four questions are asked in analyzing the adjustment for estimated depreciation.

1. What is the balance of the depreciation expense — delivery equipment account? .... zero
2. What should the balance be for this account? $1,900.00
3. What must be done to correct the account balance? ....Add $1,900.00
4. What adjusting entry is made? ....
   Debit Depreciation Expense — Delivery Equipment $1,900.00
   Credit Accumulated Depreciation — Delivery Equipment $1,900.00

The T accounts are shown on the next page after the adjustment for depreciation expense is made.

Depreciation Expense — Delivery Equipment is debited for $1,900.00 to show the increase in the balance of this expense account. The balance of this account, *$1,900.00*, is the estimated depreciation expense for the fiscal period.

AFTER ADJUSTMENT

Delivery Equipment

Jan. 1 Bal. 10,880.00	
Apr. 1 7,000.00	
Dec. 31 Bal. 17,880.00	

Depreciation Expense — Delivery Equipment

Dec. 31 Adj. 1,900.00	

Accumulated Depreciation — Delivery Equipment

	Jan. 1 Bal. 5,250.00
	Dec. 31 Adj. 1,900.00
	Dec. 31 Bal. 7,150.00

Accumulated Depreciation — Delivery Equipment is credited for $1,900.00 to show the increase in the balance of this contra account. The January 1 balance, *$5,250.00*, plus the fiscal year increase, *$1,900.00*, equals the December 31 balance, *$7,150.00*. The delivery equipment account balance, *$17,880.00*, minus the accumulated depreciation account balance, *$7,150.00*, equals the delivery equipment book value, *$10,730.00*.

The same kind of adjusting entry is made to record estimated depreciation expense for store equipment and office equipment. The book value of each kind of plant asset after the adjustments of December 31, 1983, is below.

Kind of equipment	Balance of asset account	*less*	Total accumulated depreciation	*equals*	Book value 12/31/83
Delivery equipment	$17,880.00	–	$7,150.00	=	$10,730.00
Office equipment	9,710.00	–	2,900.00	=	6,810.00
Store equipment	41,175.00	–	8,240.00	=	32,935.00

Recording depreciation expense on a work sheet

Lin's plans the adjustments for depreciation expense in the Adjustments columns of a work sheet. The December 31, 1983, adjustments for depreciation of plant assets are on the partial work sheet below.

Lin's Music Center
Work Sheet
For Year Ended December 31, 1983

	ACCOUNT TITLE	1 TRIAL BALANCE DEBIT	2 TRIAL BALANCE CREDIT	3 ADJUSTMENTS DEBIT	4 ADJUSTMENTS CREDIT
8	Delivery Equipment	17 880 00			
9	Accum. Depr.-Delivery Equip.		5 250 00		(f) 1 900 00
10	Office Equipment	9 710 00			
11	Accum. Depr.-Office Equip.		1 950 00		(g) 950 00
12	Store Equipment	41 175 00			
13	Accum. Depr.-Store Equip.		5 400 00		(h) 2 840 00
38	Depr. Exp.-Delivery Equip.			(f) 1 900 00	
39	Depr. Exp.-Office Equip.			(g) 950 00	
40	Depr. Exp.-Store Equip.			(h) 2 840 00	

Partial work sheet with adjustments for depreciation

Adjustment for depreciation of delivery equipment. On line 38, the increase in Depreciation Expense — Delivery Equipment, *$1,900.00*, is listed in the Adjustments Debit column. On line 9, the increase in Accumulated Depreciation — Delivery Equipment, *$1,900.00*, is listed in the Adjustments Credit column.

Adjustment for depreciation of office equipment. On line 39, the increase in Depreciation Expense — Office Equipment, *$950.00*, is listed in the Adjustments Debit column. On line 11, the increase in Accumulated Depreciation — Office Equipment, *$950.00*, is listed in the Adjustments Credit column.

Adjustment for depreciation of store equipment. On line 40, the increase in Depreciation Expense — Store Equipment, *$2,840.00*, is listed in the Adjustments Debit column. On line 13, the increase in Accumulated Depreciation — Store Equipment, *$2,840.00*, is listed in the Adjustments Credit column.

Journalizing adjustments for depreciation expense

Data needed to journalize adjustments for depreciation expense are obtained from the Adjustments columns of a work sheet. Lin's three adjusting entries are shown in the general journal below.

GENERAL JOURNAL PAGE 27

	DATE		ACCOUNT TITLE	POST. REF.	DEBIT	CREDIT	
1			Adjusting Entries				1
12		31	Depreciation Exp. - Delivery Equip.		1900 00		12
13			Accum. Depr. - Delivery Equip.			1900 00	13
14		31	Depreciation Exp. - Office Equip.		950 00		14
15			Accum. Depr. - Office Equip.			950 00	15
16		31	Depreciation Exp. - Store Equip.		2840 00		16
17			Accum. Depr. - Store Equip.			2840 00	17

Adjusting entries to record depreciation

Posting adjustments for estimated depreciation

After adjusting entries for depreciation expense are posted, the accounts appear as shown below and on page 512.

ACCOUNT Delivery Equipment ACCOUNT NO. 1201

DATE		ITEM	POST. REF.	DEBIT	CREDIT	BALANCE DEBIT	BALANCE CREDIT
1983 Jan.	1	Balance	✓			10880 00	
Apr.	1		CP10	7000 00		17880 00	

ACCOUNT Accumulated Depreciation - Delivery Equip. ACCOUNT NO. 1201.1

DATE		ITEM	POST. REF.	DEBIT	CREDIT	BALANCE DEBIT	BALANCE CREDIT
1983 Jan.	1	Balance	✓				5250 00
Dec.	31		G27		1900 00		7150 00

General ledger accounts after posting adjusting entries for depreciation

ACCOUNT Office Equipment — ACCOUNT NO. 1202

DATE		ITEM	POST. REF.	DEBIT	CREDIT	BALANCE DEBIT	BALANCE CREDIT
1983 Jan.	1	Balance	✓			971000	

ACCOUNT Accumulated Depreciation - Office Equip. — ACCOUNT NO. 1202.1

DATE		ITEM	POST. REF.	DEBIT	CREDIT	BALANCE DEBIT	BALANCE CREDIT
1983 Jan.	1	Balance	✓				195000
Dec.	31		G27		95000		290000

ACCOUNT Store Equipment — ACCOUNT NO. 1203

DATE		ITEM	POST. REF.	DEBIT	CREDIT	BALANCE DEBIT	BALANCE CREDIT
1983 Jan.	1	Balance	✓			3840000	
July	1		CP19	335000		4175000	

ACCOUNT Accumulated Depreciation - Store Equip. — ACCOUNT NO. 1203.1

DATE		ITEM	POST. REF.	DEBIT	CREDIT	BALANCE DEBIT	BALANCE CREDIT
1983 Jan.	1		✓				540000
Dec.	31		G27		284000		824000

ACCOUNT Depreciation Expense - Delivery Equipment — ACCOUNT NO. 6105

DATE		ITEM	POST. REF.	DEBIT	CREDIT	BALANCE DEBIT	BALANCE CREDIT
1983 Dec.	31		G27	190000		190000	

ACCOUNT Depreciation Expense - Office Equipment — ACCOUNT NO. 6106

DATE		ITEM	POST. REF.	DEBIT	CREDIT	BALANCE DEBIT	BALANCE CREDIT
1983 Dec.	31		G27	95000		95000	

ACCOUNT Depreciation Expense - Store Equipment — ACCOUNT NO. 6107

DATE		ITEM	POST. REF.	DEBIT	CREDIT	BALANCE DEBIT	BALANCE CREDIT
1983 Dec.	31		G27	284000		284000	

General ledger accounts after posting adjusting entries for depreciation

Delivery Equipment, Office Equipment, and Store Equipment have debit balances showing the original cost of equipment. The three contra accounts for the equipment accounts have credit balances showing the accumulated depreciation recorded to date. The three depreciation expense accounts have debit balances showing depreciation expense for the current fiscal period.

DISPOSAL OF A PLANT ASSET

When no longer used, a plant asset may be sold or discarded. After over five years of use, Lin's sold a delivery truck.

January 5, 1989. Received cash, $1,000.00, from the sale of a delivery truck bought on April 1, 1983, for $7,000.00. Receipt No. 106.

The plant asset record for the delivery truck is below.

PLANT ASSET RECORD

Lin's Music Center — Account No. 1201

Item: Delivery Truck — General Ledger Account: Delivery Equipment

Serial No.: 8735M96025 — Description: Model C20

From Whom Purchased: Star Motors, Dallas, TX — Cost: $7,000.00

Estimated Life: 5 years — Estimated Salvage or Trade-in Value: $1,000.00 — Depreciation per year: $1,200.00

Disposal date: January 5, 1989 — Disposal amount: $1,000.00

Date Mo. Day Yr.	Annual Depreciation Expense	Accumulated Depreciation	Book Value
4 1 83			7,000.00
12 31 83	900.00	900.00	6,100.00
12 31 84	1,200.00	2,100.00	4,900.00
12 31 85	1,200.00	3,300.00	3,700.00
12 31 86	1,200.00	4,500.00	2,500.00
12 31 87	1,200.00	5,700.00	1,300.00
12 31 88	300.00	6,000.00	1,000.00

Plant asset record showing disposal of a plant asset

When a plant asset is disposed of, a notation is made on the plant asset record. The date of disposal, *January 5, 1989*, is written on the *Disposal date* line. The amount received, *$1,000.00*, is written on the *Disposal amount* line.

Analyzing the sale of a plant asset

The delivery truck was sold for $1,000.00. The book value of the delivery truck on January 5, 1989, is $1,000.00. (Cost, $7,000.00, less accumu-

Cash	
1,000.00	

Accumulated Depreciation — Delivery Equipment	
6,000.00	

Delivery Equipment	
	7,000.00

lated depreciation, $6,000.00, equals book value, $1,000.00). The analysis of this transaction is shown in the T accounts at the left.

Cash is debited for $1,000.00 to show the increase in the balance of this asset.

Accumulated Depreciation — Delivery Equipment is debited for $6,000.00 to show the decrease in this contra account's balance. The amount, *$6,000.00*, is the total depreciation recorded during the entire life of the delivery truck.

Delivery Equipment is credited for $7,000.00 to show the decrease in the balance of this plant asset account. This entry cancels the original cost, $7,000.00, debited to the delivery equipment account when the truck was bought.

Journalizing the sale of a plant asset

The entry to record the sale of the delivery truck is shown in the cash receipts journal below.

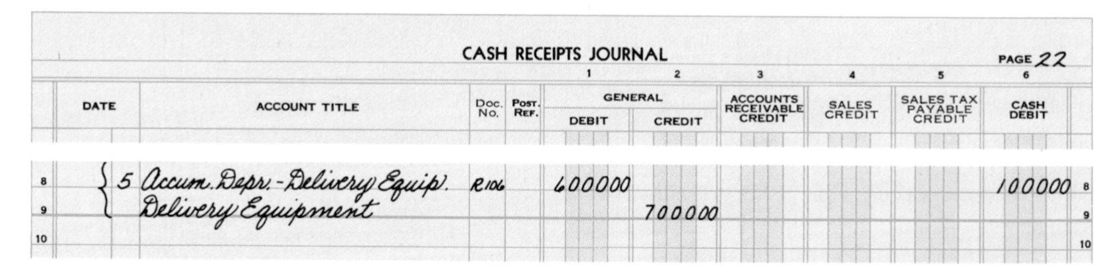

CASH RECEIPTS JOURNAL PAGE 22

	Date	Account Title	Doc. No.	Post. Ref.	1 General Debit	2 General Credit	3 Accounts Receivable Credit	4 Sales Credit	5 Sales Tax Payable Credit	6 Cash Debit	
8	5	Accum. Depr.-Delivery Equip.	R106		6000 00					1000 00	8
9		Delivery Equipment				7000 00					9
10											10

Entry to record the sale of a plant asset

Cash is debited for $1,000.00 in the Cash Debit column. Accumulated Depreciation — Delivery Equipment is debited for $6,000.00 in the General Debit column. Delivery Equipment is credited for $7,000.00 in the General Credit column.

ACCOUNTING TERMS

What is the meaning of each of the following?

1. plant assets
2. equipment
3. depreciation
4. estimated salvage value
5. straight-line method of depreciation
6. plant asset record
7. book value of a plant asset

QUESTIONS FOR INDIVIDUAL STUDY

1. What accounts are debited and credited when a plant asset is bought for cash?
2. Why are most plant assets worth less than their original cost after being used for a period of time?
3. If the expense of using a plant asset is not recorded, how will this omission affect total business expenses? How will this omission affect the net income for the period?
4. What three factors affect the amount of

depreciation of a plant asset?

5. How is the annual depreciation expense figured for a plant asset using the straight-line method of depreciation?
6. How is the book value of a plant asset figured?
7. What amount is always shown as the balance of a plant asset account?
8. What accounts are debited and credited on a work sheet in planning adjustments for depreciation of a plant asset?
9. What accounts are debited and credited to record the sale of a plant asset for its salvage value?

CASES FOR MANAGEMENT DECISION

CASE 1 Josephine Alvarez, owner of a small business, does not record depreciation expense for the business' plant assets. Ms. Alvarez says that she does not make actual cash payments for depreciation. Therefore, she records an expense for the use of plant assets only when cash is paid for a plant asset. Do you agree with Ms. Alvarez's method? Explain.

CASE 2 Kwik Delivery Service has more business than can be handled with the present number of trucks it owns. The company is investigating the cost of buying an additional delivery truck. One dealer recommends a small truck costing $8,500.00. The useful life of the truck is estimated to be 5 years with an estimated salvage value of $1,000.00. Another dealer recommends a larger truck with 50% more capacity than the smaller truck. The cost price is $12,000.00, with a useful life of 7 years, and estimated salvage value of $1,500.00. Which truck would you recommend Kwik Delivery Service buy? Why?

DRILLS FOR UNDERSTANDING

DRILL 25-D 1 Figuring depreciation expense

Instructions: Use the straight-line method of figuring depreciation described on page 506. Figure the amount of annual depreciation for each of the following plant assets.

Plant Asset	Original Cost	Estimated Salvage Value	Estimated Life
1	$ 2,850.00	$ 450.00	4 years
2	1,700.00	200.00	5 years
3	900.00	none	3 years
4	36,600.00	1,600.00	20 years
5	17,000.00	2,400.00	8 years
6	12,160.00	800.00	16 years
7	2,280.00	300.00	3 years
8	2,210.00	240.00	5 years
9	29,280.00	1,280.00	10 years
10	14,500.00	2,800.00	20 years

DRILL 25-D 2 Figuring book value of a plant asset

Instructions: Figure two amounts for each of the plant assets on page 516. (a) Figure the total amount of estimated depreciation as of December 31, 1983. (b) Figure the book value as of December 31, 1983. Figure the time of depreciation to the nearest number of months.

Plant Asset	Date Bought	Original Cost	Estimated Salvage Value	Estimated Life
1	Jan. 1, 1979	$ 2,400.00	$150.00	5 years
2	July 1, 1979	7,150.00	550.00	10 years
3	Dec. 31, 1979	10,725.00	825.00	15 years
4	Jan. 1, 1980	1,865.00	245.00	20 years
5	July 1, 1980	3,360.00	210.00	5 years
6	Nov. 1, 1980	240.00	24.00	4 years
7	Jan. 1, 1981	1,320.00	none	10 years
8	April 1, 1982	2,770.00	500.00	5 years
9	Jan. 1, 1983	2,900.00	300.00	10 years
10	Dec. 1, 1983	428.00	50.00	7 years

APPLICATION PROBLEMS

PROBLEM 25-1 Recording the buying of plant assets

Superior Company bought for cash the plant assets listed below.

Plant Asset	Date Bought	Original Cost	Asset Account Recorded In
1	Feb. 1, 1983	$1,950.00	Store Equipment
2	April 1, 1983	8,200.00	Delivery Equipment
3	May 1, 1983	975.00	Office Equipment
4	July 1, 1983	2,850.00	Store Equipment
5	Sept. 1, 1983	150.00	Office Equipment
6	Dec. 1, 1983	750.00	Store Equipment

Instructions: Record on page 5 of a cash payments journal the buying of the plant assets listed above.

PROBLEM 25-2 Figuring depreciation expense

Expressway Auto Repair owns the plant assets listed below.

Plant Asset	Date Bought	Original Cost	Estimated Salvage Value	Estimated Life
1	Jan. 1, 1976	$5,200.00	$400.00	10 years
2	July 1, 1978	1,372.00	300.00	8 years
3	July 1, 1978	1,650.00	150.00	6 years
4	Oct. 1, 1979	2,700.00	300.00	5 years
5	April 1, 1983	4,000.00	400.00	5 years
6	July 1, 1983	1,734.00	150.00	6 years

Instructions: For each plant asset above, figure the depreciation expense to be recorded for the year ended December 31, 1983. Use the straight-line method of figuring depreciation described on page 506. Figure the time of depreciation to the nearest number of months.

PROBLEM 25-3 Preparing a plant asset record

Wood Creations bought a new bench saw July 1, 1983. Other information pertaining to the bench saw is listed below and on page 517.

General ledger account: Shop Equipment
Account number: 1303

Serial number of saw: 68358M
Model number of saw: H900
From whom purchased: T & M Equipment Company, St. Louis, MO
Original cost: $2,750.00
Estimated life: 4 years
Estimated salvage value: $350.00

Instructions: Prepare a plant asset record for the bench saw similar to the record described on page 507. For each year of the plant asset's life, record year-end date, annual depreciation expense, accumulated depreciation, and book value.

PROBLEM 25-4 Recording work sheet adjustments and journal entries for depreciation expense

A partial trial balance of Edgewood Appliances is below. The accounts for depreciation of plant assets are illustrated on this partial trial balance.

Instructions: 1. Record the information in a work sheet's Trial Balance columns for the year ended December 31, 1983.

Edgewood Appliances
Trial Balance
December 31, 1983

Account	Debit	Credit
Delivery Equipment	27 810 00	
Accumulated Depreciation — Delivery Equipment		15 490 00
Store Equipment	17 160 00	
Accumulated Depreciation — Store Equipment		4 934 00
Depreciation Expense — Delivery Equipment		
Depreciation Expense — Store Equipment		

Instructions: 2. Record on the work sheet the adjustments for estimated depreciation for the year. Depreciation expenses are below.

Annual depreciation of delivery equipment, $6,330.00
Annual depreciation of store equipment, $1,020.00

3. Journalize the adjusting entries on page 24 of a general journal.

ENRICHMENT PROBLEMS

MASTERY PROBLEM 25-M Figuring depreciation expense and book value of plant assets; journalizing depreciation expense and disposal of a plant asset

Air Systems owns the plant assets listed below.

Plant Asset	Asset Account	Date Bought	Original Cost	Estimated Salvage Value	Estimated Life
1	Delivery Equip.	Oct. 1, 1976	$8,000.00	$440.00	7 years
2	Delivery Equip.	July 1, 1983	7,400.00	500.00	5 years
3	Shop Equipment	Oct. 1, 1979	1,638.00	150.00	8 years
4	Shop Equipment	Feb. 1, 1980	2,820.00	none	10 years
5	Shop Equipment	April 1, 1983	1,060.00	100.00	4 years
6	Shop Equipment	July 1, 1983	1,150.00	70.00	3 years

Instructions: 1. Figure each plant asset's depreciation expense for the year ended December 31, 1983. Use the straight-line method of figuring depreciation. Figure the time of depreciation to the nearest number of months.

2. Figure each plant asset's book value as of December 31, 1983.

3. Record on page 15 of a general journal the two adjusting entries for depreciation expense for the year ended December 31, 1983. Record delivery equipment depreciation in Depreciation Expense — Delivery Equipment. Record shop equipment depreciation in Depreciation Expense — Shop Equipment.

4. On January 25, 1984, received cash, $440.00, from the sale of delivery equipment, Plant Asset No. 1, bought October 1, 1976, for $8,000.00. Receipt No. 324. Record the sale of this asset on page 18 of a cash receipts journal.

CHALLENGE PROBLEM 25-C Figuring depreciation expense using a declining-balance method

Introductory remarks. Federal income tax regulations permit the straight-line method of figuring depreciation as described in this chapter. Regulations also permit a business to use a *declining-balance method of figuring depreciation*. For the declining-balance method, the depreciation rate may be twice the rate for the straight-line method. The rate is applied to the *book value* of the plant asset at the *beginning* of each fiscal period.

A delivery truck was bought on January 2, 1982, for $7,000.00, with an estimated life of 10 years. The rate of depreciation under the straight-line method would be 10% per year. Therefore, the rate under the declining-balance method is 20%. The remaining book value at the end of the tenth year is the estimated salvage value of the truck.

Instructions: Figure the book value at the beginning of each of the 10 years of useful life. Figure the amount of annual depreciation for each year. Figure the accumulated depreciation at the end of each year. Figure the book value at the end of each year. (The book value at the end of one year is the book value for the beginning of the next year.) Figures for the first two years are given as examples. Use a chart similar to the one below.

Year	Book value at beginning of year	Rate of depreciation	Annual depreciation this year	Accumulated depreciation at end of year	Book value at end of year
1982	$7,000.00	20%	$1,400.00	$1,400.00	$5,600.00
1983	5,600.00	20%	1,120.00	2,520.00	4,480.00

26

Accounting for Notes and Interest

ENABLING PERFORMANCE TASKS

After studying Chapter 26, you will be able to:

a. Define accounting terms related to accounting for notes and interest.
b. Explain accounting principles and practices related to accounting for notes and interest.
c. Journalize notes payable transactions.
d. Journalize notes receivable transactions.

Most businesses receive cash from sales of merchandise or services. They pay out cash to purchase merchandise, pay operating expenses, and buy new equipment. Merchandise purchased may not be sold for several months. Equipment bought may be used for several years. For these and other reasons, a business may pay out more cash some months than it receives. Therefore, many businesses borrow cash from a bank or other business when cash payments are greater than cash receipts. Then the business repays the cash in later periods when cash receipts are greater than cash payments.

A written and signed promise to pay a sum of money is called a promissory note. A promissory note is frequently referred to simply as a note.

Promissory notes are used to borrow money or to obtain an extension of time on an account. Sometimes a business requests a note from a customer who wants credit beyond the usual time given for sales on account. Notes have an advantage over oral promises and accounts receivable or payable. A note, like a check, can be endorsed and transferred to a bank. The bank then gives the business cash for the note. Thus, the business can get its money before the note is due. Notes can also be useful in a court of law as evidence of a debt.

One form of a promissory note is on the next page.

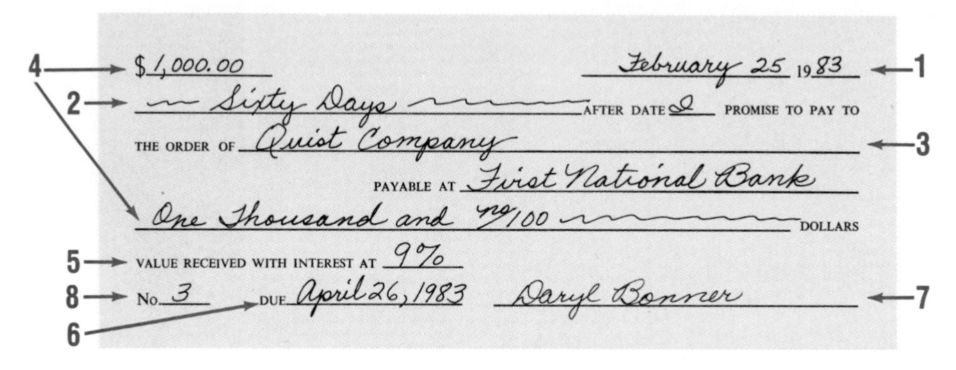
4 → $1,000.00 February 25 1983 ← 1
2 → Sixty Days AFTER DATE I PROMISE TO PAY TO
THE ORDER OF Quist Company ← 3
PAYABLE AT First National Bank
One Thousand and no/100 DOLLARS
5 → VALUE RECEIVED WITH INTEREST AT 9%
8 → No. 3 DUE April 26, 1983 Daryl Bonner ← 7
6

A promissory note

The terms defined below are used in analyzing the above note.

Term	Definition	Illustration
1 Date of a note	The day a note is issued.	February 25, 1983
2 Time of a note	The days, months, or years from the date of issue until a note is to be paid.	Sixty days
3 Payee of a note	The person to whom a note is payable.	Quist Company
4 Principal of a note	The amount a borrower promises to pay — the face of a note.	$1,000.00
5 Interest rate of a note	The percentage of the principal that is paid for use of the money.	9%
6 Maturity date of a note	The date a note is due.	April 26, 1983
7 Maker of a note	The person who signs a note and thus promises to make payment.	Daryl Bonner
8 Number of a note	The number assigned by the maker to identify a specific note.	3

INTEREST ON NOTES

An amount paid for the use of the principal of a note for a period of time is called interest. Most promissory notes require the payment of interest. Promissory notes that require interest payments are called interest-bearing notes. Promissory notes that do not contain a provision for the payment of interest are called non-interest-bearing notes.

The interest rate is stated as a percentage of the principal. Interest at 9% means that 9 cents will be paid for the use of each dollar borrowed for a full year. The interest on $100.00 for a full year at 9% is $9.00.

The principal plus the interest on a note is called the maturity value. A one-year note for $100.00 with a 9% interest rate will have a maturity value of $109.00 ($100.00 principal plus $9.00 interest).

Sometimes partial payments are made on a note each month. This is particularly true when an individual buys a car and signs a note for the amount owed. The monthly payment includes part of the money owed and part of the interest to be paid.

NOTES PAYABLE

Promissory notes that a business gives creditors are called notes payable. Notes payable are classified as current liabilities of a business.

Issuing a note payable to borrow money from a bank

On February 1, 1983, Lin's Music Center arranges to borrow money from its bank. A note payable is issued to the bank as evidence of indebtedness. The bank credits Lin's checking account for the principal amount of the note.

February 1, 1983. Issued a 6-month, 9% note to the First National Bank, $4,000.00. Note Payable No. 4.

Analyzing the issuance of a note payable for cash. A copy of the note payable is the source document used by Lin's for recording the transaction. *(CONCEPT: Objective Evidence)* In this transaction the balance of the asset account Cash is increased. The balance of the liability account Notes Payable is also increased. Therefore, Cash is debited for $4,000.00 and Notes Payable is credited for $4,000.00. No entry is made for the interest until a later date when the interest is paid.

Cash	
4,000.00	

Notes Payable	
	4,000.00

Recording the issuance of a note payable and the receipt of cash. This transaction is recorded in a cash receipts journal as shown below.

CASH RECEIPTS JOURNAL — PAGE 6

				1	2	3	4	5	6	
				GENERAL						
DATE	ACCOUNT TITLE	DOC. NO.	POST. REF.	DEBIT	CREDIT	ACCOUNTS RECEIVABLE CREDIT	SALES CREDIT	SALES TAX PAYABLE CREDIT	CASH DEBIT	
6 1	Notes Payable	NP4			400000				400000	6

The abbreviation *NP* in the Doc. No. column stands for *Note Payable.*

Entry to record cash received for a note payable

Paying principal and interest on a note payable at maturity

When cash is paid for interest, the amount paid is debited to an other expense account titled Interest Expense.

August 1, 1983. Paid the First National Bank in full for Note Payable No. 4 (principal, $4,000.00; interest, $180.00), $4,180.00. Check No. 724.

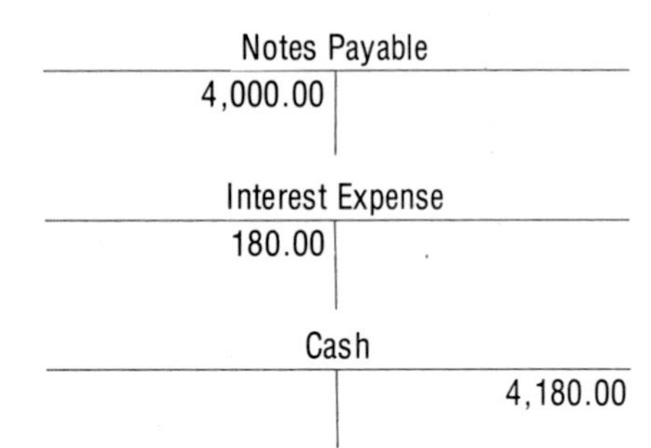

Analyzing the payment of principal and interest. The check stub is the source document for recording the transaction. *(CONCEPT: Objective Evidence)* In this transaction the balance of the liability account Notes Payable is decreased. The balance of the other expense account Interest Expense is increased. The balance of the asset account Cash is decreased. Therefore, Notes Payable is debited for $4,000.00; Interest Expense is debited for $180.00; and Cash is credited for $4,180.00.

Recording the payment of principal and interest. This transaction is recorded in a cash payments journal as shown below.

CASH PAYMENTS JOURNAL — PAGE 22

	Date	Account Title	Check No.	Post. Ref.	1 General Debit	2 General Credit	3 Accounts Payable Debit	4 Purchases Discount Credit	5 Cash Credit	
3	1	Notes Payable	724		4000 00				4180 00	3
4		Interest Expense			180 00					4

Entry to record paying principal and interest on a note payable at maturity

Issuing a note payable for an extension of time

If a business is unable to pay an account when due, the business may ask for an extension of time. Sometimes, when a request for more time is made, the business is asked to issue a note payable. The note payable does not pay the amount owed to the creditor. However, the form of the liability is changed from an account payable to a note payable.

February 25, 1983. Issued a 60-day, 8% note to Sykes Lumber Company for an extension of time on this account payable, $3,000.00. Note Payable No. 5.

Analyzing the issuance of a note payable for an extension of time. A copy of the note is the source document for recording the transaction. *(CONCEPT: Objective Evidence)* In this transaction the balance of the liability account Accounts Payable is decreased. The balance of the liability account Notes Payable is increased. The balance of the creditor's account, Sykes Lumber Company, in the accounts payable ledger, is also decreased. Therefore, Accounts Payable is debited for $3,000.00. Notes Payable is credited for $3,000.00. The creditor's account, Sykes Lumber Company, is debited for $3,000.00.

GENERAL LEDGER

Accounts Payable

Debit	Credit
3,000.00	

Notes Payable

Debit	Credit
	3,000.00

ACCOUNTS PAYABLE LEDGER

Sykes Lumber Company

Debit	Credit
3,000.00	

Whenever Accounts Payable is decreased, the creditor's account in the accounts payable ledger also is decreased by the same amount.

Recording the issuance of a note payable. This transaction is recorded in a general journal as shown below.

GENERAL JOURNAL PAGE 3

	DATE	ACCOUNT TITLE	POST. REF.	DEBIT	CREDIT	
17	25	Accts. Pay./Sykes Lumber Co.	✓	300000		17
18		Notes Payable			300000	18
19		Note Payable No. 5.				19
20						20
21						21

Entry to record issuance of a note payable for an extension of time on an account payable

When this entry is posted, the accounts payable account for Sykes Lumber Company will be closed. The account payable is replaced by the note payable.

Paying a note payable. Note Payable No. 5 is due on April 26. On that date, Lin's issues a check for $3,039.45 to Sykes Lumber Company. This check is in payment of the principal, $3,000.00, and interest, $39.45. The check is recorded in the cash payments journal as the payment of Note Payable No. 5. Notes Payable is debited for $3,000.00. Interest Expense is debited for $39.45. Cash is credited for $3,039.45. The journal entry for Note Payable No. 5 is similar to the one for Note Payable No. 4, page 522.

Bank discount

Some banks require that the interest be paid in advance of the time a borrower signs a note. Interest on a note collected in advance by a bank is called bank discount. The amount received for a note after the bank has deducted the bank discount is called proceeds. A note on which interest is paid in advance is called a discounted note.

March 25, 1983. Discounted at 10% at the First National Bank Lin's 6-month non-interest-bearing note, $2,500.00. Note Payable No. 6. The bank credited Lin's checking account for the proceeds, $2,375.00.

Analyzing the issuance of a discounted note payable. A copy of the note payable is the source document for recording the transaction. *(CONCEPT: Objective Evidence)* In this transaction the balances of the asset account Cash and the other expense account Interest Expense are increased. Therefore, Cash is debited for $2,375.00. Interest Expense is debited for $125.00. Notes Payable is credited for $2,500.00. The amount of interest is figured on the next page.

Cash	
2,375.00	

Interest Expense	
125.00	

Notes Payable	
	2,500.00

Maturity Value	×	Interest Rate	×	Time	=	Bank Discount
$2,500.00	×	10%	×	$\frac{6}{12}$ Year	=	$125.00

The proceeds are figured below.

Maturity Value	−	Bank Discount	=	Proceeds
$2,500.00	−	$125.00	=	$2,375.00

Entry to record cash received for a discounted note payable

Recording the issuance of a discounted note payable and the receipt of cash. This transaction is recorded in a cash receipts journal as shown below.

CASH RECEIPTS JOURNAL PAGE 15

	DATE	ACCOUNT TITLE	DOC. NO.	POST. REF.	1 GENERAL DEBIT	2 GENERAL CREDIT	3 ACCOUNTS RECEIVABLE CREDIT	4 SALES CREDIT	5 SALES TAX PAYABLE CREDIT	6 CASH DEBIT	
6	25	Notes Payable	NP6			250000				237500	6
7		Interest Expense			12500						7

Recording the payment of a discounted note payable. When Note Payable No. 6 is paid on September 25, Check No. 956 is issued to the First National Bank. This check is in payment of the principal. No payment of interest is necessary at this time because the bank collected the interest in advance. This transaction is recorded in a cash payments journal as shown below.

Entry to record payment of a discounted note payable

CASH PAYMENTS JOURNAL PAGE 9

	DATE	ACCOUNT TITLE	CHECK NO.	POST. REF.	1 GENERAL DEBIT	2 GENERAL CREDIT	3 ACCOUNTS PAYABLE DEBIT	4 PURCHASES DISCOUNT CREDIT	5 CASH CREDIT	
3	25	Notes Payable	956		250000				250000	3
4										4

NOTES RECEIVABLE

Promissory notes that a business accepts from customers are called notes receivable. Notes receivable are classified as current assets of a business.

Accepting a note receivable from a customer

A charge customer who is unable to pay an account on the due date may request additional time. When a request for more time is made, a business may agree to accept a note receivable. A note receivable does not pay the amount the customer owes. However, the form of the asset is changed from an account receivable to a note receivable.

> *February 15, 1983. Received a 2-month, 9% note from Dona Konich for an extension of time on her account, $500.00. Note Receivable No. 8.*

Analyzing the acceptance of a note receivable. The original copy of a note receivable is the source document for recording the transaction. *(CONCEPT: Objective Evidence)* In this transaction the balance of the asset account Notes Receivable is increased. The balance of the asset account Accounts Receivable is decreased. The balance of the customer's account, Dona Konich, in the accounts receivable ledger is also decreased. Therefore, Notes Receivable is debited for $500.00. Accounts Receivable is credited for $500.00. The customer's account, Dona Konich, is credited for $500.00.

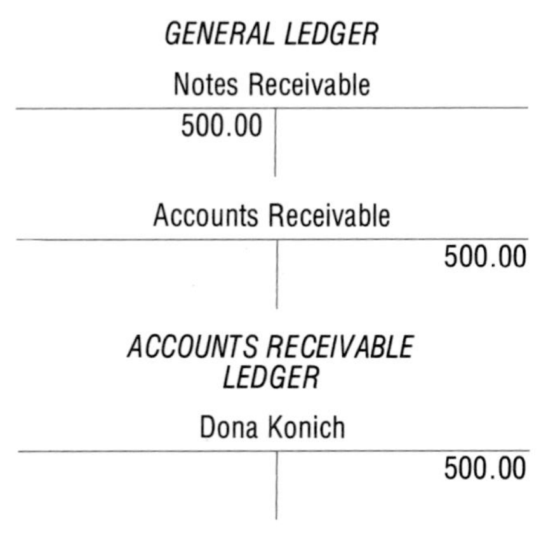

> Whenever Accounts Receivable is decreased, the named customer's account in the accounts receivable ledger must also be decreased the same amount.

Recording the acceptance of a note receivable. This transaction is recorded in a general journal as shown below.

GENERAL JOURNAL PAGE 3

	DATE		ACCOUNT TITLE	POST. REF.	DEBIT	CREDIT	
6		15	Notes Receivable		500 00		6
7			Accts. Rec./Dona Konich	✓		500 00	7
8			Note Rec. No. 8.				8
9							9

Entry to record a note received for an extension of time on an account

When this entry is posted, the account receivable account for Dona Konich will be closed. This account receivable is replaced by the note receivable.

Collecting principal and interest on a note receivable at maturity

The amount of interest received is credited to an other revenue account titled Interest Income.

> *April 15, 1983. Received cash from Dona Konich in settlement of Note Receivable No. 8 (principal, $500.00; interest, $7.50), $507.50. Receipt No. 238.*

Cash	
507.50	

Notes Receivable	
	500.00

Interest Income	
	7.50

Analyzing the receipt of principal and interest. The receipt issued for the cash received from Dona Konich is the source document for recording the transaction. *(CONCEPT: Objective Evidence)* In this transaction the balance of the asset account Cash is increased. The balance of the asset account Notes Receivable is decreased. The balance of the other revenue account Interest Income is increased. Therefore, Cash is debited for $507.50. Notes Receivable is credited for $500.00. Interest Income is credited for $7.50.

Recording the receipt of principal and interest. This transaction is recorded in a cash receipts journal as shown below.

CASH RECEIPTS JOURNAL — PAGE 18

	DATE	ACCOUNT TITLE	DOC. NO.	POST. REF.	1 GENERAL DEBIT	2 GENERAL CREDIT	3 ACCOUNTS RECEIVABLE CREDIT	4 SALES CREDIT	5 SALES TAX PAYABLE CREDIT	6 CASH DEBIT	
18	15	Notes Receivable	R238			500 00				507 50	18
19		Interest Income				7 50					19
20											20
21											21

Entry to record collection of principal and interest on a note receivable at maturity

After the entry is recorded, Note Receivable No. 8 is marked *Paid* and is returned to Dona Konich, the maker.

Dishonored note receivable

A note that is not paid when due is called a dishonored note. The balance of the notes receivable account should show only the amount of those notes that probably will be collected. The amount of a dishonored note receivable should therefore be removed from the notes receivable account. The amount of the note plus interest income earned on the note is still owed by the customer. Therefore, the amount owed should be debited to the accounts receivable account in the general ledger. The amount owed also should be debited to the customer's account in the accounts receivable ledger. The customer's account will then show the total amount owed by the customer including the amount of the dishonored note. This information may be important if the customer requests credit in the future.

February 20, 1983. John Vargo dishonored Note Receivable No. 3, a 1 month, 9% note for $400.00 plus interest due today (principal, $400.00; interest, $3.00), $403.00. Memorandum No. 36.

Analyzing a dishonored note receivable. A memorandum is the source document for recording the transaction. *(CONCEPT: Objective Evidence)*

In this transaction the balance of the asset account Accounts Receivable is increased. The balance of the asset account Notes Receivable is decreased. The balance of the other revenue account Interest Income is increased. The balance of the customer's account, John Vargo, in the accounts receivable ledger also is increased. Therefore, Accounts Receivable and John Vargo are each debited for $403.00 ($400.00 principal plus $3.00 interest). Notes Receivable is credited for $400.00, the amount of the note. Interest Income is credited for $3.00, the amount of interest earned ($400.00 × .09 × 1/12 yr. = $3.00). The interest income has been earned even though it is not paid. John Vargo owes the principal amount of the note plus the interest earned. Therefore, both principal and interest are debited to Accounts Receivable and the customer's account.

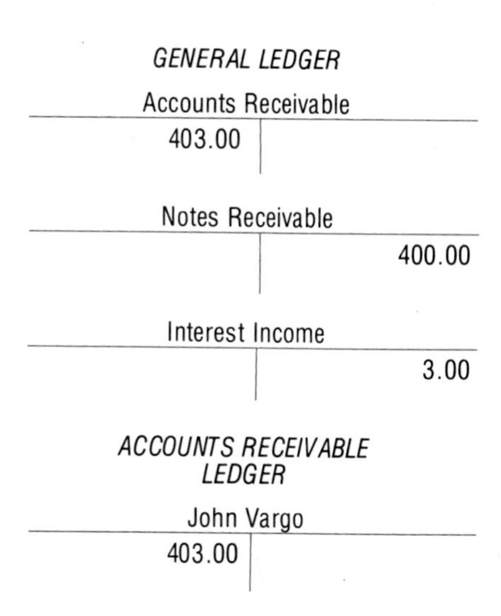

Recording a dishonored note receivable. This transaction is recorded in a general journal as shown below.

GENERAL JOURNAL PAGE 3

	DATE		ACCOUNT TITLE	POST. REF.	DEBIT	CREDIT	
9		20	Accts. Rec. / John Vargo		403 00		9
10			Notes Receivable			400 00	10
11			Interest Income			3 00	11
12			Memorandum No. 36.				12
13							13
14							14

Entry to record a dishonored note receivable

Later Lin's may decide that the account cannot be collected from Mr. Vargo. If so, the balance of the account will be written off as a bad debt. At that time Allowance for Uncollectible Accounts will be debited, and Accounts Receivable and John Vargo's account will be credited.

ACCOUNTING TERMS

What is the meaning of each of the following?

1. promissory note
2. date of a note
3. time of a note
4. payee of a note
5. principal of a note
6. interest rate of a note
7. maturity date of a note
8. maker of a note
9. number of a note
10. interest
11. interest-bearing notes
12. non-interest-bearing notes
13. maturity value
14. notes payable
15. bank discount
16. proceeds
17. discounted note
18. notes receivable
19. dishonored note

QUESTIONS FOR INDIVIDUAL STUDY

1. Why do many businesses periodically borrow cash for short periods of time?
2. Why do many businesses prefer to have a note receivable from a customer than an account receivable?
3. What is the difference between the payee and the maker of a note?
4. What does "interest at 8%" mean?
5. What is the source document for recording the issuance of a note payable?
6. When an interest-bearing note is paid, why is Cash credited for a greater amount than Notes Payable is debited?
7. What accounts are debited and credited when a business issues an interest-bearing note payable as an extension of time on its account payable?
8. How much will the maker receive for a one-year non-interest-bearing note of $2,000.00, discounted at 10%?
9. What accounts are debited and credited when a non-interest-bearing note payable is discounted at a bank?
10. What accounts are debited and credited when a discounted note payable is paid at maturity?
11. A business may accept a note receivable from a charge customer for an extension of time on the customer's account receivable. Does this acceptance change the total amount of the assets of the business?
12. What accounts are debited and credited when a business receives the principal and interest on a note receivable at maturity?
13. Why is interest income recorded at the time a note is dishonored even though cash has not been received?
14. What accounts are debited and credited when a customer dishonors an interest-bearing note receivable?

CASES FOR MANAGEMENT DECISION

CASE 1 Bonita Booker purchased $4,000.00 worth of merchandise on account from Duncan Appliances on February 1. Duncan Appliances' terms of sale require payment on accounts within 30 days. However, Mrs. Booker purchased the merchandise with the understanding that she could issue a 9 percent note payable with payment due no later than July 1. On February 1 Mrs. Booker instructed her accountant to issue the note payable to Duncan Appliances. As payments on account are due in 30 days, the accountant suggested that the note be issued on March 2. On what date would you suggest that the note be issued? Why?

CASE 2 Byers Corporation has a $3,000.00, 4-month, 9% note receivable which has been dishonored. Two company accounting clerks cannot agree on the best way to record the dishonored note. Karl Hodovan recommends Notes Receivable be credited $3,000.00 and Allowance for Uncollectible Accounts be debited for $3,000.00. Nancy Soltis recommends Accounts Receivable and the customer's account be debited for $3,090.00. Then Notes Receivable be credited for $3,000.00 and Interest Income be credited for $90.00. Which recommendation is the more desirable entry? Why?

DRILLS FOR UNDERSTANDING

DRILL 26-D 1 Recording principal, interest, and bank discount for notes payable

Instructions: Use a form such as the one on the next page. Based on the transactions given, indicate by a check mark which account(s) should be debited and which account(s) credited. Transaction 1 is shown as an example. Note payable is abbreviated NP.

Trans. No.	Cash		Notes Payable		Accounts Payable		Interest Expense	
	Debit	Credit	Debit	Credit	Debit	Credit	Debit	Credit
1.	√			√				

Transactions

1. Issued a 3-month, 9% note, $2,000.00, for cash. NP216.
2. Issued a 60-day, 9½% note, $600.00, for an extension of time on an account payable. NP217.
3. Issued a 1-year, 10% note, $3,000.00, for cash. NP218.
4. Discounted at 8% a 6-month non-interest-bearing note, $2,500.00. NP219.
5. Discounted at 9% a 90-day non-interest-bearing note, $4,000.00. NP220.
6. Discounted at 10% a 1-year non-interest-bearing note, $5,000.00. NP221.
7. Paid in full NP216.
8. Paid in full NP217.
9. Paid in full NP218.
10. Paid in full NP219.
11. Paid in full NP220.
12. Paid in full NP221.

DRILL 26-D 2 Recording principal and interest for notes receivable

Instructions: Use a form such as the one below. Based on the transactions given, indicate by a check mark which account(s) should be debited and which account(s) credited. Transaction 1 is shown as an example. Note receivable is abbreviated NR.

Trans. No.	Cash		Notes Receivable		Accounts Receivable		Interest Income	
	Debit	Credit	Debit	Credit	Debit	Credit	Debit	Credit
1.			√			√		

Transactions

1. Received a 3-month, 9% note for an extension of time on account, $800.00. NR15.
2. Received a 60-day, 8% note for an extension of time on account, $3,000.00. NR16.
3. Received a 6-month, 10% note for an extension of time on account, $4,000.00. NR17.
4. Received a 1-year, 9% note for an extension of time on account, $5,000.00. NR18.
5. Received cash in settlement of NR15.
6. Received cash in settlement of NR16.
7. Received notice that maker of NR17 has dishonored the note on this date.
8. Received cash in settlement of NR18.

APPLICATION PROBLEMS

PROBLEM 26-1 Recording notes payable, interest, and bank discount

The transactions on the next page were completed by Kresky Furniture during part of the current fiscal year.

Instructions: 1. Record the following transactions. Use a cash receipts journal (page 15), a cash payments journal (page 12), and a general journal (page 5) similar to those illustrated in this chapter. Source documents are abbreviated as: check, C; note payable, NP.

Jan. 3. Issued a 30-day, 9% note payable to Havericak Company for an extension of time on account, $1,500.00. NP111.
4. Paid Cedar River Marina for NP71 (90-day, 8½% note due today; principal, $8,000.00; interest, $167.67), $8,167.67. C62.
10. Paid Sun Bank for NP83 (60-day, 9% note due today; principal, $2,500.00; interest, $36.99), $2,536.99. C122.
17. Discounted at 10% at Friendly Bank a 45-day, non-interest-bearing note payable, $4,000.00 (bank discount, $49.32; proceeds, $3,950.68). NP112. The bank credited our checking account for the proceeds.

Feb. 2. Paid Havericak Company for NP111 (principal, $1,500.00; interest, $11.10), $1,511.10. C198.
20. Issued a 90-day, 10% note payable to First National Bank, $2,500.00. The bank credited our checking account for the principal. NP113.

Mar. 1. Paid Friendly Bank for NP112, $4,000.00. C267.
10. Issued a 30-day, 9½% note payable to Southwest Supplies for an extension of time on account, $500.00. NP114.

Apr. 9. Paid Southwest Supplies for NP114 (principal, $500.00; interest, $3.90), $503.90. C341.

May 21. Paid First National Bank for NP113 (principal, $2,500.00; interest, $61.64), $2,561.64. C401.

Instructions: 2. Prove the cash receipts and cash payments journals.

PROBLEM 26-2 Recording notes receivable and interest

The transactions below were completed by Bertram Boat Supplies during part of the current fiscal year.

Instructions: 1. Record the following transactions. Use a cash receipts journal (page 11) and a general journal (page 3) similar to those illustrated in this chapter. Source documents are abbreviated as: memorandum, M; note receivable, NR; receipt, R.

Jan. 10. Received a 60-day, 9½% note receivable from Karl Grimes for an extension of time on account, $1,000.00. NR32.
12. Received a check from Carlota Campillo in settlement of NR28 (20-day, 9% note receivable due today; principal, $300.00; interest, $1.48), $301.48. R28.
22. Received a 3-month, 9% note receivable from Fred Chaney for an extension of time on account, $750.00. NR33.

Feb. 17. Received a check from Cynthia Hill in settlement of NR21 (6-month, 8½% note receivable due today; principal, $800.00; interest, $34.00), $834.00. R31.

Mar. 11. Received a check from Karl Grimes in settlement of NR32 (principal, $1,000.00; interest, $15.62), $1,015.62. R78.

Apr. 22. Fred Chaney dishonored NR33 due today. Charged the amount of the note receivable and the interest to his account (principal, $750.00; interest, $16.88), $766.88. M145.

Instructions: 2. Prove the cash receipts journal.

ENRICHMENT PROBLEMS

MASTERY PROBLEM 26-M Recording notes, interest, and bank discount

The transactions below were completed by Mayport Corporation during part of the current fiscal year.

Instructions: 1. Record the following transactions. Use a cash receipts journal (page 15), a cash payments journal (page 9), and a general journal (page 6) like those illustrated in this chapter. Source documents are abbreviated as: check, C; memorandum, M; note payable, NP; note receivable, NR; receipt, R.

Jan. 2. Received a 2-month, non-interest-bearing note receivable from Jack Romain for an extension of time on account, $400.00. NR132.
5. Issued a 60-day, 9% note payable to Soforenko Development Company for an extension of time on account, $2,500.00. NP115.
7. Discounted at 9½% at Midwest Bank our 60-day, non-interest-bearing note payable, $8,000.00 (bank discount, $124.93; proceeds, $7,875.07). NP116. The bank credited our checking account for the proceeds.
10. Received a 45-day, 10% note receivable from Judy Elsmore for an extension of time on account, $750.00. NR133.
17. Issued a 30-day, 9% note payable to McDaniel's for an extension of time on account, $2,400.00. NP117.
27. Issued a 2-month, 9½% note payable to Security Bank, $3,000.00. NP118. The bank credited our checking account for the principal.

Feb. 14. Received a 1-month, 9% note receivable from Don Walters for an extension of time on account, $900.00. NR134.
16. Paid McDaniel's for NP117 (principal $2,400.00; interest, $17.75), $2,417.75. C318.
24. Received a check from Judy Elsmore in settlement of NR133 (principal, $750.00; interest, $9.25), $759.25. R212.

Mar. 2. Jack Romain dishonored NR132 due today, $400.00. Charged the amount of the note receivable to his account. M85.
6. Paid Soforenko Development Company for NP115 (principal, $2,500.00; interest, $36.99), $2,536.99. C329.
8. Paid Midwest Bank for NP116. C333.
14. Received a check from Don Walters in settlement of NR134 (principal, $900.00; interest, $6.75), $906.75. R296.
20. Received a 2-month, non-interest-bearing note receivable from Katharine McNeil for an extension of time on account, $450.00. NR135.
27. Paid Security Bank for NP118 (principal, $3,000.00; interest, $47.50), $3,047.50. C346.

Instructions: 2. Prove the cash receipts and cash payments journals.

CHALLENGE PROBLEM 26-C Recording notes, interest, and bank discount

Introductory remarks. Interest may be figured for a period of less than one year. To do this the principal is multiplied by the interest rate and by the fraction of the year. The interest on a 9% interest-bearing note for $600.00 for 4 months is figured on the next page.

Principal	×	Interest Rate	×	Fraction of Year	=	Interest for Fraction of Year
$600.00	×	.09	×	$\frac{4}{12}$	=	$\frac{\$216.00}{12} = \$18.00$

The time of a note is stated often as a number of days, such as 30 days or 60 days. Interest on a 9% interest-bearing note for $900.00 for 60 days is figured below. Interest is normally rounded to the nearest cent.

Principal	×	Interest Rate	×	Fraction of Year	=	Interest for Fraction of Year
$900.00	×	.09	×	$\frac{60}{365}$	=	$\frac{\$4,860.00}{365} = \$13.32$

The transactions below were completed by Helco Equipment Company during the current year.

Instructions: 1. Record the following transactions. Use a cash receipts journal (page 40), a cash payments journal (page 26), and a general journal (page 12) similar to those illustrated in this chapter. Source documents are abbreviated as: check, C; memorandum, M; note payable, NP; note receivable, NR; receipt, R.

Jan. 3. Received a 3-month, 9½% note receivable dated December 29 from Paula Ferrell for an extension of time on account, $800.00. NR62.

6. Received a 30-day, 10% note receivable dated January 5 from Daryl Seaver for an extension of time on account, $350.00. NR63.

24. Issued a 1-month, 9% note payable to Holman Distributors for an extension of time on account, $1,500.00. NP21.

Feb. 4. Received a check from Daryl Seaver in settlement of NR63. R260.

24. Paid Holman Distributors for NP21. C105.

Mar. 4. Issued a 90-day, 8½% note payable to Lee & Gates Company for an extension of time on account, $4,000.00. NP22.

11. Purchased sales display equipment from Merita Company, $2,500.00. Paid cash, $1,000.00, and issued a 60-day, 9% note payable for the balance, $1,500.00. C130; NP23.

Record the transaction in the cash payments journal in one combined entry.

29. Received notice from the bank that Paula Ferrell dishonored NR62. Charged principal and interest to her account. M72.

May 3. Discounted at 9½% at First Guaranty Bank our 30-day, non-interest-bearing note, $1,800.00. NP24. The bank credited our checking account for the proceeds.

10. Paid Merita Company for NP23. C148.

June 2. Paid First Guaranty Bank for NP24. C191.

2. Paid Lee & Gates Company for NP22. C198.

Oct. 15. Received a check from Paula Ferrell for half of the $819.00 balance charged to her account on March 29. R279. Wrote off the remainder of this account receivable as uncollectible. M124.

Record the check in the cash receipts journal. Record the write-off of the customer's account in the general journal.

Instructions: 2. Prove the cash receipts and cash payments journals.

27

End-of-Fiscal-Period Work for a Corporation

ENABLING PERFORMANCE TASKS

After studying Chapter 27, you will be able to:

a. Define accounting terms related to end-of-fiscal-period work for a corporation.
b. Explain accounting principles and practices related to end-of-fiscal-period work for a corporation.
c. Record a trial balance on a work sheet for a corporation.
d. Plan adjustments on a work sheet for a corporation.
e. Complete a work sheet for a corporation.
f. Prepare financial statements for a corporation.
g. Journalize adjusting and closing entries for a corporation.
h. Journalize the declaration and payment of a dividend.

Financial information about a corporation is needed by a number of people. *(CONCEPT: Adequate Disclosure)* Managers need information to help make sound management decisions. Owners need to know how well their investment is doing. Creditors need to know how well the corporation is meeting its credit obligations.

PREPARING A WORK SHEET FOR A CORPORATION

Work sheets for sole proprietorships, partnerships, and corporations are similar. All businesses use a work sheet to plan adjustments and provide information for financial statements. Lin's Music Center prepares a work sheet and financial statements at the end of each year. *(CONCEPT: Accounting Period Cycle)* Lin's eight-column work sheet is similar to the one used by Denim Threads in Part 3.

Recording a trial balance on a work sheet

To prepare a work sheet, a trial balance is first entered in the Trial Balance columns. General ledger accounts are listed in the same order as they appear in a general ledger. Trial Balance columns are totaled to prove equality of debits and credits.

Lin's trial balance on December 31, 1983, is shown on the work sheet, pages 536 and 537. Accounts are similar to a sole proprietorship or partnership except for a corporation's capital, federal income tax, and dividends.

Separate general ledger capital accounts are kept for each owner of a sole proprietorship or a partnership. However, for a corporation a separate capital account is not kept for each owner. Instead, a single capital account is kept for the investment of all owners. A corporation's ownership is divided into units. Each unit of ownership in a corporation is called a share of stock. An owner of one or more shares of a corporation is called a stockholder. Total shares of ownership in a corporation are called capital stock. A second capital account is used to record a corporation's earnings. An amount earned by a corporation and not yet distributed to stockholders is called retained earnings.

Preparing adjustments on a work sheet

Some general ledger accounts need to be brought up to date before end-of-fiscal-period reports are prepared. Accounts are brought up to date by planning adjustments on a work sheet as described in Chapter 14. Most corporation adjustments on a work sheet are similar to those for sole proprietorships and partnerships.

Seven expense accounts and Merchandise Inventory of Lin's need adjustments at the end of a fiscal period. Three adjustments are similar to those made by Denim Threads in Chapter 14. (1) Merchandise Inventory. (2) Supplies Expense. (3) Insurance Expense. Lin's makes adjusting entries for four other expense accounts that are also similar for corporations, sole proprietorships, and partnerships. (1) Bad Debts Expense. (2) Depreciation Expense — Delivery Equipment. (3) Depreciation Expense — Office Equipment. (4) Depreciation Expense — Store Equipment.One additional adjustment for federal income tax owed is necessary for a corporation. This adjustment is not made for sole proprietorships and partnerships because taxes are paid by the owners, not the business. Adjustments for related asset or liability accounts generally are made in the order listed on a work sheet.

Adjustment for bad debts expense. Estimated bad debts expense for a fiscal period needs to be brought up to date. Two accounts are used for a bad debts adjustment — Bad Debts Expense and Allowance for Uncollectible Accounts. An analysis of Lin's bad debts expense adjustment is described in

Chapter 24, page 491. Lin's bad debts expense adjustment is shown in the work sheet Adjustments columns, pages 536 and 537.

Steps for recording the adjustment for bad debts expense on a work sheet are described below.

1 Write the amount, *$4,740.00*, in the Adjustments Debit column on line with the title Bad Debts Expense. (Line 35)

2 Write the amount, *$4,740.00*, in the Adjustments Credit column on line with the title Allowance for Uncollectible Accounts. (Line 4)

3 Label the two parts of this adjustment with the small letter "a" in parentheses, *(a)*.

Adjustments for merchandise inventory. The merchandise inventory balance shown in a trial balance is the beginning inventory for a fiscal period. Two adjusting entries are made to bring the merchandise inventory account up to date. These adjustments are the same as described in Chapter 14.

The beginning merchandise inventory, *$182,224.00*, is credited to Merchandise Inventory and debited to Income Summary. This adjustment is shown on lines 5 and 28 of the work sheet, pages 536 and 537. After the beginning merchandise inventory adjustment is journalized and posted, Merchandise Inventory has a zero balance. The amount of the beginning merchandise inventory is a debit in the income summary account.

The merchandise inventory account is debited, *$187,462.00*, the value of the ending merchandise inventory. *(CONCEPT: Historical Cost)* The same amount is credited to the income summary account. The balance of Merchandise Inventory, after the second adjustment, is $187,462.00. The amount of the ending merchandise inventory is a credit to Income Summary. The adjustment for ending merchandise inventory is on lines 5 and 28 of the work sheet.

Adjustment for supplies. Two accounts are used in adjusting supplies: Supplies and Supplies Expense. Lin's supplies adjustment is the same as the one described in Chapter 14.

The value of supplies used, *$4,284.00*, is a credit to Supplies. Supplies Expense is debited for the same amount. The supplies adjustment is on lines 6 and 46 of the work sheet, pages 536 and 537.

Adjustment for prepaid insurance. Insurance premiums are debited to a prepaid insurance account when paid. Insurance expenses however must be recorded for the fiscal period in which they are used. *(CONCEPT: Matching Expenses with Revenue)* Therefore, Prepaid Insurance and Insurance Expense are adjusted at the end of a fiscal period.

Lin's Music Center
Work Sheet
For Year Ended December 31, 1983

	ACCOUNT TITLE	TRIAL BALANCE DEBIT (1)	TRIAL BALANCE CREDIT (2)	ADJUSTMENTS DEBIT (3)	ADJUSTMENTS CREDIT (4)	INCOME STATEMENT DEBIT (5)	INCOME STATEMENT CREDIT (6)	BALANCE SHEET DEBIT (7)	BALANCE SHEET CREDIT (8)	
1	Cash	64883 00						64883 00		1
2	Notes Receivable	2649 00						2649 00		2
3	Accounts Receivable	42135 00						42135 00		3
4	Allow. for Uncoll. Accts.		280 00		(a) 4740 00				5020 00	4
5	Merchandise Inventory	182224 00		(c) 187462 00	(b) 182224 00			187462 00		5
6	Supplies	6691 00			(d) 4284 00			2407 00		6
7	Prepaid Insurance	12662 00			(e) 7884 00			4778 00		7
8	Delivery Equipment	17880 00						17880 00		8
9	Accum. Depr.-Delivery Equip.		5250 00		(f) 1900 00				7150 00	9
10	Office Equipment	9710 00						9710 00		10
11	Accum. Depr.-Office Equip.		1950 00		(g) 950 00				2900 00	11
12	Store Equipment	41175 00						41175 00		12
13	Accum. Depr.-Store Equip.		5400 00		(h) 2840 00				8240 00	13
14	Notes Payable									14
15	Accounts Payable		16805 00						16805 00	15
16	Employees Income Tax Pay.		1162 00						1162 00	16
17	Federal Income Tax Pay.				(i) 708 00				708 00	17
18	FICA Tax Payable		1351 00						1351 00	18
19	Sales Tax Payable		4740 00						4740 00	19
20	Unemploy. Tax Pay.-Fed.		28 00						28 00	20
21	Unemploy. Tax Pay.-State		108 00						108 00	21
22	Hosp. Ins. Premiums Pay.		398 00						398 00	22
23	U.S. Savings Bonds Pay.		40 00						40 00	23
24	United Way Donations Pay.		16 00						16 00	24

25	Dividends Payable								
26	Capital Stock		20000000						20000000
27	Retained Earnings		7792900						7792900
28	Income Summary			(b) 18222400	(c) 18746200	18222400	18746200		
29	Sales		95937600				95937600		
30	Sales Returns & Allow.	1137600				1137600			
31	Purchases	68590200				68590200			
32	Purchases Returns & Allow.		250300				250300		
33	Purchases Discount		508100				508100		
34	Advertising Expense	1516600				1516600			
35	Bad Debts Expense			(a) 474000		474000			
36	Credit Card Fee Expense	959400				959400			
37	Delivery Expense	504000				504000			
38	Depr. Exp.-Delivery Equip.			(f) 190000		190000			
39	Depr. Exp.-Office Equip.			(g) 95000		95000			
40	Depr. Exp.-Store Equip.			(h) 284000		284000			
41	Insurance Expense			(e) 788400		788400			
42	Miscellaneous Expense	1041700				1041700			
43	Payroll Taxes Expense	886900				886900			
44	Rent Expense	2654400				2654400			
45	Salary Expense	11755200				11755200			
46	Supplies Expense			(d) 428400		428400			
47	Interest Income		378200				378200		
48	Interest Expense	473000				473000			
49	Federal Income Tax	1100000		(i) 70800		1170800			
50		128619900	128619900	39299200	39299200	111172000	115820400	37307900	32659500
51	Net Inc. after Fed. Inc. Tax					4648400			4648400
52						115820400	115820400	37307900	37307900

Completed work sheet for a corporation

Lin's prepaid insurance adjustment is the same as the one described in Chapter 14. The value of insurance used, *$7,884.00*, is credited to Prepaid Insurance. The same amount is debited to Insurance Expense. The prepaid insurance adjustment is on lines 7 and 41 of the work sheet, pages 536 and 537.

Adjustments for depreciation expense. Lin's depreciation expense adjustments are described in Chapter 25, pages 509–513.

Depreciation Expense — Delivery Equipment is debited for *$1,900.00*. Accumulated Depreciation — Delivery Equipment is credited for the same amount. This adjustment is on lines 9 and 38 of the work sheet, pages 536 and 537.

Depreciation Expense — Office Equipment is debited for *$950.00*. Accumulated Depreciation — Office Equipment is credited for the same amount. This adjustment is on lines 11 and 39 of the work sheet.

Depreciation Expense — Store Equipment is debited for *$2,840.00*. Accumulated Depreciation — Store Equipment is credited for the same amount. This adjustment is on lines 13 and 40 of the work sheet.

Preparing an adjustment for federal income tax and extending amounts on a work sheet

Corporations anticipating annual federal income taxes of $40.00 or more are required to estimate their tax. Estimated income tax is paid in quarterly installments in April, June, September, and December. However, the actual income tax owed is figured at the end of a fiscal year. Based on the actual tax owed for a year, a corporation must file an annual return. Tax owed but not paid in quarterly installments must be paid when the final return is sent.

Early in 1983 Lin's estimated $11,000.00 federal income tax for 1983. Lin's paid $2,750.00 in each quarterly installment for a total of $11,000.00. Each tax payment is recorded as a debit to Federal Income Tax and a credit to Cash.

Federal income tax is an expense of a corporation. However, the amount of tax depends on net income before the tax is recorded. Before federal income tax is figured, all adjustments on the work sheet are completed except the federal income tax adjustment. All amounts except the federal income tax account balance are extended to the appropriate Income Statement or Balance Sheet columns. Procedures for extending amounts are similar to those described in Chapter 14.

Two steps are followed to figure the amount of federal income tax owed.

1 Total on a separate sheet of paper the Income Statement columns of a work sheet. Figure the difference between the two totals. This difference is the net income before federal income tax. Lin's net income

before federal income tax is figured from the Income Statement columns of the work sheet, pages 536 and 537.

Total of Income Statement Credit column	$1,158,204.00
Less Total of Income Statement Debit column before federal income tax	1,100,012.00
Equals Net Income before federal income tax	$ 58,192.00

2 Figure the amount of federal income tax using a tax rate table furnished by the Internal Revenue Service. Lin's federal income tax for 1983 is $11,708.00.

Tax rate tables are distributed by the Internal Revenue Service showing income tax rates for corporations. Each corporation should check a current table to find the applicable rates. Corporation rates current when this text was written were used to figure Lin's federal income taxes.

Lin's federal income tax adjustment is shown in the T accounts at the right. Accounts are shown before and after the adjustment for federal income tax. Lin's paid quarterly federal income tax installments of $2,750.00 each. Federal Income Tax has a debit balance of $11,000.00 at the end of the fiscal period before adjustments are made.

Four questions are asked in analyzing the adjustment for federal income tax.

1. What is the balance of the federal income tax account? $11,000.00
2. What should the balance be for this account? $11,708.00
3. What must be done to correct the account balance? .... Add $ 708.00
4. What adjusting entry is made? ....
   Debit Federal Income Tax $ 708.00
   Credit Federal Income Tax Payable $ 708.00

BEFORE ADJUSTMENT

Federal Income Tax			
Apr. 15	2,750.00		
June 15	2,750.00		
Sept. 15	2,750.00		
Dec. 15	2,750.00		
Dec. 15 Bal.	*11,000.00*		

Federal Income Tax Payable			

AFTER ADJUSTMENT

Federal Income Tax			
Apr. 15	2,750.00		
June 15	2,750.00		
Sept. 15	2,750.00		
Dec. 15	2,750.00		
Dec. 15 Bal.	*11,000.00*		
Dec. 31 (i)	**708.00**		
Dec. 31 Bal.	*11,708.00*		

Federal Income Tax Payable			
		Dec. 31 (i)	708.00

Federal Income Tax is debited for $708.00 to show the increase in the balance of this expense account. The new balance of this account, *$11,708.00*, is the total federal income tax expense for the fiscal period. Federal Income Tax Payable is credited for $708.00 to show the increase in this liability account's balance. Lin's federal income tax payable account balance, *$708.00*, is the amount of income tax expense not paid at year end. Lin's federal income tax adjustment is on lines 17 and 49 of the work sheet, pages 536 and 537.

Steps in recording Lin's federal income tax adjustment on a work sheet are on the next page.

1 Write the amount, *$708.00*, in the Adjustments Debit column on line with Federal Income Tax. (Line 49)

2 Write the amount, *$708.00*, in the Adjustments Credit column on line with Federal Income Tax Payable. (Line 17)

> Federal Income Tax is an expense account. The account appears under a special heading "Income Tax" as the last item in the chart of accounts, page 392. Federal Income Tax Payable, a liability account, appears under the heading "Current Liabilities."

3 Label the two parts of this adjustment with the small letter "i" in parentheses, *(i)*.

After the federal income tax adjustment is recorded, the income tax accounts are extended to the appropriate work sheet columns. The federal income tax account balance is extended to the Income Statement Debit column. The federal income tax payable account balance is extended to the Balance Sheet Credit column.

Completing a corporate work sheet

Income Statement and Balance Sheet columns are totaled. Totals are written as shown on line 50 of the work sheet, page 537. The Income Statement Credit column total for Lin's is $46,484.00 more than the Income Statement Debit column total. (Credit column total, *$1,158,204.00*, less Debit column total, *$1,111,720.00*, equals difference, *$46,484.00*.) This amount, *$46,484.00*, is written in the Income Statement Debit column, line 51 of the work sheet. *Net Income After Federal Income Tax* is written in the Account Title column on the same line as the amount. Income Statement columns are then totaled as shown on line 52, page 537.

The net income amount after federal income tax, *$46,484.00*, is written in the Balance Sheet Credit column, line 51. Balance Sheet columns are totaled as shown on line 52, page 537. Double lines are ruled across all Income Statement and Balance Sheet columns as shown on line 52. The double lines show that the columns are in balance and assumed to be correct.

PREPARING FINANCIAL STATEMENTS FOR A CORPORATION

Financial statements are used to report financial progress and condition of a business. Corporation financial statements are similar to those prepared by sole proprietorships and partnerships. Lin's prepares three important financial statements. (1) Income statement. (2) Statement of stockholders' equity. (3) Balance sheet.

Income statement

An income statement reports financial progress of a business during a fiscal period. *(CONCEPT: Accounting Period Cycle)* Revenue, cost of merchandise sold, gross profit, operating expenses, and net income or loss are generally reported on income statements. *(CONCEPT: Adequate Disclosure)*

Lin's income statement is prepared from information on the work sheet, page 537. Procedures for preparing Lin's income statement are similar to those described in Chapter 15. Lin's income statement for the year ended December 31, 1983, is on page 542.

Lin's income statement differs from Denim Threads' income statement in four ways.

1. Income from operations is reported separately from net income. Income from operations is the income earned only from normal business activities. Lin's normal business activities are selling musical instruments and stereo equipment. Other revenue and expenses, such as interest income and interest expense, are not normal business activities. Other revenue and expenses are not used to figure income from operations.
2. Net sales is listed in the Operating Revenue section. Total sales less sales returns and allowances is called net sales. Net sales is reported in the Operating Revenue section of Lin's income statement as shown below.

Operating Revenue:		
Sales	$959,376.00	
Less Sales Returns & Allowances	11,376.00	
Net Sales		$948,000.00

3. Net purchases is reported in the Cost of Merchandise Sold section. Total purchases less purchases returns and allowances and purchases discount is called net purchases. Net purchases is reported in the Cost of Merchandise Sold section of Lin's income statement as shown below.

Purchases		$685,902.00	
Less: Purch. Ret. & Allow.	$2,503.00		
Purchases Discount . .	5,081.00	7,584.00	
Net Purchases			678,318.00

4. Net income before and net income after federal income tax are reported separately. Reporting net income before and after federal income tax is unique to corporation income statements. Corporations

pay federal income tax on their net income. However, federal income taxes are not paid by sole proprietorships and partnerships but are paid by the owners. Thus, sole proprietorships and partnerships do not report federal income tax on their income statements.

Lin's income statement for the year ended December 31, 1983, is below.

Lin's Music Center
Income Statement
For Year Ended December 31, 1983

Operating Revenue:				
Sales			$959,376.00	
Less Sales Returns & Allowances			11,376.00	
Net Sales				$948,000.00
Cost of Merchandise Sold:				
Merchandise Inventory, January 1, 1983			$182,224.00	
Purchases		$685,902.00		
Less: Purch. Ret. & Allow.	$2,503.00			
Purchases Discount	5,081.00	7,584.00		
Net Purchases			678,318.00	
Total Cost of Mdse. Avail. for Sale			$860,542.00	
Less Mdse. Inventory, Dec. 31, 1983			187,462.00	
Cost of Merchandise Sold				673,080.00
Gross Profit on Operations				$274,920.00
Operating Expenses:				
Advertising Expense			$ 15,166.00	
Bad Debts Expense			4,740.00	
Credit Card Fee Expense			9,594.00	
Delivery Expense			5,040.00	
Depreciation Exp.--Delivery Equip.			1,900.00	
Depreciation Exp.--Office Equip.			950.00	
Depreciation Exp.--Store Equip.			2,840.00	
Insurance Expense			7,884.00	
Miscellaneous Expense			10,417.00	
Payroll Taxes Expense			8,869.00	
Rent Expense			26,544.00	
Salary Expense			117,552.00	
Supplies Expense			4,284.00	
Total Operating Expenses				215,780.00
Income from Operations				$ 59,140.00
Other Revenue:				
Interest Income			$ 3,782.00	
Other Expenses:				
Interest Expense			4,730.00	
Net Deduction				948.00
Net Income Before Federal Income Tax				$ 58,192.00
Less Federal Income Tax				11,708.00
Net Income After Federal Income Tax				$ 46,484.00

Income statement for a corporation

Statement of stockholders' equity

A financial statement showing changes in a corporation's ownership for a fiscal period is called a statement of stockholders' equity. A stockholders' equity statement is similar to a capital statement for a sole proprietorship or a partnership.

A stockholders' equity statement contains two major sections. These sections relate to (a) capital stock and (b) earnings retained in a corporation. Lin's statement of stockholders' equity for the year ended December 31, 1983, is below.

Lin's Music Center
Statement of Stockholders' Equity
For Year Ended December 31, 1983

Capital Stock:			
$100.00 Per Share			
Jan. 1, 1983, 2,000 Shares Issued		$200,000.00	
Issued during 1983, None		-0-	
Balance, Dec. 31, 1983, 2,000 Shares Issued			$200,000.00
Retained Earnings:			
Jan. 1, 1983		$117,929.00	
Plus Net Income After Taxes for 1983	$ 46,484.00		
Less Dividends Declared and Paid during 1983	40,000.00		
Net Increase during 1983		6,484.00	
Balance, Dec. 31, 1983			124,413.00
Total Stockholders' Equity, Dec. 31, 1983			$324,413.00

Statement of stockholders' equity for a corporation

The first section of this statement shows that Lin's started the fiscal year, January 1, 1983, with $200,000.00 capital stock. This capital stock consisted of 2,000 shares of stock issued before January 1, 1983, for $100.00 per share. During 1983, Lin's did not issue any more capital stock. Thus, at the end of the fiscal year, Lin's still had $200,000.00 capital stock outstanding. This information is obtained from the previous year's statement and the capital stock account.

The second section of Lin's equity statement shows that Lin's started on January 1, 1983, with $117,929.00 retained earnings. This amount represents previous years' earnings that have been kept in the business. For the fiscal year ended December 31, 1983, Lin's earned net income after federal income tax of $46,484.00. This amount is obtained from line 51 on the work sheet, page 537. During the year, dividends of $40,000.00 were paid. Earnings distributed to stockholders are called dividends. The amount of dividends paid is obtained from the general ledger account Retained Earnings. Changes in Lin's retained earnings during the fiscal year, 1983, are below.

Retained earnings balance, January 1, 1983		$117,929.00
Plus net income after taxes for 1983	$46,484.00	
Less dividends paid during 1983	40,000.00	
Net increase in retained earnings during 1983		6,484.00
Retained earnings balance, December 31, 1983		$124,413.00

Lin's capital stock, *$200,000.00*, plus retained earnings, *$124,413.00*, equals total stockholders' equity on December 31, 1983, *$324,413.00*. *(CONCEPT: Adequate Disclosure)*

Balance Sheet

A corporation balance sheet reports assets, liabilities, and stockholders' equity on a specific date. *(CONCEPT: Accounting Period Cycle)*

Lin's balance sheet is prepared from information on the work sheet, pages 536 and 537, and stockholders' equity statement, page 543.

Lin's Music Center
Balance Sheet
December 31, 1983

ASSETS			
Current Assets:			
Cash		$ 64,883.00	
Notes Receivable		2,649.00	
Accounts Receivable	$ 42,135.00		
Less Allow. for Uncoll. Accounts	5,020.00	37,115.00	
Merchandise Inventory		187,462.00	
Supplies		2,407.00	
Prepaid Insurance		4,778.00	
Total Current Assets			$299,294.00
Plant Assets:			
Delivery Equipment	$ 17,880.00		
Less Accum. Depr.--Delivery Equip	7,150.00	$ 10,730.00	
Office Equipment	$ 9,710.00		
Less Accum. Depr.--Office Equip	2,900.00	6,810.00	
Store Equipment	$ 41,175.00		
Less Accum. Depr.--Store Equip.	8,240.00	32,935.00	
Total Plant Assets			50,475.00
Total Assets			$349,769.00
LIABILITIES			
Current Liabilities:			
Accounts Payable		$ 16,805.00	
Employees Income Tax Payable		1,162.00	
Federal Income Tax Payable		708.00	
FICA Tax Payable		1,351.00	
Sales Tax Payable		4,740.00	
Unemployment Tax Payable--Federal		28.00	
Unemployment Tax Payable--State		108.00	
Hospital Insurance Premiums Payable		398.00	
U.S. Savings Bonds Payable		40.00	
United Way Donations Payable		16.00	
Total Liabilities			$ 25,356.00
STOCKHOLDERS' EQUITY			
Capital Stock		$200,000.00	
Retained Earnings		124,413.00	
Total Stockholders' Equity			324,413.00
Total Liabilities and Stockholders' Equity			$349,769.00

Balance sheet for a corporation

Procedures for preparing Lin's balance sheet are similar to those described in Chapter 15. Differences between Lin's balance sheet and the one prepared for Denim Threads are described below.

Classifying assets on a balance sheet. Lin's classifies its assets in two categories: Current Assets and Plant Assets. These categories are based on the length of time the assets will be in use. A business owning both current assets and plant assets usually lists them under separate headings on a balance sheet.

Cash and assets readily exchanged for cash or consumed within a year are called current assets. Current assets include such things as cash, accounts receivable, merchandise inventory, supplies, and prepaid insurance. Current asset accounts are listed on a balance sheet under the heading *Current Assets*. Current asset accounts usually are listed with Cash first followed by the other current assets. The other current assets often are listed in the order that they can be exchanged most readily for cash.

Assets to be used for a number of years are listed on a balance sheet under the heading *Plant Assets*. Plant assets include such things as delivery equipment, office equipment, and store equipment.

Classifying liabilities on a balance sheet

Lin's classifies both liabilities and assets on a balance sheet. Liabilities are classified according to the length of time until they are due. Liabilities due within a short time, usually within a year, are called current liabilities. Examples of current liabilities are Accounts Payable, Employees Income Tax Payable, Federal Income Tax Payable, and FICA Tax Payable. All of Lin's liabilities are listed on a balance sheet as current liabilities because they become due within a year.

Liabilities owed for more than a year are called long-term liabilities. An example of a long-term liability is Mortgage Payable. On December 31, 1983, Lin's does not have any long-term liabilities.

Sav-Energy Company has both current liabilities and long-term liabilities. A portion of Sav-Energy's balance sheet is below.

Total Assets		$172,862.69
Liabilities		
Current Liabilities:		
Accounts Payable	$6,699.00	
Sales Tax Payable	1,295.27	
Total Current Liabilities		$ 25,795.00
Long-term Liabilities:		
Mortgage Payable		46,000.00
Total Liabilities		$ 71,795.00

Liabilities section of a balance sheet showing current and long-term liabilities

Reporting book value of asset accounts on a balance sheet. An asset's book value is reported on a balance sheet by listing three amounts. The amounts are (1) balance of the asset account, (2) balance of the asset's contra account, and (3) book value. Book value of Lin's accounts receivable and plant asset accounts are on the partial balance sheet on the next page.

Lin's Music Center
Balance Sheet
December 31, 1983

ASSETS			
Accounts Receivable....................	$ 42,135.00		
Less Allow. for Uncoll. Accounts......	5,020.00	37,115.00	
Plant Assets:			
Delivery Equipment.....................	$ 17,880.00		
Less Accum. Depr.--Delivery Equip.....	7,150.00	$ 10,730.00	
Office Equipment.......................	$ 9,710.00		
Less Accum. Depr.--Office Equip.......	2,900.00	6,810.00	
Store Equipment........................	$ 41,175.00		
Less Accum. Depr.--Store Equip........	8,240.00	32,935.00	
Total Plant Assets.....................			50,475.00

Book value of accounts receivable and plant assets on a partial balance sheet

The book value of accounts receivable is reported on Lin's balance sheet as follows. The total amount of accounts receivable, *$42,135.00*, is written in the first column of the balance sheet. *Less Allowance for Uncollectible Accounts* is written on the next line, indented about 1 centimeter. The amount, *$5,020.00*, is written below the $42,135.00. The difference between the two amounts, *$37,115.00*, is written in the second amount column on the same line. The amount of the difference, *$37,115.00*, is the book value of accounts receivable on December 31, 1983. Similar procedures are followed to report book values of plant asset accounts.

Reporting stockholders' equity on a balance sheet. A major difference between corporation balance sheets and sole proprietorship or partnership balance sheets is in the capital section. The capital section of Lin's balance sheet, page 544, is labeled *Stockholders' Equity*. Some corporations use the same label as sole proprietorships and partnerships: *Capital*. Either label is acceptable.

The stockholders' equity section contains accounts relating to capital stock and earnings kept in the business. For Lin's these accounts are Capital Stock and Retained Earnings. Total stockholders' equity on Lin's balance sheet, *$324,413.00*, is the same as on Lin's statement of stockholders' equity, page 543.

PREPARING ADJUSTING AND CLOSING ENTRIES

Corporations' end-of-period work is the same as for sole proprietorships and partnerships except for differences in equity accounts. After corporate financial statements are prepared, adjusting and closing entries are recorded and posted. A post-closing trial balance is then prepared.

Adjusting entries

A corporation's adjusting entries are made from the Adjustments columns of a work sheet. Each adjustment is journalized and posted to general ledger accounts. With the exception of federal income tax, adjustments are similar to those for sole proprietorships and partnerships. Lin's adjusting entries for December 31, 1983, taken from the work sheet, pages 536 and 537, are below.

GENERAL JOURNAL PAGE 27

	DATE		ACCOUNT TITLE	POST. REF.	DEBIT	CREDIT	
1			Adjusting Entries				1
2	1983 Dec.	31	Bad Debts Expense		474000		2
3			Allow. for Uncoll. Accts.			474000	3
4		31	Income Summary		18222400		4
5			Merchandise Inventory			18222400	5
6		31	Merchandise Inventory		18746200		6
7			Income Summary			18746200	7
8		31	Supplies Expense		428400		8
9			Supplies			428400	9
10		31	Insurance Expense		788400		10
11			Prepaid Insurance			788400	11
12		31	Depreciation Exp. - Delivery Equip.		190000		12
13			Accum. Depr. - Delivery Equip.			190000	13
14		31	Depreciation Exp. - Office Equip.		95000		14
15			Accum. Depr. - Office Equip.			95000	15
16		31	Depreciation Exp. - Store Equip.		284000		16
17			Accum. Depr. - Store Equip.			284000	17
18		31	Federal Income Tax		70800		18
19			Federal Income Tax Payable			70800	19
20							20
21							21
22							22

Adjusting entries for a corporation

Procedures for journalizing Lin's adjusting entries are similar to those described in Chapter 16. However, since Lin's uses special journals, adjusting entries are recorded in a general journal.

Closing entries

Closing entries for a corporation are made from a work sheet's Income Statement columns. Closing entries for revenue and expense accounts are similar to those for sole proprietorships or partnerships. However, a corporation's final closing entry differs from those previously studied. After all revenue and expense balances are closed to Income Summary, the income summary balance is closed to Retained Earnings.

Closing entry for credit balance accounts. The closing entry for Lin's credit balance accounts on December 31, 1983, is below. Credit balance accounts are revenue (*Sales* and *Interest Income*) and reduction in cost accounts (*Purchases Returns and Allowances* and *Purchases Discount*). Information needed for closing credit balance accounts is on lines 29, 32, 33, and 47 of Lin's work sheet, page 537.

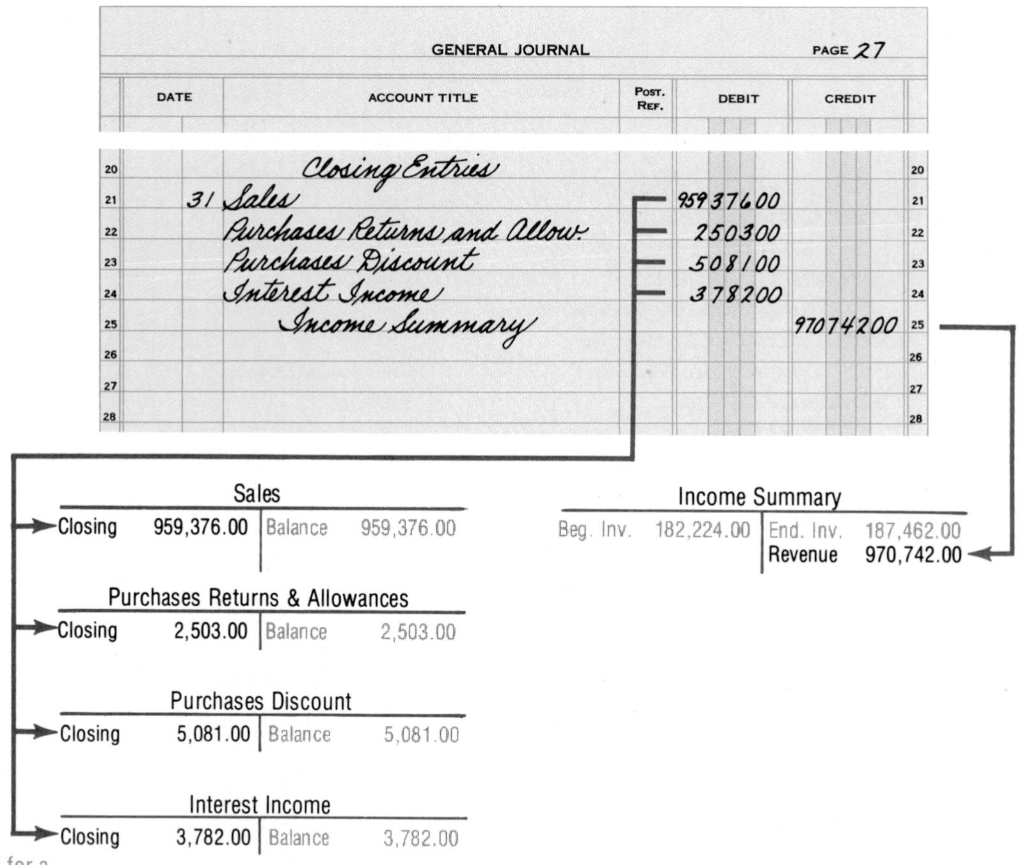
GENERAL JOURNAL PAGE 27

	DATE	ACCOUNT TITLE	POST. REF.	DEBIT	CREDIT	
20		Closing Entries				20
21	31	Sales		959376 00		21
22		Purchases Returns and Allow.		2503 00		22
23		Purchases Discount		5081 00		23
24		Interest Income		3782 00		24
25		Income Summary			970742 00	25
26						26
27						27
28						28

Closing entry for a corporation's credit balance accounts

Closing entry for debit balance accounts. The closing entry for Lin's debit balance accounts on December 31, 1983, is on page 549. Debit balance accounts are the cost and expense accounts and the reduction in revenue account (*Sales Returns and Allowances*). Information needed for closing the debit balance accounts is from lines 30–31, 34–46, and 48–49 of Lin's work sheet, page 537.

When closing entries for the income statement accounts are posted, Income Summary has a credit balance of $46,484.00. This credit balance, *$46,484.00*, is the amount of net income. This amount is the same as on line 51 of the work sheet, page 537.

GENERAL JOURNAL PAGE 28

	DATE		ACCOUNT TITLE	POST. REF.	DEBIT	CREDIT	
1			Closing Entries				1
2	1983 Dec.	31	Income Summary		929496 00		2
3			Sales Returns and Allow.			11376 00	3
4			Purchases			685902 00	4
5			Advertising Expense			15166 00	5
6			Bad Debts Expense			4740 00	6
7			Credit Card Fee Expense			9594 00	7
8			Delivery Expense			5040 00	8
9			Depr. Exp. - Delivery Equip.			1900 00	9
10			Depr. Exp. - Office Equip.			950 00	10
11			Depr. Exp. - Store Equip.			2840 00	11
12			Insurance Expense			7884 00	12
13			Misc. Expense			10417 00	13
14			Payroll Taxes Expense			8869 00	14
15			Rent Expense			26544 00	15
16			Salary Expense			117552 00	16
17			Supplies Expense			4284 00	17
18			Interest Expense			4730 00	18
19			Federal Income Tax			11708 00	19

Income Summary

Beg. Inv.	182,224.00	End. Inv.	187,462.00
Cost & Exp.	929,496.00	Revenue	970,742.00

Sales Returns & Allowances

Balance	11,376.00	Closing	11,376.00

Purchases

Balance	685,902.00	Closing	685,902.00

Advertising Expense

Balance	15,166.00	Closing	15,166.00

Bad Debts Expense

Balance	4,740.00	Closing	4,740.00

Credit Card Fee Expense

Balance	9,594.00	Closing	9,594.00

Delivery Expense

Balance	5,040.00	Closing	5,040.00

Depreciation Expense — Delivery Equipment

Balance	1,900.00	Closing	1,900.00

Depreciation Expense — Office Equipment

Balance	950.00	Closing	950.00

Depreciation Expense — Store Equipment

Balance	2,840.00	Closing	2,840.00

Insurance Expense

Balance	7,884.00	Closing	7,884.00

Miscellaneous Expense

Balance	10,417.00	Closing	10,417.00

Payroll Taxes Expense

Balance	8,869.00	Closing	8,869.00

Rent Expense

Balance	26,544.00	Closing	26,544.00

Salary Expense

Balance	117,552.00	Closing	117,552.00

Supplies Expense

Balance	4,284.00	Closing	4,284.00

Interest Expense

Balance	4,730.00	Closing	4,730.00

Federal Income Tax

Balance	11,708.00	Closing	11,708.00

Closing entry for a corporation's debit balance accounts

Closing entry for recording net income in a retained earnings account. A corporation's net income is recorded in a retained earnings account. The closing entry to record Lin's income on December 31, 1983, is below. Information needed for this entry is taken from line 51 of Lin's work sheet, page 537.

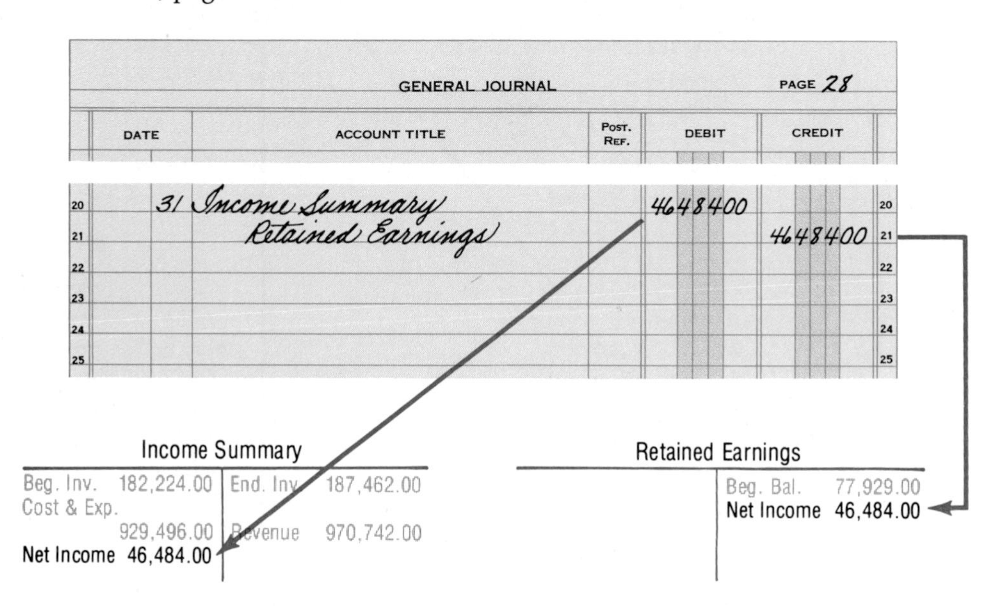

Closing entry to record a corporation's net income in a retained earnings account

When the entry to record net income is posted, Income Summary has a zero balance. The net income, *$46,484.00*, has been recorded as a credit in Retained Earnings.

If a corporation has a net loss, Income Summary has a debit balance. Retained Earnings would then be debited and Income Summary credited for the net loss amount.

After adjusting and closing entries are journalized, the entries are posted to the general ledger accounts. Lin's uses four-column general ledger account forms with separate debit balance and credit balance columns. Each time an entry is posted, the account balance is figured.

After adjusting and closing entries are posted, balance sheet accounts all have up-to-date balances. Assets, liabilities, and stockholders' equity account balances agree with amounts on the balance sheet, page 544. Revenue, cost, and expense accounts all begin the new fiscal period with zero balances.

Post-closing trial balance

A post-closing trial balance is prepared after adjusting and closing entries have been posted. Lin's post-closing trial balance, December 31, 1983, is on the next page.

Lin's Music Center
Post-Closing Trial Balance
December 31, 1983

Account Title	Debit	Credit
Cash	$ 64,883.00	
Notes Receivable	2,649.00	
Accounts Receivable	42,135.00	
Allowance for Uncoll. Accts.		$ 5,020.00
Merchandise Inventory	187,462.00	
Supplies	2,407.00	
Prepaid Insurance	4,778.00	
Delivery Equipment	17,880.00	
Accum. Depr.--Delivery Equip.		7,150.00
Office Equipment	9,710.00	
Accum. Depr.--Office Equip.		2,900.00
Store Equipment	41,175.00	
Accum. Depr.--Store Equip.		8,240.00
Accounts Payable		16,805.00
Employees Income Tax Payable		1,162.00
Federal Income Tax Payable		708.00
FICA Tax Payable		1,351.00
Sales Tax Payable		4,740.00
Unemployment Tax Payable--Federal		28.00
Unemployment Tax Payable--State		108.00
Hospital Insurance Premiums Payable		398.00
U.S. Savings Bonds Payable		40.00
United Way Donations Payable		16.00
Capital Stock		200,000.00
Retained Earnings		124,413.00
	$373,079.00	$373,079.00

Post-closing trial balance for a corporation

The equality of debits and credits is proved. Lin's general ledger is ready for the next fiscal period. *(CONCEPT: Accounting Period Cycle)*

DISTRIBUTING INCOME TO STOCKHOLDERS

Net income earned by a corporation belongs to the stockholders. Some income may be retained by a corporation for business expansion and increased needs. Some income may be given to stockholders as a return on their investments. No income can be distributed to stockholders except by formal action of a corporation's board of directors. *(CONCEPT: Business Entity)* A group of persons elected by the stockholders to manage a corporation is called a board of directors.

Declaring a dividend

Action by a board of directors to distribute corporate earnings to stockholders is called declaring a dividend. When a corporation's board of directors declares a dividend, the corporation is obligated to pay the dividend. The declared dividend is a liability. This liability must be recorded in the corporation's accounts. A memorandum is used as a source document for recording declaration of a dividend. *(CONCEPT: Objective Evidence)*

July 15, 1984. Lin's board of directors declared a dividend of $20.00 a share. Date of payment is August 15, 1984. Capital stock issued is 2,000 shares. Memorandum No. 108.

The journal entry to record Lin's declaration of a dividend is below. The amount declared is $40,000.00 ($20.00 a share for 2,000 shares).

Entry to record the declaration of a dividend by a corporation

GENERAL JOURNAL — PAGE 13

	DATE		ACCOUNT TITLE	POST. REF.	DEBIT	CREDIT	
1	1984 July	15	Retained Earnings		40 000 00		1
2			Dividends Payable			40 000 00	2
3			Memorandum No. 108.				3

Retained Earnings is debited for $40,000.00 to record the reduction in retained earnings. Dividends Payable is credited for $40,000.00 to record the liability the corporation now has for the dividend declared.

Paying a dividend

On August 15, 1984, Lin's issues one check for the amount of the total dividend.

August 15, 1984. Paid $40,000.00 cash for dividend declared July 15, 1984. Check No. 739.

This check is deposited in a special dividend checking account. A separate check for each stockholder is drawn on this special account. The special account avoids a large number of cash payments journal entries. The special dividend checking account also reserves cash specifically for paying dividends.

A check is often made payable to an agent, such as a bank. The agent then handles the details of sending dividend checks to individual stockholders.

The journal entry to record Lin's dividend payment of $40,000.00 is below.

CASH PAYMENTS JOURNAL — PAGE 26

	DATE	ACCOUNT TITLE	CHECK No.	POST. REF.	1 GENERAL DEBIT	2 GENERAL CREDIT	3 ACCOUNTS PAYABLE DEBIT	4 PURCHASES DISCOUNT CREDIT	5 CASH CREDIT	
19	15	Dividends Payable	739		40 000 00				40 000 00	19

Entry to record the payment of a dividend

Dividends Payable is debited for the amount of dividends paid, *$40,000.00.* Cash is credited for the total amount of cash paid, *$40,000.00.* When this entry is posted, the dividends payable account is closed.

ACCOUNTING TERMS

What is the meaning of each of the following?

1. share of stock
2. stockholder
3. capital stock
4. retained earnings
5. net sales
6. net purchases
7. statement of stockholders' equity
8. dividends
9. current assets
10. current liabilities
11. long-term liabilities
12. board of directors
13. declaring a dividend

QUESTIONS FOR INDIVIDUAL STUDY

1. Why do managers, owners, and creditors need financial information about how well a corporation is doing?
2. How does a work sheet for a corporation differ from a work sheet for a proprietorship?
3. In what order are general ledger accounts listed on a corporation work sheet?
4. How many capital accounts are kept for the investment of owners of Lin's Music Center?
5. Which of Lin's general ledger accounts need to be adjusted?
6. What two accounts are used in the adjustment for bad debts?
7. What are the purposes of the two adjustments for Merchandise Inventory?
8. What adjusting entry is made for the supplies account?
9. What adjusting entry is made for the prepaid insurance account?
10. What adjusting entry is made for the estimated depreciation for a plant asset?
11. Why is federal income tax not figured until all other adjustments have been planned on Lin's work sheet?
12. What entry is made to update the federal income tax expense for a fiscal period?
13. What three corporation financial statements does Lin's prepare?
14. What financial information does an income statement report?
15. Where is the information found to prepare a corporation income statement?
16. How does Lin's income statement differ from Denim Threads' income statement?
17. What financial information does a statement of stockholders' equity report?
18. What are the two main sections of a statement of stockholders' equity?
19. Where is the information found to prepare a statement of stockholders' equity?
20. What financial information does a corporation balance sheet report?
21. Where is the information found to prepare a balance sheet?
22. What three amounts are listed when the book value of an asset is reported on a balance sheet?
23. Where is the information obtained for journalizing a corporation's adjusting entries?
24. Where is the information found for journalizing a corporation's closing entries?
25. What kind of balances do income statement accounts have immediately after adjusting and closing entries are posted?
26. Why is a post-closing trial balance prepared?
27. When is a dividend recorded as a liability in a corporation's general ledger accounts?
28. What entry is made to record the declaration of a dividend?
29. What entry is made to record paying a dividend?

CASES FOR MANAGEMENT DECISION

CASE 1 Financial information for B & J Corporation for the current year is listed below.

Total revenue	$428,000.00
Total expenses	396,000.00
Net income before federal income tax	32,000.00
Federal income tax	6,400.00

The company prepared an income statement reporting $32,000.00 as net income for the year. A closing entry was prepared debiting Income Summary for $32,000.00 and crediting Retained Earnings for $32,000.00. Are the income statement and closing entry correct? If not, what should they be? Explain.

CASE 2 Graphics Company recently formed into a corporation with five stockholders. Carla Okano, the bookkeeper, is developing the accounting system. She suggested that, since there are only five stockholders, only one equity account be used. The account would be Corporation Capital. The president of Graphics questions the bookkeeper's recommendation. Is the bookkeeper's recommendation acceptable? If not, how should capital be recorded and reported? Explain your answer.

DRILLS FOR UNDERSTANDING

DRILL 27-D 1 Analyzing adjustments on a work sheet

Use a form similar to the one below.

Adjustment No.	Work Sheet Adjustment	
	(a) Account Debited	(b) Account Credited
1.	*Income Summary*	*Merchandise Inventory*

Instructions: For each adjustment below: (a) Write the name of the account debited. (b) Write the name of the account credited. Adjustment No. 1 is given as an example in the form above.

1. Adjustment for beginning merchandise inventory.
2. Adjustment for ending merchandise inventory.
3. Adjustment for bad debts expense.
4. Adjustment for supplies.
5. Adjustment for delivery equipment depreciation expense.
6. Adjustment for prepaid insurance.
7. Adjustment for office equipment depreciation expense.
8. Adjustment for additional federal income tax owed.
9. Adjustment for store equipment depreciation expense.

DRILL 27-D 2 Classifying assets, liabilities, and stockholders' equity accounts on a balance sheet

Use a form similar to the one on the next page.

Account No.	Current Assets	Contra Acct. of a Current Asset	Plant Assets	Contra Acct. of a Plant Asset	Current Liability	Long-Term Liability	Stockholders' Equity
1.	√						

Instructions: For each account below, place a check mark in the column that correctly classifies the account on a balance sheet. Account No. 1 is given as an example in the form above.

1. Cash
2. Accounts Payable
3. Supplies
4. Office Equipment
5. FICA Tax Payable
6. Merchandise Inventory
7. Allowance for Uncollectible Accounts
8. Notes Receivable
9. Accumulated Depreciation — Office Equipment
10. Retained Earnings
11. Accounts Receivable
12. Accumulated Depreciation — Delivery Equipment
13. Federal Income Tax Payable
14. Prepaid Insurance
15. Delivery Equipment
16. Capital Stock
17. Unemployment Tax Payable — State
18. Supplies
19. Mortgage Payable
20. Employees Income Tax Payable

DRILL 27-D 3 Analyzing closing entries

Use a form similar to the one below.

Closing Entry No.	Closing Entry	
	(a) Account Debited	(b) Account Credited
1.	*Income Summary*	*Delivery Expense*

Instructions: For each closing entry below and on page 556: (a) Write the name of the account debited. (b) Write the name of the account credited. Closing Entry No. 1 is given as an example in the form above.

1. Close Delivery Expense
2. Close Federal Income Tax
3. Close Purchases Returns and Allowances

4. Close Payroll Taxes Expense
5. Close Interest Income
6. Close Depreciation Expense — Office Equipment
7. Close Net Income
8. Close Sales
9. Close Sales Returns and Allowances
10. Close Insurance Expense
11. Close Purchases Discount
12. Close Bad Debts Expense

APPLICATION PROBLEMS

PROBLEM 27-1 Preparing a work sheet

The accounts and their balances in Melody Shop's general ledger appear as below on December 31 of the current year. The trial balance is recorded on the work sheet in the working papers.

Account Title	Account Balance Debits	Account Balance Credits
Cash	$ 51,906.00	
Notes Receivable	2,120.00	
Accounts Receivable	33,708.00	
Allow. for Uncoll. Accounts		$ 220.00
Merchandise Inventory	145,780.00	
Supplies	4,682.00	
Prepaid Insurance	8,880.00	
Delivery Equipment	14,300.00	
Accum. Depr. — Delivery Equip.		4,200.00
Office Equipment	7,770.00	
Accum. Depr. — Office Equip.		1,560.00
Store Equipment	32,900.00	
Accum. Depr. — Store Equip.		4,860.00
Notes Payable		1,000.00
Accounts Payable		15,120.00
Employees Income Tax Pay.		930.00
Federal Income Tax Pay.		—
FICA Tax Payable		1,081.00
Sales Tax Payable		3,792.00
Unemployment Tax Pay. — Federal		22.00
Unemployment Tax Pay. — State		86.00
Hosp. Insurance Premium Pay.		318.00
U.S. Savings Bonds Payable		50.00
United Way Donations Pay.		20.00
Dividends Payable		—
Capital Stock		150,000.00
Retained Earnings		67,134.00
Income Summary	—	—
Sales		767,500.00
Sales Returns and Allow	9,100.00	
Purchases	548,722.00	
Purch. Returns and Allow		2,000.00
Purchases Discount		4,065.00
Advertising Expense	12,133.00	
Bad Debts Expense	—	

Account Title	Account Balance Debits	Credits
Delivery Expense	$ 4,032.00	
Depr. Exp. — Delivery Equip.	—	
Depr. Exp. — Office Equip.	—	
Depr. Exp. — Store Equip.	—	
Insurance Expense	—	
Miscellaneous Expense	14,408.00	
Payroll Taxes Expense	7,095.00	
Rent Expense	24,000.00	
Salary Expense	94,042.00	
Supplies Expense	—	
Interest Income		3,404.00
Interest Expense	3,784.00	
Federal Income Tax	8,000.00	
	$1,027,362.00	$1,027,362.00

Instructions: Complete the eight-column work sheet for the fiscal year ended December 31 of the current year. Use as a guide the work sheet, pages 536 and 537. Information needed for the adjustments is below.

Bad debts expense is estimated as 1.0% of charge sales. Charge sales were $307,000.00.

Merchandise inventory, December 31	$149,970.00
Supplies inventory, December 31	1,872.00
Value of insurance policies, December 31	2,960.00
Annual depreciation expense on delivery equipment	1,716.00
Annual depreciation expense on office equipment	777.00
Annual depreciation expense on store equipment	2,632.00
Federal income tax for the year	8,634.00

The solution to Problem 27-1 is needed to complete Problem 27-2 and Problem 27-3.

PROBLEM 27-2 Preparing financial statements

The work sheet prepared in Problem 27-1 is needed to complete Problem 27-2.

Instructions: 1. From the work sheet, prepare an income statement for the fiscal year ended December 31 of the current year.

2. Prepare a statement of stockholders' equity. Additional information needed is below.

January 1 balance of capital stock account (1,500 shares issued for $100.00 per share.)	$150,000.00
January 1 balance of retained earnings account	97,134.00
Dividends declared and paid during the current year	30,000.00

3. Prepare a balance sheet for December 31 of the current year.

PROBLEM 27-3 Recording adjusting and closing entries

The work sheet prepared in Problem 27-1 is needed to complete Problem 27-3.

Instructions: 1. From the work sheet prepared in Problem 27-1, record the adjusting entries on page 18 of a general journal.

2. Record the closing entries on page 19 of a general journal.

PROBLEM 27-4 Distributing income to stockholders

On January 10 following the current year, the board of directors of Melody Shop declared a dividend of $24.00 a share to stockholders. Date of payment is January 31. Capital stock issued is 1,500 shares.

Instructions: 1. Record the dividend declared on January 10 on page 20 of a general journal. Source document is Memorandum No. 126.

2. Record payment of the dividend on page 36 of a cash payments journal. Source document is Check No. 486.

ENRICHMENT PROBLEMS

MASTERY PROBLEM 27-M Preparing end-of-fiscal-period work for a corporation

The accounts and their balances in RSD Corporation's general ledger appear as below on December 31 of the current year. The trial balance is recorded on the work sheet in the working papers.

Account Title	Account Balance
Cash	$ 44,120.10
Notes Receivable	1,800.00
Accounts Receivable	28,653.80
Allow. for Uncoll. Accounts	187.00
Merchandise Inventory	123,913.00
Supplies	3,991.70
Prepaid Insurance	7,560.00
Delivery Equipment	12,155.00
Accum. Depr. — Delivery Equip.	3,570.00
Office Equipment	6,604.50
Accum. Depr. — Office Equip.	1,326.00
Store Equipment	27,965.00
Accum. Depr. — Store Equip.	4,131.00
Accounts Payable	13,702.00
Employees Income Tax Payable	790.50
Federal Income Tax Payable	—
FICA Tax Payable	918.85
Sales Tax Payable	3,223.20
Unemployment Tax Pay. — Federal	18.70
Unemployment Tax Pay. — State	73.10
Hosp. Insurance Premium Pay	270.30
U.S. Savings Bonds Payable	44.50
United Way Donations Payable	15.00
Dividends Payable	—
Capital Stock	150,000.00
Retained Earnings	34,587.85
Income Summary	—
Sales	652,375.00
Sales Returns and Allow.	7,735.00
Purchases	466,413.70
Purch. Returns and Allow.	1,700.00
Purchases Discount	3,455.20
Advertising Expense	10,313.00
Bad Debts Expense	—
Delivery Expense	3,427.20
Depr. Exp. — Delivery Equip.	—
Depr. Exp. — Office Equip.	—
Depr. Exp. — Store Equip.	—

Account Title	Account Balance
Insurance Expense	—
Miscellaneous Expense	$ 12,246.80
Payroll Taxes Expense	6,030.70
Rent Expense	20,400.00
Salary Expense	79,935.70
Supplies Expense	—
Interest Income	2,893.40
Interest Expense	3,216.40
Federal Income Tax	6,800.00

Instructions: 1. Prepare an eight-column work sheet for the fiscal year ended December 31 of the current year. Use as a guide the work sheet, pages 536 and 537. Information needed for the adjustments is below.

Bad debts expense is estimated as 1.5% of charge sales. Charge sales were $163,100.00.	
Merchandise inventory, December 31	$130,108.60
Supplies inventory, December 31	849.40
Value of insurance policies, December 31	3,150.00
Annual depreciation expense on delivery equipment	2,431.00
Annual depreciation expense on office equipment	660.45
Annual depreciation expense on store equipment	2,796.50
Federal income tax for the year	7,452.79

2. Prepare an income statement similar to the one on page 542.

3. Prepare a statement of stockholders' equity similar to the one on page 543. Additional information needed is below.

January 1 balance of capital stock account (15,000 shares issued for $10.00 per share.)	$150,000.00
January 1 balance of retained earnings account	64,587.85
Dividends declared and paid during the current year	30,000.00

4. Prepare a balance sheet for December 31 of the current year.

5. Record the adjusting entries on page 15 of a general journal.

6. Record the closing entries on page 16 of a general journal.

7. On January 20 following the current year, the board of directors declared a dividend of $2.00 a share to stockholders. Record the dividend declared on page 18 of a general journal. Source document is Memorandum No. 98.

8. The dividend declared in Instruction 7 was paid on February 10. Record payment of the dividend on page 32 of a cash payments journal. Source document is Check No. 339.

CHALLENGE PROBLEM 27-C Preparing end-of-fiscal-period work for a corporation

The accounts and their balances in Aquarian Electronics' general ledger appear as below and on the next page on December 31 of the current year. The trial balance is recorded on the work sheet in the working papers.

Account Title	Account Balance
Cash	$ 28,937.20
Notes Receivable	4,134.00
Accounts Receivable	31,316.36
Allow. for Uncoll. Accounts	31.00
Merchandise Inventory	86,331.00
Supplies	1,772.40

Account Title	Account Balance
Prepaid Insurance	$ 6,300.00
Delivery Equipment	8,240.00
Accum. Depr. — Delivery Equip.	2,472.00
Office Equipment	4,820.00
Accum. Depr. — Office Equip.	1,205.00
Store Equipment	6,480.00
Accum. Depr. — Store Equip.	1,944.00
Notes Payable	10,000.00
Accounts Payable	9,173.70
Employees Income Tax Payable	1,240.00
Federal Income Tax Payable	——
FICA Tax Payable	327.00
Sales Tax Payable	2,751.16
Unemployment Tax Pay. — Federal	15.00
Unemployment Tax Pay. — State	58.00
Hosp. Insurance Premium Pay.	222.50
Dividends Payable	7,500.00
Capital Stock	75,000.00
Retained Earnings	4,638.69
Income Summary	——
Sales	660,053.40
Sales Returns and Allow.	4,968.90
Purchases	438,978.50
Purch. Returns and Allow.	1,617.40
Purchases Discount	3,252.56
Advertising Expense	9,493.00
Bad Debts Expense	——
Delivery Expense	3,225.60
Depr. Exp. — Delivery Equip.	——
Depr. Exp. — Office Equip.	——
Depr. Exp. — Store Equip.	——
Insurance Expense	——
Miscellaneous Expense	5,763.20
Payroll Taxes Expense	6,615.00
Rent Expense	19,200.00
Salary Expense	94,622.00
Supplies Expense	——
Interest Income	1,723.20
Interest Expense	3,027.45
Federal Income Tax	19,000.00

Instructions: 1. Prepare an eight-column work sheet for the fiscal year ended December 31 of the current year. Use as a guide the work sheet, pages 536 and 537.

Bad debts expense is estimated as 1.5% of charge sales. Charge sales were $660,053.40.

Merchandise inventory, December 31	$104,212.80
Supplies inventory, December 31	227.80
Value of insurance policies, December 31	2,100.00
Annual depreciation expense on delivery equipment	1,030.00
Annual depreciation expense on office equipment	482.00
Annual depreciation expense on store equipment	518.40

Federal income tax for the year is figured at the following rates:

17% of the first $25,000.00 net income before taxes.
20% of the next $25,000.00 net income before taxes.
30% of the next $25,000.00 net income before taxes.
40% of the next $25,000.00 net income before taxes or amount above $75,000.00.

2. Prepare an income statement similar to the one on page 542.

3. Prepare a statement of stockholders' equity similar to the one on page 543. Additional information needed is below.

January 1 balance of capital stock account	$75,000.00
(750 shares issued for $100.00 per share.)	
January 1 balance of retained earnings account	12,138.69
Dividend declared December 31 of the current year	7,500.00

4. Prepare a balance sheet for December 31 of the current year.

5. Record the adjusting entries on page 20 of a general journal.

6. Record the closing entries on page 21 of a general journal.

7. The dividend declared on December 31 was paid on January 10 following the current year. Record payment of the dividend on page 40 of a cash payments journal. Source document is Check No. 667.

Reinforcement Activity 4

PART B

An Accounting Cycle for a Corporation Using Special Journals

The general ledger and general journal prepared in Part A are needed to complete Part B.

Reinforcement Activity 4, Part B, includes the accounting activities needed to complete an accounting cycle for a corporation. In Part A, Electronic Emporium's transactions were recorded for the month of December. The general ledger account balances of Electronic Emporium now include transactions for the fiscal year ended December 31. (Beginning account balances given in Part A included transactions from the first eleven months of the fiscal year.)

In Part B, end-of-fiscal-period work will be completed for Electronic Emporium.

Preparing end-of-fiscal-period work for a corporation

Instructions: 1. Prepare an eight-column work sheet for the fiscal year ended December 31 of the current year. Information needed for the adjustments is below. Bad debts expense is estimated as 2.0% of charge sales. Charge sales were $79,206.50 for the fiscal year.

Merchandise inventory, December 31	$75,033.20
Supplies inventory, December 31	182.20
Value of insurance policies, December 31	1,680.00
Annual depreciation expense on office equipment	434.00
Annual depreciation expense on store equipment	622.00
Federal income tax for the year	8,075.56

2. Prepare an income statement for the year ended December 31.

3. Prepare a statement of stockholders' equity. Additional information needed is below.

January 1 balance of capital stock account (6,000 shares issued for $10.00 per share.)	$60,000.00
January 1 balance of retained earnings account	45,622.00
Dividends declared and paid during the current year	30,000.00

4. Prepare a balance sheet for December 31 of the current year.

5. Record the adjusting entries on pages 8 and 9 of the general journal. Post to the general ledger accounts.

6. Record the closing entries on page 9 of the general journal. Post to the general ledger accounts.

7. Prepare a post-closing trial balance.

FIRE PLACE, INC., is a merchandising business organized as a corporation. This business simulation covers the realistic transactions completed by a corporation that sells fireplaces and inserts, wood stoves, and gas grills. Transactions are recorded in special journals from source documents. In addition, a payroll register, employee's earnings records, a general journal, a general ledger, an accounts receivable ledger, and an accounts payable ledger are used. A pictorial flowchart of the accounting cycle of FIRE PLACE, INC., is shown on the next two pages. This business simulation is available from the publisher.

Flowchart of the
Accounting Cycle of
FIRE PLACE, INC.

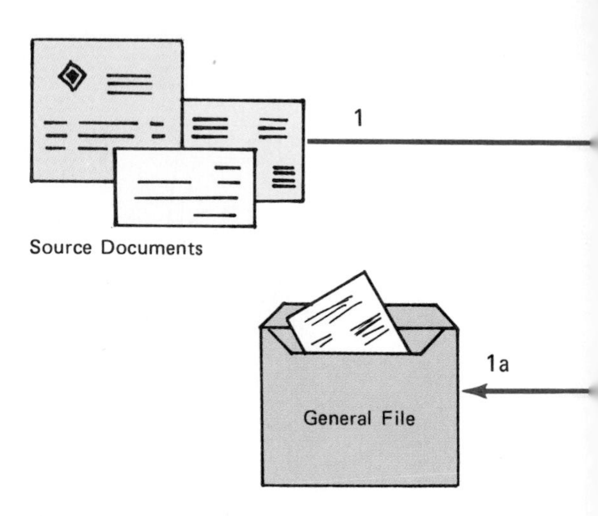

1 Record transactions in the appropriate special journals from source documents.
1a File source documents.
2 Post items to be posted individually to the general ledger and subsidiary ledgers.
3 Prepare the payroll and record the entries. Update the employee's earnings records.
4 Post column totals to the general ledger.
5 Prepare schedules of accounts receivable and accounts payable from subsidiary ledgers.
6 Prepare the trial balance on the work sheet.
7 Plan adjustments and complete the work sheet.
8 Prepare financial statements.
9 Record adjusting and closing entries from the work sheet.
10 Post adjusting and closing entries to the general ledger.
11 Prepare a post-closing trial balance from the general ledger.

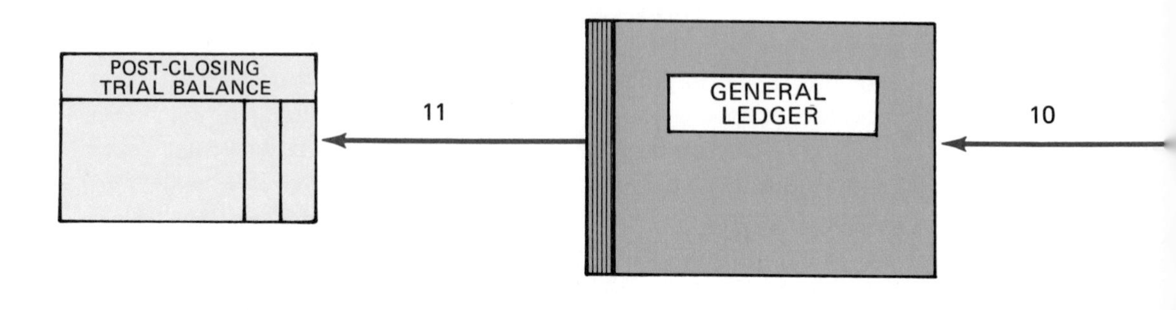

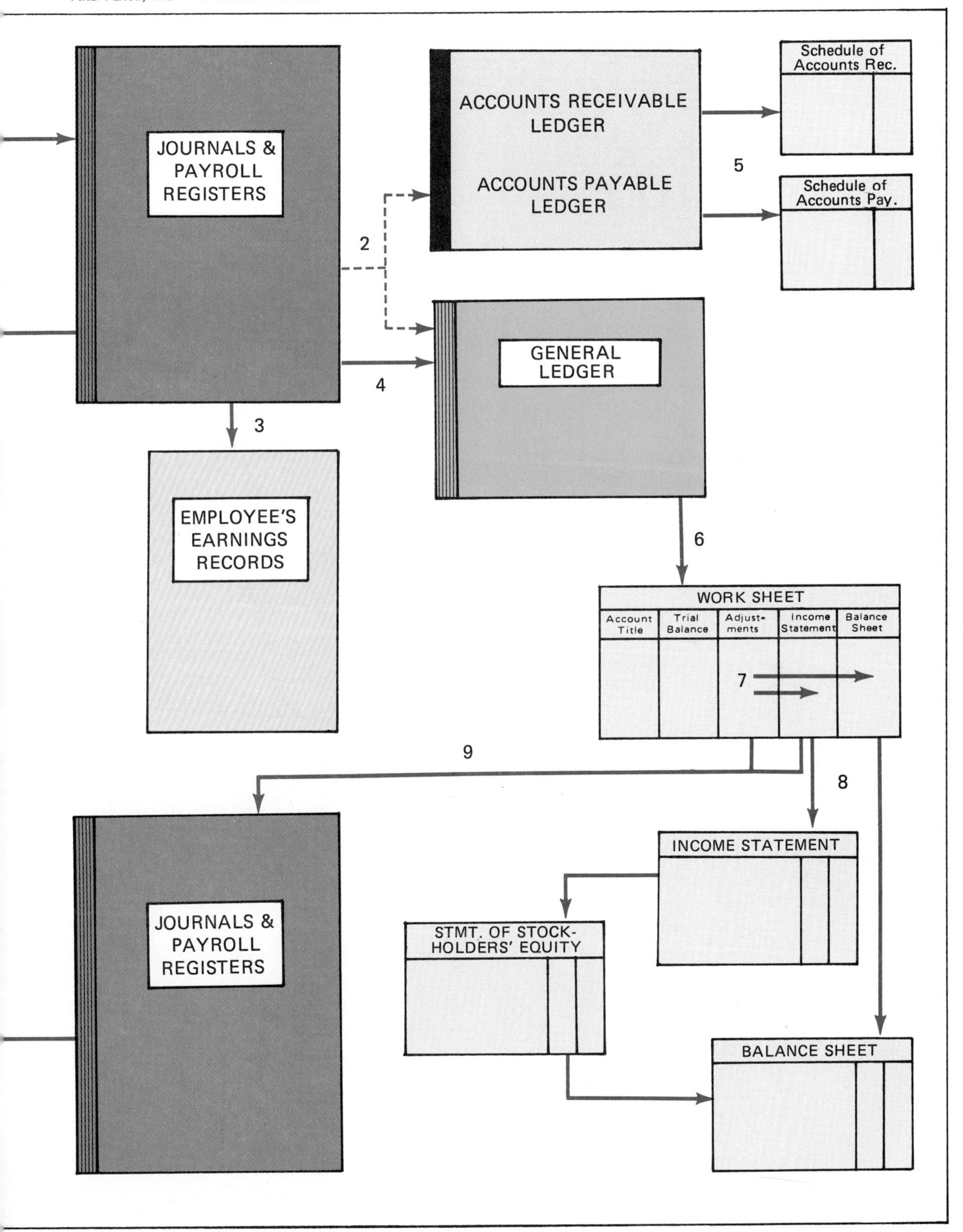
JOURNALS & PAYROLL REGISTERS
2
ACCOUNTS RECEIVABLE LEDGER
ACCOUNTS PAYABLE LEDGER
Schedule of Accounts Rec.
5
Schedule of Accounts Pay.
GENERAL LEDGER
4
3
EMPLOYEE'S EARNINGS RECORDS
6
WORK SHEET
Account Title
Trial Balance
Adjust-ments
Income Statement
Balance Sheet
7
9
8
JOURNALS & PAYROLL REGISTERS
INCOME STATEMENT
STMT. OF STOCK-HOLDERS' EQUITY
BALANCE SHEET

6 ACCOUNTING CONTROL SYSTEMS

GENERAL BEHAVIORAL GOALS

1. Know accounting terminology related to accounting control systems for a merchandising business organized as a corporation.
2. Understand accounting principles and practices for accounting control systems of a merchandising business organized as a corporation.
3. Demonstrate accounting procedures for control systems of a merchandising business organized as a corporation.

Solar Power, the business for Part 6, sells solar equipment.

SOLAR POWER
Chart of Accounts

Balance Sheet Accounts

(1) ASSETS	Account Number
11 Current Assets	
Cash	1101
Petty Cash	1102
Notes Receivable	1103
Accounts Receivable	1104
Allowance for Uncollectible Accounts	1104.1
Merchandise Inventory	1105
Supplies	1106
Prepaid Insurance	1107
12 Plant Assets	
Delivery Equipment	1201
Accumulated Depreciation — Delivery Equipment	1201.1
Office Equipment	1202
Accumulated Depreciation — Office Equipment	1202.1
Store Equipment	1203
Accumulated Depreciation — Store Equipment	1203.1
(2) LIABILITIES	
21 Current Liabilities	
Notes Payable	2101
Vouchers Payable	2102
Employees Income Tax Payable — Federal	2103
Employees Income Tax Payable — State	2104
FICA Tax Payable	2105
Income Tax Payable — Federal	2106
Income Tax Payable — State	2107
Sales Tax Payable	2108
Unemployment Tax Payable — Federal	2109
Unemployment Tax Payable — State	2110
Hospital Insurance Premiums Payable	2111
Dividends Payable	2112
(3) STOCKHOLDERS' EQUITY	
Capital Stock	3101
Retained Earnings	3201
Income Summary	3301

Income Statement Accounts

(4) OPERATING REVENUE	Account Number
Sales	4101
Sales Returns and Allowances	4101.1
(5) COST OF MERCHANDISE	
Purchases	5101
Purchases Returns and Allowances	5101.1
Purchases Discount	5101.2
(6) OPERATING EXPENSES	
Advertising Expense	6101
Bad Debts Expense	6102
Delivery Expense	6103
Depreciation Expense — Delivery Equipment	6104
Depreciation Expense — Office Equipment	6105
Depreciation Expense — Store Equipment	6106
Insurance Expense	6107
Miscellaneous Expense	6108
Payroll Taxes Expense	6109
Rent Expense	6110
Salary Expense	6111
Supplies Expense	6112
(7) OTHER REVENUE	
Interest Income	7101
(8) OTHER EXPENSES	
Interest Expense	8101
Cash Short and Over	8102
(9) INCOME TAX	
Federal Income Tax	9101
State Income Tax	9102

The chart of accounts for Solar Power is illustrated above for ready reference as you study Part 6 of this textbook.

28

A Voucher System

ENABLING PERFORMANCE TASKS

After studying Chapter 28, you will be able to:

a. Define accounting terms related to a voucher system.
b. Explain accounting principles and practices related to a voucher system.
c. Prepare a voucher.
d. Record vouchers in a voucher register.
e. Record cash transactions in a check register.
f. Record purchases returns and allowances and payroll transactions in a voucher system.

Business transactions affect the cash account more often than any other general ledger account. Cash also is more often subject to misuse because ownership is so easy to transfer. Thus, a procedure is needed that places accounting controls on the asset cash.

Many businesses use a control procedure that requires all cash payments to be approved by someone in authority. In small businesses, usually the owner or manager approves cash payments. In large businesses, more than one person may have authority to approve cash payments. A voucher system is frequently used for controlling cash payments when several persons are authorized to approve cash payments. Controlling cash payments by preparing and approving vouchers before payments are made is called a voucher system.

USING A VOUCHER SYSTEM

A business form showing approval by an authorized person for a cash payment is called a voucher. A business paper used to authorize an accounting entry often is referred to as a voucher. When a voucher system is used however *voucher* refers only to the cash payment approval form.

A journal in which vouchers are recorded is called a voucher register. A journal used in a voucher system to record cash payments is called a check register.

Major steps in using a voucher system are listed below.

1 Verify amounts and data on invoice.

2 Prepare voucher. Determine accounts and amounts to be debited and credited.

3 Obtain approval of voucher.

4 Record voucher in voucher register and make notation on voucher.

5 File unpaid voucher in "unpaid vouchers file."

6 Obtain approval for payment of voucher. Issue check. Make notation on voucher.

7 File voucher in "paid vouchers file."

8 Record check in check register. Make notation in voucher register.

PREPARING VOUCHERS

Solar Power, a solar equipment business, uses a voucher system to control all cash payments. A voucher is prepared for each cash payment to be made.

Verifying an invoice

When Solar Power receives an invoice, a verification form is stamped on the invoice as shown on the next page.

The invoice is verified for such details as quantities received, terms, prices, and amounts. Account or accounts to be debited and credited are also shown. The person doing each part of this work initials the verification form to show the responsibility for that part.

Preparing a voucher

A verified invoice is used to prepare a voucher. The voucher prepared for the verified invoice, page 571, is on the next page.

Four kinds of information are listed in Section 1 of Solar Power's voucher. (1) Voucher number. (2) Date on which the voucher is being prepared. (3) Date on which payment is to be made. (4) Name and address of the person or business to which money is to be paid.

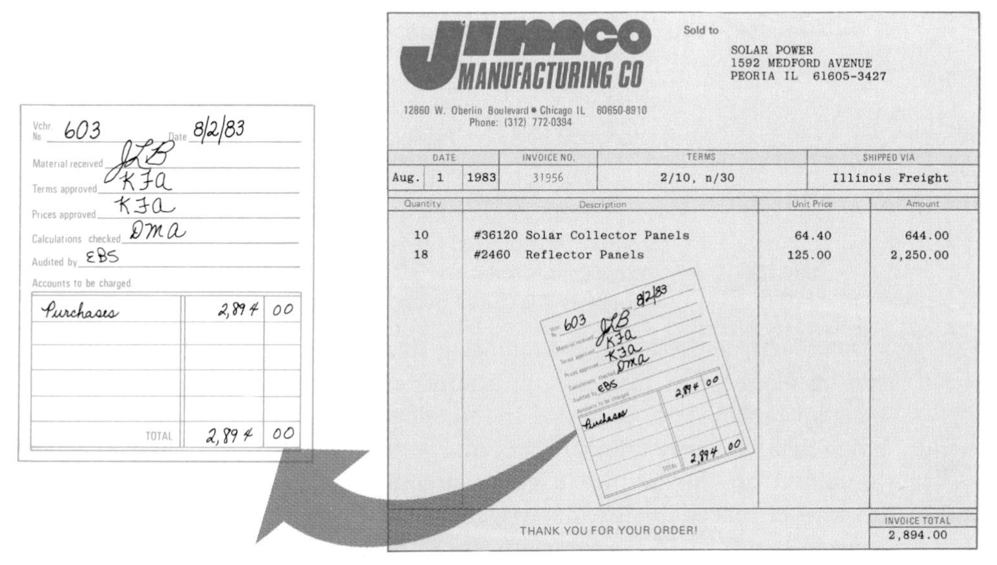

Vchr. No. 603 Date 8/2/83
Material received JLB
Terms approved KJa
Prices approved KJa
Calculations checked DMa
Audited by EBS
Accounts to be charged

Purchases	2,894	00
TOTAL	2,894	00

JIMCO MANUFACTURING CO
12860 W. Oberlin Boulevard • Chicago IL 60650-8910
Phone: (312) 772-0394

Sold to
SOLAR POWER
1592 MEDFORD AVENUE
PEORIA IL 61605-3427

DATE	INVOICE NO.	TERMS	SHIPPED VIA
Aug. 1 1983	31956	2/10, n/30	Illinois Freight

Quantity	Description	Unit Price	Amount
10	#36120 Solar Collector Panels	64.40	644.00
18	#2460 Reflector Panels	125.00	2,250.00

THANK YOU FOR YOUR ORDER!

INVOICE TOTAL 2,894.00

Verification of invoice

1 — Vchr. No. 603 Date 8/2/83 Due Date 8/10/83
To Jimco Manufacturing Company
Address 12860 W. Oberlin Blvd. (Street)
Chicago, IL 60650-8910 (City, State, ZIP)

2 —

ACCOUNTS DEBITED	AMOUNT	
PURCHASES	2,894	00
SUPPLIES		
ADVERTISING EXPENSE		
DELIVERY EXPENSE		
INSURANCE EXPENSE		
MISCELLANEOUS EXPENSE		
PAYROLL TAXES EXPENSE		
RENT EXPENSE		
SALARY EXPENSE		
TOTAL DEBITS	2,894	00

ACCOUNTS CREDITED	AMOUNT	
VOUCHERS PAYABLE	2,894	00
EMPLOYEES INC. TAX PAY. – FED.		
EMPLOYEES INC. TAX PAY. – STATE		
FICA TAX PAYABLE		
TOTAL CREDITS	2,894	00

3 — Voucher Approved by Louis Zink

4 — Recorded in Voucher Register Page ________ by ________

5 — Paid { Date ________ Check No. ________ Amount $ ________ Approved by ________ }

Outside of voucher for an invoice

Vouchers are numbered consecutively to identify and account for all vouchers.

Accounts and amounts to be debited and credited, total debits, and total credits are listed in Section 2. Account titles not printed on a voucher form are written on blank lines in Section 2.

August 2, 1983. Purchased merchandise on account from Jimco Manufacturing Company, $2,894.00. Voucher No. 603.

Purchases	
2,894.00	

Vouchers Payable	
	2,894.00

The cost account Purchases is debited, $2,894.00. The liability account Vouchers Payable is credited, $2,894.00.

In a voucher system, Vouchers Payable is used as the liability account rather than Accounts Payable. Also, no accounts payable ledger is kept. An unpaid vouchers file shows amounts owed. A paid vouchers file shows amounts that have been paid.

A voucher is folded and becomes a folder in which related documents can be placed. For this reason, a voucher is sometimes referred to as a voucher jacket. The inside of the voucher, page 571, contains space for other details about the transaction. For Voucher No. 603, all details are contained on the invoice used to prepare the voucher. Therefore, the invoice is placed inside the voucher. No further information need be recorded on the inside of the voucher.

A separate voucher is usually prepared for each invoice received. However, several invoices received at the same time from the same creditor may be combined into one voucher.

After a voucher is completed, the voucher is sent to a person authorized to approve it. Louis Zink, manager, is the person who approves vouchers for Solar Power. He checks the voucher and indicates approval by signing the voucher in Section 3 as on page 571. The approved voucher is then recorded.

PAGE 24 VOUCHER REGISTER

	DATE	PAYEE	VCHR. NO.	PAID DATE	CK. NO.	1 VOUCHERS PAYABLE CREDIT	
1	1983 Aug. 2	Jimco Manufacturing Company	603	Aug. 10	741	2894 00	1
2	3	Trinity Motors	604			7950 00	2
3	4	Energy Electronics	605	Aug. 11	742	826 50	3
4	5	Solano Company	606			372 00	4
5	8	Colonial Service Center	607			47 50	5
6	8	Moreno's, Inc.	608	See Vchr. No. 611		136 00	6
7	10	Central Supply	609			73 25	7
8	11	Mandarin, Inc.	610	Aug. 21	748	248 40	8
9	12	Moreno's, Inc.	611			90 00	9
10							10
30	31	Payroll	628	Aug. 31	755	4126 73	30
31							31
32							32
33							33
34	31	Totals				91865 10	34
35						(2102)	35

Voucher register (left page)

RECORDING VOUCHERS IN A VOUCHER REGISTER

A voucher register is similar to and replaces a purchases journal described in Chapter 20. The source document for an entry in a voucher register is a voucher. *(CONCEPT: Objective Evidence)* Vouchers are recorded in numerical order. A missing number shows that a voucher has not been recorded.

Solar Power's voucher register is below and on page 572. Special columns are used for Purchases Debit, Delivery Expense Debit, Supplies Debit, and Vouchers Payable Credit. For accounts with no special amount columns, amounts are recorded in the General columns.

Recording a voucher in special amount columns of a voucher register

The entry on line 1 of the voucher register, page 572, is for Voucher No. 603, page 571. The date of the voucher, *1983, Aug. 2*, is written in the Date column. The name of the creditor, *Jimco Manufacturing Company*, is written in the Payee column. The number of the voucher, *603*, is written in the Vchr. No. column. The total amount to be paid for this voucher, *$2,894.00*, is written in the Vouchers Payable Credit column. As the total amount of the voucher is debited to Purchases, $2,894.00 is also written in the Purchases Debit column. This information is obtained from Sections 1 and 2 of the voucher.

After Voucher No. 603 is recorded in the voucher register, a notation is made on the voucher jacket, Section 4. The illustration on the next page

FOR MONTH OF *August* 19 *83* PAGE *24*

	2	3	4			5	6	
	DISTRIBUTION			GENERAL				
	PURCHASES DEBIT	DELIVERY EXPENSE DEBIT	SUPPLIES DEBIT	ACCOUNT	POST REF.	DEBIT	CREDIT	
1	2894 00							1
2				Delivery Equipment	1201	7950 00		2
3	826 50							3
4	372 00							4
5		47 50						5
6	136 00							6
7			73 25					7
8	248 40							8
9				Vouchers Payable	2102	136 00		9
10				Purchases Returns + Allow.	5101.1		46 00	10
30				Salary Expense	6111	5072 80		30
31				Employees Inc. Tax Pay. - Fed.	2103		558 00	31
32				Employees Inc. Tax Pay. - State	2104		83 70	32
33				FICA Tax Payable	2106		304 37	33
34	67830 00	504 00	428 40			25644 80	2542 10	34
35	(5101)	(6103)	(1105)			(✓)	(✓)	35

Voucher register (right page)

shows that Voucher No. 603 was recorded on page 24 of the voucher register. The voucher is initialed in this section to show who recorded the entry. The voucher is then filed in an unpaid vouchers file. The voucher is filed by the date payment should be made, August 10, 1983.

Voucher clerk's notation on the voucher to show that the voucher has been recorded

Recording a voucher in the General columns of a voucher register

August 3, 1983. Bought delivery truck on account from Trinity Motors, $7,950.00. Voucher No. 604.

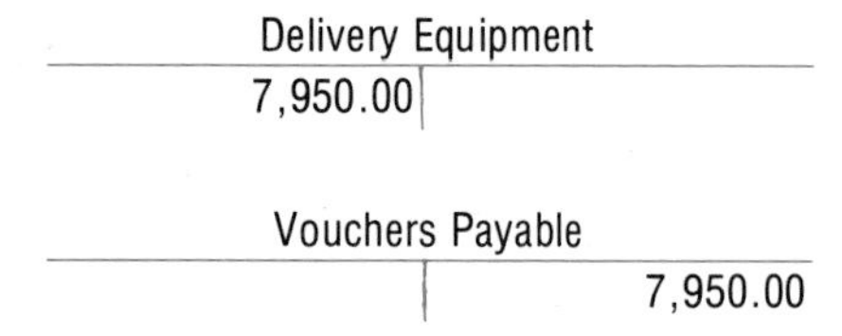

The plant asset account Delivery Equipment is debited and the liability account Vouchers Payable is credited, $7,950.00.

The entry on line 2 of the voucher register, pages 572 and 573, is made from information on Voucher No. 604. *(CONCEPT: Objective Evidence)* The total voucher amount, *$7,950.00*, is written in the Vouchers Payable Credit column. No special amount column is provided to record a debit to the delivery equipment account. *Delivery Equipment* is written in the General Account column. The amount, *$7,950.00*, is written in the General Debit column.

Posting from a voucher register

Only items recorded in the General Debit or General Credit columns are posted individually from a voucher register. As each amount is posted, an account number is written in the voucher register's Post. Ref. column.

At the end of each month, a voucher register is totaled, proved, and ruled as on pages 572 and 573.

Totals of special amount columns are posted to general ledger accounts named in the column headings. The number of the account to which each special amount column total is posted is written in parentheses below the total. Check marks are placed below the General Debit and General Credit columns to show that these totals are not posted.

PAYING VOUCHERS

When a voucher system is used, each voucher is paid by a check. Each day all vouchers to be paid that day are removed from the unpaid vouchers file. A check is prepared for the amount of each voucher less any deductions for cash discounts. Checks are issued only for approved vouchers.

Preparing a voucher check

A check with space for writing the purpose of the payment is called a voucher check. A voucher check is below.

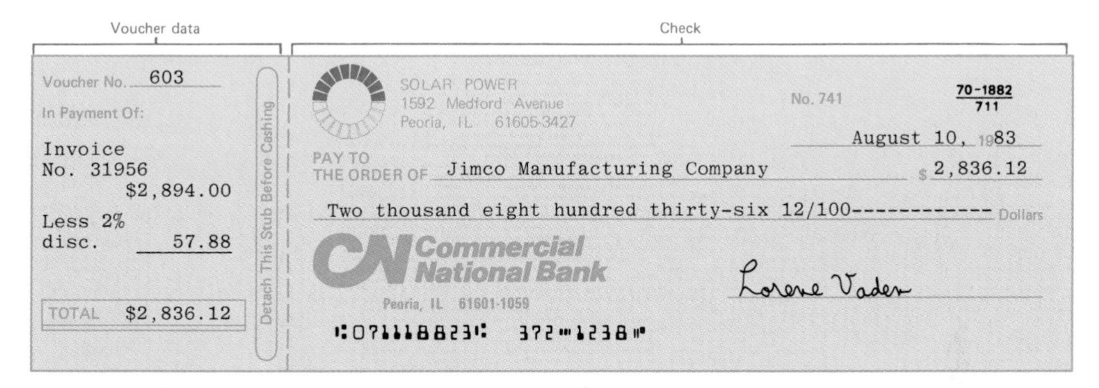

Voucher data | Check

Voucher No. 603
In Payment Of:
Invoice
No. 31956
$2,894.00
Less 2%
disc. 57.88
TOTAL $2,836.12

Detach This Stub Before Cashing

SOLAR POWER
1592 Medford Avenue
Peoria, IL 61605-3427

No. 741

70-1882
711

August 10, 1983

PAY TO THE ORDER OF Jimco Manufacturing Company $ 2,836.12

Two thousand eight hundred thirty-six 12/100------------ Dollars

Commercial National Bank
Peoria, IL 61601-1059

Lorene Vaden

⑆071118823⑆ 372⑈1238⑈

Voucher check

Voucher checks can be used when a voucher system is not used. For example, the check on page 451, Chapter 22, is a voucher check.

The check above is issued by Solar Power in payment of Voucher No. 603. The items listed below are recorded in the space provided for voucher data.

1. Voucher number.
2. Invoice number.
3. Amount of the invoice.
4. Amount of the discount, if any.
5. Net amount for which the check is written.

The main portion of the check is prepared in the usual manner.

Recording a payment on a voucher

After a voucher check is written, a notation is made in Section 5 of the voucher. The notation on Voucher No. 603, below, shows that Check No. 741 was issued on August 10, 1983. The payment is approved and the check is signed by Lorene Vaden.

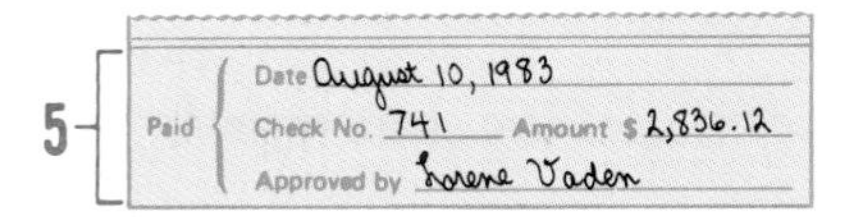

5
Paid
Date August 10, 1983
Check No. 741 Amount $ 2,836.12
Approved by Lorene Vaden

Notation on a voucher to show that a voucher has been paid

When a voucher is paid, the date and check number are written in a voucher register's Paid columns. This gives a cross-reference from a voucher register to a check register.

After payment is noted on a voucher, the voucher is filed in numerical order in a paid vouchers file. The voucher is then available for future reference.

RECORDING CASH TRANSACTIONS IN A CHECK REGISTER

Solar Power's check register is below. The check register is similar to and replaces the cash payments journal described in Chapter 20.

CHECK REGISTER — PAGE 28

	DATE		PAYEE	CK. No.	VCHR. No.	1 VOUCHERS PAYABLE DEBIT	2 PURCHASES DISCOUNT CREDIT	3 CASH CREDIT	4 BANK DEPOSITS	5 BANK BALANCE	
1	1983 Aug.	10	Brought Forward		✓	1788210	17780	1770430		8940260	1
2		10	Jimco Manufacturing Co.	741	603	289400	5788	283612		8656648	2
3		11	Energy Electronics	742	605	82650	1653	80997		8575651	3
4		15	Payroll	743	612	378284		378284		8197367	4
5		15	Ebensberger Supply	744	582	14625		14625		8182742	5
6		15	Deposit		✓				1632140	9814882	6
18		31	Payroll	755	628	412673		412673		8358480	18
19		31	Deposit		✓				1527480	9885960	19
20		31	Totals			8941020	50810	8890210			20
21						(2102)	(5101.2)	(1101)			21
22											22

Check register

A check is written each time a voucher is paid. Solar Power prepares each voucher check in duplicate. The duplicate copy is the source document for the entry in the check register. *(CONCEPT: Objective Evidence)* Source document for cash payments transactions, described in Chapter 20, is a check stub. Each check is recorded in a check register in numerical order.

Each check is recorded in a check register as a debit to Vouchers Payable and a credit to Cash. If a discount is earned for prompt payment, the amount is recorded in the Purchases Discount Credit column. In a voucher system, these general ledger accounts are the only ones affected by cash payments transactions. All other accounts are debited or credited when a voucher is recorded in a voucher register. Special amount columns are used in a check register only for Vouchers Payable Debit, Purchases Discount Credit, and Cash Credit.

Maintaining bank balance columns in a check register

The check register above has two columns headed *Bank*. These two columns are used to keep an up-to-date record of cash in the bank account. The Bank Deposit column is used to record the amounts deposited in the bank account. The Bank Balance column shows the bank account balance after each check is issued and after each deposit is made. Solar Power uses these columns instead of check stubs to maintain a record of deposits and bank balance. Solar Power's check register combines a cash payments journal and check stub information.

Recording checks in a check register

On August 10, 1983, Solar Power's check register column totals are forwarded from page 27 to page 28. Amounts brought forward are shown on line 1 of the check register, page 576.

> *August 10, 1983. Paid Voucher No. 603, $2,894.00, less Purchases Discount of $57.88. Check No. 741.*

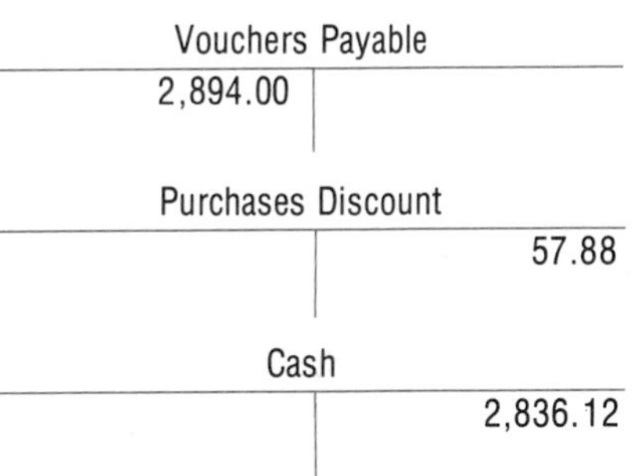

The liability account Vouchers Payable is debited for $2,894.00. The contra account, Purchases Discount, is credited for $57.88. Cash is credited for $2,836.12.

The entry to record this check is on line 2 of the check register, page 576. The date, *10*, is entered in the Date column. The payee's name, *Jimco Manufacturing Company*, is written in the Payee column. The check number, *741*, is written in the Ck. No. column, and the voucher number, *603*, is written in the Vchr. No. column. The total voucher amount, *$2,894.00*, is written in the Vouchers Payable Debit column. The discount amount, *$57.88*, is written in the Purchases Discount Credit column. The check amount, *$2,836.12*, is written in the Cash Credit column. The check amount is subtracted from the balance in the Bank Balance column on line 1. The amount of the new balance, *$86,566.48*, is written in the Bank Balance column on line 2.

On August 15, 1983, Solar Power made a bank deposit of $16,321.40. The entry to record this deposit is on line 6 of the check register, page 576. The date, *15*, is written in the Date column. The word, *Deposit*, is written in the Payee column. A check mark is placed in the Vchr. No. column to show that no voucher is used for this entry. The amount of the deposit, *$16,321.40*, is written in the Bank Deposits column. The deposit amount is then added to the previous bank balance shown in the Bank Balance column on line 5. The new bank balance, *$98,148.82*, is written in the Bank Balance column. Information to record this entry is taken from the bank deposit slip.

Posting from a check register

Solar Power's check register has only special amount columns. Individual items in the check register are not posted. At the end of each month, the check register's debit and credit columns are totaled, proved, and ruled as on page 576.

Totals of special amount columns are posted to the accounts named in the column headings. The account number to which each amount column total is posted is written in parentheses below the total.

Bank Deposits and Bank Balance columns show only the current balance of the bank account. These columns are neither totaled, ruled, nor posted.

USING A VOUCHER SYSTEM FOR SELECTED BUSINESS TRANSACTIONS

For transactions described previously, a voucher was prepared from each invoice and each voucher was paid in full when due. Some transactions however require different procedures. Examples are purchases returns and allowances and payroll payments.

Recording purchases returns and allowances

A purchases returns and allowances transaction reduces the total invoice amount owed. A voucher for an original invoice must be changed to show reduction in the amount owed.

August 12, 1983. Issued Debit Memorandum No. 64 to Moreno's, Inc., for the return of merchandise purchased, $46.00. Canceled Voucher No. 608 and issued Voucher No. 611.

Vouchers Payable

Vchr. 611	136.00	Vchr. 608	136.00
		Vchr. 611	90.00

Purchases Returns and Allowances

		Vchr. 611	46.00

The liability account Vouchers Payable is debited for the amount of Voucher No. 608, *$136.00*. Vouchers Payable is credited for the amount of the new Voucher No. 611, *$90.00*. The contra account, Purchases Returns and Allowances, is credited for $46.00. The following procedure is used to change the amount owed on Voucher No. 608.

1 Remove Voucher No. 608 from the unpaid vouchers file. Write *Canceled* across the outside of the voucher.

2 Prepare a new voucher and have it approved. Voucher No. 611 is prepared for the new amount, $90.00. (Original voucher amount, $136.00, less amount of purchases return, $46.00.) The canceled copy of Voucher No. 608, original invoice, and debit memorandum are placed inside Voucher No. 611.

3 Write *See Vchr. No. 611* in the voucher register's Paid columns on the line for Voucher No. 608. This notation is on line 6 of the voucher register, page 572.

4 Record the new voucher in the voucher register. This entry is on the voucher register, lines 9–10, pages 572 and 573. The date, *12*, is entered in the Date column. The payee's name, *Moreno's, Inc.*, is written in the Payee column. The voucher number, *611*, is written in the Vchr. No. column. The account debited, *Vouchers Payable*, is written in the General Account column. The canceled voucher's amount, *$136.00*, is written in the General Debit column. The amount of the

new voucher, *$90.00*, is written in the Vouchers Payable Credit column. This is the amount of the original voucher less the purchases return. ($136.00 − 46.00 = $90.00) On the next voucher register line, the account credited, *Purchases Returns and Allowances*, is written in the General Account column. The amount of purchases return, *$46.00*, is written in the General Credit column.

5 File Voucher No. 611 in the unpaid vouchers file by the due date.

Paying a payroll

Solar Power pays its employees semimonthly. A payroll register is prepared to show the details of each payroll. Information from a payroll register is used in preparing a payroll voucher.

August 31, 1983. Recorded semimonthly payroll for period ending August 31, 1983, $5,072.80. Voucher No. 628.

Data from a payroll register are recorded in summary form on the inside of a voucher. Solar Power's August 31, 1983, payroll summary is recorded on the inside of the voucher below. The outside of the voucher is completed as shown below at the right.

VOUCHER

Vchr. No. 628 Date August 31, 1983 Terms ____ Due August 31, 1983

To Payroll

Address

City ____ State ____ Zip ____

For the following: Attach all invoices or other papers permanently to voucher.

DATE	VOUCHER DETAILS		AMOUNT
Aug. 31	Payroll for period ended 8/31/83		
	Salary Expense		$5,072.80
	Deductions:		
	Employees Inc. Tax Pay.-Federal	$558.00	
	Employees Inc. Tax Pay.-State	83.70	
	FICA Tax Payable	304.37	946.07
	Net cash payment		$4,126.73

SOLAR POWER

Inside of voucher for a payroll

Vchr. No. 628 Date 8/31/83 Due Date 8/31/83

To Payroll

Address ____ Street

City State ZIP

ACCOUNTS DEBITED	AMOUNT	
PURCHASES		
SUPPLIES		
ADVERTISING EXPENSE		
DELIVERY EXPENSE		
INSURANCE EXPENSE		
MISCELLANEOUS EXPENSE		
PAYROLL TAXES EXPENSE		
RENT EXPENSE		
SALARY EXPENSE	5,072	80
TOTAL DEBITS	5,072	80
ACCOUNTS CREDITED	**AMOUNT**	
VOUCHERS PAYABLE	4,126	73
EMPLOYEES INC. TAX PAY. – FED.	558	00
EMPLOYEES INC. TAX PAY. – STATE	83	70
FICA TAX PAYABLE	304	37
TOTAL CREDITS	5,072	80

Voucher Approved by *Louis Zink*

Recorded in Voucher Register Page 24 by *DRD*

Paid: Date *August 31, 1983* Check No. 755 Amount *$4,126.73* Approved by *Lorene Vader*

Outside of voucher for a payroll

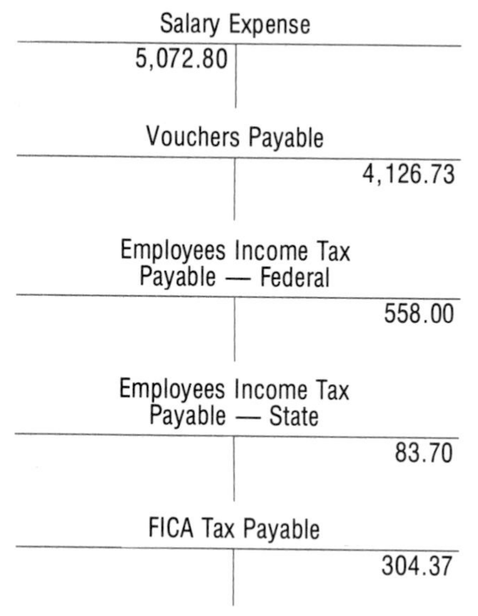

The amounts for each of Solar Power's payroll accounts are shown on the outside of Voucher No. 628. Salary Expense is debited for $5,072.80. The total of the debits, *$5,072.80*, is entered on the Total Debits line. Vouchers Payable is credited for $4,126.73, the net payroll amount to be paid to the employees. Employees Income Tax Payable — Federal is credited for $558.00. Employees Income Tax Payable — State is credited for $83.70. FICA Tax Payable is credited for $304.37. These amounts are the withholding taxes for the employees' salaries. The four credits are added and the total, *$5,072.80*, is entered on the Total Credits line. The voucher's total debits must equal the total credits.

The voucher is approved by Louis Zink. Mr. Zink signs the outside of Section 3. The approved voucher is then recorded in the voucher register. The entry to record Voucher No. 628 is in the voucher register, lines 30–33, pages 572 and 573. After this entry is recorded, a notation is made in Section 4 on the outside of Voucher No. 628. The voucher register page number and the recording clerk's initials are recorded.

Since Voucher No. 628 is to be paid immediately, the voucher is not placed in the unpaid vouchers file. Rather, Check No. 755 is issued for the payroll voucher. The paid section of Voucher No. 628 is completed. The payment is approved and the check is signed by Lorene Vaden. The paid voucher is then filed in the paid vouchers file.

August 31, 1983. Paid Voucher No. 628, $4,126.73. Check No. 755.

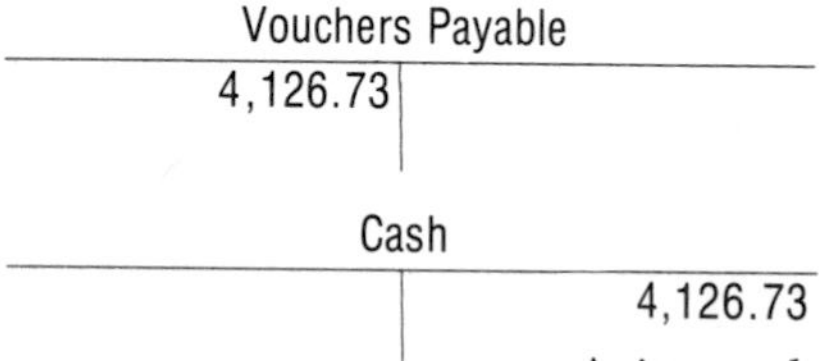

The entry to record Check No. 755 is in the check register, line 18, page 576. Vouchers Payable is debited and Cash is credited for $4,126.73. The date and check number are written in the voucher register's Paid columns, line 30, page 572.

A journal entry to record an employer's payroll taxes is described in Chapter 23. When payroll taxes are due to a government, a voucher is prepared and approved. The approved voucher is recorded in the voucher register. A check is then issued for the voucher.

SUMMARIZING THE ADVANTAGES OF A VOUCHER SYSTEM

A voucher system has advantages for businesses that make many cash payments. Some of these advantages are listed below and on the next page.

1. Responsibility for authorizing and approving all expenditures is limited to a few persons.

2. A voucher jacket provides a convenient method of filing invoices for reference. This is especially true when invoices received from creditors may be of different sizes.
3. Filing vouchers according to their due dates helps assure invoice payments within discount periods.
4. A paid vouchers file and an unpaid vouchers file replace the accounts payable ledger.
5. The voucher system eliminates all posting to creditors' accounts.

ACCOUNTING TERMS

What is the meaning of each of the following?

1. voucher system
2. voucher
3. voucher register
4. check register
5. voucher check

QUESTIONS FOR INDIVIDUAL STUDY

1. Why is a procedure needed that places accounting controls on the asset Cash?
2. What are the major steps in using a voucher system?
3. Why are vouchers numbered consecutively?
4. In a voucher system what liability account is used in place of accounts payable?
5. What ledger is usually not kept when a voucher system is used?
6. When an invoice is received for merchandise purchased on account, which accounts are debited and credited in a voucher system?
7. What journal does the voucher register replace when a voucher system is used?
8. In the voucher register, pages 572–573, which amount columns are posted individually?
9. In the voucher register, page 572, why is there no entry in the Paid columns on line 2?
10. What five items does Solar Power include in the voucher space on its voucher checks?
11. What journal does the check register replace in Solar Power's voucher system?
12. Why does Solar Power's check register have Bank Deposits and Bank Balance columns?
13. Why are no amounts posted individually from any of the columns in the check register used by Solar Power?
14. How is a purchases return recorded on a voucher?
15. What is the source of data for a payroll voucher?
16. What are five advantages of a voucher system?

CASES FOR MANAGEMENT DECISION

CASE 1 Barbara Vornberg owns and operates two sportswear stores. Mrs. Vornberg keeps most of the accounting records herself. She employs a public accountant part time to assist her. Mrs. Vornberg is considering using a voucher system for her business. What questions should she answer before deciding whether to install a voucher system?

CASE 2 Alan Rodgers owns a hardware store. He uses a voucher system involving four steps. (1) An invoice is received and verified and a voucher is prepared. (2) The voucher is filed in an unpaid vouchers file by the due date. (3) When the voucher is due, a check is issued. A notation of the payment is made on the voucher and it is filed in the paid vouchers file. (4) The check issued is recorded in a cash payments journal. Mr. Rodgers does not record a voucher in any journal. The check is recorded as the only entry. For example, payment for purchases with a discount is entered in a cash payments journal. This transaction debits Purchases and credits Purchases Discount and Cash. What are the advantages and disadvantages of this procedure?

DRILLS FOR UNDERSTANDING

DRILL 28-D 1 Analyzing transactions using a voucher register

Use a form similar to the one below.

Trans. No.	Name of Amount Column Used in Voucher Register	
	(a) For Amount Debited	(b) For Amount Credited
1.	*Supplies Debit*	*Vouchers Payable Credit*

Instructions: Complete the following steps for each transaction given below. (a) Write the name(s) of the voucher register amount column(s) in which the debit amount(s) will be recorded. (b) Write the name(s) of the voucher register amount column(s) in which the credit amount(s) will be recorded. Amount columns are like those on voucher register, pages 572 and 573. Transaction 1 is given as an example in the form above.

1. Bought supplies on account.
2. Purchased merchandise on account.
3. Received a statement for delivery expenses for the month.
4. Bought a desk (office equipment).
5. Purchased merchandise on account.
6. Received monthly bill from telephone company (miscellaneous expense).
7. Issued debit memorandum for the return of merchandise purchased earlier. Canceled original voucher and issued new voucher.
8. Payroll register showed entries in the following accounts: Salary Expense, Employees Income Tax Payable — Federal, FICA Tax Payable, and Vouchers Payable.
9. Bought supplies on account.
10. Bought new delivery truck.

DRILL 28-D 2 Analyzing transactions using a check register

Use a form similar to the one below.

Trans. or Activity No.	Vouchers Payable Debit	Purchases Discount Credit	Cash Credit	Bank	
				Deposits	Balance
1.	√		√		√

Instructions: For each transaction or activity given below, place a check mark in each column that should have an amount recorded. Transaction 1 is given as an example in the form, page 582.

1. Paid a voucher; no discount.
2. Made a deposit in the bank.
3. Paid a voucher less discount.
4. Recorded the cash balance on the first day of the month.
5. Paid a voucher; no discount.
6. Paid a voucher less discount.
7. Brought forward account balances from previous page of check register.
8. Paid voucher less discount.
9. Totaled, proved, and ruled the check register.

APPLICATION PROBLEMS

PROBLEM 28-1 Preparing a voucher

Capri Building Supplies uses a voucher form similar to the one on pages 572 and 573.

Instructions: 1. Record in Sections 1 and 2 of the outside of a voucher the following selected transactions. Use July of the current year. Voucher is abbreviated as V.

July 6. Purchased merchandise on account from Four Seasons Inc., 5925 Beechmont Avenue, St. Louis, MO 63121-3789, $1,890.00. V123. Due date is July 14.

8. Bought supplies on account from Elder Supplies, 1208 Harris Road, St. Joseph, MO 64505-2431, $258.25. V124. Due date is July 18.

11. Received a statement from Custom Delivery Service, 1480 Parkhill Road, St. Louis, MO 63143-5103, $127.50. Statement is for delivery expenses. V125. Due date is July 12.

Instructions: 2. Check the accuracy of each completed voucher. Then sign your name on the "Voucher Approved by" line.

PROBLEM 28-2 Recording vouchers in a voucher register

Airco Energy uses a voucher register similar to the one on pages 572 and 573.

Instructions: 1. Record on page 7 of a voucher register the following selected transactions completed during March of the current year. Voucher is abbreviated as V.

Mar. 1. Received bill for March rent owed to Katz Real Estate, $1,000.00. V63.

4. Purchased merchandise on account from Kohler Company, $2,338.40. V64.
7. Purchased merchandise on account from Fox Corporation, $2,987.25. V65.
7. Bought supplies on account from Office Center, $296.50. V66.
8. Received monthly bill from Southwestern Telephone Company, $136.80. V67.
11. Received monthly statement from Daily Herald for newspaper advertising, $78.30. V68.
14. Purchased merchandise on account from DiLeo Equipment, $4,577.40. V69.
18. Bought supplies on account from Office Center, $137.60. V70.
21. Bought a desk from Herkes Office Equipment, $600.00. V71.
26. Purchased merchandise on account from Energy Search, $2,445.00. V72.
28. Bought supplies on account from Ryan Supplies, $325.50. V73.
30. Purchased merchandise on account from Zeff Enterprises, $1,890.30. V74.

Instructions: 2. Total, prove, and rule the voucher register.

The voucher register prepared in Problem 28-2 is needed to complete Problem 28-3.

PROBLEM 28-3 Recording cash transactions in a check register

The voucher register prepared in Problem 28-2 is needed to complete Problem 28-3.

Airco Energy uses a check register similar to the one on page 576 to record all cash payments.

Instructions: 1. Record on page 5 of a check register the following cash payments made during March of the current year. Source documents are abbreviated as: check, C; voucher, V.

2. Vouchers paid are for transactions in Problem 28-2. Record the date and check number for each transaction in the Paid columns of the voucher register completed in Problem 28-2.

Mar. 1. Recorded cash balance on March 1, $15,532.90.
1. Paid V63, $1,000.00. C56.
8. Paid V67, $136.80. C57.
11. Paid V68, $78.30. C58.
14. Paid V65, $2,987.25, less purchases discount, $59.75. C59.
14. Paid V64, $2,338.40, less purchases discount, $23.38. C60.
14. Made a deposit in the bank, $5,979.60.
15. Paid V66, $296.50; no discount. C61.
21. Paid V69, $4,577.40, less purchases discount, $45.77. C62.
26. Paid V70, $137.60; no discount. C63.
28. Paid V71, $600.00; no discount. C64.
30. Made a deposit in the bank, $9,130.25.

Instructions: 3. Total, prove, and rule the check register.

PROBLEM 28-4 Preparing payroll vouchers

Airco Energy's payroll register shows the following information. Voucher is abbreviated as V.

May 15. The payroll register shows the following: Salary Expense, $2,588.60; Employees Income Tax Payable — Federal, $345.40; Employees Income Tax Payable — State, $112.50; FICA Tax Payable, $155.32. V120.

31. The payroll register shows the following: Salary Expense, $2,735.70; Employees Income Tax Payable — Federal, $372.50; Employees Income Tax Payable — State, $119.00; FICA Tax Payable, $164.14. V139.

Instructions: Prepare a voucher for each of the payroll entries above.

PROBLEM 28-5 Recording purchases returns and allowances and payroll transactions in a voucher system

Airco Energy uses a voucher register similar to the one on pages 572 and 573. The company uses a check register similar to the one on page 576.

Instructions: 1. Record the following selected transactions completed during May of the current year. Use page 9 of a voucher register and page 7 of a check register. Source documents are abbreviated as: check, C; debit memorandum, DM; voucher, V.

May 1. Recorded cash balance on May 1, $14,235.50.
5. Purchased merchandise on account from Yetka Corporation, $2,565.00. V104.
9. Issued DM48 to Yetka Corporation for the return of merchandise purchased, $125.00. Canceled V104 and issued V107.
15. The payroll register for the semimonthly payroll showed the following information. Salary Expense, $2,588.60; Employees Income Tax Payable — Federal, $345.40; Employees Income Tax Payable — State, $112.50; FICA Tax Payable, $155.32. V120.
15. Paid V120, $1,975.38. C94.
18. Paid V107, $2,440.00; no discount. C98.
24. Purchased merchandise on account from LiteRite Company, $1,315.00. V130.
28. Issued DM49 to LiteRite Company for the return of merchandise purchased, $165.00. Canceled V130 and issued V136.
31. The payroll register for the semimonthly payroll showed the following information. Salary Expense, $2,735.70; Employees Income Tax Payable — Federal, $372.50; Employees Income Tax Payable — State, $119.00; FICA Tax Payable, $164.14. V139.
31. Paid V139, $2,080.06. C124.

Instructions: 2. Total, prove, and rule the voucher register and check register.

ENRICHMENT PROBLEMS

MASTERY PROBLEM 28-M Recording transactions in a voucher system

Carson Company uses a voucher system. A voucher register and a check register similar to those on pages 572–573 and 576 are used.

Instructions: 1. Record the following transactions completed during June of the current year. Use page 15 of a voucher register and page 12 of a check register. Source documents are abbreviated as: check, C; debit memorandum, DM; voucher, V.

All purchases of merchandise on account are subject to a 2% purchases discount if paid within 10 days. No discounts are allowed on other payments.

June 1. Recorded the cash balance on June 1, $10,636.44.
2. Purchased merchandise on account from Merriam Supplies, $400.40. V223.
9. Purchased merchandise on account from Western Enterprises, $1,797.04. V224.
9. Made a deposit in the bank, $3,763.66.
12. Paid V223 less discount. C176.
20. Purchased merchandise on account from Gonzalez Wholesale Company, $610.66. V225.
21. Made a deposit in the bank, $3,178.22.
22. Bought supplies from Jericho Supplies, $373.24. V226.
22. Paid V226; no discount. C177.
24. Issued DM39 to Western Enterprises for the return of merchandise purchased, $324.04. Canceled V224 and issued V227.

June 27. Paid V227. Since this voucher was not paid within the discount period, no discount is to be taken. C178.
28. Received a statement from Northpark Delivery Service for delivery expenses for the month, $402.50. V228.
28. Paid V228; no discount. C179.
28. Paid V225 less discount. C180.
29. Purchased merchandise on account from Western Enterprises, $921.48. V229.
29. Paid V229 less discount. C181.
30. The payroll register for the monthly payroll showed the following information. Salary Expense, $6,918.24; Employees Income Tax Payable — Federal, $865.70; Employees Income Tax Payable — State, $187.35; FICA Tax Payable, $415.09. V230.
30. Paid V230. C182.
30. Made a deposit in the bank, $3,174.47.

Instructions: 2. Total, prove, and rule the voucher register and check register.

CHALLENGE PROBLEM 28-C Recording purchase invoices at the net amount in a voucher system

Introductory remarks. Some businesses make a practice of paying all invoices within the discount period. These businesses can record invoices at the net amount to be paid at the time the invoice is received. For example, a $1,000.00 invoice with a 2% discount allowed if paid within 10 days would be recorded at $980.00. At the time the voucher is prepared and recorded in the voucher register, Purchases is debited for $980.00. Vouchers Payable is credited for the same amount. The purchases discount amount is not recorded.

If an invoice is not paid within the discount period, Discounts Lost is debited for the amount of discount lost. For example, if the invoice described above were not paid within the discount period, $1,000.00 would have to be paid. The entry would be debits to Vouchers Payable, $980.00, and Discounts Lost, $20.00. Cash would be credited for the amount paid, $1,000.00.

If the invoice above is recorded at the net amount, a purchases return also is recorded at the net amount. If a debit memorandum is issued for $100.00, the purchases return is recorded at $98.00. (Purchases return, $100.00, less 2% discount.) The entry is a debit to Vouchers Payable, $980.00, to cancel the original voucher. Vouchers Payable is credited for the amount of the new voucher, $882.00. (Original voucher amount, $980.00, less amount of purchases return, $98.00.) Purchases Returns and Allowances is credited for $98.00. If the invoice is not paid within the discount period, $900.00 would have to be paid. The entry would be debits to Vouchers Payable, $882.00, and Discounts Lost, $18.00. Cash would be credited for the amount paid, $900.00.

This system uses a check register with special amount columns for Vouchers Payable Debit, Discounts Lost Debit, and Cash Credit.

Instructions: 1. Use the transactions and information given in Mastery Problem 28-M. In the check register, record the beginning cash balance, $10,636.44.

2. Record the transactions for June on page 17 of a voucher register and on page 14 of a check register. Record all vouchers at the net amount to be paid. If the discount is lost, record this in the check register at the time the voucher is paid.

3. Total, prove, and rule the voucher register and the check register.

29

A Petty Cash System

ENABLING PERFORMANCE TASKS

After studying Chapter 29, you will be able to:

a. Define accounting terms related to a petty cash system.
b. Explain accounting principles and practices related to a petty cash system.
c. Establish a petty cash fund using a voucher system.
d. Record payments from a petty cash fund in a petty cash record.
e. Prepare a voucher to replenish a petty cash fund.
f. Determine if a petty cash fund is short or over.
g. Establish and replenish a petty cash fund using a cash payments journal.

Good cash control requires that businesses deposit all cash receipts in a bank account. Good control also requires that checks be written for all major cash payments. Most businesses however make small cash payments for items such as postage, delivery charges, collect telegrams, and some supplies.

Writing a separate check for each small purchase becomes a time-consuming and expensive process. To avoid writing many checks for small amounts, some businesses establish a special cash fund. These small payments are then made from this fund. An amount of cash kept on hand and used for making small payments is called petty cash. Making such payments from petty cash avoids issuing checks for small amounts.

Using a petty cash fund enables a business to practice good cash control. A business can then deposit all receipts and write checks for all payments except petty cash payments. When this practice is followed, most small payments made by a business are from petty cash. Special procedures may then be used to control the petty cash fund. These cash control procedures permit a business to use monthly bank statements to prove its cash records. A specific employee should be assigned responsibility for safekeeping and maintaining the fund. This person generally is referred to as petty cash custodian or petty cash cashier.

ESTABLISHING A PETTY CASH FUND

In establishing a petty cash fund, an estimate is made of an amount of cash needed for small payments. An amount should be sufficient to last for a period of time, usually a month. Solar Power establishes a petty cash fund on September 1, 1983. Based on past experience, the company determines that $250.00 will be an adequate petty cash fund.

If a voucher system is used, a voucher is prepared for the amount of the petty cash fund to be established. A memorandum is used as authorization to prepare a voucher to establish Solar Power's petty cash fund. *(CONCEPT: Objective Evidence)*

September 1, 1983. Established a petty cash fund, $250.00. Voucher No. 629.

Petty Cash	
250.00	

Vouchers Payable	
	250.00

The asset account Petty Cash is debited, *$250.00*. The liability account Vouchers Payable is credited, *$250.00*.

The voucher prepared to establish Solar Power's petty cash fund is on the next page.

The voucher register below and on page 589 shows the entry to record the establishment of a petty cash fund for Solar Power. The voucher register payee is Petty Cash Custodian, Solar Power. The debit is to Petty Cash, *$250.00*. The credit is to Vouchers Payable, *$250.00*.

Voucher register entry establishing a petty cash fund (left page)

PAGE 25 VOUCHER REGISTER

	DATE		PAYEE	VCHR. NO.	PAID DATE	CK. NO.	1 VOUCHERS PAYABLE CREDIT	
1	1983 Sept.	1	Petty Cash Custodian, Solar Power	629	Sept. 1	756	250 00	1

The check for establishing Solar Power's petty cash fund is made payable to Petty Cash Custodian, Solar Power. The check is recorded in a check register below as a debit to Vouchers Payable and a credit to Cash, *$250.00*.

Solar Power now has two general ledger accounts for cash. The account Cash includes all cash in Solar Power's bank account. The new account Petty Cash includes cash kept in the business to pay small amounts. Petty Cash is placed immediately after Cash in the general ledger as on the chart of accounts, page 568.

Check register entry establishing a petty cash fund

CHECK REGISTER PAGE 29

	DATE		PAYEE	CK. NO.	VCHR. NO.	1 VOUCHERS PAYABLE DEBIT	2 PURCHASES DISCOUNT CREDIT	3 CASH CREDIT	4 BANK DEPOSITS	5 BANK BALANCE	
1	1983 Sept.	1	Balance on hand		✓					9885960	1
2		1	Petty Cash Custodian, Solar Power	756	629	250 00		250 00		9860960	2

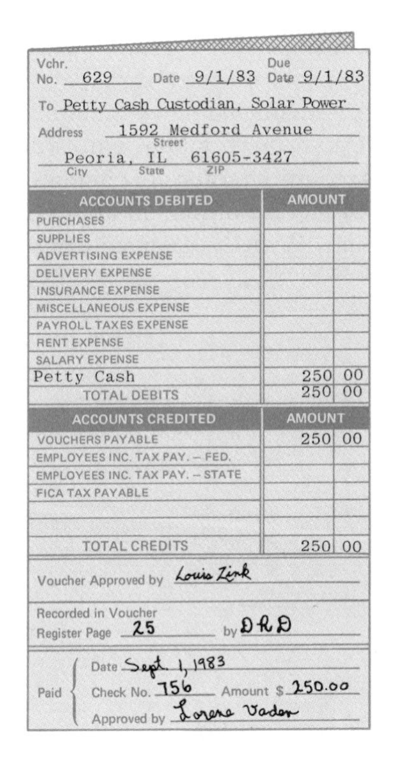

Vchr. No. 629 Date 9/1/83 Due Date 9/1/83

To Petty Cash Custodian, Solar Power

Address 1592 Medford Avenue (Street)

Peoria, IL 61605-3427 (City, State, ZIP)

ACCOUNTS DEBITED	AMOUNT
PURCHASES	
SUPPLIES	
ADVERTISING EXPENSE	
DELIVERY EXPENSE	
INSURANCE EXPENSE	
MISCELLANEOUS EXPENSE	
PAYROLL TAXES EXPENSE	
RENT EXPENSE	
SALARY EXPENSE	
Petty Cash	250 00
TOTAL DEBITS	250 00

ACCOUNTS CREDITED	AMOUNT
VOUCHERS PAYABLE	250 00
EMPLOYEES INC. TAX PAY. – FED.	
EMPLOYEES INC. TAX PAY. – STATE	
FICA TAX PAYABLE	
TOTAL CREDITS	250 00

Voucher Approved by *Louis Zink*

Recorded in Voucher Register Page 25 by *DRD*

Paid: Date *Sept. 1, 1983* Check No. *756* Amount $ *250.00* Approved by *Lorene Vader*

Voucher to establish a petty cash fund

FOR MONTH OF *September* 19*83* PAGE *25*

	2	3	4			5	6	
	DISTRIBUTION			GENERAL				
	PURCHASES DEBIT	DELIVERY EXPENSE DEBIT	SUPPLIES DEBIT	ACCOUNT	POST REF.	DEBIT	CREDIT	
1				*Petty Cash*	*1102*	*250 00*		1

Voucher register entry establishing a petty cash fund (right page)

Solar Power appointed its cashier, George Hernandez, Petty Cash Custodian. Mr. Hernandez cashed the check payable to Petty Cash Custodian. He placed the $250.00 in a petty cash box in the office safe. Mr. Hernandez is responsible for keeping the petty cash secure and separate from all other cash.

MAKING PAYMENTS FROM A PETTY CASH FUND

Before the business opens each day, Solar Power's petty cash custodian removes the petty cash box from the office safe. The petty cash box is placed in a separate compartment of the cash register. Petty cash payments are made from the cash box. The custodian is authorized to make petty cash payments up to $30.00 for a single payment. Petty cash payments more than $30.00 must have the manager's approval.

Each time a petty cash payment is made, a petty cash voucher is prepared. A form showing proof of petty cash payments is called a petty cash voucher. A petty cash voucher shows the following information. (a) Voucher number. (b) Date. (c) To whom paid. (d) Reason for payment. (e) Amount paid. (f) Account charged. (g) Signature of person to whom payment is made. (h) Signature of person approving payment, normally the petty cash custodian. A petty cash voucher for cash paid to buy stamps on September 2 is below.

PETTY CASH VOUCHER

Date 9/2/83 No. 1

Paid to U.S. Postal service

For Postage stamps

Account Charged Supplies

Amount 30 00

SOLAR POWER

Phylis Brown
Received by

George Hernandez
Approved by

Petty cash voucher

After each petty cash payment, the voucher is recorded in a petty cash record and placed in the petty cash box. A form on which petty cash receipts and payments are recorded is called a petty cash record. Solar Power's petty cash record showing a payment, line 2, for postage stamps is on the next page.

A petty cash record usually is a supplementary record, not a journal from which accounts are posted. Solar Power uses its petty cash record to summarize petty cash receipts and payments for a month. The record is totaled monthly to summarize the amounts for an entry in a voucher register.

At the end of each day *all* vouchers in the petty cash box are added and all money is counted. The vouchers plus cash in the petty cash box should always equal the original amount of the petty cash fund. The total of all vouchers plus cash in the petty cash box must equal $250.00. For example, on September 8, four vouchers totaling $54.95 and the remaining cash, *$195.05*, are in the petty cash box. The vouchers total, *$54.95*, plus cash, *$195.05*, equals $250.00. This total amount, *$250.00*, is the amount placed in the petty cash fund originally.

REPLENISHING A PETTY CASH FUND

As money is paid out of petty cash, the vouchers amount increases and the cash amount decreases. Therefore, petty cash is replenished periodically.

A petty cash fund should be replenished at two different times. (1) Petty cash is replenished when only a small amount of cash remains in the petty cash box. (2) Petty cash is always replenished at the end of each fiscal period. Vouchers in a petty cash box represent transactions that must be journalized and posted. If accounting records are to be accurate, a petty cash fund must be replenished at the end of fiscal periods. If a fund is not replenished at the end of each fiscal period, the following inaccuracies occur. The balance of Petty Cash in the general ledger is not an accurate statement of cash on hand. The balance sheet is not an accurate statement of assets. The income statement expenses are not an accurate statement of expenses.

Solar Power replenishes its petty cash fund when cash in the cash box is reduced not lower than $50.00. This practice assures cash available for unexpected cash payments. Solar Power also replenishes its fund at the end of each fiscal period. This practice assures that all petty cash payments will be posted before financial statements are prepared.

Solar Power's procedures for replenishing its petty cash fund are described below.

1 The custodian totals, proves, and rules the petty cash record amount columns as shown on line 13 of the record below.

Petty cash record at the end of a fiscal period

PETTY CASH RECORD

MONTH OF *September 1983* PAGE 1

	DATE	EXPLANATION	PETTY CASH VCHR. NO.	RECEIPTS	PAYMENTS	DISTRIBUTION OF PAYMENTS: SUPPLIES	DELIVERY EXPENSE	MISC. EXPENSE	OTHER PAYMENTS: ACCOUNT	AMOUNT	
1	1983 Sept. 1	Established fund		250 00							1
2	2	Postage stamps	1		30 00	30 00					2
3	5	Collect telegram	2		3 50			3 50			3
4	7	Postage on a sale	3		6 85		6 85				4
5	8	Typewriter ribbons	4		14 60	14 60					5
6	12	Repair of calculator	5		22 50			22 50			6
7	14	Ad in school yearbook	6		25 00				Advertising Expense	25 00	7
8	15	Postage on a sale	7		6 25		6 25				8
9	19	Postage stamps	8		30 00	30 00					9
10	20	Special envelopes	9		16 50	16 50					10
11	26	Award certificates	10		10 80			10 80			11
12	30	Coffee for conference	11		8 50			8 50			12
13		Totals		250 00	174 50	91 10	13 10	45 30		25 00	13
14		Cash balance			75 50						14
15		Totals		250 00	250 00						15
16	Sept. 30	Cash balance		75 50							16
17	30	Replenished fund		174 50							17

The sum of Distribution of Payments column totals, *$174.50*, must be equal to Payments column total, *$174.50*. Payments column total, *$174.50*, is subtracted from Receipts column total, *$250.00*. The difference, *$75.50*, is recorded as shown on line 14 of the petty cash record. *Cash balance* is written in the Explanation column. The cash balance, *$75.50*, should be the same as the amount in the petty cash box, $75.50. The Receipts and Payments columns are then ruled as shown on line 15 of the petty cash record.

2 A voucher is prepared to replenish the petty cash fund for the amount paid out, *$174.50*. This amount will restore the cash balance of the fund to its original amount, *$250.00*. Voucher debit entry accounts and amounts are from the Distribution of Payments column totals, line 13 of the record, page 591. The supporting petty cash vouchers are enclosed in the voucher. *(CONCEPT: Objective Evidence)*

Supplies	
91.10	

Delivery Expense	
13.10	

Miscellaneous Expense	
45.30	

Advertising Expense	
25.00	

Vouchers Payable	
	174.50

September 30, 1983. Replenished petty cash fund. Charge the following accounts: Supplies, $91.10; Delivery Expense, $13.10; Miscellaneous Expense, $45.30; Advertising Expense, $25.00; total, $174.50. Voucher No. 665.

The debit entries are Supplies, *$91.10*, Delivery Expense, *$13.10*, Miscellaneous Expense, *$45.30*, Advertising Expense, *$25.00*. The liability account Vouchers Payable is credited, *$174.50*.

The voucher prepared to replenish Solar Power's petty cash fund is on the next page.

3 The voucher to replenish the petty cash fund is recorded in a voucher register as shown below and on page 593. The voucher register payee is Petty Cash Custodian, Solar Power. The following accounts are debited. Supplies, *$91.10*. Delivery Expense, *$13.10*. Miscellaneous Expense, *$45.30*. Advertising Expense, *$25.00*. Vouchers Payable is credited for $174.50.

PAGE 26 VOUCHER REGISTER

	DATE	PAYEE	VCHR. NO.	PAID DATE	CK. NO.	1 VOUCHERS PAYABLE CREDIT	
10	30	Petty Cash Custodian, Solar Power	665	Sept. 30	790	174 50	10
11							11
12							12
13							13
14							14

Voucher register entry replenishing a petty cash fund (left page)

Vchr. No. 665 Date 9/30/83 Due Date 9/30/83

To Petty Cash Custodian, Solar Power

Address 1592 Medford Avenue (Street)

Peoria, IL 61605-3427 (City, State, ZIP)

ACCOUNTS DEBITED	AMOUNT
PURCHASES	
SUPPLIES	91 10
ADVERTISING EXPENSE	25 00
DELIVERY EXPENSE	13 10
INSURANCE EXPENSE	
MISCELLANEOUS EXPENSE	45 30
PAYROLL TAXES EXPENSE	
RENT EXPENSE	
SALARY EXPENSE	
TOTAL DEBITS	174 50

ACCOUNTS CREDITED	AMOUNT
VOUCHERS PAYABLE	174 50
EMPLOYEES INC. TAX PAY. – FED.	
EMPLOYEES INC. TAX PAY. – STATE	
FICA TAX PAYABLE	
TOTAL CREDITS	174 50

Voucher Approved by *Louis Zink*

Recorded in Voucher Register Page *26* by *DRD*

Paid: Date *Sept. 30, 1983* Check No. *790* Amount $ *174.50* Approved by *Lorene Vaden*

Voucher to replenish a petty cash fund

4 The check for replenishing Solar Power's petty cash fund is made payable to Petty Cash Custodian, Solar Power. The check is recorded in Solar Power's check register. The custodian cashes the check and places the cash in the petty cash box.

5 The custodian records the cash balance, *$75.50*, and replenished fund, *$174.50*, in the Receipts column of the petty cash record. This entry for Solar Power is on lines 16 and 17 of a petty cash record, page 591. The cash balance plus replenished fund equals the original fund balance ($75.50 plus $174.50 equals $250.00). This amount, *$250.00*, is the beginning balance for the next fiscal period.

FOR MONTH OF *September* 19*83* PAGE *26*

	2	3	4			5	6	
	DISTRIBUTION			GENERAL				
	PURCHASES DEBIT	DELIVERY EXPENSE DEBIT	SUPPLIES DEBIT	ACCOUNT	POST REF.	DEBIT	CREDIT	
10		13 10	91 10	*Advertising Expense*		25 00		10
11				*Miscellaneous Expense*		45 30		11
12								12
13								13
14								14

Voucher register entry replenishing a petty cash fund (right page)

RECORDING PETTY CASH THAT IS SHORT OR OVER

Errors may be made when making payments from a petty cash fund. These errors cause a difference between actual cash on hand and the cash balance in the petty cash record. Differences are discovered at the end of each day when petty cash vouchers and cash are totaled. To keep the petty cash fund at a constant amount, differences are recorded at the end of a fiscal period. Differences for a fiscal period are determined by comparing the payments record with the cash box amount before replenishment.

Petty cash short

Cash in the petty cash box may be less than the cash balance shown in the petty cash record. A petty cash on hand amount less than a recorded amount is called cash short. Column totals for Solar Power's petty cash record prior to replenishment on October 31 are below, line 10. Receipts total, *$250.00*, less Payments total, *$156.40*, equals the balance, *$93.60*. The balance, *$93.60*, should equal the amount in the petty cash box. A count shows $89.85 in the petty cash box. Cash on hand, *$89.85*, is $3.75 less than the record shows, *$93.60* ($250.00 − $156.40). Therefore, the petty cash fund is short.

PETTY CASH RECORD

MONTH OF *October 1983* PAGE *2*

	DATE		EXPLANATION	PETTY CASH VCHR. NO.	RECEIPTS	PAYMENTS	DISTRIBUTION OF PAYMENTS					
							SUPPLIES	DELIVERY EXPENSE	MISC. EXPENSE	OTHER PAYMENTS ACCOUNT	OTHER PAYMENTS AMOUNT	
1	1983 Oct.	1	Beginning balance		250 00							1
10			Totals		250 00	156 40	78 75	28 50	38 10		11 05	10
11			Cash short			3 75				Cash Short and Over	3 75	11
12			Cash balance			89 85						12
13			Totals		250 00	250 00						13
14	Oct.	31	Cash balance		89 85							14
15		31	Replenished fund		160 15							15

Petty cash record with a cash short entry

Cash short, *$3.75*, is recorded on line 11 of the record above. *Cash short* is written in the Explanation column. The cash shortage, *$3.75*, is entered in the Payments column and Other Payments Amount column. The account *Cash Short and Over* is written in the Other Payments Account column. Actual cash on hand, *$89.85*, is then recorded in the Payments column, on line 12. The Receipts and Payments columns are totaled and ruled as shown on the record, line 13.

A voucher is prepared when the fund is replenished for the amount paid out, *$156.40*, plus cash short, *$3.75*. This amount, *$160.15*, will restore the fund's cash balance to its original amount, *$250.00* ($156.40 + $3.75 + $89.85 cash on hand).

October 31, 1983. Replenished petty cash fund. Charge the following accounts: Supplies, $78.75; Delivery Expense, $28.50; Miscellaneous Expense, $38.10; Advertising Expense, $11.05; Cash Short and Over, $3.75; total, $160.15. Voucher No. 705.

Supplies	
78.75	

Delivery Expense	
28.50	

Miscellaneous Expense	
38.10	

Advertising Expense	
11.05	

Cash Short and Over	
3.75	

Vouchers Payable	
	160.15

A voucher is prepared with entries shown at the right to replenish Solar Power's petty cash fund. Debit entries include each account in the petty cash record's Distribution of Payments columns plus Cash Short and Over. The credit entry, Vouchers Payable, is the sum of the debit entries. Procedures for preparing the voucher and completing the replenishment process are the same as steps 2–5, pages 592 and 593.

Petty cash over

Cash in the petty cash box may be more than the cash balance shown in the petty cash record. An error in making change generally causes this difference. A petty cash on hand amount more than a recorded amount is called cash over.

Column totals for Solar Power's petty cash record on January 31, 1984, are below, line 12.

PETTY CASH RECORD

MONTH OF January 1984 PAGE 5

	DATE	EXPLANATION	PETTY CASH VCHR. NO.	RECEIPTS	PAYMENTS	DISTRIBUTION OF PAYMENTS: SUPPLIES	DELIVERY EXPENSE	MISC. EXPENSE	OTHER PAYMENTS: ACCOUNT	AMOUNT	
1	1984 Jan. 1	Beginning balance		250 00							1
12		Totals		250 00	166 25	88 50	36 40	41 35		0 00	12
13		Cash over			(1 00)				Cash Short and Over	(1 00)	13
14		Cash balance			84 75						14
15		Totals		250 00	250 00						15
16	Jan. 31	Cash balance		84 75							16
17	31	Replenished fund		165 25							17

Petty cash record with a cash over entry

Receipts column total, *$250.00*, less Payments column total, *$166.25*, equals $83.75, the amount of cash that should be on hand. However, a cash count shows $84.75 in the cash box. Cash on hand, *$84.75*, is $1.00 more than the record shows, $83.75 ($250.00 − $166.25). Therefore, the petty cash fund is over.

Cash over is recorded as shown on line 13 of the record above. *Cash over* is written in the Explanation column. Cash over amount, *$1.00*, is written within parentheses in the Payments column and Other Payments Amount column to indicate subtraction from other amounts. The account *Cash Short and Over* is written in the Other Payments Account column. Actual cash on hand, *$84.75*, is entered in the Payments column, on line 14. The Receipts and Payments columns are totaled and ruled as shown on line 15 of the record, page 595.

A voucher is prepared replenishing the petty cash fund to its original amount, *$250.00*. The vouchers payable amount, $165.25, is the amount paid out, $166.25, less cash over, *$1.00*.

January 31, 1984. Replenished petty cash fund. Debit the following accounts: Supplies, $88.50; Delivery Expense, $36.40; Miscellaneous Expense, $41.35. Credit Vouchers Payable, $165.25; Cash Short and Over, $1.00. Voucher No. 832.

Supplies	
88.50	

Delivery Expense	
36.40	

Miscellaneous Expense	
41.35	

Vouchers Payable	
	165.25

Cash Short and Over	
	1.00

A voucher is prepared with entries shown at the left. Debit entries are the accounts in the petty cash record's Distribution of Payments columns. Credit entries are Vouchers Payable and Cash Short and Over. Procedures for preparing the voucher and completing the replenishment process are the same as steps 2–5, pages 592 and 593.

Any balance in a cash short and over account is closed to Income Summary at the end of a fiscal period. A Cash Short and Over debit balance is reported on an income statement as other expenses. A credit balance is reported as other revenue.

USING A PETTY CASH FUND WITH A CASH PAYMENTS JOURNAL

Businesses using a cash payments journal follow similar petty cash fund procedures as businesses using a voucher system. In a voucher system, a voucher and voucher register are used to establish and replenish a petty cash fund. Other businesses may use a cash payments journal to establish and replenish a petty cash fund.

Way Station Appliances, using a cash payments journal, maintains and replenishes its petty cash fund as described below.

1 Petty cash vouchers are recorded in a petty cash record for each payment similar to Solar Power, page 591.

2 Before replenishing the fund, the petty cash record is totaled, proved, and ruled similar to Solar Power's step 1, page 591.

3 From the petty cash record's column totals, a request to replenish petty cash fund is prepared. On October 31, 1983, the following column totals were listed on Way Station's petty cash record. Receipts, $150.00. Payments, $113.05. Supplies, $64.20. Delivery Expense, $32.75.

Miscellaneous Expense, $16.10. A cash count shows $36.95 in the petty cash box. Receipts, *$150.00*, less payments, *$113.05*, equals cash balance, *$36.95*. Equality of the fund is proven. Way Station's October 31 request form to replenish petty cash is below.

REQUEST TO REPLENISH PETTY CASH FUND

PAYMENTS	
Account	Amount
Supplies	64.20
Delivery Expense	32.75
Miscellaneous Expense	16.10
Total needed to replenish	113.05

Requested by:	Approved by:
Jan Rogue, Custodian	Paul Whitaker
October 31, 1983	October 31, 1983
	Issued Check No. 316

Request form for replenishing a petty cash fund

October 31, 1983. Issued a check to replenish the petty cash fund. Charge the following accounts: Supplies, $64.20; Delivery Expense, $32.75; Miscellaneous Expense, $16.10; total, $113.05. Check No. 316.

A check for $113.05 is approved and issued to the petty cash custodian. The petty cash fund is restored to $150.00, the original amount.

4 Information for a cash payments journal entry is from the completed form Request to Replenish Petty Cash Fund. The check stub is the source document for the entry. *(CONCEPT: Objective Evidence)* Each account listed on the form is debited for the amount shown. Cash is credited for the total amount. The entry for petty cash fund replenishment is recorded in a cash payments journal as shown below.

Cash payments journal entry to replenish a petty cash fund

CASH PAYMENTS JOURNAL PAGE 19

	DATE	ACCOUNT TITLE	CHECK No.	POST. REF.	1 GENERAL DEBIT	2 GENERAL CREDIT	3 ACCOUNTS PAYABLE DEBIT	4 PURCHASES DISCOUNT CREDIT	5 CASH CREDIT	
12	31	Supplies	316		64 20				113 05	12
13		Delivery Expense			32 75					13
14		Miscellaneous Expense			16 10					14

ACCOUNTING TERMS

What is the meaning of each of the following?

1. petty cash
2. petty cash voucher
3. petty cash record
4. cash short
5. cash over

QUESTIONS FOR INDIVIDUAL STUDY

1. What practices are a required part of a business' good cash control?
2. How can a business avoid writing checks for very small purchases and still practice good cash control?
3. What amount of cash should be placed in a petty cash fund?
4. What accounts did Solar Power debit and credit in the voucher register to establish a petty cash fund?
5. To whom is a check for establishing a petty cash fund made payable?
6. Where is a petty cash account located in a general ledger?
7. What are the principal responsibilities of a petty cash custodian?
8. What form does Solar Power prepare each time a payment is made from petty cash?
9. Why does Solar Power use a petty cash record?
10. How can a custodian determine if, at the end of any day, the cash in the petty cash box is the correct amount?
11. When should a petty cash fund be replenished?
12. Why must the petty cash fund be replenished at the end of each fiscal period?
13. What accounts are debited and credited to replenish a petty cash fund?
14. What is the amount for which a fund is replenished?
15. If cash is short when a fund is replenished, what account is used to record the shortage?
16. If cash is over when a fund is replenished, what account is used to record the overage?
17. How is a balance in the cash short and over account treated at the end of a fiscal period?
18. How is a Cash Short and Over debit balance reported on the financial statements?
19. How is a Cash Short and Over credit balance reported on the financial statements?
20. What is the difference between a petty cash fund using a voucher system and one using a cash payments journal?

CASES FOR MANAGEMENT DECISION

CASE 1 Fairmont Company has decided to establish a petty cash fund. Estimated weekly expenditures from the fund are $50.00. Roy Dorries, the accountant, recommends the fund amount be established at $50.00. Mr. Dorries states that this amount will permit frequent review of the expenditures and better cash control. Mary Yarbro, the manager, prefers the fund be established for $2,500.00 to "avoid writing so many checks." Is Mr. Dorries' or Ms. Yarbro's recommendation better? Or do you recommend an amount not suggested by either Dorries or Yarbro? Give the reason for your recommendation.

CASE 2 Delta Company has established a $200.00 petty cash fund. During a routine review of the petty cash records, you discover small shortages totaling $15.00 have occurred over the past four months. The fund custodian, Deb Hopkins, has not listed Cash Short and Over on any of the vouchers prepared for replenishment. When asked about this practice, Miss Hopkins said she always waited until the amount of shortage was significant, approximately $50.00. Then she requested replenishment for the amount of shortage. What is your opinion of this practice? What action do you recommend?

DRILL FOR UNDERSTANDING

DRILL 29-D 1 Replenishing a petty cash fund

Petty cash is replenished for the amounts and on the dates shown in the table below.

Date on which Replenished	Totals of Petty Cash Record Amount Columns			
	Supplies	Delivery Expense	Miscellaneous Expense	Advertising Expense
March 31	$47.25	$23.60	$32.15	$15.25
April 30	$68.40	$41.90	$24.25	$20.00
May 31	$36.95	$28.20	$20.25	$32.50
June 30	$73.16	$51.22	$36.93	$28.75

Instructions: For each date, prepare T accounts for the accounts affected by the voucher register entry to replenish petty cash. Record the amounts on the debit or credit side of each T account to show how accounts are affected.

APPLICATION PROBLEMS

PROBLEM 29-1 Establishing and making payments from a petty cash fund

Metro Company decided to establish a petty cash fund on June 1 of the current year. The amount of the fund is to be $200.00.

Instructions: 1. Record on a voucher register like the one on pages 588 and 589 the establishment of the petty cash fund. Voucher number is 336. Voucher register page is 12. Payee is Petty Cash Custodian.

2. Record on a check register like the one on page 588 the check to establish the petty cash fund. June 1 cash balance on hand is $84,623.50. Check number is 381. Check register page is 10.

3. Record the beginning balance and the following payments from Metro's petty cash fund during June of the current year. Record the transactions on page 1 of a petty cash record like the one on page 591. Source document petty cash voucher is abbreviated PV.

June 2. Paid for typing paper, $10.50. PV1. (Supplies)
6. Paid collect telegram, $5.40. PV2. (Miscellaneous Expense)
7. Paid repair of typewriter, $26.50. PV3. (Miscellaneous Expense)
9. Paid postage on a sale, $7.35. PV4. (Delivery Expense)
13. Paid for postage stamps, $15.00. PV5. (Supplies)
15. Paid for ad in school paper, $20.00. PV6. (Advertising Expense)
17. Paid postage on a sale, $8.90. PV7. (Delivery Expense)
20. Paid for telegram, $7.25. PV8. (Miscellaneous Expense)
21. Paid for carbon paper, $10.60. PV9. (Supplies)
23. Paid postage on a sale, $12.75. PV10. (Delivery Expense)
27. Paid for postage stamps, $30.00. PV11. (Supplies)
30. Paid for postage on a sale, $7.75. PV12. (Delivery Expense)

The petty cash record prepared in Problem 29-1 is needed to complete Problem 29-2.

PROBLEM 29-2 Replenishing a petty cash fund

The petty cash record prepared in Problem 29-1 is needed to complete Problem 29-2.

Instructions: 1. Total and rule the Distribution of Payments columns in the petty cash record prepared in Problem 29-1.

2. The petty cash box has $38.00 at the end of the day, June 30. Compare for equality the sum of cash and payments with the petty cash beginning balance.

3. Record the cash balance. Total and rule the Receipts and Payments columns.

4. Prepare a voucher like the one on page 593 to replenish Metro's petty cash fund on June 30. Additional information on the voucher is listed below.

Voucher No.: 392
Metro's address: 4232 Sikes Avenue, Waco, KY 40385-9321
Voucher approved by: Mari Tanaka
Voucher register page: 14
Recorded by: LBK
Check No.: 423
Payment approved by: Michael MacIver

5. Record Voucher No. 392 on page 14 of a voucher register like the one on pages 592 and 593.

6. Record Check No. 423 on page 12 of a check register like the one on page 588. June 30 cash balance brought forward is $87,019.27.

7. Record the June 30 cash balance and amount of replenished fund in the petty cash record. Use lines 16 and 17 of petty cash record, page 591, as a model.

PROBLEM 29-3 Establishing and replenishing a petty cash fund using a cash payments journal

On May 1 of the current year, Datascribe issued Check No. 49 for $200.00 to establish a petty cash fund. During May the custodian made payments from the petty cash fund. On May 31, the custodian submitted the request form below.

REQUEST TO REPLENISH PETTY CASH FUND

PAYMENTS	
Account	Amount
Supplies	73.25
Delivery Expense	42.30
Miscellaneous Expense	27.60
Total needed to replenish	143.15

Requested by:	Approved by:
Joe Mendel, Custodian	________
May 31, 1983	________ 19__
	Issued Check No. ________

Instructions: 1. Record Check No. 49 on page 8 of a cash payments journal to establish Datascribe's petty cash fund. Record the transaction in a journal like the one on page 597.

2. The petty cash box has $56.85 at the end of the day, May 31. Compare for equality the sum of cash and payments with the petty cash beginning balance.

3. Record Check No. 84 in the cash payments journal to replenish the petty cash fund May 31.

ENRICHMENT PROBLEMS

MASTERY PROBLEM 29-M Establishing and replenishing a petty cash fund

Audio Alert Company established a $250.00 petty cash fund on July 1 of the current year.

Instructions: 1. Record on page 20 of a voucher register establishment of a petty cash fund. Voucher number is 483. Payee is Petty Cash Custodian.

2. Record on page 14 of a check register Check No. 469 to establish the petty cash fund. July 1 cash balance on hand is $96,739.40.

Totals of the petty cash record's amount columns on July 31 are listed below.

			Distribution of Payments			
	Receipts	Payments	Supplies	Delivery Expense	Misc. Expense	Other Payments Amount
Totals	250.00	202.15	86.45	38.50	42.20	35.00

Instructions: 3. Record the totals above on line 11 of a petty cash record. Petty cash record page is 16.

4. The petty cash box has $46.35 at the end of the day July 31. Compare for equality the sum of cash and payments with the petty cash beginning balance (Receipts column total).

5. Record any cash short or cash over and the cash balance, then total and rule the Receipts and Payments columns. Make entries like those in petty cash record, page 594 or 595.

6. From information in petty cash record, record voucher register entry to replenish petty cash fund on July 31. Amount in the Other Payments column is Advertising Expense. Voucher number is 544.

7. Record Check No. 530 in the check register to replenish the fund.

8. Record the July 31 cash balance and amount of replenished fund on the petty cash record. Use lines 16 and 17 of petty cash record, page 595, as a model.

CHALLENGE PROBLEM 29-C Establishing, making payments from, and replenishing a petty cash fund

Continental Company established a $200.00 petty cash fund on August 1 of the current year.

Instructions: 1. Record on page 24 of a voucher register establishment of a petty cash fund. Voucher number is 579. Payee is Petty Cash Custodian.

2. Record on page 17 of a check register Check No. 563 to establish the petty cash fund. August 1 cash balance on hand is $86,598.25.

3. Record the beginning balance and the payments below from Continental's petty cash fund during August of the current year. Record the transactions on page 1 of a petty cash record like the one on page 591. Source document petty cash voucher is abbreviated PV.

Aug. 2. Paid postage on a sale, $8.50. PV1
4. Paid for typewriter ribbons, $21.40. PV2
8. Paid for telegram, $6.90. PV3
10. Paid for ad in community newspaper, $20.00. PV4 (Advertising Expense)
11. Paid for postage stamps, $30.00. PV5
15. Paid for calculator repair, $22.50. PV6
18. Paid postage on a sale, $9.45. PV7
22. Paid for calculator paper tape, $12.75. PV8
25. Paid a collect telegram, $5.70. PV9
29. Paid for ad in local high school paper, $15.00. PV10 (Advertising Expense)
31. Paid postage on a sale, $9.60. PV11

Instructions: 4. Total and rule the Distribution of Payments columns in the petty cash record.

5. The petty cash box has $40.00 at the end of the day August 31. Compare for equality the sum of cash and payments with the petty cash beginning balance.

6. Record any cash short or cash over and the cash balance, then total and rule the Receipts and Payments columns. Make entries like those in petty cash record, page 594 or 595.

7. Prepare a voucher like the one on page 593 to replenish Continental's petty cash fund on August 31. Additional information on the voucher is listed below.

Voucher No.: 661
Continental's address: 5229 Elm Street, Salina, KS 67401-1128
Voucher Approved by: Jean Lebel
Voucher register page: 24
Recorded by: AML
Check No.: 641
Payment approved by: Patrick Yeager

8. Record Voucher No. 661 in the voucher register.

9. Record Check No. 641 in the check register.

10. Record the August 31 cash balance and amount of replenished fund on the petty cash record. Use lines 16 and 17 of petty cash record, page 595, as a model.

30

An Inventory System

ENABLING PERFORMANCE TASKS

After studying Chapter 30, you will be able to:

a. Define accounting terms related to an inventory system.
b. Explain accounting principles and practices related to an inventory system.
c. Determine the cost of merchandise inventory using the fifo and lifo methods.
d. Determine the valuation of merchandise inventory using the lower of cost or market method.
e. Estimate the value of merchandise inventory using the gross profit method.

Merchandise purchases are a large part of total costs of a merchandising business. Therefore, an effective inventory system is needed to control merchandise inventory.

Sale of merchandise provides a major source of revenue for a merchandising business. To encourage sales, a business must have merchandise available for sale that customers want. A business therefore needs controls that help maintain a merchandise inventory of sufficient quantity, variety, and price.

The value of merchandise on hand is reported on both the balance sheet and the income statement. If merchandise inventory is recorded incorrectly, current assets and retained earnings will be misstated on the balance sheet. The inventory error also will cause a misstatement of gross profit and net income reported on the income statement. *(CONCEPT: Adequate Disclosure)*

CONTROLLING THE QUANTITY OF MERCHANDISE INVENTORY

Knowing the size of inventory to maintain requires frequent analyses of purchases, sales, and inventory records. Many businesses fail because too much or too little merchandise inventory is kept on hand. Sometimes the wrong merchandise is kept on hand. If the merchandise is not sold, the result is less revenue. In addition, greater expense results from storing merchandise that sells slowly.

Merchandise inventory larger than needed

Merchandise inventory that is larger than needed may decrease net income of a business for several reasons.

1. Store and warehouse space used by the unneeded part of inventory is expensive.
2. Part of the capital invested in excess inventory could be invested to better advantage in other assets.
3. Taxes and insurance premiums must be paid on excess merchandise inventory.
4. Excess merchandise may become obsolete and unsaleable.

Merchandise inventory smaller than needed

Merchandise inventory that is smaller than needed may decrease net income of a business for several reasons.

1. Sales will be lost to competitors if items wanted by customers are not on hand.
2. Sales will be lost if there is insufficient variety of merchandise that customers want.
3. Merchandise reordered often and in small quantities costs more than if ordered in larger quantities.

DETERMINING THE QUANTITIES OF MERCHANDISE INVENTORY

A merchandising business needs to know the quantity of merchandise on hand. Two principal methods are used to determine the quantity of each type of merchandise on hand.

1. Quantities may be determined by counting, weighing, or measuring each kind of merchandise on hand.
2. A continuous record may be kept of increases, decreases, and the current balance of each kind of merchandise on hand.

Merchandise inventory determined by counting, weighing, or measuring items of merchandise on hand is called a periodic inventory. A periodic inventory is sometimes known as a physical inventory. Merchandise inventory determined by keeping a continuous record of increases, decreases, and balance on hand is called a perpetual inventory. A perpetual inventory is sometimes known as a book inventory.

Periodic inventory

Counting, weighing, or measuring a periodic inventory is commonly known as "taking an inventory." Inventories on hand at the end of a fiscal period must be known to figure the cost of merchandise sold. However, taking a periodic inventory is usually a large task. Therefore, periodic inventories normally are taken only at the end of a fiscal year.

Businesses frequently set their end of fiscal period when inventory is at a low point. A lower inventory thus takes less time to count. For example, a department store may take a periodic inventory at the end of January. The amount of merchandise on hand is low because of Christmas sales. January clearance sales have been held and few purchases of additional merchandise are made in January. All of these activities make the merchandise inventory low at the end of January.

Solar Power takes its periodic inventory during the last week of December. Solar Power has found from past experience that relatively few sales are made during that week. Few customers start energy improvement or new construction projects during the holiday season. Also, the stock of merchandise is relatively low at that time.

Solar Power uses a form to record important information about each major item of merchandise. The form has space to record stock number, unit of count, number of units, unit cost, and total value. The form used by Solar Power is below.

Information is typed in the Stock No. column and Unit of Count column before the count is begun. Employees taking the periodic inventory write the actual count in the No. of Units on Hand column. Inventory forms are then sent to the accounting department where the Unit Cost and Total Value columns are completed.

Merchandise Inventory

Form No. 2

Date December 31, 1983

Item Solar Collector Panels

Stock No.	Unit of Count	No. of Units on Hand	Unit Cost Price	Total Value
6212	.5 x 1.5m panels	20	8.00	160.00
6213	1.0 x 1.5m panels	50	15.50	775.00
6215	1.5 x 1.5m panels	30	23.00	690.00
6216	.5 x 2.0m panels	100	60 @ 10.00 40 @ 11.25	1,050.00
6640	1.0 x 2.0m panels	60	21.00	1,260.00
6696	2.0 x 4.0m panels	120	68.50	8,220.00
				23,155.00

Inventory record form

Perpetual inventory

Some businesses keep inventory records that show continuously the quantity on hand for each kind of merchandise. A form used to show kind of merchandise, quantity received, quantity sold, and balance on hand is called a stock record. The form also may be known as an inventory card. A file of stock records for all merchandise on hand is called a stock ledger.

A perpetual inventory system provides day-to-day information about the quantity of merchandise on hand. On each stock record is shown the minimum balance allowed before a reorder must be placed. When the minimum balance is reached, additional merchandise should be ordered. The minimum balance is the amount of merchandise that will last until additional merchandise can be received from the suppliers. For example, daily reports of merchandise on hand may be necessary to determine when to reorder specific items that are selling rapidly. These daily reports may be prepared from information on perpetual inventory records.

When a perpetual inventory of merchandise is kept, entries are made on stock records to show the following information.

1. Increases in the quantity on hand when additional merchandise is received.
2. Decreases in the quantity on hand when merchandise is sold.
3. The balance on hand after each increase or decrease is recorded.

A stock record in card form is below.

Description Solenoid Solar Switch Stock No. C460
Maximum 20 Minimum 4 Location Aisle 2

INCREASES			DECREASES			BALANCE
DATE	PURCHASE NO.	QUANTITY	DATE	SALES INVOICE NO.	QUANTITY	QUANTITY
1983 Jan. 1						6
			1983 Jan. 18	4387	2	4
Jan. 19	633	16				20
			Feb. 3	4705	2	18

Stock record card

Usually a stock record shows quantity but not value of merchandise.

A separate stock record card is prepared for each kind of merchandise carried in stock. Each time additional merchandise is purchased, an entry is recorded in the Increases columns. Then the balance on hand is updated in the Balance column. Each time merchandise is sold, an entry is recorded in the Decreases columns and the balance is updated. The quantity of merchandise on hand is the last amount in the Balance column of a stock record card.

When a perpetual inventory is kept manually, errors may be made in recording or figuring amounts. Also, some records may be incorrect because merchandise is taken from stock and not recorded on stock record cards. A customary practice is to take a periodic inventory at least once a year. The periodic inventory is then compared with the perpetual inventory records. If errors are discovered, they are corrected on the stock record cards.

Perpetual inventory with a cash register and automated equipment

Businesses keeping a computerized perpetual inventory may use a special cash register as part of the system. Each item of merchandise has a code number on the price tag. The code number is recorded on the cash register when the sale is recorded. As a result, a punched paper tape is prepared inside the cash register with a coded record of items sold. Each day the punched paper tape is used to bring the perpetual inventory in a computer up to date.

Special cash registers may also be connected directly to a computer. As a sale is recorded on a cash register, information is fed directly to a computer. Thus, inventory records are brought up to date immediately.

DETERMINING THE COST OF MERCHANDISE INVENTORY

Costs often are not recorded on inventory forms at the time a periodic inventory is taken. After the quantities of merchandise on hand are counted, purchase invoices or catalogs are used to find merchandise costs. Costs are recorded on the inventory forms and necessary extensions made. Total cost value of the inventory is then figured.

First-in, first-out method

Solar Power takes a periodic inventory at the end of each fiscal period. The company assumes that the merchandise purchased first is also the merchandise sold first. Solar Power also assumes that the ending inventory consists of the most recently purchased merchandise. Only the most recent invoices for purchases are used in recording costs for each item on the inventory forms. For example, the most recently received filters are placed on the shelves behind older filters. Therefore, the merchandise purchased first is also the merchandise sold first.

The first-in, first-out method is frequently abbreviated as *fifo* (the first letter of each of the four words). On December 31, a periodic count of solar collector panels, Stock No. 6650, showed 80 panels on hand. Cost information for this item is on the next page.

	Units	Unit Cost
January 1, beginning inventory	20 panels	$20.00
March 10, purchases	30 panels	20.00
May 18, purchases	30 panels	21.00
July 7, purchases	50 panels	22.00
November 18, purchases	50 panels	24.00

Under the fifo method, the 80 units are priced at the most recent costs. The most recent costs are $24.00 and $22.00. Computations are summarized below.

Most recent costs, November 18, 50 units @ $24.00	$1,200.00
Next most recent costs, July 7, 30 units @ $22.00	660.00
Total value of 80 units	$1,860.00

On the inventory forms the 80 panels would be shown as having a total value of $1,860.00.

Last-in, first-out method

The last-in, first-out method is frequently abbreviated as *lifo*. In the lifo method, an inventory is recorded at the amount paid for the merchandise purchased first. This method is based on the idea that the most recent costs of merchandise should be charged against current revenue. *(CONCEPT: Matching Expenses with Revenue)*

Under the lifo method, each item on the inventory forms is recorded at the earliest costs paid for the merchandise. Inventory value for the 80 panels described above is figured below using the lifo method.

Earliest costs, January 1, 20 units @ $20.00	$ 400.00
Next earliest costs, March 10, 30 units @ $20.00	600.00
Next earliest costs, May 18, 30 units @ $21.00	630.00
Total value of 80 units	$1,630.00

On the inventory forms, the 80 units of this kind of merchandise would therefore show a total value of $1,630.00.

A comparison of fifo and lifo pricing methods

The figures above show inventory cost for 80 solar collector panels using both fifo and lifo methods during rising prices. To show the effect of falling prices, the cost figures for the items are reversed as shown below.

	Units	Unit Cost
January 1, beginning inventory	20 panels	$24.00
March 10, purchases	30 panels	22.00
May 18, purchases	30 panels	21.00
July 7, purchases	50 panels	20.00
November 18, purchases	50 panels	20.00

Under the fifo method, the 80 units are priced at the most recent costs. The most recent costs are $20.00 and $20.00. The figures are summarized below.

Most recent costs, November 18, 50 units @ $20.00..............	$1,000.00
Next most recent costs, July 7, 30 units @ $20.00.................	600.00
Total value of 80 units..	$1,600.00

Under the lifo method, the 80 units are priced at the earliest costs. The earliest costs are $24.00, $22.00, and $21.00. The figures are summarized below.

Earliest costs, January 1, 20 units @ $24.00..........................	$ 480.00
Next earliest costs, March 10, 30 units @ $22.00..................	660.00
Next earliest costs, May 18, 30 units @ $21.00......................	630.00
Total value of 80 units..	$1,770.00

A comparison of the fifo and lifo methods in determining gross profit with net sales of $4,000.00 is below.

	RISING PRICES				FALLING PRICES			
	FIFO		LIFO		FIFO		LIFO	
Revenue:								
Net Sales		$4,000.00		$4,000.00		$4,000.00		$4,000.00
Cost of Merchandise Sold:								
Merchandise Inventory, Jan. 1 .	$ 400.00		$ 400.00		$ 480.00		$ 480.00	
Net Purchases	3,530.00		3,530.00		3,290.00		3,290.00	
Merchandise Available for Sale .	3,930.00		3,930.00		3,770.00		3,770.00	
Less Ending Inventory, Dec. 31	1,860.00		1,630.00		1,600.00		1,770.00	
Cost of Merchandise Sold		2,070.00		2,300.00		2,170.00		2,000.00
Gross Profit on Operations		$1,930.00		$1,700.00		$1,830.00		$2,000.00

In a year of rising prices, the fifo method gives the highest possible valuation of ending inventory. The lifo method gives the lowest possible valuation during rising prices. Therefore, the fifo method gives the highest and lifo method the lowest net income during a year of rising prices.

In a year of falling prices, the fifo method gives the lowest possible valuation of ending inventory. The lifo method gives the highest possible valuation during falling prices. Therefore, the fifo method gives the lowest and lifo method the highest net income during a year of falling prices.

DETERMINING THE VALUATION OF MERCHANDISE INVENTORY AT LOWER OF COST OR MARKET

Another inventory valuation method uses both the cost and market price of each item of merchandise. This method is referred to as the *lower of cost or market*. "Market" as used in this phrase means the cost to replace the merchandise on the date of inventory. This method applies a conservative approach to valuing merchandise inventory. If the market value of an inventory declines, the loss is recognized even though the merchandise has not been sold. *(CONCEPT: Conservatism)*

When this inventory valuation method is applied to the pricing of each inventory item, the rules below are followed.

1. When the cost is lower than the current market price, use the cost.
2. When the market price is lower than the cost, use the market price.

When the lower of cost or market method is used, the inventory form has four amount columns.

1. The cost of each item is recorded in one column.
2. The market price of each item is recorded in one column.
3. The unit price to be used is recorded in one column.
4. The total value of all identical items using the lower of cost or market price is recorded in one column.

One form of inventory record form using this inventory pricing method is below.

KOOL AIR CO.

MERCHANDISE INVENTORY — ITEM Filters

DATE December 31, 1983 — SHEET NO. 3

Item No.	No. of Units on Hand	Unit Price		Unit Price to be Used	Value at Lower of Cost or Market
		Cost	Current Market		
G1010	24	$ 6.00	$ 4.00	$ 4.00	$ 96.00
H1221	32	9.60	11.50	9.60	307.20
I2342	70	9.50	12.00	9.50	665.00
J3425	12	2.25	2.25	2.25	27.00
K5748	18	21.80	13.90	13.90	250.20
V9053	120	7.15	6.90	6.90	828.00
W7532	40	3.60	3.70	3.60	144.00
X5937	8	131.95	139.80	131.95	1,055.00
Y4908	9	35.90	33.30	33.30	299.70
					$10,326.30

Inventory record form for pricing at lower of cost or market

The first item on the inventory form above, *G1010*, has a lower market price, *$4.00*, than the cost price, *$6.00*. Therefore, the market price is used for this item on the inventory form. The number of items on hand, *24*, times the price to be used, *$4.00*, equals the value, *$96.00*. The value, *$96.00*, is recorded in the column headed "Value at Lower of Cost or Market."

Each business decides which method to use in pricing merchandise inventory. However, the method selected (fifo, lifo, lower of cost or market) is used consistently from year to year. *(CONCEPT: Consistent Reporting)* The Internal Revenue Service requires that a business use the same method from year to year. If a business wishes to change inventory pricing methods, permission of the IRS must be obtained.

ESTIMATING THE VALUE OF MERCHANDISE INVENTORY

Estimating inventory by using previous years' percent of gross profit on operations is called gross profit method of estimating inventory. Solar Power prepares an income statement at the end of each month. *(CONCEPT: Accounting Period Cycle)* The gross profit method of estimating the ending merchandise inventory is used. To estimate the ending merchandise inventory on September 30, 1983, the following information is obtained.

Beginning inventory, January 1, 1983	$ 58,140.00
Net purchases for the period, January 1 to September 30	434,112.40
Net sales for the period, January 1 to September 30	657,378.50
Gross profit on operations (percentage based on records of previous years' operations)	30% of sales

Three steps are followed to estimate the ending merchandise inventory for Solar Power on September 30, 1983.

1 Determine the value of the cost of merchandise available for sale.

Beginning inventory, January 1	$ 58,140.00
Plus net purchases, January 1 to September 30	434,112.40
Equals value of merchandise available for sale	$492,252.40

2 Determine the estimated value of the cost of merchandise sold.

Net sales for January 1 to September 30	$657,378.50
Less estimated gross profit on operations ($657,378.50 × 30%)	197,213.55
Equals estimated cost of merchandise sold	$460,164.95

3 Subtract the estimated cost of merchandise sold from the value of the merchandise available for sale. This step determines the estimated ending merchandise inventory.

Merchandise available for sale (from step 1)	$492,252.40
Less estimated cost of merchandise sold (from step 2)	460,164.95
Equals estimated ending merchandise inventory	$ 32,087.45

The estimated merchandise inventory for Solar Power on September 30, 1983, is $32,087.45. This value is used on the monthly income statement.

An estimated inventory is not completely accurate. The rate of gross profit on operations may not be exactly the percentage used in the estimate. Also, some merchandise may have been stolen or damaged. However, estimated ending inventory is accurate enough for a monthly income statement without taking the time to count the inventory.

Solar Power's income statement prepared on September 30, 1983, is below. The beginning inventory recorded is the estimated ending inventory from the income statement for August 31, 1983.

Income statement with estimated ending inventory

The estimated ending inventory is used on Solar Power's monthly income statements. However, a periodic inventory is used for the end-of-fiscal-period income statement for greater accuracy.

Solar Power
Income Statement
For Month Ended September 30, 1983

Revenue:		
Net Sales..................................		$73,045.00
Cost of Merchandise Sold:		
Estimated Merchandise Inventory, Sept. 1..	$34,957.25	
Net Purchases..........................	48,265.70	
Merchandise Available for Sale...........	$83,222.95	
Less Estimated Ending Inventory, Sept. 30.	32,087.45	
Cost of Merchandise Sold.................		51,135.50
Gross Profit on Operations.................		$21,909.50
Operating Expenses.........................		13,245.70
Net Income.................................		$ 8,663.80

ACCOUNTING TERMS

What is the meaning of each of the following?

1. periodic inventory
2. perpetual inventory
3. stock record
4. stock ledger
5. gross profit method of estimating inventory

QUESTIONS FOR INDIVIDUAL STUDY

1. What item is a large part of total costs of a merchandising business?
2. Why does a business need controls for its merchandise inventory?
3. What effect does an error in determining the value of the merchandise inventory have on the balance sheet and income statement?
4. If the merchandise inventory is larger than needed, what effect may this value have on the net income of a business? Why?
5. If the inventory is smaller than needed, what effect may this have on the net income of a business? Why?
6. What two methods can be used to determine the quantity of each item of merchandise on hand?
7. How often are periodic inventories taken?
8. When should a business use a perpetual inventory system?
9. How may the balance on hand of an item of merchandise be determined when a manual perpetual inventory is used?

10. How is the accuracy of a perpetual inventory checked?
11. When the fifo method is used, how is the value of each kind of merchandise determined?
12. When the lifo method is used, how is the value of each kind of merchandise determined?
13. In a year of rising prices, which inventory method, fifo or lifo, gives the highest net income?
14. In a year of falling prices, which inventory method, fifo or lifo, gives the highest net income?
15. Why is the lower of cost or market method considered a conservative approach to valuing inventory?
16. When neither a perpetual nor a periodic inventory is taken, how can an ending merchandise inventory be determined that is accurate enough for a monthly income statement?

CASES FOR MANAGEMENT DECISION

CASE 1 Thermtron Company recently started a perpetual inventory system. Mr. Nadolski, the manager, asks you if there is any reason for the company to continue with periodic inventories now that a perpetual inventory system is used. How would you answer Mr. Nadolski?

CASE 2 Valentino's uses the lifo method of valuing its merchandise inventory. The manager is considering a change to the fifo method. Prices have increased steadily over the past three years. What effect will the change have on the following items? (1) The amount of net income as shown by the income statement. (2) The amount of income taxes to be paid. (3) The quantity of each item of merchandise that must be kept in stock? Why?

CASE 3 Garratt Hardware has many small and large items of merchandise. The store has always taken a periodic inventory at the end of a fiscal year. The store has not kept a perpetual inventory because of the cost. However, the manager wants a reasonably accurate inventory at the end of each month. The manager needs the inventory to prepare monthly income statements and to help in making decisions about the business. What would you recommend?

DRILL FOR UNDERSTANDING

DRILL 30-D 1 Determining the quantities of merchandise on hand using perpetual inventory

Accounting records at Garland Supply showed inventory increases and decreases for Item 16-Z as listed below. Beginning inventory on May 1 was 136 units.

Increases		Decreases	
Date	Quantity	Date	Quantity
		May 5	52
		May 9	45
May 10	125		
		May 16	62
		May 23	75
May 25	150		
		May 31	65

Use a stock record with the column headings below.

Increases		Decreases		Balance
Date	Quantity	Date	Quantity	Quantity
May 1				136

Instructions: 1. Record the increases and decreases.
2. Figure the balance of units on hand for each date a transaction occurred.
3. Record the balance of units on hand in the Balance Quantity column.

APPLICATION PROBLEMS

PROBLEM 30-1 Determining cost of inventory using the fifo and lifo methods

Accounting records at Energy-Wise showed the purchases and periodic inventory counts listed below.

Model	Beginning Inventory January 1	First Purchase	Second Purchase	Third Purchase	Periodic Inventory Count December 31
A 36	16 @ $ 38	25 @ $ 39	10 @ $ 40	20 @ $ 41	24
A 49	7 @ $ 85	12 @ $ 87	10 @ $ 88	24 @ $ 89	22
C 17	22 @ $ 21	25 @ $ 24	30 @ $ 25	30 @ $ 20	28
C 72	10 @ $ 41	12 @ $ 42	15 @ $ 38	10 @ $ 44	15
F 96	5 @ $140	5 @ $142	6 @ $148	8 @ $150	18
G 12	85 @ $ 16	20 @ $ 18	25 @ $ 19	40 @ $ 20	35
J 78	36 @ $ 50	40 @ $ 54	44 @ $ 55	50 @ $ 58	32
M 61	72 @ $ 60	48 @ $ 58	50 @ $ 54	60 @ $ 50	75

Use a form with the column headings below.

Model	No. of Units on Hand	Unit Cost	Inventory Value December 31
A 36	*24*	*20 @ $41* *4 @ 40*	*$980*

Instructions: 1. Figure the total amount of the inventory on December 31 according to the *fifo* method. Determining the inventory value for Model A36 is given as an example. Use the following procedure.

(a) Record the model number and the number of units of each model on hand December 31.

(b) Record the unit cost of each model. When more than one unit cost is used, list the units and unit costs on separate lines.

(c) Figure the total inventory value of each model and write the amount in the Value column.

(d) Add the Value column to determine the total amount of inventory.

2. On another form, figure the total amount of inventory using the *lifo* method. Follow the steps given in Instruction 1.

3. Compare the total amount of the inventory obtained in Instructions 1 and 2. Which method, *fifo* or *lifo*, resulted in the lower total amount for the inventory?

PROBLEM 30-2 Determining valuation of inventory at lower of cost or market

Part of the inventory form of Stonegate Company on December 31 of the current year is below.

1	2	3	4
Item	No. of Units on Hand	Unit Cost	Current Unit Market Price
14 C	48	$ 16.50	$ 17.25
28 L	125	11.20	11.25
11 M	72	36.60	34.40
96 N	90	25.00	26.36
42 Q	12	322.50	296.40
56 R	256	26.75	24.70
38 S	60	43.40	48.60
73 T	85	18.20	19.20
21 U	30	51.50	49.35
99 W	105	12.50	12.60

Instructions: 1. Record the inventory information from Columns 1–4 on an inventory form with the column headings below.

1	2	3	4	5	6
Item	No. of Units on Hand	Unit Cost	Current Unit Market Price	Unit Price to be Used	Value at Lower of Cost or Market

Instructions: 2. Record the unit price to be used in Column 5.

3. Figure the value of each kind of merchandise at lower of cost or market. Record the value in Column 6.

4. Total Column 6 to determine the value of the ending merchandise inventory.

PROBLEM 30-3 Estimating the value of inventory using the gross profit method

The following information is available from the accounting records of Sundrops Corporation for January of the current year.

Beginning inventory, January 1	$ 69,900.00
Net purchases for January	76,400.00
Net sales for January	121,700.00
Gross profit on operations	30% of sales
Operating expenses for January	30,870.00

Instructions: 1. Estimate the value of the ending inventory for January of the current year. Use the gross profit method of estimating an inventory.

2. Prepare an income statement similar to the one on page 612 for the month ended January 31 of the current year.

ENRICHMENT PROBLEMS

MASTERY PROBLEM 30-M Determining cost of inventory using the fifo and lifo methods

Accounting records at Manatee Company showed the purchases and periodic inventory counts listed below.

Model	Beginning Inventory January 1	First Purchase	Second Purchase	Third Purchase	Periodic Inventory Count December 31
250	40 @ $10.50	50 @ $10.00	90 @ $ 8.50	40 @ $ 8.10	60
251	10 @ $32.50	30 @ $32.50	60 @ $33.30	50 @ $31.80	60
252	20 @ $10.00	40 @ $10.00	60 @ $10.50	60 @ $10.80	20
360	60 @ $12.00	30 @ $12.50	20 @ $13.00	40 @ $13.50	70
361	80 @ $15.50	30 @ $14.50	120 @ $15.00	60 @ $15.50	80
362	20 @ $17.50	40 @ $18.00	20 @ $19.50	70 @ $20.00	100
470	25 @ $46.00	30 @ $48.50	40 @ $50.00	50 @ $45.00	35
471	10 @ $82.00	40 @ $85.00	60 @ $81.00	70 @ $79.00	40

Use a form with the column headings below.

Model	No. of Units on Hand	Unit Cost	Inventory Value December 31

Instructions: 1. Figure the total amount of the inventory on December 31 according to the *fifo* method. Use the following procedure.

(a) Record the model number and number of units of each model on hand on December 31.

(b) Record the unit cost of each model. When more than one unit cost is used, list the units and unit costs on separate lines.

(c) Figure the total inventory value of each model and write the amount in the Value column.

(d) Add the Value column to determine the total amount of the inventory.

2. On another form, figure the total amount of inventory using the *lifo* method. Follow the steps given in Instruction 1.

3. Compare the total amount of the inventory obtained in Instructions 1 and 2. Which method, *fifo* or *lifo*, resulted in the lower total amount for the inventory?

CHALLENGE PROBLEM 30-C Determining cost of inventory using the lifo method with perpetual inventory

Accounting records at Orbit Company showed inventory increases (purchases) and decreases (sales) for Product 32-X as listed on page 617. Beginning inventory on June 1 was $1,000.00 (50 units at $20.00 each).

Date	Increases		Decreases
	No. of Units	Unit Cost	Units
June 2	20	$22.00	
6			25
9			15
13	50	23.00	
16			25
20			20
24	50	24.00	
28			30

Use a form with the column headings below. *Beginning inventory and the first two transactions are given as examples.*

Date	Increases			Decreases			Balance		
	No. of Units	Unit Cost	Total Cost	No. of Units	Unit Cost	Total Cost	No. of Units	Unit Cost	Total Cost
June 1							*50*	*$20.00*	*$1,000.00*
2	*20*	*$22.00*	*$440.00*				*50* *20*	*20.00* *22.00*	*1,440.00*
6				*20* *5*	*$22.00* *20.00*	*$540.00*	*45*	*20.00*	*900.00*

Instructions: Figure the amount of increase or decrease and the inventory balance for each transaction. Orbit keeps a perpetual cost inventory. Therefore, the amount of inventory is figured after each transaction. Orbit uses the *lifo* method. Therefore, purchases (increases) that are added most recently (last in) are removed first (first out) when a sale occurs.

Use the following procedures.

(a) Record the beginning inventory date, number of units, unit cost, and total cost.

(b) Record each transaction in the order it occurs.

(c) For each increase, record the number of units, unit cost, and total cost. Record the inventory balance (previous balance plus this transaction increase), number of units, unit cost, and total cost. When inventory has more than one unit cost, list the units and unit costs on separate lines. Bracket the unit cost lines and record a combined total inventory cost.

(d) For each decrease, record the number of units, unit cost, and total cost. Decreases are taken from the "last-in" units. When the decrease includes more than one unit cost, list the units and unit costs on separate lines. Bracket the unit cost lines and record a combined total decrease cost. Record the balance number of units, unit cost, and total cost after subtracting the "decrease" units and costs. Remember the decrease is subtracted from the "last-in" units and costs in the balance.

Balancing and Ruling Ledger Accounts

Appendix A

A practice in decreasing use is the balancing and ruling of two-column ledger accounts. There is an increased use of three-column and four-column ledger account forms. The use of these account forms is described in Part 3. The three-column and four-column account forms do not require balancing and ruling.

BALANCING AND RULING LEDGER ACCOUNTS

As a result of posting the closing entries, each revenue and expense account has a zero balance. To specifically separate information from one fiscal period to another, two-column ledger accounts may be balanced and ruled.

Ruling an account with a zero balance

Putt Around's utilities expense account ruled after the closing entries are posted is below.

ACCOUNT Utilities Expense — ACCOUNT NO. 54

DATE		ITEM	POST. REF.	DEBIT	DATE		ITEM	POST. REF.	CREDIT
1982 July	2		C1	25 00	1982 July	31		G1	117 00
	5		C1	60 00					
	20		C2	32 00					
				117 00					
				117 00					117 00

A single line is drawn across both amount columns. The two amount columns are added. The two total amounts must be the same. The totals are written immediately below the single lines. Double lines are drawn immediately below the total amounts. Entries for the next fiscal period are posted to the account starting below the double lines. The double lines definitely separate information from one fiscal period to the next.

Ruling an account with only one debit and one credit

If an account has only one debit and one credit amount, the account does not need to be totaled before ruling. Putt Around's rent expense account after ruling is below.

ACCOUNT *Rent Expense* ACCOUNT NO. *53*

DATE		ITEM	POST. REF.	DEBIT	DATE		ITEM	POST. REF.	CREDIT
1982 *July*	*1*		*C1*	*600 00*	*1982* *July*	*31*		*G1*	*600 00*

The single debit and credit amounts show that debits equal credits. Double lines are ruled immediately below the two amounts.

Balancing and ruling accounts that have balances

After closing entries are posted, most asset and liability accounts still have balances. The owner's capital account also has a balance. These accounts may be balanced and ruled to separate information from one fiscal period to another.

Accounts with entries on only one side are footed but not balanced and ruled. The supplies account, page 621, is an account that is not balanced and ruled.

Putt Around's cash account after it has been balanced and ruled is below.

ACCOUNT *Cash* ACCOUNT NO. *11*

DATE		ITEM	POST. REF.	DEBIT	DATE		ITEM	POST. REF.	CREDIT
1982 *July*	*1*	*Balance*	*G1*	*1100 00*	*1982* *July*	*31*		*C2*	*1887 00*
	31	*2192.00*	*C2*	*2979 00* *4079 00*		*31*	*Balance*	✓	*2192 00*
				4079 00					*4079 00*
Aug.	*1*	*Balance*	✓	*2192 00*					

Putt Around's cash account is balanced and ruled as described below.

1. Write the account balance on the side having the smaller total. (For the account above, the smaller total is on the credit side.) The balance, *$2,192.00*, is written on the credit side. The date, *31*, is written in the Date column. A check mark is placed in the Post. Ref. col-

umn. The check mark shows that this amount is not posted from a journal.

2. The account is totaled and ruled in the same manner as for any account. A single line is drawn across both amount columns. The two columns are totaled. The two totals must be the same. Double lines are drawn immediately below the two totals.
3. The account balance is written below the double lines on the balance's original side. (For Putt Around's cash account, the balance was originally a debit.) The amount of the balance, *$2,192.00*, is written in the debit column. The word *Balance* is written in the Item column. The date, *August 1*, is written in the Date column. (Use the first day of the next fiscal period.) A check mark is placed in the Post. Ref. column. The check mark shows that the amount is not posted from a journal.

Complete ledger after balancing and ruling

Putt Around's ledger after all accounts are balanced and ruled is below.

Ledger accounts after balancing and ruling

ACCOUNT *Cash* ACCOUNT NO. *11*

DATE		ITEM	POST. REF.	DEBIT	DATE		ITEM	POST. REF.	CREDIT
1982					*1982*				
July	*1*	*Balance*	*G1*	*1100 00*	*July*	*31*		*C2*	*1887 00*
	31		*C2*	*2979 00*		*31*	*Balance*	✓	*2192 00*
		2192.00		*4079 00*					
				4079 00					*4079 00*
Aug.	*1*	*Balance*	✓	*2192 00*					

ACCOUNT *Supplies* ACCOUNT NO. *12*

DATE		ITEM	POST. REF.	DEBIT	DATE	ITEM	POST. REF.	CREDIT
1982								
July	*1*	*Balance*	*G1*	*500 00*				
	2		*C1*	*50 00*				
	12		*C1*	*75 00*				
	24		*C2*	*100 00*				
				725 00				

ACCOUNT *Golf Equipment* ACCOUNT NO. *13*

DATE		ITEM	POST. REF.	DEBIT	DATE	ITEM	POST. REF.	CREDIT
1982								
July	*1*	*Balance*	*G1*	*2200 00*				
	12		*C1*	*100 00*				
				2300 00				

ACCOUNT *Maintenance Equipment* ACCOUNT NO. 14

DATE		ITEM	POST. REF.	DEBIT	DATE		ITEM	POST. REF.	CREDIT
1982 July	1	Balance	G1	900 00	1982 July	1		C1	50 00
	2		C1	400 00		31	Balance	✓	1250 00
		1250.00		1300 00					
				1300 00					1300 00
Aug.	1	Balance	✓	1250 00					

ACCOUNT *Melcor Equipment Company* ACCOUNT NO. 21

DATE		ITEM	POST. REF.	DEBIT	DATE		ITEM	POST. REF.	CREDIT
					1982 July	1	Balance	G1	650 00

ACCOUNT *Sasson Supply Company* ACCOUNT NO. 22

DATE		ITEM	POST. REF.	DEBIT	DATE		ITEM	POST. REF.	CREDIT
1982 July	1		C1	200 00	1982 July	1	Balance 350.00	G1	550 00
	31	Balance	✓	350 00					
				550 00					550 00
					Aug.	1	Balance	✓	350 00

ACCOUNT *Harry Rossi, Capital* ACCOUNT NO. 31

DATE		ITEM	POST. REF.	DEBIT	DATE		ITEM	POST. REF.	CREDIT
1982 July	31		G1	150 00	1982 July	1	Balance	G1	3500 00
	31	Balance	✓	5467 00		1		C1	500 00
									4000 00
						31	5467.00	G1	1617 00
									5617 00
				5617 00					5617 00
					Aug.	1	Balance	✓	5467 00

ACCOUNT *Harry Rossi, Drawing* ACCOUNT NO. 32

DATE		ITEM	POST. REF.	DEBIT	DATE		ITEM	POST. REF.	CREDIT
1982 July	2		C1	100 00	1982 July	31		G1	150 00
	23		C2	50 00					
				150 00					
				150 00					150 00

Ledger accounts after balancing and ruling (continued)

ACCOUNT *Income Summary* ACCOUNT NO. 33

DATE		ITEM	POST. REF.	DEBIT	DATE		ITEM	POST. REF.	CREDIT
1982 July	31		G1	812 00	1982 July	31		G1	2429 00
	31		G1	1617 00					
				2429 00					2429 00

ACCOUNT *Sales* ACCOUNT NO. 41

DATE		ITEM	POST. REF.	DEBIT	DATE		ITEM	POST. REF.	CREDIT
1982 July	31		G1	2429 00	1982 July	31		C2	2429 00

ACCOUNT *Advertising Expense* ACCOUNT NO. 51

DATE		ITEM	POST. REF.	DEBIT	DATE		ITEM	POST. REF.	CREDIT
1982 July	6		C1	25 00	1982 July	31		G1	25 00

ACCOUNT *Miscellaneous Expense* ACCOUNT NO. 52

DATE		ITEM	POST. REF.	DEBIT	DATE		ITEM	POST. REF.	CREDIT
1982 July	2		C1	10 00	1982 July	31		G1	70 00
	7		C1	10 00					
	15		C2	15 00					
	22		C2	18 00					
	27		C2	5 00					
	30		C2	12 00					
				70 00					
				70 00					70 00

ACCOUNT *Rent Expense* ACCOUNT NO. 53

DATE		ITEM	POST. REF.	DEBIT	DATE		ITEM	POST. REF.	CREDIT
1982 July	1		C1	600 00	1982 July	31		G1	600 00

ACCOUNT *Utilities Expense* ACCOUNT NO. 54

DATE		ITEM	POST. REF.	DEBIT	DATE		ITEM	POST. REF.	CREDIT
1982 July	2		C1	25 00	1982 July	31		G1	117 00
	5		C1	60 00					
	20		C2	32 00					
				117 00					
				117 00					117 00

Ledger accounts after balancing and ruling (concluded)

Appendix B

Accrued Revenue and Accrued Expenses

Most journal entries that record revenue are made when the revenue is received. However, some revenue may be earned before it is actually received. For example, interest is earned for each day an interest-bearing note receivable is held. The interest is not received however until the maturity date of the note.

Most entries recording expenses are also made when the expense is paid. Some expenses though are incurred before they are actually paid. For example, salary expense is incurred for each day that an employee works. The payment for salary expense is not made however until the regular payday.

To record the revenue that has been earned but not yet received, an adjusting entry is made at the end of the fiscal period. Because of this adjustment, the revenue is reported for the fiscal period in which the revenue is actually earned. *(CONCEPT: Realization of Revenue)* An adjusting entry also is made at the end of a fiscal period to record the amount of an expense that has been incurred but not yet paid. As a result of this adjustment, the expense is reported for the fiscal period in which the expense is actually incurred. *(CONCEPT: Matching Expenses with Revenue)*

ACCRUED REVENUE

Revenue earned in one fiscal period but not received until the next fiscal period is called accrued revenue. Accrued revenue is a receivable that is classified as an asset. At the end of a fiscal period, each type of accrued revenue is recorded by an adjusting entry. *(CONCEPT: Realization of Revenue)* The income statement will then show all the revenue for the period even though some has not been received. The balance sheet will show all the assets, including the accrued revenue receivable. *(CONCEPT: Adequate Disclosure)*

Adjusting entry for accrued interest income

At the end of each fiscal period, Furniture Mart examines the notes receivable on hand. The amount of interest income earned but not collected is determined. Interest earned on notes receivable but not yet collected is called accrued interest income. On December 31, 1983, there is only one note receivable on hand. This is Note Receivable No. 41, a 60-day, 9% note for $1,000.00 from Susan Price, dated December 1, 1983. The accounting records should show all the interest income for the fiscal period. Therefore, an adjusting entry must be made to record the amount of interest earned to date on this note.

Analyzing the adjusting entry for accrued interest income. Interest on $1,000.00 at 9% for 30 days (December 1 to 31) is $7.40. The adjustment for accrued interest income is analyzed in the T accounts at the right.

Interest Receivable is debited for $7.40. The balance of the interest receivable account is the amount of interest income that has accrued at the end of the fiscal period. However, this revenue is not received until the next fiscal period.

Interest Income is credited for $7.40 to show the increase in the balance of this account. The new balance of the interest income account is the amount of interest income earned during the fiscal period.

Interest Receivable	
7.40	

Interest Income	
	7.40

Adjustment for accrued interest income on a work sheet. The adjusting entry for accrued interest income is planned on a work sheet. The adjustment is below.

	Account Title	Trial Balance Debit (1)	Trial Balance Credit (2)	Adjustments Debit (3)	Adjustments Credit (4)	Income Statement Debit (5)	Income Statement Credit (6)	Balance Sheet Debit (7)	Balance Sheet Credit (8)	
4	Interest Receivable			(a) 740				740		4
42	Interest Income		7860		(a) 740		8600			42

Accrued interest income on a work sheet

Interest Receivable is debited for $7.40. This amount is extended to the Balance Sheet Debit column. Interest Income is credited for $7.40. This amount, $7.40, is added to the amount in the Trial Balance Credit column, $78.60. The new balance, $86.00, is extended to the Income Statement Credit column.

Recording and posting the adjustment for accrued interest income. Data needed to journalize the adjustment for accrued interest income are obtained from the Adjustments columns of the work sheet. The adjusting entry in the general journal is on the next page.

10			Adjusting Entries			10
11	Dec.	31	Interest Receivable	7 40		11
12			Interest Income		7 40	12

Adjusting entry for accrued interest income

After the adjusting entry is posted, the interest receivable and interest income accounts appear as shown below.

ACCOUNT Interest Receivable ACCOUNT NO. 1103

DATE		ITEM	POST. REF.	DEBIT	CREDIT	BALANCE DEBIT	BALANCE CREDIT
1983 Dec.	31		G42	7 40		7 40	

ACCOUNT Interest Income ACCOUNT NO. 7101

DATE		ITEM	POST. REF.	DEBIT	CREDIT	BALANCE DEBIT	BALANCE CREDIT
Dec.	1		CR48		5 00		78 60
	31		G42		7 40		86 00

Accounts after posting the adjusting entry for accrued interest income

The interest receivable account has a debit balance of $7.40. This is the accrued interest income earned but not collected at the end of the fiscal period. The interest income account has a credit balance of $86.00. This is the total interest income for the fiscal period.

Reporting accrued interest income on financial statements

The asset account Interest Receivable is listed on a balance sheet in the Current Assets section. The account Interest Income is listed on an income statement in the Other Revenue section.

Closing entry for the interest income account

One closing entry is recorded for accounts listed in the Income Statement Credit column of a work sheet. Interest Income is closed into the income summary account. The closing entry in the general journal on December 31, 1983, is below. After the closing entry is posted, the interest income account is closed.

1	1983 Dec.	31	Closing Entries			1
2			Sales	856 16 00		2
3			Purchases Returns + Allow.	12 91 00		3
4			Purchases Discount	29 76 00		4
5			Interest Income	86 00		5
6			Income Summary		899 69 00	6
7						7

Closing entry for the interest income account

Need for readjusting the interest receivable and interest income accounts

When cash is received for Note Receivable No. 41 on January 30, 1984, the cash will include principal, $1,000.00, plus interest, $14.79. To record the cash receipt, Cash will be debited for the amount received, $1,014.79. Notes Receivable will be credited for the principal, $1,000.00. Interest Income will be credited for the interest received, $14.79. But $7.40 of this interest was credited to Interest Income as accrued revenue at the end of the 1983 fiscal period. Only $7.39 applies to the 1984 fiscal period.

Accrued interest income recorded in one fiscal period should not be credited to Interest Income a second time when actually received in the following fiscal period. To avoid this double credit, the interest receivable and interest income accounts are readjusted at the beginning of the new fiscal period. An entry made at the beginning of one fiscal period to reverse an adjusting entry made in a previous fiscal period is called a reversing entry.

After the reversing entry has been recorded and posted, all interest income transactions during the new fiscal period are recorded in the usual way. That is, the full amount of interest is credited to Interest Income. Using reversing entries makes it unnecessary to analyze each receipt of interest to determine how much was earned during a previous fiscal period.

Reversing entry for accrued interest income

A reversing entry is exactly the opposite of the original adjusting entry. Furniture Mart's adjusting entry for accrued interest income on December 31, 1983, debited Interest Receivable for $7.40 and credited Interest Income for $7.40. The reversing entry on January 1, 1984, reverses this adjusting entry.

Analyzing the reversing entry for accrued interest income. The reversing entry for accrued interest income is analyzed in the T accounts at the right.

Interest Income is debited for $7.40 and Interest Receivable is credited for $7.40. This reversing entry closes the interest receivable account and transfers the original debit balance to the debit side of the interest income account. The debit to Interest Income is a temporary balance that represents uncollected interest income earned and recorded during the previous fiscal period.

Interest Income			
Closing	86.00	Balance	78.50
Reversing	7.40	Adjusting	7.40

Interest Receivable			
Adjusting	7.40	Reversing	7.40

During the new fiscal period, receipts of interest income are credited to Interest Income. The portion of each receipt of interest that applies to the previous fiscal period will automatically be deducted because of the debit balance.

Recording and posting the reversing entry for accrued interest income. The reversing entry is recorded in the general journal as of January 1, 1984, under the centered heading *Reversing Entries* as shown below.

Reversing entry for accrued interest income

	Date		Account Title	Post. Ref.	Debit	Credit	
1	1984 Jan.	1	Reversing Entries				1
2			Interest Income		740		2
3			Interest Receivable			740	3

After the reversing entry is posted, the interest receivable and interest income accounts appear as shown below.

Accounts after posting the reversing entry for accrued interest income

ACCOUNT Interest Receivable — ACCOUNT NO. 1103

Date		Item	Post. Ref.	Debit	Credit	Balance Debit	Balance Credit
1983 Dec.	31		G42	740		740	
1984 Jan.	1		G44		740	—	—

ACCOUNT Interest Income — ACCOUNT NO. 7101

Date		Item	Post. Ref.	Debit	Credit	Balance Debit	Balance Credit
	31		G43	8600		—	—
1984 Jan.	1		G44	740		740	

Interest Receivable has a zero balance at the beginning of the new 1984 fiscal period. Interest Receivable will not be used again until it is needed for an adjusting entry at the end of the 1984 fiscal period. Interest Receivable is needed for only one day each period to prepare complete financial reports. *(CONCEPT: Adequate Disclosure)*

Interest Income has a debit balance of $7.40 on January 1, 1984. This balance on the first day of the new fiscal year is the result of posting the reversing entry for accrued interest income. During 1984 Interest Income will be credited each time cash is received for interest income. At the end of the 1984 fiscal period, the credit balance will show the amount of interest income that belongs to the 1984 fiscal period. *(CONCEPT: Realization of Revenue)* At the end of the 1984 fiscal period there will be new accrued interest income, earned in 1984 but not collected in 1984. The accrued interest income on December 31, 1984, will be recorded in the same manner as the accrued interest income on December 31, 1983.

ACCRUED EXPENSES

Expenses incurred in one fiscal period but not paid until the next fiscal period are called accrued expenses. An example of an accrued expense is interest expense incurred during one fiscal period but not paid until the next fiscal period. Another example is salaries earned by employees in one fiscal period but not paid until the next fiscal period. At the end of a fiscal period, each type of accrued expense is recorded by an adjusting entry. *(CONCEPT: Matching Expenses with Revenue)* The income statement will show all expenses for the period even though some have not been paid. The balance sheet will show all liabilities, including amounts owed for accrued expenses. *(CONCEPT: Adequate Disclosure)*

Adjusting entry for accrued interest expense

At the end of each fiscal period, Furniture Mart examines the notes payable on hand to determine the amount of interest expense incurred but not paid. Interest incurred on notes payable but not yet paid is called accrued interest expense. On December 31, 1983, there is only one note payable on hand. This is Note Payable No. 11, a 90-day, 8% note for $3,000.00 issued to the Davis Company on November 1, 1983. An adjusting entry is made to record the amount of interest expense incurred to date on this note.

Analyzing the adjusting entry for accrued interest expense. The interest on $3,000.00 at 8% for 60 days (November 1 to December 31) is $39.45. The adjustment for accrued interest expense is analyzed in the T accounts at the right.

Interest Expense is debited for $39.45 to show the increase in the balance of this account. The new balance of Interest Expense is the total amount of interest expense incurred during the fiscal period. Interest Payable is credited for $39.45. The balance of Interest Payable is interest expense that has accrued at the end of the fiscal period but that is not paid until the next fiscal period.

Interest Expense	
39.45	

Interest Payable	
	39.45

Adjustment for accrued interest expense on a work sheet. The adjusting entry for accrued interest expense is planned on a work sheet. The adjustment is below.

	Account Title	1 Trial Balance Debit	2 Trial Balance Credit	3 Adjustments Debit	4 Adjustments Credit	5 Income Statement Debit	6 Income Statement Credit	7 Balance Sheet Debit	8 Balance Sheet Credit	
15	Interest Payable				(i) 3945				3945	15
44	Interest Expense	19055		(i) 3945		23000				44

Accrued interest expense on a work sheet

Interest Expense is debited for $39.45. This amount, $39.45, is added to the amount in the Trial Balance Debit column, $190.55. The new balance, $230.00, is extended to the Income Statement Debit column.

Interest Payable is credited for $39.45. This amount is extended to the Balance Sheet Credit column.

Recording and posting the adjustment for accrued interest expense. Data needed to journalize the adjustment for accrued interest expense are obtained from the Adjustments columns of the work sheet. The adjusting entry in the general journal is below.

Adjusting entry for accrued interest expense

17	31	Interest Expense		39 45		17
18		Interest Payable			39 45	18

After the adjusting entry is posted, the interest payable and interest expense accounts appear as shown below.

ACCOUNT Interest Payable ACCOUNT NO. 2102

DATE		ITEM	POST. REF.	DEBIT	CREDIT	BALANCE DEBIT	BALANCE CREDIT
1983 Dec.	31		G42		39 45		39 45

ACCOUNT Interest Expense ACCOUNT NO. 8101

DATE		ITEM	POST. REF.	DEBIT	CREDIT	BALANCE DEBIT	BALANCE CREDIT
Dec.	15		CP37	20 00		190 55	
	31		G42	39 45		230 00	

Accounts after posting the adjusting entry for accrued interest expense

Interest Payable has a credit balance of $39.45. This balance is the accrued interest expense incurred in the current fiscal period but to be paid in the next fiscal period. Interest Expense has a debit balance of $230.00, which is the total interest expense for the fiscal period.

Reporting accrued interest expense on financial statements

The liability account Interest Payable is listed on the balance sheet in the Current Liabilities section. The expense account Interest Expense is listed on the income statement in the Other Expenses section.

Closing entry for the interest expense account

One closing entry is recorded for accounts listed in the Income Statement Debit column of the work sheet. Interest Expense is closed into the income summary account. The closing entry in Furniture Mart's general journal on December 31, 1983, is on the next page. After the closing entry is posted, the interest expense account is closed.

Need for readjusting interest payable and interest expense accounts

When Furniture Mart pays Note Payable No. 11 on January 30, 1984, it will pay the principal, $3,000.00, plus the interest, $59.18. To record the

7	31	Income Summary	75 892 00		7
8		Sales Returns + Allow.		2 107 10	8
9		Purchases		227 160 00	9
10		Bad Debts Expense		428 40	10
11		Delivery Expense		1 873 00	11
12		Depr. Expense-Office Equip.		2 246 00	12
13		Depr. Expense-Store Equip.		4 115 50	13
14		Insurance Expense		180 00	14
15		Miscellaneous Expense		647 15	15
16		Payroll Taxes Expense		2 968 60	16
17		Rent Expense		600 00	17
18		Salary Expense		37 108 00	18
19		Supplies Expense		672 25	19
20		Interest Expense		230 00	20
21					21

Closing entry including the interest expense account

payment Notes Payable will be debited for the principal of the note, $3,000.00. Interest Expense will be debited for the interest paid, $59.18. Cash will be credited for the total amount paid, $3,059.18. But $39.45 of the interest paid has been debited to Interest Expense as accrued expense at the end of the 1983 fiscal period. Only $19.73 applies to the 1984 fiscal period.

Accrued interest expense recorded in one fiscal period should not be debited to Interest Expense a second time when actually paid in the following fiscal period. To avoid this double debit, Interest Payable and Interest Expense are readjusted at the beginning of the new fiscal period by a reversing entry. After the reversing entry has been recorded and posted, all interest expense transactions during the new fiscal period are recorded in the usual way.

Reversing entry for accrued interest expense

Furniture Mart's adjusting entry for accrued interest expense on December 31, 1983, debited Interest Expense for $39.45 and credited Interest Payable for $39.45. The reversing entry on January 1, 1984, reverses this adjusting entry.

Analyzing the reversing entry for accrued interest expense. The reversing entry for accrued interest expense is analyzed in the T accounts at the right.

Interest Payable is debited for $39.45 and Interest Expense is credited for $39.45. This reversing entry closes the interest payable account and transfers the original credit balance to the credit side of the interest expense account. The credit to Interest Expense is a temporary balance that represents unpaid interest expense incurred and recorded during the previous fiscal period.

Interest Payable

Reversing	39.45	Adjusting	39.45

Interest Expense

Balance	190.55	Closing	230.00
Adjusting	39.45	Reversing	39.45

During the new fiscal period, payments of interest expense are debited to Interest Expense. The portion of each interest payment that applies to the previous fiscal period will automatically be deducted because of the credit balance. *(CONCEPT: Matching Expenses with Revenue)*

Recording and posting the reversing entry for accrued interest expense. The reversing entry is recorded in the general journal as of January 1, 1984, as shown below.

Reversing entry for accrued interest expense

4	1	Interest Payable	3945		4
5		Interest Expense		3945	5

After the reversing entry is posted, the interest payable and interest expense accounts appear as shown below.

ACCOUNT Interest Payable — ACCOUNT NO. 2102

DATE		ITEM	POST. REF.	DEBIT	CREDIT	BALANCE DEBIT	BALANCE CREDIT
1983 Dec.	31		G42		3945		3945
1984 Jan.	1		G44	3945		—	—

ACCOUNT Interest Expense — ACCOUNT NO. 8101

DATE		ITEM	POST. REF.	DEBIT	CREDIT	BALANCE DEBIT	BALANCE CREDIT
	31		G43		23000	—	—
1984 Jan.	1		G44		3945		3945

Accounts after posting the reversing entry for accrued interest expense

Interest Payable has a zero balance at the beginning of the new 1984 fiscal period. Interest Payable will not receive any entries until the end of the 1984 fiscal period. Interest Payable is needed for only one day each period to prepare complete financial reports.

Interest Expense has a credit balance of $39.45 on January 1, 1984. This balance on the first day of the new fiscal year is the result of posting the reversing entry for accrued interest expense. During 1984 Interest Expense will be debited each time cash is paid for interest expense. At the end of the 1984 fiscal period, the debit balance will show the amount of interest expense that belongs to the 1984 fiscal period. Then, at the end of the 1984 fiscal period there will be new accrued interest expense, incurred in 1984 but not paid in 1984. The new accrued interest expense on December 31, 1984, will be handled in the same manner as the accrued interest expense on December 31, 1983.

Adjusting entry for accrued salary expense

Furniture Mart pays its employees weekly on Friday. At the end of the fiscal period on Saturday, December 31, 1983, one day's salary amounting to $120.00 is owed to employees for work performed on Saturday. This salary expense will not be paid until the next regular payday on Friday, January 6, 1984. The $120.00 owed is a salary expense of the 1983 fiscal period. The accounting records must show all the salary expense for the 1983 fiscal period. *(CONCEPT: Matching Expenses with Revenue)* An adjusting entry is made to record the amount of salary owed at the end of December, 1983, but to be paid in January, 1984. Salary owed but not yet paid is called accrued salary expense.

Analyzing the adjusting entry for accrued salary expense. The amount of salary owed but not paid on December 31, 1983, is $120.00. The adjustment for accrued salary expense is analyzed in the T accounts at the right.

Salary Expense is debited for $120.00 to show the increase in the balance of this account. The new balance of Salary Expense is the total amount of salary expense incurred during the fiscal period.

Salaries Payable is credited for $120.00. The balance of Salaries Payable is the amount of accrued salary expense at the end of the fiscal period.

Salary Expense	
120.00	

Salaries Payable	
	120.00

Adjustment for accrued salary expense on a work sheet. The adjusting entry for accrued salary expense is planned on a work sheet. The adjustment is below.

	Account Title	1 Trial Balance Debit	2 Trial Balance Credit	3 Adjustments Debit	4 Adjustments Credit	5 Income Statement Debit	6 Income Statement Credit	7 Balance Sheet Debit	8 Balance Sheet Credit	
16	Salaries Payable				(f) 120 00				120 00	16
39	Salary Expense	36 988 00		(f) 120 00		37 108 00				39

Accrued salary expense on a work sheet

Salary Expense is debited for $120.00. This amount, $120.00, is added to the amount in the Trial Balance Debit column, $36,988.00. The new balance, $37,108.00, is extended to the Income Statement Debit column.

Salaries Payable is credited for $120.00. This amount is extended to the Balance Sheet Credit column.

Recording and posting the adjustment for accrued salary expense. Data needed to journalize the adjustment for accrued salary expense are obtained from the Adjustments columns of the work sheet. The adjusting entry in the general journal is on the next page.

Adjusting entry for accrued salary expense

19	31	Salary Expense		120 00	
20		Salaries Payable			120 00

After the adjusting entry is posted, the salaries payable and salary expense accounts appear as shown below.

ACCOUNT Salaries Payable ACCOUNT NO. 2103

DATE		ITEM	POST. REF.	DEBIT	CREDIT	BALANCE DEBIT	BALANCE CREDIT
1983 Dec.	31		G42		120 00		120 00

ACCOUNT Salary Expense ACCOUNT NO. 6112

DATE		ITEM	POST. REF.	DEBIT	CREDIT	BALANCE DEBIT	BALANCE CREDIT
	30		CP37	720 00		36,988 00	
	31		G42	120 00		37,108 00	

Accounts after posting the adjusting entry for accrued salary expense

Salaries Payable has a credit balance of $120.00. This is the accrued salary expense incurred in the current fiscal period but to be paid in the next fiscal period. Salary Expense has a debit balance of $37,108.00, which is the total salary expense for the fiscal period. *(CONCEPT: Matching Expenses with Revenue)*

Reporting accrued salary expense on financial statements

The liability account Salaries Payable is listed on the balance sheet in the Current Liabilities section. The expense account Salary Expense is listed on the income statement in the Operating Expenses section.

Closing entry for the salary expense account

Salary expense is included in the closing entry made for the accounts listed in the Income Statement Debit column of the work sheet. Furniture Mart's closing entry on December 31, 1983, for the salary expense account is on page 631. After this closing entry is posted, the salary expense account is closed.

Need for readjusting the salaries payable and salary expense accounts

Furniture Mart's next weekly payroll is January 6, 1984. The entire amount of salaries for the week, $720.00, is debited to Salary Expense. This entry is the same as that for each weekly payroll in 1983. But $120.00 of these salaries has already been debited to Salary Expense as accrued expense at the end of the 1983 fiscal period. Therefore, only $600.00 applies to the 1984 fiscal period.

Accrued salary expense recorded in one fiscal period should not be debited to Salary Expense a second time when actually paid in the following fiscal period. To avoid this double debit, the salaries payable and salary expense accounts are readjusted at the beginning of the new fiscal period by a reversing entry.

Reversing entry for accrued salary expense

Furniture Mart's adjusting entry for accrued salary expense on December 31, 1983, debited Salary Expense for $120.00 and credited Salaries Payable for $120.00. The reversing entry on January 1, 1984, reverses this adjusting entry.

Analyzing the reversing entry for accrued salary expense. The reversing entry for accrued salary expense is analyzed at the right.

Salaries Payable is debited for $120.00 and Salary Expense is credited for $120.00. This reversing entry closes the salaries payable account and transfers the original credit balance to the credit side of the salary expense account. The credit to Salary Expense is a temporary balance that represents unpaid salary expense incurred and recorded during the previous fiscal period.

Salaries Payable

Debit		Credit	
Reversing	120.00	Adjusting	120.00

Salary Expense

Debit		Credit	
Balance	36,988.00	Closing	37,108.00
Adjusting	120.00	Reversing	120.00

Recording and posting the reversing entry for accrued salary expense. The reversing entry is recorded in the general journal as of January 1, 1984, as shown below.

	Date	Account Title	Post. Ref.	Debit	Credit	
6	1	Salaries Payable		120 00		6
7		Salary Expense			120 00	7

Reversing entry for accrued salary expense

After the reversing entry is posted, the salaries payable and salary expense accounts appear as shown below.

ACCOUNT Salaries Payable ACCOUNT NO. 2103

Date		Item	Post. Ref.	Debit	Credit	Balance Debit	Balance Credit
1983 Dec.	31		G42		120 00		120 00
1984 Jan.	1		G44	120 00		—	—

ACCOUNT Salary Expense ACCOUNT NO. 6112

Date		Item	Post. Ref.	Debit	Credit	Balance Debit	Balance Credit
	31		G43		37,108 00	—	—
1984 Jan.	1		G44		120 00		120 00

Accounts after posting the reversing entry for accrued salary expense

Salaries Payable has a zero balance at the beginning of the new 1984 fiscal period. Like Interest Payable, Salaries Payable will not receive any entries until the end of the 1984 fiscal period.

Salary Expense is credited at the beginning of the new 1984 fiscal period for the amount of salary expense that belongs to the 1983 fiscal period. This amount will be paid in 1984. During 1983 Salary Expense will be debited each time the weekly payroll is paid.

ACCOUNTING TERMS

What is the meaning of each of the following?

1. accrued revenue
2. accrued interest income
3. reversing entry
4. accrued expenses
5. accrued interest expense
6. accrued salary expense

QUESTIONS FOR INDIVIDUAL STUDY

1. When are most journal entries made that record revenue?
2. Why should revenue that has been earned but not received be recorded before financial statements are prepared at the end of a fiscal period?
3. What accounts are debited and credited to record the adjusting entry for accrued interest income?
4. Under what heading on the balance sheet is the balance of the interest receivable account listed?
5. Why are the interest receivable and interest income accounts readjusted at the beginning of a new fiscal period?
6. What accounts are debited and credited to record the reversing entry for accrued interest income?
7. Why should expenses that have been incurred but not paid be recorded before financial statements are prepared at the end of a fiscal period?
8. What accounts are debited and credited to record the adjusting entry for accrued interest expense?
9. Under what heading on the income statement is the balance of the interest expense account listed?
10. Why are the interest payable and interest expense accounts readjusted at the beginning of a new fiscal period?
11. What accounts are debited and credited to record the reversing entry for accrued interest expense?
12. Why are the salaries payable and salary expense accounts readjusted at the beginning of a new fiscal period?

CASES FOR MANAGEMENT DECISION

CASE 1 At the end of the fiscal period, Lawson Company failed to record accrued interest income amounting to $300.00 on notes receivable. What effect does this omission have on (a) the income statement and (b) the balance sheet?

CASE 2 At the end of the fiscal period, Scott Company failed to record accrued interest expense amounting to $100.00 on notes payable. They also failed to record accrued salary expense amounting to $200.00. What effect do these omissions have on (a) the income statement and (b) the balance sheet?

DRILL FOR UNDERSTANDING

DRILL Recording adjusting and reversing entries for accrued revenue and accrued expenses

Instructions: 1. Prepare a form similar to the one below. Enter each number and item on the form.

No.	Item	Account Titles Affected By			
		Adjusting Entry		Reversing Entry	
		Account Debited	Account Credited	Account Debited	Account Credited
1.	Accrued interest income				
2.	Accrued interest expense				
3.	Accrued salary expense				

Instructions: 2. For each item, indicate the titles of the accounts debited and credited to record the adjusting entry on December 31 of the current year.

3. For each item, indicate the titles of the accounts debited and credited to record the reversing entry on January 1 of the following year.

APPLICATION PROBLEM

APPLICATION PROBLEM Recording and posting adjusting, closing, and reversing entries for accrued revenue and accrued expenses

Selected accounts from Brook's ledger are below. The balances are for December 31 of the current fiscal year before adjusting entries.

Account Title	Acct. No.	Balance	Account Title	Acct. No.	Balance
Interest Receivable	1103	—	Salary Expense	6112	$8,918.00
Interest Payable	2102	—	Interest Income	7101	296.80
Salaries Payable	2103	—	Interest Expense	8101	122.50
Income Summary	3301	—			

On December 31, accrued interest income on notes receivable is $27.30. Accrued salaries are $169.40. Accrued interest expense on notes payable is $61.00.

Instructions: 1. Open the general ledger accounts and record the balances.
2. Use page 14 of a general journal. Record the adjusting entries for accrued revenue and accrued expenses on December 31 of the current year.
3. Post the adjusting entries.
4. Record the entries to close (a) the interest income account and (b) the salary expense and interest expense accounts.
5. Post the closing entries.
6. Record the reversing entries on January 1 of the next year.
7. Post the reversing entries.

ENRICHMENT PROBLEMS

MASTERY PROBLEM Recording and posting adjusting, closing, and reversing entries for accrued revenue and accrued expenses

Selected accounts from Hoffman's ledger are below. The balances are for December 31 of the current fiscal year before adjusting entries.

Account Title	Acct. No.	Balance	Account Title	Acct. No.	Balance
Interest Receivable	1103	—	Salary Expense	6112	$18,952.50
Interest Payable	2102	—	Interest Income	7101	72.00
Salaries Payable	2103	—	Interest Expense	8101	165.00
Income Summary	3301	—			

Adjustment data at the end of the fiscal period on December 31:
Accrued interest income on notes receivable, $33.75.
Accrued salaries payable, $372.00.
Accrued interest expense on notes payable, $60.00.

Instructions: 1. Open the general ledger accounts and record the balances.
2. Use page 8 of a general journal. Record the adjusting entries for accrued revenue and accrued expenses on December 31 of the current year. Post the adjusting entries.
3. Record the entries to close the revenue and expense accounts. Post the closing entries.
4. Record the reversing entries for the accruals as of January 1 of the next year. Post the reversing entries.

CHALLENGE PROBLEM Recording and posting adjusting, closing, and reversing entries for accrued revenue and accrued expenses

Selected accounts from Jackson's ledger are below. The balances are for December 31 of the current fiscal year before adjusting entries.

Account Title	Acct. No.	Balance	Account Title	Acct. No.	Balance
Interest Receivable	1103	—	Salary Expense	6112	$36,468.00
Rent Receivable	1104	—	Interest Income	7101	225.00
Interest Payable	2102	—	Rent Income	7102	1,500.00
Salaries Payable	2103	—	Interest Expense	8101	90.00
Income Summary	3301	—			

Adjustment data at the end of the fiscal period on December 31:

Accrued interest income has been earned on a 60-day, 9% note for $6,000.00 dated November 21.

Accrued interest expense has been incurred on a 120-day, 8% note for $4,000.00 dated December 16.

Accrued rent receivable, $300.00.

Accrued salaries payable, $280.00.

Instructions: 1. Open the general ledger accounts and record the balances.

2. Use page 23 of a general journal. Record the adjusting entries for accrued revenue and accrued expenses on December 31 of the current year. Post the adjusting entries.

3. Record the entries to close the revenue and expense accounts. Post the closing entries.

4. Record the reversing entries on January 1 of the new year. Post the reversing entries.

Recycling Problems

NOTE: No recycling problems are provided for Chapter 1.

RECYCLING PROBLEM 2-R 1 Preparing a beginning balance sheet; recording and posting an opening entry

The following financial information is listed by Lucia Sanchez for a new business, Sanchez Company.

Assets: Cash, $2,430.00; Supplies, $570.00; Equipment, $4,770.00.

Liabilities: Menington Supply Company, $800.00; Ramon's Equipment Company, $2,880.00.

Instructions: 1. Prepare a beginning balance sheet using the date October 1 of the current year.

2. Record the opening entry for Sanchez Company using page 1 of a general journal.

3. Open the following ledger accounts for the partial chart of accounts below.

Account Title	Account Number	Account Title	Account Number
Cash	11	Menington Supply Company	21
Supplies	12	Ramon's Equipment Company	22
Equipment	13	Lucia Sanchez, Capital	31

Instructions: 4. Post the opening entry recorded in Instruction 2 above.

RECYCLING PROBLEM 3-R 1 Determining how transactions change the expanded accounting equation

The transactions below were completed for Kawoski Cleaning Service, operated by Josef Kawoski. Use a form similar to the one below.

Trans. No.	Assets			=	Liabilities	+	Capital
	Cash	Supplies	Equipment		Showse Supply & Service Co.		
Bal. 1.	9,000 *−500*	600	6,600	=	1,550	+	14,650 *−500*
Bal. 2.	*8,500*	*600*	*6,600*	=	*1,550*	+	*14,150*

Transactions

1. Paid cash for gasoline bill, $500.00.
2. Paid cash for supplies, $150.00.
3. Paid cash for a new piece of equipment, $450.00.
4. Received cash from day's sales, $600.00.
5. Paid cash for part of amount owed Showse Supply & Service Company, $450.00.
6. Paid cash for the telephone bill, $130.00.
7. Received cash from day's sales, $375.00.
8. Paid cash for repairs to station wagon used by the business, $155.00.
9. Paid cash for a new piece of cleaning equipment, $600.00.
10. Paid cash to the owner for personal use, $300.00.
11. Received cash from the sale of an old piece of equipment, $75.00.
12. Received cash from day's sales, $450.00.
13. Paid cash for the electric bill, $100.00.
14. Paid cash for next month's rent, $400.00.
15. Received cash from day's sales, $325.00.

Instructions: 1. Complete steps a, b, and c for each transaction. (a) Analyze the transaction and show the amount increased (+) and decreased (−) for the items affected on the equation. Transaction 1 is shown as an example. (b) Figure the new balance for each item and write it on the next line. (c) Check that *Assets* = *Liabilities* + *Capital* for each new balance line.

2. Prepare a balance sheet using the information on the last balance line of the solution to Instruction 1. Use the date October 15 of the current year.

RECYCLING PROBLEM 4-R 1 Analyzing transactions into debit and credit parts

Mrs. Rosa Benitez operates a private swimming club. She pays a monthly rent for the use of the swimming pool and facilities. Revenue for the business comes from two sources. (a) Annual membership dues. (b) Daily swim fees paid by non-members. The ledger of the club includes the accounts below on October 1 of the current year.

Cash, $2,360.00
Supplies, $600.00.
Pool Equipment, $965.00
Swim-set Equipment Company (liability), $675.00
Rosa Benitez, Capital, $3,250.00
Rosa Benitez, Drawing

Admissions Revenue
Membership Revenue
Electricity Expense
Maintenance Expense
Miscellaneous Expense
Rent Expense
Water Expense

Instructions: 1. Prepare T accounts for the accounts listed above. Record the account balance for those accounts that have a balance.

2. Analyze each of the following transactions into debit and credit parts. Record the amounts in the correct T accounts for each transaction. The T accounts at the right show the accounts affected by Transaction 1 as an example.

Rent Expense

	Debit		Credit
(1)	375.00		

Cash

	Debit		Credit
Balance	2,360.00	(1)	375.00

Transactions

1. Paid cash for month's rent, $375.00.
2. Paid cash for the water bill, $85.00.
3. Received cash from membership dues, $860.00.

4. Paid cash for maintaining the pool, $52.00.
5. Received cash from daily pool admissions, $45.00.
6. Paid cash to Swim-set Equipment Company for part payment of amount owed, $150.00.
7. Received cash from membership dues, $520.00.
8. Received cash from the sale of a used pool pump and filter, $390.00.
9. Paid cash for a new pool pump and filter, $1,500.00.
10. Paid cash for the electric bill, $85.00.
11. Received cash from daily pool admissions, $120.00.
12. Paid cash for a new diving board, $130.00.
13. Received cash from daily pool admissions, $135.00.
14. Paid cash for general supplies, $25.00.
15. Paid cash for folding chairs to be used around the poolside, $100.00.
16. Paid cash to Swim-set Equipment Company for part payment of amount owed, $200.00.
17. Paid cash to the owner for personal use, $200.00.
18. Received cash from daily pool admissions, $165.00.
19. Paid cash for minor repair to a leak in pool filtering equipment, $25.00.

RECYCLING PROBLEM 5-R 1 Recording transactions in a cash journal

Carl Johnson operates a hunting lodge. The lodge is open only during the hunting season. The lodge opened on October 1 of the current year. The business' cash journal is similar to the one described on page 71.

The following are some of the accounts in the business' ledger. *Assets*: Cash, Supplies, Equipment. *Liabilities*: Ackerman Plumbing Company, Commercial Furniture Company. *Capital*: Carl Johnson, Capital; Carl Johnson, Drawing. *Revenue*: Room Sales. *Expenses*: Advertising Expense, Laundry Expense, Miscellaneous Expense, Rent Expense, Utilities Expense.

Instructions: 1. Record the cash balance on hand, $819.00, on page 1 of a cash journal.

2. Record the following transactions. All payments are made by check beginning with Check No. 1. All cash received is recorded on a cash register. Number all cash register tapes with the letter T plus the date.

Oct. 1. Paid cash for having the lodge cleaned, $85.00.
1. Paid cash for month's rent of lodge, $300.00.
2. Received cash from sale of old furniture, $45.00.
3. Received cash from room sales, $145.00.
6. Paid cash to Ackerman Plumbing Company for amount owed, $58.00.
9. Received cash from room sales, $147.00.
13. Paid cash for laundry, $44.10.
15. Received cash from sale of old piece of equipment, $32.00.
16. Received cash from room sales, $270.00.
19. Paid cash for installing road signs advertising the lodge, $115.00.
23. Received cash from room sales, $230.00.
27. Paid cash for telephone bill, $78.50.
28. Paid cash for laundry, $25.00.
29. Paid cash for electric bill, $45.00.
30. Received cash from room sales, $294.00.
30. Paid cash for advertisement in local newspaper, $75.00.

Instructions: 3. Prove cash. The ending balance on Check Stub No. 9 is $1,156.40.
4. Prove the cash journal.
5. Rule the cash journal.

RECYCLING PROBLEM 6-R 1 Journalizing and posting using a cash journal

Rachael Moser, an attorney, uses the ledger accounts below.

Account Title	Acct. No.	Account Balance	Account Title	Acct. No.	Account Balance
Cash	11	$8,587.00	Professional Fees	41	—
Supplies	12	125.00	Miscellaneous Expense	51	—
Office Furniture	13	870.00	Rent Expense	52	—
Law Library	14	645.00	Utilities Expense	53	—
Castle Garage (liability)	21	685.00			
Huffer Company (liability)	22	110.00			
Rachael Moser, Capital	31	9,432.00			
Rachael Moser, Drawing	32	—			

Instructions: 1. Open a ledger account for each account listed above. Write the account title and number at the top of the form. Record the balance for each account that has a balance. Write the word *Balance* in the Item column and place a check mark in the Post. Ref. column. Use October 1 of the current year.

2. Record the following transactions on page 10 of a cash journal similar to the one on page 96. Use the revenue column heading *Professional Fees Credit* instead of Sales Credit. Source documents are abbreviated as: check, C; receipts, R.

Oct. 1. Record cash balance on hand, $8,587.00.
1. Paid cash for October rent, $350.00. C150.
4. Received cash for legal services, $50.00. R45.
6. Paid cash for new office furniture, $145.00. C151.
8. Received cash for sale of old office furniture, $12.00. R46.
8. Received cash for legal services, $100.00. R47.
11. Paid cash to Huffer Company, $50.00. C152.
12. Paid cash for supplies, $240.00. C153.
15. Paid cash for miscellaneous expense, $6.00. C154.
18. Paid cash for the miscellaneous expense of taking a client to dinner, $28.50. C155.
19. Paid cash for telephone bill, $25.80. C156.
21. Received cash for legal services, $360.00. R48.
22. Paid cash to Castle Garage, $300.00. C157.
25. Received cash from sale of old office furniture, $20.00. R49.
26. Received cash for legal services, $150.00. R50.
27. Received cash for legal services, $95.00. R51.
29. Paid cash for gas bill, $32.00. C158.
31. Paid cash for electric bill, $38.00. C159.
31. Paid cash for supplies, $200.00. C160.
31. Paid cash to Miss Moser for personal use, $500.00. C161.

Instructions: 3. Prove cash. The balance on Check Stub No. 161 is $7,458.70.
4. Total, prove, and rule the cash journal.
5. Post from the cash journal to the ledger.

RECYCLING PROBLEM 7-R 1 Completing a work sheet

Lanahan Insurance Agency's ledger accounts and balances on July 31 of the current year are below.

Account Title	Account Balance	Account Title	Account Balance
Cash	$2,860.00	Premiums Revenue	$2,600.00
Automobiles	9,000.00	Advertising Expense	182.00
Office Furniture	1,440.00	Automobile Expense	250.00
Office Equipment	1,321.00	Miscellaneous Expense	72.00
Nichols Company (liability)	753.00	Rent Expense	450.00
Poldark Motors (liability)	2,800.00	Utilities Expense	302.00
Richards Products Co. (liability)	1,481.00		
Teresa Lanahan, Capital	8,443.00		
Teresa Lanahan, Drawing	200.00		
Income Summary	——		

Instructions: 1. Complete the heading on a work sheet. The Agency uses a one-month fiscal period. Prepare a trial balance on the work sheet.

2. Extend the asset, liability, and capital account balances to the Balance Sheet columns.

3. Extend the revenue and expense account balances to the Income Statement columns.

4. Figure the net income or net loss and complete the Income Statement columns.

5. Complete the Balance Sheet columns.

RECYCLING PROBLEM 8-R 1 Preparing a work sheet and financial statements

The ledger accounts and balances for Midtown Cinema are below.

Account Title	Account Balance	Account Title	Account Balance
Cash	$ 3,994.71	Admissions Revenue	$ 4,701.76
Air Conditioning Equipment	4,080.00	Advertising Expense	262.40
Projection Equipment	10,560.00	Film Rental Expense	1,624.00
Sound Equipment	5,207.99	Maintenance Expense	132.80
Allied Studios (liability)	171.68	Miscellaneous Expense	42.10
Bader Films Company (liability)	52.96	Projection Expense	367.68
Gibson Sound Service (liability)	212.80	Rent Expense	600.00
Elisa Downs, Capital	23,065.60	Utilities Expense	333.12
Elisa Downs, Drawing	1,000.00		
Income Summary	——		

Instructions: 1. Prepare a work sheet for the month ending October 31 of the current year.

2. Prepare an income statement.

3. Prepare a balance sheet.

RECYCLING PROBLEM 9-R 1 Recording closing entries

Parts of Manor Car Wash's work sheet are given on the next page. The balance of the account David Filipe, Drawing on December 31 is $150.00.

Instructions: Record the closing entries. Use page 1 of a general journal.

Manor Car Wash
Work Sheet
For Month Ended December 31, 19--

Account Title	Income Statement Debit	Income Statement Credit
Sales		1 366 00
Advertising Expense	112 84	
Miscellaneous Expense	98 80	
Rent Expense	650 00	
Repairs Expense	48 10	
Utilities Expense	239 36	
	1 149 10	1 366 00
Net Income	216 90	
	1 366 00	1 366 00

RECYCLING PROBLEM 10-R 1 Reconciling a bank statement; recording a bank service charge and a dishonored check

On November 1 of the current year, Mason's Miniature Golf receives a bank statement dated October 29. A comparison of the bank statement and the checkbook shows the information below.

The outstanding checks are: No. 251, $25.52; No. 252, $11.40; No. 257, $29.28.
An outstanding deposit was made on October 31, $66.88.
The bank service charge is $1.10.
The bank statement balance is $256.67.
The checkbook balance on Check Stub No. 258 is $258.45.

Instructions: 1. Prepare a bank reconciliation. Use November 1 of the current year.

2. Record the bank service charge on page 6 of a cash journal. Memorandum No. 12.

3. Record a dishonored check on page 6 of a cash journal. Use November 2 of the current year. Amount of check, $15.00; bank fee, $1.00. Memorandum No. 13.

RECYCLING PROBLEM 11-R 1 Journalizing transactions in a combination journal

Raymond Anthony and Jack Almond, partners in a sporting goods store, completed the transactions below for November of the current year. The cash balance on November 1 was $5,200.00.

Instructions: 1. Record the cash balance on hand on page 8 of a combination journal like the one on pages 192 and 193.

2. Record the following transactions. Source documents are abbreviated as: check, *C*; purchase invoice, *P*; memorandum, *M*.

Nov. 1. Paid November rent, $650.00. C260.
1. Paid salaries, $1,250.00. C261.
1. Purchased merchandise on account from Kramer Sporting Goods, $725.00. P72.
2. Paid on account to Greenville Supply, $82.00. C262.
3. Raymond Anthony, partner, withdrew cash, $450.00. C263.

Nov. 3. Jack Almond, partner, withdrew cash, $450.00. C264.
5. Purchased merchandise on account from Schultz Co., $525.00. P73.
6. Jack Almond, partner, withdrew merchandise, $33.00. M22.
8. Paid advertising bill, $26.00. C265. (Miscellaneous Expense)
9. Bought supplies on account from Hillsdale Supply, $43.00. M23.
11. Purchased merchandise for cash, $175.00. C266.
12. Paid on account to Kramer Sporting Goods, $460.00. C267.
15. Purchased merchandise on account from Stevens Sportswear, $280.00. P74.
15. Purchased merchandise for cash, $185.00. C268.
16. Bought supplies for cash, $26.00. C269.
16. Paid on account to Schultz Co., $410.00. C270.
17. Raymond Anthony, partner, withdrew merchandise, $26.00. M24.
19. Purchased merchandise for cash, $115.00. C271.
20. Bought supplies on account from Eastside Supply, $44.00. M25.
22. Purchased merchandise on account from Berry, Inc., $235.00. P75.
23. Bought supplies for cash, $74.00. C272.
25. Discovered that supplies bought last month had been recorded in error as a debit to Purchases instead of Supplies, $64.00. M26.
27. Bought supplies on account from Janer Supply, $29.00. M27.
29. Paid on account to Kramer Sporting Goods, $725.00. C273.
30. Purchased merchandise for cash, $135.00. C274.
30. Paid on account to Schultz Co., $525.00. C275.

RECYCLING PROBLEM 12-R 1 Journalizing sales and cash receipts in a combination journal

David Franklin and Lu Chi, partners in a retail shoe store, completed the transactions below for December of the current year. The cash balance on December 1 was $3,750.00.

Instructions: 1. Record the cash balance on page 12 of a combination journal like the one on pages 218 and 219.

2. Record the following transactions. Credit card sales are recorded as cash sales. Source documents are abbreviated as: sales invoice, *S*; receipt, *R*; cash register tape, *T*; adding machine tape, *CT*.

Dec. 1. Sold merchandise on account to Martha Howard, $35.00, plus sales tax, $1.75. Total, $36.75. S53.
1. Received on account from Mary Hopkins, $42.00. R72.
2. Received on account from Jerry Shields, $63.00. R73.
4. Cash sales for the week, $1,460.00, plus sales tax, $73.00. Total, $1,533.00. T4.
4. Credit card sales for the week, $540.00, plus sales tax, $27.00. Total, $567.00. CT4.
6. Sold merchandise on account to Phillip Kane, $45.00, plus sales tax, $2.25. Total, $47.25. S54.
7. Sold merchandise on account to Sandra King, $72.00, plus sales tax, $3.60. Total, $75.60. S55.
9. Received on account from Robert Davis, $68.25. R74.
11. Cash sales for the week, $1,830.00, plus sales tax, $91.50. Total, $1,921.50. T11.
11. Credit card sales for the week, $715.00, plus sales tax, $35.75. Total, $750.75. CT11.
14. Sold merchandise on account to James Barrett, $45.00, plus sales tax, $2.25. Total, $47.25. S56.
17. Received on account from Martha Howard, $36.75. R75.

Dec. 18. Sold merchandise on account to Phillip Kane, $30.00, plus sales tax, $1.50. Total, $31.50. S57.
20. Cash sales for the week, $1,920.00, plus sales tax, $96.00. Total, $2,016.00. T20.
20. Credit card sales for the week, $760.00, plus sales tax, $38.00. Total, $798.00. CT20.
21. Sold merchandise on account to Charlotte Reynolds, $92.00, plus sales tax, $4.60. Total, $96.60. S58.
22. Received on account from Phillip Kane, $47.25. R76.
24. Sold merchandise on account to Mary Hopkins, $42.00, plus sales tax, $2.10. Total, $44.10. S59.
24. Cash sales for the week, $2,160.00, plus sales tax, $108.00. Total, $2,268.00. T24.
24. Credit card sales for the week, $830.00, plus sales tax, $41.50. Total, $871.50. CT24.
27. Received on account from Sandra King, $75.60. R77.
31. Cash sales for the week, $1,340.00, plus sales tax, $67.00. Total, $1,407.00. T31.
31. Credit card sales for the week, $240.00, plus sales tax, $12.00. Total, $252.00. CT31.

Instructions: 3. Total the amount columns on the combination journal. Prove the equality of debits and credits.

4. Rule the combination journal. Use the illustration on pages 220 and 221 as a guide.

RECYCLING PROBLEM 13-R 1 Posting to ledgers from a combination journal

Instructions: 1. Open the following creditors' accounts in the accounts payable ledger. Record the balances as of November 1 of the current year.

Creditor	Address	Account Balance
Eastern Distributors	2230 West Shire, Bay Shore, NY 11706-1485	——
Grayling Building Supply	1610 Preston Street, Fulton, NY 13069-8372	$1,780.00
R & J Manufacturing	3360 Providence, Belmont, NH 03220-3961	——

2. Open the following customers' accounts in the accounts receivable ledger. Record the balances as of November 1 of the current year.

Customer	Address	Account Balance
Theresa Harris	620 West Elm Street, Belford, NJ 07718-2943	$1,250.00
Louise Hamagami	367 Lake Street, Belford, NJ 07718-3104	——
Rodney Paxton	320 Park Avenue, Belford, NJ 07718-2872	1,500.00
Julio Ruiz	883 Chester Avenue, Belford, NJ 07718-3019	——

3. Open the following accounts in the general ledger of James Home Improvement Center. Record the balances as of November 1 of the current year.

Account Title	Acct. No.	Account Balance
Cash	11	$ 5,400.00
Accounts Receivable	12	2,750.00
Merchandise Inventory	13	84,000.00
Supplies	14	800.00
Prepaid Insurance	15	300.00
Accounts Payable	21	1,780.00
Sales Tax Payable	22	364.00

Account Title	Acct. No.	Account Balance
Marcus Fields, Capital	31	$45,553.00
Marcus Fields, Drawing	32	——
Randolph Pearson, Capital	33	45,553.00
Randolph Pearson, Drawing	34	——
Income Summary	35	——
Sales	41	——
Purchases	51	——
Credit Card Fee Expense	61	——
Delivery Expense	62	——
Insurance Expense	63	——
Miscellaneous Expense	64	——
Rent Expense	65	——
Salary Expense	66	——
Supplies Expense	67	——

Instructions: 4. Record the following transactions on page 17 of a combination journal similar to the one on pages 242 and 243. The beginning cash balance is $5,400.00. Add a 5% sales tax to all sales transactions. Credit card sales are recorded as cash sales. Source documents are abbreviated as: check, *C*; memorandum, *M*; purchase invoice, *P*; sales invoice, *S*; cash register tape, *T*; adding machine tape, *CT*.

Nov. 1. Paid delivery expense, $83.00. C121.
1. Paid rent expense, $950.00. C122.
1. Paid salaries, $1,830.00. C123.
3. Purchased merchandise on account from R & J Manufacturing, $1,380.00. P64.
4. Purchased merchandise for cash, $750.00. C124.
6. Sold merchandise on account to Julio Ruiz, $260.00. S48.
6. Cash sales for the week, $2,360.00. T6.
6. Credit card sales for the week, $506.00. CT6.
8. Paid for advertising, $36.00. C125. (Miscellaneous Expense)
8. Purchased merchandise on account from Eastern Distributors, $1,480.00. P65.
9. Received on account from Theresa Harris, $1,250.00. R32.
13. Cash sales for the week, $2,050.00. T13.
13. Credit card sales for the week, $580.00. CT13.
15. Received on account from Rodney Paxton, $1,500.00. R33.
16. Sold merchandise on account to Louise Hamagami, $1,100.00. S49.
17. Marcus Fields, partner, withdrew cash, $700.00. C126.
17. Randolph Pearson, partner, withdrew cash, $700.00. C127.
18. Bought supplies for cash, $200.00. C128.
20. Paid on account to Grayling Building Supply, $1,780.00. C129.
20. Cash sales for the week, $2,240.00. T20.
20. Credit card sales for the week, $615.00. CT20.
21. Discovered that supplies bought on account had been recorded as a debit to Purchases instead of Supplies, $345.00. M23.
23. Marcus Fields, partner, withdrew merchandise, $40.00. M24.
25. Sold merchandise on account to Theresa Harris, $880.00. S50.
27. Cash sales for the week, $2,550.00. T27.
27. Credit card sales for the week, $740.00. CT27.
29. Sold merchandise on account to Julio Ruiz, $1,250.00. S51.
30. Cash sales for the week, $925.00. T30.
30. Credit card sales for the week, $180.00. CT30.

Instructions: 5. Total the columns of the combination journal on an adding machine or on paper. Prove that the sum of the debit totals equals the sum of the credit totals.

6. Prove cash. The balance on Check Stub No. 130 is $14,504.30.

7. Write the column totals in the combination journal.

8. Rule the combination journal.

9. Post the individual items recorded in the following columns of the combination journal. (a) General Debit and Credit. (b) Accounts Receivable Debit and Credit. (c) Accounts Payable Debit and Credit.

10. Post the totals of the special columns of the combination journal.

11. Prepare a schedule of accounts payable and a schedule of accounts receivable. Prove the accuracy of the subsidiary ledgers. Compare the schedule totals with the balances of the controlling accounts in the general ledger. If the totals are not the same, find and correct the errors.

12. Prove the equality of debits and credits in the general ledger. On an adding machine or on paper, add the balances of all accounts with debit balances. Then add the balances of all accounts with credit balances. If the two totals are not the same, find and correct the errors.

RECYCLING PROBLEM 14-R 1 Preparing a work sheet

The accounts and their balances in Teen Fashions' general ledger appear below. Ending inventories and the value of insurance policies are also given.

Instructions: Prepare Teen Fashions' eight-column work sheet for the monthly fiscal period ending December 31 of the current year. Use as a guide the eight-column work sheet, page 272.

Account Title	Account Balance	Account Title	Account Balance
Cash	$ 9,350.00	Todd Drake, Drawing	$ 830.00
Accounts Receivable	620.00	Income Summary	—
Merchandise Inventory	83,700.00	Sales	14,800.00
Supplies	460.00	Purchases	4,400.00
Prepaid Insurance	340.00	Credit Card Fee Expense	230.00
Accounts Payable	3,610.00	Insurance Expense	—
Sales Tax Payable	592.00	Miscellaneous Expense	92.00
Susan Casper, Capital	42,300.00	Rent Expense	750.00
Susan Casper, Drawing	750.00	Salary Expense	1,300.00
Todd Drake, Capital	41,520.00	Supplies Expense	—

Adjustment Information, December 31

Merchandise inventory	$80,600.00
Supplies inventory	330.00
Value of insurance policies	258.00

RECYCLING PROBLEM 15-R 1 Preparing financial statements

The work sheet for Gift Gallery for the month ended November 30 of the current year is on the next page.

Instructions: 1. Prepare an income statement similar to one on page 283.

2. Prepare a distribution of net income statement similar to one on page 285. The net income is to be shared equally.

3. Prepare a capital statement similar to one on page 288. No additional investments were made during November.

4. Prepare a balance sheet in report form similar to the one on page 292.

Gift Gallery
Work Sheet
For Month Ended November 30, 19--

	Account Title	1 Trial Balance Debit	2 Trial Balance Credit	3 Adjustments Debit	4 Adjustments Credit	5 Income Statement Debit	6 Income Statement Credit	7 Balance Sheet Debit	8 Balance Sheet Credit
1	Cash	6 400 00						6 400 00	
2	Accounts Receivable	280 00						280 00	
3	Merchandise Inventory	56 000 00		(b)54 500 00	(a)56 000 00			54 500 00	
4	Supplies	260 00			(c) 140 00			120 00	
5	Prepaid Insurance	320 00			(d) 60 00			260 00	
6	Accounts Payable		2 580 00						2 580 00
7	Sales Tax Payable		626 00						626 00
8	Stella Sanders, Capital		27 811 50						27 811 50
9	Stella Sanders, Drawing	650 00						650 00	
10	Silvia Wicks, Capital		27 811 50						27 811 50
11	Silvia Wicks, Drawing	600 00						600 00	
12	Income Summary			(a)56 000 00	(b)54 500 00	56 000 00	54 500 00		
13	Sales		12 520 00				12 520 00		
14	Purchases	4 600 00				4 600 00			
15	Credit Card Fee Expense	275 00				275 00			
16	Insurance Expense			(d) 60 00		60 00			
17	Miscellaneous Expense	74 00				74 00			
18	Rent Expense	750 00				750 00			
19	Salary Expense	1 140 00				1 140 00			
20	Supplies Expense			(c) 140 00		140 00			
21		71 349 00	71 349 00	110 700 00	110 700 00	63 039 00	67 020 00	62 810 00	58 829 00
22	Net Income					3 981 00			3 981 00
23						67 020 00	67 020 00	62 810 00	62 810 00

RECYCLING PROBLEM 16-R 1 Completing the work at the end of a fiscal period

Recycling Problem 15-R 1 above shows the completed work sheet for Gift Gallery. Use this completed work sheet to complete this problem.

Instructions: 1. On page 3 of a combination journal record the adjusting entries shown in the Adjustments columns of the work sheet.

2. Record in the combination journal the closing entries from the information on the work sheet. The distribution of net income statement showed equal distribution of earnings.

RECYCLING PROBLEM 17-R 1 Preparing a general ledger chart of accounts and financial statement setup forms

The general ledger chart of accounts for Kimura Furniture is on the next page.

Instructions: 1. Prepare a general ledger chart of accounts setup form dated February 23 of the current year for the accounts given on page 651. Kimura Furniture's client number is 262. Use chart of accounts setup form, page 335, as a guide.

2. Prepare the following financial statement setup forms for Kimura Furniture dated February 24 of the current year. (1) Income statement. (2) Distribution of net income statement. Net income is to be shared equally. (3) Capital statement. (4) Balance sheet. Use financial statement setup forms, pages 337–339, as a guide.

Account Number	ASSETS	Account Number	REVENUE
11000	Cash	41000	Sales
11500	Accounts Receivable		
12000	Merchandise Inventory		COST OF MERCHANDISE SOLD
12500	Supplies	51000	Purchases
13000	Prepaid Insurance		
13500	Office Equipment		EXPENSES
14000	Store Equipment	61000	Advertising Expense
	LIABILITIES	61500	Credit Card Fee Expense
21000	Accounts Payable	62000	Insurance Expense
		62500	Miscellaneous Expense
	CAPITAL	63000	Rent Expense
31000	Emi Kimura, Capital	63500	Salary Expense
31500	Emi Kimura, Drawing	64000	Supplies Expense
32000	Saburo Kimura, Capital		
32500	Saburo Kimura, Drawing		
33000	Income Summary		

RECYCLING PROBLEM 18-R 1 Recording an opening entry in an EDP general ledger accounting system

The chart of accounts given in Recycling Problem 17-R 1, Chapter 17, is needed to complete Recycling Problem 18-R 1.

Kimura Furniture's balance sheet for February 28 of the current year is below.

Kimura Furniture
Balance Sheet
February 28, 19--

Assets		
Cash	9 460 00	
Accounts Receivable	780 00	
Merchandise Inventory	265 650 00	
Supplies	730 00	
Prepaid Insurance	880 00	
Office Equipment	1 340 00	
Store Equipment	950 00	
Total Assets		279 790 00
Liabilities		
Accounts Payable		4 830 00
Capital		
Emi Kimura, Capital	140 160 00	
Saburo Kimura, Capital	134 800 00	
Total Capital		274 960 00
Total Liabilities and Capital		279 790 00

Instructions: Record the opening entry for Kimura Furniture, Client No. 262, on a journal entry transmittal. Use March 1 of the current year as the date of the opening entry. Use account numbers from the chart of accounts shown in Recycling Problem 17-R 1.

RECYCLING PROBLEM 19-R 1 Recording weekly batched transactions for EDP using a journal entry transmittal

The chart of accounts given in Recycling Problem 17-R 1, Chapter 17, is needed to complete Recycling Problem 19-R 1.

Kimura Furniture arranges source documents into five batches. (1) Accounts payable. (2) Cash payments. (3) Accounts receivable. (4) Cash receipts. (5) General. Reference numbers are assigned to transaction source documents within each batch. The batched transactions are recorded as combined entries weekly. Batched transactions for week ended March 6 of the current year are below.

Accounts payable		
Bought supplies on account	$ 200.00.	Ref. No. 1000.
Purchased merchandise on account	$ 450.00.	Ref. No. 1001.
Total accounts payable	$ 650.00.	
Cash payments		
Bought supplies for cash	$ 50.00.	Ref. No. 2000.
Paid on account	$ 180.00.	Ref. No. 2001.
Emi Kimura, partner, withdrew cash	$ 600.00.	Ref. No. 2002.
Saburo Kimura, partner, withdrew cash	$ 600.00.	Ref. No. 2003.
Paid March rent	$ 750.00.	Ref. No. 2004.
Paid salaries	$1,000.00.	Ref. No. 2005.
Total cash payments	$3,180.00.	
Accounts receivable		
Sold merchandise on account	$ 140.00.	Ref. No. 3000.
Total accounts receivable	$ 140.00.	
Cash receipts		
Cash received on account	$ 250.00.	Ref. No. 4000.
Cash received from sales	$2,830.00.	Ref. No. 4001.
Total cash receipts	$3,080.00.	
General		
Emi Kimura, partner, withdrew merchandise	$ 75.00.	Ref. No. 5000.
Total withdrawals of merchandise by partners	$ 75.00.	

Instructions: Record the batched transactions for Kimura Furniture, Client No. 262, on a journal entry transmittal. Use March 6 of the current year as the date of the last business day for the week's transactions. Use account numbers from the chart of accounts shown in Recycling Problem 17-R 1, page 651. Use the journal entry transmittal, page 365, as your model.

RECYCLING PROBLEM 19-R 2 Recording adjusting and closing entries for EDP using a journal entry transmittal

The chart of accounts given in Recycling Problem 17-R 1, Chapter 17, is needed to complete Recycling Problem 19-R 2.

Kimura Furniture's trial balance is shown in the partial work sheet printout on the next page. Ending inventories and the value of insurance policies are also given.

	TRIAL BALANCE	
	DEBIT	CREDIT
CASH....................	$ 15,500.00	
ACCOUNTS RECEIVABLE......	380.00	
MERCHANDISE INVENTORY....	265,650.00	
SUPPLIES................	930.00	
PREPAID INSURANCE........	880.00	
OFFICE EQUIPMENT.........	1,340.00	
STORE EQUIPMENT..........	950.00	
ACCOUNTS PAYABLE.........		$ 2,290.00
EMI KIMURA, CAPITAL......		140,160.00
EMI KIMURA, DRAWING......	675.00	
SABURO KIMURA, CAPITAL...		134,800.00
SABURO KIMURA, DRAWING...	600.00	
INCOME SUMMARY...........		
SALES....................		15,830.00
PURCHASES................	3,540.00	
ADVERTISING EXPENSE......	60.00	
CREDIT CARD FEE EXPENSE..	233.00	
INSURANCE EXPENSE........		
MISCELLANEOUS EXPENSE....	92.00	
RENT EXPENSE.............	950.00	
SALARY EXPENSE...........	1,300.00	
SUPPLIES EXPENSE.........		
	$293,080.00	$293,080.00

Adjustment Information, March 31

Merchandise inventory	$262,140.00
Supplies inventory	700.00
Value of insurance policies	800.00

Instructions: 1. Enter adjustments and complete work sheet printout for month ended March 31 of the current year. Use as a guide the work sheet printout, page 371.

2. Record adjusting entries for Kimura Furniture, Client No. 262, on a journal entry transmittal. Use account numbers from the chart of accounts shown in Recycling Problem 17-R 1, page 651. Use the journal entry transmittal, page 365, as your model.

3. Record closing entries for Kimura Furniture on a journal entry transmittal. Distribution of net income statement printout shows net income shared equally: Emi Kimura, $2,917.50; Saburo Kimura, $2,917.50.

RECYCLING PROBLEM 20-R 1 Journalizing and posting transactions affecting purchases and cash payments

Instructions: 1. Open the creditors' accounts, page 654, in the accounts payable ledger of Cantrell Company. Record the balances as of July 1 of the current year.

Creditor	Account Balance
Conley Supply Company, 466 Broadmeadow Court, Richmond, VA 23202-4437	—
Gaither Company, 27 Industrial Drive, Petersburg, VA 23803-9227	—
Iverson Exports, 3494 Englewood Drive, Hampton, VA 23661-2920	—
Ivory Company, 7978 Central Parkway, Petersburg, VA 23803-4464	$1,440.00
Perlich Company, 2480 Fairview Avenue, Richmond, VA 23201-6213	675.00
Zeigler Company, 5941 Wolfcreek Pike, Richmond, VA 23202-7883	—

Instructions: 2. Open the following partial list of accounts in the general ledger of Cantrell Company. Record the balances as of July 1 of the current year.

Account Title	Account No.	Account Balance
Cash	1101	$17,400.00
Supplies	1105	778.70
Accounts Payable	2102	2,115.00
Purchases	5101	—
Purchases Returns and Allowances	5101.1	—
Purchases Discount	5101.2	—
Delivery Expense	6103	—
Miscellaneous Expense	6108	—
Rent Expense	6110	—

Instructions: 3. The following transactions affecting purchases and cash payments were completed by Cantrell Company during July of the current year. Record these transactions in a purchases journal, general journal, and cash payments journal similar to those in Chapter 20. Use page 12 for each journal. Source documents are abbreviated as: check, C; memorandum, M; purchase invoice, P; debit memorandum, DM.

July 1. Paid July rent, $1,500.00. C240.
2. Purchased merchandise on account from Gaither Company, $900.00. P122.
2. Returned merchandise to Perlich Company, $42.00. DM37.
5. Purchased merchandise on account from Iverson Exports, $270.00. P123.
6. Paid on account to Perlich Company, $633.00, covering P118 for $675.00 less DM37 for $42.00; no discount. C241.
Posting. Post the items that are to be posted individually. Post from the journals in this order: Purchases journal, general journal, and cash payments journal.
8. Paid on account to Ivory Company, $1,425.60, covering P104 for $1,440.00 less a 1% discount of $14.40. C242.
11. Purchased merchandise for cash, $396.00. C243.
13. Paid on account to Iverson Exports, $267.30, covering P123 for $270.00 less a 1% discount of $2.70. C244.
13. Bought supplies on account from Conley Supply Company, $216.00. M76.
Posting. Post the items that are to be posted individually.
15. Purchased merchandise on account from Zeigler Company, $684.00. P124.
15. Purchased merchandise on account from Iverson Exports, $360.00. P125.
18. Paid miscellaneous expense, $36.00. C245.
20. Returned merchandise to Gaither Company, $108.00. DM38.
Posting. Post the items that are to be posted individually.
22. Purchased merchandise on account from Zeigler Company, $720.00. P126.
22. Paid on account to Gaither Company, $792.00, covering P122 for $900.00 less DM38 for $108.00; no discount. C246.
22. Paid delivery expense, $54.00. C247.
22. Paid on account to Zeigler Company, $670.32, covering P124 for $684.00 less a 2% discount of $13.68. C248.

July 25. Paid miscellaneous expense, $60.00. C249.
27. Paid on account to Conley Supply Company, $216.00; no discount. C250.
28. Returned merchandise to Zeigler Company, $30.00. DM39.
29. Purchased merchandise on account from Perlich Company, $528.00. P127.
Posting. Post the items that are to be posted individually.

Instructions: 4. Total and rule the purchases journal. Post the total.

5. Total, prove, and rule the cash payments journal. Post the totals of the special columns.

6. Prepare a schedule of accounts payable similar to the one on page 250. Compare the schedule total with the balance of the accounts payable account in the general ledger. The total and the balance should be the same.

RECYCLING PROBLEM 21-R 1 Journalizing and posting sales and cash receipts transactions

Instructions: 1. Open the charge customers' accounts given below in the accounts receivable ledger of Johnston Company. Record the balance as of March 1 of the current year.

Charge Customer	Account Balance
Stephanie Cook, 680 Starfish Avenue, Portland, ME 04110-1902	$325.00
Ron Kennedy, 530 Silverston Pike, Portland, ME 04107-1784	235.00
Luis Livermore, 5233 South Plaza, Portland, ME 04105-1521	489.00
Pam Pembrook, 4251 Brach Boulevard, Portland, ME 04102-1241	284.00
Steven Phillips, 892 Arthur Avenue, Portland, ME 04109-2047	390.00

Instructions: 2. Open the following partial list of accounts in the general ledger of Johnston Company. Record the balances as of March 1 of the current year.

Account Title	Acct. No.	Account Balance
Cash	1101	$4,800.00
Accounts Receivable	1103	1,723.00
Sales Tax Payable	2106	—
Sales	4101	—
Sales Returns and Allowances	4101.1	—

Instructions: 3. The following transactions affecting sales and cash receipts were completed by Johnston Company during March of the current year. Record these transactions in a sales journal, general journal, and cash receipts journal similar to those illustrated in Chapter 21. Use page 12 of each journal. Source documents are abbreviated: sales invoice, S; receipt, R; cash register tape, T; credit card sales adding machine tape, CT; credit memorandum, CM.

Mar. 1. Recorded the cash balance on hand in the cash receipts journal, $4,800.00.
2. Received cash on account from Ron Kennedy, $235.00. R41.
4. Sold merchandise on account to Pam Pembrook, $531.00, plus sales tax, $26.55. S73.
4. Credited Luis Livermore's account for merchandise returned, $80.00, plus sales tax, $4.00. CM18.
5. Recorded cash sales for the week, $653.00, plus sales tax, $32.65. T5.
5. Recorded credit card sales for the week, $535.00, plus sales tax, $26.75. CT5.
Posting. Post the items that are to be posted individually. Post from the journals in this order: sales journal, general journal, and cash receipts journal.

Mar. 7. Received cash on account from Luis Livermore, $405.00. R42.
8. Received cash on account from Pam Pembrook, $284.00. R43.
10. Received cash on account from Steven Phillips, $390.00. R44.
12. Recorded cash sales for the week, $701.00, plus sales tax, $35.05. T12.
12. Recorded credit card sales for the week, $589.00, plus sales tax, $29.45. CT12.
Posting. Post the items that are to be posted individually.
14. Sold merchandise on account to Luis Livermore, $250.00, plus sales tax, $12.50. S74.
15. Credited Pam Pembrook's account for merchandise returned, $25.00, plus sales tax, $1.25. CM19.
15. Received cash on account from Stephanie Cook, $325.00. R45.
17. Sold merchandise on account to Ron Kennedy, $750.00, plus sales tax, $37.50. S75.
19. Recorded cash sales for the week, $654.00, plus sales tax, $32.70. T19.
19. Recorded credit card sales for the week, $592.00, plus sales tax, $29.60. CT19.
Posting. Post the items that are to be posted individually.
21. Sold merchandise on account to Steven Phillips, $340.00, plus sales tax, $17.00. S76.
22. Sold merchandise on account to Stephanie Cook, $376.00, plus sales tax, $18.80. S77.
24. Received cash on account from Pam Pembrook, $504.75. R46.
26. Recorded cash sales for the week, $690.00, plus sales tax, $34.50. T26.
26. Recorded credit card sales for the week, $605.00, plus sales tax, $30.25. CT26.
Posting. Post the items that are to be posted individually.
28. Received cash on account from Luis Livermore, $262.50. R47.
28. Received cash on account from Ron Kennedy, $750.00. R48.
31. Recorded cash sales for the week, $590.00, plus sales tax, $29.50. T31.
31. Recorded credit card sales for the week, $435.00, plus sales tax, $21.75. CT31.
Posting. Post the items that are to be posted individually.

Instructions: 4. Total, prove, and rule the sales journal. Post the totals of the special columns.

5. Prove the equality of debits and credits for the cash receipts journal.

6. Prove cash. The total of the Cash Credit column of the cash payments journal for Johnston Company is $10,345.25. The balance on the last check stub on March 31 is $3,957.20.

7. Rule the cash receipts journal. Post the special column totals to the appropriate general ledger accounts.

8. Prepare a schedule of accounts receivable similar to the one on page 250. Compare the schedule total with the balance of the accounts receivable account in the general ledger. The total and the balance should be the same.

RECYCLING PROBLEM 22-R 1 Preparing a semimonthly payroll

Information from employee time cards for the semimonthly pay period March 16–31 of the current year is on the next page.

Instructions: 1. Prepare for the semimonthly pay period March 16–31 a payroll register similar to the illustration, page 447. The date of payment is April 1. Use the income tax withholding tables on pages 448 and 449. Deduct 6% of each employee's total earnings for FICA taxes.

2. Prepare Check No. 904 for the total net pay. Make the check payable to *Payroll Account* and sign your name. The beginning check stub balance is $9,545.00.

3. Prepare payroll checks for Gary Jackson, Check No. 104, and Diane Simpson, Check No. 105. Sign your name as treasurer of the company. Record the payroll check numbers in the payroll register.

Ling Company

Employee		Marital Status	No. of Allowances	Time card amounts for period March 16–31		Deductions
No.	Name			Regular	Overtime	Hospital Insurance
1	Banks, Harvey	M	2	$702.00	$20.25	$25.00
2	Barton, Melvin	M	1	516.00	13.50	
3	Cox, Mark	S	1	754.00		
4	Jackson, Gary	S	1	696.00	13.50	
5	Simpson, Diane	M	4	712.50	28.14	28.00
6	Van Norren, Agnes	M	3	725.00		14.00
7	Webber, Vickie	S	1	580.00		

RECYCLING PROBLEM 23-R 1 Recording payroll transactions

Jackson Stationers completed the payroll transactions given below.

Feb. 28. Paid monthly payroll, $3,792.00 (less deductions: employees' income tax, $417.10; FICA tax, $227.52). C88.

28. Recorded the employer's payroll taxes at the following rates: FICA tax, 6%; federal unemployment tax, 0.7%; state unemployment tax, 2.7%. M22.

Mar. 15. Paid deposit for February payroll liabilities (employees' income tax, $417.10; FICA tax, $455.04; total deposit, $872.14). C103.

31. Paid monthly payroll, $3,806.00 (less deductions: employees' income tax, $418.70; FICA tax, $228.36). C145.

31. Recorded the employer's payroll taxes at the same rates as in February. M25.

Apr. 15. Paid deposit for March payroll liabilities (employees' income tax, $418.70; FICA tax, $456.72; total deposit, $875.42). C178.

30. Paid federal unemployment tax for the quarter ended March 31, $79.80. C218.

30. Paid state unemployment tax for the quarter ended March 31, $307.80. C219.

Instructions: 1. Record the selected transactions on page 5 of a cash payments journal and page 2 of a general journal. Use the current year in the date.

2. Prove the cash payments journal.

RECYCLING PROBLEM 24-R 1 Recording entries for bad debts expense

Brett Associates has general ledger accounts for Allowance for Uncollectible Accounts and Bad Debts Expense. On January 1 of the current year, the credit balance of Allowance for Uncollectible Accounts was $220.50. Selected entries affecting uncollectible accounts are given on page 658.

Instructions: Record all the necessary entries for the transactions, page 658, on page 24 of a general journal like the one on page 495.

Feb. 18. Wrote off past-due account of Willie Iverson as uncollectible, $167.64. M17.
Mar. 31. *End of the first quarterly fiscal period.* Make adjusting entry for estimated bad debts expense. Bad debts expense is estimated as ½% (.005) of the total charge sales. Total charge sales for the first quarterly fiscal period were $40,833.15.
Apr. 11. Wrote off past-due account of W. C. Causey as uncollectible, $220.95. M88.
June 30. *End of the second quarterly fiscal period.* Make adjusting entry for estimated bad debts expense. Total charge sales for the second quarterly fiscal period were $45,856.23.
July 20. Wrote off past-due account of Ray Hammond as uncollectible, $243.15. M125.
Sept. 30. *End of third quarterly fiscal period.* Make adjusting entry for estimated bad debts expense. Total charge sales for the third quarterly fiscal period were $42,212.20.
Dec. 31. Wrote off past-due account of Frank Ikard as uncollectible, $232.20. M340.
Dec. 31. *End of the fourth quarterly fiscal period.* Make adjusting entry for estimated bad debts expense. Total charge sales for the fourth quarterly fiscal period were $54,048.36.

RECYCLING PROBLEM 25-R 1 Figuring depreciation expense and book value of plant assets; journalizing depreciation expense and disposal of a plant asset

Discount Music owns the plant assets listed below.

Plant Asset	Asset Account	Date Bought	Original Cost	Estimated Salvage Value	Estimated Life
1	Delivery Equipment	July 1, 1977	$7,500.00	$300.00	6 years
2	Delivery Equipment	June 1, 1983	8,600.00	500.00	5 years
3	Store Equipment	April 1, 1976	2,840.00	200.00	10 years
4	Store Equipment	Jan. 1, 1980	3,000.00	300.00	15 years
5	Store Equipment	Oct. 1, 1983	1,000.00	100.00	3 years

Instructions: 1. Figure each plant asset's depreciation expense for the year ended December 31, 1983. Use the straight-line method of figuring depreciation. Figure the time of depreciation to the nearest number of months.

2. Figure each plant asset's book value as of December 31, 1983.

3. Record on page 12 of a general journal the two adjusting entries for depreciation expense for the year ended December 31, 1983. Record delivery equipment depreciation in Depreciation Expense — Delivery Equipment. Record store equipment depreciation in Depreciation Expense — Store Equipment.

4. On February 2, 1984, received cash, $300.00, from the sale of delivery equipment, Plant Asset No. 1, bought July 1, 1977, for $7,500.00. Receipt No. 189. Record the sale of this plant asset on page 15 of a cash receipts journal.

RECYCLING PROBLEM 26-R 1 Recording notes, interest, and bank discount

The transactions below were completed by Brockway Corporation during March of the current year.

Instructions: 1. Record the transactions on page 659. Use a cash receipts journal (page 15) and a cash payments journal (page 7) similar to those illustrated in Chapter 26. Source documents are abbreviated as: check, C; note payable, NP; note receivable, NR; receipt, R.

Mar. 3. Paid Liehr Supply Company for NP71 (60-day, 8% note payable due today; principal, $1,200.00; interest, $15.78), $1,215.78. C122.

7. Discounted at 9½% at the First National Bank our 30-day, non-interest-bearing note payable, $4,000.00 (bank discount, $31.23; proceeds, $3,968.77). NP75. The First National Bank credited our checking account for the proceeds.

8. Received a check from Doris Ellefson in settlement of NR98 (20-day, 9% note receivable due today; principal, $650.00; interest, $3.21), $653.21. R88.

10. Paid Security Bank for NP66 (90-day, 8½% note payable due today; principal, $4,200.00; interest, $88.03), $4,288.03. C128.

16. Issued a 30-day, 9% note payable to Security Bank, $2,500.00. NP76. The bank credited our checking account for the principal.

17. Received a check from Marilyn McClure in settlement of NR81 (6-month, 9% note receivable due today; principal, $1,100.00; interest, $49.50), $1,149.50. R91.

18. Paid Equipment Sales Company for NP52 (60-day, 9½% note payable due today; principal, $1,800.00; interest, $28.11), $1,828.11. C136.

24. Discounted at 10% at First National Bank, our 20-day, non-interest-bearing note payable, $1,500.00 (bank discount, $8.22; proceeds, $1,491.78). NP77. The First National Bank credited our checking account for the proceeds.

25. Received a check from Larry Rothermel in settlement of NR99 (30-day, 9% note receivable due today; principal, $850.00; interest, $6.29), $856.29. R93.

28. Paid Hailey Corporation for NP68 (90-day, 9½% note payable due today; principal, $3,000.00; interest, $70.27), $3,070.27. C145.

Instructions: 2. Prove the cash receipts and cash payments journals.

RECYCLING PROBLEM 27-R 1 Preparing end-of-fiscal-period work for a corporation

The accounts and their balances in Bike Mart's general ledger appear as below and on page 660 on December 31 of the current year.

Account Title	Account Balance
Cash	$ 41,339.00
Accounts Receivable	39,145.00
Allow. for Uncoll. Accounts	22.00
Merchandise Inventory	107,914.00
Supplies	2,212.00
Prepaid Insurance	7,875.00
Delivery Equipment	7,350.00
Accum. Depr. — Delivery Equip.	1,470.00
Office Equipment	6,020.00
Accum. Depr. — Office Equip.	626.00
Store Equipment	8,100.00
Accum. Depr. — Store Equip.	2,167.00
Accounts Payable	23,966.00
Employees Income Tax Payable	1,550.00
Federal Income Tax Payable	—
FICA Tax Payable	1,039.00
Sales Tax Payable	3,984.00
Unemployment Tax Pay. — Federal	36.00
Unemployment Tax Pay. — State	196.00
Hosp. Insurance Premium Pay	980.00
Dividends Payable	—
Capital Stock	150,000.00
Retained Earnings	29,995.00
Income Summary	—

Account Title	Account Balance
Sales	$796,800.00
Sales Returns and Allow.	2,023.00
Purchases	633,127.00
Purch. Returns and Allow.	2,180.00
Purchases Discount	2,849.00
Advertising Expense	2,394.00
Bad Debts Expense	—
Delivery Expense	11,352.00
Depr. Exp. — Delivery Equip.	—
Depr. Exp. — Office Equip.	—
Depr. Exp. — Store Equip.	—
Insurance Expense	—
Miscellaneous Expense	1,318.00
Payroll Taxes Expense	9,449.00
Rent Expense	25,200.00
Salary Expense	106,604.00
Supplies Expense	—
Interest Income	1,082.00
Interest Expense	2,520.00
Federal Income Tax	5,000.00

Instructions: 1. Prepare an eight-column work sheet for the fiscal year ended December 31 of the current year. Use as a guide the work sheet, pages 536 and 537. Information needed for the adjustments is below.

Bad debts expense is estimated as 1.5% of charge sales. Charge sales were $199,200.00.	
Merchandise inventory, December 31	$144,740.00
Supplies inventory, December 31	288.00
Value of insurance policies, December 31	2,835.00
Annual depreciation expense on delivery equipment	1,470.00
Annual depreciation expense on office equipment	602.00
Annual depreciation expense on store equipment	810.00
Federal income tax for the year	5,833.00

2. Prepare an income statement similar to the one on page 542.

3. Prepare a statement of stockholders' equity similar to the one on page 543. Additional information needed is below.

January 1 balance of capital stock account (1,500 shares issued for $100.00 per share.)	$150,000.00
January 1 balance of retained earnings account	52,495.00
Dividend declared and paid during the current year	22,500.00

4. Prepare a balance sheet for December 31 of the current year.

5. Record the adjusting entries on page 12 of a general journal.

6. Record the closing entries on page 13 of a general journal.

7. On January 10 following the current year, the board of directors declared a dividend of $15.00 a share to stockholders. Record the dividend declared on page 14 of a general journal. Source document is Memorandum No. 189.

8. The dividend declared in Instruction 7 was paid on January 31. Record payment of the dividend on page 28 of a cash payments journal. Source document is Check No. 246.

RECYCLING PROBLEM 28-R 1 Recording transactions in a voucher system

Innovation Products uses a voucher system. A voucher register and a check register similar to those on pages 572–573 and 576 are used.

Instructions: 1. Record the following transactions completed during May of the current year. Use page 14 of a voucher register and page 11 of a check register. Source documents are abbreviated as: check, C; debit memorandum, DM; voucher, V.

May 1. Recorded cash balance on May 1, $15,940.80.
2. Purchased merchandise on account from Kalman Exchange, $551.30. V216.
4. Purchased merchandise on account from Homestead Corporation, $2,348.20. V217.
5. Bought supplies from Kwik Supplies, $107.30. V218.
5. Paid V218, $107.30; no discount. C183.
8. Issued DM62 to Kalman Exchange for the return of merchandise purchased, $43.00. Canceled V216 and issued V219.
10. Paid V219, $508.30, less purchases discount, $5.08. C184.
11. Bought supplies from Camacho Supplies, $206.60. V220.
12. Paid V217, $2,348.20; no discount. C185.
16. Made a deposit in the bank, $7,516.40.
16. Purchased merchandise on account from Constellation, $2,103.10. V221.
19. Paid V221, $2,103.10, less purchases discount, $42.06. C186.
26. Paid V220, $206.60; no discount. C187.
29. Bought gasoline for delivery truck from Mohawk Service Station, $186.00. V222. (Delivery Expense)
29. Paid V222, $186.00; no discount. C188.
30. Made a deposit in the bank, $7,012.70.
31. The payroll register for the monthly payroll showed the following information. Salary Expense, $4,207.90; Employees Income Tax Payable — Federal, $689.50; Employees Income Tax Payable — State, $173.25; FICA Tax Payable, $252.47. V223.
31. Paid V223, $3,092.68. C189.

Instructions: 2. Total, prove, and rule the voucher register and check register.

RECYCLING PROBLEM 29-R 1 Establishing and replenishing a petty cash fund

LaRoche, Inc., established a $150.00 petty cash fund on April 1 of the current year.

Instructions: 1. Record on page 12 of a voucher register establishment of a petty cash fund. Voucher number is 289. Payee is Petty Cash Custodian.

2. Record on page 8 of a check register Check No. 281 to establish the petty cash fund. April 1 cash balance on hand is $65,482.50.

Totals of the petty cash record's amount columns on April 30 are listed below.

			Distribution of Payments			
	Receipts	Payments	Supplies	Delivery Expense	Misc. Expense	Other Payments Amount
Totals	$150.00	121.30	51.90	23.10	25.30	21.00

Instructions: 3. Record the totals above on line 10 of a petty cash record. Petty cash record page is 14.

4. The petty cash box has $27.70 at the end of the day April 30. Compare for equality the sum of cash and payments with the petty cash beginning balance.

5. Record any cash short or cash over and the cash balance, then total and rule the Receipts and Payments columns. Make entries like those in petty cash record, pages 594 and 595.

6. From information in petty cash record, record voucher register entry to replenish petty cash fund on April 30. Amount in the Other Payments column is Advertising Expense. Voucher number is 326.

7. Record Check No. 318 in the check register to replenish the fund.

8. Record the April 30 cash balance and amount of replenished fund on the petty cash record. Use lines 16 and 17 of the petty cash record, page 595, as a model.

RECYCLING PROBLEM 30-R 1 Determining cost of inventory using the fifo and lifo methods

Accounting records at Chaparral Company showed the purchases and periodic inventory counts listed below.

Model	Beginning Inventory January 1	First Purchase	Second Purchase	Third Purchase	Periodic Inventory Count December 31
S 32	320 @ $ 8.40	150 @ $8.75	200 @ $9.00	150 @ $9.20	280
S 34	210 @ $ 7.60	200 @ $8.00	200 @ $8.20	200 @ $7.80	250
M 36	300 @ $ 9.00	250 @ $9.20	200 @ $9.20	250 @ $9.20	180
M 38	250 @ $10.00	225 @ $9.80	225 @ $9.50	200 @ $9.40	200
L 42	160 @ $ 5.60	150 @ $5.20	180 @ $5.75	120 @ $6.00	160
L 44	800 @ $ 4.80	100 @ $5.00	100 @ $5.25	100 @ $5.50	400
XL 48	50 @ $ 6.00	300 @ $6.20	300 @ $6.40	400 @ $6.50	200
XL 50	120 @ $ 8.50	250 @ $8.60	500 @ $8.00	250 @ $8.90	260

Use a form with the column headings below.

Model	Number of Units on Hand	Unit Cost	Inventory Value December 31
S 32	280	150 @ $9.20 130 @ $9.00	$2,550.00

Instructions: 1. Figure the total amount of the inventory on December 31 according to the *fifo* method. Determining the inventory value for model S32 is given as an example. Use the following procedure.

(a) Record the model number and number of units of each model on hand on December 31.

(b) Record the unit cost of each model. When more than one unit cost is used, list the units and unit costs on separate lines.

(c) Figure the total inventory value of each model and write the amount in the Value column.

(d) Add the value column to determine the total amount of the inventory.

2. On another form, figure the total amount of inventory using the *lifo* method. Follow the steps given in Instruction 1.

3. Compare the total amount of the inventory obtained in Instructions 1 and 2. Which method, *fifo* or *lifo*, resulted in the lower total amount for the inventory?

Index

A

B

D

E

H

I

J

K

L

T

U

V

W